EXODUS;

OR,

THE SECOND BOOK OF MOSES,

WITH AN EXPLANATORY AND CRITICAL

𝕮ommentary.

EDITED

By F. C. COOK, M.A., Canon of Exeter.

(This volume forms part of the Speaker's Commentary on the Pentateuch.)

WIPF & STOCK · Eugene, Oregon

Wipf and Stock Publishers
199 W 8th Ave, Suite 3
Eugene, OR 97401

Exodus
Or, the Second Book of Moses, with an Explanatory and Critical Commentary
By Cook, F. C.
Softcover ISBN-13: 979-8-3852-0639-1
Hardcover ISBN-13: 979-8-3852-0640-7
eBook ISBN-13: 979-8-3852-0641-4
Publication date 10/23/2023
Previously published by Scribner, Armstrong & Co., 1874

This edition is a scanned facsimile of the original edition published in 1874.

This volume is part of a multi-volume set

PUBLISHERS' NOTE.

This volume includes all of "The Speaker's Commentary" which relates to Exodus. It is printed in this form for the convenience of teachers and scholars who are now engaged in the study of the International Uniform Series of Sunday School Lessons, and it is hoped that it may prove as widely useful as the Commentary on Genesis did when that part of the Scripture occupied attention.

Besides the comment proper on the text, which is throughout so clear and compact as to make the volume exceptionally available among works of its class for popular use, there is here given an important essay "On the Bearings of Egyptian History on the Pentateuch"—a sketch map of the part of the Peninsula of Sinai through which the Israelites must have passed, and several illustrations explaining the Construction of the Tabernacle, &c. As the notes and maps embody the results of the most recent researches, they alone give this Commentary a freshness and value not possessed by any other similar work now before the public.

PREFACE.

IT is about seven years since the Speaker of the House of Commons, the Right Hon. J. Evelyn Denison, conceived the idea of the present Commentary, and suggested its execution.

It appeared to him that in the midst of much controversy about the Bible, in which the laity could not help feeling a lively interest, even where they took no more active part, there was a want of some Commentary upon the Sacred Books, in which the latest information might be made accessible to men of ordinary culture. It seemed desirable that every educated man should have access to some work which might enable him to understand what the original Scriptures really say and mean, and in which he might find an explanation of any difficulties which his own mind might suggest, as well as of any new objections raised against a particular book or passage. Whilst the Word of God is one, and does not change, it must touch, at new points, the changing phases of physical, philological, and historical knowledge, and so the Comments that suit one generation are felt by another to be obsolete.

The Speaker, after mentioning this project to several prelates and theologians, consulted the Archbishop of York upon it. Although the difficulties of such an undertaking were very great, it seemed right to the Archbishop to make the attempt to meet a want which all confessed to exist; and accordingly he undertook to form a company of divines, who, by a judicious distribution of the labour amongst them, might expound, each the portion of Scripture for which his studies might best have fitted him.

The difficulties were indeed many. First came that of

treating a great and almost boundless subject upon a limited scale. Let any one examine the most complete Commentaries now in existence, and he will find that twenty or thirty ordinary volumes are not thought too many for the exhaustive treatment of the Scripture text. But every volume added makes a work less accessible to those for whom it is intended; and it was thought that eight or ten volumes ought to suffice for text and notes, if this Commentary was to be used by laymen as well as by professed divines. Omission and compression are at all times difficult; notes should be in proportion to the reader's needs, whereas they are more likely to represent the writer's predilections. The most important points should be most prominent; but the writer is tempted to lay most stress on what has cost him most labour.

Another difficulty lay in the necessity of treating subjects that require a good deal of research, historical and philological, but which could not be expected to interest those who have had no special preparation for such studies. In order to meet this, it was resolved that subjects involving deep learning and fuller illustration should be remitted to separate essays at the end of each Chapter, Book or division; where they can be found by those who desired them.

The general plan has been this. A Committee was formed to select the Editor and the Writers of the various sections. The Rev. F. C. Cook, Canon of Exeter, and Preacher of Lincoln's Inn, was chosen Editor. The work has been divided into Eight Sections, of which the present volume contains the Pentateuch. Each book has been assigned to some writer who has paid attention to the subject of it. The Editor thought it desirable to have a small Committee of reference, in cases of dispute; and the Archbishop of York with the Regius Professors of Divinity of Oxford and Cambridge agreed to act in this capacity. But in practice it has rarely been found necessary to resort to them.

The Committee were called upon, in the first place, to consider the important question, which has since received a much fuller discussion, whether any alterations should be made in the authorized English Version. It was decided to reprint that Version, without alteration, from the edition of 1611, with the marginal references and renderings; but to supply in the notes amended translations[1] of all passages proved to be incorrect. It was thought that in this way might be reconciled the claims of accuracy and truth with that devout reverence, which has made the present text of the English Bible so dear to all Christians that speak the English tongue. When the Prayer Book was revised, the earlier Psalter of Coverdale and Cranmer was left standing there, because those who had become accustomed to its use would not willingly attune their devotions to another, even though a more careful, Version: the older Psalter still holds its place, and none seem to desire its removal. Since then, knowledge of the Bible has been much diffused, and there seems little doubt that the same affection, which in the middle of the seventeenth century clung to the Psalter and preserved it, has extended itself by this time to the Authorized Version of 1611. Be that as it may, those who undertook the present work desired that the layman should be able to understand better the Bible which he uses in Church and at home; and for this purpose that Bible itself gives the best foundation, altered only where alteration is required to cure an error, or to make the text better understood.

This volume is sent forth in no spirit of confidence, but with a deep sense of its imperfections. Those who wish to condemn will readily extract matter on which to work. But those who receive it willing to find aid in it, and ready to admit that it is no easy matter to expound, completely, fully and popularly, that Book which has been the battle-field of all sects and parties, which has been interpreted by all the ages, each according to its measure of light, will do justice to the spirit that has guided the writers. Such will find in it something that may help them better to appreciate the Sacred Text.

[1] These emendations are printed throughout in a distinctive type, darker than the rest of the note.

"As for the commendation," says Coverdale, "of God's holy Scripture, I would fain magnify it as it is worthy, but I am far insufficient thereto, and therefore I thought it better for me to hold my tongue than with few words to praise or commend it." Our English Bible has come down to us, won for us by much devoted labour, by persecution, by exile, even by blood of martyrdom. It has still much work to do, and when we consider the peoples to whom we have given our language, and the vast tracts over which English-speaking peoples rule, we feel how impossible it is for us to measure the extent of that work. We humbly desire to further it in some small measure, by removing a stumblingblock here, and by shedding light upon some dark places there. Such human efforts are needed, but the use of them passes, whilst the Word of God of which they treat will endure to the end. Yet it is permitted to offer them with an aspiration after the same result that attends the Word of God itself; and that result is, in the words of inspiration, "that ye might believe that Jesus is the Christ, the Son of God; and that believing ye might have life through His name." (John xx. 31.)

More than seven years have elapsed since this Commentary was first projected. It will, doubtless, be admitted that this period is not longer than might be reasonably demanded for the preparation of any considerable portion of such a work: but it is due to all concerned with this volume to state that but for unforeseen circumstances it would have been published much earlier. We have to deplore the premature death of no less than three contributors, two of whom had undertaken the commentary on Exodus and Numbers. All the writers in this volume had, in consequence of this and of other circumstances, a much larger amount of work imposed upon them than they were prepared for, long after the commencement of the undertaking. For one book they had to write the entire commentary; for another to re-write, with a special view to condensation, notes which had been prepared with great ability and learning by Mr Thrupp. This statement is made simply to account for the delay in the publication. The other parts of the work are now far advanced, and two volumes, including the historical and poetical books, will probably be printed within twelve months.

CONTENTS.

INTRODUCTION. BY F. C. COOK, M.A., CANON OF EXETER.

	PAGE		PAGE
§ 1. Division of the Book	237	sula of Sinai shown by the author	244
§ 2. Mosaic authorship	239	§ 5. Argument from the account of the	
§ 3. Miracles in Egypt	241	Tabernacle	247
§ 4. Personal knowledge of the Penin-		§ 6. Chronology	248

COMMENTARY AND CRITICAL NOTES, CHAP. i.—xix.
BY CANON COOK. pp. 253—329.

On Manna. Chap. xvi. 320

COMMENTARY AND CRITICAL NOTES, CHAP. xx.—xl.
BY SAMUEL CLARK, M.A., VICAR OF BREDWARDINE. pp. 330—434.

On the Ten Commandments. Chap. xx. 1—17 335
§ 1. The Name. § 2. What was written on the stones? § 3. The Division into Ten. § 4. The Two Tables. § 5. The Commandments as A TESTIMONY. § 6. Breadth of their meaning.
On the Sabbath Day. Chap. xx. 8 . . 339
§ 1. The Sabbath according to the Law; § 2. according to Tradition. § 3. Its connection with the Creation. § 4. Its relation to Sunday. § 5. Its connection with the deliverance from Egypt. § 6. Its meaning.
On the Colours of the Tabernacle. Chap. xxv. 4 366
On the Mercy Seat. Chap. xxv. 17 . . 368
On the Construction of the Tabernacle. Chap. xxvi. 374
§ 1. The Mishkan, its Tent and its Covering. § 2. Common view of the arrangement of the parts. § 3. Mr Fergusson's theory. § 4. The place of the tabernacle cloth. § 5. Symmetry of the proposed arrangement. § 6. The Court.
On the Urim and the Thummim. Chap. xxviii. 30 390
§ 1. Their Names. § 2. They were previously known and distinct from the Breastplate. § 3. Their purpose and history. § 4. Their origin. § 5. Theories.
On the Groves. Ch. xxxiv. 13 . . . 416
On the Sanctuary as a whole. Chap. xl. 432
§ 1. The Altar and the Tabernacle. § 2. Names of the Tabernacle. § 3. Order of the Sacred things. § 4. The Ark and its belongings. § 5. Allegorical explanations. § 6. Originality of the Tabernacle.

ON THE ROUTE OF THE ISRAELITES FROM RAMESES TO SINAI. By CANON COOK. Chap. xvi. xvii. xix. 435

TWO ESSAYS. BY CANON COOK.

I. ON THE BEARINGS OF EGYPTIAN HISTORY UPON THE PENTATEUCH . 443
II. ON EGYPTIAN WORDS IN THE PENTATEUCH 476

N. B. As this volume is designed to meet a special and temporary demand, it has not been thought necessary to alter the folios. They remain as they were in the Commentary of which it is a part.

EXODUS.

INTRODUCTION.

	PAGE		PAGE
Divisions of the Book, § 1	. 237	Sinai shown by the author, § 4	. 244
Mosaic Authorship, § 2	. 239	Argument from the account of the	
Miracles in Egypt, § 3	. 241	Tabernacle, § 5	. 247
Personal knowledge of the Peninsula of		Chronology, § 6	. 248

§ 1. THE Book of Exodus consists of two distinct portions. The former (cc. i—xix) gives a detailed account of the circumstances under which the deliverance of the Israelites was accomplished. The second (cc. xx—xl) describes the giving of the law, and the institutions which completed the organization of the people as "a kingdom of priests, and an holy nation," c. xix. 6.

These two portions are unlike in style and structure, as might be expected from the difference of their subject-matter: but their mutual bearings and interdependence are evident, and leave no doubt as to the substantial unity of the book. The historical portion owes all its significance and interest to the promulgation of God's will in the law. The institutions of the law could not, humanly speaking, have been established or permanently maintained but for the deliverance which the historical portion records.

The name Exodus, *i.e.* "the going forth," applies rather to the former portion than to the whole book. It was very naturally assigned to it by the Alexandrian Jews, by whom the most ancient translation was written. Like their forefathers they were exiles in Egypt, and looked forward to their departure from that land as the first condition of the accomplishment of their hopes. The Hebrews of Palestine simply designated the book by its first words Elleh Shemoth, *i.e.* "these are the names," regarding it not as a separate work, but as a section of the Pentateuch.

The narrative, indeed, is so closely connected with that of Genesis as to shew not only that it was written by the same author, but that it formed part of one general plan. Still it is a distinct section; the first events which it relates are separated from the last chapter in Genesis by a considerable interval, and it presents the people of Israel under totally different circumstances. Its termination is marked with equal distinctness, winding up with the completion of the tabernacle.

The book is divided into many smaller sections; each of which has the marks which throughout the Pentateuch indicate a subdivision. They are of different lengths, and were probably written on separate parchments or papyri, the longest not exceeding the dimensions of contemporary documents in Egypt[1]. They

---

[1] A single page of Egyptian papyrus contains very frequently as much subject-matter as is found in any section of the Pentateuch. Thus, for instance, the 17th chapter of the Ritual in a papyrus, of which a facsimile has been published by M. de Rougé, occupies one page of 49 lines: each line is equivalent to three lines of Hebrew, as may be proved by transcription of the two languages in Egyptian and Phœnician

were apparently so arranged for the convenience of public reading. This is a point of importance, accounting to a great extent for apparent breaks in the narrative, and for repetitions, which have been attributed to the carelessness of the compiler, who is supposed to have brought separate and unconnected fragments into a semblance of order.

The first seven verses are introductory to the whole book. In accordance with the almost invariable custom of the writer, we find a brief recapitulation of preceding events, and a statement of the actual condition of affairs. The names of the Patriarchs and the number of distinct families at the time of the immigration into Egypt are stated in six verses: a single paragraph then records the rapid and continuous increase of the Israelites after the death of Joseph and his contemporaries.

The narrative begins with the 8th verse, c. i. The subdivision which includes the first two chapters relates very briefly the events which prepared the way for the Exodus: the accession of a new king, followed by a change of policy and measures of extreme cruelty towards the Israelites; and the birth and early history of Moses, destined to be their deliverer. The second division, from c. iii. 1 to vi. 1, opens after an interval of some forty years. From this point the narrative is full and circumstantial.

letters. The longest section in the Pentateuch scarcely exceeds 150 lines in Van der Hooght's edition. Several papyri of the 18th dynast, are of considerable length. Thus, the papyrus called Anastasi I., in the British Museum, contains 28 pages, each page of 9 lines, equal to three lines of ancient Hebrew characters. This exceeds the length of any one division of the Pentateuch. The papyrus in question is undoubtedly of the age in which the generality of modern critics hold the Exodus to have occurred. The assertion that Moses probably used parchment rests on the fact that it was commonly employed at an early time, and more especially, as it would seem, for sacred compositions. Thus, in an inscription of Thotmes III., either contemporary with Moses, or much older, we read that an account of his campaigns was written on parchment, and hung up in the temple of Ammon. See Brugsch, 'Dictionnaire Hieroglyphique,' p. 208. A far more ancient instance of the use of parchment in sacred writings is given by M. Chabas and Mr Goodwin in the 'Egyptische Zeitschrift' for Nov. 1865 and June 1867.

It describes the call of Moses; the **revelation of God's will and purpose; the return of Moses to Egypt, and his first application to Pharaoh, of which the immediate result was a treatment of the Israelites, which materially advanced the work, on the one hand preparing them for departure from their homes, and on the other attaching them more closely to their native officers by the bonds of** common suffering.

c. vi. 2—27 forms a distinct portion. Moses is instructed to explain the bearings of the Divine name (of which the meaning had been previously intimated, see iii. 14) upon the relations of God to the people. He then receives a renewal of his mission to the Israelites and to Pharaoh, Aaron being formally appointed as his coadjutor: the genealogy of both is then introduced, marking their position as leaders of the people.

This portion stands in its right place. It is necessary to the full understanding of the following, and is closely connected with the preceding, section; but it stands apart from both, it begins with a solemn declaration and ends with a distinct announcement.

c. vi. 28 to the end of c. xi. In this division the narrative makes a fresh start. It begins, as usual in a new section, with a brief statement to remind the reader of the relative position of Moses and Aaron and of the work appointed to them. Then follows in unbroken order the history of nine plagues, in three groups, each increasing in severity. At the close of this division the tenth and most terrible plague is denounced, and the failure of the other nine, in turning Pharaoh, is declared in the often recurring form, "the Lord hardened Pharaoh's heart, so that he would not let the children of Israel go out of his land" (xi. 10).

The next section, xii. 1—42, gives an account of the institution of the Passover, and the departure of the Israelites from Rameses: the close of the section is distinctly marked by the chronological statement. This important section is closely connected with the preceding narrative, but it was evidently intended to be read as a separate lesson, and may possibly have been rewritten or revised for that purpose towards the close of the life of Moses. From xii. 43 to xiii. 16 special injunctions touching the Passover are recorded; they may have been inserted here as the most appropriate place when the separate documents were put together.

The narrative begins again c. xiii. 17. After a brief introduction, stating the general direction of the journey, comes the history of the march towards the Red Sea, the passage across it, and the destruction of Pharaoh's host. This subdivision extends to the end of the xivth chapter.

The Song of Moses[1] is inserted here: it does not interrupt the narrative, which proceeds without a break until, in the third month after the Exodus, Israel came to the Wilderness of Sinai and camped before the Mount: c. xix. In this chapter and the next the promulgation of the law is described. The remainder of the book gives the directions received by Moses touching the Tabernacle and its appurtenances, and the institution of the Aaronic priesthood. It then relates the sin of the Israelites, and their forgiveness at the intercession of Moses: and concludes with an account of the making of the tabernacle, and a description of the symbolical manifestation of God's Presence with His people.

This general view of the structure of the book meets several questions which have been raised as to its integrity. That the several portions are distinct, forming complete subdivisions, may not only be admitted without misgiving, but this fact is best accounted for by the circumstances under which the work must have been composed, if Moses was its author. It was the form in which a man engaged in such an undertaking would naturally present at intervals an account of each series of transactions, and in which such an account would be best adapted for the instruction of the people. The combination of all the documents into a complete treatise might naturally occupy the period of comparative leisure towards the end of his life, and, while it involved some few additions and explanations, would be effected without any substantial change.

§ 2. The principal arguments for the Mosaic authorship have been stated in the Introduction to the Pentateuch: but many objections apply especially to this book; and some of the most convincing evidences are supplied by its contents. This might be expected. On the one hand the question of authorship is inseparably bound up with that of the miraculous character of many transactions which are recorded. Critics who reject miracles as simply incredible under any circumstances, have ever felt that the narrative before us could scarcely have been written by a man in the position and with the character of Moses, and could not certainly have been addressed to eye-witnesses or contemporaries of the events which it relates. It is a foregone conclusion with writers of this school. On the other hand a narrative of the personal history of Moses, of the circumstances under which the greatest work in the world's annals was accomplished, if it be authentic and veracious, must abound in internal coincidences and evidences sufficient to convince any inquirer not shut up to the opposite theory. In fact no critic of any weight, either in France or Germany, who admits the supernatural character of the transactions, rejects the authorship of Moses.

[1] The length and structure of this great hymn have been represented as proofs of a later origin. A comparison with Egyptian poems of the age of Moses, or much earlier, gives these results. The hymn to the Nile, in the 'Pap. Sallier,' II., was written at the time when the Exodus is fixed by most Egyptologers. It is more than twice the length of the Song of Moses. The structure is elaborate and the cadences resemble the Hebrew. It begins thus, "Hail, O Nile, thou comest forth over this land, thou comest in peace, giving life to Egypt, O hidden God." Again, a poem inscribed on the walls of a temple built by Thotmes III. is about twice as long as the Song. Its style is artificial and the cadences even more strongly marked. It is some two centuries older than the hymn to the Nile. We have also exact information as to the time which it would take to write out such a hymn. An Egyptian scribe writing, with the greatest care, with rubrical headings, &c. would have done it in half a day: a few hours would suffice in the simpler characters used by the Semitic races. This comparison leaves no doubt as to the possibility of such a hymn being written by Moses, who was trained in the schools of Egypt; and no one denies his genius.

One argument is drawn from the representation of the personal character and qualifications of Moses. In its most important features it is such as could never have been produced by a writer collecting the traditional reminiscences or legends of a later age: not such even as might have been drawn by a younger contemporary. To posterity, to Israelites of his own time, Moses was simply the greatest of men: but it is evident that the writer of this book was unconscious of the personal greatness of the chief actor. He was indeed thoroughly aware of the greatness of his mission, and consequently of the greatness of the position, which was recognized at last by the Egyptians, see ch. xi. 3; but as to his personal qualifications, the points which strike him most forcibly are the deficiencies of natural gifts and powers, and the defects of character, which he is scrupulously careful to record, together with the rebukes and penalties which they brought upon him, and the obstacles which they opposed to his work. His first attempt to deliver the people is described as a complete failure; an act which, however it might be palliated by the provocation, is evidently felt by the writer to have been wrongful, punished by a long exile extending over the best years of his life. When he receives the Divine call he is full of hesitation, and even when his unbelief is overcome by miracles he still recoils from the work, dwelling with almost irreverent pertinacity upon his personal disqualifications, ch. iii. 10—13. On his homeward journey he is severely chastised for neglect of a religious duty, ch. iv. 24—26. When his first application to Pharaoh brings increased suffering to his people, he bursts out into passionate remonstrance. The courage and magnanimity of his conduct to Pharaoh are never the subject of direct commendation. No act is attributed to his personal character. Even in the passage over the Red Sea and in the journeying through the wilderness, nothing recalls his individuality. Each step is under Divine guidance: no intimation is given of wisdom, skill, or foresight in the direction of the march. The first conflict with assailants is conducted by Joshua. The only important act in the organization of the nation, which is not distinctly assigned to a Divine revelation, is attributed to the wisdom, not of Moses, but of his kinsman Jethro. The few notices of personal character in the other books accord with this portraiture: the repugnance to all self-assertion in the controversy with Aaron and Miriam; the hasty and impetuous temper which, manifested on one important occasion, brought upon him the lasting displeasure of God, and ultimately transferred the execution of his great work to the hands of his successor Joshua.

Such a representation is perfectly intelligible, as proceeding from Moses himself: but what in him was humility would have been obtuseness in an annalist: such as never is found in the accounts of other great men, nor in the notices of Moses in later books[1]. What other men have seen in Moses is the chief agent in the greatest work ever intrusted to man, an agent whose peculiar and unparalleled qualifications are admitted alike by those who accept and by those who deny the Divine interposition[2]: what the writer himself sees in Moses is a man whose only qualification is an involuntary and reluctant surrender to the will of God. The only rational account of the matter is, that we have Moses' own history of himself and of his work.

The next argument is even less open to objection, since it rests not on subjective impressions, but on external facts. The book of Exodus could not have been written by any man who had not passed many years in Egypt, and who had not also a thorough knowledge, such as could only be acquired by personal observation, of the Sinaitic Peninsula. But it is improbable that any Israelite between the time of Moses and Jeremiah could have possessed either of these qualifications; it is not credible, or even possible, that any should have

[1] See especially the three last verses of Deuteronomy, added either by a younger contemporary of Moses, or at a later time by a reviser.

[2] The two writers by whom the greatness of the character and work of Moses are perhaps most thoroughly appreciated and developed with greatest power are Ewald, 'G. I.' vol. II., and Salvador, 'Histoire des Institutions de Moïse et du peuple Hebréu.'

combined both. Israelites may have been, and probably were, brought into Egypt as captives by the Pharaohs in their not unfrequent invasions of Syria, but in that position they were not likely to become acquainted with the institutions of Egypt: still less likely is it that any should have returned to their native land. Again, no Israelite, for centuries after the occupation of Palestine, is likely to have penetrated into the Sinaitic Peninsula, occupied as it was by hostile tribes, while it is certain that none could have had any motive, or opportunity, for traversing the route from Egypt to Horeb, with which no one doubts the writer of the Pentateuch was personally familiar. The notices are too numerous, and interwoven with the narrative too intimately, to be accounted for as mere traditional reminiscences, or even as derived from scanty records in the possession of the Israelites at a later period. We have no probable alternative but to admit that the narrative in its substance came from Moses, or from a contemporary. Either alternative might suffice so far as regards the accuracy and trustworthiness of the narrative, and consequently the miraculous character of the transactions which it records; but we can have little hesitation as to our choice between these alternatives, when we consider that none of the contemporaries of Moses had equal opportunities of observation, and that none were likely to have received the education and training[1] which would have enabled them to record the events.

§ 3. A weighty argument is drawn from the accounts of the miracles, by which Moses was expressly bidden to attest his mission, and by which he was enabled to accomplish the deliverance of his people. One characteristic, common to all scriptural miracles, but in none more conspicuous than in those recorded in the book of Exodus, is their strongly marked, and indeed unmistakeable, local colouring. They are such as no later writer living in Palestine could have invented for Egypt. From beginning to end no miracle is recorded which does not strike the mind by its peculiar suitableness to the place, time, and circumstances under which it was wrought. The plagues are each and all Egyptian; and the modes by which the people's wants are supplied in the Sinaitic Peninsula recall to our minds the natural conditions of such a journey in such a country. We find nature everywhere, but nature in its master's hand.

Detailed accounts of the plagues and of the natural phenomena in Egypt with which they were severally connected will be found in the notes; but it may be well to bring together a few points which shew the effects produced both by the miracles, and by the apparent failure of all but the last in determining the immediate deliverance of the people. The direct and indirect effects were in fact equally necessary, humanly speaking, for the accomplishment of that event.

In the first place it must be remarked, that the delay occasioned by Pharaoh's repeated refusals to listen to the commands afforded ample time for preparation. Two full months elapsed between the first and second interview of Moses with the king; see notes on v. 7 and vii. 17. During that time the people, uprooted for the first time from the district in which they had been settled for centuries, were dispersed throughout Egypt, subjected to severe suffering, and impelled to exertions of a kind differing altogether from their ordinary habits, whether as herdsmen or bondsmen. This was the first and a most important step in their training for a migratory life in the desert.

Towards the end of June, at the beginning of the rise of the annual inundation, the first series of plagues began. The Nile was stricken. Egypt was visited in the centre both of its physical existence, and of its national superstitions. Pharaoh did not give way, and no intimation as yet was made to the people that permission for their departure would be extorted; but the intervention of their Lord was now certain, the people, on their return wearied and exhausted from the search for stubble, had an interval of suspense. Three

---

[1] On the education of Moses see note at the end of ch. ii.

Vol. I.

months appear to have intervened between this and the next plague. There must have been a movement among all the families of Israel; as they recapitulated their wrongs and hardships, the sufferings of their officers, and their own position of hopeless antagonism to their oppressors, it is impossible that they should not have looked about them, calculated their numbers and resources, and meditated upon the measures which, under the guidance of a leader of ability and experience, might enable them to effect their escape from Egypt. Five months might not be too much, but were certainly sufficient, to bring the people so far into a state of preparation for departure.

The plague of frogs followed. It will be shewn in the notes that it coincided in time with the greatest extension of the inundation in September. Pharaoh then gave the first indication of yielding; the permission extorted from him, though soon recalled, was not therefore ineffectual. On the one hand native worship in one of its oldest and strangest forms was attacked[1]; on the other hand Moses was not likely to lose any time in transmitting instructions to the people. The first steps may have been then taken towards an orderly marshalling of the people.

The third plague differed from the preceding in one important point. There was no previous warning[2]. It must have followed soon after that of frogs, early in October. It marks the close of the first series of inflictions, none of them causing great suffering, but quite sufficient on the one hand to make the Egyptians conscious of danger, and to confirm in the Israelites a hope of no remote deliverance.

The second series of plagues was far more severe; it began with swarms of poisonous insects, probably immediately after the subsidence of the inundation. It is a season of great importance to Egypt; from that season to the following June the land is uncovered; cultivation begins; a great festival (called Chabsta) marks the period for ploughing. At that time there was the first separation between Goshen and the rest of Egypt. The impression upon Pharaoh was far deeper than before, and then, in November, the people once more received instructions for departure; there was occasion for a rehearsal, so to speak, of the measures requisite for the proper organization of the tribes and families of Israel.

The cattle plague broke out in December, or at the latest in January. It was thoroughly Egyptian both in season[3] and in character. The exemption of the Israelites was probably attributed by Pharaoh to natural causes; but the care then bestowed by the Israelites upon their cattle, the separation from all sources of contagion, must have materially advanced their preparation for departure.

Then came the plagues of boils, severe but ineffectual, serving however to make the Egyptians understand that continuance in opposition would be visited on their persons. With this plague the second series ended. It appears to have lasted about three months.

The hailstorms followed, just when they now occur in Egypt, from the middle of February to the early weeks of March. The time was now drawing near. The Egyptians for the first time shew that they are seriously impressed. There was a division among them, many feared the word of the Lord, and took the precautions, which, also for the first time, Moses then indicated. This plague

---

[1] This has been shewn by Lepsius; see note in loc. There is a curious vignette in Mariette's work, 'Fouilles d'Abydos,' Part II. Vol. I. p. 30, No. CVIII. It represents Seti, the father of Rameses II., offering two vases of wine to a frog inshrined in a small chapel, with the legend, 'The Sovereign Lady of both worlds.' Mariette's work has been withdrawn from circulation.

[2] This peculiarity, which applies to the third plague in each group, was pointed out by Maimonides.

[3] In an Egyptian calendar, written in the reign of Rameses II., and lately translated by M. Chabas, the 22nd of Tobi, corresponding to January, has this notice, "Il y a des ouragans dans le ciel ce jour-là, la contagion annuelle s'y mêle abondamment." 'Pap. Sallier,' IV. pp. 14, 15. This applies even more specially to the following plague.

THE BOOK OF EXODUS.

drew from Pharaoh the first confession of guilt; and now for the third time, between one and two months before the Exodus, the Israelites receive permission to depart, when formal instructions for preparation were of course given by Moses. The people now felt also for the first time that they might look for support or sympathy among the very servants of Pharaoh.

The plague of locusts, when the leaves were green, towards the middle of March, was preceded by another warning, the last but one. The conquest over the spirit of Egypt was now complete. All but the king gave way; see x. 7. Though not so common in Egypt as in adjoining countries, the plague occurs there at intervals, and is peculiarly dreaded. Pharaoh once more gives permission to depart; once more the people are put in an attitude of expectation.

The ninth plague concludes the third series. Like the third and the sixth, each closing a series, it was preceded by no warning. It was peculiarly Egyptian. Though causing comparatively but little suffering, it was felt most deeply as a menace and precursor of destruction. It took place most probably a very few days before the last and crowning plague, a plague distinct in character from all others, the first and the only one which brought death home to the Egyptians, and accomplished the deliverance of Israel.

We have thus throughout the characteristics of local colouring, of adaptation to the circumstances of the Israelites, and of repeated announcements followed by repeated postponements, which enabled and indeed compelled the Israelites to complete that organization of their nation, without which their departure might have been, as it has been often represented, a mere disorderly flight.

There are some who fear to compromise the miraculous character of events by admitting any operation of natural causes to a share of them. Yet the inspired writer does not fail to record that it was by the east wind that the Lord brought the locusts (Exod. x. 12) and sent back the sea (xiv. 21), and by the mighty strong west wind (x. 19) took back the plague that he had sent. Nor is the miracle at all lessened, because the winds of heaven were made God's messengers and instruments in the doing it. In order to guard against misapprehensions from such readers, let us state with some precision the view we take of the miracles in Egypt. They were supernatural in their greatness, in their concentration upon one period, in their coming and going according to the phases of the conflict between the tyrant and the captive race, in their measured gradation from weak to strong, as each weaker wonder failed to break the stubborn heart. And king and people so regarded them; they were accustomed perhaps to frogs and lice and locusts; but to such plagues, so intense, so threatened, and accomplished, and withdrawn, as it were so disciplined to a will, they were not accustomed; and they rightly saw them as miraculous and divinely sent. This being clearly laid down it is most desirable to notice that the phenomena that are put to this use are such as mark the country where this great history is laid. No Jewish writer, who had lived in Palestine alone, could have imagined a narrative so Egyptian in its marks. Much evidence will appear in the course of the Commentary tending this way; that the history was written by some one well conversant with Egypt; and we shall look in vain for any one, other than Moses himself, who possessed this qualification for writing under divine guidance the history of the emancipation of the Israelites.

A point of subordinate, but in the present state of biblical criticism of practical importance, is suggested by the view here presented. The two facts that between all the miracles there is an intimate connection, and that each and all are shewn to be nearly allied to analogous phenomena recorded in ancient and modern accounts of Egypt, leave no place for interpolations of any considerable extent, none certainly for the introduction of any single visitation. In the commentaries of some scholars, to whose learning and ability the student of Holy Scripture is deeply indebted, some of the accounts are attributed to the Elohistic, others to the Jehovistic writer. The arguments based upon language are considered in their proper places[1]; those resting on merely subjective impressions, varying to a most remarkable extent in writers of the same school, are too vague and indefinite to be capable of disproof, as they are incapable of demonstration, and will probably leave no trace in biblical literature; but the characteristics here pointed out are common to all the plagues, and they are conclusive. In fact no one plague could be omitted without dislocating the whole narrative, and breaking the order distinctly intimated, though nowhere formally stated, by the writer. The results were brought about by the combined operation of all the plagues; they could never have been produced by a merely fortuitous concurrence of natural events, and the narrative which records them, remarkable as it is for artlessness and simplicity, is certainly not one which could have been concocted from documents of different ages, constructed on different principles, and full of internal discrepancies and contradictions. It is the production of one mind, written by one man, and by one who had alone witnessed all the events which it records, who alone was at that time likely to possess the knowledge or ability required to write the account.

§ 4. The portion of the book, which follows the account of the departure from Egypt, has characteristics marked with equal distinctness, and bearing with no less force upon the question of authorship. It has never occurred to any traveller who has traversed the route from Suez to Sinai, or from Sinai to Palestine, to doubt that the chapters of Exodus which touch that ground were written by one to whom the localities were known from personal observation. It is not merely that the length of each division of the journey, the numerous halting places are distinctly marked; for although such notices could not possibly have been invented, or procured at any later period by a dweller in Palestine, the fact might be accounted for by the supposition, gratuitously made, but hard to be rebutted, that some ancient records of the journey had been preserved by written or oral tradition; but the chapters which belong either to the early sojourn of Moses, or to the wanderings of the Israelites, are pervaded by a peculiar tone, a local colouring, an atmosphere so to speak of the desert, which has made itself felt by all those who have explored the country, to whatever school of religious thought they may have belonged. And this fact is the more striking when we bear in mind that, although the great general features of the Peninsula, the grouping of its arid heights and the direction of its innumerable wadys are permanent, still changes of vast, and scarcely calculable importance in matters which personally affect the traveller and modify his impressions, have taken place since the time of Moses; changes to which, for obvious reasons, it is necessary to call special attention.

At present one great difficulty felt by all travellers is the insufficiency of the resources of the Peninsula to support such a host as that which is described in

---

[1] The attention of scholars is specially called to the following list of words. They are either found only in this book and marked ἁ. λ., or in the Pentateuch and later Psalms taken directly from it, marked P. All marked E. have Egyptian equivalents, and are derived from roots either common to Egyptian and Hebrew, or found only in Egyptian.
Ch. i. 7, were fruitful, E., increased exceedingly, P. E. v. 11, taskmasters, ἁ. λ., E. Pithon and Rameses, E. v. 16, the stools, ἁ. λ. ii. 3, ark, P. E. bulrushes, E. pitch, E. flags, E. river's brink, E. v. 5, wash, E. v. 10, drew out, P. E. v. 16, troughs, P., once in Cant. iii. a bush, P. E. v. 12, stubble and straw, E. vii. 3, magicians, sorcerers, E. v. 22, enchantments, ἁ. λ., E. v. 27, frogs, P. E. viii. 13, lice, ἁ. λ., i.e. here and Ps. cv. 31, E. v. 17, swarms of flies, ἁ. λ., E. ix. 8, ashes, ἁ. λ., E. furnace, P. E. v. 9, a boil, E. breaking forth, E., blains, ἁ. λ., E. x. 31, flax, E. bolled, ἁ. λ., E. v. 32, spelt, E. not grown up, ἁ. λ., E. xii. 4, number, ἁ. λ. v. 6, two evenings, ἁ. λ. v. 7, lintel, ἁ. λ. vv. 8, 11, passover, E. v. 15, leaven, ἁ. λ., E. xiii. 16, frontlets, P. xiv. horse, E. xv. 1, hath triumphed gloriously, E. v. 2, I will prepare him an habitation? ἁ. λ. v. 7, heaped up, ἁ. λ. v. 8, congealed: in this sense, ἁ. λ., E. v. 20, timbrel, E. xvi. 3, flesh-pots, E. v. 15, manna, E. v. 16, omer, P. E. v. 33, pot, P. E.
It is to be observed that these words occur indiscriminately in the so-called Jehovistic and Elohistic passages. The list may be extended.

the narrative; a difficulty not wholly removed by the acceptance of the accounts of providential interventions, which appear to have been not permanent, but limited to special occasions. But facts can be adduced which confirm, and indeed go far beyond, the conjectures of travellers, who have pointed out that the supply of water, and the general fertility of the district, must have been very different before the process of denudation, which has been going on for ages, and is now in active progress, had commenced. We have now proofs from inscriptions coeval with the pyramids, both in Egypt and in the Peninsula, that under the Pharaohs of the third to the eighteenth dynasty, ages before Moses, and up to his time, the whole district was occupied by a population, whose resources and numbers must have been considerable, since they were able to resist the forces of the Egyptians, who sent large armies in repeated, but unsuccessful, attempts to subjugate the Peninsula. Their principal object however was effected, since they established permanent settlements at Sarbet el Khadim, and at Mughara, to work the copper-mines[1]. These settlements were under the command of officers of high rank, and are proved by monuments and inscriptions to have been of an extent, which implies the existence of considerable resources in the immediate neighbourhood. It is well known that the early Egyptian kings were careful to provide for the security and sustentation of the caravans and bodies of troops, by which the communications with settlements under such circumstances were carried on: and every spot where the modern traveller still finds water on the route was doubtless then the object of special attention[2]. The vegetation which even now protects the wells of Moses, from which the dwellers at Suez obtain a supply of brackish water, must have been then far more luxuriant; and the seventy palm-trees, which Moses found at Elim, doubtless sheltered fountains, from which streams far more copious than those which now water the wady, flowed over the adjoining district. See note, ch. xv. 27. Where the superficial water was insufficient, it was customary in that early age to dig wells of whatever depth might be needed[3]; and every tree, now recklessly destroyed, was the object of special care, and even superstitious reverence. During the long ages which have elapsed since the Egyptian power passed away, the Peninsula has never been subjected to an Empire which has had a sufficient motive, or sufficient wisdom and resources, to arrest the process of deterioration: and every horde of Arabs, who have since been virtually its masters, bent only on supplying their own limited wants, cut down without remorse the shrubs and trees, on which the water supply, and consequently the general fertility of the district, mainly depend. The aspect of the whole country when

---

[1] Brugsch differs from all Egyptian scholars in a point of secondary importance, holding that the mines here were worked chiefly for the sake of turquoises (see Leps. 'Zeits.' 1866, p. 74, n. 3); but his treatise, entitled 'Wanderung nach den Türkis Minen,' gives a good account of the inscriptions. They are very numerous in the Wady Mughara; the earliest dates from Snefru, of the third dynasty; 8 Pharaohs of the three following dynasties have left many inscriptions, a considerable number belong to Amenemha III., dating from his 2nd to his 42nd year; and one of great importance describes an expedition under Ramaaka, i.e. Hatasu, the widow of Thotmes II. These inscriptions repeatedly speak of victories over native tribes: the very earliest inscription in existence, earlier than any in Egypt, records a victory achieved by Snefru over the Mentu, the general designation of the mountaineers of the Peninsula. The mines were lately worked by an Englishman, Major Macdonald, of whom Brugsch gives a full and very interesting account.

[2] In one of the most ancient papyri we find a notice of a place called She-Snefru, that is, the reservoir of Snefru, named after Snefru, the earliest Pharaoh who is known to have established an Egyptian settlement in the Peninsula of Sinai. M. Chabas remarks " She-Snefru était sans doute l'une des stations qu'il avait disposées au desert d'Arabie, sur la route de la Mer-Rouge." 'Les Papyrus Hiératiques de Berlin,' p. 39.

[3] See, for instance, the inscription relating to the gold mines near Dakkeh, explained by Mr B rch. It mentions a well 180 feet deep, and another still deeper, on a route where water could not be procured, dug by the order of Seti I. and Rameses II. The works of preceding Pharaohs, especially under the 12th dynasty, were equally remarkable for forethought.

it was first visited by Christian pilgrims who have left us accounts of their journeyings, must have differed greatly from that which it presented to the Israelites, when, under the guidance of Moses, they found pasturage for their flocks and herds. But far greater is the difference at present. Under Turkish misrule the Arabs carry on the work of desolation with no effective interference; no plantations are made, no wells are dug, the fountains are unprotected; and as though natural causes were insufficient, the annual tribute demanded by the Pasha consists in charcoal, each contribution laying waste a whole district. The devastation which began ages ago has in fact continued without cessation, and if it goes on at the present rate of increase, will ere long reduce the whole district to a state of utter aridity and barrenness. When Niebuhr visited the country, at the beginning of the last century, large supplies of vegetable produce were exported regularly to Egypt, shewing that the original fertility was not even then exhausted. Those supplies have ceased; and the only wonder is that so much remains to satisfy a careful inquirer of the possibility of the events recorded in Exodus.

Taking summarily the points in this part of the argument, we find the following coincidences between the narrative and accounts of travellers. Absence of water where no sources now exist, abundance of water where fountains are still found, and indications of a far more copious supply in former ages; tracts, occupying the same time in the journey, in which food would not be found; and in some districts a natural production similar to manna, most abundant in rainy seasons (such as several notices shew the season of the Exodus to have been), but not sufficient for nourishment, nor fit for large consumption, without such modifications in character and quantity as are attributed in the narrative to a divine intervention. We have the presence of Nomad hordes, and an attack made by them precisely in the district, and under the circumstances when their presence and attack might be expected. We have a route which the late exploration of the Peninsula, of which an account will be found at the end of the notes on this book, will shew to have been probably determined by conditions agreeing with incidental notices in the history; and when we come to the chapters in which the central event in the history of Israel, the delivery of God's law, is recorded, we find localities and scenery which travellers concur in declaring to be such as fully correspond to the exigencies of the narrative, and which in some accounts (remarkable at once for scientific accuracy and graphic power) are described in terms which shew they correspond, so far as mere outward accessories can correspond, to the grandeur of the manifestation.

Throughout this portion it will be observed that the notices on which the argument mainly rests are interwoven with the narrative and inseparable from it. It is easy to assert that any single notice may have been retained by oral tradition, or preserved for ages in scanty documents, such as were formerly supposed to be alone likely or possible to have been produced in the time of Moses; and such is the course generally adopted when any coincidence is pointed out too clear to be explained away; a course which, were it applied to any secular history, would be condemned as disingenuous or uncritical, making it in fact impossible to establish the authenticity of any ancient writing. But in addition to the positive arguments thus adduced, a negative argument at least equally conclusive demands attention. No history or composition in existence, which is known to have been written long after the events which it describes, is without internal indications which conclusively prove its later origin; contemporary documents may be interwoven with it, and great pains taken in ages of literary refinement and artifice to disguise its character, but even when anachronisms and errors of detail are avoided, which is seldom, if ever, effectually done, the genuine touch of antiquity, the χνοῦς ἀρχαιοπρεπής, is invariably and inevitably absent. Whether we look at the general tone of this narrative, the style equally remarkable for artlessness and power, or at the innumerable points of contact with external facts capable of exact determination, we are impressed by the weight of this internal evidence, supported as it has been shewn to be by the unbroken and unvarying tradition of the nation to whom the narrative was addressed, and by whom it was held too sacred not to be preserved from wilful mutilation or interpolation.

§ 5. An argument which many readers may feel to be even less open to objection is drawn from the account of the Tabernacle. In the notes on this part of the work the following facts are demonstrated.

In form, structure, and materials, the tabernacle belongs altogether to the wilderness. The wood used in the structure is found there in abundance. It appears not to have been used by the Israelites in Palestine; when the temple was rebuilt it was replaced by cedar. (See note on xxv. 10.) The whole was a tent, not a fixed structure, such as would naturally have been set up, and in point of fact was very soon set up, in Palestine; where wooden doors and probably a surrounding wall existed under the Judges of Israel. The skins and other native materials belong equally to the locality. One material which entered largely into the construction, the skin of the Tachash, was in all probability derived from the Red Sea; with the exception of one reference in Ezekiel xvi. 10, no traces of its use are found at a later period, or in any other district. The metals, bronze, silver and gold, were those which the Israelites knew, and doubtless brought with them from Egypt; nor is it probable that they possessed equal resources for a long time after their settlement in Palestine. The names of many of the materials and implements which they used, and the furniture and accessories of the tabernacle, the dress and ornaments of the priests, are shewn to have been Egyptian. It is also certain that the arts required for the construction of the tabernacle, and for all its accessories, were precisely those for which the Egyptians had been remarkable for ages; such as artizans who had lived under the influence of Egyptian civilization would naturally have learned. The rich embroidery of the hangings, the carving of the cherubic forms, the ornamentation of the capitals, the naturalistic character of the embellishments, were all things with which the Israelites had been familiar in Egypt; but which for ages after their settlement in Palestine, in which the traces of Canaanitish culture had been destroyed as savouring of idolatry, and where the people were carefully separated from the contagious influences of other nations on a par with Egypt, must have died out, if not from their remembrance, yet from all practical application. There are exceedingly few indications of any such arts among the Israelites during the period from the occupation of Palestine to the accession of Solomon; the ephod of Micah, and the teraphim in David's bed, being scarcely noticeable exceptions. It is improbable that any portion of the decorations of the tabernacle could have been produced, even had the rich materials been forthcoming; and it is to be noted as a fact of very special importance in this inquiry, that when Solomon, in the height of his prosperity, with the resources of a vast empire at his disposal, erected the temple which was to replace the tabernacle, he was compelled to seek the aid of foreigners, and to bring Tyrian artists to accomplish the work which Bezaleel had produced, when his native genius, trained in the school of Egypt, was developed by the Spirit of God.

The peculiar way in which the history of the erection of the Tabernacle is recorded suggests another argument, which has not hitherto received due attention. Two separate accounts are given. In the first Moses relates the instructions which he received, in the second he describes the accomplishment of the work. Nothing would be less in accordance with the natural order of a history written at a later period than this double account. It has been represented as an argument for a double authorship, as though two sets of documents had been carelessly or superstitiously adopted by a compiler. It is however fully accounted for by the obvious hypothesis, adopted throughout this part of the commentary, that each part of the narrative was written at the time, and on the occasion, to which it immediately refers. When Moses received these instructions he wrote a full account of them for the information of the people. This was on all accounts probable and necessary: among other obvious reasons it was necessary in order that the people might learn exactly what amount of materials and what amount of work would be required of them. When again he had executed his task, it was equally proper, and doubtless also in accordance with the habits of a people keen and jealous in the management of their affairs, and at no time free from tendencies to suspicion, that he should give a formal account of every detail in its execution[1]: a proof, to such as might call for proof, that all their precious offerings had been devoted to the purpose; and what was of far more importance, that the divine instructions had been completely and literally obeyed. It is a curious fact, that in the two accounts the order of the narrative is systematically reversed. In the instructions given to Moses and recorded for the information of the people, the most important objects stand first. The ark, the mercy-seat, the cherubs, the table of shew-bread, the golden candlestick, the whole series of symbolic forms by which the national mind was framed to comprehend the character of the divine revelation, are presented at once to the worshippers. Then come instructions for the tabernacle, its equipments and accessories; and when all else is completed, the dress and ornaments of the officiating priests. But when the work of Bezaleel and his assistants is described, the structure of the tabernacle comes first, as it naturally would do when the work was commenced, the place was first prepared, and then the ark and all the sacred vessels, according to all that the Lord commanded Moses.

§ 6. The Chronology of Exodus involves two questions, the duration of the sojourn of the Israelites in Egypt, and the date of their departure. So far as regards the direct statements in the Hebrew text, the answers to both questions are positive and unambiguous. Exodus xii. 40 gives 430 years for the sojourn, Genesis xv. 13 gives 400 years for the whole, or the greater portion of the same period. Again, the 1st book of Kings, c. vi. 1, fixes the Exodus at 480 years before the building of the Temple in the fourth year of Solomon's reign. This would settle the date within a few years, about 1490 B.C. See note on c. xii. 40.

Both statements are taken in their obvious and literal meaning by critics of different schools in Germany and England. The latter statement presents some difficulties. On the one hand it involves a longer period than appears to be consistent with the genealogies, especially with the genealogy of David. This objection loses its weight if the omission of several links in the genealogies be admitted as probable: in some cases of the highest importance it is certain, *e.g.* in that of Ezra and of our Lord. On the other hand it involves a shorter period than is deduced from notices in the book of Judges; an objection met by the probable hypothesis that many transactions in that book may have taken place at the same period in different parts of Palestine. Egyptian chronology is too uncertain to determine the question, as is shewn in the Appendix. The date appears on the whole to be reconcileable with the facts of history, and to rest on higher authority than any other which has been proposed.

The grounds on which the duration of the sojourn is determined are considered in the note at the end of c. xii. It is especially important with reference to the number of the Israelites, which amounted to 600,000 males at the time of the Exodus. Such an increase of a patriarchal family within 215 years, the

---

[1] It is also to be observed that a very large portion of the papyri, written at nearly the same period in Egypt, consist of minute accounts of the work done, and the sums expended under the superintendence of the writers. In an inscription on the statue of an Egyptian architect, Bokenchons, who lived under Sethos I. and Rameses II., special note is made of his accuracy in accounting for expensive buildings.

period deduced by the Rabbins from genealogical computations, and adopted by many theologians, presents great, if not insuperable difficulties, which are removed if we accept the statement of Moses in the sense attached to it by most commentators. It needs no elaborate calculation to shew that in a period extending over more than four centuries, a family which counted 70 males with their households, probably amounting to many hundreds, occupying the most fertile district in Egypt, under circumstances most favourable to rapid and continuous increase specially recorded in this book, should become a mighty nation, such as they are represented in the narrative, and as critics admit they must have been to effect the conquest of Canaan and to retain their national integrity in the midst of a hostile population.

The commentary on this book was originally assigned to the Rev. R. C. Pascoe, Principal of the Theological college at Exeter. His death in June 1868 was preceded by a long illness, which prevented him from preparing notes which could be used for this work. In consequence of this very serious loss the first 19 chapters, together with the Introduction and appendices on Egyptian subjects, were undertaken by the Editor, and the remainder by the Rev. S. Clarke.

THE SECOND BOOK OF MOSES,

CALLED

EXODUS.

CHAPTER I.

1 *The children of Israel, after Joseph's death, do multiply.* 8 *The more they are oppressed by a new king, the more they multiply.* 15 *The godliness of the midwives, in saving the men children alive.* 22 *Pharaoh commandeth the male children to be cast into the river.*

NOW these *are* the names of the ^achildren of Israel, which came into Egypt; every man and his household came with Jacob.

2 Reuben, Simeon, Levi, and Judah,
3 Issachar, Zebulun, and Benjamin,
4 Dan, and Naphtali, Gad, and Asher.

5 And all the souls that came out of the †loins of Jacob were *b*seventy souls: for Joseph was in Egypt already.

6 And Joseph died, and all his brethren, and all that generation.

7 ¶ *c*And the children of Israel were fruitful, and increased abundantly, and multiplied, and waxed exceeding mighty; and the land was filled with them.

8 Now there arose up a new king over Egypt, which knew not Joseph.

a Gen. 46. 8. chap. 6. 14.

† Heb. *thigh.*
b Gen. 46. 27. Deut. 10. 22.

c Acts 7. 17.

CHAP. I. 1. *Now*] Literally "and." This conjunction is omitted by the LXX. but it is commonly used at the beginning of the historical books after Genesis, and here indicates a close connection with the preceding narrative. This chapter in fact contains a fulfilment of the predictions recorded in Gen. xlvi. 3, that God would make of Jacob "a great nation" in Egypt: and in Gen. xv. 13, that the people of that land would "afflict them four hundred years."

every man and his household] It may be inferred from various notices that the total number of dependents was considerable, a point of importance in its bearings upon the history of the Exodus. See Gen. xiii. 6, xiv. 14, from which we learn that Abram had 318 trained servants born in his house. The daughters are not mentioned, nor are the names of their husbands given; it is more likely that they were married to their near relations, or to dependents than to heathens; and in that case they with their families would form part of the patriarchal households.

5. *seventy*] This number includes Joseph, his two sons, and by a mode of reckoning not uncommon, Jacob himself; see Gen. xlv. 11, xlvi. 27; Deut. x. 22. The object of the writer in this introductory statement is to give a complete list of the heads of separate families at the time of their settlement in Egypt. See note on Num. xxvi. 5. The LXX. place the last clause, "Joseph was in Egypt," at the beginning of the verse, an arrangement which seems preferable, and is defended by Egli; see 'Zeitschrift für wissenschaftliche Theologie,' 1870, p. 326.

7. The narrative begins, properly speaking, with this paragraph. This is clearly shewn by the construction of the Hebrew, which does not connect the word "was fruitful" with the preceding verse. Egypt was always celebrated for its fruitfulness, and in no province does the population increase so rapidly as in that occupied by the Israelites. See notes on Gen. xlvii 6. At present it has more flocks and herds than any province in Egypt, and more fishermen, though many villages are deserted; it is calculated that another million might be sustained in it. (See Robinson, Vol. I. p. 55.) Until the accession of the new king, the relations between the Egyptians and the Israelites were undoubtedly friendly. The expressions used in this verse imply the lapse of a considerable period after the death of Joseph.

the land was filled with them] *i.e.* the district allotted to them, extending probably from the Eastern branch of the Nile to the borders of the desert. It appears from other passages (see iii. 22) that they did not occupy this land exclusively, but were intermingled with the native Egyptians.

8. The expressions in this verse are peculiar, and emphatic. "A new king" is a phrase not found elsewhere. It is understood by most commentators to imply that he did not succeed his predecessor in natural order of descent and inheritance. He "arose up over Egypt," occupying the land, as it would seem, on different terms from the king whose place he took, either by usurpation or conquest. The fact that he knew not Joseph implies a complete separation from the tradi-

9 And he said unto his people, Behold, the people of the children of Israel *are* more and mightier than we:

10 Come on, let us deal wisely with them; lest they multiply, and it come to pass, that, when there falleth out any war, they join also unto our enemies, and fight against us, and *so* get them up out of the land.

11 Therefore they did set over them taskmasters to afflict them with their burdens. And they built for Pharaoh treasure cities, Pithom and Raamses.

12 †But the more they afflicted them, the more they multiplied and grew. And they were grieved because of the children of Israel.

† Heb. *And as they afflicted them, so they multiplied, &c*

---

tions of Lower Egypt. At present the generality of Egyptian scholars identify this Pharaoh with Rameses II. The question is discussed in the Appendix, where it is shewn that all the conditions of the narrative are fulfilled in the person of Amosis I., the head of the 18th Dynasty. He was the descendant of the old Theban sovereigns, but his family resided for many years at Eileithyia, (El Kab, south of Thebes,) and was tributary to the Dynasty of the Shepherds, the Hyksos of Manetho, then ruling in the North of Egypt. Amosis married an Ethiopian princess, Nephertari, and in the third year of his reign captured Avaris, or Zoan, the capital of the Hyksos, and completed the expulsion of that race.

9. *unto his people*] This expression has a peculiar fitness as addressed by the representative of the old Egyptian kings to his countrymen immediately after their emancipation from the dominion of aliens.

more and mightier] This may have been literally true, if, as was natural, the king compared the Israelites of Goshen with the population of the North Eastern district after the expulsion of the shepherds. The first impression made upon his mind would be the insecurity of a frontier occupied by a foreign race.

10. *any war*] The king had good cause to anticipate war. The North Eastern frontier was infested by the neighbouring tribes, the Shasous of Egyptian monuments, and war was waged with Egypt by the confederated nations of Western Asia under the reigns of his successors. These incursions were repulsed with extreme difficulty. In language, features, costume, and partly also in habits, the Israelites probably resembled those enemies of Egypt, and were regarded by the Egyptians as their natural allies.

out of the land] This is important as the first indication of a motive which determined the policy of the Pharaohs in dealing with the Israelites: they apprehended the loss of revenue and power, which would result from the withdrawal of a peaceful and industrious race.

11. *taskmasters*] The writer uses the proper Egyptian designation for these officers, viz. Chiefs of tributes (see Note at the end of the Chapter). They were men of rank,

superintendents of the public works (LXX. ἐπιστάται τῶν ἔργων), such as are often represented on Egyptian monuments, and carefully distinguished from the subordinate overseers. The Israelites were employed in forced labours, probably in detachments, each under an Egyptian "taskmaster:" but they were not reduced to slavery, properly speaking, nor treated as captives of war. They continued to occupy and cultivate their own district, and they retained possession of their houses, flocks, herds, and other property until they emigrated from Egypt. Amosis had special need of such labourers. He restored the temples and other buildings destroyed by the shepherds, employing foreigners, either as subjects or mercenaries, for the transport of materials. This is proved by an inscription, dated in his 22nd year, see 'Æg. Zeitschrift,' November 1867.

treasure cities] The Hebrew word corresponds very closely both in form and meaning with "magazines," depots of ammunition and provisions: the same word is used 1 Kings ix. 19; 2 Chron. viii. 4 and xxxii. 28. Captives were employed in great numbers for building and enlarging such depots under the Egyptian kings of the 18th and 19th dynasties.

Pithom and Raamses] Both cities were situate on the canal, which had been dug or enlarged long before, under Osertasen, of the 12th dynasty. The names of both cities are found on Egyptian monuments: the former is known to have existed under the 18th dynasty: both were in existence in the beginning of the reign of Rameses II., by whom they were fortified and enlarged. The name "Pithom" means "House or temple of Tum," the Sun God of Heliopolis. The name of Raamses, or Rameses is generally assumed to have been derived from Rameses II., the Sesostris of the Greeks, but it was previously known as the name of the district. See Genesis xlvii. 11, and Appendix. The LXX. add "On, which is Heliopolis:" a reading commended by Egli, l.c. but On existed long before that age.

12. *they were grieved*] The Hebrew expresses a mixture of loathing and alarm. For "they" the LXX. read "the Egyptians."

13 And the Egyptians made the children of Israel to serve with rigour:

14 And they made their lives bitter with hard bondage, in morter, and in brick, and in all manner of service in the field: all their service, wherein they made them serve, *was* with rigour.

15 ¶ And the king of Egypt spake to the Hebrew midwives, of which the name of the one *was* Shiphrah, and the name of the other Puah:

16 And he said, When ye do the office of a midwife to the Hebrew women, and see *them* upon the stools; if it *be* a son, then ye shall kill him: but if it *be* a daughter, then she shall live.

17 But the midwives feared God, and did not as the king of Egypt commanded them, but saved the men children alive.

18 And the king of Egypt called for the midwives, and said unto them, Why have ye done this thing, and have saved the men children alive?

19 And the midwives said unto Pharaoh, Because the Hebrew women *are* not as the Egyptian women; for they *are* lively, and are delivered ere the midwives come in unto them.

20 Therefore God dealt well with the midwives: and the people multiplied, and waxed very mighty.

21 And it came to pass, because

---

13. *with rigour*] The word is repeated v. 14; but does not occur elsewhere.

14. *morter and brick*] The use of brick, at all times common in Egypt, was especially so under the 18th dynasty. An exact representation of the whole process of brickmaking is given in a small temple at Thebes, erected by Thotmes III., the fourth in descent from Amosis. The persons there employed are captives, taken by that Pharaoh in his Asiatic campaigns. They are under a general superintendent, or "taskmaster," and are driven to work by overseers, armed with heavy lashes, who cry out "work without fainting." A report from a scribe at a later date, under the 19th dynasty, shews the rigour with which the labour, generally assigned to captives or to slaves, was enforced. See Brugsch, 'Histoire d'Egypte,' p. 174, and Chabas, 'Mélanges égyptologiques,' II. p. 121. Immense masses of brick are found at Belbeis, the modern capital of Sharkiya, *i.e.* Goshen, and in the adjoining district. There is no intimation that the Israelites were employed in building pyramids, which were erected by kings of Lower Egypt, with few exceptions, long before this period.

all manner of service in the field] Not merely agricultural labours to which the Israelites were accustomed, but probably the digging of canals and processes of irrigation which are peculiarly onerous and unhealthy, and on both accounts likely to have been imposed upon the Israelites. The word used throughout by the Targumist (see Note at the end of the Chapter) is interesting; the designation Fellahs, forced workers, is derived from it.

15. *Hebrew midwives*] Or "midwives of the Hebrew women." This measure at once attested the inefficacy of the former measures, and was the direct cause of the event which issued in the deliverance of Israel, viz. the exposure of Moses. Two midwives only are named. They may have been the two chief midwives, but it is not improbable that they were the only ones in Goshen. At present all travellers state that midwives are very seldom employed by Egyptian women, never by the common people, and by women of station only in cases of peculiar difficulty. Two might therefore have sufficed for the Israelites. It may perhaps be inferred from this statement that the object of the king was not to destroy all the male infants, a course obviously contrary to his interests, but those of the chiefs, whose wives were alone likely to call in the midwives. Both midwives bear names which are supposed by some to be of Hebrew origin, signifying personal beauty. They were however probably Egyptians, as would seem to be implied in the expressions in *vv.* 17 and 19: an Egyptian etymology of each name may be suggested: Puah from a word which means "child bearing," and Shiphrah, "prolific." See Note below.

16. *upon the stools*] The Hebrew means literally "two stones." The meaning is doubtful, as the expression does not occur elsewhere, but it probably denotes a peculiar seat, such as is represented on monuments of the 18th dynasty, and according to Lane is still used by Egyptian midwives. So it is understood by our translators, by the Targumist, and the Arabian translator, Saadia, a resident in Egypt and a man of great learning, whose authority on such a point has considerable weight. Gesenius, however, takes it to mean the stone

the midwives feared God, that he made them houses.

22 And Pharaoh charged all his people, saying, Every son that is born ye shall cast into the river, and every daughter ye shall save alive.

---

laver in which the newborn infant was washed, and he quotes a striking passage from Thevenot, stating that the Persian kings order the newborn male infants of their relatives to be killed in the stone basin in which they are washed. See Note below.

21. made them houses] *i.e.* they married Hebrews and became mothers in Israel. The expression is proverbial. See 2 Sam. vii. 11, 27.

22. Pharaoh thus made the people agents in the crime. The command, though general, may have been understood to apply to the leading families by whom the midwives had been employed, or to be in force until the population was reduced, so as to remove all apprehensions for the security of the frontier. The extreme cruelty of the measure does not involve improbability. Hatred of strangers was always a characteristic of the Egyptians, see Gen. xliii. 32, and was likely to be stronger than ever after the expulsion of an alien race. Before Psammetichus chance visitors were taken as slaves or put to death, see Diod. Sic. I. 67. Under the 12th dynasty, in the time of Abraham, the wives and children of foreigners were the property of the king (Chabas, 'Pap. Hier.' p. 14). The Spartans were even more guilty; they systematically murdered their Helots when their increased numbers excited alarm; on one occasion they slew 2,000, who had offered themselves as volunteers at the invitation of the state. Plut. 'Lyc.' § 28, and Thuc. IV. 80.

NOTES on vv. 11, 14, 15, 16.

11. The Hebrew is שרי־מסים, Sare massim. Sar means chief, or prince in Semitic languages, in Assyrian it has lately been shewn to be the proper phonetic for king; and it is common in Hebrew: but it is an Egyptian title, found on very ancient monuments, and it is the title specially given to the head of the works in the representation of brick making under Thotmosis III., to which allusion is more than once made in these notes. The word *massim* has no satisfactory etymology in Hebrew. Gesenius supposes it to be a contracted form, Michaelis suggests an improbable derivation from Arabic. The Egyptian *mas*, gives a good and natural sense, it means to bring tribute, *mas-mas* to divide or number in portions. See the Egyptian forms in the Appendix.

14. The Chaldee paraphrase of Onkelos is always meant when reference is made to the Targum in these notes; it is of great antiquity and authority. The Targum attributed to Jonathan is of late date and comparatively of little value. Saadia, who is often mentioned, was a Jew of great learning, a native of Fayoum in Egypt, towards the end of the 9th century. His Arabic translation is printed in Walton's Polyglott.

15. The Hebrew derivations of the two names are not satisfactory. Simonis makes פועה equivalent to יפועה, splendid, from יפע, a form for which there is no authority. Gesenius suggests the Arabic فوهة, countenance; this would require a change of letters, and is quite improbable. The Egyptian gives a simple and very satisfactory etymology; pā = פע with one determinative or explanatory sign means "splenduit" (coinciding in sense with Simonis' conjecture); with another and equally common sign it means "parturio, accoucher d'un enfant." Brugsch, 'D. H.' p. 463. Shiphra is rendered "child of Ra," by Bunsen, 'Bibelwerk.' This is inadmissible; "sefi" means "child," but the transcription of both syllables is inexact. The sense "prolific" given above is derived from one of the commonest words in Egyptian, Cheper; the transcription is very close, the ch and sh being regularly interchanged; the meaning "esse, fieri, nasci, procreare," with the additional notion of rapid increase and reproduction.

16. Professor Selwyn proposes an emendation which would entirely remove the difficulty; instead of אבנים he would read בנים, when ye look upon the children. The insertion of *them* in the Authorised Version is unauthorised. The only objection to the conjecture is that the change from so plain and intelligible a reading can scarcely be accounted for. Hirsch, chief Rabbi at Frankfort, whose commentary has appeared since these notes were printed, observes very truly that there is no authority for the interpretation most commonly received of אבנים, but the explanation which he suggests is forced and improbable. Like many other words it belongs to the age of Moses.

CHAPTER II.

1 *Moses is born,* 3 *and in an ark cast into the flags.* 5 *He is found, and brought up by Pharaoh's daughter.* 11 *He slayeth an Egyptian.* 13 *He reproveth an Hebrew.* 15 *He fleeth into Midian.* 21 *He marrieth Zipporah.* 22 *Gershom is born.* 23 *God respecteth the Israelites' cry.*

a pp. 6.
20.
Ni ub. 26.
59.

AND there went *a* man of the house of Levi, and took *to wife* a daughter of Levi.

2 And the woman conceived, and bare a son: and when she saw him that he *was a* goodly *child*, she *b*hid him three months.

b ;ts 7.
23
Pр). 11.
23.

3 And when she could not longer hide him, she took for him an ark of bulrushes, and daubed it with slime and with pitch, and put the child therein; and she laid *it* in the flags by the river's brink.

4 And his sister stood afar off, to wit what would be done to him.

5 ¶ And the daughter of Pharaoh came down to wash *herself* at the river; and her maidens walked along by the river side; and when she saw the ark among the flags, she sent her maid to fetch it.

CHAP. II. 1. *a man of the house of Levi*] The marriage of Amram and Jochebed took place so long after the immigration of the Israelites, that it seems scarcely possible that Amram should have been the grandson, and Jochebed the daughter of Levi. The idiom which calls even a remote descendant the son or daughter is common to the Old and New Testament, and this passage may be understood to mean that both parents of Moses were of the house and lineage of Levi. Thus the Vulgate renders the verse, "and he took a wife of his own family;" the LXX. has "a wife of the daughters of Levi." See the Introduction, and note on ch. vi. 20, and on Num. xxvi. 59.

2. *bare a son*] Not her firstborn, Aaron and Miriam were older than Moses. In this part of the book the object of the writer is simply to narrate the events which led to the Exodus, and, as usual, he omits to notice what had no direct bearing upon that object. It is remarkable that any critic conversant with the style of the sacred writers should have drawn from this omission an argument against the accuracy or veracity of the writer.

a goodly child] This is the only allusion in the Pentateuch to the personal appearance of Moses, upon which much stress is laid by later tradition. Jochebed probably did not call in a midwife, see note on ch. i. 15, and she was of course cautious not to shew herself to Egyptians. The hiding of the child is spoken of as an act of faith, see Heb. xi. 23. It was done in the belief that God would watch over the child.

3. *an ark of bulrushes*] Both of these words, like the other words used in this description, are either common to Hebrew and Egyptian, or simply Egyptian. See Appendix. The ark was made of the papyrus which was commonly used by the Egyptians for light and swift boats. The species is no longer found in the Nile below Nubia. It is a strong rush, like the bamboo, about the thickness of a finger, not quite cylindrical but three cornered, and attains the height of 10 to 15 feet. It is represented with great accuracy on the most ancient monuments of Egypt; as for instance in the tomb of Tei under the 6th dynasty. An article on the Papyrus is given in the 'Mémoires de l'Académie des Inscriptions et de belles lettres,' Tom. XIX. p. 156.

slime and pitch] The "slime" is understood by most critics to be asphalt, but it more probably means the mud, of which bricks were usually made in Egypt, and which in this case was used to bind the stalks of the papyrus into a compact mass, and perhaps also to make the surface smooth for the infant. The pitch or bitumen (commonly used in Egypt, bearing the name here used by Moses,) made the small vessel watertight.

in the flags] This is another species of the papyrus, called tufi, or sufi, (an exact equivalent of the Hebrew *suph*,) which was less in size and height than the rush of which the ark was made. The brink, or "lip of the river" is an expression common to Egyptian and Hebrew; both words correspond in meaning and form. That which is rendered "river," viz. *Jor* is not used in the Bible of any river out of Egypt, except once by Daniel xii. 5, on which see Ges. 'Thes.' s.v.

5. *the daughter of Pharaoh*] The traditions which give a name to this princess are probably of late origin, and merely conjectural. Josephus calls her Thermuthis; which means "the great Mother," a designation of Neith, the special deity of Lower Egypt: but it does not occur as the name of a princess. The names Pharia, Merris, and Bithia are also found in Syncellus, Eusebius, and the Rabbins. It is of more importance to observe that the Egyptian princesses held a very high and almost independent position under the ancient and middle empire, with a separate household and numerous officials. This was espe-

6 And when she had opened *it*, she saw the child: and, behold, the babe wept. And she had compassion on him, and said, This *is one* of the Hebrews' children.

7 Then said his sister to Pharaoh's daughter, Shall I go and call to thee a nurse of the Hebrew women, that she may nurse the child for thee?

8 And Pharaoh's daughter said to her, Go. And the maid went and called the child's mother.

9 And Pharaoh's daughter said unto her, Take this child away, and nurse it for me, and I will give *thee* thy wages. And the woman took the child, and nursed it.

10 And the child grew, and she brought him unto Pharaoh's daughter, and he became her son. And she called his name [1] Moses: and she said, Because I drew him out of the water.

[1] That is, *Drawn out.*

11 ¶ And it came to pass in those days, when Moses was grown, that he went out unto his brethren, and looked on their burdens: and he spied an Egyptian smiting an Hebrew, one of his brethren.

---

cially the case with the daughters of the first sovereigns of the 18th dynasty: in two instances at least they were regents or co-regents with their brothers. See Appendix.

The facts recorded in these verses, according to M. Quatremère, suggest a satisfactory answer as to the residence of the daughter of Pharaoh and of the family of Moses. It must have been in the immediate neighbourhood of the Nile, and therefore not at On or Heliopolis, at which place Amosis put down human sacrifices offered by the Hyksos: it must have been near a branch of the Nile not infested by crocodiles, or the child would not have been exposed, nor would the princess have bathed there: therefore not near Memphis, where Amosis rebuilt the great temple of Ptah, from which the city took its name. At present crocodiles are not often found below the cataracts, but under the ancient empire they were common as far north as Memphis. These and other indications agreeing with the traditions recorded by Eutychius (see Milman, 'H. J.' I. p. 68), point to Zoan, Tanis, now San, the ancient Avaris, on the Tanitic branch of the river, near the sea, where crocodiles are never found, which was probably the western boundary of the district occupied by the Israelites. Avaris was captured by Amosis, and was the most suitable place for the head quarters of the Pharaohs, both as commanding the districts liable to incursions from Asiatic nomads, and as well adapted for carrying out the measures for crushing the Israelites. The field of Zoan was always associated by the Hebrews with the marvels which preceded the Exodus. See Ps. lxxviii. 43.

to wash] It is not customary at present for women of rank to bathe in the river, but it was a common practice in ancient Egypt. See Wilkinson, III. p. 389. The Nile was worshipped as an emanation (ἀπορροή) of Osiris, and a peculiar power of imparting life and fertility was attributed to its waters, a superstition still prevalent in the country. (Thus Strabo, Ælian, and Pliny and Seetzen, Vol. III. p. 204. See also Brugsch, 'Zeitschrift,' 1868, p. 123, and 'D. H.' p. 413.) The habits of the princess, as well as her character, must have been well known to the mother of Moses, and probably decided her choice of the place.

6. *she had compassion on him*] A touch of natural feeling, to which throughout the narrative Moses is careful to direct attention. The Egyptians indeed regarded such tenderness as a condition of acceptance on the day of reckoning. In the presence of the Lord of truth each spirit had to answer, "I have not afflicted any man, I have not made any man weep, I have not withheld milk from the mouths of sucklings." See the 'Funeral Ritual,' c. 125. There was special ground for mentioning the feeling, since it led the princess to save and adopt the child in spite of her father's commands.

10. *he became her son*] This expression leaves no doubt as to the formal adoption of Moses. He became a member of the royal household, where the training and education which he received would be such as St Stephen describes, he became learned in all the wisdom of the Egyptians. (See Note at the end of the Chapter.) Such a preparation was indeed humanly speaking all but indispensable to the efficient accomplishment of his work as the predestined leader and instructor of his countrymen. Moses probably passed the early years of his life in Lower Egypt, where the princess resided; all the notices in this book indicate a thorough familiarity with that portion of the country, and scarcely refer to the Thebaid. There may however be substantial grounds for the tradition in Josephus that he was engaged in a campaign against the Ethiopians, thus shewing himself, as St Stephen says, "mighty in word and deed." See 'Excursus' I. at the end of the volume.

Moses] The Egyptian origin of this word is generally admitted. The name itself is not uncommon in ancient documents. The exact

12 And he looked this way and that way, and when he saw that *there was* no man, he slew the Egyptian, and hid him in the sand.

13 And when he went out the second day, behold, two men of the Hebrews strove together: and he said to him that did the wrong, Wherefore smitest thou thy fellow?

14 And he said, Who made thee ¹a prince and a judge over us? intendest thou to kill me, as thou killedst the Egyptian? And Moses feared, and said, Surely this thing is known.

15 Now when Pharaoh heard this thing, he sought to slay Moses. But Moses fled from the face of Pharaoh, and dwelt in the land of Midian: and he sat down by a well.

16 Now the ¹priest of Midian had

¹ Heb. *a man, a prince.*

¹ Or, *prince.*

---

meaning is "son," but the verbal root of the word signifies "produce," "draw forth." The whole sentence in Egyptian would exactly correspond to our version. She called his name Moses, *i.e.* "son," or "brought forth," because she brought him forth out of the water. See Appendix.

11. Moses records no incident of his life during the following years. His object, as Ranke observes, was not to write his own biography, but to describe God's dealings with his people. Later tradition would have been full of details. At the end of 40 years, when according to St Stephen, Moses visited his brethren, the princess was probably dead, as Syncellus relates, and the events which follow took place under another Pharaoh.

went out unto his brethren] This shews that the Egyptian princess had not concealed from him the fact of his belonging to the oppressed race, nor is it likely that she had debarred him from intercourse with his foster-mother and her family, whether or not she became aware of the true relationship.

an Egyptian] This man was probably one of the overseers of the workmen, natives under the chief superintendent, who are represented in the well-known picture of brickmakers under Thotmes III. See note on c. i. 13. They were armed with long heavy scourges, made of a tough pliant wood imported from Syria. See Chabas, 'Voyage d'un Égyptien,' pp. 119 and 136. The discipline of the Egyptian services, both military and civil, was maintained by punishments of excessive severity, even in the case of native officers. Hence the proverbial saying, "the child grows up and his bones are broken like the bones of an ass," and again, "the back of a lad is made that he may hearken to him that beats it." (Chabas, l. c. p. 136, and 'Pap. Anast.' v. 8, 6.) The "smiting" must have been unusually cruel to excite the wrath of Moses. The slaying of the Egyptian is not to be justified, or attributed to a divine inspiration, which Moses would not have omitted to mention; but it is to be judged with reference to the provocation, the impetuosity of Moses' natural character, perhaps also to the habits developed by his training at the court of Pharaoh.

See the excellent remarks of St Augustine, 'c. Faust.' XXII. 70. The act involved a complete severance from the Egyptians; but far from expediting, it delayed for many years the deliverance of the Israelites. Forty years of a very different training prepared Moses for the execution of that appointed work.

13. *did the wrong*] Lit. "the wicked one," *i.e.* the aggressor.

thy fellow] **Thy neighbour:** so the word should be rendered: the reproof was that of a legislator who established moral obligations on a recognized principle. Hence in the following verse the offender is represented as feeling that the position claimed by Moses was that of a Judge. The act could only have been known by the Hebrew on whose behalf Moses had committed it.

14. *a prince*] lit. as in the margin, a man, a prince. The Hebrew for Prince is *Sar*, used in i. 11. The word "Sar" implies the power, "judge" the right, of interfering.

15. *Pharaoh heard it*] No Egyptian king would have left such an offence unpunished, even had it been committed by a native of high rank: it is not even necessary to assume the death of the princess (see note on *v.* 2) to rebut the objection that her adopted son found no defender. It is observed however (by Hirsch) that the expression "sought to kill him" implies that the position of Moses, as adopted son of a princess, made it necessary even for a despotic sovereign to take unusual precautions.

the land of Midian] The Midianites occupied an extensive district from the eastern coast of the Red Sea to the borders of Moab. It is not improbable that in the time of Moses they may have had a settlement in the peninsula, at Sherm, where the two harbours, the only safe ones on that coast, offered peculiar advantages to them, engaged as they were from the earliest times in the transport of merchandize. (See Note at the end of the Chapter.)

by a well] **The well.** The well is spoken of as well known, the chief feature of the locality; such was the case whichever site be accepted as the residence of Reuel.

16. *the Priest of Midian*] Not "the prince" as in the margin. The word *Cohen*

seven daughters: and they came and drew *water*, and filled the troughs to water their father's flock.

17 And the shepherds came and drove them away: but Moses stood up and helped them, and watered their flock.

18 And when they came to Reuel their father, he said, How *is it that* ye are come so soon to day?

19 And they said, An Egyptian delivered us out of the hand of the shepherds, and also drew *water* enough for us, and watered the flock.

20 And he said unto his daughters, And where *is* he? why *is* it *that* ye have left the man? call him, that he may eat bread.

21 And Moses was content to dwell with the man: and he gave Moses Zipporah his daughter.

22 And she bare *him* a son, and he called his name ^c Gershom: for he said, ^{c chap 18.} I have been a stranger in a strange land. ^{3.}

---

may have that meaning in some passages, but there is no reason for assuming it in this. Josephus and most of the ancient versions render it "priest." A Jewish tradition, derived probably from the Targum (which styles him Rabba, or Lord), represents Reuel as the prince, or probably as combining, like Melchizedek, the hereditary offices of chieftain and priest of the tribe, the Imam, the word used in the Arabic Version. The name of Reuel, and the detailed notices in c. xviii. (where see notes), prove that he was a priest of the one true God, known to the patriarchs especially under the name El; although the great bulk of the tribe, certainly those who lived farther north and more closely in contact with the Hamites of Canaan, were already plunged in idolatry. The conduct of the shepherds may indicate that his person and office were lightly regarded by the idolatrous tribes in his immediate neighbourhood.

drew water] This act would not be unbecoming or uncommon for the daughters of a priest whether chief of his tribe or not. At present the watering of cattle in that district is a work of maidens, from which even the daughters of sheickhs are not exempt. See Burckhardt, 'Syria,' p. 531. Thus Dr Stanley speaks of flocks climbing the rocks or gathered round the brooks and springs of the valleys under the charge of the black-vested Bedouin women of the present day.

18. *Reuel*] Or as in Num. x. 29, Raguel. The name means "friend of God." It appears to have been not uncommon among Hebrews and Edomites; see Gen. xxxvi. 4, 10; 1 Chron. ix. 8; Tobit vi. 10. Commentators, who identify Reuel with Jethro, a point open to grave objections (see Note at the end of the Chapter), generally accept the conjecture of Josephus, viz. that Reuel was his proper name, and Jether or Jethro, which means "excellency" (corresponding, as Knobel observes, to Imam), was his official designation. Moses naturally used the former name when he first mentioned his father-in-law, on other occasions he might take that by which the Priest was probably best known to the Israelites.

19. *An Egyptian*] Of course they spoke judging from his costume, or language, which must have been Egyptian at that time; a slight coincidence, but such as may be looked for only in a narrative of facts. Had Moses lived long among the Israelites, the Midianitish maidens would not have mistaken him for an Egyptian: a later writer would scarcely have noted the occurrence.

21. *was content to dwell with the man*] This conveys the true sense of the Hebrew. It implies that Moses recognized in Reuel a man in whom he could confide; and in his family a fitting home. So quietly, and yet so impressively, Moses records the entrance upon a long period, extending over forty years of mature life. Moses tells us nothing of what he may have learned from his father-in-law, but he must have found in him a man conversant with the traditions of the family of Abraham; nor is there any improbability in the supposition that, as hereditary priest, Reuel may have had written documents concerning their common ancestors. The use of letters was well known to the Phœnicians, whose trade with the dwellers in that very district is recorded on Egyptian monuments of the 13th dynasty, long anterior to the age of Moses: (see Brugsch, 'Histoire d'E-gypte,' p. 74,) and inscriptions which record the campaigns of Pharaohs of the 18th and 19th dynasties, make express mention of scribes and historians of nations, *e.g.* of the Kheta or Hittites, who were probably not in advance of the Midianites.

22. *Gershom*] According to most Hebrew scholars the name is derived from a word meaning "expulsion." This, however, is scarcely reconcileable with Moses' own account, of which the Egyptian supplies an exact and satisfactory explanation. The first syllable "Ger" is common to Hebrew and Egyptian, and means "sojourner." The second syllable "Shom" answers exactly to the Coptic "Shemmo," which means "a foreign or strange land." For the old Egyptian forms, see Appendix.

Vol. I.

R

EXODUS. II. [v. 23—25.

23 ¶ And it came to pass in process of time, that the king of Egypt died: and the children of Israel sighed by reason of the bondage, and they cried, and their cry came up unto God by reason of the bondage.

24 And God heard their groaning, and God remembered his *d* covenant with Abraham, with Isaac, and with Jacob.

25 And God looked upon the children of Israel, and God † had respect unto *them*.

d Gen. 15. 14. & 46. 4.

† Heb. *knew*.

---

23. *in process of time*] Nearly forty years: some delay intervened between the call of Moses and his departure for Egypt. This verse marks the beginning of another section. We now enter at once upon the history of the Exodus.

their cry came up unto God] This statement, taken in connection with the two following verses, proves that the Israelites retained their faith in the God of their Fathers. The divine name God, Elohim, is chosen because it was that which the Israelites must have used in their cry for help, that under which the covenant had been ratified with the Patriarchs. Dr Stanley would illustrate this by an account of the cries of the Fellahs in Egypt: but the distinction ought to be marked between their execrations, and the prayers which reached God from the Israelites.

24. *remembered*] This means that God was moved by their prayers to give effect to the covenant, of which an essential condition was the faith and contrition involved in the act of supplication. The whole history of Israel is foreshadowed in these words. The accumulation of so called anthropomorphic terms in this passage is remarkable. God heard, remembered, looked upon, and knew them. It evidently indicates the beginning of a crisis marked by a personal intervention of God.

25. *had respect unto them*] lit. and God knew. The LXX. "and was known unto them." This involves only a change of punctuation and may be preferable.

NOTES on vv. 10, 13, 18.

10. The education which would be given to a youth belonging to the royal household, and destined for military or civil service under the Middle Empire, has lately been illustrated by the labours of Goodwin, Chabas, and other Egyptologers, from the select papyri published in 1844 by the Trustees of the British Museum. These documents belong for the most part to the reigns of Rameses II. and his immediate successors, but the literary habits and attainments which they describe are known to have been far more ancient; collections of manuscripts, and scribes holding high offices of state, are frequently mentioned in the monuments of the early dynasties (see M. de Rougé, 'Recherches,' p. 73), and some of the most valuable papyri are productions of the ancient empire. M. Maspero has lately collected the most important facts in the introduction to his work on a portion of a papyrus of the 19th dynasty, entitled 'Hymne au Nil.'

He observes that we know for certain that a literary education was the first condition for admission to the public service; the title of scribe was necessary in order to obtain the lowest appointment in the civil administration or in the army. Hence a real enthusiasm for study is manifested by men of letters, such as Enna and Pentaour, whose compositions, indeed whose autographs are preserved. We have addresses to Thoth, the Hermes of the Greeks, the god of learning, in which the superiority of his work to all works is passionately maintained. "Thy works are better than all works; he who devotes himself to them becomes a noble; all successes achieved in life are due to thee; under thy inspiration a man becomes great, powerful, rich; of him all the world, all generations of men cry out, 'Great is he, great is the work of Thoth.'"

The education so highly valued began at a tender age; the infant, when it was weaned, was sent to school, and there instructed by scribes officially appointed. The discipline was severe, but due care was taken for the child's maintenance: the mother brought his food daily from his home, and in the upper schools rations of bread and salt fish seem to have been supplied regularly by the government: the register of distribution being, as in our colleges, accepted as proofs of the scholars' attendance (see Chabas, 'Voyage d'un Egyptien,' p. 23).

The scholar learned the elements of letters, the rules of orthography and grammar; and as he advanced, the art of expressing his thoughts in simple and perspicuous prose, of which the story of the two brothers in the D'Orbiney papyrus is a fair specimen; or in the epistolary style adapted for official communications, which occupy a large portion of the papyri; or in poetical composition, in which extant examples shew a genuine feeling for art; resembling Hebrew poetry in the carefully balanced parallelisms, and skilful combination of antitheses, though differing from it as markedly in the absence of the essential characteristics of simplicity and grace. It was indeed no slight thing to master the qualifications of a man of letters. The mere art of writing presented difficulties so serious that we find scribes boasting of a thorough knowledge of the mysteries of sacred letters as a rare and wonderful attainment. According to Diodorus special pains were bestowed upon arithmetic and geometry, an assertion borne out by late inquiries, which shew that the system of notation was remarkably clear, and that exact accounts were kept in every large household; a treatise on geometry in the British Museum now engages the attention of scholars, and will probably be published by Mr Birch. The mystic writings, in which ancient truths were imbedded in dark and dreary superstitions, occupied much of the time, not only of the priests, but of all men of learning. Schools of interpretation existed at an age long before Moses, which have left abundant traces in various readings, glosses, and mystic explanations of the so-called Funeral Ritual or Book of the Dead, a work which the literal translation of Mr Birch, remarkable for learning and ingenuity, has made to some extent accessible to English readers. The earliest extant copy of the chapter (the 17th) which gives the deepest insight into the ancient theosophy of Egypt dates from the 11th dynasty, and has even in that form numerous glosses bearing witness to a remote antiquity. In an address to an officer of rank, whose adventures in Syria have been illustrated by Goodwin and Chabas, the scribe whose autograph is before us, says, "Thou art a scribe skilful above thy equals, learned in the sacred writings, chastened in heart, disciplined in tongue; thy words pierce me, one phrase has thrice gone forth, thou hast broken me with terror." In a work just published ('Moses der Hebräer') M. Lauth attempts to identify this personage so remarkable for talents, learning, and bold speculations on religion, with Moses the Hebrew; an identification not likely to approve itself to scholars, but which serves to show the course of thought, and to some extent the state of mental development, in Egypt at a time not far remote from that in which Moses became learned in all the wisdom of the Egyptians, and mighty in word and deed.

13. The question whether the residence of Reuel was on the eastern or western coast of the Ælanitic gulf is not easily settled. The older and more general tradition is in favour of the former. The ruins of the city of Madian, described by Edrisi and Abul-feda and visited by Seetzen, lay on the east of the gulph, five days' journey from Aila, *i. e.* Akaba, and a well was shewn there as that from which Moses watered the flocks of his father-in-law. It would seem scarcely probable that Moses would be secure from pursuit within the peninsula, which was frequented by the Egyptians, who long before that time worked the copper mines and carried on a considerable traffic. Under the 18th and 19th dynasties the power of the Pharaohs appears to have extended over the whole country. It is also to be observed that the Israelites did not come into contact with the Midianites while they were in the peninsula, and that Jethro appears from the notices in ch. xviii. vv. 1, 5, 27 to have come from some considerable distance to meet Moses. It is objected that the distance of this city would have been too great for Moses to have pastured the flocks of Jethro in the peninsula, but we find instances of much longer distances in the history of Jacob and Laban, and at present in the accounts of the Bedouins. Thus Bochart, D'Anville, Mannert, and Quatremère, 'Mémoires de l'Académie des Inscriptions et Belles Lettres.'

On the other hand it is argued by Laborde, Knobel and others, that Reuel must have lived on the west of the gulf. The communications between the two coasts have always been frequent; at present sheep and goats are brought in great numbers from Mukna, near Madian, for sale in the peninsula, and at different times settlements have been made by Bedouins from the Hedjaz. The Towara, who are now the most powerful and most civilized tribe in the Peninsula, and have been recognized as the true descendants of the Midianites by most geographers (see Ritter, 'Sinai,' p. 936), occupied Madian in the time of Mahomet, who received one of their chieftains with the exclamation, "welcome to the brothers-in-law of Moses, welcome to the race of Shoeib, *i. e.* Jethro." If Reuel lived in this district, it must have been at Sherm, about 10 miles from Ras Mohammed, the southern headland. There are proofs that peculiar sanctity attached to that place at a very early period. The notices of ancient geographers (Strabo, Artemidorus, and Agatharchides, ap. Diodor. Sic., collected and examined by Knobel) speak of extensive palm-groves, abundant sources of fresh water, and a sanctuary under the charge of an hereditary priest and priestess, who held their office for life. The same writers testify to the existence of an ancient tribe in that neighbourhood bearing a name (Μαριανεῖς) nearly resembling and probably identical with Midianites; the d and r are frequently interchanged, or confounded owing to the similarity of ד and ר, a similarity even more striking in the most archaic forms of the two letters. The place, though sharing the general desolation of Turkish provinces, is at present of some importance. "There are two large bays affording the only safe anchorage for large ships; on the southern bay is the tomb of an unknown sheickh, near the northern bay are several copious wells of brackish water, deep, and lined with ancient stones, apparently an ancient work of considerable labour." Burckhardt, 'Syria,' p. 52.

18. The identity of Reuel with Jethro rests chiefly on the assumption that חתן, which is applied to Jethro repeatedly in the 3rd and 18th chapters, means "father-in-law." If Jethro were the father-in-law of Moses he would of course be the same person as Reuel. But in all other passages when the word חתן occurs, it means simply a "relation by marriage." In the Pentateuch it is applied to the sons-in-law of Lot, Gen. xix. 12, 14: to the brother-in-law of Moses, Hobab, Num. x. 29: to Moses himself, as husband of Zipporah, Exod. iv. 25, 26. In the book of Judges it is used once (xix. 4) of "a father-in-law," twice of "a son-in-law," twice of "a brother-in-law." The meaning in other passages is far more commonly son-in-law. The LXX. uses πενθερὸς and γαμβρός. The usage in Hebrew, Syriac, and Arabic is the same. Thus Freytag, خَتَن socer, vel omnis propinquus ab uxoris parte, scil. pater ejus, aut frater, &c.: ita apud genuinos Arates: vulgo autem est gener. Our rendering follows the Targums and Saadia. The Coptic word "Shom" has the same range of meaning. The meaning "circumcidit" has no authority in Hebrew, unless the very improbable explanation of ch. iv. 21, proposed by Gesenius, were admitted. The relationship therefore between Jethro and Moses cannot be decided by this word: it depends upon the internal evidence of the narrative. But Reuel must have been advanced in years, having seven grown up daughters when Moses arrived in Midian. When Moses was eighty years old, it is more probable that Reuel's son had succeeded him in his hereditary priesthood than that he was still living: and no difficulty is presented by the supposition that Jethro was the brother-in-law, not the father-in-law of Moses. The identity in that case of Jethro and Hobab, see Numb. x. 29, may be regarded as possible, but by no means as certain. Jethro returned to his own land before the promulgation of the law on Sinai, nor does his name occur afterwards. Hobab appears to have accompanied Moses on his journey, casting in his lot with the Israelites (see Judges iv. 11). He may have been, and very probably was, a younger brother of Jethro, not bound, like him, to his own tribe by the duties of an hereditary priesthood. This combination seems to meet all the conditions of the narrative, which would otherwise present serious, if not insuperable, difficulties.

CHAPTER III.

1 *Moses keepeth Jethro's flock.* 2 *God appeareth to him in a burning bush.* 9 *He sendeth him to deliver Israel.* 14 *The name of God.* 15 *His message to Israel.*

NOW Moses kept the flock of Jethro his father in law, the priest of Midian: and he led the flock to the backside of the desert, and

CHAP. III: The connection between this chapter and the preceding is very close, although many years intervened between the arrival of Moses in Midian and the transactions described in it. It marks however a distinct epoch, the commencement of the series of events which immediately preceded the Exodus. Hitherto the narrative has been studiously brief, stating only what was necessary to be known as preparatory to those events; but from this point Moses dwells minutely on the details, and enables us to realize the circumstances of the catastrophe which in its immediate and remote consequences stands alone in the world's history. This chapter is attributed by some writers to the so-called Jehovist; by others it is broken up into fragments, in order to meet the obvious objection that the name Elohim is found in it seventeen times, that of Jehovah six times only. But the internal evidence of unity is irresistible, and the fact that both the divine names occur far more frequently than in the preceding chapters is sufficiently accounted for by our having here a record of the personal intervention of the Lord God.

1. *the flock*] The expression is precise in Hebrew as in English, meaning not the cattle, but the sheep and goats. At present neither oxen nor horses are kept in the Peninsula, which does not supply fodder for them, under ordinary circumstances. It was however far more fertile in the time of Moses.

Jethro his father-in-law] Or "brother-in-law," see note above. An indefinite word such as affinis, signifying relation by marriage, would be preferable, but Jethro was probably the brother-in-law of Moses.

the backside] Gesenius explains this to mean "to the west of the district." This follows from the Hebrew system of orientation. The East is the region which is looked upon as before a man, the west behind him, the south and north as the right and left hand.

desert] Or **wilderness**. The word here used does not mean a barren waste, but a district supplying pasturage. The district near

came to the mountain of God, *even* to Horeb.

2 And the angel of the LORD appeared unto him in a *a* flame of fire out of the midst of a bush: and he looked, and, behold, the bush burned with fire, and the bush *was* not consumed.

3 And Moses said, I will now turn aside, and see this great sight, why the bush is not burnt.

a Acts 7. 30.

4 And when the LORD saw that he turned aside to see, God called unto him out of the midst of the bush, and said, Moses, Moses. And he said, Here *am* I.

5 And he said, Draw not nigh hither: *b* put off thy shoes from off thy feet, for the place whereon thou standest *is* holy ground.

6 Moreover he said, *c* I *am* the God of thy father, the God of Abraham,

b Josh 5. 15. Acts 7. 33.

c Matt. 22. 32. Acts 7. 32.

Sherm, where Jethro may have resided, is described by ancient and modern travellers as barren and parched; on the west and east are rocky tracts, but to the north-west, at a distance of three or four days' journey, lies the district of Sinai, where the pasturage is good and water abundant. The Bedouins drive their flocks thither from the lowlands at the approach of summer. From this it may be inferred that the events here recorded took place at that season.

the mountain of God, even to Horeb] More exactly, **To the mountain of God, towards Horeb**. The meaning is that Moses came to the mountain of God, *i.e.* Sinai, on his way towards Horeb. The name Horeb appears to belong to the northern part of the Sinaitic range, and to reach it Moses probably followed the road from Sherm, which passes through the deep valley between the Gebel ed Deir and the range terminated on the south by the commanding height called Gebel Musa. The tract which leads to the height is half way between the two extremities, about three miles distant from each other: this would bring Moses to the lower part of the range towards the north, which is best adapted for pasturage. An argument is drawn from the expression "mountain of God" against the Mosaic authorship: but Moses, who appears to have written, or to have revised, this book towards the end of his life, may naturally have given this name by anticipation, with reference to the manifestation of God. The paraphrase in the Targum gives the true meaning, "the mountain in which the glory of Jah was revealed to him." On the other hand, it is assumed that the spot was previously held sacred. For this there is no ancient authority; though it has been lately shewn that the whole Peninsula was regarded by the Egyptians as specially consecrated to the gods from a very early time. An inscription at Sarbut el Chadem, dated the 25th year of Thotmes III., speaks of an officer charged to bring copper from the land of the gods.

2. *the angel of the LORD*] Or **an angel of Jehovah**; the article is not in the Hebrew. On the meaning and usage of the expression see note on Gen. xii. 7. In this passage it appears to designate a manifestation of God by the agency, or instrumentality of a created being. What Moses saw was the flame of fire in the bush; what he recognised therein was an intimation of the presence of God, who maketh "a flame of fire His angel." Ps. civ. 4. The words which Moses heard were those of God Himself, as all ancient and most modern divines have held, manifested in the Person of the Son.

out of the midst of a bush] Literally "**of the bush**, or seneh," a word which ought perhaps to be retained as the proper name of a thorny shrub common in that district, a species of acacia according to Dr Stanley. The name is very ancient, in Coptic *Sheno*; it is found in papyri of the 19th dynasty and in inscriptions quoted by Brugsch, 'D. H.' p. 1397, who translates it Dorn-Acacia, thorny acacia. The use of the article is peculiar: it seems to mean that bush of which Moses must have spoken frequently to the Israelites.

4. *the LORD saw*] The interchange of the two divine names is to be observed; *Jehovah* saw, *God* called.

5. *put off thy shoes*] The reverence due to holy places thus rests on God's own command. The custom itself is well known from the observances of the Temple, it was almost universally adopted by the ancients, and is retained in the East.

holy ground] This passage is almost conclusive against the assumption that the place was previously a sanctuary. Moses knew nothing of its holiness after some 40 years spent on the Peninsula. It became holy by the presence of God.

6. *Moreover*] Literally **And**.

thy father] The word seems to be used collectively for the forefathers of Moses; it may, however, refer specially to Abraham, the father of the faithful; with whom the covenant was first made.

Our Saviour adduces the passage as a proof that the doctrine of the resurrection was taught in the Old Testament, and he calls this

the God of Isaac, and the God of Jacob. And Moses hid his face; for he was afraid to look upon God.

7 ¶ And the LORD said, I have surely seen the affliction of my people which *are* in Egypt, and have heard their cry by reason of their taskmasters; for I know their sorrows;

8 And I am come down to deliver them out of the hand of the Egyptians, and to bring them up out of that land unto a good land and a large, unto a land flowing with milk and honey; unto the place of the Canaanites, and the Hittites, and the Amorites, and the Perizzites, and the Hivites, and the Jebusites.

9 Now therefore, behold, the cry of the children of Israel is come unto me: and I have also seen the oppression wherewith the Egyptians oppress them.

10 Come now therefore, and I will send thee unto Pharaoh, that thou mayest bring forth my people the children of Israel out of Egypt.

11 ¶ And Moses said unto God, Who *am* I, that I should go unto Pharaoh, and that I should bring forth the children of Israel out of Egypt?

12 And he said, Certainly I will be with thee; and this *shall be* a token unto thee, that I have sent thee:

---

book the book of Moses (see marg.), two points to be borne in mind by readers of the Pentateuch.

7. *taskmasters*] A different word from that used in ch. i. 11. It means oppressors.

I know] The expression implies a personal feeling, tenderness, and compassion.

8. *a good land*, &c.] The natural richness of Palestine, the variety and excellence of its productions, are attested by all ancient writers, whose descriptions are strongly in contrast with those of later travellers. The expression "flowing with milk and honey" is used proverbially by Greek poets. Knobel assumes very unnecessarily, that the honey of wine, not of bees, is meant; Euripides, describing a paradisiacal state, says: "It flows with milk, it flows with the honey of bees," 'Bacchæ,' l. 142. On the abundance of honey in Palestine see Tristram, 'Land of Israel,' p. 88.

the place of the Canaanites] This is the first passage in this book where the enumeration, so often repeated, of the nations then in possession of Palestine, is given. Moses was to learn at once the extent of the promise, and the greatness of the enterprise. In Egypt, the forces, situation, and character of these nations were then well known. Aahmes I. had invaded the south of Palestine in his pursuit of the Shasous; Thotmes I. had traversed the whole land on his campaign in Syria and Mesopotamia; representations of Canaanites, of the Cheta, identified by most Egyptologers with the Hittites, are common on monuments of the 18th and 19th dynasties, and give a strong impression of their civilization, riches, and especially of their knowledge of the arts of war. In this passage, the more general designations come first—"Canaanites" probably includes all the races; the Hittites, who had great numbers of chariots (892 were taken from them by Thotmes III. in one battle), occupied the plains; the Amorites were chiefly mountaineers, but gave their name to the whole country in Egyptian inscriptions; the name Perizzites probably denotes the dwellers in scattered villages, the half-nomad population; the Hivites, a comparatively unwarlike, but influential people, held 4 cities in Palestine proper, but their main body dwelt in the north-western district, from Hermon to Hamath (see Josh. xi. 3, and Judg. iii. 3); the Jebusites at that time appear to have occupied Jerusalem and the adjoining district. Soon after their expulsion by Joshua, they seem to have recovered possession of part of Jerusalem, probably Mount Zion, and to have retained it until the time of David.

11. *Who am I*] The change in the character of Moses since his first attempt, is strongly marked by these words, which, however, indicate humility, not fear. Among the grounds which he alleges for his hesitation, in no instance is there any allusion to personal danger; what he feared was failure owing to incompetency, especially in the power of expression. This shrinking from self-assertion is the quality which seems to be specially intimated by the word rendered "meek" in Numbers ch. xii. 3.

12. *a token unto thee*] Or **the sign**. This passage illustrates a peculiar use of the word. It generally means any act, whether supernatural or not, which is made the pledge of some future event; but sometimes, as undoubtedly in this place, it means a declaration or promise of God, which rests absolutely on His word, and demands faith. The promise that God would have the people serve Him in that place was an assurance, if fully believed, that all intervening obstacles would be removed by His power.

When thou hast brought forth the people out of Egypt, ye shall serve God upon this mountain.

13 And Moses said unto God, Behold, *when* I come unto the children of Israel, and shall say unto them, The God of your fathers hath sent me unto you; and they shall say to me, What *is* his name? what shall I say unto them?

14 And God said unto Moses, I AM THAT I AM: and he said, Thus shalt thou say unto the children of Israel, I AM hath sent me unto you.

15 And God said moreover unto Moses, Thus shalt thou say unto the children of Israel, The LORD God of your fathers, the God of Abraham, the God of Isaac, and the God of Jacob, hath sent me unto you: this *is* my name for ever, and this *is* my memorial unto all generations.

16 Go, and gather the elders of Israel together, and say unto them, The LORD God of your fathers, the God of Abraham, of Isaac, and of Jacob, appeared unto me, saying, I have surely visited you, and *seen* that which is done to you in Egypt:

17 And I have said, I will bring you up out of the affliction of Egypt unto the land of the Canaanites, and the Hittites, and the Amorites, and the Perizzites, and the Hivites, and the Jebusites, unto a land flowing with milk and honey.

18 And they shall hearken to thy voice: and thou shalt come, thou and the elders of Israel, unto the king of Egypt, and ye shall say unto him, The LORD God of the Hebrews hath

---

13. *What is his name*] The meaning of this question is evidently: By which name shall I tell them the promise is confirmed? Each name of the Deity represented some aspect or manifestation of His attributes. El, Elohim, or Shaddai would speak of majesty, or might; either would probably have sufficed for Moses, but he would not use any one of them without God's special permission. What he needed was not a new name, but direction to use that Name which would bear in itself a pledge of accomplishment. It is not probable that Moses alluded to the multitudinous gods of Egypt; but he was familiar with the Egyptian habit of choosing from their many names that which bore specially upon the wants and circumstances of their worshippers (see especially the formulæ in the 'Papyrus magique d'Harris,' Chabas), and this may possibly have suggested the question which he was of course aware would be the first his own people would expect him to answer.

14. *I am that I am*] That is "I am what I am." The words express absolute, and therefore unchanging and eternal Being. So they are understood by ancient and modern interpreters (On the meaning and use of the name see the General Introduction). To Moses and the Israelites this was an explanation of the name Jehovah, which had been known from the beginning, but of which probably the meaning, certainly the full import, was not comprehended. The word "I am" in Hebrew is equivalent in meaning to Jehovah, and differs from it very slightly in form. This is much obscured by our substitution of Lord for Jehovah. The name, which Moses was thus commissioned to use, was at once new and old; old in its connection with previous revelations; new in its full interpretation, and in its bearing upon the covenant of which Moses was the destined mediator.

15. *The LORD God*] In this passage it is of great importance to keep the divine name **Jehovah God of your fathers, God of Abraham, God of Isaac, and God of Jacob**. It corresponds exactly to the preceding verse, the words **I am** and **Jehovah** being equivalent. This enables us to omit the article before "God," which is not in the Hebrew, and may be misunderstood, as though distinguishing Jehovah from other gods. The name met all the requirements of Moses, involving a twofold pledge of accomplishment; the pledges of ancient benefits and of a new manifestation.

name...memorial] The name signifies that by which God makes himself known, the *memorial* that by which His people worship Him; or as Bishop Wordsworth, following Keil, expresses it "the name declares the objective manifestation of the Divine Nature; the memorial, the subjective recognition by man."

18. *hath met with us*] This translation has been questioned, but it is now generally adopted. The Ancient Versions generally have "hath commanded or called us."

met with us: and now let us go, we beseech thee, three days' journey into the wilderness, that we may sacrifice to the Lord our God.

19 ¶ And I am sure that the king of Egypt will not let you go, ¹no, not by a mighty hand.

20 And I will stretch out my hand, and smite Egypt with all my wonders which I will do in the midst thereof: and after that he will let you go.

21 And I will give this people favour in the sight of the Egyptians: and it shall come to pass, that, when ye go, ye shall not go empty:

22 ᵈBut every woman shall borrow of her neighbour, and of her that sojourneth in her house, jewels of silver, and jewels of gold, and raiment: and ye shall put *them* upon your sons, and upon your daughters; and ye shall spoil ¹the Egyptians.

¹ Or, *but by strong hand.*

ᵈ chap. 11. 2. & 12. 35

¹ Or, *Egypt.*

---

three days' journey] i.e. A journey which would occupy three days in going and returning. The request which the Israelites were instructed to make was therefore most probably not a permission to go beyond the frontier, but into the part of the desert adjoining Goshen. In this there was no deception. The Israelites were to ask what could not reasonably be refused, being a demand quite in accordance with Egyptian customs. The refusal of Pharaoh and his subsequent proceedings led to the accomplishment of the ultimate purpose of God, which was revealed to Moses at once, since without it his mission would have had no adequate object. It is important to observe that the first request which Pharaoh rejected could have been granted without any damage to Egypt, or any risk of the Israelites passing the strongly fortified frontier. The point is well drawn out by M. de Quatremère. See 'Mémoires de l'Académie des Inscriptions et Belles Lettres,' Vol. XIX.

19. *And I am sure*] Or, **I know.**

no, not] The marginal rendering "but by a mighty hand" probably gives the true meaning, but the construction presents some difficulty. The LXX. have ἐὰν μή, unless. Keil renders the phrase "not even by a mighty hand," and explains it to mean Pharaoh will not let the people go even when severely smitten. This is a satisfactory explanation, and is borne out by the history; even after the 8th plague, we read "Pharaoh would not let them go."

22. *shall borrow*] or **shall ask.** (See Note at the end of the Chapter.) Our translation is unfortunate. The word is exceedingly common, and always means **ask** or demand. Setting aside this passage no proof or justification of the rendering "borrow" is adduced, except 1 Sam. i. 28, and 2 Kings vi. 5. In the former passage the meaning is "asked," and granted, not "borrowed." In the latter the meaning "borrowed" is true, but secondary. Of course "asked" may apply either to a gift or a loan, a sense to be determined by the context, **as** in Exod. xxii. 14, where the construction **is** different. In this case there is no indication that the jewels which were demanded when the final departure of the Israelites was settled, and strongly urged upon their acceptance by the Egyptians, were expected to be returned. The Egyptians had made the people serve "with rigour, in all manner of service in the fields," and the Israelites when about to leave the country for ever were to ask, or claim the jewels as a just, though very inadequate remuneration for services which had made "their lives bitter." The Egyptians doubtless would have refused had not their feelings towards Moses (see ch. xi. 3) and the people been changed under God's influence, by calamities in which they recognized a divine interposition, which also they rightly attributed to the obstinacy of their own king, (see ch. x. 7). The Hebrew women were to make the demand, and were to make it to women, who would of course be specially moved to compliance by the loss of their children, the fear of a recurrence of calamity, perhaps also by a sense of the fitness of the request in connection with a religious festival.

jewels] The Hebrew may be rendered more generally "vessels" or simply "articles." (The Vulgate has vasa, the LXX. σκεύη.) But the word probably refers chiefly to trinkets. The ornaments of gold and silver worn at that time by Egyptian women were beautiful and of great value. It is probable that, as at present, husbands invested their earnings in jewels. The wife of a tradesman or of a dragoman is thus often in possession of bracelets and collars of gold which in Europe would indicate wealth or high station. It is to be observed that these ornaments were actually applied to the purpose for which they were probably demanded, being employed in making the vessels of the sanctuary.

sojourneth in her house] This indicates a degree of friendly and neighbourly intercourse, which could scarcely be inferred from the preceding narrative, but it is in accordance with several indirect notices, and was a natural result of long and peaceable sojourn in the district. The Egyptians did not all necessarily share the feelings of their new king.

NOTE on CHAP. III. V. 22.

The true translation is important. The word has in fact but one true meaning, 'ask.' The ancient Versions take it in this sense. The LXX. has αἰτήσει, the Vulgate, postulabit. The Syriac and the Targum use the same word, in the same sense as the Hebrew. Thus too the Samaritan paraphrase. Saadia has تشتوهب, which is incorrectly rendered in Walton's Polyglott, mutuabitur. Freytag, 'Lex. Arab.' s. v., gives the true sense, rogavit donum, aut petiit dono sibi dari quid. See also the note on c. xii. 36.

CHAPTER IV.

1 *Moses's rod is turned into a serpent.* 6 *His hand is leprous.* 10 *He is loth to be sent.* 14 *Aaron is appointed to assist him.* 18 *Moses departeth from Jethro.* 21 *God's message to Pharaoh.* 24 *Zipporah circumciseth her son.* 27 *Aaron is sent to meet Moses.* 31 *The people believeth them.*

AND Moses answered and said, But, behold, they will not believe me, nor hearken unto my voice: for they will say, The LORD hath not appeared unto thee.

2 And the LORD said unto him, What *is* that in thine hand? And he said, A rod.

3 And he said, Cast it on the ground. And he cast it on the ground, and it became a serpent; and Moses fled from before it.

4 And the LORD said unto Moses, Put forth thine hand, and take it by the tail. And he put forth his hand, and caught it, and it became a rod in his hand:

5 That they may believe that the LORD God of their fathers, the God of Abraham, the God of Isaac, and the God of Jacob, hath appeared unto thee.

6 ¶ And the LORD said furthermore unto him, Put now thine hand into thy bosom. And he put his hand into his bosom: and when he took it out, behold, his hand *was* leprous as snow.

7 And he said, Put thine hand into thy bosom again. And he put his hand into his bosom again; and plucked it out of his bosom, and, behold, it was turned again as his *other* flesh.

8 And it shall come to pass, if they will not believe thee, neither hearken to the voice of the first sign, that they will believe the voice of the latter sign.

CHAP. IV. With this chapter begins the series of miracles which resulted in the deliverance of Israel. Long intervals of sacred history pass without any notice of miracle; not one, properly speaking, is recorded in connection with the previous history of the children of Jacob; but they cluster around great and critical events, occurring where they are demonstrably necessary. It is clear that unless a spiritual miracle transcending outward marvels had been wrought in the hearts both of the Israelites and of their oppressors, some special manifestations of divine power were indispensable. The first miracle was wrought to remove the first obstacle, viz. the reluctance of Moses, conscious of his own weakness, and of the enormous power with which he would have to contend. The LXX. add, "what shall I say unto them?" a probable, but not a necessary reading.

2. *A rod*] The word seems to denote the long staff which on Egyptian monuments is borne by men in positions of authority. See Wilkinson, III. pp. 367 and 386. It was usually made of acacia wood, such as is still sold for that purpose by the monks of the convent of Mount Sinai.

3. *a serpent*] This miracle had a meaning which Moses could not mistake. The serpent was probably the basilisk or Uræus, the Cobra. See Tristram, 'Nat. Hist.' p. 271. This was the symbol of royal and divine power on the diadem of every Pharaoh. It was a poisonous snake, as is shown by the flight of Moses and by most passages in which the same word occurs, *nahash*, derived from hissing. This snake never attacks without first inflating its neck, and then hissing; on the monuments it is always represented with its neck enormously swollen. The conversion of the rod was not merely a portent ($\tau\epsilon\rho as$), it was a sign ($\sigma\eta\mu\epsilon\hat{\iota}ov$), at once a pledge and representation of victory over the king and gods of Egypt.

6. *leprous*] The instantaneous production and cure of the most malignant and subtle disease known to the Israelites was a sign of their danger if they resisted the command, and of their deliverance if they obeyed it. The infliction and cure were always regarded as special proofs of a divine intervention.

9 And it shall come to pass, if they will not believe also these two signs, neither hearken unto thy voice, that thou shalt take of the water of the river, and pour *it* upon the dry *land:* and the water which thou takest out of the river †shall become blood upon the dry *land.*

10 ¶ And Moses said unto the Lord, O my Lord, I *am* not †eloquent, neither †heretofore, nor since thou hast spoken unto thy servant: but I *am* slow of speech, and of a slow tongue.

11 And the Lord said unto him, Who hath made man's mouth? or who maketh the dumb, or deaf, or the seeing, or the blind? have not I the Lord?

12 Now therefore go, and I will be *a*with thy mouth, and teach thee what thou shalt say.

13 And he said, O my Lord, send, I pray thee, by the hand *of him whom* thou ¹wilt send.

14 And the anger of the Lord was kindled against Moses, and he said, *Is* not Aaron the Levite thy brother? I know that he can speak well. And also, behold, he cometh forth to meet thee: and when he seeth thee, he will be glad in his heart.

15 And thou shalt speak unto him, and put words in his mouth: and I will be with thy mouth, and with his mouth, and will teach you what ye shall do.

16 And he shall be thy spokesman

† Heb. *shall be and shall be.*
† Heb. *a man of words.*
† Heb. *since yesterday, nor since the third day.*

a Matt 10. 19. Mark 13. 11. Luke 1. 11.
¹ Or, *shouldest.*

---

9. *shall become*] This rendering is preferable to that in the margin.

10. *eloquent*] Lit. **a man of words,** as in margin. The expressions which Moses uses do not imply a natural defect or impediment, but an inability to speak fluently. "Slow of speech," literally **heavy,** is specially used of persons speaking a foreign language imperfectly (see Ezek. iii. 5). The double expression slow of speech and of a slow tongue seems to imply a difficulty both in finding words and in giving them utterance, a very natural result of so long a period of a shepherd's life, passed in a foreign land, and as such to be counted among the numerous latent coincidences of the narrative.

since thou hast spoken] This expression seems to imply that some short time had intervened between this address and the first communication of the divine purpose to Moses.

12. Compare with this our Lord's promise to His Apostles; Matt. x. 19, Mark xiii. 11. It applies to both difficulties; "be with thy mouth" giving prompt utterance, and "teach thee" supplying or eliciting the best expression of the right thought.

13. *And he said*] The reluctance of Moses is a point of great moment. It had a permanent effect, for it caused the transfer of a most important part of his work to his brother, and its record supplies a strong evidence of the Mosaic authorship of this portion, attributed by Knobel to the so-called Jehovist. Like every other circumstance in the narrative it is in accordance with the inner law of man's spiritual development, and specially with the character of Moses; but under the circumstances it indicates a weakness of faith, such as no late writer would have attributed to the greatest of the descendants of Abraham.

send...by the hand] The Hebrew phrase is curt, so to speak, and ungracious; literally "send I pray by hand, thou wilt send," *i.e.* by whomsoever thou wilt; an expression which has scarcely a precedent and which may serve to illustrate Moses' own account of his heavy and awkward utterance: cf. Note on Numb. xiv. 13—17.

14. *anger*] This proves that the words of Moses indicated more than a consciousness of infirmity; somewhat of the vehemence and stubbornness, characteristic failings of strong, concentrated natures, which had previously been displayed in the slaying of the Egyptian.

Aaron] This is the first mention of Aaron. The exact meaning of the words "he can speak well," lit. "speaking he can speak," has been questioned, but they probably imply that Aaron had both the power and will to speak. Aaron is here called "the Levite," with reference, it may be, to the future consecration of this tribe; but not, as Knobel assumes, as though at that time the office and duties of the priesthood were assigned to him.

he cometh forth] *i.e.* is on the eve of setting forth. The Hebrew does not imply that Aaron was already on the way, but that he had the intention of going to his brother, probably because the enemies of Moses were now dead, see v. 19. The divine intimation was given afterwards, v. 27; it told Aaron where his brother was to be found. The expression "glad in his heart" should be noted as one of many indications of the divine sympathy with strong and pure natural affections.

15. *thou shalt speak*] Moses thus retains his position as "mediator;" the word comes to him first, he transmits it to his brother.

unto the people: and he shall be, *even* he shall be to thee instead of a mouth, and *ᵇ*thou shalt be to him instead of God.

^a chap. 7. 1.

17 And thou shalt take this rod in thine hand, wherewith thou shalt do signs.

18 ¶ And Moses went and returned to †Jethro his father in law, and said unto him, Let me go, I pray thee, and return unto my brethren which *are* in Egypt, and see whether they be yet alive. And Jethro said to Moses, Go in peace.

19 And the LORD said unto Moses in Midian, Go, return into Egypt: for all the men are dead which sought thy life.

20 And Moses took his wife and his sons, and set them upon an ass, and he returned to the land of Egypt: and Moses took the rod of God in his hand.

21 And the LORD said unto Moses, When thou goest to return into Egypt, see that thou do all those wonders before Pharaoh, which I have put in thine hand: but I will harden his heart, that he shall not let the people go.

22 And thou shalt say unto Pharaoh, Thus saith the LORD, Israel *is* my son, *even* my firstborn:

---

16. *instead of a mouth*] We may bear in mind Aaron's unbroken habitude of speaking Hebrew and his probable familiarity with Egyptian. The Arabic translator (Saadia) uses the word tarjaman, *i.e.* dragoman, interpreter. Thus also the Syriac and the Targum.

instead of God] The word God is used of persons who represent the Deity, as kings, or judges, and it is understood in this sense by the Targumist and Saadia: "Thou shalt be to him a master."

18. *Jethro*] In the Hebrew Jether, see note on ch. 11. Moses says nothing of his divine mission to Jethro; it was a secret thing between him and God.

19. *in Midian*] The LXX. insert before this verse "but after those many days the king of Egypt died." Egli, l. c., holds this to be the ancient reading, but it was probably introduced to explain the following statement, which is clear without it. There was apparently some delay on the part of Moses, who did not set out until he received a distinct assurance that all his enemies were removed. Such notices would never have occurred to a later writer, nor could they have originated in popular impressions. They show moreover how entirely Moses acted under an influence overruling the feelings, in which some would find the key to his acts.

20. *an ass*] Lit. "the ass," which according to Hebrew idiom means that he set them upon asses, not upon one ass, which would imply that they were both infants. This is the first notice of other sons besides Gershom.

the rod of God] The reference to the miracle recorded in v. 2, and to the express command in v. 17, is so obvious that it would be unnecessary to point it out but for the strange statement (Knobel) that the rod is here first mentioned. The staff of Moses was consecrated by the miracle and became the rod of God.

21. *see that thou do*, &c.] The Hebrew has, See all the wonders which I have put into thy hand, and do them before Pharaoh. Moses is called upon to consider the signs and to be prepared to produce them. The construction however is not certain; and the old Versions for the most part agree with our Authorised Version, which gives the general sense.

I will harden] Calamities which do not subdue the heart harden it; and the effects of God's judgments being foreknown are willed by Him. We should not therefore adopt a forced interpretation of this expression in order to explain away its apparent harshness. The hardening itself is judicial, and just, when it is a consequence of previously formed habits; in the case of Pharaoh it was at once a righteous judgment, and a natural result of a long series of oppressions and cruelties. Theodoret thus deals with the question: "The sun by the action of heat makes wax moist, and mud dry, hardening the one while it softens the other, by the same operation producing exactly opposite results; thus from the long-suffering of God some derive benefit and others harm, some are softened while others are hardened." 'Quæst. XII. in Exod.' The reason why the action of God rather than the character of Pharaoh is dwelt on in this passage would seem to be that it was necessary to sustain the spirit of Moses and the people during the process of events, which they were thus taught were altogether foreseen and predetermined by God.

22. *my firstborn*] The expression would be perfectly intelligible to Pharaoh, whose official designation was Si Ra, son of Ra. In numberless inscriptions the Pharaohs are styled "own sons" or "beloved sons" of the deity. It is here applied for the first time to Israel; and as we learn from *v.* 23, emphatically in antithesis to Pharaoh's own firstborn. The menace however was not uttered until it was called forth by Pharaoh's sin. See ch. xi. 5.

23 And I say unto thee, Let my son go, that he may serve me: and if thou refuse to let him go, behold, I will slay thy son, *even* thy firstborn.

24 ¶ And it came to pass by the way in the inn, that the LORD met him, and sought to kill him.

25 Then Zipporah took a sharp ¹stone, and cut off the foreskin of her son, and †cast *it* at his feet, and said, Surely a bloody husband *art* thou to me.

¹ Or, knife.
† Heb. made it touch.

26 So he let him go: then she said, A bloody husband *thou art*, because of the circumcision.

27 ¶ And the LORD said to Aaron, Go into the wilderness to meet Moses. And he went, and met him in the mount of God, and kissed him.

28 And Moses told Aaron all the words of the LORD who had sent him, and all the signs which he had commanded him.

29 ¶ And Moses and Aaron went

---

24. *in the inn*] Or "resting place," it probably does not mean a building, but the place where they rested for the night, whether under a tent, or in the open air. The khans or caravanserais, now common in the East, appear to have been unknown to the ancient Israelites and Egyptians.

met him, and sought to kill him] The expression is obscure, but is understood to mean that Moses was attacked by a sudden and dangerous illness, which he knew was inflicted by God. The word 'sought to kill' implies that the sickness, whatever might be its nature, was one which threatened death had it not been averted by a timely act. We are not told for what cause the visitation came; but from the context it may be inferred that it was because Moses had neglected the duty of an Israelite and had not circumcised his son. From the words of Zipporah it is evident that she believed the illness of Moses was to be thus accounted for; the delay was probably owing to her own not unnatural repugnance to a rite, which though practised by the Egyptians under the 19th dynasty, and perhaps earlier, was not adopted generally in the East, even by the descendants of Abraham and Keturah. Moses appears to have been utterly prostrate and unable to perform the rite himself.

25. *sharp stone*] Not "knife," as in the margin. Zipporah used a piece of flint, in accordance with the usage of the patriarchs. The Egyptians never used bronze or steel in the preparation of mummies because stone was regarded as a purer and more sacred material than metal. See Wilkinson, Vol. II. p. 164; and M. de Rougemont, 'Age du Bronze,' p. 152.

cast it at his feet] The Hebrew is obscure, but the Authorised Version probably gives the true meaning. Zipporah threw it at the feet of Moses, not of her son, as some commentators suppose; showing at once her abhorrence of the rite, and her feeling that by it she had saved her husband's life.

a bloody husband] Lit. "A husband of blood;" or "bloods:" the plural form signifies effusion of blood; the word (חתן) rendered husband (as in Psalm xix. 5, bridegroom) includes all relations by marriage; see note at the end of c. ii. The meaning is, the marriage bond between us is now sealed by blood. In the next verse Zipporah repeats the expression, as though she would say, thou art bound to me by a second covenant of which this bloody rite is the sign and pledge. By performing it Zipporah had recovered her husband; his life was purchased for her by the blood of her child. See the remarks of Hooker, 'E. P.' v. 62. The Targum Onk. gives a paraphrase, "had it not been for the blood of this circumcision my husband had been condemned to death." This appears to be the true explanation of a very obscure passage; other interpretations, which make the words refer to the child, or to the Angel of the Covenant, are generally admitted to be untenable.

26. *So he let him go*] i.e. God withdrew His visitation from Moses. The Hebrew allows no other interpretation.

We learn from ch. xviii. 2, that Moses sent Zipporah and her children back to Jethro before he went to Egypt. It was probably on this occasion. The journey would have been delayed had he waited for the healing of the child.

27. *And the LORD said*] See v. 14. Aaron now receives direct intimation where he is to meet his brother. He might otherwise have undertaken a long and fruitless journey to the residence of Jethro.

in the mount of God] Horeb lies on the direct route from Sherm to Egypt; this passage is therefore in favour of the supposition that Jethro's residence was on the west of the gulf. See note on c. ii.

28. *who had sent him*] The meaning is, probably, "which God had charged him to do." Thus the Vulgate, LXX., Knobel, and other commentators; but it is not necessary to alter the translation, which is literal and supported by Rosenmüller, who renders it, "qui eum miserat."

and gathered together all the elders of the children of Israel:

30 And Aaron spake all the words which the LORD had spoken unto Moses, and did the signs in the sight of the people.

31 And the people believed: and when they heard that the LORD had visited the children of Israel, and that he had looked upon their affliction, then they bowed their heads and worshipped.

CHAPTER V.

1 *Pharaoh chideth Moses and Aaron for their message.* 5 *He increaseth the Israelites' task.* 15 *He checketh their complaints.* 20 *They cry out upon Moses and Aaron.* 22 *Moses complaineth to God.*

AND afterward Moses and Aaron went in, and told Pharaoh, Thus saith the LORD God of Israel, Let my people go, that they may hold a feast unto me in the wilderness.

2 And Pharaoh said, Who *is* the LORD, that I should obey his voice to let Israel go? I know not the LORD, neither will I let Israel go.

3 And they said, *a* The God of the Hebrews hath met with us: let us go, we pray thee, three days' journey into the desert, and sacrifice unto the LORD our God; lest he fall upon us with pestilence, or with the sword.

4 And the king of Egypt said unto

a chap. 3. 18.

---

29. *all the elders*] The Israelites retained their own national organization; their affairs were administered by their own elders.

31. *the people*] This implies that the elders called a public assembly to hear the message brought by Moses and Aaron.

and worshipped] There is no reason to doubt that this act of worship was addressed to God, not to Moses and Aaron. It is important to remark that in this narrative there is no indication of ignorance of the history of the patriarchs, or of abandonment of the worship of God, sometimes attributed to the Israelites.

CHAP. V. **1.** *Pharaoh*] This king, probably (see Appendix) Thotmes II. the great grandson of Aahmes, the original persecutor of the Israelites, must have been resident at this time in a city of lower Egypt, situate on the Nile. It could not therefore have been Heliopolis, and we have to choose between Memphis and Tanis; and there can be little doubt that most of the events which follow occurred at the latter city, the Zoan of Scripture. The notice in Psalm lxxviii. 12, 43, is admitted by all critics to be of great weight, and all the circumstances confirm it. See on ix. 31 and on i. 5. Tanis was a very large city, and strongly fortified. The remains of buildings and the obelisks are numerous; they bear for the most part the name of Rameses II.; but it was the place of rendezvous for the armies of the Delta, and an imperial city in the 12th dynasty; it is identified by M. de Rougé with Avaris the capital of the Hyksos, who probably gave it its Hebrew name; both Avaris and Zoan mean "going out." This Pharaoh had waged a successful war in the beginning of his reign against the Shasous, the nomad tribes of the adjoining district, and his residence in the north-west of Egypt would be of importance at that time.

the LORD God] This version rather obscures the meaning; **Jehovah God of Israel** demanded the services of his people. The demand according to the general views of the heathens was just and natural; the Israelites could not offer the necessary sacrifices in the presence of Egyptians.

2. *I know not the LORD*] This may mean either that Pharaoh had not heard of Jehovah, or that he did not recognize Him as a God. The former is possible, for though the name was ancient, it was apparently less used by the Israelites than other designations of God. The Targum thus paraphrases: "the name of Jah has not been revealed to me."

3. *three days' journey*] This would not suffice for the journey to the "Mountain of God." See note on iii. 18. All that Moses was instructed to ask for was permission to go into a part of the desert where the people might offer sacrifices without interruption from the Egyptians; and that might be found on the frontiers of Egypt, or, at least, in a district commanded by the king's army. It is evident from Pharaoh's answer that he did not see in the request any indication of an intention to escape from Egypt. Ewald (Vol. II. pp. 84, 85) recognizes the reasonableness and modesty of this demand, which he represents as a manifest proof that the sober and noble spirit of prophecy in its best age has interpenetrated the narrative; words which do but express the old truth that the transaction and record bear equally the marks of divine governance and inspiration.

with pestilence, or with the sword] This notice is important as shewing that the plague was well known to the ancient Egyptians. It

them, Wherefore do ye, Moses and Aaron, let the people from their works? get you unto your burdens.

5 And Pharaoh said, Behold, the people of the land now *are* many, and ye make them rest from their burdens.

6 And Pharaoh commanded the same day the taskmasters of the people, and their officers, saying,

7 Ye shall no more give the people straw to make brick, as heretofore: let them go and gather straw for themselves.

8 And the tale of the bricks, which they did make heretofore, ye shall lay upon them; ye shall not diminish *ought* thereof: for they *be* idle; therefore they cry, saying, Let us go *and* sacrifice to our God.

9 †Let there more work be laid upon the men, that they may labour therein; and let them not regard vain words.

† Heb. *Let the work be heavy upon the men.*

10 ¶ And the taskmasters of the people went out, and their officers, and they spake to the people, saying, Thus saith Pharaoh, I will not give you straw.

11 Go ye, get you straw where ye can find it: yet not ought of your work shall be diminished.

12 So the people were scattered abroad throughout all the land of Egypt to gather stubble instead of straw.

13 And the taskmasters hasted them, saying, Fulfil your works, †your daily tasks, as when there was straw.

† Heb. *a matter of a day in his day.*

---

was probably less common than at present under the ancient Pharaohs, who bestowed great care on the irrigation and drainage of the country, but there are other indications of its ravages. See Chabas, 'Mél. Eg.' I. p. 40. The reference to the sword is equally natural, since the Israelites occupied the eastern district, which was frequently disturbed by the neighbouring Shasous. See note on v. 1.

6. *the taskmasters*] This word, which means "exactors" or "oppressors," designates the Egyptian overseers, who were subordinate to the officers called "taskmasters" in ch. i. 11, but whose name is different in Hebrew. See note on ch. i. 11, and 14.

their officers] Or **scribes**. These were Hebrews, appointed by the Egyptian superintendents, and responsible to them for the work; see v. 14. The Hebrew name *shoter* is equivalent to "scribe;" and it is probable that persons were chosen who were able to keep accounts in writing. Subordinate officers are frequently represented on Egyptian monuments giving in written accounts to their immediate superiors. Rosellini (II. 3, p. 272) observes that Egyptians made more use of writing on ordinary occasions than modern Europeans. "Shoterim" are often mentioned in the Old Testament, generally in connection with judges or leaders, by whom they were employed to transmit orders to the people and superintend the execution. It is evident how much this measure must have advanced the organization of the Israelites, and prepared them for their departure. See Note at the end of the Chapter.

7 *straw*] Some of the most ancient buildings in Egypt were constructed of bricks not burned, but dried in the sun; they were made of clay, or more commonly of mud, mixed with straw chopped into small pieces. Baked bricks are seldom found in ruins more ancient than the Exodus, never, according to Sir G. Wilkinson, (see Quarterly Review, 1859, April, p. 421), but there is a specimen in the British Museum belonging to the reign of Thotmosis III. An immense quantity of straw must have been wanted for the works on which the Israelites were engaged, and their labours must have been more than doubled by this requisition. In a papyrus of the 19th dynasty ('Anast.' IV. 12, 16) the writer complains: "I have no one to help me in making bricks, no straw." The expression at that time was evidently proverbial, whether or not as a reminiscence of the Israelites may be questioned, but it shows the thoroughly Egyptian character of the transaction.

9. *may labour therein*] The LXX. have "that they may attend to it and not attend to vain words:" a good and probable reading.

12. *stubble instead of straw*] Rather, **for the straw**. See Note at the end of the Chapter. The Israelites had to go into the fields after the reaping, was done, to gather the stubble left by the reapers, who then, as at present in Egypt, cut the stalks close to the ears. They had then to chop it into morsels of straw before it could be mixed with the clay: see the previous note. This implies that some time must have elapsed before Moses again went to Pharaoh; and it also marks the season of the year, viz. early spring, after the barley or wheat harvest, towards the end of April. Their suffering must have been severe, since at that season the pestilential sand-wind blows over Egypt some 50 days, hence its name Chamsin.

14 And the officers of the children of Israel, which Pharaoh's taskmasters had set over them, were beaten, *and* demanded, Wherefore have ye not fulfilled your task in making brick both yesterday and to day, as heretofore?

15 ¶ Then the officers of the children of Israel came and cried unto Pharaoh, saying, Wherefore dealest thou thus with thy servants?

16 There is no straw given unto thy servants, and they say to us, Make brick: and, behold, thy servants *are* beaten; but the fault *is* in thine own people.

17 But he said, Ye *are* idle, *ye are* idle: therefore ye say, Let us go *and* do sacrifice to the LORD.

18 Go therefore now, *and* work; for there shall no straw be given you, yet shall ye deliver the tale of bricks.

19 And the officers of the children of Israel did see *that* they *were* in evil *case*, after it was said, Ye shall not minish *ought* from your bricks of your daily task.

20 ¶ And they met Moses and Aaron, who stood in the way, as they came forth from Pharaoh:

21 And they said unto them, The LORD look upon you, and judge; because ye have made our savour †to be abhorred in the eyes of Pharaoh, and in the eyes of his servants, to put a sword in their hand to slay us.

† Heb. *to stink.*

22 And Moses returned unto the LORD, and said, Lord, wherefore hast thou so evil entreated this people? why *is* it *that* thou hast sent me?

23 For since I came to Pharaoh to speak in thy name, he hath done evil to this people; neither hast thou †delivered thy people at all.

† Heb. *delivering thou hast not delivered*

---

13. *hasted them*] See the words of the overseer quoted above on ch. i. 14. In a passage of the papyrus 'Anast.' III. translated by M. Chabas, 'Mél. Eg.' II. p. 122, twelve labourers employed in the same district are punished for negligence in failing to make up their daily tale of bricks.

14. *Were beaten*] The beating of these officers is quite in accordance with Egyptian customs; even natives of rank in civil and military service were subject to severe corporal punishments. See note on ch. ii. 11.

16. *the fault is in thine own people*] Lit. **thy people sin**: which may possibly mean thy subjects, *i.e.* the Israelites, are made guilty and punished: but the Authorised Version probably gives the true meaning; thus the Vulg., Targ. and Saadia. The LXX. and Syr. have "thou hast sinned against thy people."

17. *Ye are idle*] The old Egyptian language abounds in epithets which shew contempt for idleness. The charge was equally offensive and ingenious; one which would be readily believed by Egyptians who knew how much public and private labours were impeded by festivals and other religious ceremonies. Among the great sins which involved condemnation in the final judgment, idleness is twice mentioned; see funeral ritual in Bunsen's 'Egypt,' ed. 2, Vol. V. pp. 254, 255.

19. *in evil case*] They saw plainly that the object of Pharaoh was to find a pretext for further cruelty; probably for cutting off the leaders of the Israelites; see v. 21. The effect, however, would be to bring them into closer union and sympathy with the people.

20. *who stood in the way*] Or "waiting to meet them," *i.e.* Moses and Aaron stood without the palace to learn the result of the interview.

21. *in the eyes*] The change of metaphor shows that the expression was proverbial. Thus an Egyptian of rank complains to the scribe, who writes his history, "Thou hast made my name offensive, stinking, to all men." 'Anast.' I. 27, 7.

23. The earnestness of this remonstrance, and even its approach to irreverence, are quite in keeping with other notices of Moses' naturally impetuous character, see especially, ch. iii. 13; but such a speech would certainly not have been put into his mouth by a later writer. See note on ch. iv. 10.

NOTES on CHAP. V. *vv.* 6 and 12.

6. The question whether the שֹׁטְרִים were Egyptians or Hebrews is important in its bearings on the narrative. The word is common, and always denotes the class of persons described in the foot-note. Gesenius finds its root in the Arabic سطر, he wrote. The LXX. render it τοῖς γραμματεῦσιν: the Syr. ܣܦܪܐ, writer or scribe. Thus also the Samaritan version. The Targum Onk. uses the word סָרְכָא, which is incorrectly rendered "exactor" in Walton's Polyglott. It corresponds exactly to *shoter*, and is applied to the native officers of Israel: see Buxtorf, 'Lex. Chal.' s. v. Saadia uses a word which Walton renders "exactor;" but its true meaning is "cognitor, qui suos cognitos habet;" a very apt expression for these Hebrew officials.

12. The Hebrew has קַשׁ, stubble, and לְתֶבֶן, which does not mean instead of, but "for," *i.e.* to be prepared as תֶבֶן. "straw chopped small:" stramenta minutim concisa. Thus the ancient versions and Targ. Onk., which is incorrectly translated in Walton. The etymology of תֶבֶן is doubted; no Semitic root is found. The Egyptian has *tebu*, chaff. 'Pap. Sallier,' v. 6. *Kash* also is Egyptian for stubble, or stalk.

CHAPTER VI.

1 *God reneweth his promise by his name JEHOVAH.* 14 *The genealogy of Reuben,* 15 *of Simeon,* 16 *of Levi, of whom came Moses and Aaron.*

THEN the LORD said unto Moses, Now shalt thou see what I will do to Pharaoh: for with a strong hand shall he let them go, and with a strong hand shall he drive them out of his land.

2 And God spake unto Moses, and said unto him, I *am* ¹the LORD:

3 And I appeared unto Abraham, unto Isaac, and unto Jacob, by *the name of* God Almighty, but by my name JEHOVAH was I not known to them.

4 And I have also established my covenant with them, to give them the land of Canaan, the land of their pilgrimage, wherein they were strangers.

5 And I have also heard the groaning of the children of Israel, whom the Egyptians keep in bondage; and I have remembered my covenant.

6 Wherefore say unto the children of Israel, I *am* the LORD, and I will bring you out from under the burdens of the Egyptians, and I will rid you out of their bondage, and I will redeem you with a stretched out arm, and with great judgments:

7 And I will take you to me for a people, and I will be to you a God: and ye shall know that I *am* the LORD

CHAP. VI. 1. *with a strong hand*] Or, **by a strong hand**, *i.e.* compelled by the power of God, manifested in judgments. In the 2nd clause the LXX. have "by a stretched out arm:" a probable reading, adopted by Egli, l. c.

2, 3. There appears to have been an interval of some months between the preceding events and this renewal of the promise to Moses. The oppression in the mean time was not merely driving the people to desperation, but preparing them by severe labour, varied by hasty wanderings in search of stubble, for the exertions and privations of the wilderness. Hence the formal and solemn character of the announcements in the whole chapter.

2. *I am the* LORD] See General Introduction, p. 25. The meaning, as is there shewn, seems to be this. I am Jehovah, and I appeared to Abraham, Isaac, and Jacob as El Shaddai, but as to my name Jehovah, I was not made known to them. In other words, the full import of that name was not disclosed to them. On the one hand it is scarcely possible to doubt, and it is in fact admitted by most critics, that the sacred name Jehovah **was** known from very early times; on the other, the revelation on Mount Sinai clearly states that the derivation and full meaning of the name were then first declared. On this special occasion it was important or necessary, for the support and encouragement of Moses and the people to whom he gave the announcement, to repeat the declaration as a pledge of the fulfilment of the promises made on the "Mountain of God."

3. *God Almighty*] Rather, "**El Shaddai**," it is better to keep this as a proper name; the meaning is correctly given in the text.

4. *And I have also*] The connection between this and the following verse is marked by the repetition of these words. Two reasons are assigned for the promise, viz. the old covenant with the patriarchs, and the divine compassion for the sufferings of Israel.

6. *with a stretched out arm*] The figure is common and quite intelligible; it may have struck Moses and the people the more forcibly since they were familiar with the hieroglyphic which represents might by two outstretched arms. On the obelisk at Heliopolis, Moses had been from infancy familiar with the symbol in the official name of Osertasen Racheperka, *i.e.* Ra is might.

your God, which bringeth you out from under the burdens of the Egyptians.

8 And I will bring you in unto the land, concerning the which I did †swear to give it to Abraham, to Isaac, and to Jacob; and I will give it you for an heritage: I *am* the LORD.

9 ¶ And Moses spake so unto the children of Israel: but they hearkened not unto Moses for †anguish of spirit, and for cruel bondage.

10 And the LORD spake unto Moses, saying,

11 Go in, speak unto Pharaoh king of Egypt, that he let the children of Israel go out of his land.

12 And Moses spake before the LORD, saying, Behold, the children of Israel have not hearkened unto me; how then shall Pharaoh hear me, who *am* of uncircumcised lips?

13 And the LORD spake unto Moses and unto Aaron, and gave them a charge unto the children of Israel, and unto Pharaoh king of Egypt, to bring the children of Israel out of the land of Egypt.

14 ¶ These *be* the heads of their fathers' houses: *a* The sons of Reuben the firstborn of Israel; Hanoch, and Pallu, Hezron, and Carmi: these *be* the families of Reuben.

15 *b* And the sons of Simeon; Jemuel, and Jamin, and Ohad, and Jachin, and Zohar, and Shaul the son of a Canaanitish woman: these *are* the families of Simeon.

† Heb. *lift up my hand.*

† Heb. *shortness, or, straitness.*

a Gen. 46. *1* Chron. 5. 3.

b 1 Chro. 4. 24.

---

8. *I am the* LORD] Rather, **I the Lord**: the word "am" obscures the construction.

9. *they hearkened not*] The contrast between the reception of this communication and that recorded in ch. iv. 31, is dwelt upon by some critics as indicating different authors, but it is distinctly accounted for by the change of circumstances. On the former occasion the people were comparatively at ease, accustomed to their lot, sufficiently afflicted to long for deliverance, and sufficiently free in spirit to hope for it.

for anguish] Literally as in the margin, **for shortness of spirit**; out of breath, as it were, after their cruel disappointment, they were quite absorbed by their misery, unable and unwilling to attend to any fresh communication; an effect which might seem recorded expressly to preclude the notion that the deliverance of Israel was the result of a religious struggle, such as is assumed in some accounts of the transaction.

11. *go out of his land*] There is now a change in the demand; the first of a series of changes. Moses is now bidden to demand not a permission for a three days' journey, which might be within the boundaries of Egypt, but for departure from the land.

12. *uncircumcised lips*] An uncircumcised ear is one that does not hear clearly; an uncircumcised heart one slow to receive and understand warnings; uncircumcised lips, such as cannot speak fluently. Thus LXX., Syr., Targ., &c. There is no ground for assuming a natural defect. See note on ch. iv. 10. The recurrence of Moses' hesitation is natural; great as was the former trial this was far more severe; yet his words as ever imply fear of failure, not of personal danger.

13. *unto Moses and unto Aaron*] The final and formal charge to the two brothers is given, as might be expected, before the plagues are denounced. With this verse begins a new section of the history, and as in the book of Genesis "there is in every such case a brief repetition of so much of the previous account as is needed to make it an intelligible narrative in itself; a peculiarity which extends to the lesser subdivisions also." Quarry 'On Genesis,' p. 322.

14. *These be the heads*] We have in the following verses, not a complete genealogy, but a summary account of the family of the two brothers. It has been objected to as out of place, interrupting the narrative, and therefore probably an interpolation; but, as Rosenmüller and other unbiassed critics have observed, the reason is clear why Moses should have recorded his own genealogy and that of his brother, when they were about to execute a duty of the highest importance which had been imposed upon them; just then it was right and natural to state, for the satisfaction of Hebrew readers, to whom genealogical questions were always interesting, the descent and position of the designated leaders of the nation.

The sons of Reuben] Moses mentions in the first place the families of the elder brothers of Levi, in order to shew the exact position of his own tribe and family. Thus Rashi and Rosenmüller.

VOL. I.

S

16 ¶ And these *are* the names of the ͨsons of Levi according to their generations; Gershon, and Kohath, and Merari: and the years of the life of Levi *were* an hundred thirty and seven years.

17 The sons of Gershon; Libni, and Shimi, according to their families.

18 And ͩthe sons of Kohath; Amram, and Izhar, and Hebron, and Uzziel: and the years of the life of Kohath *were* an hundred thirty and three years.

19 And the sons of Merari; Mahali and Mushi: these *are* the families of Levi according to their generations.

20 And ͤAmram took him Jochebed his father's sister to wife; and she bare him Aaron and Moses: and the years of the life of Amram *were* an hundred and thirty and seven years.

21 ¶ And the sons of Izhar; Korah, and Nepheg, and Zithri.

22 And the sons of Uzziel; Mishael, and Elzaphan, and Zithri.

23 And Aaron took him Elisheba, daughter of Amminadab, sister of Naashon, to wife; and she bare him Nadab, and Abihu, Eleazar, and Ithamar.

24 And the sons of Korah; Assir, and Elkanah, and Abiasaph: these *are* the families of the Korhites.

25 And Eleazar Aaron's son took him *one* of the daughters of Putiel to wife; and ͟she bare him Phinehas: these *are* the heads of the fathers of the Levites according to their families.

26 These *are* that Aaron and Moses, to whom the LORD said, Bring out the children of Israel from the land of Egypt according to their armies.

Marginal references: ͨ Numb. 3. 17; 1 Chron. 6. 1. ͩ Numb. 5. 57; 1 Chron. 6. ͤ chap 2. 2. unt. 26. ͟ Num. 25. 11.

---

16. *sons of Levi*] Thus Moses shews that of the three great divisions of the tribe, the one to which he and Aaron belonged, and to which the priesthood was afterwards confined, was the second, not the first. Again, he does not trace the descent of other families, but passes at once from Kohath, the son of Levi, to the heads of Kohath's family in his own time.

the years of the life of Levi] It is usual throughout Genesis in each genealogy to give the age of the chief person in each principal family, and to omit it in the case of secondary families.

20. *Amram*] This can scarcely be the same person who is mentioned in *v.* 18; but his descendant and representative in the generation immediately preceding that of Moses. The intervening links are omitted, as is the rule where they are not needed for some special purpose, and do not bear upon the history. Between the death of Amram and the birth of Moses was an interval which can scarcely be brought within the limits assigned by any system of chronology to the sojourn in Egypt. Thus Tiele, quoted by Keil: "According to Numbers iii. 27, &c. in the time of Moses the Kohathites were divided into four branches, that of Amram, Izhar, Hebron, and Uzziel: their number amounted to 8600 males; of these the Amramites were about one fourth, *i.e.* more than 2000 males. This would be impossible were Amram the son of Kohath identical with Amram the father of Moses. We must therefore admit an omission of several links between the two." Thus in the genealogy of Ezra (Ezra vii. 3, compared with 1 Chron. v. 33—35) five descents are omitted between Azariah the son of Meraioth and Azariah son of Johanan, and several between Ezra himself and Seraiah, who was put to death by Nebuchadnezzar 150 years before the time of Ezra."

Jochebed] Here named for the first time, and, as might be expected, not in the general narrative but in a genealogical statement. The name means "the glory of Jehovah," one clear instance of the usage of the sacred name before the Exodus.

father's sister] This was within the prohibited degrees after the law was given, but not previously.

23. *Elisheba*] Her brother Naashon was at that time captain of the children of Judah, Num. ii. 3. Theodoret remarks, τῆς βασιλικῆς καὶ τῆς ἱερατικῆς φυλῆς τὴν ἐπιμιξίαν διδάσκει. 'Quæst. in Exod.' *i.e.* (Moses) shews the intermixture of the royal and priestly tribes.

25. *Putiel*] This name is remarkable, being compounded of Puti, or Poti, in Egyptian "devoted to," and "El," the Hebrew name of God. See De Vogué, 'Inscriptions sémitiques,' p. 125.

26, 27. This emphatic repetition shews the reason for inserting the genealogy. The names of Moses and Aaron are given twice and in a different order; in the 26th verse probably to mark Aaron as the elder in the genealogy, and in the 27th to denote the leadership of Moses.

27 These *are* they which spake to Pharaoh king of Egypt, to bring out the children of Israel from Egypt: these *are* that Moses and Aaron.

28 ¶ And it came to pass on the day *when* the Lord spake unto Moses in the land of Egypt,

29 That the Lord spake unto Moses, saying, I *am* the Lord: speak thou unto Pharaoh king of Egypt all that I say unto thee.

30 And Moses said before the Lord, Behold, I *am* of uncircumcised lips, and how shall Pharaoh hearken unto me?

CHAPTER VII.

1 *Moses is encouraged to go to Pharaoh.* 7 *His age.* 8 *His rod is turned into a serpent.* 11 *The sorcerers do the like.* 13 *Pharaoh's heart is hardened.* 14 *God's message to Pharaoh.* 19 *The river is turned into blood.*

AND the Lord said unto Moses, See, I have made thee a god to Pharaoh: and Aaron thy brother shall be thy prophet.

---

28. This and the following verses belong to the next chapter. They mark distinctly the beginning of a subdivision of the narrative, and according to the general rule in the Pentateuch (see note on ver. 14), begin with a brief recapitulation. Moses once more, like other sacred writers, dwells strongly upon his personal deficiencies and faults of character (see Ewald, II. p. 84), an all but certain indication of autobiography in the case of great and heroic personages.

Chap. VII. With this chapter begins the series of miracles wrought in Egypt. They are progressive. The first miracle is wrought to accredit the mission of the brothers; it is simply credential, and unaccompanied by any infliction. Then come signs which shew that the powers of nature are subject to the will of Jehovah, each plague being attended with grave consequences to the Egyptians, yet not inflicting severe loss or suffering; then in rapid succession come ruinous and devastating plagues, murrain, boils, hail and lightning, locusts, darkness, and lastly, the death of the firstborn. Each of the inflictions has a demonstrable connection with Egyptian customs and phenomena; each is directly aimed at some Egyptian superstition; all are marvellous, not, for the most part, as reversing, but as developing forces inherent in nature, and directing them to a special end. The effects correspond with these characteristics; the first miracles are neglected; the following plagues first alarm, and then for a season, subdue, the king, who does not give way until his firstborn is struck. Even that blow leaves him capable of a last effort, which completes his ruin, and the deliverance of the Israelites.

It is admitted by critics that the deliverance of the Israelites must have been the result of heavy calamities inflicted upon the Egyptians, who certainly would never have submitted to so great a loss had they been in a state to prevent it. Nor could it have been effected by a successful uprising of the Israelites, who were not in a position to resist the power of Egypt, and who, had such been the case, would certainly have preserved the record of a war issuing in so glorious a result. It is also generally admitted that the calamities, whatever they might have been, did not include an overthrow of Egyptian power by foreign enemies, or national insurrections. No notice of either, as Knobel remarks, is found in Hebrew traditions; and it may be added, that in neither of the reigns to which the Exodus has been assigned, are there any indications of either calamity. Egypt was in the highest state of power and prosperity through the whole period within which all agree that the Exodus took place. The reign of Thotmes II., which has been shewn in the Appendix to be that which tallies best with all ascertained facts, intervened between two of the ablest and most successful sovereigns in Egypt, and though obscure and uneventful, it gives no indications of loss or disturbance; the only war recorded was one that extended or confirmed his power. Late investigations have also shewn that the reigns of Merneptah and his successor (under whom these events are supposed by most critics to have occurred), were on the whole prosperous; one only invasion is recorded in the beginning of that period and it was completely repelled. A succession of such plagues as are described in Exodus must therefore be assumed, and is in fact accepted by critics, as the only conceivable cause of the result. The question whether it was miraculous, depends upon the ulterior question, whether miracles under any circumstances are conceivable; if in any case possible no case can be imagined in which the necessity of a divine interposition, and its direct and permanent results upon the whole state of humanity, could be more satisfactorily shewn.

1. *I have made thee*] Or "appointed thee." The expression "a god" is not unfrequently used of an appointed representative of God; but here it implies that Moses will stand in this peculiar relation to Pharaoh, that he will address him by a prophet, *i.e.* by one appointed to speak in his name. The pas-

2 Thou shalt speak all that I command thee: and Aaron thy brother shall speak unto Pharaoh, that he send the children of Israel out of his land.

3 And I will harden Pharaoh's heart, and multiply my signs and my wonders in the land of Egypt.

4 But Pharaoh shall not hearken unto you, that I may lay my hand upon Egypt, and bring forth mine armies, *and* my people the children of Israel, out of the land of Egypt by great judgments.

5 And the Egyptians shall know that I *am* the LORD, when I stretch forth mine hand upon Egypt, and bring out the children of Israel from among them.

6 And Moses and Aaron did as the LORD commanded them, so did they.

7 And Moses *was* fourscore years old, and Aaron fourscore and three years old, when they spake unto Pharaoh.

8 ¶ And the LORD spake unto Moses and unto Aaron, saying,

9 When Pharaoh shal speak unto you, saying, Shew a miracle for you: then thou shalt say unto Aaron, Take thy rod, and cast *it* before Pharaoh, *and* it shall become a serpent.

10 ¶ And Moses and Aaron went in unto Pharaoh, and they did so as the LORD had commanded: and Aaron cast down his rod before Pharaoh, and before his servants, and it became a serpent.

11 Then Pharaoh also called the wise men and the sorcerers: now the magicians of Egypt, they also did in like manner with their enchantments.

12 For they cast down every man his rod, and they became serpents: but Aaron's rod swallowed up their rods.

---

sage is an important one as illustrating the primary and essential characteristic of a prophet, he is the declarer of God's will and purpose.

3. *and my wonders*] The distinction between signs and the word here rendered "wonders," according to Kimchi, is that the former is used more generally, the latter only of portents wrought to prove a divine interposition; they were the credentials of God's messengers.

9. *thy rod*] Apparently the rod before described, which Moses on this occasion gives to Aaron as his representative.

a serpent] A different word is used in ch. iv. 3, when the rod of Moses is changed. In that passage the snake is called "Nahash," which corresponds to the Egyptian Ara, or Uræus. Here another and more general term, "Tannin," is employed, which in other passages includes all sea or river monsters, and is more specially applied to the crocodile as a symbol of Egypt. It occurs in the Egyptian ritual, c. 163, nearly in the same form, "Tanem," as a synonym of the monster serpent which represents the principle of antagonism to light and life. The ancient versions either render the word coluber, δράκων, or simply transcribe the Hebrew; thus Syr., Targ., Sam., and Saadia.

11. *magicians*] See Note at the end of the chapter.

with their enchantments] The derivation of the original expression is ambiguous. It may come from a word meaning "flame," or from another meaning "conceal;" in either case it implies a deceptive appearance, an illusion, a juggler's trick, not an actual putting forth of magic power. It bears a very near resemblance to an Egyptian term for a magic formula, sc. Ra, or La, ap. Chabas, 'P. M.' p. 170. Moses describes the act of the sorcerers as it appeared to Pharaoh and the spectators; living serpents may have been thrown down by the jugglers, a feat not transcending the well-known skill of their modern representatives, with whom it is a common trick to handle venomous serpents, and benumb them so that they are motionless and stiff as rods. Pharaoh may or may not have believed in a real transformation; probably he did, for the jugglers have always formed a separate caste, and have kept their arts secret; but in either case he would naturally consider that if the portent wrought by Aaron differed from theirs, it was a difference of degree only, implying merely superiority in a common art. The miracle which followed was sufficient to convince him had he been open to conviction. The accounts in the Koran, Sur. VII. and x x., are curious. They represent the magicians as deceiving the spectators by acting upon their imagination.

12. *swallowed up their rods*] The miracle here is distinctly stated, and is bound up with the very substance of the narrative. Its meaning is obvious. Ewald remarks truly that this miracle was the clearest expression of the truth which underlies all these stories, as he is pleased to call the miracles, viz. the truth and power of the religion of Jehovah in contrast with others.

13 And he hardened Pharaoh's heart, that he hearkened not unto them; as the LORD had said.

14 ¶ And the LORD said unto Moses, Pharaoh's heart *is* hardened, he refuseth to let the people go.

15 Get thee unto Pharaoh in the morning; lo, he goeth out unto the water; and thou shalt stand by the river's brink against he come; and the rod which was turned to a serpent shalt thou take in thine hand.

16 And thou shalt say unto him, The LORD God of the Hebrews hath sent me unto thee, saying, Let my people go, that they may serve me in the wilderness: and, behold, hitherto thou wouldest not hear.

17 Thus saith the LORD, In this thou shalt know that I *am* the LORD: behold, I will smite with the rod that *is* in mine hand upon the waters which *are* in the river, and they shall be turned to blood.

18 And the fish that *is* in the river shall die, and the river shall stink; and the Egyptians shall lothe to drink of the water of the river.

19 ¶ And the LORD spake unto Moses, Say unto Aaron, Take thy rod, and stretch out thine hand upon the waters of Egypt, upon their streams, upon their rivers, and upon their ponds, and upon all their †pools of water, that they may become blood; and *that* there may be blood

† Heb. *gathering of their waters.*

---

13. *And he hardened*] Or **Pharaoh's heart was hardened.** The word is here used intransitively, as in many passages: thus all the Ancient Versions.

15. *he goeth out unto the water*] The Nile was worshipped under various names and symbols, at Memphis especially, as Hapi, *i.e.* Apis, the sacred bull, or living representation of Osiris, of whom the river was regarded as the embodiment or manifestation. See 'Zeitschrift Eg.' 1868, p. 123. It is therefore probable that the king went in the morning to offer his devotions. This gives a peculiar force and suitableness to the miracle. The reason which Knobel assigns is not incompatible with this. It was the season of the yearly overflowing, about the middle of June. (The Arabic almanacs give the 18th of Payni, *i.e.* the 12th of June, for the festival of the rising of the Nile.) The daily rise of the water was accurately recorded, probably in the time of Moses, as some centuries later, under the personal superintendence of the king. In early inscriptions the Nilometer is the symbol of stability and providential care. According to Diodorus a Nilometer was erected at Memphis under the ancient Pharaohs; one is described by Lepsius which bears the name of Amenemha III., of the 12th dynasty, by whom the system of irrigation was completed. See Appendix.

The First Plague.

17. *turned to blood*] In accordance with the general character of the narrative it might be expected that this miracle would bear a certain resemblance to natural phenomena, and therefore be one which Pharaoh might see with amazement and dismay, yet without complete conviction. It is well known that before the rise the water of the Nile is green and unfit to drink. About the 25th of June it becomes clear, and then yellow, and gradually reddish like ochre; this effect has been generally attributed to the red earth brought down from Sennaar, but Ehrenberg proves that it is owing to the presence of microscopic cryptogams and infusoria. The depth of the colour varies in different years; when it is very deep the water has an offensive smell. Late travellers say that at such seasons the broad turbid tide has a striking resemblance to a river of blood. The supernatural character of the visitation was attested by the suddenness of the change; by its immediate connection with the words and act of Moses, and by its effects. It killed the fishes, and made the water unfit for use, neither of which results follows the annual discoloration.

18. *shall lothe*] Lit. "be weary of," but the Authorised Version expresses the meaning. The word has a special force as applied to the water of the Nile, which has a certain sweetness when purified of the slime, and has always been regarded by Egyptians as a blessing peculiar to their land. It is the only pure and wholesome water in their country, since the water in wells and cisterns is unwholesome, while rain water seldom falls, and fountains are extremely rare. Maillet, ap. Kalisch.

19. The expressions in this verse shew an accurate knowledge of Egypt, where the water system was complete at a period long before Moses. Lepsius ('Zeitschrift,' 1865) describes it carefully. *Their streams* mean the natural branches of the Nile in Lower Egypt. The word *rivers* should rather be *canals*. Moses uses the Egyptian word explained above (ch. ii.). It includes canals. They were of great extent, running parallel to the Nile, and

throughout all the land of Egypt, both in *vessels of* wood, and in *vessels of* stone.

20 And Moses and Aaron did so, as the LORD commanded; and he *a*lifted up the rod, and smote the waters that *were* in the river, in the sight of Pharaoh, and in the sight of his servants; and all the *b*waters that *were* in the river were turned to blood.

21 And the fish that *was* in the river died; and the river stank, and the Egyptians could not drink of the water of the river; and there was blood throughout all the land of Egypt.

22 *c*And the magicians of Egypt did so with their enchantments: and Pharaoh's heart was hardened, neither did he hearken unto them; as the LORD had said.

23 And Pharaoh turned and went into his house, neither did he set his heart to this also.

24 And all the Egyptians digged round about the river for water to drink; for they could not drink of the water of the river.

25 And seven days were fulfilled, after that the LORD had smitten the river.

a chap. 17. 5.
b Psal. 78. 44.
c Wisd. 17. 7.

---

communicating with it by sluices, which were opened at the rise, and closed at the subsidence of the inundation. The word rendered "*ponds*" refers either to natural fountains, or more probably to cisterns or tanks found in every town and village. The "*pools*," lit. "gathering of waters," were the reservoirs, always large and some of enormous extent, containing sufficient water to irrigate the country in the dry season.

in vessels of wood] Lit. "in wood and stone;" but the word "vessels" is understood and should be retained. This also marks the familiarity of the writer with Egyptian customs. The Nile water is kept in vessels and is purified for use by filtering, and by certain ingredients such as the paste of almonds. At present the vessels are generally earthenware. The words in the text appear to include all household vessels in which the water was kept.

21. *the fish*, &c.] The expression may not necessarily mean "all the fish;" but a great mortality is of course implied, and would be a most impressive warning. The Egyptians subsisted to a great extent on the fish of the Nile, though salt-water fish was regarded as impure. A mortality among the fish was a plague much dreaded. In a hymn to the Nile written by the scribe Enna it is said that the wrath of Hapi the Nile-God is a calamity for the fishes. See Maspero, 'Hymne au Nil,' p. 27.

22. *did so*] From this it must be inferred that the plague though general was not universal. In numberless instances the Hebrew terms which imply universality must be understood in a limited sense.

24. *digged round about the river*] This statement corroborates the explanation given above on *v.* 17. The discoloured water would be purified by a natural filtration.

25. *seven days*] This marks the duration of the plague. The natural discoloration of the Nile water lasts generally much longer, about 20 days.

NOTE on CHAP. VII. 11.

11. Three names for the magicians of Egypt are given in this verse. The first and last occur in Genesis, ch. v. The word (חכמים), wise men, is used specifically of men who know occult arts. Corresponding expressions in Arabic are well known, as araph, alam, &c. Thus in the Acts the sorcerer Bar-jesus is called Elymas, "the knowing one." In ancient Egyptian the most general name is Rechiu Chetu, *i.e.* people who know things, the word "things" being applied technically to secret and curious things. The word rendered "sorcerers" (מכשפים) occurs first in this passage. It is used in the sense "muttering magic formulæ." According to Gesenius the original meaning, as retained in Syriac and Ethiopic, is simply to worship or pray. No exact parallel is found for this word among the numerous designations for sorcerers in Egyptian documents; but it seems not improbable that it may be connected with "Chesef," a very common word used specially in the sense of repelling, driving away, conjuring all noxious creatures by magic formulæ. Thus in the funeral ritual there are no less than 11 chapters (32—42) containing forms for "stopping" or driving away crocodiles, snakes, asps, &c. It was natural that Pharaoh should have sent especially for persons armed with such formulæ on this occasion. The more general word "chartummim," which corresponds in meaning to ἱερογραμ-

ματεὺς or ἐξηγητής, "sacred scribe" or "interpreter," has not been yet traced in Egyptian. If however it is resolved into its probable elements, the first syllable חר (char) answers exactly to "cher," one of the commonest Egyptian words, used in compound terms as "bearing," "having," "possessing;" the second part corresponds to "temu" or "tum," "to speak. utter," which is applied specifically to uttering a sacred name, and apparently as "a spell." Thus on certain days of the calendar it was unlawful to utter (temu) the name of Set or Sutech, the Typhon, or spirit of force and destruction. See 'Papyrus Sallier,' IV. p. 12, last line; and Brugsch, 'D. H.' s. v. In the trilingual inscription lately discovered at San, "tum" means to recite a sacred hymn, l. 34. Cher-tum would thus mean "bearer of sacred words."

The most complete and interesting account of Egyptian magic is given by M. Chabas in his work called 'Le Papyrus Magique,' Harris, 1866. Books containing magic formulæ belonged exclusively to the king; no one was permitted to consult them but the priests and wise men, who formed a council or college, and were called in by the Pharaoh on all occasions of difficulty. These "wise men" are called "scribes" (see Brugsch, 'D. H.' p. 1576), "scribes of the sacred house," or "te-ameni," *i.e.* "scribes of occult writings," &c. Under the 20th dynasty, the use of these books was interdicted under pain of death. Two curious documents (the Papyrus Lee and Rollin explained by M. Chabas, and lately edited by Pleyte) give a full account of the trial and execution of a criminal who fraudulently obtained possession of some books kept in the archives of the palace. No formulæ are more common than those which were used to fascinate, or to repel serpents.

The names of the two principal magicians, Jannes and Jambres, who "withstood Moses" are preserved by S. Paul, 2 Tim. iii. 8. Both names are Egyptian, in which language An, or Anna, identical with Jannes, means scribe. It was also a proper name borne by a writer well known in Papyri of the time of Rameses II. Jambres may mean Scribe of the South. The tradition was widely spread. It is found in the Talmud, in the later Targum, and in other Rabbinical writings quoted by Buxtorf, 'Lex. H. C.' p. 946. Pliny, who makes Moses, Jamnes, and Jotape heads of magic factions, seems to have derived his information from other sources, and he is followed by Apuleius. Numenius, a Pythagorean, quoted by Eusebius, comes nearer to the truth, though according to Greek habit he transforms Moses into Musæus.

CHAPTER VIII.

1 *Frogs are sent.* 8 *Pharaoh sueth to Moses,* 12 *and Moses by prayer removeth them away.* 16 *The dust is turned into lice, which the magicians could not do.* 20 *The swarms of flies.* 25 *Pharaoh inclineth to let the people go,* 32 *but yet is hardened.*

AND the LORD spake unto Moses, Go unto Pharaoh, and say unto him, Thus saith the LORD, Let my people go, that they may serve me.

2 And if thou refuse to let *them* go, behold, I will smite all thy borders with frogs:

3 And the river shall bring forth frogs abundantly, which shall go up and come into thine house, and into

---

The Second Plague.

CHAP. VIII. 2. *with frogs*] The annoyance and suffering caused by frogs are described by ancient writers, quoted by Bochart, 'Hier.' III. In Egypt they sometimes amount at present to a severe visitation. Some months appear to have elapsed between this and the former plague, if they made their appearance at the usual time, that is (according to Seetzen, who gives the fullest and most accurate account of them, Vol. III. p. 492) in September. He describes two species, the rana Nilotica, and the rana Mosaica, called by the natives "Dofda," which exactly corresponds to the Hebrew word used in this and no other passage, except in the psalms taken from it; it is not a general designation, but restricted to the species, and probably of Egyptian origin. See Appendix and end of volume. They are small, do not leap much, are much like toads, and fill the whole country with their croakings. They are generally consumed rapidly by the Ibis (ardea Ibis), which thus preserves the land from the stench described *v.* 14. This plague was thus, like the preceding, in general accordance with natural phenomena, but marvellous both for its extent and intensity, and for its direct connection with the words and acts of God's messengers. It had also apparently, like the other plagues, a direct bearing upon Egyptian superstitions. A female deity with a frog's head, named Heka, was worshipped in the district of Sah (*i.e.* Benihassan) as the wife of Chnum, the god of the cataracts, or of the inundation; see Brugsch, 'Geog.' p. 224. Lepsius has shewn that the frog was connected with the most

thy bedchamber, and upon thy bed, and into the house of thy servants, and upon thy people, and into thine ovens, and into thy ⁿkneadingtroughs:

Or, dough.

4 And the frogs shall come up both on thee, and upon thy people, and upon all thy servants.

5 ¶ And the LORD spake unto Moses, Say unto Aaron, Stretch forth thine hand with thy rod over the streams, over the rivers, and over the ponds, and cause frogs to come up upon the land of Egypt.

6 And Aaron stretched out his hand over the waters of Egypt; and the frogs came up, and covered the land of Egypt.

a Wisd. 17. 7.

7 *ᵃ* And the magicians did so with their enchantments, and brought up frogs upon the land of Egypt.

8 ¶ Then Pharaoh called for Moses and Aaron, and said, Intreat the LORD, that he may take away the frogs from me, and from my people; and I will let the people go, that they may do sacrifice unto the LORD.

Or, Have this honour over me, &c.
Or, against when.

9 And Moses said unto Pharaoh, ⁿGlory over me: ⁿwhen shall I in-treat for thee, and for thy servants, and for thy people, †to destroy. the frogs from thee and thy houses, that they may remain in the river only?

† Heb. *to cut off.*

10 And he said, ⁿTomorrow. And he said, *Be it* according to thy word: that thou mayest know that *there is* none like unto the LORD our God.

ⁿOr, *Against to morrow.*

11 And the frogs shall depart from thee, and from thy houses, and from thy servants, and from thy people; they shall remain in the river only.

12 And Moses and Aaron went out from Pharaoh: and Moses cried unto the LORD because of the frogs which he had brought against Pharaoh.

13 And the LORD did according to the word of Moses; and the frogs died out of the houses, out of the villages, and out of the fields.

14 And they gathered them together upon heaps: and the land stank.

15 But when Pharaoh saw that there was respite, he hardened his heart, and hearkened not unto them; as the LORD had said.

---

ancient forms of nature-worship in Egypt. See also Duemichen, 'Æg. Zeitschrift,' 1869, p. 6. According to Chæremon (see Bunsen's 'Egypt,' Vol. v. p. 736) the frog was regarded as a symbol of regeneration. See the note, p. 242, on the adoration of the frog by the father of Rameses II.

3. *into thine house*] This appears to have been peculiar to the plague, as such. No mention is made of it by travellers. It was specially the visitation which would be felt by the scrupulously clean Egyptians.

kneadingtroughs] Not "dough," as in the margin.

7. The magicians would seem to have been able to increase the plague, but not to remove it; hence Pharaoh's application to Moses, the first symptom of yielding. An explanation, which is certainly ingenious and not improbable, is suggested by a late commentator (Hirsch, 1869). He assumes that the words "the magicians did so," mean that they imitated the action of Aaron, stretching out their rods, but using magic formulæ with the intention of driving away the frogs, the result being not only a frustration of their object, but an increase of the plague.

9. *Glory over me*] The expression is rather obscure, but it is supposed by most of the later, and by some early commentators, to mean, as the margin renders it, "have honour over me," *i.e.* have the honour, or advantage over me, directing me when I shall entreat God for thee and thy servants, &c. Moses thus accepts the first intimation of a change of mind in Pharaoh, and expresses himself, doubtless in accordance with Egyptian usage, at once courteously and deferentially. It is, however, obvious that such an expression would not have been attributed to him by a later writer. The old versions, LXX., Vulg., Saadia, who are followed by Gesenius, generally render the word, appoint for me, determine for me when, &c., the Syriac has "ask for me a time when;" this agrees well with the answer "to-morrow."

when] Or **by when**; *i.e.* for what exact time. Pharaoh's answer in *v.* 10 refers to this, **by to-morrow**. The shortness of the time would, of course, be a test of the supernatural character of the transaction.

13. *villages*] Lit. "inclosures, or courtyards."

16 ¶ And the LORD said unto Moses, Say unto Aaron, Stretch out thy rod, and smite the dust of the land, that it may become lice throughout all the land of Egypt.

17 And they did so; for Aaron stretched out his hand with his rod, and smote the dust of the earth, and it became lice in man, and in beast; all the dust of the land became lice throughout all the land of Egypt.

18 And the magicians did so with their enchantments to bring forth lice, but they could not: so there were lice upon man, and upon beast.

19 Then the magicians said unto Pharaoh, This *is* the finger of God: and Pharaoh's heart was hardened, and he hearkened not unto them; as the LORD had said.

20 ¶ And the LORD said unto Moses, Rise up early in the morning, and stand before Pharaoh; lo, he cometh forth to the water; and say unto him, Thus saith the LORD, Let my people go, that they may serve me.

21 Else, if thou wilt not let my people go, behold, I will send ¹swarms *of flies* upon thee, and upon thy servants, and upon thy people, and into thy houses: and the houses of the Egyptians shall be full of swarms *of flies*, and also the ground whereon they *are*.

¹ Or, *a mixture of noisome beasts, &c.*

The Third Plague.

It is observed by Hebrew commentators that the nine plagues are divided into three groups: distinct warnings are given of the first two plagues in each group; the third in each is inflicted without any previous notice, the third, *lice*, the sixth, *boils*, the ninth, *darkness*.

16. *the dust of the land*] The two preceding plagues fell upon the Nile. This fell on the earth, which was worshipped under the name Seb, its personification, regarded, in the pantheistic system of Egypt, as the father of the gods. See Brugsch, 'Zeitschrift,' 1868, p. 123. An especial sacredness was attached to the black fertile soil of the basin of the Nile, called Chemi, from which the ancient name of Egypt is supposed to be derived.

lice] In Hebrew "Kinnim." The word occurs only in connection with this plague. These insects are generally identified with mosquitos, a plague nowhere greater than in Egypt. They are most troublesome towards October, *i.e.* soon after the plague of frogs, and are dreaded not only for the pain and annoyance which they cause, but also because they are said to penetrate into the body through the nostrils and ears. Thus the LXX. (σκνίφες), Philo, and Origen, whose testimony as residents in Egypt is of great weight. The mosquito net is an indispensable article to Egyptian travellers. There are however some grave objections to this interpretation. Mosquitos are produced in stagnant waters where their larvæ are deposited, whereas these kinnim spring from the dust of the earth. The word in our version may be nearer to the original, which is probably Egyptian; see Appendix. Late travellers (*e.g.* Sir S. Baker) describe the visitation of vermin in very similar terms, " it is as though the very dust were turned into lice." The lice which he describes are a sort of tick, not larger than a grain of sand, which when filled with blood expands to the size of a hazel nut. Saadia renders the word "lice."

17. *all the dust*] The sense is here necessarily limited: the meaning being, the dust swarmed with lice in every part of the land.

19. *the finger of God*] This expression is thoroughly Egyptian; it need not imply that the magicians recognised Jehovah as the God who wrought the marvel, which they attributed generally to the act of the Deity. They may possibly have referred it to a god hostile to their own protectors, such as Set, or Sutech, the Typhon of later mythology, to whom such calamities were attributed by popular superstition.

The Fourth Plague.

20. *cometh forth to the water*] See note ch. vii. 15. It is not improbable that on this occasion Pharaoh went to the Nile with a procession in order to open the solemn festival, which was held 120 days after the first rise, at the end of October or early in November, when the inundation is abating and the first traces of vegetation are seen on the deposit of fresh soil.

The plague now denounced may be regarded as connected with the atmosphere, each element in turn being converted into a scourge. The air was an object of worship, personified in the deity Shu, the son of Ra, the sun-god; or in Isis, queen of heaven.

21. *swarms of flies*] The Hebrew has the word "Arob," which most of the ancient, and some modern interpreters, understand to mean a mixture of beasts and insects, a sense

22 And I will sever in that day the land of Goshen, in which my people dwell, that no swarms *of flies* shall be there; to the end thou mayest know that I *am* the LORD in the midst of the earth.

23 And I will put ¹a division between my people and thy people: ‖ to morrow shall this sign be.

24 And the LORD did so; and *b* there came a grievous swarm *of flies* into the house of Pharaoh, and *into* his servants' houses, and into all the land of Egypt: the land was ¹ corrupted by reason of the swarm *of flies*.

25 ¶ And Pharaoh called for Moses and for Aaron, and said, Go ye, sacrifice to your God in the land.

26 And Moses said, It is not meet so to do; for we shall sacrifice the abomination of the Egyptians to the LORD our God: lo, shall we sacrifice the abomination of the Egyptians before their eyes, and will they not stone us?

27 We will go three days' journey into the wilderness, and sacrifice to the LORD our God, as *c* he shall command us.

¹ Heb. *a redemption.*
‖ Or, *by to morrow.*
b Wisd. 16. 9.
¹ Or *destroyed.*
c chap. 18.

---

derived from the Arabic "Arab," "mixed." (Thus the Vulg., Targ., Saadia, Syr., and Aquila.) It is now, however, more generally supposed that a particular species of fly is described, the dog-fly (κυνόμυια, LXX.), which at certain seasons is described as a far worse plague than mosquitos. The bite is exceedingly sharp and painful, causing severe inflammation, especially in the eyelids. Coming in immense swarms they cover all objects in black and loathsome masses and attack every exposed part of a traveller's person with incredible pertinacity. Some commentators however adopt the opinion of Œdmann, who identifies the species here described with the blatta orientalis, or the kakerlaque, a species of beetle, of which Munk ('Palestine,' p. 120) says: "Ceux qui ont voyagé sur le Nil savent combien cet insecte est incommode: les bateaux en sont infestés, et on les y voit souvent par milliers." Kalisch quotes passages which prove that they inflict painful bites and consume all sorts of materials. There would be a special fitness in this plague, since the beetle was reverenced by the Egyptians as the symbol of life, of reproductive or creative power. No object is more common in hieroglyphics, where it represents the word "cheper," "to exist," or "to become." The sun-god, as creator, bore the name Chepera, and is represented in the form, or with the head, of a beetle. The word "arob," which occurs nowhere else, moreover bears a very near resemblance to an old Egyptian word, retained in Coptic, which designates a species of beetle. See Brugsch, 'D. H.' p. 178, s.v. 'Abeb.'

22. *I will sever*, &c.] This severance constituted a specific difference between this and the preceding plagues. Pharaoh could not of course attribute the exemption of Goshen from a scourge, which fell on the valley of the Nile, to an Egyptian deity, certainly not to Chepera (see the last note), a special object of worship in lower Egypt

in the midst]. Literally "heart." The idiom is common in Hebrew, but there may possibly be an allusion to the Egyptian "heart" used specially to designate lower Egypt.

25. *to your God*] Pharaoh now admits the existence and power of the God whom he had professed not to know; but, as Moses is careful to record, he recognises Him only as the national Deity of the Israelites.

in the land] *i.e.* In Egypt, not beyond the frontier.

26. *the abomination*] The expression may mean either the object of an abominable worship (as Chemosh is called the abomination of Moab, and Moloch the abomination of Ammon, see 1 Kings xi. 7), or an animal which the Egyptians held it sacrilegious to slay. The latter meaning seems more probable, considering that the words were addressed to Pharaoh. Thus Ros., Knob., but the former meaning is preferred by Bp. Wordsworth, and is given by the LXX., Targ., Vulg., and Syr. In either case the ox, bull, or cow, is meant. The cow was never sacrificed in Egypt, being sacred to Isis; but as a general rule, no animal was slaughtered in a district where it represented a local deity. From a very early age the ox was worshipped throughout Egypt, and more especially at Heliopolis and Memphis under various designations, Apis, Mnevis, Amen-Ehe, as the symbol or manifestation of their greatest deities, Osiris, Atum, Ptah, and Isis.

27. *three days' journey*] See note on ch. iii. 18. The demand does not refer to a journey to Sinai, which would have occupied much longer time. In the next verse Pharaoh grants the permission, not however without imposing a condition which would have enabled him to take effectual measures to prevent the final emigration of the Israelites. The power of the Pharaohs extended far beyond the frontier, especially on the road to

28 And Pharaoh said, I will let you go, that ye may sacrifice to the LORD your God in the wilderness; only ye shall not go very far away: intreat for me.

29 And Moses said, Behold, I go out from thee, and I will intreat the LORD that the swarms *of flies* may depart from Pharaoh, from his servants, and from his people, to morrow: but let not Pharaoh deal deceitfully any more in not letting the people go to sacrifice to the LORD.

30 And Moses went out from Pharaoh, and intreated the LORD.

31 And the LORD did according to the word of Moses; and he removed the swarms *of flies* from Pharaoh, from his servants, and from his people; there remained not one.

32 And Pharaoh hardened his heart at this time also, neither would he let the people go.

CHAPTER IX.

1 *The murrain of beasts.* 8 *The plague of boils and blains.* 13 *His message about the hail.* 22 *The plague of hail.* 27 *Pharaoh sueth to Moses,* 35 *but yet is hardened.*

THEN the LORD said unto Moses, Go in unto Pharaoh, and tell him, Thus saith the LORD God of the Hebrews, Let my people go, that they may serve me.

2 For if thou refuse to let *them* go, and wilt hold them still,

3 Behold, the hand of the LORD is upon thy cattle which *is* in the field, upon the horses, upon the asses, upon the camels, upon the oxen, and upon the sheep: *there shall be* a very grievous murrain.

4 And the LORD shall sever between the cattle of Israel and the cattle of Egypt: and there shall nothing die of all *that is* the children's of Israel.

5 And the LORD appointed a set time, saying, To morrow the LORD shall do this thing in the land.

6 And the LORD did that thing on the morrow, and all the cattle of Egypt died: but of the cattle of the children of Israel died not one.

7 And Pharaoh sent, and, behold, there was not one of the cattle of the Israelites dead. And the heart of Pharaoh was hardened, and he did not let the people go.

8 ¶ And the LORD said unto Moses and unto Aaron, Take to you

Palestine, which was commanded by fortresses erected by the early sovereigns of the 18th dynasty.

The Fifth Plague.

CHAP. IX. 3. *a very grievous murrain*] Or "pestilence;" but the word murrain, *i.e.* a great mortality, exactly expresses the meaning. This terrible visitation struck far more severely than the preceding, which had caused distress and suffering; it attacked the resources of the nation. The disease does not appear to have been common in ancient times, no distinct notice is found on the monuments, unless it is included, as seems not improbable, under the term "Aat," which, as M. Chabas shews, applies to the contagious or epidemic pestilence which frequently, as it would almost seem annually, broke out after the subsidence of the inundation; see 'Mélanges Egyptologiques,' I. p. 39. Within the last few years the murrain has thrice fallen upon Egypt, in 1842, 1863, and 1866 (also 60 years previously); when nearly the whole of the herds have been destroyed. The disease appears to have been of the same kind as that which lately fell so severely upon England. The exact time of the infliction is not mentioned; but in Egypt the cattle are in the fields from December to the end of April, and the disease may have broken out in the former month when the cattle were predisposed to it by the change from confinement to the open air, and from old to fresh pastures; a change more dangerous than usual in so exceptional a year. In 1863 the murrain began in November, and was at its height in December.

the camels] These animals are only twice mentioned, here and Gen. xii. 16, in connection with Egypt. In this passage the enumeration of cattle is studiously complete. It is shewn in the Appendix, that though camels are never represented on the monuments, they were known to the Egyptians and were probably used on the frontier bordering on the desert.

7. *was hardened*] Pharaoh may have attributed to natural causes both the severity of the plague and even the exemption of the Israelites, a pastoral race well acquainted with all that appertained to the care of cattle; and dwelling in a district probably far more healthy than the rest of lower Egypt.

handfuls of ashes of the furnace, and let Moses sprinkle it toward the heaven in the sight of Pharaoh.

9 And it shall become small dust in all the land of Egypt, and shall be a boil breaking forth *with* blains upon man, and upon beast, throughout all the land of Egypt.

10 And they took ashes of the furnace, and stood before Pharaoh; and Moses sprinkled it up toward heaven; and it became a boil breaking forth *with* blains upon man, and upon beast.

11 And the magicians could not stand before Moses because of the boils; for the boil was upon the magicians, and upon all the Egyptians.

12 And the LORD hardened the heart of Pharaoh, and he hearkened not unto them; *a*as the LORD had spoken unto Moses. *a* chap. 4. 21.

13 ¶ And the LORD said unto Moses, Rise up early in the morning, and stand before Pharaoh, and say unto him, Thus saith the LORD God of the Hebrews, Let my people go, that they may serve me.

14 For I will at this time send all my plagues upon thine heart, and upon thy servants, and upon thy people; that thou mayest know that *there is* none like me in all the earth.

15 For now I will stretch out my hand, that I may smite thee and thy people with pestilence; and thou shalt be cut off from the earth.

The Sixth Plague.

This marks a distinct advance and change in the character of the visitations. Hitherto the Egyptians had not been attacked directly in their own persons. It is the second plague which was not preceded by a demand and warning, probably on account of the peculiar hardness shewn by Pharaoh in reference to the murrain.

8. *ashes of the furnace*] The Hebrew word occurs only in the Pentateuch, and is probably of Egyptian origin. The act was evidently symbolical: the ashes were to be sprinkled towards heaven, challenging, so to speak, the Egyptian Deities, and specially it may be Neit, who bore the designation "The Great Mother Queen of highest heaven," and was worshipped as the tutelary Goddess of lower Egypt. There may possibly be a reference to an Egyptian custom of scattering to the winds ashes of victims offered to Sutech, or Typhon. Human sacrifices said to have been offered at Heliopolis under the Shepherd dynasty were abolished by Amosis I., but some part of the rite may have been retained, and the memory of the old superstition would give a terrible significance to the act. Thus Burder, Hævernick and Kurtz.

9. *a boil breaking forth with blains*] The word rendered boil is derived from "burning inflammation," and is used elsewhere of plague-boils, of the leprosy, and elephantiasis. See Deut. xxviii. 27, and 35, which may specially refer to this passage. Here it means probably a burning tumour or carbuncle breaking out in pustulous ulcers. Cutaneous eruptions of extreme severity are common in the valley of the Nile, some bearing a near resemblance to the symptoms described in this passage. The date is not marked. It was probably soon after the last plague. In an old Egyptian calendar mention is made of severe contagious diseases in December, Pap. Sall. IV. The analogy of natural law is still preserved, the miracle consisting in the severity of the plague and its direct connection with the act of Moses.

11. This verse seems to imply that the magicians now formally gave way and confessed their defeat.

The Seventh Plague.

13—34. The plague of hail: with this begins the last series of plagues, which differ from the former both in their severity and their effects. Each produced a temporary, but real change in Pharaoh's feelings.

14. *all my plagues*] This applies to all the plagues which follow; the effect of each was foreseen and foretold. The words "at this time" are understood by some to limit the application to the plague of hail, but they point more probably to a rapid and continuous succession of blows. The plagues which precede appear to have been spread over a considerable time; the first message of Moses was delivered after the early harvest of the year before, when the Israelites could gather stubble, *i.e.* in April and May: the second mission, when the plagues began, was probably towards the end of June, and they went on at intervals until the winter; this plague was in February; see note on *v.* 31.

15. *For now*, &c.] This verse (as scholars are agreed, *e.g.* Rosenmüller, Ewald, Knobel, Keil) should be rendered thus: **For now in**

16 And in very deed for ^bthis cause have I †raised thee up, for to shew *in* thee my power; and that my name may be declared throughout all the earth.

17 As yet exaltest thou thyself against my people, that thou wilt not let them go?

18 Behold, to morrow about this time I will cause it to rain a very grievous hail, such as hath not been in Egypt since the foundation thereof even until now.

19 Send therefore now, *and* gather thy cattle, and all that thou hast in the field; *for upon* every man and beast which shall be found in the field, and shall not be brought home, the hail shall come down upon them, and they shall die.

20 He that feared the word of the LORD among the servants of Pharaoh made his servants and his cattle flee into the houses:

21 And he that †regarded not the word of the LORD left his servants and his cattle in the field.

22 ¶ And the LORD said unto Moses, Stretch forth thine hand toward heaven, that there may be hail in all the land of Egypt, upon man, and upon beast, and upon every herb of the field, throughout the land of Egypt.

23 And Moses stretched forth his rod toward heaven: and the LORD sent thunder and hail, and the fire ran along upon the ground; and the LORD rained hail upon the land of Egypt.

24 So there was hail, and fire mingled with the hail, very grievous, such as there was none like it in all the land of Egypt since it became a nation.

25 And the hail smote throughout all the land of Egypt all that *was* in the field, both man and beast; and the hail smote every herb of the field, and brake every tree of the field.

26 Only in the land of Goshen, where the children of Israel *were*, was there no hail.

27 ¶ And Pharaoh sent, and called for Moses and Aaron, and said unto them, I have sinned this time: the

---

deed had I stretched forth my hand and smitten thee and thy people with the pestilence then hadst thou been cut off from the earth. The next verse gives the reason why God had not thus inflicted a summary punishment once for all.

16. *have I raised thee up*] The margin made thee stand is correct: the meaning is, not that God raised Pharaoh to a position of rank and power, but that he kept him standing, *i.e.* permitted him to live and hold out until His own purpose was accomplished.

18. *a very grievous hail*] This verse distinctly states that the miracle consisted in the magnitude of the infliction and in its immediate connection with the act of Moses. Travellers in lower Egypt speak of storms of snow, thunder and lightning in the winter months; and Seetzen and Willman (quoted by Knobel) describe storms of thunder and hail in March. A friend (Rev. T. H. Tooke) describes a storm of extreme severity, which lasted 24 hours, in the middle of February, at Benihassan. The natives spoke of it as not uncommon at that season.

19. *thy cattle*] In Egypt the cattle are sent to pasture in the open country from January to April, when the grass is abundant; see note on *v.* 3. They are kept in stalls the rest of the year. The word "gather" does not exactly express the meaning of the original, "cause to flee," *i.e.* bring them rapidly under cover.

20. *the word of the* LORD] This gives the first indication that the warnings had a salutary effect upon the Egyptians. See ch. xi. 3.

22. *in all the land of Egypt*] The storms described above fell on lower Egypt: the expression here may imply that this extended to the upper valley of the Nile, but it is possible that the land of Mizraim is used specially to designate the Delta and the adjoining district.

23. *and the fire ran along upon the ground*] The expression is peculiar (literally "fire walked earthwards"), and appears to describe a succession of flashes mingled with the hail: our Authorised Version seems to present a true and graphic account of the phenomenon.

25. *smote*] The words imply heavy damage both to herbs and trees, but not total destruction: the loss however must have been enormous.

27. *this time*] *i.e.* I acknowledge now that I have sinned.

286   EXODUS. IX. X.   [v. 28—1.

LORD *is* righteous, and I and my people *are* wicked.

28 Intreat the LORD (for *it is* enough) that there be no *more* †mighty thunderings and hail; and I will let you go, and ye shall stay no longer.

† Heb. *voices of God.*

29 And Moses said unto him, As soon as I am gone out of the city, I will spread abroad my hands unto the LORD; *and* the thunder shall cease, neither shall there be any more hail; that thou mayest know how that the *c* earth *is* the LORD'S.

c Psal. 24. I.

30 But as for thee and thy servants, I know that ye will not yet fear the LORD God.

31 And the flax and the barley was smitten: for the barley *was* in the ear, and the flax *was* bolled.

32 But the wheat and the rie were not smitten: for they *were* †not grown up.

† Heb. *hidden,* or, *dark.*

33 And Moses went out of the city from Pharaoh, and spread abroad his hands unto the LORD: and the thunders and hail ceased, and the rain was not poured upon the earth.

34 And when Pharaoh saw that the rain and the hail and the thunders were ceased, he sinned yet more, and hardened his heart, he and his servants.

35 And the heart of Pharaoh was hardened, neither would he let the children of Israel go; as the LORD had spoken †by Moses.

† Heb. *by the hand of Moses.*

CHAPTER X.

1 *God threateneth to send locusts.* 7 *Pharaoh, moved by his servants, inclineth to let the Israelites go.* 12 *The plague of the locusts.* 16 *Pharaoh sueth to Moses.* 21 *The plague of darkness.* 24 *Pharaoh sueth unto Moses,* 27 *but yet is hardened.*

AND the LORD said unto Moses, Go in unto Pharaoh: for *a* I have hardened his heart, and the heart of his servants, that I might shew these my signs before him:

a chap. 4. 21.

---

the LORD] Thus for the first time Pharaoh explicitly recognizes Jehovah as God.

28. *for it is enough*] The Authorised Version is not literal, but it probably expresses the meaning of the original, which is somewhat obscure, and it is much, *i.e.* enough, that there should be voices of God (thunderings) and hail, no more are needed now.

29. *the earth is the* LORD'S] This declaration has a direct reference to Egyptian superstition. Each God was held to have special power within a given district; Pharaoh had learned that Jehovah was *a* God, he was now to admit that his power extended over the whole earth. The unity and universality of the Divine power are tenets distinctly promulgated in the Pentateuch, and though occasionally recognized in ancient Egyptian documents (*e.g.* in the early copies of the 17th chapter of the Funeral Ritual under the 11th dynasty), were overlaid at a very early period by systems alternating between Polytheism and Pantheism.

31. *the flax was bolled*] *i.e.* in blossom. This is a point of great importance. It marks the time. In the north of Egypt the barley ripens and flax blossoms about the middle of February, or at the latest early in March, and both are gathered in before April, when the wheat harvest begins (Forskal and Seetzen ap. Knobel). The cultivation of flax must have been of great importance; linen was preferred to any material and exclusively used by the priests. It is frequently mentioned on Egyptian monuments. Four kinds are noted by Pliny (XIX. 1) as used in Egypt. He makes special mention of Tanis, *i.e.* Zoan, as one of the places famous for flax. The texture was remarkably fine, in general quality equal to the best now made, and for the evenness of the threads, without knot or break, superior to any of modern manufacture. Wilkinson on Herod. II. c. 37, p. 54.

32. *rie*] Rather **spelt**, triticum spelta, the common food of the ancient Egyptians, now called doora by the natives: the only grain, according to Wilkinson (on Herod. II. c. 36), represented on the sculptures: the name however occurs on the monuments very frequently in combination with other species. See Brugsch, 'D. H.' p. 442.

34. *hardened*] Different words are used in this and the following verse: here the word means "heavy," *i.e.* obtuse, incapable of forming a right judgment; the other, which is more frequently used in this narrative, is stronger and implies a stubborn resolution. The LXX. render the former word ἐβάρυνε, the latter ἐσκλήρυνθη. The other old Versions mark the distinction with equal clearness.

The Eighth Plague.

CHAP. X. 1—20. *I have hardened*] Literally "made heavy." This state of mind, though judicial, may be accounted for psychologically by the fact that the corn, to

2 And that thou mayest tell in the ears of thy son, and of thy son's son, what things I have wrought in Egypt, and my signs which I have done among them; that ye may know how that I *am* the LORD.

3 And Moses and Aaron came in unto Pharaoh, and said unto him, Thus saith the LORD God of the Hebrews, How long wilt thou refuse to humble thyself before me? let my people go, that they may serve me.

4 Else, if thou refuse to let my people go, behold, to morrow will I bring the *b*locusts into thy coast:

5 And they shall cover the *f*face of the earth, that one cannot be able to see the earth: and they shall eat the residue of that which is escaped, which remaineth unto you from the hail, and shall eat every tree which groweth for you out of the field:

6 And they shall fill thy houses, and the houses of all thy servants, and the houses of all the Egyptians; which neither thy fathers, nor thy fathers' fathers have seen, since the day that they were upon the earth unto this day. And he turned himself, and went out from Pharaoh.

7 And Pharaoh's servants said unto him, How long shall this man be a snare unto us? let the men go, that they may serve the LORD their God: knowest thou not yet that Egypt is destroyed?

8 And Moses and Aaron were brought again unto Pharaoh: and he

b Wisd. 16 9.
f Heb. *eye.*

---

which he and his people attached most importance had been spared in the visitation. The word "I" is emphatic, equivalent to "as for me I have," &c.

2. *thou*] Moses is addressed as the representative of Israel.

wrought] The Hebrew word is not very commonly used. It implies an action which brings shame and disgrace upon its objects, making them, so to speak, playthings of divine power (התעלל, LXX. ἐμπέπαιχα). Ges. 'Thes.' interprets it with reference to 1 Sam. xxxi. 4, "animum explevit illudendo," which appears to be the true meaning in this passage, as in most others.

4. *the locusts*] The locust is less common in Egypt than in many eastern countries, yet it is well known, and dreaded as the most terrible of scourges. In the papyrus Anast. v. p. 10, it is mentioned as a common enemy of the husbandmen. Niebuhr and Forskal witnessed two visitations; Tischendorf describes one of unusual extent in March which covered the whole country: they come generally from the western deserts, but sometimes from the east and the south-east. Denon saw an enormous cloud of locusts in May, which came from the east, settling upon every blade of grass, and after destroying the vegetation of a district passing on to another. No less than nine names are given to the locust in the Bible, the word here used is the most common; it signifies "multitudinous," and whenever it occurs reference is made to its terrible devastations. See notes on Leviticus xi. 12.

5. *the face*] Literally "the eye of the earth," alluding doubtless to the darkness when, as Olivier describes it, "the whole atmosphere is filled on all sides and to a great height by an innumerable quantity of these insects—in a moment all the fields are covered by them."

shall eat every tree] Not only the leaves, but the branches and even the wood are attacked and devoured. Pliny says, XI. 29, "omnia morsu erodentes et fores quoque tectorum." The Egyptians were passionately fond of trees; in hieroglyphics one of the most ancient names of Egypt is "the land of the sycomore:" see De Rougé, 'Recherches,' p. 80, under the 5th dynasty; Saneha, *i.e.* "son of the sycomore," is found as a name given to a court favourite under the 12th dynasty. The widow of Thotmes II. a few years after his death, imported a large number of trees from Arabia Felix; a singular coincidence if, as seems probable, that was the date of the Exodus. See Duemichen's 'Fleet of an Egyptian Queen.'

6. *fill thy houses*] The terraces, courts, and even the inner apartments are said to be filled in a moment by a locust storm. Cf. Joel ii. 9.

7. *Pharaoh's servants*] This marks a very considerable advance in the transaction. For the first time the officers of Pharaoh intervene before the scourge is inflicted, shewing at once their belief in the threat, and their special terror of the infliction. Pharaoh also for the first time takes measures to prevent the evil; he does not indeed send for Moses and Aaron, but he permits them to be brought into his presence.

let the men go] *i. e.* the men only, not all the people; the officers assumed that the women and children would remain as hostages, and Pharaoh was now ready to consent to the proposal so limited.

said unto them, Go, serve the LORD your God: but *who are they that shall go?*

Heb. who and who, &c.

9 And Moses said, We will go with our young and with our old, with our sons and with our daughters, with our flocks and with our herds will we go; for we *must hold* a feast unto the LORD.

10 And he said unto them, Let the LORD be so with you, as I will let you go, and your little ones: look *to it;* for evil *is* before you.

11 Not so: go now ye *that are* men, and serve the LORD; for that ye did desire. And they were driven out from Pharaoh's presence.

12 ¶ And the LORD said unto Moses, Stretch out thine hand over the land of Egypt for the locusts, that they may come up upon the land of Egypt, and eat every herb of the land, *even* all that the hail hath left.

13 And Moses stretched forth his rod over the land of Egypt, and the LORD brought an east wind upon the land all that day, and all *that* night; and when it was morning, the east wind brought the locusts.

14 And the locusts went up over all the land of Egypt, and rested in all the coasts of Egypt: very grievous *were they;* before them there were no such locusts as they, neither after them shall be such.

15 For they covered the face of the whole earth, so that the land was darkened; and they did eat every herb of the land, and all the fruit of the trees which the hail had left: and there remained not any green thing in the trees, or in the herbs of the field, through all the land of Egypt.

16 ¶ Then Pharaoh ✝called for Moses and Aaron in haste; and he said, I have sinned against the LORD your God, and against you.

✝ *Heb. hastened to call.*

17 Now therefore forgive, I pray thee, my sin only this once, and intreat the LORD your God, that he may take away from me this death only.

18 And he went out from Pharaoh, and intreated the LORD.

19 And the LORD turned a mighty strong west wind, which took away

---

9. *with our young, &c.*] The demand was not contrary to Egyptian usage, as great festivals were kept by the whole population: see Herod. II. 58, "the numbers who attend (*i.e.* the festival at Bubastis) counting only the men and women, and omitting the children, amounted, according to the native reports, to seven hundred thousand."

10. *evil is before you*] The meaning is ambiguous. It may be a threat, but most commentators (LXX., Vulg., Rosen., Knobel, &c.) render it, "for your intentions are evil," and this doubtless expresses the exact motive of the king: great as the possible infliction might be, he held it to be a less evil than the loss of so large a population.

13. *an east wind*] Moses is careful to record the natural and usual cause of the evil, portentous as it was in its extent, and in its connection with his denouncement. The east wind sometimes brings locusts into Egypt, see note on *v.* 4, nor is there any reason for departing from the common meaning of the word which is given in the Authorised Version.

14. *went up*] The expression is exact and graphic; at a distance the locusts appear hanging, as it were, like a heavy cloud over the land; as they approach they seem to rise, and they fill the atmosphere overhead on their arrival.

over all the land] The expression may be taken in the broadest sense. Accounts are given by Major Moore of a cloud of locusts extending over 500 miles, and so compact while on the wing that, like an eclipse, it completely hid the sun. Brown states ('Travels in Africa'), that an area of nearly two thousand square miles was literally covered by them. This passage describes a swarm unprecedented in extent.

17. *this death only*] Pliny calls locusts "Pestis iræ Deorum," a pestilence brought on by divine wrath. Pharaoh now recognizes the justice of his servants' apprehensions, *v.* 7.

19. *west wind*] Literally "a sea wind," which in Palestine of course is from the west: but in this passage it may, and probably does, denote a wind blowing from the sea on the north-west of Egypt. A direct westerly wind would come from the Lybian desert and be far less effectual than one rushing transversely over the whole surface of lower Egypt (which was doubtless the main centre of the visitation), and driving the locusts into the Red

the locusts, and †cast them into the Red sea; there remained not one locust in all the coasts of Egypt.

20 But the LORD hardened Pharaoh's heart, so that he would not let the children of Israel go.

21 ¶ And the LORD said unto Moses, Stretch out thine hand toward heaven, that there may be darkness over the land of Egypt, †even darkness *which* may be felt.

22 And Moses stretched forth his hand toward heaven; and there was a thick darkness in all the land of Egypt three days:

23 They saw not one another, neither rose any from his place for three days: *c*but all the children of Israel had light in their dwellings.

24 ¶ And Pharaoh called unto Moses, and said, Go ye, serve the LORD; only let your flocks and your herds be stayed: let your little ones also go with you.

25 And Moses said, Thou must give †us also sacrifices and burnt offerings, that we may sacrifice unto the LORD our God.

26 Our cattle also shall go with us; there shall not an hoof be left behind; for thereof must we take to serve the LORD our God; and we know not with what we must serve the LORD, until we come thither.

27 ¶ But the LORD hardened Pharaoh's heart, and he would not let them go.

28 And Pharaoh said unto him, Get thee from me, take heed to thyself, see my face no more; for in *that* day thou seest my face thou shalt die.

29 And Moses said, Thou hast spoken well, I will see thy face again no more.

† Heb. *fastened.*

† Heb. *that one may feel darkness.*

c Wisd. 18 1.

† Heb. *into our hands*

Sea. The rendering "cast" in the text is preferable to that in the margin; the Hebrew word means to drive in by a sharp stroke or blow.

Red sea] The Hebrew has the Sea of Suph: the exact meaning of Suph is disputed. Gesenius renders it "rush" or "sea-weed;" but it is probably an Egyptian word. A sea-weed resembling wool is thrown up abundantly on the shores of the Red Sea. The origin of the modern name is uncertain. The Egyptians called it the sea of Punt, *i.e.* of Arabia. The sudden and complete disappearance of the locusts, generally effected by a strong wind (gregatim sublatæ vento in maria aut stagna decidunt, Plin. 'H. N.' XI. 35), is a phenomenon scarcely less remarkable than their coming; the putrefaction of such immense masses not unfrequently causes a terrible pestilence near the coasts of the sea into which they fall.

The Ninth Plague.

21. *darkness*] This infliction was specially calculated to affect the spirits of the Egyptians, whose chief object of worship was Ra, the Sun-god, and its suddenness and severity in connection with the act of Moses mark it as a preternatural withdrawal of light. Yet it has an analogy in physical phenomena. After the vernal equinox the south-west wind from the desert blows some fifty days, see note on v. 12, not however continuously but at intervals, lasting generally some two or three days. (Thus Lane, Willman and others quoted by Knobel.) It fills the atmosphere with dense masses of fine sand, bringing on a darkness far deeper than that of our worst fogs in winter. While it lasts no man "rises from his place; men and beasts hide themselves: people shut themselves up in the innermost apartments or vaults." "So saturated is the air with the sand that it seems to lose its transparency, so that artificial light is of little use." The expression "even darkness which might be felt," has a special application to a darkness produced by such a cause. The consternation of Pharaoh proves that, familiar as he may have been with the phenomenon, no previous occurrence had prepared him for its intensity and duration, and that he recognized it as a supernatural visitation. The rendering, which has been questioned, is correct, LXX. ψηλαφητὸν σκότος, Vulg. tam densæ ut palpari queant. Thus Rosen., Maurer, Knobel, &c.

23. *had light in their dwellings*] The sandstorm, if such were the cause, may not have extended to the district of Goshen; but the expression clearly denotes a miraculous intervention, whether accomplished or not by natural agencies.

24. *your flocks and your herds*] Pharaoh still exacts what would of course be a complete security for their return: but the demand was wholly incompatible with the object assigned for the journey into the wilderness. Every gradation in the yielding of Pharaoh and in the demands of Moses is distinctly noted: but it should be observed that these do not yet

VOL. I.   T

CHAPTER XI.

1 *God's message to the Israelites to borrow jewels of their neighbours.* 4 *Moses threateneth Pharaoh with the death of the firstborn.*

AND the Lord said unto Moses, Yet will I bring one plague more upon Pharaoh, and upon Egypt; afterwards he will let you go hence: when he shall let *you* go, he shall surely thrust you out hence altogether.

2 Speak now in the ears of the people, and let every man borrow of his neighbour, and every woman of her neighbour, ^{*a*} jewels of silver, and jewels of gold.

^{*a*} chap. 3. 22. & 12. 35.

3 And the Lord gave the people favour in the sight of the Egyptians. Moreover the man ^{*b*}Moses *was* very great in the land of Egypt, in the sight of Pharaoh's servants, and in the sight of the people.

^{*b*} Ecclus. 45. 1.

4 And Moses said, Thus saith the Lord, ^{*c*}About midnight will I go out into the midst of Egypt:

^{*c*} chap. 12. 29.

---

extend to a permission to emigrate from the country. Had Pharaoh even then yielded he could have taken measures to compel them to come back, a result only at last rendered impossible by the destruction of the whole army stationed on the frontier of lower Egypt.

Chap. XI. 1. *the* Lord *said*] Or "the Lord had said." Commentators generally agree that the first three verses of this chapter are parenthetical. The most probable account of their insertion in this place appears to be that, before Moses relates the last warning given to Pharaoh, he feels it right to recall to his readers' minds the revelation and command which had been previously given to him by the Lord. Thus Aben-Ezra, who proposes the rendering "had said," which is adopted by Rosenmüller, Keil, Kalisch, Ranke, Smith ('Pentateuch,' pp. 557—560), who completely disposes of the objections of German and English critics. No grammatical objection is made to this construction, which is common in the Old Testament and belongs to the simple and inartificial style of the Pentateuch. The command may have been given immediately before the last interview with Pharaoh; such repetition when a work is on the eve of accomplishment is customary in Holy Writ. Here it accounts "both for the confidence with which Moses, remembering the words of Jehovah, had just told the king that he would no more see his face, and for the prediction which immediately follows, that Pharaoh's court would come humbly to entreat him to depart." Smith, *l. c.*

when he shall let you go, &c.] The original is obscure, but it may probably be rendered **when he lets you go altogether he will surely thrust you out hence**; see note below. The meaning is, when at last he lets you depart with children, flocks, herds, and all your possessions, he will compel you to depart in haste. This part of the command is important, as shewing that Moses was already aware that the last plague would be followed by an immediate departure, and, therefore, that measures had probably been taken to prepare the Israelites for the journey. In fact on each occasion when Pharaoh relented for a season, immediate orders would of course be issued by Moses to the heads of the people, who were thus repeatedly brought into a state of more or less complete organization for the final movement. See Introduction.

2. *every man*] In ch. iii. 22 women only were named; the command is more explicit when the time is come for its execution.

borrow] Or "demand." See note on ch. iii. 22.

3. *gave the people favour*] See note on iii. 22.

Moreover the man Moses was very great] No objection would have been taken to this statement had it been found in any other book. It does not assert, however, what was perfectly true, that Moses was a great man by reason of personal qualifications, but that he was great in the estimation of Pharaoh, of his servants, and of all the Egyptians. This has a very important bearing upon the narrative, shewing the effect produced upon the Egyptians by the previous visitations, and by the conduct of Moses, especially by the care he had taken to warn them, and, so far as was practicable, to save them from suffering. See ch. ix. 19, 20. It accounts for their ready compliance with the demand of the Israelites. God gave them a kindly feeling, by an inward act, not changing their nature, but eliciting their better feelings, the sense of obligation, and gratitude for benefits which Diodorus specially mentions as a characteristic of the Egyptians. The reasons above assigned appear sufficient to account for the introduction of these verses, which undoubtedly interrupt the narrative; but there would be no objection in point of principle to the supposition that they may have been inserted either by Moses at a later period, when he probably put together and revised the detached portions of the books; or by one of his younger contemporaries, who must have been equally conversant with the facts, and aware of the

5 And all the firstborn in the .and of Egypt shall die, from the firstborn of Pharaoh that sitteth upon his throne, even unto the firstborn of the maidservant that *is* behind the mill; and all the firstborn of beasts.

6 And there shall be a great cry throughout all the land of Egypt, such as there was none like it, nor shall be like it any more.

7 But against any of the children of Israel shall not a dog move his tongue, against man or beast: that ye may know how that the LORD doth put a difference between the Egyptians and Israel.

8 And all these thy servants shall come down unto me, and bow down themselves unto me, saying, Get thee out, and all the people †that follow thee: and after that I will go out. And he went out from Pharaoh in †a great anger.

† Heb. *that is at thy feet.*
† Heb. *heat of anger.*

9 And the LORD said unto Moses, Pharaoh shall not hearken unto you; that my wonders may be multiplied in the land of Egypt.

10 And Moses and Aaron did all these wonders before Pharaoh: and the LORD hardened Pharaoh's heart, so that he would not let the children of Israel go out of his land.

---

importance of the statement in its bearings upon the whole transaction.

4. *And Moses said*] The following words must be read in immediate connection with the last verse of the preceding chapter. It is not there stated that Moses left the presence of Pharaoh; this passage tells us what took place after his declaration that this would be his last interview.

About midnight] This marks the hour, but not the day, on which the visitation would take place. There may have been, and probably was, an interval of some days, during which preparations might be made both for the celebration of the Passover, and the departure of the Israelites: in the meantime Egypt remained under the shadow of the menace.

5. *the firstborn*] Two points are to be noticed: 1, The extent of the visitation: the whole land suffers in the persons of its firstborn, not merely for the guilt of the sovereign, but for the actual participation of the people in the crime of infanticide. 2, The limitation. Pharaoh's command had been to slay all the male children of the Israelites, one child only in each Egyptian family was to die. If Thotmes II. was the Pharaoh (see Appendix) the visitation fell with special severity on his family. He left no son, but was succeeded by his widow.

the mill] The mill used by the Israelites, and probably by the Egyptians, consisted of two circular stones, one fixed in the ground, the other turned by a handle. The work of grinding was extremely laborious, and performed by women of the lowest rank.

firstborn of beasts] This visitation has a peculiar force in reference to the worship of beasts, which was universal in Egypt; each nome having its own sacred animal, adored as a manifestation or representative of the local tuteiary deity.

8. *in great anger*] Or **in heat of anger**, as in the margin.

9, 10. These two verses refer to the whole preceding narrative, and mark the close of one principal division of the book.

NOTE on *v.* 1.

The force of the word כלה appears to have been overlooked by our translators, who misplace it, as also by the Vulgate, which takes no notice of it. The Targum of Onkelos renders it correctly גמירא. The LXX. σὺν παντί: the Syriac less accurately, "all of you." It reads also in both clauses, "I will dismiss you." The Arabic forcibly and correctly جَمْلَة

CHAPTER XII.

1 *The beginning of the year is changed.* 3 *The passover is instituted.* 11 *The rite of the passover.* 15 *Unleavened bread.* 29 *The firstborn are slain.* 31 *The Israelites are driven out of the land.* 37 *They come to Succoth.* 43 *The ordinance of the passover.*

AND the LORD spake unto Moses and Aaron in the land of Egypt, saying,

2 This month *shall be* unto you the beginning of months: it *shall be* the first month of the year to you.

3 ¶ Speak ye unto all the congregation of Israel, saying, In the tenth day of this month they shall take to them every man a ¹lamb, according to the house of *their* fathers, a lamb for an house:

¹ Or, *kid.*

4 And if the household be too little for the lamb, let him and his neighbour next unto his house take *it* according to the number of the souls; every man according to his eating shall make your count for the lamb.

5 Your lamb shall be without blemish, a male † of the first year: ye

† Heb. *son of a year.*

CHAP. XII. 1. *in the land of Egypt*] It seems evident that this verse, and consequently the rest of the chapter, was written some time after the Exodus, probably when Moses put together the portions of the book towards the end of his life. The statements that these instructions were given in the land of Egypt, and that they were given to Moses and Aaron, are important: the one marks the peculiar dignity of this ordinance, which was established before the Sinaitic code, the other marks the distinction between Moses and Aaron and all other prophets. They alone, as Aben-Ezra observes, were prophets of the Law, *i.e.* no law was promulgated by any other prophets.

2. *This month*] The name of the month, Abib, is given xiii. 4. It was called by the later Hebrews Nisan, a name found in early Syrian inscriptions, De Vogüé, 'Syrie centrale,' p. 5, and derived from the Nisannu of the Assyrians and Babylonians, with whom it was the first month of the year. It corresponds nearly to our April, since the last full moon in March or the first in April fell in the middle of the month. It is clear that in this passage the Israelites are directed to take Abib henceforth as the beginning of the year; the year previously began with the month Tisri, when the harvest was gathered in; see xxiii. 16. They do not appear to have adopted the Egyptian division, in which the fixed year began in June, at the rise of the Nile. The injunction touching Abib or Nisan referred only to religious rites; in other affairs they retained the old arrangement, even in the beginning of the Sabbatic year; see Levit. xxv. 9; and Josephus, 'Ant.' I. 25. 9. The assumption that an ancient festival was previously held at this season to celebrate the ripening of the wheat has no grounds in history or tradition.

3. *a lamb*] The Hebrew word, used in the same way in Arabic and Chaldee, is general, meaning either a sheep or goat, male or female, and of any age; the age and sex are therefore specially defined in the following verse. The direction to select the lamb on the tenth day, the fourth day before it was offered, is generally assumed to have applied to the first institution only, but there is no indication of this in the text, and it seems more probable that the injunction was intended to secure due care in the preparation for the greatest national festival. The custom certainly fell into desuetude at a later period, but probably not before the destruction of the Temple. The later Targum, which asserts that the rule was not intended to be of permanent obligation, records the traditions of Rabbins of the sixth century.

the house of their fathers] Lit. a house of fathers, or parents; *i.e.* for each family.

4. *if the household be too little, &c.*] The meaning is clear, if there be not persons enough to consume a lamb at one meal: tradition specifies ten as the least number; thus Josephus says, not less than ten attend this sacrifice, and twenty are generally assembled, 'De B. J.' VI. 9. 3. The later Targum paraphrases the passage thus: "If the men of the household be less than ten in number." There is, however, no indication of such a rule earlier than Josephus, and it was probably left altogether to the discretion of the heads of families. The women and children were certainly not excluded, though the Rabbins held their attendance to be unnecessary, and the Karaites permitted none but adult males to be partakers.

The last clause should be rendered: "let him and his neighbour who is near to his house take according to the number of souls, each man according to his eating ye shall count for the lamb." Our Version only requires the insertion of *ye*, or *you*, before "shall make your count." See note below.

5. *without blemish*] This is in accordance with the general rule laid down in Levit. xxii. 20: so also is the choice of a male, Levit. i. 3: although in this case there is a special reason, since the lamb was in place of the firstborn male in each household. The re-

shall take *it* out from the sheep, or from the goats:

6 And ye shall keep it up until the fourteenth day of the same month: and the whole assembly of the congregation of Israel shall kill it †in the evening.

7 And they shall take of the blood, and strike *it* on the two side posts and on the upper door post of the houses, wherein they shall eat it.

8 And they shall eat the flesh in that night, roast with fire, and unleavened bread; *and* with bitter *herbs* they shall eat it.

† Heb. *between the two evenings*

---

striction to the first year is peculiar, and refers apparently to the condition of perfect innocence in the antitype, the Lamb of God.

or from the goats] There is no indication of a preference, but the Hebrews have generally held that a lamb was the more acceptable offering.

6. *ye shall keep it up*] The Hebrew implies that it was to be kept with great care, which appears to be the meaning of the expression "keep it up."

until the fourteenth day] It should be observed that the offering of our Lord on the selfsame day is an important point in determining the typical character of the transaction. Masius on Josh. v. 10 quotes a remarkable passage from the Talmud: "It was a famous and old opinion among the ancient Jews that the day of the new year which was the beginning of the Israelites' deliverance out of Egypt should in future time be the beginning of the redemption by the Messiah."

in the evening] The Hebrew has **between the two evenings**. The meaning of the expression is disputed. The most probable explanation is that it includes the time from afternoon, or early eventide, until sunset. This accords with the ancient custom of the Hebrews, who slew the paschal lamb immediately after the offering of the daily sacrifice, which on the day of the passover took place a little earlier than usual, between two and three p.m. This would allow about two hours and a half for slaying and preparing all the lambs. It is clear that they would not wait until sunset, at which time the evening meal would take place. This interpretation is supported by Rashi, Kimchi, Bochart, Lightfoot, Clericus, and Patrick. Thus Josephus: "they offer this sacrifice from the ninth to the eleventh hour." The Greeks had the same idiom, distinguishing between the early and late evening. Other interpreters understand it to mean the interval between sunset and total darkness, an exceedingly short time in the East, and quite insufficient for the work. Rosenmüller shews from the Talmud that the twilight as strictly defined did not last longer than it would take to walk half a mile, *i.e.* about ten minutes. If, moreover, the lamb were slain after sunset, it would not have been on the fourteenth day of the month, since the day was reckoned from sunset to sunset. Knobel observes that the expression is peculiar to the so-called Elohist; it is in fact peculiar to the Pentateuch, and its meaning was evidently ascertained only by conjecture at a later period. It is to be observed that the slaying of the lamb on the former hypothesis coincides exactly with the death of our Saviour, at the ninth hour of the day.

7. *the upper door post*] Or **lintel**, as it is rendered v. 23. This meaning is generally accepted, but the word occurs only in this passage; it is derived from a root which means to "look out," and may signify a lattice above the door: thus Aben-Ezra and Rosenmüller. This direction was understood by the Hebrews to apply only to the first Passover: it was certainly not adopted in Palestine. The meaning of the sprinkling of blood is hardly open to question. It was a representation of the offering of the life, substituted for that of the firstborn in each house, as an expiatory and vicarious sacrifice.

8. *in that night*] The night is thus clearly distinguished from the evening when the lamb was slain. It was slain before sunset, on the 14th, and eaten after sunset, the beginning of the 15th.

with fire] Among various reasons given for this injunction the most probable and satisfactory seems to be the special sanctity attached to fire from the first institution of sacrifice. The memory of this primeval sanctity is preserved by universal tradition, *e.g.* among the Aryans, as is shewn by the hymns in the Rig Veda to Agni, the fire-god, and by the whole system of the Zend Avesta.

and unleavened bread] Or, **and they shall eat unleavened cakes with bitter herbs**. See note below. The Hebrew word is certain in meaning, but of doubtful origin; see note below. Like many others in this account it is archaic, found only in the Pentateuch, except in passages which refer to the Passover. The importance of the injunction is admitted; the unleavened cakes give one of the two general designations to the festival. This may in part be accounted for by its being a lasting memorial of the circumstances

9 Eat not of it raw, nor sodden at all with water, but roast *with* fire; his head with his legs, and with the purtenance thereof.

10 And ye shall let nothing of it remain until the morning; and that which remaineth of it until the morning ye shall burn with fire.

11 ¶ And thus shall ye eat it; *with your loins girded, your shoes on your*

---

of the hasty departure, allowing no time for the process of leavening: but the meaning discerned by St Paul, 1 Cor. v. 7, and recognized by the Church in all ages, was assuredly implied, though not expressly declared in the original institution; and though our Lord may not directly refer to the Passover, yet His words, Matt. xiii. 33, are conclusive as to the symbolism of leaven.

bitter herbs] The word occurs only here and in Numbers ix. 11, in reference to herbs. The symbolical reference to the previous sufferings of the Israelites is generally admitted. Various kinds of bitter herbs are enumerated in the Mishna; but the expression should be taken generally; the bitter herbs of Egypt would of course differ in kind from those of other countries where the Passover was to be eaten.

9. *raw*] Another obsolete word, probably Egyptian, found only in this passage: the corresponding root in Arabic means "half-cooked," and this appears to be the sense here: raw meat was not likely to be eaten, though some interpreters find here a reference to the ὠμοφαγία, "feasting on raw food," in some Gentile festivals. The prohibition of eating it sodden with water has been considered in reference to "roast with fire:" it was probably more common to seethe than to roast meat; hence the regrets expressed by the Israelites for the seething pots of Egypt; on other occasions the flesh of sin and peace-offerings, whether consumed by the people or the priests, was ordered to be sodden: see Lev. vi. 28; Num. vi. 19.

sodden...with water] or "sodden," omitting "water," which is added in Hebrew because the word in that language may be used either of roasting (as in 2 Chron. xxxv. 13) or boiling.

the purtenance thereof] **or its intestines.** This verse directs that the lamb should be roasted and placed on the table whole. No bone was to be broken (see v. 46, and Num. ix. 12, an injunction which the LXX. insert in the next verse). According to Rashi and other Rabbins the bowels were taken out, washed and then replaced. The Talmud prescribes the form of the oven of earthenware, in which the lamb was roasted, open above and below with a grating for the fire. Lambs and sheep are roasted whole in Persia, nearly in the same manner. Thevenot describes **the process,** Vol. II. p. 180, ed. 1674.

This entire consumption of the lamb constitutes one marked difference between the Passover and all other sacrifices, in which either a part or the whole was burned, and thus offered directly to God. The whole substance of the sacrificed lamb was to enter into the substance of the people, the blood only excepted, which was sprinkled as a propitiatory and sacrificial offering. Another point of subordinate importance is noticed. The lamb was slain and the blood sprinkled by the head of each family: no separate priesthood as yet existed in Israel; its functions belonged from the beginning to the father of the family: when the priesthood was instituted the slaying of the lamb still devolved on the heads of families, though the blood was sprinkled on the altar by the priests; an act which essentially belonged to their office. The typical character of this part of the transaction is clear. Our Lord was offered and His blood shed as an expiatory and propitiatory sacrifice, but His whole humanity is transfused spiritually and effectually into His Church, an effect which is at once symbolized and assured in Holy Communion, the Christian Passover.

10. *And ye shall let nothing*, &c.] This was afterwards a general law of sacrifices; at once preventing all possibility of profanity, and of superstitious abuse, such as was practised among some ancient heathens, who were wont to reserve a portion of their sacrifices; see Herod. I. 132; and Baruch vi. 28. The injunction is on both accounts justly applied by our Church to the Eucharist.

burn with fire] Not being consumed by man, it was thus offered, like other sacrifices, to God.

11. *with your loins girded*, &c.] These instructions are understood by the Jews to apply only to the first Passover, when they belonged to the occasion. There is no trace of their observance at any later time; a striking instance of good sense and power of distinguishing between accidents and substantial characteristics. Each of the directions marks preparation for a journey; the long flowing robes are girded round the loins; shoes or sandals, not worn in the house or at meals, were fastened on the feet; and the traveller's staff was taken in hand.

the LORD'*s passover*] A most important statement. It gives at once the great and most significant name to the whole ordinance. The word Passover renders as nearly as pos-

feet, and your staff in your hand; and ye shall eat it in haste: it *is* the LORD's passover.

12 For I will pass through the land of Egypt this night, and will smite all the firstborn in the land of Egypt, both man and beast; and against all the ¹gods of Egypt I will execute judgment: I *am* the LORD.

13 And the blood shall be to you for a token upon the houses where ye *are:* and when I see the blood, I will pass over you, and the plague shall not be upon you †to destroy you, when I smite the land of Egypt.

14 And this day shall be unto you for a memorial; and ye shall keep it a feast to the LORD throughout your generations; ye shall keep it a feast by an ordinance for ever.

¹ Or, *princes.*

† Heb. *for a destruction.*

---

sible the true meaning of the original, of which the primary sense is generally held to be "pass rapidly," like a bird with outstretched wings, but it undoubtedly includes the idea of sparing. See Ges. 'Thes.' s.v. It is a word which occurs very seldom in other books, twice in one chapter of 1 K., xviii. 21, where it is rendered "halt," and seems to mean "waver," flitting like a bird from branch to branch, and 26, where our A. V. has in the margin "leaped up and down." A passage in Isaiah xxxi. 5 is of more importance, since it combines the two great ideas involved in the word: "As birds flying, so will the LORD of hosts defend Jerusalem; defending also he will deliver it; and PASSING OVER he will preserve it." This combination of ideas is recognized by nearly all ancient and modern critics. It is remarkable that the word is not found in other Semitic languages, except in passages derived from the Hebrew Bible. In Egyptian the word Pesh, which corresponds to it very nearly in form, means to "spread out the wings over," and "to protect;" see Brugsch, 'D. H.' p. 512.

12. *I will pass through*] The word rendered "pass through" is wholly distinct from that which means "pass over." The passing through was in judgment, the "passing over" in mercy.

against all the gods of Egypt] The meaning of this and of the corresponding passage, Num. xxxiii. 4, is undoubtedly that the visitation reached the gods of Egypt, not "the princes" as in the margin. The true explanation in this case is that in smiting the firstborn of all living beings, man and beast, God smote the objects of Egyptian worship. It is not merely that the bull and cow and goat and ram and cat were worshipped in the principal cities of Egypt as representatives, or, so to speak, incarnations, of their deities, but that the worship of beasts was universal; every nome, every town had its sacred animal, including the lowest forms of animal life; the frog, the beetle, being especial objects of reverence as representing the primeval deities of nature. In fact not a single deity of Egypt was unrepresented by some beast. This explanation, which is adopted by many critics, *e.g.* Michaelis, Rosenmüller, forces itself upon our minds in proportion to our closer and more accurate knowledge of Egyptian superstitions. It would not however have occurred to an Israelite living in Palestine, and the Rabbins in course of time adopted a different view, which approved itself to some of the early Fathers of the Church. Thus Jerome, 'Ep. ad Fabiolam,' says: "The Hebrews think that in the night when the people went forth all the temples in Egypt were destroyed either by earthquake or lightning:" and the second Targum, which gives the traditions of a still later time, asserts that each and every idol was destroyed. The explanation given above meets the whole requirement of the text.

13. *a token*] A sign to you, so to speak, a sacramental pledge of mercy.

I will pass over you] The same word as in *v.* 11. The sense of sparing is clear. The Targum renders it "I will spare you," and the LXX. "I will protect you."

to destroy you] or "to destruction," but our version gives the true sense and may be retained.

14. *a memorial*] The following verses to end of *v.* 20 contain explicit instructions for the future celebration of the Passover. They appear from *v.* 17 to have been given to Moses after the departure from Egypt, but are inserted here in their proper place, in connection with the history. The passover was to be a memorial, a commemorative and sacramental ordinance of perpetual obligation. As such it has ever been observed by the Hebrews. By the Christian it is spiritually observed; its full significance is recognized, and all that it foreshadowed is realized, in the Sacrament of Holy Communion. It is not therefore necessary to limit the meaning of the words "throughout your generations" and "for ever," although both expressions are frequently used with reference to an existing dispensation, or to a limited period.

ye shall keep it a feast] The word *chag* is used twice in this passage, for "keep a feast." The radical meaning is festivity, expressed in outward demonstrations of joy.

15 Seven days shall ye eat unleavened bread; even the first day ye shall put away leaven out of your houses: for whosoever eateth leavened bread from the first day until the seventh day, that soul shall be cut off from Israel.

16 And in the first day *there shall be* an holy convocation, and in the seventh day there shall be an holy convocation to you; no manner of work shall be done in them, save *that* which every †man must eat, that only may be done of you.

17 And ye shall observe *the feast of* unleavened bread; for in this selfsame day have I brought your armies out of the land of Egypt: therefore shall ye observe this day in your generations by an ordinance for ever.

18 ¶ *a*In the first *month*, on the fourteenth day of the month at even, ye shall eat unleavened bread, until the one and twentieth day of the month at even.

19 Seven days shall there be no leaven found in your houses: for whosoever eateth that which is leavened, even that soul shall be cut off from the congregation of Israel, whether he be a stranger, or born in the land.

20 Ye shall eat nothing leavened; in all your habitations shall ye eat unleavened bread.

21 ¶ Then Moses called for all the elders of Israel, and said unto them, Draw out and take you a ‖lamb according to your families, and kill the passover.

† Heb. *soul*

a Lev. 23. 5. Numb. 28. 16.

‖ Or. *kid*

---

15. *Seven days*] From the evening of the fourteenth of Nisan to the end of the 21st day. The leaven was removed from the houses before the paschal lamb was slain, in accordance with the general instruction, "Thou shalt not offer the blood of my sacrifice with leavened bread;" xxiii. 18. The unleavened bread was an essential element in the celebration: see note on *v.* 8. The penalty inflicted on those who transgressed the command may be accounted for on the ground that it was an act of rebellion; but additional light is thrown upon it by the typical meaning assigned to leaven by our Lord, Matt. xvi. 6. The period of seven days does not settle the question as to the previous observance of the week, since this command may have been first given after the institution of the Sabbath, but it adds considerable weight to the argument in its favour.

16. *an holy convocation*] This rendering exactly expresses the sense of the original; an assembly called by proclamation for a religious solemnity. The proclamation was directed to be made on some occasions by the blowing of the silver trumpets. See Num. x. 2. 3. In the East the proclamation is made by the Muezzins from the minarets of the mosques.

save that, &c.] In this the observance of the festival differed from the Sabbath, when the preparation of food was prohibited. The same word for " work " is used here and in the 4th Commandment: it is very general, and includes all laborious occupation, not however all bodily exercise, as it is understood by the stricter sects of the Rabbins.

17. *the feast of unleavened bread*] lit. "the unleavened bread;" which may mean either the festival, or the instructions relating to the unleavened bread. The Samaritan Pentateuch and the LXX. read "the precept," taking a word which differs slightly in form in the unpunctuated Hebrew: but our reading and translation are accepted by most critics.

18. *In the first month*] or "in the beginning," which may mean at the beginning of the festival, on the evening of the 14th Nisan. Thus the LXX.; but the other ancient versions agree with our own, and their rendering is supported by Rosenmüller.

19. *leaven*] The Hebrew word used here occurs only in the Pentateuch. It denotes the leaven itself; the word in the next clause, which is also found only in the Pentateuch, means the leavened dough, or bread.

born in the land] or "a native of the land;" a stranger or foreigner might be born in the land, but the word here used means indigenous, belonging to the country in virtue of descent, that descent being reckoned from Abraham, to whom Canaan was promised as a perpetual inheritance. The Hebrews had no tinge of the opinion which takes human races to be autochthonous. It is indeed remarkable that that opinion was entertained most strongly of old by the Athenians, a people whose foreign origin is incontestably proved by their language, customs and religion.

21. *Then Moses called*] From this verse to end of the 28th Moses records the directions

22 *b*And ye shall take a bunch of hyssop, and dip *it* in the blood that *is* in the bason, and strike the lintel and the two side posts with the blood that *is* in the bason; and none of you shall go out at the door of his house until the morning.

23 For the LORD will pass through to smite the Egyptians; and when he seeth the blood upon the lintel, and on the two side posts, the LORD will pass over the door, and will not suffer the destroyer to come in unto your houses to smite *you*.

24 And ye shall observe this thing for an ordinance to thee and to thy sons for ever.

25 And it shall come to pass, when ye be come to the land which the LORD will give you, according as he hath promised, that ye shall keep this service.

26 *c*And it shall come to pass, when your children shall say unto you, What mean ye by this service?

27 That ye shall say, It *is* the sacrifice of the LORD'S passover, who passed over the houses of the children of Israel in Egypt, when he smote the Egyptians, and delivered our houses. And the people bowed the head and worshipped.

28 And the children of Israel went away, and did as the LORD had commanded Moses and Aaron, so did they.

29 ¶ *d*And it came to pass, that at midnight the LORD smote all the firstborn in the land of Egypt, *e*from the firstborn of Pharaoh that sat on his throne unto the firstborn of the captive that *was* in the †dungeon; and all the firstborn of cattle.

Heb. 11. 28.
b
c Josh. 4. 6.
d chap. 11. 4.
e Wisd. 18. 11.
† Heb. *house of the pit.*

---

which, in obedience to the command, he gave at the time to the people. This method of composition occurs frequently in the Pentateuch: it involves of course some repetition, from which no very ancient writer would shrink, but it would scarcely have been adopted by a compiler. Moses is ever careful to record first the commands which he receives, and afterwards the way in which he executed them.

Draw out] The expression is clear, but the sense has been questioned. Moses directs the elders to draw the lamb from the fold and then to take it to their houses.

the passover] The word is here applied to the lamb; an important fact, marking the lamb as the sign and pledge of the exemption of the Israelites.

22. *a bunch of hyssop*] The word rendered hyssop occurs only in the Pentateuch, with two exceptions, Ps. li. 7, which refers to the Mosaic rite, and 1 K. iv. 33, where it is applied to a herb growing on the wall, probably a small species of fern, mentioned as the smallest of plants and therefore not likely to be used for the sprinkling. The species here designated does not appear to be the plant now bearing the name. If we follow the Hebrew tradition, which in such matters is of weight, and is supported by most critics, it would seem to be a species of origanum, common in Palestine and near Mount Sinai, an aromatic plant with a long straight stalk and leaves well adapted for the purpose. See note on Lev. xiv. 4.

bason] The rendering rests on good authority and gives a good sense: but the word means threshold in some other passages and in Egyptian, and is taken here in that sense by the LXX. and Vulgate. If that rendering were correct it would imply that the lamb was slain on the threshold.

none...shall go out, &c.] There is no safety outside of the precincts protected by the blood of the lamb; a symbolism too obvious to require pointing out.

23. *the destroyer*] The word certainly denotes a personal agent; see note on *v*. 29.

24. *this thing*] The injunction would seem to apply specially to the sprinkling of blood on the lintel and doorposts; but the authority for changing the rite is unquestioned; see note on *v*. 9; and the Hebrew tradition is uniform. It may therefore be admitted, with Aben-Ezra and Knobel, who represent very different schools, that this charge refers to the general observance of the Passover.

27. *It is the sacrifice of the* LORD'*s passover*] or **This is the sacrifice of the Passover to Jehovah.** The most formal and exact designation of the festival is thus given: but "the Passover" may mean either the act or God's mercy in sparing the Israelites, or the lamb which is offered in sacrifice: more probably the latter, as in *v*. 21, "and kill the passover." This gives a clear sense to the expression "to Jehovah;" it was a sacrifice offered to Jehovah by His ordinance.

The Tenth and Last Plague.

29. *smote all the firstborn*] This plague is distinctly attributed here and in *v*. 23 to

30 And Pharaoh rose up in the night, he, and all his servants, and all the Egyptians; and there was a great cry in Egypt; for *there was* not a house where *there was* not one dead.

31 ¶ And he called for Moses and Aaron by night, and said, Rise up, *and* get you forth from among my people, both ye and the children of Israel; and go, serve the LORD, as ye have said.

32 Also take your flocks and your herds, as ye have said, and be gone; and bless me also.

33 And the Egyptians were urgent upon the people, that they might send them out of the land in haste; they said, We *be* all dead *men*.

34 And the people took their dough before it was leavened, their ¹knead- ingtroughs being bound up in their clothes upon their shoulders.

¹ Or, *dough.*

35 And the children of Israel did according to the word of Moses; and they borrowed of the Egyptians *ƒ*jewels of silver, and jewels of gold, and raiment:

ƒ chap. 3 22. & 11. 2.

36 And the LORD gave the people favour in the sight of the Egyptians, so that they lent unto them *such things as they required*. And they spoiled the Egyptians.

---

the personal intervention of THE LORD; but it is to be observed that although the Lord Himself passed through to smite the Egyptians, He employed the agency of "the destroyer," in whom, in accordance with Heb. xi. 28, all the Ancient Versions, and most critics, recognize an angel. Such indeed is the express statement of Holy Writ with reference to other visitations, as 2 Kings xix. 35, and more especially 2 Sam. xxiv. 16. The employment of angelic agency, however, does not always exclude the operation of physical causes. In the same chapter of 2 Sam. which describes the destruction of 70,000 Israelites by an angel, whose personality is distinctly attested, see *vv.* 15—17, it is no less distinctly declared to have been effected by a pestilence; see *vv.* 13 and 25. Nature accomplishes God's purposes under His control. As in every other case the hand of God was distinctly shewn by the previous announcement, the suddenness, intensity, and limitation of the calamity. No house of the Egyptians escaped; the firstborn only perished in each; the Israelites were unscathed.

the captive] In ch. xi. 5, the woman at the mill is mentioned. Such variations are common in Holy Writ, and are to be noticed as shewing the disregard of slight or apparent discrepancies. The notices of captives under the 18th dynasty are numerous on the monuments: they were generally employed in brick-making and building, and this passage implies that they were treated to some extent as settlers in the land. The word "dungeon" translated more literally in the margin "house of the pit," corresponds to the Egyptian "Rar," or "Lar," in meaning; the same word for "pit" is found in both languages. See Brugsch, 'D. H.' p. 402, who considers it to be Semitic.

31. *the* LORD] The LXX. add " your God," a very probable reading.

32. *bless me also*] No words could shew more strikingly the complete, though temporary submission of Pharaoh.

34. *kneadingtroughs*] Not "dough" as in the margin. The same word is used in ch. viii. 3, and Deut. xxviii. 5. The troughs were probably small, such as are now used by the Arabians; wooden bowls in which the cakes when baked are preserved for use. The Hebrews used their outer garment, or mantle, in the same way as the Bedouins at present, who make a bag of the voluminous folds of their haiks or burnous. See Ruth iii. 15; 2 Kings iv. 39.

35. *borrowed*] Or "asked of." See note ch. iii. 22.

36. *lent*] Or **gave**. The word here used in the Hebrew means simply "granted their request." Whether the grant is made as a loan, or as a gift, depends in every instance upon the context. In this case the question is whether the Israelites asked for the jewels and the Egyptians granted them as a loan with reference to the festival in the wilderness; or whether this was regarded on both sides as a moderate remuneration for long service, and a compensation for cruel wrongs. The word "spoiling" (iii. 22) ought to be regarded as conclusive for the latter sense. The Arabic translator, Saadia, uses the word "gave." The Syriac and the Targum Onk. have the exact equivalent of the Hebrew. Rosenmüller says truly, in Hebrew the word means simply "to give;" often with the idea of willingness or readiness. Thus too Knobel, who altogether rejects the notion of lending; and Kalisch. Even if the word were taken, as it is by some distinguished scholars, in the sense "lent," it must be remembered that the actual cause which prevented the Egyptians from recovering their property was, that the return of the

f Numb. 33. 3.

† Heb. *a great mixture.*

37 ¶ And ᵍ the children of Israel journeyed from Rameses to Succoth, about six hundred thousand on foot *that were* men, beside children.

38 And †a mixed multitude went up also with them; and flocks, and herds, *even* very much cattle.

39 And they baked unleavened cakes of the dough which they brought forth out of Egypt, for it was not leavened; because they were thrust out of Egypt, and could not tarry, neither had they prepared for themselves any victual.

40 ¶ Now the sojourning of the children of Israel, who dwelt in Egypt, *was* ʰ four hundred and thirty years.

41 And it came to pass at the end of the four hundred and thirty years, even the selfsame day it came to pass, that all the hosts of the LORD went out from the land of Egypt.

42 It *is* †a night to be much observed unto the LORD for bringing them out from the land of Egypt: this *is* that night of the LORD to be observed of all the children of Israel in their generations.

ʰ Gen. 15. 13.
Acts 7. 6.
Gal. 3. 17

† Heb. *a night of observations.*

Israelites was cut off by the treachery of Pharaoh. Thus Ewald, 'G. I.' II. p. 87. Ewald also accepts the application of the transaction found so commonly in the Fathers, who see in it a figure of the appropriation by the Israelites of Egyptian rites and ceremonies, and of the truths thereby represented.

The Departure of the Israelites.

37. *Rameses*] See note on ch. i. 11. Rameses was evidently the place of general rendezvous, well adapted for that purpose as the principal city of Goshen. The Israelites, by whom it had been built, were probably settled in considerable numbers in it and about it. Pharaoh with his army and court were at that time near the frontier, and Rameses, where a large garrison was kept, was probably the place where the last interview with Moses occurred. Under the 19th dynasty the Pharaohs received foreign embassies, transacted treaties, and held their court in this city, which was considerably enlarged and embellished by Rameses II. A discussion on the route of the Israelites from Rameses to Sinai will be found in the Appendix to this book. The first part of the journey appears to have followed the course of the ancient canal. The site of Succoth cannot be exactly determined, but it lay about half-way between Rameses and Etham. It could not therefore have been on the road to Palestine which ran north-east of the lake of crocodiles (Birket Timseh), but to the south of that lake by the road which led by the shortest way to the edge of the wilderness. The frontier to the east of the road appears to have been covered in ancient times by the so-called bitter lakes, which extended to the Gulf of Suez. The name Succoth (*i.e.* "tents" or "booths" in Hebrew), may have been given by the Israelites, but the same, or a similar word, occurs in Egyptian in connection with the district. Thus in De Rougé, 'Recherches,' p. 50, we find an officer of state in possession of a domain called Sechet, or Sochot, in the time of Chufu. That domain was certainly in lower Egypt, and probably at no great distance from Memphis.

600,000] This includes all the males who could march. The total number of the Israelites should therefore be calculated not from the men above twenty years old, but from the males above twelve or fourteen, and would therefore amount to somewhat more than two millions. This is not an excessive population for Goshen, nor does it exceed a reasonable estimate of the increase of the Israelites, including their numerous dependents. See Payne Smith's 'Bampton Lectures,' 1869, L. III. p. 88. The number 600,000 is confirmed by many distinct statements and details, and is accepted by Ewald and other critics.

38. *a mixed multitude*] They consisted probably of remains of the old Semitic population, whether or not first brought into the district by the Hyksos is uncertain. As natural objects of suspicion and dislike to the Egyptians who had lately become masters of the country, they would be anxious to escape, the more especially after the calamities which preceded the Exodus.

very much cattle] This is an important fact, both as shewing that the oppression of the Israelites had not extended to confiscation of their property, and as bearing upon the question of their maintenance in the Wilderness.

40. *who dwelt*] Read, **which they sojourned**. The obvious intention of Moses is to state the duration of the sojourn in Egypt. On the interpretation and chronology see note below.

41. At the end of this verse the LXX. add "by night."

43 ¶ And the LORD said unto Moses and Aaron, This *is* the ordinance of the passover: There shall no stranger eat thereof:

44 But every man's servant that is bought for money, when thou hast circumcised him, then shall he eat thereof.

45 A foreigner and an hired servant shall not eat thereof.

i Numb. 9. 12.

46 *ⁱ* In one house shall it be eaten; thou shalt not carry forth ought of the flesh abroad out of the house;

k John 19. 36.

ᵏ neither shall ye break a bone thereof.

47 All the congregation of Israel shall † keep it.

† Heb. *do it.*

48 And when a stranger shall sojourn with thee, and will keep the passover to the LORD, let all his males be circumcised, and then let him come near and keep it; and he shall be as one that is born in the land: for no uncircumcised person shall eat thereof.

49 One law shall be to him that is homeborn, and unto the stranger that sojourneth among you.

50 Thus did all the children of Israel; as the LORD commanded Moses and Aaron, so did they.

51 And it came to pass the selfsame day, *that* the LORD did bring the children of Israel out of the land of Egypt by their armies.

---

43. *And the LORD said*] The following passage, from this verse to *v.* 16 of the next chapter, contains additional instructions regarding the Passover. Such instructions were needed when the Israelites were joined by the "mixed multitudes" of strangers; and they were probably given at Succoth, on the morning following the departure from Rameses. The antiquity of this section is admitted by critics of all schools. The first point which required to be determined was the condition of participation in the rite; it is simple and complete. No one was to be admitted without being circumcised: all were to be admitted who were qualified by that rite.

no stranger] lit. "son of a stranger." The term is general; it includes all who were aliens from Israel, until they were incorporated into the nation by circumcision. The Arabic translator is probably right in using a word which involves the idea of persistence in a false religion; the Targum goes farther, and takes a word which means apostate.

44. *servant*] or "slave." It seems better to retain the word "servant," for although the servant was, strictly speaking, a slave, being the property of his master, his condition differed very widely from that of a slave in heathen countries, or those Christian nations wherein slavery is legalized. The circumcision of the slave, thus enjoined formally on the first day that Israel became a nation, in accordance with the law given to Abraham Gen. xvii. 12, made him a true member of the family, equally entitled to all religious privileges. In the household of a priest the slave was even permitted to eat the consecrated food: Lev. xxii. 11.

45. *A foreigner*] or **sojourner**. The Hebrew means one who resides in a country, not having a permanent home, nor being attached to an Israelitish household. A different word is used *v.* 43.

46. *In one house*] The Targum renders this "in one company," a translation which, though not literal, expresses the true meaning of the injunction. Each lamb was to be entirely consumed by the members of one company, whether they belonged to the same household or not.

break a bone] The typical significance of this injunction is recognized by St John; see marginal reference. It is not easy to assign any other satisfactory reason for it. This victim alone was exempt from the general law by which the limbs were ordered to be separated from the body.

48. *when a stranger shall sojourn*] or "when a stranger shall settle with thee." It is not easy to express in English the exact meaning of these words. The sojourner and the hired servant did not come under the definition of a permanent settler. When circumcised any foreigner became one of the chosen race.

50. *Thus did*, &c.] This verse and the following apply apparently to the stay of the people at Succoth, where they may have remained a short time, completing their preparation for final departure from Egypt.

EXODUS. XII. 301

NOTES on vv. 4, 8, 40.

4. The variations in translating this verse do not affect the general sense, but indicate some difficulty in the construction. "Each man according to his eating" is understood by the Vulg. to mean the number which may be sufficient to consume the lamb: but the evident sense is that the head of the family must judge what quantity each person will probably consume, a quantity varying of course according to age, strength, and other circumstances. The Hebrew root כסס, with its derivatives, does not occur in any book but the Pentateuch, and with one exception, Num. xxxi., only in connection with this special transaction, nor is it found in any of the Semitic languages. It is evidently archaic, unknown to later Hebrews except from this book. Gesenius points out the analogy with other roots with the same or similar initials, and Fuerst compares the Sanscrit *ças, kshi*, which however differ, having, as well as the Egyptian *kesha*, the sense of cutting, wounding, &c.

8. Hebrew מצות; derived by Gesenius from מצץ, "cum voluptate hausit, gustavit." Brugsch, 'D. H.' s. v., suggests an Egyptian etymology. The cakes offered at the festival of the New Year to Osiris were called *mest*, or *mesī-t*. It is possible that the word was commonly used while the Israelites were in Egypt to denote sweet, or unleavened, cakes used exclusively for sacred purposes. Knobel and Keil agree in referring *mazzoth* to a word extant in Arabic, in the sense "pure:" but that sense is secondary and probably not ancient; the root has the meaning assigned above to מצץ. At the end of this verse the LXX. and Vulg. omit "it" after "eat." This gives a preferable construction to that of our A.V.; and the authority of the LXX., always high in the Pentateuch, is especially so in this book.

40. The rendering of the Authorised Version, "who dwelt," is peculiar. It has no support in the Ancient Versions: (the LXX. have ἣν κατῴκησαν; the Vulg. qua manserunt; thus also the Arabic, Syriac, Chaldee and Samaritan;) nor does it appear to be adopted by any modern commentator. In fact the mention of the sojourning without reference to its duration would be beside the mind of the writer. If the Hebrew text be taken as it stands, it fixes that duration to 430 years; and this is accepted by the majority of critics of all schools. It agrees substantially with Genesis xv. 13, 14, when the announcement was first made to Abraham, "know of a surety that thy seed shall be a stranger in a land that is not theirs, and shall serve them; and they shall afflict them four hundred years; and also that nation, whom they shall serve, will I judge: and afterwards shall they come out with great substance." The expressions here used apply to Egypt and not to Canaan, in which the Patriarchs were certainly not made to serve. The additional statement in *v.* 16 of the same chapter "in the fourth generation they shall come hither again" presents some difficulty; it is however probably identical in sense with the preceding one, referring to the time during which the people would serve in a strange land; the term generation is understood by Gesenius and other Hebrew scholars to be equivalent to a century.

The correctness of the Hebrew text has however been questioned. The LXX. according to the Vatican codex inserts after Egypt, "and in the land of Canaan:" or according to the Alexandrian codex and Coptic Version, ed. De Lagarde, "which they and their fathers dwelt in the land of Egypt and the land of Canaan." The Samaritan Pentateuch has "which they dwelt in the land of Canaan and the land of Egypt." This is supposed by some to represent a various reading in the original: but the authority of both witnesses is impaired by the variations which indicate an intention to meet a difficulty, and by the fact that the most ancient Greek codices omit the words altogether and agree with the Hebrew text. For this we have the evidence of Theophilus Ant. who states twice, 'ad Aut.' III. § 9 and 24, that the Israelites sojourned 430 years in Egypt: the Samaritan text and that of one late Hebrew MS. which agrees with it are suspected of interpolation. Scholars at present generally accept the Hebrew as genuine, differing only in the interpretation.

There can be no doubt that at an early time the Jews felt the difficulty of reconciling this statement with the genealogies, which they held to be complete. If Levi were the grandfather of Moses on the mother's side through Jochebed, and separated only by two descents on the father's, through Kohath and Amram, it is clear that a space of 430 years could not be accounted for. Levi was past middle age when he went into Egypt; Moses was born 80 years before the Exodus. The difficulty however appears to be insuperable even on the hypothesis that 430 years included the whole interval between Abraham and the Exodus. Isaac was born 25 years after Abraham's arrival in Canaan, Jacob was born in Isaac's 60th year, and was 130 years old when he entered Egypt. This accounts for 215 years, leaving 215 for the sojourn. But in order to make out 215 years it is necessary to assume that Levi was 95 years old when Jochebed was born, and that Jochebed was 85 years old when she became mother of Moses. This is said by a commentator of great weight not to be improbable; but it involves two miracles, for which there is no authority in Scripture.

In the later Targum on Exodus ii. 1 a rabbinical tradition is recorded that Jochebed was miraculously restored to youth at the age of 130 years. But even these assumptions would not remove the objection, that the male descendants of Kohath (the grandfather of Moses on this hypothesis) amounted to 8600 at the time of the Exodus; see Num. iii. 28. The Kohathites were then divided into four families, each of which must have numbered, including females, about 4300, when Moses was 80 years of age. Whether the longer or shorter period be adopted it is equally necessary either to assume a succession of miracles, or to admit that an indefinite number of links in the genealogies are omitted; a fact for which we have positive evidence in the most important of all genealogies, that of our Lord, and in that of Ezra, which therefore there can be no irreverence in assuming in a case when it clears up every difficulty in the narrative.

The Jewish tradition is assumed to be in favour of 215 years; this may be true in reference to the later Rabbis: but it is far from being uniform. Josephus adopts in one passage, 'Ant.' II. 15. 2, but in others he distinctly asserts that the period of affliction in Egypt after the death of Joseph lasted 400 years; see 'Ant.' II. 9. 1 and 'B. J.' v. 9. 4. The evidence is worth little, being self-contradictory, but it shews that both opinions were held at his time. In the New Testament St Stephen's speech, Acts vii. 6, recognizes 400 years as the period when the seed of Abraham should be in bondage and evil entreated, terms which could only apply to Egypt. St Paul however seems to support the other view, Gal. iii. 17, when he says that the law was given 430 years after Abraham: but the period accepted generally by the Jews in his time sufficed for his purpose, and a discussion upon a point which did not affect his argument would have been out of place.

It may be possible to reconcile the number of the Israelites at the time of the Exodus with the shorter period; but it certainly is far more probable if we accept without any reserve the statement of Moses in this passage, made as it is in the most formal and precise terms, with the express purpose of fixing the length of the sojourn permanently upon the national mind.

The determination of the date of the Exodus rests mainly upon the statement in 1 K. vi. 1, that 480 years elapsed between the fourth year of Solomon and the time when the children of Israel came out of the land of Egypt. That date is supported by all the ancient versions (the slight deviation in the LXX., 440 for 480, being accounted for by Winer and Thenius in loc. as a lapsus calami, מ=40 for פ=80), it is accepted by able critics, and it appears to the writer of this note to accord best with the indications of time in the historical books; but the subject belongs properly to the commentatary on Kings.

CHAPTER XIII.

1 *The firstborn are sanctified to God.* 3 *The memorial of the passover is commanded.* 11 *The firstlings of beasts are set apart.* 17 *The Israelites go out of Egypt, and carry Joseph's bones with them.* 20 *They come to Etham.* 21 *God guideth them by a pillar of a cloud, and a pillar of fire.*

AND the LORD spake unto Moses, saying,

2 ^aSanctify unto me all the firstborn, whatsoever openeth the womb among the children of Israel, *both* of man and of beast: it *is* mine.

3 ¶ And Moses said unto the people, Remember this day, in which ye came out from Egypt, out of the house of †bondage; for by strength of hand the LORD brought you out

^a chap. 22. 29.
& 34. 19.
Lev. 27.26.
Numb. 3. 13.
& 8. 16.
Luke 2. 23.

† Heb. *servants.*

CHAP. XIII. The instructions in the first part of this chapter are not necessarily connected with the rest of the narrative, and there may have been special reasons for adding some of them, together with the grounds for their observance, when the people were preparing for the invasion of Palestine. This might have been before the beginning of their long wandering in the wilderness of Tih, at the same time when Moses sent the spies to explore Canaan. Whether written later or not, this section contains much which must have been orally given at the first celebration of the Passover.

2. *Sanctify unto me*] The command is addressed to Moses. It was to declare the will of God that all firstborn were to be consecrated to him, set apart from all other creatures. The command is expressly based upon the Passover. The firstborn exempt from the destruction became in a new and special sense the exclusive property of the Lord: the firstborn of man as His ministers, the firstborn of cattle as victims. In lieu of the firstborn of men the Levites were devoted to the temple services. The consecration of all firstborn is admitted to be peculiar to the Hebrews; nor can any satisfactory reason for such a law be assigned by those who refuse to accept the Scriptural statement, which they admit to be explicit. Knobel refutes the theories of other writers.

from this *place:* there shall no leavened bread be eaten.

4 This day came ye out in the month Abib.

5 ¶ And it shall be when the LORD shall bring thee into the land of the Canaanites, and the Hittites, and the Amorites, and the Hivites, and the Jebusites, which he sware unto thy fathers to give thee, a land flowing with milk and honey, that thou shalt keep this service in this month.

6 Seven days thou shalt eat unleavened bread, and in the seventh day *shall be* a feast to the LORD.

7 Unleavened bread shall be eaten seven days; and there shall no leavened bread be seen with thee, neither shall there be leaven seen with thee in all thy quarters.

8 ¶ And thou shalt shew thy son in that day, saying, *This is done* because of that *which* the LORD did unto me when I came forth out of Egypt.

9 And it shall be for a sign unto thee upon thine hand, and for a memorial between thine eyes, that the LORD's law may be in thy mouth: for with a strong hand hath the LORD brought thee out of Egypt.

10 Thou shalt therefore keep this ordinance in his season from year to year.

11 ¶ And it shall be when the LORD shall bring thee into the land of the Canaanites, as he sware unto thee and to thy fathers, and shall give it thee,

12 *b*That thou shalt †set apart unto the LORD all that openeth the matrix, and every firstling that cometh of a beast which thou hast; the males *shall be* the LORD's.

13 And every firstling of an ass thou shalt redeem with a ‖lamb; and

b chap. 22. 29. & 34. 19. Ezek. 44. 30.
† Heb. *cause to pass over.*
‖ Or, *kid.*

---

4. *Abib*] It is uncertain whether this name was ancient or given then for the first time. It is found only in the Pentateuch, twice in the sense of young wheat, six times as the name of the first month. The two former instances leave little doubt as to the etymology, viz. the month when the wheat began to ripen. Thus the LXX., Targ. and Saadia. In Arabic *abbon* means green herbs. The name resembles the Egyptian Epiphi, April, and may possibly have been derived from it; that name is ancient. See Brugsch, 'H. E.' p. 162.

5. *the Canaanites*] Five nations only are named in this passage, whereas six are named in iii. 8, and ten in the original promise to Abraham, Gen. xv. 19—21. The LXX. add the Perizzites and Girgashites, probably on MSS. authority. The first word Canaanite is generic, and includes all the Hamite races of Palestine.

9. *And it shall be for a sign unto thee,* &c.] Hebrew writers have generally regarded this as a formal injunction to write the precepts on slips of parchment, and to fasten them on the wrists and forehead; but other commentators are generally agreed that it is to be understood metaphorically. The words appear to be put into the mouths of the parents. They were to keep all the facts of the passover constantly in mind, and, referring to a custom prevalent ages before Moses in Egypt, to have them present as though they were inscribed on papyrus or parchment fastened on the wrists, or on the face between the eyes. It is improbable that Moses should have adopted that custom, which was scarcely separable from the Egyptian superstition of amulets; but modern Israelites generally allege this precept as a justification for the use of phylacteries. Moses states distinctly the object of the precept, which was that the law of Jehovah should be in their mouth: see *v.* 16. The expression may have been proverbial in the time of Moses, as it certainly was at a later period; see Proverbs vi. 20—22, vii. 3, where the metaphorical sense is not questioned. Jerome gives a clear and rational interpretation in his commentary on Matthew xxiii. 5, "Præcepta mea sint in manu tua, ut opere compleantur, sint ante oculos tuos ut nocte et die mediteris in illis."

12. *thou shalt set apart*] lit. as in the margin "cause to pass over," but the sense is correctly expressed in the text, which follows the Old Versions, and is preferable to the marginal rendering, which suggests a reference to the word "Passover."

13. *an ass*] The reason of the injunction is evidently that the ass could not be offered in sacrifice, being an unclean animal: possibly the only unclean animal domesticated among the Israelites at the time of the Exodus. The principle of the law being obvious, it was extended to the horse and camel, and generally to every unclean beast; see Num. xviii. 15. The mention of the ass only would scarcely have occurred to an Israelite of a

304   EXODUS. XIII.   [v. 14—19.

if thou wilt not redeem it, then thou shalt break his neck: and all the firstborn of man among thy children shalt thou redeem.

14 ¶ And it shall be when thy son asketh thee †in time to come, saying, What *is* this? that thou shalt say unto him, By strength of hand the LORD brought us out from Egypt, from the house of bondage:

15 And it came to pass, when Pharaoh would hardly let us go, that the LORD slew all the firstborn in the land of Egypt, both the firstborn of man, and the firstborn of beast: therefore I sacrifice to the LORD all that openeth the matrix, being males; but all the firstborn of my children I redeem.

16 And it shall be for a token upon thine hand, and for frontlets between thine eyes: for by strength of hand the LORD brought us forth out of Egypt.

17 ¶ And it came to pass, when Pharaoh had let the people go, that God led them not *through* the way of the land of the Philistines, although that *was* near; for God said, Lest peradventure the people repent when they see war, and they return to Egypt:

18 But God led the people about, *through* the way of the wilderness of the Red sea: and the children of Israel went up ‖harnessed out of the land of Egypt.

19 And Moses took the bones of Joseph with him: for he had straitly sworn the children of Israel, saying,

† Heb. *to morrow.*

‖ Or, *by five in a rank.*

---

later age. It has been observed that the ass was held by the Egyptians to be typhonic, *i.e.* in a peculiar sense unclean: but that feeling appears to belong to a comparatively later period; in early monuments the ass is frequently represented, and in the 'Ritual,' c. 40, it is even a type of Osiris.

thou shalt redeem] The lamb, or sheep, was given to the priest for the service of the sanctuary.

firstborn of man] The price of redemption was fixed at five shekels of the sanctuary: Num. iii. 47, where see note.

16. *it shall be*] This passage confirms the interpretation given above on *v.* 9.

17—19. These verses do not appear to be a continuation of the narrative, which is resumed at *v.* 20. It is not improbable that some short time was passed at Succoth, and that Moses then gave final injunctions touching the celebration of the Passover, and received general instructions as to the ultimate direction of the journey. Succoth may very probably have been the head-quarters of the Hebrews in Goshen. The name in Hebrew indicates an assemblage of booths, or moveable huts (see ch. xii. 37), such as were probably used by the Israelites, ever mindful of their condition as sojourners in a strange land: the notice in *v.* 19 naturally leaves the impression that the bones of Joseph were kept there, of course in the charge of his own descendants.

17. *the way of the land of the Philistines*] The occupancy of southern Palestine by the Philistines, at a much earlier period than is assigned by any critics to the Exodus, is attested by the narrative in Genesis xxvi. 1. It has lately been questioned on the ground that the inhabitants of Ascalon, when it was captured by Rameses II. did not wear the well-known costume of the Philistines, but that of the ancient Canaanites, and that the name Pulisha, *i.e.* Philistines, occurs first in monuments of the time of Rameses III. Brugsch, 'Geog. Ins.' II. p. 86. The objection is answered in the Appendix at the end of the volume: here it may suffice to notice that the persons represented on the monuments of Rameses II. were probably Israelites; for they actually took possession of the cities of the Philistines, who did not recover the territory until a considerable time had elapsed after the death of Joshua. The warlike character of the Philistines is equally conspicuous in the Egyptian and Hebrew records.

18. *harnessed*] This interpretation of the Hebrew word rests on the authority of some ancient versions, and a possible etymology is suggested by Rabbinical writers. It seems, however, more probable that the meaning is marshalled or in orderly array. See note below. The objection (grounded on the rendering in our version) that the Israelites were not likely to have been armed is unreasonable. There is not the least indication that they were disarmed by the Egyptians, and as occupying a frontier district frequently assailed by the nomads of the desert they would of necessity be accustomed to the use of arms. The fear expressed by Pharaoh (see ch. i. 10) that they might at any time join the invaders and fight against Egypt was the avowed and doubtless the true motive for the crafty measures by which he hoped to subdue their spirit and prevent their increase.

*Gen. 50.
25.
Josh. 24.
32.
*Numb.
33. 6.
*Numb.
14. 14.
Deut. 1.
33.
Psal. 78. 14.
1 Cor. 10. 1.

*God will surely visit you; and ye shall carry up my bones away hence with you.

20 ¶ And *they took their journey from Succoth, and encamped in Etham, in the edge of the wilderness.

21 And *the LORD went before them by day in a pillar of a cloud, to lead them the way; and by night in a pillar of fire, to give them light; to go by day and night:

22 He took not away the pillar of the cloud by day, *nor the pillar of fire by night, *from* before the people.

*Neh. 9. 19.

20. *Etham*] The Egyptian notices of Etham will be found in the Appendix at the end of this volume. The most probable result of those notices is that Etham, which means the house or sanctuary of Tum (the Sun God worshipped specially by that name in lower Egypt), was in the immediate vicinity of Heroopolis, called by the Egyptians the fortress of Zar, or Zalu (*i.e.* of foreigners); the frontier city where the Pharaohs of the 18th dynasty reviewed their forces when about to enter upon a campaign on Syria. The name Pithom has precisely the same meaning with Etham, and may possibly be identified with it. It was at this point that the Bedouins of the adjoining wilderness came into contact with the Egyptians. Under the 19th dynasty we find them applying in a time of famine for admission to the fertile district commanded by the fortress called the sanctuary of Tum.

21. *pillar of cloud*] The Lord Himself did for the Israelites by preternatural means that which armies were obliged to do for themselves by natural agents. Passages are quoted from classical writers which shew that the Persians and Greeks used fire and smoke as signals in their marches. Curtius describes the practice of Alexander, who gave the signal for departure by a fire on a tall pole over his tent, and says, observabatur ignis noctu fumus interdiu. Vegetius and Frontinus mention it as a general custom, especially among the Arabians. The success of some important expeditions, as of Thrasybulus and Timoleon, was attributed by popular superstition to a divine light guiding the leaders. To these well-known instances may be added two of peculiar interest, as bearing witness to a custom known to all the contemporaries of Moses. In an inscription of the Ancient Empire an Egyptian general is compared to "a flame streaming in advance of an army." (See Chabas 'V. E.' p. 54; the inscription is in the Denkmæler, II, pl. 150, 2). Thus too in a wellknown papyrus, (Anast. 1) the commander of an expedition is called "A flame in the darkness at the head of his soldiers." By this sign then of the pillar of cloud, the Lord shewed Himself as their leader and general. "The Lord is a man of war... thy right hand, O Lord, hath dashed in pieces the enemy" (xv.).

NOTE on *v.* 18.

The Hebrew חמשים is rendered "armati" by the Vulg., מזרזין by Onkelos, *i.e.* accincti, expediti, rather than armati, as it is rendered in Walton's Polyglott. This would suit the etymology proposed by Abulwalid, Kimchi, and Tanchum, and adopted by Kalisch, viz. חמש, ilia, abdomen. The sense however would be *not* "full-armed," but simply "with their loins girded," as men prepared for a journey. Thus in Joshua i. 14 it is rendered εὔζωνοι by the LXX. The Arabic in Walton (by Saadia) has مُسَيَّـٮ. *i.e.* instructi, marshalled; and this meaning is adopted by many critics, though different etymologies are proposed. Knobel says that it *must* signify assembled, arranged in orderly divisions, in contradistinction from a disorganised rabble. He derives it from Arabic roots, such as خمس &c. It seems however preferable to take the obvious Hebrew etymology from חמש, *i.e.* five, probably connected with خمس, agmen instructum, pr. quinquepartitum, which is pointed at by the singular rendering of the LXX. "in the fifth generation." Ewald, 'G. I.' explains it "arranged in five divisions," *i.e.* van, centre, two wings and rear-guard. The promptitude with which so vast a multitude was marshalled and led forth justifies admiration, but is not marvellous, nor without parallels in ancient and modern history (see Introduction). The Israelites had been prepared for departure, some preliminary measures must have been taken after each of the plagues when Pharaoh had given a temporary assent to the request of Moses, see viii. 8, 28, ix. 28, x. 16, four several occasions on which notice must have been given to the people. It must also be borne in mind that the despotism of Pharaoh had supplied the Israelites with native officers whom they were accustomed to obey, and with whom they were united by the bond of a common suffering (see ch. v. 14—21). Their leader had the experience of an early life at a warlike court, and of long years passed among the fierce tribes of the desert. The nation moreover has shewn in every age a remarkable talent for prompt and systematic organization.

VOL. I.

CHAPTER XIV.

1 *God instructeth the Israelites in their journey.* 5 *Pharaoh pursueth after them.* 10 *The Israelites murmur.* 13 *Moses comforteth them.* 15 *God instructeth Moses.* 19 *The cloud removeth behind the camp.* 21 *The Israelites pass through the Red sea,* 23 *which drowneth the Egyptians.*

AND the Lord spake unto Moses, saying,

2 Speak unto the children of Israel, that they turn and encamp before *a* Pi-hahiroth, between Migdol and the sea, over against Baal-zephon: before it shall ye encamp by the sea.

3 For Pharaoh will say of the children of Israel, They *are* entangled in the land, the wilderness hath shut them in.

a Numb. 33. 7.

The Passage over the Red Sea.

CHAP. XIV. 2. *That they turn*] The narrative is continued from *v.* 20 of the preceding chapter. The people were then at Etham, or Pithom, the frontier city towards the wilderness: they are now commanded to change the direction of their march, and to go southwards, to the west of the Bitter Lakes, which completely separated them from the desert: see note on c. xii. 37.

Pi-hahiroth] The derivation of this name is doubtful. If it is Semitic, like the two other names mentioned in connection with it, the meaning may be "mouth, or entrance of the holes or caverns," but it is more probably Egyptian, with the common prefix Pi, *i. e.* house. In an ancient papyrus, we read of a place called Hir, or Pe-Hir, where there was a large well, at no great distance from Rameses, which it supplied with garlands. See Chabas, 'Mél. Eg.' II. p. 123. The place is generally identified with Ajrud, a fortress with a very large well of good water (see Niebuhr, 'Voyage,' I. p. 175), situate at the foot of an elevation commanding the plain which extends to Suez, at a distance of four leagues. The journey from Etham might occupy two, or even three days; had however Etham been, as many geographers suppose, half-way between Mukfar and Ajrud (see Robinson's 'Chart'), Pharaoh could not possibly have overtaken the Israelites, whether his head-quarters were at Zoan, or even at Rameses, which was two days' journey from Etham.

Migdol] The word means a tower, or fort: it is probably to be identified with Bir Suweis, about two miles from Suez. The water is said by Niebuhr to be scarcely drinkable; according to Robinson, p. 45, it is used only for cooking and washing. This traveller observes justly, that if the wells were in existence at the time of the Exodus they would mark the site of a town. Now M. Chabas has lately shewn that Maktal, or Magdal, an Egyptian fort (which on other grounds he identifies with Migdol), visited by Sethos I. on his return from a campaign in Syria, was built over a large well: see 'Voyage d'un Egyptien,' p. 286. This leaves scarcely any room for doubt as to the locality; it is a point of importance with reference to the passage over the sea.

Baal-zephon] This appears to have been the name under which the Phœnicians, who had a settlement in lower Egypt at a very ancient period, worshipped their chief Deity. The corresponding Egyptian Deity was Sutech, who is often called Bal on monuments of the 19th dynasty. Sethos I. gave a name closely connected with this to a city in the same neighbourhood, which Chabas, l. c., holds to be Baal-Zephon. There can be no doubt it was near Kolsum, or Suez. In the time of Niebuhr there were considerable ruins close to Suez on the north. From the text it is clear that the encampment of the Israelites extended over the plain from Pi-hahiroth: their head-quarters being between Bir Suweis and the sea opposite to Baal-Zephon. At Ajrud the road branches off in two directions, one leading to the wilderness by a tract, now dry, but in the time of Moses probably impassable, see next note; the other leading to Suez, which was doubtless followed by the Israelites.

3. *They are entangled,* &c.} The meaning evidently is, in that direction they have no egress from Egypt: the latter part of the verse is generally rendered as in our Version, "the wilderness has shut them in," but the sense would rather seem to be "the wilderness is closed to them;" see note below. The original intention of Moses was to go towards Palestine by the wilderness: when that purpose was changed by God's direction and they moved southwards, Pharaoh on receiving information was of course aware that they were completely shut in, since the waters of the Red Sea then extended to the bitter lakes. It is known that the Red Sea at some remote period extended considerably further towards the north than it does at present. In the time of Moses the water north of Kolsum joined the bitter lakes, though at present the constant accumulation of sand has covered the intervening space to the extent of 8000 to 10000 yards, not however rising higher than six feet above the level of the lakes, and from 40 to 50 feet below the level of the Red Sea. Mr Malan, p. 217, observes that the lake Timseh, still further north, is full of

4 And I will harden Pharaoh's heart, that he shall follow after them; and I will be honoured upon Pharaoh, and upon all his host; that the Egyptians may know that I *am* the LORD. And they did so.

5 ¶ And it was told the king of Egypt that the people fled: and the heart of Pharaoh and of his servants was turned against the people, and they said, Why have we done this, that we have let Israel go from serving us?

6 And he made ready his chariot, and took his people with him:

7 And he took six hundred chosen chariots, and all the chariots of Egypt, and captains over every one of them.

8 And the LORD hardened the heart of Pharaoh king of Egypt, and he pursued after the children of Israel: and the children of Israel went out with an high hand.

9 But the *b* Egyptians pursued after them, all the horses *and* chariots of Pharaoh, and his horsemen, and his army, and overtook them encamping by the sea, beside Pi-hahiroth, before Baal-zephon.

10 ¶ And when Pharaoh drew nigh, the children of Israel lifted up their eyes, and, behold, the Egyptians marched after them; and they were sore afraid: and the children of Israel cried out unto the LORD.

11 And they said unto Moses, Be-

b Josh. 24. 6.
1 Mac. 4. 9.

---

the Saris or Shari, the arundo Egyptiaca, from which the Red Sea takes its local name.

5. *the people fled*] This was a natural inference from the change of direction, which could have no object but escape from Egypt by the pass at Suez. Up to the time when that information reached Pharaoh both he and his people understood that the Israelites would return after keeping a festival in the district adjoining Etham. From Etham the intelligence would be forwarded by the commander of the garrison to Rameses in less than a day, and the cavalry, a highly disciplined force, would of course be ready for immediate departure.

7. *six hundred chosen chariots*] The Egyptian army comprised large numbers of chariots, each drawn by two horses, with two men, one bearing the shield and driving, the other fully armed. The horses were thoroughbred, renowned for strength and spirit. Chariots are first represented on the monuments of the 18th dynasty: they were used by Amosis I. in the expedition against the shepherd kings, by Thotmes I. against Syria and Mesopotamia: under Thotmes III. we have the record of a battle at Megiddo in which 897 war-chariots were captured from the confederated forces of northern Palestine and Syria. By "all the chariots of Egypt" we are to understand all that were stationed in lower Egypt, most of them probably at Rameses and other frontier garrisons near the head-quarters of Pharaoh. According to Diodorus Siculus, I. 54, the Egyptians had 27000 chariots in the time of Rameses II.

captains over every one of them] Rather **captains over the whole of them.** Thus the LXX., Vulg., Saadia, Syr. The word rendered captains (Shalishim, lit. third or thirtieth) is supposed by Rœdiger, Ges. 'Thes.' s. v., to mean the warriors in the chariots, but the Egyptians never put more than two men in a chariot. The true meaning is captains or commanders. The word may represent an Egyptian title. The king had about him a council of thirty, each of whom bore a title corresponding to the Roman decemvir, viz. Mapu, a "thirty man." See Pleyte, 'Æg. Zeitschrift,' 1866, p. 12, and Chabas, 'Voyage d'un Égyptien.' The word occurs frequently in the books of Kings. David seems to have organized the Shalishim as a distinct corps, see 2 Sam. xxiii. 8, where it is translated, as in this passage, captains. He probably retained the old name, though it is possible that he may have adopted the Egyptian system, being on friendly terms with the contemporary dynasty, which gave a queen to Israel.

9. *and his horsemen*] Horsemen are not represented on Egyptian monuments, even on those of a later age, when they were employed in great numbers; the omission is probably connected with the strict regulations of Egyptian art; but Diodorus Siculus, whose authority is not questioned on this point, states that Rameses II. had a force of 24000 cavalry, independent of the chariotry; Isaiah makes the same distinction between the chariots and horsemen of Egypt, c. xxxi. 1. The technical expression for mounting on horseback is found in ancient papyri.

beside Pi-hahiroth] This statement is urged as an objection to the identification with Ajrud; but the encampment of the great host of Israel extended over many miles.

U 2

cause *there were* no graves in Egypt, hast thou taken us away to die in the wilderness? wherefore hast thou dealt thus with us, to carry us forth out of Egypt? 12 ᶜ*Is* not this the word that we did tell thee in Egypt, saying, Let us alone, that we may serve the Egyptians? For *it had been* better for us to serve the Egyptians, than that we should die in the wilderness.

13 ¶ And Moses said unto the people, Fear ye not, stand still, and see the salvation of the LORD, which he will shew to you to day: ¹for the Egyptians whom ye have seen to day, ye shall see them again no more for ever.

14 The LORD shall fight for you, and ye shall hold your peace.

15 ¶ And the LORD said unto Moses, Wherefore criest thou unto me? speak unto the children of Israel, that they go forward:

16 But lift thou up thy rod, and stretch out thine hand over the sea, and divide it: and the children of Israel shall go on dry *ground* through the midst of the sea.

17 And I, behold, I will harden the hearts of the Egyptians, and they shall follow them: and I will get me honour upon Pharaoh, and upon all his host, upon his chariots, and upon his horsemen.

18 And the Egyptians shall know that I *am* the LORD, when I have gotten me honour upon Pharaoh, upon his chariots, and upon his horsemen.

19 ¶ And the angel of God, which went before the camp of Israel, removed and went behind them; and the pillar of the cloud went from before their face, and stood behind them:

20 And it came between the camp of the Egyptians and the camp of Israel; and it was a cloud and darkness *to them*, but it gave light by night *to these:* so that the one came not near the other all the night.

21 And Moses stretched out his hand over the sea; and the LORD caused the sea to go *back* by a strong east wind all that night, and made the sea dry *land*, and the waters were ᵈdivided.

ᵃ chap. 6. 9.

¶ Or, *for whereas you have seen the Egyptians to day, &c.*

ᵈ Josh 4 23. Psal. 114 3.

---

11. *no graves in Egypt*] This bitter taunt was probably suggested by the vast extent of cemeteries in Egypt, which might not improperly be called the land of tombs: it would scarcely have been imagined by one who had not dwelt there.

12. *Let us alone*] This is a gross exaggeration, yet not without a semblance of truth: for although the Israelites welcomed the message of Moses at first, they gave way completely at the first serious trial. See the reference in marg. The whole passage foreshadows the conduct of the people in the wilderness.

13. *for the Egyptians whom*, &c.] Rather **for as ye have seen the Egyptians** to-day ye shall see them again no more for ever. Our A.V. follows the Vulg., but the LXX., Targ., Saad. give the true sense, ye shall never see the Egyptians in the same way, under the same circumstances.

15. *Wherefore criest thou unto me?*] Moses does not speak of his intercession, and we only know of it from this answer to his prayer. This is a characteristic of the narrative, important to be observed with reference to other omissions less easily supplied.

19. *the angel of God*] Compare ch. xiii. 21; and see note on ch. iii. 2.

20. The words in Italics are accepted as explanatory by some commentators; but the LXX. read "and the night passed" instead of "it gave light by night." The sense is good and the reading not improbable.

21. *a strong east wind*] It is thus distinctly stated that the agency by which the object was effected was natural. It is clear that Moses takes for granted that a strong east wind blowing through the night, under given circumstances, would make the passage quite possible. It would seem to be scarcely practicable, when the wind blows from other quarters (see Tischendorf's account, 'Aus dem heiligen Lande,' p. 21). Of course this would not explain the effect, if the passage had been made, as was formerly supposed, through the deep sea near the Wady Musa, some leagues south of Suez. All the conditions of the narrative are satisfied by the hypothesis, that the passage took place near Suez.

the waters were divided] *i. e.* there was a complete separation between the water of the gulf and the water to the north of Kolsum.

e Psal. 78.
13.
1 Cor. 10.
1.
Heb. 11.
29.

22 And *the children of Israel went into the midst of the sea upon the dry ground: and the waters *were* a wall unto them on their right hand, and on their left.

23 ¶ And the Egyptians pursued, and went in after them to the midst of the sea, *even* all Pharaoh's horses, his chariots, and his horsemen.

24 And it came to pass, that in the morning watch the LORD looked unto the host of the Egyptians through the pillar of fire and of the cloud, and troubled the host of the Egyptians,

25 And took off their chariot wheels, ¹that they drave them heavily: so that the Egyptians said, Let us flee from the face of Israel; for the LORD

¹ Or, *made them to go heavily*.

fighteth for them against the Egyptians.

26 ¶ And the LORD said unto Moses, Stretch out thine hand over the sea, that the waters may come again upon the Egyptians, upon their chariots, and upon their horsemen.

27 And Moses stretched forth his hand over the sea, and the sea returned to his strength when the morning appeared; and the Egyptians fled against it; and the LORD †overthrew the Egyptians in the midst of the sea.

28 And the waters returned, and covered the chariots, and the horsemen, *and* all the host of Pharaoh that came into the sea after them; there remained not so much as *f* one of them.

† Heb. *shook off*.

f Psal. 106. 11.

---

22. *were a wall unto them*] The waters served the purpose of an intrenchment and wall; the people could not be attacked on either flank during the transit; to the north was the water covering the whole district; to the south was the Red Sea. For the idiom, compare Nahum iii. 8.

23. *the Egyptians pursued*] The Egyptians might be aware that under ordinary circumstances there would be abundant time for the passage of the chariots and cavalry, of which the force chiefly consisted.

24. *in the morning watch*] At sunrise, a little before 6 A.M. in April.

troubled] Threw them into confusion by a sudden panic.

25. *And took off their chariot wheels*] This translation is generally accepted. The LXX. however render the word "bound" or clogged (συνέδησε = אָסַר), a probable reading, and perhaps more suited to the context.

26. *that the waters may come*] A sudden cessation of the wind at sunrise, coinciding with a spring tide (it was full moon) would immediately convert the low flat sand-banks first into a quicksand, and then into a mass of waters, in a time far less than would suffice for the escape of a single chariot, or horseman loaded with heavy corslet.

27. *overthrew the Egyptians*] Better as in the margin, **The Lord shook them off**, hurled them from their chariots into the sea. Thus in the papyrus quoted above, when the chariot is broken the warrior is hurled out with such force that his armour is buried in the sand.

28. *not so much as one of them*] The statement is explicit, all the chariots and horsemen and that portion of the infantry which followed them into the bed of the sea. In fact, as has been shewn, escape would be impossible. A doubt has been raised whether Pharaoh himself perished: but independent of the distinct statement of the Psalmist, Ps. cxxxvi. 15, his destruction is manifestly assumed, and was in fact inevitable. The station of the king was in the vanguard: on every monument the Pharaoh is represented as the leader of the army, and allowing for Egyptian flattery on other occasions, that was his natural place in the pursuit of fugitives whom he hated so intensely. The death of the Pharaoh, and the entire loss of the chariotry and cavalry accounts for the undisturbed retreat of the Israelites through a district then subject to Egypt and easily accessible to their forces. The blow to Egypt was not fatal, for the loss of men might not amount to many thousands; but falling upon their king, their leaders and the portion of the army indispensable for the prosecution of foreign wars, it crippled them effectually. If, as appears probable, Tothmosis II. were the Pharaoh, the first recorded expedition into the Peninsula took place 17 years after his death; and twenty-two years elapsed before any measures were taken to recover the lost ascendancy of Egypt in Syria. So complete, so marvellous was the deliverance: thus the Israelites were baptized to Moses in the cloud and in the sea. When they left Baal-Zephon they were separated finally from the idolatry of Egypt: when they passed the Red Sea their independence of its power was sealed; their life as a nation then began, a life inseparable henceforth from belief in Jehovah, and His servant Moses, only to be merged in the higher life revealed by His Son.

29 But the children of Israel walked upon dry *land* in the midst of the sea; and the waters *were* a wall unto them on their right hand, and on their left.

30 Thus the Lord saved Israel that day out of the hand of the Egyptians; and Israel saw the Egyptians dead upon the sea shore.

31 And Israel saw that great †work which the Lord did upon the Egyptians: and the people feared the Lord, and believed the Lord, and his servant Moses.

† Heb. *hand.*

NOTE on *v.* 3.

The Hebrew has סגר עליהם המדבר. The LXX. and Vulg. render סגר συγκέκλεικε, conclusit: but it is not followed by an accusative in the Hebrew, and must be intransitive, as it is taken by Saadia انغلق, and the Syr. ܐܣܬܟܪ, *i.e.* conclusum est. Thus in Judges iii. 22, "The fat closed upon the blade." The correct rendering seems to be the wilderness is closed to them. In no sense could the wilderness be a barrier; the direct route led them into it, the change of route shut them out from it.

CHAPTER XV.

1 *Moses' song.* 22 *The people want water.* 23 *The waters at Marah are bitter.* 25 *A tree sweeteneth them.* 27 *At Elim are twelve wells, and seventy palm trees.*

a Wisd. 1. 20.

THEN sang *a* Moses and the children of Israel this song unto the Lord, and spake, saying, I will sing unto the Lord, for he hath triumphed gloriously: the horse and his rider hath he thrown into the sea.

2 The Lord *is* my strength and song, and he is become my salvation: he *is* my God, and I will prepare him

---

Chap. XV. 1—18. With the deliverance of Israel is associated the development of the national poetry, which finds its first and perfect expression in this magnificent hymn. It is said to have been sung by Moses and the people, an expression which evidently points to him as the author. That it was written at the time is an assertion expressly made in the text, and it is supported by the strongest internal evidence. The style is admitted, even by critics who question its genuineness, to be archaic, both in the language, which is equally remarkable for grandeur, and severe simplicity, and in the general structure, which, though rhythmical and systematic, differs materially from later compositions, in which the divisions are more numerous and the arrangement more elaborate. The subject matter and the leading thoughts are such as belong to the time and the occasion; unlike the imitations in the later Psalms, the song abounds in allusions to incidents passing under the eye of the composer: it has every mark of freshness and originality. The only objections are founded on the prophetic portion (15—17): but if ever there was a crisis calculated to elicit the spirit of prophecy, it was that of the Exodus, if ever a man fitted to express that spirit, it was Moses. Even objectors admit that the invasion of Palestine was contemplated by Moses: if so what more natural than that after the great catastrophe, which they accept as an historical fact, he should anticipate the terror of the nations through whose territories the Israelites would pass, and whose destruction was an inevitable condition of their success. In every age this song gave the tone to the poetry of Israel; especially at great critical epochs of deliverance. In the book of Revelation (xv. 3) it is associated with the final triumph of the Church, when the saints "having the harps of God" will sing "the Song of Moses the servant of God, and the Song of the Lamb."

The division of the Song into three parts is distinctly marked: 1—5, 6—10, 11—18: each begins with an ascription of praise to God; each increases in length and varied imagery unto the triumphant close.

First Division. 1—10. Ascription of praise and brief statement of the transaction.

1. *He hath triumphed gloriously*] This gives the true meaning, but not the force and grandeur of the Hebrew, literally He is gloriously glorious. Among the Ancient Versions the LXX, ἐνδόξως δεδόξασται, comes near, the Arabic of Saadia is very fine اقتدر اقتدارا.

an habitation; my father's God, and I will exalt him.

3 The LORD *is* a man of war: the LORD *is* his name.

4 Pharaoh's chariots and his host hath he cast into the sea: his chosen captains also are drowned in the Red sea.

5 The depths have covered them: they sank into the bottom as a stone.

6 Thy right hand, O LORD, is become glorious in power: thy right hand, O LORD, hath dashed in pieces the enemy.

7 And in the greatness of thine excellency thou hast overthrown them that rose up against thee: thou sentest forth thy wrath, *which* consumed them as stubble.

8 And with the blast of thy nostrils the waters were gathered together, the floods stood upright as an heap, *and*

---

the horse and his rider] The word "rider" may include horseman, but applies properly to the charioteer: the Egyptian word for horse which corresponds exactly to the Hebrew, always designates the swift, high-bred horses used for the war-cars of nobles. Thus in the papyrus 'Anast.' 1, "The horses of my chariot are swift as jackals: their eyes like fire: they are like a hurricane when it bursts."

2. *The LORD is my strength and song*] **My strength and song is Jah.** This name is specially associated with victory by the Psalmist, Ps. lxviii. 4. It was doubtless chosen here by Moses to draw attention to the promise ratified by the name "I am." The form of the word "song" in Hebrew is archaic.

I will prepare Him an habitation] **I will glorify Him.** Scholars agree that the Hebrew word means to celebrate with grateful, loving adoration. In fact this sense is given by most of the ancient Versions. Our Authorised Version is open to serious objection, as suggesting a thought (viz. of erecting a temple) which could hardly have been in the mind of Moses at that time, and unsuited to the occasion. It is one of many instances of undue deference to Rabbinical authorities on the part of our translators. The Targum of Onkelos, who is followed by Kimchi, has "I will build Him a sanctuary." Thus too the interlinear Latin in Walton's Polyglott. The LXX., Vulg. and Syr. render the word correctly. Saadia has "I will take refuge with Him."

3. *a man of war*] Compare Ps. xxiv. 8. The name has on this occasion a peculiar fitness; man had no part in the victory: the battle was the Lord's.

the LORD is his name] A pregnant expression, implying that the manifestation of might, by which the salvation of Israel was effected, accorded with the name Jehovah, the most perfect expression of the Divine Essence.

4. *hath He cast*] The Hebrew is very forcible, "hurled," as from a sling. See note on ch. xiv. 27. All the words which describe the fall of the mailed warriors of Egypt are such as one who actually witnessed their overthrow would naturally employ. See note on the next verse.

his chosen captains] The same expression is used in ch. xiv. 7, where see note. It designates officers of the highest rank, chosen specially to attend on the person of Pharaoh: probably commanders of the 2000 Calasirians who alternatively with the Hermotybians formed his body-guard. They may have been for the most part personally known to Moses.

drowned] The original is more graphic, "plunged, submerged," describing the overthrow in the rushing tide.

5. *as a stone*] The warriors on chariots are always represented on the monuments with heavy coats of mail; the corslets of "chosen captains" consisted of plates of highly tempered bronze, with sleeves reaching nearly to the elbow, covering the whole body and the thighs nearly to the knee; see the engraving of the corslet of Rameses III. in Sir G. Wilkinson, 'M. and C.' I. p. 366. They must have sunk at once like a stone, or as we read in v. 10, like lumps of lead. Touches like these come naturally from an eye-witness.

SECOND DIVISION. 6—10. This division presents the details more fully, and completes the picture by describing the mode in which the destruction was effected, and the arrogance of the Egyptians by which it was provoked.

6. *is become glorious*] The translation is correct, but inadequately represents the force and beauty of the Hebrew word, which is archaic in form and usage.

7. *thy wrath*] lit. Thy burning, *i.e.* the fire of Thy wrath, a word chosen expressly with reference to the effect: it consumed the enemy suddenly, completely, like fire burning up stubble. The simile is not uncommon in Egyptian: thus in the poem of Pentaour addressed to Rameses II. "The people were as stubble before thy chariot:" but the superiority of the Hebrew is obvious—it represents the

the depths were congealed in the heart of the sea.

9 The enemy said, I will pursue, I will overtake, I will divide the spoil; my lust shall be satisfied upon them; I will draw my sword, my hand shall ¹destroy them.

10 Thou didst blow with thy wind, the sea covered them: they sank as lead in the mighty waters.

11 Who *is* like unto thee, O LORD, among the ¹gods? who *is* like thee, glorious in holiness, fearful *in* praises, doing wonders?

¹ Or, *repossess*.

¹ Or, *mighty ones!*

---

flame going forth from the Presence of God. The Hebrew for stubble is also Egyptian.

8. This description has been strangely misrepresented as though it were irreconcileable with the preceding narrative. It differs from that as lyric poetry differs in its imagery from prose; and as inspired poetry it brings us into contact with the hidden and effectual causes of the natural phenomena, which it still distinctly recognizes. The blast of God's nostrils corresponds to the natural agency, the east wind (ch. xiv. 21), which drove the waters back. On each side the Psalmist describes what he must actually have seen: on the north the waters rising high, overhanging the sands, but kept back by the strong wind: on the south lying in massive rollers, kept down by the same agency in the heart, or deep bed of the Red Sea. In both descriptions we have precisely the same effects; in the former the bearings upon the passage of the Israelites are most prominent; in this the scenery is presented in the form which impressed the seer's imagination most vividly, and which fixes itself most strongly on the spirit of the reader.

as an heap] The LXX. render this "as a wall," ὡσεὶ τεῖχος. The Hebrew word probably means "a dam." It corresponds to wall, xiv. 22.

9. *The enemy said*] The abrupt, gasping utterances; the haste, cupidity and ferocity of the Egyptians, the confusion and disorder of their thoughts, are described in terms recognized by critics of all schools as belonging to the highest order of poetry; it must not be forgotten that they enable us to realize the feelings which induced Pharaoh and his host to pursue the Israelites over the treacherous sandbanks.

destroy them] Thus Vulg., Targ., Saad. and most modern critics. The margin follows the LXX. and is defensible.

10. *Thou didst blow with thy wind*] The solemn majesty of these few words, in immediate contrast with the tumult and confusion of the preceding verse, needs scarcely be noticed: it is important to observe that Moses here states distinctly the natural agency by which the destruction was effected. In the direct narrative, xiv. 28, we read only, "the waters returned," here we are told that it was because the wind blew. A sudden change in the direction of the wind would bring back at once the masses of water heaped up on the north. If the tide rose at the same time, the waters of the Red Sea would meet and overwhelm the host: but this is not said, and the Egyptians, who were close observers of natural phenomena, would probably have been aware of the danger of attempting the passage had flood-time been near at hand. One cause is assigned and it suffices for the effect.

they sank as lead] See note on *v.* 4. The sudden drowning of the charioteers as they fell headlong in their heavy panoply must have been one of the most striking features of the scene: hence the repetition, not without a variation, which gives a more exact simile: they fell like masses of lead, helpless, motionless, unable for a moment to struggle with the waters.

THIRD AND LAST DIVISION. After the ascription of praise the seer turns to the remoter, but certain consequences of this unparalleled event. It was impossible that a man in the position and with the feelings of Moses should not revert to them, and at once present them in clear strong language to His people. The deliverance was the earnest of a complete fulfilment of old promises, it was a pledge also that enemies, whom the Israelites could not but dread as their superiors in the arts and resources of war, would be disheartened, and speedily overcome, and that they themselves would be put in possession of the inheritance of Abraham.

11. *among the gods*] The marg. has "mighty ones," which is a possible rendering, adopted in the Vulg. But the translation is quite correct, and justified by other unmistakeable passages; thus in Ps. lxxxvi. 8, "Among the gods there is none like unto Thee," an expression which by no means admits the substantial power of the objects of heathen worship, in which the Israelite recognized either evil spirits or mere phantoms of superstitious imagination; see especially Deut. xxxii. 16, 17. A Hebrew just leaving the land in which Polytheism attained its highest development, with gigantic statues and temples of incomparable grandeur, might well on such an occ-

12 Thou stretchedst out thy right hand, the earth swallowed them.

13 Thou in thy mercy hast led forth the people *which* thou hast redeemed: thou hast guided *them* in thy strength unto thy holy habitation.

14 The *b*people shall hear, *and* be afraid: sorrow shall take hold on the inhabitants of Palestina.

15 Then the dukes of Edom shall be amazed; the mighty men of Moab, trembling shall take hold upon them; all the inhabitants of Canaan shall melt away.

16 *c*Fear and dread shall fall upon them; by the greatness of thine arm they shall be *as* still as a stone; till thy people pass over, O Lord, till the people pass over, *which* thou hast purchased.

a Deut. 2.
25
Josh. a. 9.

b Deut. 2.
25
Josh. a. 9.

c Deut. 2.
29.
Josh. a. 9.

---

sion dwell upon this consummation of the long series of triumphs by which the "greatness beyond compare" of Jehovah was once for all established.

12. *the earth swallowed them*] The statement is general, not dwelling on the special mode of the Egyptian overthrow, which had already been fully treated, but serving to mark the transition to a different subject, viz. the effects of the deliverance upon Israel.

13. *thou hast guided them*, &c.] Two objections are made to this, as indicating a later origin; (1) the use of the past tense; but Moses naturally and correctly speaks of the guidance as already begun, God had redeemed the Israelites, and placed them in the way towards Canaan. (2) The words "thy holy habitation" are supposed to refer to the temple at Jerusalem. It would not however be an unsuitable designation for Palestine, regarded as the land of promise, sanctified by manifestations of God to the Patriarchs, and destined to be both the home of God's people, and the place where His glory and purposes were to be perfectly revealed. It is clear that no Hebrew writing before the time of Solomon would have introduced a reference to the temple, and improbable that any one writing afterwards would have put an expression with that meaning into the mouth of Moses. But it is possible that Moses had Mount Moriah in his mind, whether in remembrance of Abraham's offering, or as the result of an immediate inspiration. If so it would be an instance of that not uncommon and most interesting form of prediction in which events separated by a wide interval from the seer's time are realized as impending. Of all predictions such are least likely to be attributed to any writer after their long deferred fulfilment.

14. *The people*] or **the peoples**, an expression now justified by usage, and necessary in this passage to give the true meaning.

the inhabitants of Palestina] In Hebrew Pelasheth, *i.e.* the country of the Philistines. They were the first who would expect an invasion, and the first whose district would have been invaded but for the faintheartedness of the Israelites. It is obvious that the order of thoughts would have been very different had the song been composed at a later period, since in fact Philistia was the last district occupied by the Israelites.

15. *the dukes of Edom*] The specific name used in Genesis xxxvi. 15, where see note It denotes the chieftains, not the kings of Edom: see also Dr W. Smith, 'The Pentateuch,' p. 385.

the mighty men of Moab] The physical strength and great stature of the Moabites are noted in other passages: see Jer. xlviii. 29, 41.

Canaan] The name in this, as in many passages of Genesis, designates the whole of Palestine: and is used of course with reference to the promise to Abraham. It was known to the Egyptians, and occurs frequently on the monuments as Pa-kanana, which according to M. Chabas designates only a large fortress in Syria, but as most Egyptologers hold, and on very solid grounds, applies, if not to the whole of Palestine, yet to the northern district under Lebanon, which the Phœnicians occupied and called Canaan.

16. *shall fall upon them*] Most of the ancient versions use the optative form. Let fear and dread fall upon them, let them be still, *i.e.* motionless, as a stone: thus LXX, Vulg. Such undoubtedly may be the meaning of the Hebrew, but the future is equally, if not more forcible; and the prediction is so general that even those, who reject specific announcements of future events, might accept it as a natural expression of the anticipations of Moses. An objection is taken by some critics to the expression "pass over" as applying specially to the passage over Jordan; the prophecy was doubtless then fulfilled, but that event could not have been in the mind of Moses, since he expected that the entrance would be by the southern frontier; and the term which he uses would be equally applicable to any passing over the physical barriers of Canaan; had indeed the song been composed after that passage it is scarcely possible that some allusion would not have been made to the resemblance between the two miracles.

17 Thou shalt bring them in, and plant them in the mountain of thine inheritance, *in* the place, O LORD, *which* thou hast made for thee to dwell in, *in* the Sanctuary, O Lord, *which* thy hands have established.

18 The LORD shall reign for ever and ever.

19 For the horse of Pharaoh went in with his chariots and with his horsemen into the sea, and the LORD brought again the waters of the sea upon them; but the children of Israel went on dry *land* in the midst of the sea.

20 ¶ And Miriam the prophetess, the sister of Aaron, took a timbrel in her hand; and all the women went out after her with timbrels and with dances.

21 And Miriam answered them, Sing ye to the LORD, for he hath triumphed gloriously; the horse and his rider hath he thrown into the sea.

22 So Moses brought Israel from the Red sea, and they went out into the wilderness of Shur; and they went three days in the wilderness, and found no water.

---

17. *in the mountain of thine inheritance*] See note on v. 13. The expressions in this verse, especially the word Sanctuary, are in favour of the explanation given in the latter part of that note; but some critics (as Smith 'Pentateuch,' p. 403, and Bleek, 'Einleitung,' p. 274) consider that Palestine is meant.

The psalm closes, not with the conquest of Canaan, but with its ultimate and crowning result, the settlement of the people of Jehovah in the inheritance which he had promised, and in the place which he destined for His Sanctuary.

19. *For the horse,* &c.] This verse does not belong to the hymn, but marks the transition from it to the narrative. Writers, who attribute different portions of the book to various authors, consider that it belongs to the original composition. It is however obviously a summary statement of the cause and subject-matter of the preceding hymn, and as such, assumes its existence.

20 *And Miriam the prophetess*] The part here assigned to Miriam and the women of Israel is in accordance both with Egyptian and Hebrew customs. The men are represented as singing the hymn in chorus, under the guidance of Moses; at each interval Miriam and the women sang the refrain, marking the time with the timbrel, and with the measured rhythmical movements always associated with solemn festivities. Compare Judg. xi. 34, 1 Sam. xviii. 6, and 2 Sam. vi. 5. A representation of women dancing, some with boughs in their hand, others playing on timbrels, or tambourines of various shapes, some square and some round, is given by Wilkinson, 'M. and C.' 1. p. 93. The word used in this passage for the timbrel is Egyptian, and judging from its etymology and the figures which are joined with it in the inscriptions, it was probably the round instrument. See Brugsch, 'D. H.' p. 1323, and 1534.

Miriam is called a prophetess, evidently, as appears from Numbers xii. 2, because she and Aaron had received divine communications. The word is used here in its proper sense of uttering words suggested by the Spirit of God. On the use and meaning of the word see note on Genesis xx. 7. She is called the sister of Aaron, most probably to indicate her special position as co-ordinate, not with Moses the leader of the nation, but with his chief aid and instrument. It is evident, however, that this designation, most natural in the mouth of Moses, who would be careful to record the names of his brother and sister on such an occasion, was not likely to have been applied to Miriam by a later writer.

22. *So Moses*] Lit. **And Moses**. The word *so* gives the impression of a closer connection with the preceding verse than is suggested by the Hebrew. The history of the journey from the Red Sea to Sinai begins in fact with this verse, which would more conveniently have been the commencement of another chapter.

from the Red sea] The station where Moses and his people halted to celebrate their deliverance is generally admitted to be the Ayoun Musa, *i.e.* the fountains of Moses. It is the only green spot near the passage over the Red Sea. There are several wells there (17 according to Dr Stanley, p. 67, 7 according to Robinson, p. 62). Tischendorf, whose description is fuller than that of other travellers and gives a more pleasing impression, counted 19, and observes that the vegetation indicates a still larger number. 'Aus dem heiligen Lande,' p. 22. The water, like all the water on the western coast of the Peninsula, is dark-coloured and brackish, but it is drinkable, and is said to be highly prized by the people of Suez, whose richer inhabitants formerly built country houses, and laid out gardens in the place. At present the German consul has a garden of

23 ¶ And when they came to Marah, they could not drink of the waters of Marah, for they *were* bitter: therefore the name of it was called [1] Marah.

[1] That is, *bitterness*.

24 And the people murmured against Moses, saying, What shall we drink?

25 And he cried unto the LORD; and the LORD shewed him a *d*tree, which when he had cast into the waters, the waters were made sweet:

d Ecclus. 38. 5.

there he made for them a statute and an ordinance, and there he proved them,

26 And said, If thou wilt diligently hearken to the voice of the LORD thy God, and wilt do that which is right in his sight, and wilt give ear to his commandments, and keep all his statutes, I will put none of these diseases upon thee, which I have brought upon the Egyptians: for I *am* the LORD that healeth thee.

---

considerable extent and beauty, described by Tischendorf. Wellsted found there about twenty clumps of palm-trees, the branches of which were so closely interwoven that they formed a dense impervious shade, affording shelter to the Arabs. According to M. Monge (quoted by Robinson, p. 62) there was formerly an aqueduct extending to the sea so as to form a watering place for ships. In the time of Moses the wells were probably inclosed and kept with great care by the Egyptians, for the use of the frequent convoys to and from their ancient settlements at Sarbut el Khadem and the Wady Mughara.

the wilderness of Shur] This name belongs to the whole district between the north-eastern frontier of Egypt and Palestine. The word is undoubtedly Egyptian, whether derived from the name of the fortress on the frontier, called the Fort of Zor, or more probably from the word Khar, which designated all the country between Egypt and Syria proper. Thus in a papyrus of the 19th dynasty ('Anast.' III. 1, l. 7) we read "The land of Khar from Zor to Aup," a city in Syria. 'Kh' and 'Sh' are constantly interchanged in transcription: see Chabas, 'V. E.' p. 97. In Numbers xxxiii. 8, the more special designation is used, viz. "the wilderness of Etham," a strong corroboration of the view that Etham was not on the west of the Bitter lakes, but at their northern extremity.

three days] The distance between Ayoun Musa and Huwara, the first spot where any water is found on the route, is 33 geographical miles. A small fountain Abu Suweira, near the sea, and another called the Cup of Sudr on the east, some hours distant from the road, were of course known to Moses, but would be of little, if any use to the host. The whole district is a tract of sand, or rough gravel; the wadys are depressions in the desert, with only a few scattered herbs and shrubs, withered and parched by drought: the road afterwards continues through hills of limestone equall, destitute of vegetation, some exhibit-

ing an abundance of crystallized sulphate of lime.

23. *Marah*] The identification of Marah with the fount of Huwara, first proposed by Burckhardt, is now generally accepted. The fountain rises from a large mound, a whitish petrifaction, deposited by the water. At present no water flows, but there are traces of a running stream, and in the time of Moses, when the road was kept by the Egyptians and vegetation was more abundant, the source was probably far more copious. The water is considered by the Arabians to be the worst in the whole district. Two stunted palm-trees now stand near it, and the ground is covered by thickets of the ghurkud (Peganum retusum, Forskal), a low bushy thorny shrub, producing a small fruit which ripens in June, not unlike the barberry, very juicy and slightly acidulous; see Robinson, p. 66. Burckhardt, 'Syria,' p. 474, suggested that the juice might possibly be used to sweeten the water, but no such process is known to the Bedouins, and the fruit would not be ripe about Easter, when the Israelites reached the place. Wellsted observes that when he tasted the water and muttered the word "Marah" his Bedouin said "You speak the word of truth: they are indeed Mara." The Arabic word Huwara means "ruin," "destruction" (Freytag); but "bitter" and "deadly" are with the Arabs, as with the Hebrews, convertible terms.

25. *a tree*] The statement evidently points to a natural agency. The miracle was not wrought without the tree. This is in accordance with the whole spirit of the narrative. There may possibly have been some resemblance to a mode of purifying stagnant waters, such as Josephus and Du Boys Aimé describe, by thrusting long sticks into the bottom of a spring and eliciting a fresh supply: but the result was manifestly supernatural.

he made, &c.] The Lord then set before them the fundamental principle of implicit trust, to be shewn by obedience. The healing of the water was a symbol of deliverance from physical and spiritual evils.

27 ¶ *And they came to Elim, where *were* twelve wells of water, and three score and ten palm trees: and they encamped there by the waters.

*Numb. 13. 9.

CHAPTER XVI.

1 *The Israelites come to Sin.* 2 *They murmur for want of bread.* 4 *God promiseth them bread from heaven.* 11 *Quails are sent,* 14 *and manna.* 16 *The ordering of manna.* 25 *It was not to be found on the sabbath.* 32 *An omer of it is preserved.*

AND they took their journey from Elim, and all the congregation of the children of Israel came unto the wilderness of Sin, which *is* between Elim and Sinai, on the fifteenth day of the second month after their departing out of the land of Egypt.

2 And the whole congregation of the children of Israel murmured against Moses and Aaron in the wilderness:

3 And the children of Israel said unto them, Would to God we had died by the hand of the Lord in the land of Egypt, when we sat by the flesh pots, *and* when we did eat bread to the full; for ye have brought us forth into this wilderness, to kill this whole assembly with hunger.

4 ¶ Then said the Lord unto Moses, Behold, I will rain bread from heaven for you; and the people shall go out and gather †a certain rate every day, that I may prove them, whether they will walk in my law, or no.

5 And it shall come to pass, that

† Heb. *the portion of a day in his day.*

---

27. *Elim*] At a distance of two hours' journey south of Huwara is the large and beautiful valley of Gharandel (Girondel, Niebuhr, p. 183). In the rainy season a considerable torrent flows through it, discharging its waters in the Red Sea. Even in the dry season water is still found, which though somewhat brackish after long drought (Robinson), is generally good, and according to all travellers the best on the whole journey from Cairo to Sinai. The grass there grows thick and high, there is abundance of brushwood, with tamarisks and acacias; a few palm-trees still remain, relics of the fair grove which once covered this Oasis of the western side of the Peninsula. The only objection to the identification of this valley with Elim is the shortness of the distance, but the inducement for the encampment is obvious, and no other site corresponds with the main conditions of the narrative. The Israelites remained a considerable time in this neighbourhood, since they did not reach the wilderness of Sin till two months and a half after leaving Suez. They would find water and pasturage in the district between Elim and the station on the Red Sea, mentioned in Numbers xxxiii. 10: which appears to have been at the further end of the Wadi Tayibe, a journey of eight hours, near the headland of Ras Selima. The whole valley is said to be beautiful, full of tamarisks and other shrubs, the Tarfa-tree and the Palm. Water is found in it, though far inferior to that in Gharandel. The station at the Red Sea then visited by the Israelites was of considerable importance, the starting point for the roads to the copper-mines of the Wadi Mughara, Sarbut el Khalem, and the Wadi Nasb.

twelve wells] Read **springs**; the Hebrew denotes natural sources. These springs may have been perennial when a richer vegetation clothed the adjacent heights. They certainly supplied copious streams when the Israelites "encamped there by the waters."

Chap. XVI. 1. *the wilderness of Sin*] The desert tract, called Debbet er Ramleh, extends nearly across the peninsula from the Wady Nasb in a south-easterly direction, between the limestone district of El Tih and the granite of Sinai. The journey from the station at Elim, or even from that on the Red Sea, could be performed in a day: at that time the route was kept in good condition by the Egyptians who worked the copper-mines at Sarbut el Khadim. The text seems to imply that the Israelites proceeded in detachments, and were first assembled as a complete host when they reached the wilderness of Sin.

2. *murmured*] The want of food was first felt after six weeks from the time of the departure from Egypt, see *v.* 1: we have no notice previously of any deficiency of bread.

3. *by the hand of the Lord*] This evidently refers to the plagues, especially the last, in Egypt: the death which befell the Egyptians appeared to the people preferable to the sufferings of famine.

flesh pots, and...bread] These expressions prove that the servile labours to which they had been subjected did not involve privation: they were fed abundantly, either by the officials of Pharaoh, or more probably by the produce of their own fertile district. The word used for flesh-pots is Egyptian, the name and representation are given in Brugsch, 'D. H.' p. 1264.

4. *rain bread from heaven*] This marks at the outset the strictly supernatural character of the supply. Without such supply the vast host of the Israelites could not have subsisted

on the sixth day they shall prepare *that* which they bring in; and it shall be twice as much as they gather daily.

6 And Moses and Aaron said unto all the children of Israel, At even, then ye shall know that the LORD hath brought you out from the land of Egypt:

7 And in the morning, then ye shall see the glory of the LORD; for that he heareth your murmurings against the LORD: and what *are* we, that ye murmur against us?

8 And Moses said, *This shall be*, when the LORD shall give you in the evening flesh to eat, and in the morning bread to the full; for that the LORD heareth your murmurings which ye murmur against him: and what *are* we? your murmurings *are* not against us, but against the LORD.

9 ¶ And Moses spake unto Aaron, Say unto all the congregation of the children of Israel, Come near before the LORD: for he hath heard your murmurings.

10 And it came to pass, as Aaron spake unto the whole congregation of the children of Israel, that they looked toward the wilderness, and, behold, the glory of the LORD *a*appeared in the cloud. *a* chap. 13. 21.

11 ¶ And the LORD spake unto Moses, saying,

12 I have heard the murmurings of the children of Israel: speak unto them, saying, At even ye shall eat flesh, and in the morning ye shall be filled with bread; and ye shall know that I *am* the LORD your God.

13 And it came to pass, that at even *b*the quails came up, and covered the camp: and in the morning the dew lay round about the host.

b Numb. 11. 31. *c* Numb. 11. 7. Psal. 78. 24. Wisd. 16. 20.

14 And when *c*the dew that lay was gone up, behold, upon the face of

---

for a considerable time in any part of the Peninsula.

a certain rate every day] Lit. as in the margin, "the portion of a day in its day:" *i.e.* the quantity sufficient for one day's consumption: this may be better expressed "a day's portion each day."

that I may prove them] The trial consisted in the restriction to the supply of their daily wants.

5. *it shall be twice as much*] The meaning evidently is that they should collect and prepare a double quantity, not (as has been assumed, in order to make out a contradiction with *v.* 22) that the quantity collected would be miraculously increased afterwards.

7. *the glory of the LORD*] Some commentators understand this to mean the manifestation of His power and goodness in supplying the people with food; but it refers to the visible appearance described in *v.* 10.

8. *not against us*] *i.e.* according to a common Hebrew idiom, not so much against us as against the Lord; the murmuring implied a distrust of the people in the divine mission of their leaders, notwithstanding the previous miracles.

9. The preceding paragraph from *v.* 3 describes the conference between the people and their leaders: the result was a summons to meet Him whom they represented, *i. e.* to assemble in the open space before the tabernacle.

10. *appeared in the cloud*] Or, "was seen in a cloud." The definite article would imply that the cloud was the same which is often mentioned in connection with the tabernacle. The people saw the cloud here spoken of beyond the camp.

12. *flesh...bread*] These expressions refer to the previous murmuring of the people, *v.* 3. God gives them in His own way that which they longed for: this is a clear proof that the narrative is continuous and that the preceding passage is not (as Knobel assumes) an interpolation: see also notes on *vv.* 16 and 27.

13. *quails*] The identification of the Hebrew, "slav," with the common quail may be assumed as certain. The name is applied in Arabic to that bird: it migrates in immense numbers in spring from the south: it is nowhere more common than in the neighbourhood of the Red Sea. When exhausted by a long flight it is easily captured even with the hand. The flesh is palatable and not unwholesome when eaten in moderation. In this passage we read of a single flight so dense that it covered the encampment. The miracle consisted in the precise time of the arrival and its coincidence with the announcement. Other explanations of the name have been given, but this alone meets all the conditions.

the dew lay round] Lit. "a lying of dew

the wilderness *there lay* a small round thing, *as* small as the hoar frost on the ground.

15 And when the children of Israel saw *it*, they said one to another, ¹It is manna: for they wist not what it was. And Moses said unto them, ᵈThis *is* the bread which the LORD hath given you to eat.

16 ¶ This *is* the thing which the LORD hath commanded, Gather of it every man according to his eating, an omer † for every man, *according to* the number of your † persons; take ye every man for *them* which *are* in his tents.

17 And the children of Israel did so, and gathered, some more, some less.

18 And when they did mete *it* with an omer, ᵉhe that gathered much had nothing over, and he that gathered little had no lack; they gathered every man according to his eating.

19 And Moses said, Let no man leave of it till the morning.

20 Notwithstanding they hearkened not unto Moses; but some of them

¹ Or, *What is this?* or, *It is a portion.*
ᵈ John 6. 31.
1 Cor. 10. 3.
† Heb. *by the poll, or, head.*
† Heb. *souls.*
ᵉ 2 Cor. 8. 15.

---

round the camp." This is generally understood to mean there was a heavy fall of dew round the encampment. Knobel explains it to be a dense mist, but the usage seems to be that which is recognized by the Authorised Version and all the ancient versions. There are many indications that the season was unusually humid, natural agencies concurring with supernatural interpositions. Manna is found in abundance in wet seasons, in dry seasons it ceases altogether.

On Manna, see note at the end of the chapter.

14. *a small round thing*] The meaning of the Hebrew is questioned (see note below), but there is good authority for our version, which is true to nature: manna appears in small, compact grains. Here we have a resemblance in shape and appearance, but natural manna is not found on the open plain, "the face of the wilderness," but on dry leaves, or the ground under the tamarisk, from the trunk and branches of which it exudes.

15. *It is manna*] This rendering is disputed. The Old Versions concur in rendering the phrase "What is this?" But oriental scholars are generally agreed that this explanation is not borne out by ancient usage, and that the Israelites said "this is *man*." The word "man" they explain by reference to the Arabic, in which it means "gift." The Egyptian language seems to afford the true solution. It has been very lately shown that "man" or man-hut, *i. e.* white manna, was the name under which the substance was known to the Egyptians, and therefore to the Israelites; see note below. When they saw it on the ground they would of course at once recognize it. They wist not what it was: for in fact it was not natural manna, but a heavenly gift. Our Version should therefore be retained, and the passage may be thus explained. When the Israelites saw the small round thing, they said at once "this is manna," but with an exclamation of surprise at finding it on the open plain, in such immense quantities, under circumstances so unlike what they could have expected: in fact they did not know what it really was, only what it resembled.

16. *according to his eating*] This refers to *v.* 4; it was a trial of the faith of the people, since they were to gather just enough for a day's consumption. The reference is noticeable as an additional argument against Knobel's assumption of an interpolation; see note on *v.* 12.

an omer] *i. e.* the tenth part of an Ephah, see *v.* 36. The exact quantity cannot be determined, since the measures varied at different times. Josephus makes the omer equal to six cotylæ, or half-pints. The ephah was an Egyptian measure, supposed to be about a bushel or one-third of a hin. See Brugsch, 'D. H.' pp. 49, 50. The word omer, in this sense, occurs in no other passage. It was probably not used at a later period, belonging, like many other words, to the time of Moses. It is found in old Egyptian, but with the meaning "storehouse" (see Birch, 'D. H.' p. 363. Brugsch does not give it). See Lev. xix. 36.

man...persons] Lit. as in the margin, **head**, and **souls**, which should be retained as in many other passages.

17. *some more, some less*] It is evidently implied that the people were in part at least disobedient and failed in this first trial.

18. *had nothing over*] The result is undoubtedly represented as miraculous. The Jewish interpreters understand by this statement that whatever quantity each person had gathered, when he measured it in his tent, he found that he had just as many omers as he needed for the consumption of his family: and this is probably the true meaning. It is adopted by Knobel and Keil.

20. *it bred worms*] This result was super-

left of it until the morning, and it bred worms, and stank: and Moses was wroth with them.

21 And they gathered it every morning, every man according to his eating: and when the sun waxed hot, it melted.

22 ¶ And it came to pass, *that* on the sixth day they gathered twice as much bread, two omers for one *man*: and all the rulers of the congregation came and told Moses.

23 And he said unto them, This is *that* which the LORD hath said, To morrow *is* the rest of the holy sabbath unto the LORD: bake *that* which ye will bake *to day*, and seethe that ye will seethe; and that which remaineth over lay up for you to be kept until the morning.

24 And they laid it up till the morning, as Moses bade: and it did not stink, neither was there any worm therein.

25 And Moses said, Eat that to day; for to day *is* a sabbath unto the LORD: to day ye shall not find it in the field.

26 Six days ye shall gather it; but on the seventh day, *which is* the sabbath, in it there shall be none.

27 ¶ And it came to pass, *that* there went out *some* of the people on the seventh day for to gather, and they found none.

28 And the LORD said unto Moses, How long refuse ye to keep my commandments and my laws?

29 See, for that the LORD hath given you the sabbath, therefore he giveth

---

natural: no such tendency to rapid decomposition is recorded of common manna.

21. *it melted*] This refers to the manna which was not gathered. It is noted in all accounts of common manna that it is melted by the heat of the sun.

22. *twice as much bread*] This was in accordance with God's command to Moses *v.* 5, which it is not probable he had omitted to communicate to the people, though the fact is unnoticed in the narrative. The rulers of the congregation appear to have applied to Moses for instructions as to what was to be done under these circumstances, fearing possibly the recurrence of the result mentioned above, *v.* 20. Knobel supposes that the people acted unconsciously, God permitting them to gather a double quantity, but the other explanation is far more natural.

From this passage and from *v.* 5 it is inferred that the seventh day was previously known to the people as a day separate from all others, and if so, it must have been observed as an ancient and primeval institution. No other account of the command (given without any special explanation), or of the conduct of the people, who collected the manna, is satisfactory: thus Rosenmüller, and others. It is at the same time evident that Moses took this opportunity of enforcing a strict and more solemn observance of the day.

23. *To morrow is the rest of the holy sabbath unto the LORD*] Or, **To-morrow is a rest, a Sabbath holy to Jehovah**: *i.e.* to-morrow must be a day of rest, observed strictly as a sabbath, or festal rest, holy to Jehovah. It is at once a statement, and an injunction. The people knew it as the Sabbath, they were to observe it as a great festival.

bake, &c.] These directions shew that the manna thus given differed essentially from the natural product. Here and in Numbers xi. 8 it is treated in a way which shews it had the properties of corn, could be ground in a mortar, baked and boiled. Ordinary manna is used as honey, it cannot be ground, it melts when exposed to a moderate heat forming a substance like barley sugar, called manna tabulata. In Persia it is boiled with water and brought to the consistency of honey. The Arabs also boil the leaves to which it adheres, and the manna thus dissolved floats on the water as a glutinous or oily substance (Rosenmüller, Niebuhr, &c.). It is obvious that these accounts are inapplicable to the manna from heaven, which had the characteristics and nutritive properties of bread.

25. *Eat that to day*] The practical observance of the Sabbath was thus formally instituted before the giving of the law. The people were to abstain from the ordinary work of every-day life: they were not to collect food, nor, as it would seem, even to prepare it as on other days.

27. *there went out some of the people*] This was an act of wilful disobedience. It is remarkable, being the first violation of the express command, that it was not visited by a signal chastisement: the rest and peace of the "Holy Sabbath" were not disturbed by a manifestation of wrath.

28. *How long*] The reference to *v.* 4 is obvious. The prohibition involved a trial of

you on the sixth day the bread of two days; abide ye every man in his place, let no man go out of his place on the seventh day.

30 So the people rested on the seventh day.

31 And the house of Israel called the name thereof Manna: and it *was* like coriander seed, white; and the taste of it *was* like wafers *made* with honey.

32 ¶ And Moses said, This *is* the thing which the Lord commandeth, Fill an omer of it to be kept for your generations; that they may see the bread wherewith I have fed you in the wilderness, when I brought you forth from the land of Egypt.

33 And Moses said unto Aaron, Take a pot, and put an omer full of manna therein, and lay it up before the Lord, to be kept for your generations.

34 As the Lord commanded Moses, so Aaron laid it up before the Testimony, to be kept.

35 And the children of Israel did eat manna forty years, *until* they came to a land inhabited; they did eat manna, until they came unto the borders of the land of Canaan. *Josh. 5. 12. Neh. 9. 15.*

36 Now an omer *is* the tenth *part* of an ephah.

---

faith, in which as usual the people were found wanting. Every miracle formed some part, so to speak, of an educational process.

29. *abide ye every man in his place*] This is an additional injunction. They were to remain within the camp. The expression in Hebrew is peculiar and seems almost to enjoin a position of complete repose, "in his place," lit. under himself, as the Oriental sits with his legs drawn up under him. The prohibition must however be understood with reference to its immediate object; they were not to go forth from their place in order to gather manna, which was on other days without the camp. The spirit of the law is sacred rest. The Lord gave them this Sabbath, as a blessing and privilege. It was "made for man." A Jewish sect called Masbothei, *i.e.* Sabbatarians, took this text as a command that no man should change his position from the morning to the evening of the Sabbath; see Routh on 'Hegesippus,' R. S. 1. p. 225.

31. *Manna*] This refers of course to their first exclamation, confirmed after a week's experience. It was not indeed the common manna, as they then seem to have believed, but the properties which are noted in this passage are common to it and the natural product: in size, form and colour it resembled the seed of the white coriander, a small round grain of a whitish or yellowish grey. The wafer made with honey is called by the LXX. ἐγκρὶς ἐν μέλιτι, *i.e.* according to Athenæus a cake of meal, oil and honey.

32. *Fill an omer*] This was probably done at the end of the first week; but the order to Aaron may have been repeated when the tabernacle was fitted up with its appurtenances.

33. *a pot*] The word here used occurs in no other passage. It corresponds in form and use to the Egyptian for a casket or vase in which oblations were presented. Br. D. H. p. 1644.

35. *did eat manna forty years*] This does not necessarily imply that the Israelites were fed exclusively on manna, or that the supply was continuous during forty years: but that whenever it might be needed, owing to the total or partial failure of other food, it was given until they entered the promised land. They had numerous flocks and herds, which were not slaughtered (see Numbers xi, 22), but which gave them milk, cheese and of course a limited supply of flesh: nor is there any reason to suppose that during a considerable part of that time they may not have cultivated some spots of fertile ground in the wilderness. We may assume, as in most cases of miracle, that the supernatural supply was commensurate with their actual necessity. Dr W. Smith, p. 365, observes the peculiarity of the expression. Moses gives a complete history of manna till the end of his own life. The manna was not withheld in fact until the Israelites had passed the Jordan. Moses writes as a historian, not as a prophet. What he knew as fact was that it lasted until he penned this passage. A later writer would have been more specific.

36. *an omer*] This definition of an omer has been attributed to a later hand, a gloss inserted to explain an obsolete word, "omer" occurring only in this passage as the name of a measure; on the other hand, it has been argued that Moses, as a legislator, would be careful to define what was probably a new measure; both omer and ephah are Egyptian words.

NOTE ON MANNA.

It is well to bring together the facts which are certainly known from ancient and modern authorities. They leave no doubt, on the one hand, as to the connection between the manna of Exodus and the natural production: or on the other, as to the supernatural character of the former. Both points are admitted alike by critics who believe, or disbelieve the sacred narrative: the only question between them is the truth of the writer; his intention and meaning are unmistakeable.

The manna of the Peninsula of Sinai is the sweet juice of the Tarfa, a species of tamarisk. It exudes from the trunk and branches in hot weather, and forms small round white grains. In cool weather it preserves its consistency, in hot weather it melts rapidly. It is either gathered from the twigs of the tamarisk, or from the fallen leaves underneath the tree. The colour is a greyish yellow. It begins to exude in May, and lasts about six weeks. The Arabs cleanse it from leaves and dirt, boil it down, strain it through coarse stuff and keep it in leather bags: they use it as honey with bread. Its taste is sweet, with a slight aromatic flavour: travellers generally compare it with honey. According to Ehrenberg it is produced by the puncture of an insect. It is abundant in rainy seasons, many years it ceases altogether. The whole quantity now produced in a single year does not exceed 600 or 700 pounds. It is found in the district between the Wady Gharandel, *i.e.* Elim, and Sinai, in the Wady Sheich, and in some other parts of the Peninsula. For each of these statements we have the concurrent testimony of travellers. Seetzen in 1807 was the first who described the natural product with scientific accuracy: see Kruse's notes on Seetzen, Vol. IV. p. 416. The resemblance in colour, shape, taste, and in the time and place of the appearance is exact. The name is also that now given to the product, well known as its Arabic designation, and, as we have shewn, found also on Egyptian monuments.

The differences however are equally unmistakeable. 1. The manna of Exodus was not found under the tamarisk tree, but on the surface of the wilderness, after the disappearance of the morning dew. 2. The quantity which was gathered in a single day far exceeded the annual produce at present, and probably at the time of Moses. 3. The supply ceased on the Sabbath-day. 4. The properties differed from common manna; it could be ground, baked, and in other respects treated like meal. It was not used merely as a condiment, or medicine, but had the nutritive qualities of bread. 5. It was found after leaving the district where it is now produced, until the Israelites reached the land of Canaan.

It is to be observed that we have all the conditions and characteristics of Divine interpositions. (1) The condition of a recognized necessity: for all writers agree that under any conceivable circumstances the preservation of the Israelites would otherwise have been impossible. (2) The condition of a harmony with a Divine purpose, the preservation of a peculiar people on which the whole scheme of providential government and the salvation of mankind depended. (3) We have the usual characteristics of harmony between the natural order of events and the supernatural transaction. God fed His people not with the food which belonged to other regions, but with such as appertained to the district. The local colouring is unmistakeable. We may not attempt to give an explanation how the change was effected; to such a question we have but to answer that we know nothing. One thing certain is, that if Moses wrote this narrative, it is impossible that he could be deceived, and equally impossible that he could have deceived contemporaries and eye-witnesses. As for ourselves, we must be content to bear the reproach that we are satisfied with a reference to the Almightiness of Jehovah, in which alone faith finds any explanation of the mystery of the universe.

מְחֻסְפָּס. LXX. ὡσεὶ κόριον λευκόν, Vulg. quasi pilo tusum. Ch. מְקֻלָּף, and Syr. ܡܩܠܦܐ, decorticatum. Saad. ܡܚܪܔ, round. These renderings seem to be conjectural. Gesenius derives the word from حسف, Chal. חסף to peel: and explains the phrase "a small thing, as something peeled." This explanation has in its favour the Egyptian usage, in which "heseb" means "peel." Brugsch, 'D. H.' p. 994. Knobel points out that in that case a particle of comparison would be required, and compares حسفة, frost, hoar-frost, understanding it to describe a small compact granular substance. In this he is followed by Keil.

מָן is the Chaldaic form for מָה, what? but there is no vestige of the use in the ancient language. Thus Gesenius and Knobel; Keil assumes it to be the popular, and old Semitic form, but gives no proof. The meaning "gift" was first suggested by Kimchi, מתנה וחלק, gift and portion. Gesenius derives it from מנה, to distribute or apportion. The Arabic مَنّ (mann) is adduced in support of the meaning "gift," but as Keil points out it is probably taken from the Hebrew Manna. Kalisch mentions the conjecture of Rashbam that the word was probably Egyptian, for which, as he observes truly, no proof could be adduced. The conjecture was a happy one, and the proof is now found. Brugsch gives the word, see 'D. H.' p. 655. "Mennu," "identical with the Hebrew מָן, Arabic مَنّ." It is found among other articles in a basket of oblations at Apollinopolis. Under another form it appears as Mannu-hut, *i.e.* white Manna, and is described as the product of a tree, probably a species of Tamarisk.

VOL. I.   X

CHAPTER XVII.

1 *The people murmur for water at Rephidim.* 5 *God sendeth him for water to the rock in Horeb.* 8 *Amalek is overcome by the holding up of Moses' hands.* 15 *Moses buildeth the altar Jehovah-nissi.*

AND all the congregation of the children of Israel journeyed from the wilderness of Sin, after their journeys, according to the commandment of the LORD, and pitched in Rephidim: and *there was* no water for the people to drink.

2 Wherefore *a* the people did chide with Moses, and said, Give us water that we may drink. And Moses said unto them, Why chide ye with me? wherefore do ye tempt the LORD?

3 And the people thirsted there for water; and the people murmured against Moses, and said, Wherefore *is* this *that* thou hast brought us up out of Egypt, to kill us and our children and our cattle with thirst?

4 And Moses cried unto the LORD, saying, What shall I do unto this people? they be almost ready to stone me.

5 And the LORD said unto Moses, Go on before the people, and take with thee of the elders of Israel; and thy rod, wherewith *b* thou smotest the river, take in thine hand, and go.

6 *c* Behold, I will stand before thee there upon the rock in Horeb; and thou shalt smite the rock, and there shall come water out of it, that the people may drink. And Moses did so in the sight of the elders of Israel.

7 And he called the name of the place ¹ Massah, and ¹ Meribah, because of the chiding of the children of Israel,

a Numb. 20. 4.
b chap. 7. 20.
c Numb. 20. 9. Psal. 78. 15. & 105. 41. Wisd. 11. 4. 1 Cor. 10. 4.

¹ That is, *Tentation.*
¹ That is, *Chiding,* or, *Strife.*

CHAP. XVII. 1. *according to their journeys*] The Israelites rested at two stations before they reached Rephidim, viz. Dophkah and Alush: see Numbers xxxiii. 12—14. According to Knobel, whose view is adopted by Keil, and appears, on the whole, to accord best with the Biblical notices and the accounts of travellers, Dophkah was in the Wady Seih, a day's journey from the Wady Nasb: traces of the ancient name were found by Seetzen at a place called El Tabbacha in a rocky pass, El Kineh, where Egyptian antiquities still remain, indicating the ancient route. The wilderness of Sin properly speaking ends here, the sandstone ceases, and is replaced by the porphyry and granite which belong to the central formation of the Sinaitic group. Alush lay on the way towards Rephidim; the identification with Ash is doubtful, the distance from Horeb exceeding a day's march. Alush may have been near the entrance to the Wady Sheich.

Rephidim] On the identification of Rephidim see note at the end of this book.

2. *tempt the* LORD] It is a general characteristic of the Israelites that the miracles, which met each need as it arose, failed to produce a habit of faith: but the severity of the trial, the faintness and anguish of thirst in the burning desert, must not be overlooked in appreciating their conduct. "I thirst" was the only expression of bodily suffering wrung from our Lord on the Cross.

4. *they be almost ready to stone me*] Lit. **yet a little and they will stone me.** The Authorised Version gives the meaning, but not the liveliness and force of the Hebrew.

6. *the rock in Horeb*] The name Horeb signifies "dry, parched," and evidently points to a distinct miracle. At what point Moses struck the rock cannot be determined; but it would seem to have been in the presence of the Elders as selected witnesses, not in the sight of the people, and therefore not near the summit.

It is questioned whether the water thus supplied ceased with the immediate occasion. St Paul calls it "a spiritual drink," and adds, "that all the Israelites drank of the spiritual rock which followed them, and that rock was Christ." 1 Cor. x. 4. The interpretation of that passage belongs to the New Testament: but the general meaning appears to be that their wants were ever supplied from Him, of whom the rock was but a symbol, and who accompanied them in all their wanderings. Two traditions of the Rabbins are noticeable: one, that the rock thus smitten actually followed the Israelites, another, that the stream of water went with them. There is no justification for these fables in the sacred narrative. The repetition of the miracle (see Numbers xx. 11) excludes the second, the first needs no refutation.

7. *Massah*] The word is derived from that which is used by Moses, *v.* 2. Meribah, as is stated in the margin, means "chiding," referring also to *v.* 2. The names were retained from that time, nor are Rephidim and Kadesh mentioned by later writers: they belong to the time of Moses. On the im-

v. 8—13.] EXODUS. XVII. 323

and because they tempted the LORD, saying, Is the LORD among us, or not?

8 ¶ *d*Then came Amalek, and fought with Israel in Rephidim.

9 And Moses said unto *e*Joshua, Choose us out men, and go out, fight with Amalek: to morrow I will stand on the top of the hill with the rod of God in mine hand.

10 So Joshua did as Moses had said to him, and fought with Amalek: and Moses, Aaron, and Hur went up to the top of the hill.

11 And it came to pass, when Moses held up his hand, that Israel prevailed: and when he let down his hand, Amalek prevailed.

12 But Moses' hands *were* heavy; and they took a stone, and put *it* under him, and he sat thereon; and Aaron and Hur stayed up his hands, the one on the one side, and the other on the other side; and his hands were steady until the going down of the sun.

13 And Joshua discomfited Amalek and his people with the edge of the sword.

d Deut. 25. 17.
Wisd. 11. 3.
e Called Jesus, Acts 7. 45.

---

portance of this lesson see our Lord's words, Matt. iv. 7.

8. *Then came Amalek*] The attack upon the Israelites was made under circumstances, at a time and place, fully explained by what is known of the Peninsula. It occurred about two months after the Exodus, towards the end of May or early in June, when the Bedouins leave the lower plains in order to find pasture for their flocks on the cooler heights. The approach of the Israelites to Sinai would of course attract notice, and no cause of warfare is more common than a dispute for the right of pasturage. The Amalekites were at that time the most powerful race in the Peninsula, which from the earliest ages was peopled by fierce and warlike tribes, with whom the Pharaohs, from the third dynasty downwards, were engaged in constant struggles. It may be conjectured that reports of the marvellous supply of water may have reached the natives and accelerated their movements. On this occasion Amalek took the position, recognized in the Sacred History, as the chief of the heathens, Num. xxiv. 20; the first among the heathens who attacked God's people, and as such marked out for punishment, see 1 Sam. xv. 2, especially merited by them as descendants of the elder brother of Jacob, and therefore near kinsmen of the Israelites.

9. *Joshua*] This is the first mention of the great follower and successor of Moses. He died at the age of 110, some 65 years after this transaction. His original name was Hosea, but Moses calls him by the full name, which was first given about forty years afterwards, as that by which he was to be known to succeeding generations. From this it may perhaps be inferred that this portion of Exodus was written, or revised, towards the end of the sojourn in the wilderness. A later writer, mindful of the change of name, would probably have avoided the appearance of an anachronism.

the rod of God] By using the same rod Moses gave the people an unmistakeable and much needed proof that victory over human enemies was to be attributed altogether to the divine power which had delivered them from Egypt, and saved them from perishing in the wilderness. The hill, on which Moses stood during the combat, Knobel supposed to be the height now called Feria on the north side of the plain Er Rahah; on its top is a level tract with good pasturage and plantations. The conjecture may shew the vivid impression of reality made by the narrative upon a critic who believes this very portion to be the product of a later age.

10. *Hur*] Hur is mentioned in one other passage in connection with Aaron, ch. xxiv. 14. He was grandfather of Bezaleel, the great sculptor and artificer of the tabernacle, see ch. xxxi. 2—5, and belonged to the tribe of Judah. From the book of Chronicles we learn that the name of his father was Caleb, of his mother, Ephrath. That he was a person of high station and of advanced years is evident, but the traditions that he was the husband of Miriam (Josephus), or her son by Caleb (Jarchi), would seem to be mere conjecture; such a connection would scarcely have been unnoticed in the account of Bezaleel.

11. The act represents the efficacy of intercessory prayer—offered doubtless by Moses—a point of great moment to the Israelites at that time and to the Church in all ages. This interpretation would seem too obvious to insist upon, but it has been contested by Kurtz, who regards the lifting of Moses' hands as the attitude of a general directing the battle.

12. *until the going down of the sun*] The length of this first great battle indicates the strength and obstinacy of the assailants. It was no mere raid of Bedouins, but a deliberate attack of the Amalekites, who, as we have seen, were thoroughly trained in warfare by their struggles with Egypt.

13. *with the edge of the sword*] This

X 2

EXODUS. XVII. [v. 14—16.]

14 And the Lord said unto Moses, Write this *for* a memorial in a book, and rehearse *it* in the ears of Joshua: for *f*I will utterly put out the remembrance of Amalek from under heaven.

15 And Moses built an altar, and called the name of it ¹Jehovah-nissi:

16 For he said, ¹Because †the Lord hath sworn *that* the Lord *will have* war with Amalek from generation to generation.

f Numb. 24. 20. 1 Sam. 15. 3.

¹ That is, The LORD my banner.

‖ Or, Because the hand of Amalek is against the throne of the LORD, therefore, &c. † Heb. *the hand upon the throne of the* LORD.

---

expression always denotes a great slaughter of the enemy.

14. *in a book*] It should be rendered **in the book**. The plain and obvious meaning is that the account of this battle, and of the command to destroy the Amalekites, was to be recorded in the book which contained the history of God's dealings with His people. In this explanation nearly all critics are agreed. See Introduction to the Pentateuch, p. 1, and note below. Moses was further instructed to impress the command specially on the mind of Joshua, as the leader to whom the first step towards its accomplishment would be entrusted on the conquest of Canaan. The work was not actually completed until the reign of Hezekiah, when 500 of the tribe of Simeon "smote the rest of the Amalekites that were escaped" and retained possession of Mount Seir, when the book of Chronicles was written, 1 Chron. iv. 43. This is a point to be especially noticed. True prophecy deals often with the remote future, regardless of delays in its fulfilment; but certainly no one writing at a later time, while the Amalekites still existed as a nation, would have invented the prediction.

15. *Jehovah-nissi*] *i.e.* as in the margin, " Jehovah my banner." As a proper name the Hebrew word is rightly preserved. The meaning is evidently that the name of Jehovah is the true banner under which victory is certain; so to speak, the motto or inscription on the banners of the host. Inscriptions on the royal standard were well known. Each of the Pharaohs on his accession adopted one in addition to his official name.

16. *Because the* LORD *hath sworn*] This rendering is incorrect, but the Hebrew is obscure and the true meaning is very doubtful. As the Hebrew text now stands the literal interpretation is "for hand on throne of Jah," which may mean, as our margin and as Clericus and Rosenmüller explain it, "because his hand (*i.e.* the hand of Amalek) is against the throne of God, therefore the Lord hath war with Amalek from generation to generation;" and this on the whole, seems to be the most satisfactory explanation. It expresses a certain fact, and keeps most closely to the Hebrew. The word rendered "throne" occurs in the exact form in no other passage, but it may be an archaic form of the very common word from which it differs but slightly (כס for כסא), and which is found in the Samaritan. Our translators follow the general sense given by the Targum of Onkelos and Saadia, who agree in regarding the expression as a solemn asseveration by the throne of God. To this however the objections are insuperable; it has no parallel in Scriptural usage: God swears by Himself, not by His Throne.

An alteration, slight in form, but considerable in meaning, has been proposed with much confidence, viz. "Nes," standard for "Kes," throne; thus connecting the name of the altar with the sentence. But conjectural emendations are not to be adopted without necessity, and the obvious a priori probability of such a reading makes it improbable that one so far more difficult should have been substituted for it. One of the surest canons of criticism militates against its reception. The text as it stands was undoubtedly that which was alone known to the Targumists, the Samaritan, the Syriac, the Latin and the Arabic translators. The LXX. appear to have had a different reading, ἐν χειρὶ κρυφαίᾳ πολεμεῖ.

NOTE on *v.* 14.

Rosenmüller expresses himself without any doubt. In his note on the passage he says "Memoriale in libro quem scribere incepisti:" and in the Prolegg. p. 5, "Moses dicit se divino jussu (insidias) inscripsisse libro, incœpto haud dubie, et in quo jam plura exaraverat, quod cum articulo בַּסֵּפֶר (non בְּסֵפֶר) scripsit, quo innuit se de certo quodam et satis noto libro loqui." Thus Keil, "the book appointed for the record of the glorious works of God;" and Kalisch, who renders it "the book:" he quotes Aben-Ezra to prove that a particular book was referred to, and compares other passages (Exod. xxiv. 4, 7, xxxiv. 27; Num. xxxiii. 1, 2, xxxvi. 13; Deut. xxviii. 61). Knobel however proposes a different interpretation, taking "in the book" to mean simply, "in writing." He refers to Num. v. 23; 1 S. x. 25; Jer. xxxii. 10; and Job xix. 23: which prove that this expression might mean "a book" generally, provided no particular book were already in existence. It is not however by any means equivalent to our expression "in writing," which would be a strange tautology "write in writing," but in each case a book or schedule is meant: whether a book already begun, or then to be begun, is a question to be determined by the context. The argument for the positive existence of "a book" is not materially affected by the proposed change: but all probability is in favour of the natural and obvious impression that Moses was commanded to record this particular transaction in "the book" which related the history of God's dealings with His people. The evidence for the existence of books of considerable extent is stated in the Introduction to the Pentateuch. To this it may be added that under the ancient Empire, functionaries of the highest rank held the office of governor of the Palace and of the "house of manuscripts;" see De Rougé, 'Recherches,' pp. 73, 85. The tutelary Deity of writing was called Saph or Sapheh (a name apparently connected with the Hebrew "sepher"): a Pharaoh of the 5th Dynasty bears the style "beloved of Saph." l.c. p. 84.

CHAPTER XVIII.

1 *Jethro bringeth to Moses his wife and two sons.* 7 *Moses entertaineth him.* 13 *Jethro's counsel is accepted.* 27 *Jethro departeth.*

^a chap. 2. 16.

WHEN ^a Jethro, the priest of Midian, Moses' father in law, heard of all that God had done for Moses, and for Israel his people, *and* that the LORD had brought Israel out of Egypt;

2 Then Jethro, Moses' father in law, took Zipporah, Moses' wife, after he had sent her back,

3 And her two sons; of which the ^b name of the one *was* ‖ Gershom; for he said, I have been an alien in a strange land:

^b chap. 2. 22.
‖ That is, *A stranger there.*

4 And the name of the other *was* ‖ Eliezer; for the God of my father, *said he, was* mine help, and delivered me from the sword of Pharaoh:

‖ That is, *My God is an help.*

5 And Jethro, Moses' father in law, came with his sons and his wife unto Moses into the wilderness, where he encamped at the mount of God:

6 And he said unto Moses, I thy father in law Jethro am come unto thee, and thy wife, and her two sons with her.

7 ¶ And Moses went out to meet his father in law, and did obeisance, and kissed him; and they asked each other of *their* † welfare; and they came into the tent.

† Heb. *peace.*

8 And Moses told his father in law all that the LORD had done unto Pharaoh and to the Egyptians for Israel's sake, *and* all the travail that had † come upon them by the way, and how the LORD delivered them.

† Heb. *found them.*

9 And Jethro rejoiced for all the goodness which the LORD had done

CHAP. XVIII. The events recorded in this chapter could not have occupied many days, fifteen only elapsed between the arrival of the Israelites in the wilderness of Sin and their final arrival at Sinai, see ch. xvi. 1, and xix. 1. This leaves however sufficient time for the interview and transactions between Moses and Jethro.

1. *Jethro*] See note on ch. ii. 18. For "father in law" the Vulgate has cognatus, an indefinite expression. Jethro was in all probability the "brother in law" of Moses. On the parting from Zipporah, see note on ch. iv. 26.

This chapter, which abounds in personal reminiscences (and gives a vivid impression of the affectionate and confiding character of Moses), stands rather apart from the general narrative. It may have been and probably was written on a separate roll. The repetition of particulars well known to the reader is a general characteristic of such distinct portions.

5. *into the wilderness*] i.e. according to the view which seems on the whole most probable, on the plain near the northern summit of Horeb, the mount of God. It is described by Robinson, I. p. 88, as a naked desert,—wild and desolate. The exact specification of the locality may indicate a previous engagement between Moses and Jethro to meet at this place. The valley which opens upon Er Rahah on the left of Horeb is called by the Arabs Wady Shueib, *i.e.* the vale of Hobab.

6. The LXX. read, "And it was told to Moses, saying, Lo, thy father in law Jether is come." This suits the context, and is probably the true reading.

7. *did obeisance*] As to an elder, the priest, if not the chief, of a great tribe.

asked each other of their welfare] Or, addressed each other with the customary salutation, "Peace be unto you."

to Israel, whom he had delivered out of the hand of the Egyptians.

10 And Jethro said, Blessed *be* the LORD, who hath delivered you out of the hand of the Egyptians, and out of the hand of Pharaoh, who hath delivered the people from under the hand of the Egyptians.

11 Now I know that the LORD *is* greater than all gods: ^cfor in the thing wherein they dealt proudly *he was* above them.

^c chap. i. 10, 16, 22. & 5. 7. & 14. 18.

12 And Jethro, Moses' father in law, took a burnt offering and sacrifices for God: and Aaron came, and all the elders of Israel, to eat bread with Moses' father in law before God.

13 ¶ And it came to pass on the morrow, that Moses sat to judge the people: and the people stood by Moses from the morning unto the evening.

14 And when Moses' father in law saw all that he did to the people, he said, What *is* this thing that thou doest to the people? why sittest thou thyself alone, and all the people stand by thee from morning unto even?

15 And Moses said unto his father in law, Because the people come unto me to inquire of God:

16 When they have a matter, they come unto me; and I judge between †one and another, and I do make *them* know the statutes of God, and his laws.

† Heb. *a man and his fellow.*

---

11. *greater than all gods*] This does not prove that Jethro recognized the existence or power of other Deities, for the expression is not uncommon in the mouth of Hebrew monotheists, and corresponds exactly to the terms in which Moses had himself celebrated the overthrow of the Egyptians; see note on ch. xv. 11. It simply indicates a conviction of the incomparable might and majesty of Jehovah.

for in...above them] Lit. **For** (*this is shewn*) **in the matter wherein they dealt proudly against them.** The construction depends upon the previous clause; the meaning is, I know the greatness of Jehovah by the very transaction wherein the Egyptians dealt haughtily and cruelly against the Israelites. Jethro refers especially to the destruction of the Egyptian host in the Red Sea, and very probably to the words in which Moses himself had celebrated that event; see ch. xv. 11.

12. *a burnt offering and sacrifices*] This verse clearly shews that Jethro was recognized as a priest of the true God. The identity of religious faith could not be more conclusively proved than by the participation in the sacrificial feast. This passage is of great importance in its bearings upon the relation between the Israelites and their congeners, and upon the state of religion among the descendants of Abraham.

13. In the following passage the change in the organization of the people, by which the burden of judicial proceedings was transferred in great part from Moses to subordinate officers, is attributed entirely to the counsel of Jethro. This is important for several reasons. It is certain that no late writer would have invented such a story, and most improbable that tradition would have long preserved the memory of a transaction which to Israelites might naturally seem derogatory to their legislator. Nothing however can be more characteristic of Moses, who combines on all occasions distrust of himself, and singular openness to impressions, with the wisdom and sound judgment which chooses the best course when pointed out. It is remarkable that an institution so novel and important should have preceded the promulgation of the Sinaitic law.

from the morning unto the evening] It may be assumed as at least probable that numerous cases of difficulty arose out of the division of the spoil of the Amalekites: this was moreover the first station at which the Israelites appear to have rested long after their departure from Elim, and causes would of course accumulate during the journey.

15. *to inquire of God*] The decisions of Moses were doubtless accepted by the people as oracles. There is no reason to suppose that he consulted, or that the people expected him to consult, the Lord by Urim and Thummim, which are first mentioned xxviii. 30, where see note. The internal prompting of the Spirit was a sufficient guidance for him, and a sufficient authority for the people.

16. *the statutes of God, and his laws*] This would seem to imply that in deciding each particular case Moses explained the principles of right and justice on which his decision rested. It became, so to speak, a precedent; he can scarcely be supposed to refer to any existing code, the necessity for which must, however, have soon become apparent, preparing the people for the legislation given within a few days at Sinai.

17 And Moses' father in law said unto him, The thing that thou doest is not good.

18 ⁺Thou wilt surely wear away, both thou, and this people that *is* with thee: for this thing *is* too heavy for thee; *ᵈ*thou art not able to perform it thyself alone.

19 Hearken now unto my voice, I will give thee counsel, and God shall be with thee: Be thou for the people to God-ward, that thou mayest bring the causes unto God:

20 And thou shalt teach them ordinances and laws, and shalt shew them the way wherein they must walk, and the work that they must do.

21 Moreover thou shalt provide out of all the people able men, such as fear God, men of truth, hating covetousness; and place *such* over them, *to be* rulers of thousands, *and* rulers of hundreds, rulers of fifties, and rulers of tens:

22 And let them judge the people at all seasons: and it shall be, *that* every great matter they shall bring unto thee, but every small matter they shall judge: so shall it be easier for thyself, and they shall bear *the burden* with thee.

23 If thou shalt do this thing, and God command thee *so*, then thou shalt be able to endure, and all this people shall also go to their place in peace.

24 So Moses hearkened to the voice of his father in law, and did all that he had said.

25 And Moses chose able men out of all Israel, and made them heads over the people, rulers of thousands, rulers of hundreds, rulers of fifties, and rulers of tens.

26 And they judged the people at all seasons: the hard causes they brought unto Moses, but every small matter they judged themselves.

27 ¶ And Moses let his father in law depart; and he went his way into his own land.

† Heb. *Fading thou wilt fade.*

ᵈ Deut. i. 9.

---

18. *Thou wilt surely wear away*] This expresses the true sense: the Hebrew word implies decay and exhaustion.

19. *counsel*] In this counsel Jethro draws a distinction, probably not previously recognized, between the functions of the legislator and the judge. Moses as legislator stands between the people and God. He brings the cause to God, and learns from Him the principle by which it is to be determined: and in the next place, sets before the people the whole system of ordinances and laws by which they are to be henceforth guided. As judge Moses decides all difficult cases in the last resort, leaving questions of detail to officers chosen by himself from the people.

to God-ward] lit. "before God," standing between them and God, both as His minister, or representative: and also as the representative of the people, their agent, so to speak, or deputy before God.

20. *teach them*] The Hebrew word is emphatic, and signifies "enlightenment." The text gives four distinct points, (*a*) the "ordinances," or specific enactments, (*b*) "the laws," or general regulations, (*c*) "the way," the general course of duty, (*d*) "the work," each specific act.

21. *able men*] This gives the true force of the Hebrew, literally "men of might;" *i.e* strength of character and ability. The qualifications are remarkably complete, ability, piety, truthfulness and unselfishness. The recommendation leaves no doubt as to the faith of Jethro, though, with the usual care observed by Moses in relating the words of pious Gentiles, he is represented as using the general expression God, not the revealed name Jehovah. From Deut. i. 13, it appears that Moses left the selection of the persons to the people, an example followed by the Apostles; see Acts vi. 3.

rulers of thousands, &c.] This minute classification of the people is thoroughly in accordance with the Semitic character, and was retained in after ages. The numbers appear to be conventional, corresponding nearly, but not exactly, to the military, or civil divisions of the people. The number "ten" denotes in Arabic, and may have denoted in Hebrew, a family; the largest division 1000 is used as an equivalent of a *gens* under one head, Num. i. 16, x. 4; Josh. xxii. 14.

The word "rulers," sometimes rendered "princes," is general, including all ranks of officials placed in command. The same word is used regularly on Egyptian monuments of the time of Moses: see note on ch. i. 11.

23. *to their place*] *i.e.* to Canaan, which is thus recognized by Jethro as the appointed and true home of Israel.

27. *into his own land*] Midian. This

CHAPTER XIX.

1 *The people come to Sinai.* 3 *God's message by Moses unto the people out of the mount.* 8 *The people's answer returned again.* 10 *The people are prepared against the third day.* 12 *The mountain must not be touched.* 16 *The fearful presence of God upon the mount.*

IN the third month, when the children of Israel were gone forth out of the land of Egypt, the same day came they *into* the wilderness of Sinai.

2 For they were departed from Rephidim, and were come *to* the desert of Sinai, and had pitched in the wilderness; and there Israel camped before the mount.

3 And ^aMoses went up unto God, and the LORD called unto him out of the mountain, saying, Thus shalt thou say to the house of Jacob, and tell the children of Israel;

4 ^bYe have seen what I did unto the Egyptians, and *how* I bare you on eagles' wings, and brought you unto myself.

5 Now ^ctherefore, if ye will obey my voice indeed, and keep my covenant, then ye shall be a peculiar treasure unto me above all people: for ^dall the earth *is* mine:

6 And ye shall be unto me a ^ekingdom of priests, and an holy nation. These *are* the words which thou shalt speak unto the children of Israel.

^a Acts 7. 38.
^b Deut 29. 2.
^c Deut. 5. 2.
^d Deut. 10. 14. Psal. 24. 1.
^e 1 Pet. 2. 9. Rev. 1. 6.

---

expression is favourable to the view that the home of Midian was on the east of the Red Sea, and not in the Peninsula of Sinai. If the identity of Jethro with Hobab be assumed, he must have returned and met Moses once more after the departure from Sinai. See Numbers x. 29—32. It seems however far more probable that Hobab was his brother. See note on ch. ii. 18.

CHAP. XIX. 1. *In the third month*] This expression does not determine the exact day: the word "month" is not found in the Pentateuch in the sense of new moon, or the first day of the month, which has been attributed to it in this passage by many eminent critics. Still the natural impression made by this statement is that the arrival of the Israelites coincided with the beginning of the third month.

the wilderness of Sinai] See note at the end of the book.

3. *Moses went up unto God*] This seems to imply that the voice was heard by Moses as he was ascending the mount.

house of Jacob] This expression does not occur elsewhere in the Pentateuch. It has a peculiar fitness here, referring doubtless to the special promises made to the Patriarch.

4. *on eagles' wings*] Bochart, after quoting passages from Ælian, Appian and other writers, observes that Moses gives a perfect explanation of the simile in Deuteronomy xxxii. 11. He adds "It is to be observed that both in the law and in the gospel the Church is compared to fledgelings which the mother cherishes and protects under her wings: but in the law that mother is an eagle, in the gospel a hen; thus shadowing forth the diversity of administration under each Covenant: the one of power, which God manifested when He brought His people out of Egypt with a mighty hand and an outstretched arm, and led them into the promised land; the other of grace, when Christ came in humility and took the form of a servant and became obedient unto death, even the death of the Cross." Bochart however, remarks, that the simile of an eagle is applied to Christ when He vindicates His people from the Dragon, Rev. xii. 14. See Hierozoicon, lib. II. ch. 22, § 3 and 4.

5. *a peculiar treasure*] This expresses the true sense of the Hebrew word, which designates a costly possession acquired with exertion, and carefully guarded. The peculiar relation in which Israel stands, taken out of the Heathen world and consecrated to God, as his slaves, subjects, and children, determines their privileges, and is the foundation of their duties. The same principle applies even in a stronger sense to the Church. See Acts xx. 28; 1 Cor. vi. 20; 1 Pet. ii. 9.

all the earth is mine] This is added, as we may believe, to impress upon the Jews that their God was no mere national Deity, a point of great practical importance.

6. *a kingdom of priests*] The exact meaning of this expression, as it was understood by all the ancient translators, and as it is explained in the New Testament, is that Israel collectively is a royal and priestly race: a dynasty of priests, each true member uniting in himself the attributes of a king and priest. The word "kingdom" is not taken in the modern sense, as a collective name for the subjects of a king, but in the old Hebrew sense of "royalty," or "dynasty." Thus nearly all ancient and modern commentators explain the words. (The LXX. βασίλειον ἱεράτευμα, Targum Onk. kings and priests; Jonathan, crowned kings and ministering priests.)

7 ¶ And Moses came and called for the elders of the people, and laid before their faces all these words which the LORD commanded him.

8 And *ᶠ*all the people answered together, and said, All that the LORD hath spoken we will do. And Moses returned the words of the people unto the LORD.

9 And the LORD said unto Moses, Lo, I come unto thee in a thick cloud, that the people may hear when I speak with thee, and believe thee for ever. And Moses told the words of the people unto the LORD.

10 ¶ And the LORD said unto Moses, Go unto the people, and sanctify them to day and to morrow, and let them wash their clothes,

11 And be ready against the third day: for the third day the LORD will come down in the sight of all the people upon mount Sinai.

12 And thou shalt set bounds unto the people round about, saying, Take heed to yourselves, *that ye* go not up into the mount, or touch the border of it: ᵍwhosoever toucheth the mount shall be surely put to death:

13 There shall not an hand touch it, but he shall surely be stoned, or shot through; whether *it be* beast or man, it shall not live: when the ⁱtrumpet soundeth long, they shall come up to the mount.

14 ¶ And Moses went down from the mount unto the people, and sanctified the people; and they washed their clothes.

15 And he said unto the people, Be ready against the third day: come not at *your* wives.

16 ¶ And it came to pass on the third day in the morning, that there were thunders and lightnings, and a thick cloud upon the mount, and the voice of the trumpet exceeding loud; so that all the people that *was* in the camp trembled.

ᶠ chap. 24. 3, 7. Deut. 5. 27. v. 26, 17.

ᵍ Heb. 12. 20.

ⁱ Or, cornet.

---

an holy nation] The holiness of Israel consisted in its special consecration to God: it was a sacred nation, sacred by adoption, by covenant, and by participation in all means of grace. The radical meaning of the Hebrew "Khodesh" appears to be "pure, clean, clear from all pollution bodily or spiritual," rather than, as many critics have assumed, "separate and set apart." The distinction between official consecration, and internal holiness is secondary, and scarcely seems to have lain within the scope of the Hebrew mind: the ideas were inseparable.

8. *All that the LORD*, &c.] By this answer the people accepted the covenant. It was the preliminary condition of their complete admission into the state of a royal priesthood.

9. *in a thick cloud*] Or "in the darkness of cloud," *i.e.* in the midst of the dense cloud which indicated the Presence of Jehovah. The people were to hear the voice of God, distinctly announcing the fundamental principles of the eternal law.

10. *sanctify them*] The injunction involves bodily purification and undoubtedly also spiritual preparation. Thus Heb. x. 22, "our hearts sprinkled from an evil conscience, and our bodies washed with pure water." The washing of the clothes was an outward symbol well understood in all nations. The supply of water in the region about Sinai is repeatedly stated by Burckhardt and other travellers to be abundant. In Deut. ix. 21, we read of the brook descending from the mount.

11. *the third day*] The significance of the expression "third day" scarcely needs to be pointed out; whether this third day fell on the Jewish or Christian Sabbath is quite uncertain; but it can scarcely have corresponded to the day of Pentecost, as Bp. Wordsworth holds on the authority of an ancient and widely accredited tradition: more than 60 days had elapsed since the Passover. See the article on Pentecost in Smith's 'Dict.'

12. *set bounds unto the people*] The access to the base of the mountain is evidently shewn to have been otherwise unimpeded. Dr Stanley speaks of the low line of alluvial mounds at the foot of the cliff of Ras Safsafeh as exactly answering to the bounds which were to keep the people off from touching the mount: but the bounds here spoken of were to be set up by Moses.

13. *touch it*] Rather "touch him." The person was not to be touched, since the contact would be pollution. He was to be stoned or shot with an arrow; or probably with a javelin, as was customary in later times.

when the trumpet, &c.] When the trumpet sounded those who were specially called might ascend.

17 And Moses brought forth the people out of the camp to meet with God; and they stood at the nether part of the mount.

Deut. 4.

18 And ⁿmount Sinai was altogether on a smoke, because the LORD descended upon it in fire: and the smoke thereof ascended as the smoke of a furnace, and the whole mount quaked greatly.

19 And when the voice of the trumpet sounded long, and waxed louder and louder, Moses spake, and God answered him by a voice.

20 And the LORD came down upon mount Sinai, on the top of the mount: and the LORD called Moses *up* to the top of the mount; and Moses went up.

† Heb. *contest.*

21 And the LORD said unto Moses, Go down, †charge the people, lest they break through unto the LORD to gaze, and many of them perish.

22 And let the priests also, which come near to the LORD, sanctify themselves, lest the LORD break forth upon them.

23 And Moses said unto the LORD, The people cannot come up to mount Sinai: for thou chargedst us, saying, Set bounds about the mount, and sanctify it.

24 And the LORD said unto him, Away, get thee down, and thou shalt come up, thou, and Aaron with thee: but let not the priests and the people break through to come up unto the LORD, lest he break forth upon them.

25 So Moses went down unto the people, and spake unto them.

CHAPTER XX.

1 *The ten commandments.* 18 *The people are afraid.* 20 *Moses comforteth them.* 22 *Idolatry is forbidden.* 24 *Of what sort the altar should be.*

AND God spake all these words, saying,

2 ᵃI am the LORD thy God, which have brought thee out of the land of Egypt, out of the house of †bondage.

a Deut. 5. 6.
Psal. 81. 10.
† Heb. *servants.*

---

17. *out of the camp*] The encampment must have extended far and wide over the plain in front of the mountain. From one entrance of the plain to the other there is space for the whole host of the Israelites. This is a point which has been determined by accurate measurement of the valley. See note at the end of Exodus.

18. *a furnace*] The word is Egyptian, and occurs only in the Pentateuch.

22. *the priests also*] The Levitical priesthood was not yet instituted, but sacrifices had hitherto been offered by persons who were recognized as having the right or authority: according to the very probable account of Rabbinical writers these were the firstborn, or the heads of families, until they were superseded by the Aaronic priesthood.

THE TEN COMMANDMENTS.
CHAP. XX. 1—17.

On the Ten Commandments, taken as a whole, see Note after *v.* 21. The account of the delivery of them in chap. xix. and in *vv.* 18—21 of this chap. is in accordance with their importance as the recognized basis of the Covenant between Jehovah and His ancient people (Exod. xxxiv. 27, 28; Deut. iv. 13; 1 K. viii. 21, &c.), and as the Divine testimony against the sinful tendencies in man for all ages. Jewish writers have speculated as to the mode in which the Divine communication was made to the people (Philo, 'de Orac.' c. 9; Palestine Targum, &c.). It may be noticed that, while it is here said that "God spake all these words," and in Deut. v. 4, that He "spake face to face," in the New Testament the giving of the Law is spoken of as having been through the ministration of angels (Acts vii. 53; Gal. iii. 19; Heb. ii. 2). We can only reconcile these contrasts of language by keeping in mind that God is a Spirit, and that He is essentially present in the agents who are performing His will. A similar difficulty was felt by some in St Augustin's time in reconciling Gen. i. 1 with John i. 3. ('Cont. Adimant. Man.' c. 1.)—Josephus appears as the only witness for the superstition, which was probably common amongst the Pharisees of his day, that it was not lawful to utter the very words in which the Ten Commandments were originally expressed ('Ant.' III. 5, § 4). It is remarkable that there seems to be no trace of this in the rabbinists,—The Two Tables of stone on which the Commandments were inscribed are mentioned ch. xxiv. 12, xxxi. 18.

2. *which have brought thee out of the land of Egypt, out of the house of bondage*] It was a rabbinical question, Why, on this occasion, was not THE LORD rather proclaimed as "the Creator of Heaven and Earth"? The true answer evidently is, That the Ten Commandments were at this time addressed by Jehovah

v. 3—5.] EXODUS. XX. 331

3 Thou shalt have no other gods before me.

*Lev. 26.
Psal. 97. 7.

4 *b* Thou shalt not make unto thee any graven image, or any likeness of any thing that *is* in heaven above, or that *is* in the earth beneath, or that *is* in the water under the earth:

5 Thou shalt not bow down thyself to them, nor serve them: for I the LORD thy God *am* a jealous God, visiting the iniquity of the fathers upon the children unto the third and fourth *generation* of them that hate me;

---

not merely to human creatures, but to the people whom He had redeemed, to those who had been in bondage, but were now free men. (Exod. vi. 6, 7, xix. 5.) The Commandments are expressed in absolute terms. They are not sanctioned by outward penalties, as if for slaves, but are addressed at once to the conscience, as for free men. The well-being of the nation called for the infliction of penalties, and therefore statutes were passed to punish offenders who blasphemed the name of Jehovah, who profaned the Sabbath, or who committed murder or adultery. (See on Lev. xviii. 24—30.) But these penal statutes were not to be the ground of obedience for the true Israelite according to the Covenant. He was to know Jehovah as his Redeemer, and was to obey Him as such. (Cf. Rom. xiii. 5; see Note after *v.* 21, § V.)

3. *before me*] Literally, *before my face*. The meaning is that no god should be worshipped in addition to Jehovah. Cf. *v.* 23. The rendering in our Prayer-Book, *but me*, with that of the LXX. πλὴν ἐμοῦ, does not so well represent the Hebrew. The polytheism which was the besetting sin of the Israelites in later times did not exclude Jehovah, but it associated Him with false deities. See Note on xxxiv. 13.

4. *graven image*] Any sort of image is here intended. The Hebrew word (*pesel*) strictly means a carved image, mostly denoting one of wood or stone, and in some places it is distinguished from a molten image of metal (*massēkāh*): but as molten images were finished up with a graver or carving tool, *pesel* is sometimes applied to them (Is. xl. 19, xliv. 10; Jer. x. 14, &c.), and is frequently used, as it is here, for a general name for images of all sorts.

or any likeness] This may be rendered, **even any likeness**. What follows in the verse expresses the whole material creation; it is expanded in detail in Deut. iv. 16—19.

5. *Thou shalt not bow down thyself to them, nor serve them*] The antecedent to *them* in each clause appears to be the likenesses of things in heaven and earth spoken of in the preceding verse. It has been observed that, according to the Hebrew idiom, these clauses may have a strict grammatical connection with "Thou shalt not make," &c. in *v.* 4. The meaning certainly is to prohibit the making of the likeness of any material thing, *in order to* worship it. For a similar form of expression, see Num. xxii. 12. As the First Commandment forbids the worship of any false god, seen or unseen, it is here forbidden to worship an image of any sort, whether the figure of a false deity or one in any way symbolical of Jehovah (see on xxxii. 4). The spiritual acts of worship were symbolized in the furniture and ritual of the Tabernacle and the Altar, and for this end the forms of living things might be employed as in the case of the Cherubim (see on xxv. 18): but the presence of the invisible God was to be marked by no symbol of Himself, but by His words written on stones, preserved in the Ark in the Holy of Holies and covered by the Mercy-seat. On the repudiation of images of the Deity by the ancient Persians, see Herodot. I. 131; Strabo, XV. p. 732; and by the earliest legislators of Rome, see Plut. 'Numa,' 8; Augustin. 'de Civ. Dei,' IV. 31.

The Jews, not recognizing the connection between *vv.* 4 and 5, have imagined *v.* 4 to be a prohibition of the exercise of the arts of painting and sculpture. Considering the Cherubim of the Mercy-seat and of the curtains of the Tabernacle, the pomegranates of the High-priest's robe, and the fruits and flowers of the Candlestick, to say nothing of the sculptures of the Temple in later times (1 K. vi. 23 sq., vii. 27 sq.), any such notion as this must show the prejudiced and fragmentary way in which they were tempted to study the Scriptures. Philo declares that Moses condemned to perpetual banishment the cheating arts (ἐπιβούλοι τέχναι) of painters and sculptors ('Quis div. rer. heres.' c. 35; 'de Orac.' c. 29). Josephus charges Solomon with a breach of the Law, on account of the oxen which supported the brazen sea, and the lions which adorned his throne ('Ant.' VIII. 7, § 5): and in direct contradiction of Exod. xxvi. 31, he denies that the vail which concealed the Most Holy Place was ornamented with living creatures. ('Ant.' III. 6, § 4.) This prejudice, from the time when the pharisaic tendency began to work on the mind of the nation, must have effectually checked the progress of the imitative arts.

for I the LORD thy God am a jealous God] Deut. vi. 15; Josh. xxiv. 19; Is. xlii. 8, xlviii. 11; Nahum i. 2. This reason applies to the First, as well as to the Second Commandment. The truth expressed in it was declared more fully

6 And shewing mercy unto thousands of them that love me, and keep my commandments.

7 ᶜThou shalt not take the name of the LORD thy God in vain; for the LORD will not hold him guiltless that taketh his name in vain.

8 Remember the sabbath day, to keep it holy.

ᶜ Lev. 19. 12. Deut. 5. 11. Matt. 5. 33.

---

to Moses when the name of Jehovah was proclaimed to him after he had interceded for Israel on account of the golden calf (xxxiv. 6, 7; see note).

visiting the iniquity of the fathers upon the children] The visitation here spoken of can hardly be any other than that which we are accustomed to witness in the common experience of life. (Cf. xxxiv. 7; Jer. xxxii. 18.) Sons and remote descendants inherit the consequences of their fathers' sins, in disease, poverty, captivity, with all the influences of bad example and evil communications. (See Lev. xxvi. 39; Lam. v. 7 sq.) The "inherited curse" seems to fall often most heavily on the least guilty persons, as is abundantly proved in all history and is pointedly illustrated in Greek tragedy. But such suffering must always be free from the sting of conscience; it is not like the visitation for sin on the individual by whom the sin has been committed. The suffering, or loss of advantages, entailed on the unoffending son, is a condition under which he has to carry on the struggle of life, and, like all other inevitable conditions imposed upon men, it cannot tend to his ultimate disadvantage, if he struggles well and perseveres to the end. He may never attain in this world to a high standard of knowledge, or of outward conduct, compared with others, but the Searcher of hearts will regard him with favour, not in proportion to his visible conduct, but to his unseen struggles. As regards the administration of justice by earthly tribunals, the Law holds good, "The fathers shall not be put to death for the children, neither shall the children be put to death for the fathers; every man shall be put to death for his own sin" (Deut. xxiv. 16). The same principle is carried out in spiritual matters by the Supreme Judge. The Israelites in a later age made a confusion in the use of their common proverb, "The fathers have eaten sour grapes, and the children's teeth are set on edge." There would have been truth in this saying had it been used only in reference to the mere natural consequences of their fathers' sins. In this sense their teeth were set on edge by the sour grapes their fathers had eaten. But the Prophets pointed out the falsehood involved in the proverb as it was understood by the people. They showed that it was utterly false when applied to the spiritual relation in which each person stands in the judgment of Him who is no respecter of persons. (Jer. xxxi. 29, 30; Ezek. xviii. 2—4 sq.)

Another explanation of the words appears in the Targums, and is favoured by some of the Fathers and other commentators, Christian and Jewish. It assumes that the words refer only to the children who go on sinning so as to fill up the measure of their fathers' iniquities in the manner spoken of Lev. xxvi. 39; Is. lxv. 7; Jer. xvi. 10—13; Matt. xxiii. 29—32. (See Hengst. 'Pent.' Vol. II. p. 446.) But this seems unworthily to reduce the Divine words to a mere truism. It makes them say in an awkward mannner no more than that the guilty sons shall be punished as well as the guilty fathers.

6. *unto thousands*] **unto the thousandth generation.** Jehovah's visitations of chastisement extend to the third and fourth generation, his visitations of mercy to the thousandth; that is, for ever. That this is the true rendering seems to follow from Deut. vii. 9. Cf. 2 S. vii. 15, 16. So Syr., Onk., Leo Juda, Geneva French, Rosen., Zunz, Schott. Knobel, Keil, Herx., and Wogue. Our version is supported by the LXX., Vulg., Saadia, Luther, and de Wette.

7. Our translators have followed the LXX., Aquila, the Vulgate, Augustin ('Serm.' VIII.), and Theodoret ('Quæst. in Exod.' 41), in making the Third Commandment bear upon any profane and idle utterance of the name of God. Saadia, the Syriac, some of the Rabbinists, and the greater number of the critics of our day, give it the sense, *Thou shalt not swear falsely by the name of Jehovah thy God*. The Hebrew word which answers to *in vain* may be rendered either way. The two abuses of the sacred name seem to be distinguished in Lev. xix. 12. Our Version is probably right in giving the rendering which is more inclusive. To swear falsely is undoubtedly a profanation of the name of God; and looking at the matter on its practical side, the man who, in a right spirit, avoids the idle use of the Name will be incapable of swearing falsely. Hence there may be a reference to this Commandment, as well as to Lev. xix. 12, in Matt. v. 33. The caution that a breach of this Commandment incurs guilt in the eyes of Jehovah is especially appropriate, in consequence of the ease with which the temptation to take God's name in vain besets men in their common intercourse with each other.

8. *Remember the sabbath day*] These words have been taken to refer to the observance of the Sabbath day as an old usage dating back

EXODUS. XX.

d chap. 23.
12.
Ezek. 20.
12.
Luke 13.
14.

9 *d* Six days shalt thou labour, and do all thy work:

10 But the seventh day *is* the sabbath of the LORD thy God: in it thou shalt not do any work, thou, nor thy son, nor thy daughter, thy manservant, nor thy maidservant, nor thy cattle, nor thy stranger that *is* within thy gates:

11 For *e in* six days the LORD made heaven and earth, the sea, and all that in them *is*, and rested the seventh day: wherefore the LORD blessed the sabbath day, and hallowed it.

12 ¶ *f* Honour thy father and thy mother: that thy days may be long upon the land which the LORD thy God giveth thee.

e Gen. 2. 2
f Deut. 5. 16.
Matt. 15.
Eph. 6. 2.

---

to the Patriarchs, or even to the creation of the world. There is however no distinct evidence that the Sabbath, as a formal ordinance, was recognized before the time of Moses. The expressions of Nehemiah (ix. 14), of Ezekiel (xx. 10, 11, 12), and, perhaps, of Moses himself (Deut. v. 15), may be taken to intimate that the observance was regarded as originating in the Law given on Mount Sinai. The most ancient testimonies favour this view. (See Note at end of this Chapter. Also note on Gen. ii. 2.) It is now generally admitted that the attempts to trace the observance in heathen antiquity have failed. It has been alleged that the word *remember* may be reasonably explained in one of two ways without adopting the inference that has been mentioned; it may either be used in the sense of *keep in mind* what is here enjoined for the first time, or it may refer back to what is related in ch. xvi. where the Sabbath day is first noticed, in giving the law for collecting the manna.

to keep it holy] See Note after *v.* 21, § I.

10. *the sabbath of the LORD thy God*] a Sabbath to Jehovah thy God. It may be observed that the word *sabbath* (more properly, *shabbath*) has no etymological connection with *sheba'*, the Hebrew for *seven*. The proper meaning of *sabbath* is, *rest after labour*.

thy stranger that is within thy gates] The Hebrew word *geer* does not mean a *stranger* (that is an unknown person), but, according to its mere derivation, a *lodger*, or *sojourner*. In this place it denotes one who had come from another people to take up his permanent abode among the Israelites, and who might have been well known to his neighbours. Our word *foreigner*, in its common use, seems best to answer to it here. The LXX. renders *geer* by προσήλυτος (*proselyte*), πάροικος, and ξένος. That the word did not primarily refer to foreign domestic servants (though all such were included under it) is to be inferred from the term used for gates (*sha'arim*), signifying not the doors of a private dwelling, but the gates of a town or camp.

11. *wherefore the LORD blessed the sabbath day*] Our Communion Service and Catechism follow the reading of the LXX. and the earlier English Versions, in calling this the *seventh day* instead of the *sabbath day*. On the meaning of the verse, see Note after *v.* 21.

12. *Honour thy father and thy mother*] According to our usage, the Fifth Commandment is placed as the first in the second table; and this is necessarily involved in the common division of the Commandments into our duty towards God and our duty towards men. But the more ancient, and probably the better, division allots five Commandments to each Table. The connection between the first four Commandments and the Fifth exists in the truth that all faith in God centres in the filial feeling. Our parents stand between us and God in a way in which no other beings can. It is worthy of note that the honouring of parents and the keeping of the Sabbath day, which is the same as honouring God, are combined in one precept in Lev. xix. 3.—In connection with this, it may be observed that the Fifth Commandment and the first part of the Fourth are the only portions of the Decalogue which are expressed in a positive form. See Note after *v.* 21, § IV. On the maintenance of parental authority, see xxi. 15, 17; Deut. xxi. 18—21.

that thy days may be long upon the land] Filial respect is the ground of national permanence. When the Jews were about to be cast out of their land, the rebuke of the prophet was, that they had not walked in the old paths and had not respected the voice of their fathers as the sons of Jonadab had done (Jer. vi. 16, xxxv. 18, 19). And when in later times the land had been restored to them, and they were about to be cast out of it a second time, the great sin of which they were convicted was, that they had set aside this Fifth Commandment for the sake of their own traditions. (Matt. xv. 4—6; Mark vii. 10, 11.) Every other nation that has a history bears witness to the same truth. Rome owed her strength, as well as the permanence of her influence after she had politically perished, to her steady maintenance of the *patria potestas* (Maine, 'Ancient Law,' p. 135). China has mainly owed her long duration to the simple way in which she has uniformly acknowledged the authority of fathers. The Divine words were addressed emphatically to Israel, but they

13 *Thou shalt not kill.

14 Thou shalt not commit adultery.

15 Thou shalt not steal.

16 Thou shalt not bear false witness against thy neighbour.

17 *Thou shalt not covet thy neighbour's house, thou shalt not covet thy neighbour's wife, nor his manservant, nor his maidservant, nor his ox, nor his ass, nor any thing that *is* thy neighbour's.

18 ¶ And *all the people saw the thunderings, and the lightnings, and the noise of the trumpet, and the mountain smoking: and when the people saw *it*, they removed, and stood afar off.

19 And they said unto Moses, *Speak thou with us, and we will

---

set forth a universal principle of national life. St Paul calls this Commandment, "the first commandment with promise" (Eph. vi. 2); the promise is fulfilled in God's government of the whole world. The narrow view which Selden and others have taken of the Commandment, that it implied no more than a prediction that the children of Israel should possess the land of Canaan on the condition stated, is alien to the spirit of the Decalogue. (See Note after *v.* 21, § VI.)

13, 14. The Sixth and Seventh Commandments are amongst those utterances of the Law which our Saviour, in the Sermon on the Mount, took to illustrate the relation in which the Gospel stands to the Law. Whatever range of meaning we are to give to the expression in Matt. v. 17, that Christ came not to destroy but to *fulfil* (πληρῶσαι), we can hardly exclude from it, in its bearing on the discourse that follows in *vv.* 18—48, the sense, to *set forth perfectly* in the way of teaching. (Cf. Rom. xv. 19; Col. i. 25.) The Scribes and Pharisees failed perfectly to set forth the Law, in their teaching as well as in their practice; they taught the mere words in their dry external relations; "they gave the husk without the kernel." Their righteousness, both that which they taught and that which they practised, therefore fell short of the true standard (Matt. v. 20). If this view of the word *fulfil* is admitted, our Saviour's words respecting these Commandments (*vv.* 21—32) cannot be taken as an external supplement to the Law, or as a new adaptation of it to a changed order of things, but as a perfect unfolding, in the most practical form, of the meaning which the Commandments had from the beginning, and which had been, with different degrees of distinctness, shadowed forth to all who wisely and devoutly obeyed the Law under the Old Dispensation. The passage in St Matthew (v. 21—32) is therefore the best comment on these two verses of Exodus. St Augustin says that the purpose of Christ's coming was, *non ut Legi adderentur quæ deerant, sed ut fierent quæ scripta erant.* 'Cont. Faust.' XVII. 6.

15. The right of property is sanctioned in the Eighth Commandment by an external rule: its deeper meaning is involved in the Tenth Commandment.

17. As the Sixth, Seventh, and Eighth Commandments forbid us to injure our neighbour in deed, the Ninth forbids us to injure him in word, and the Tenth, in thought. No human eye can see the coveting heart; it is witnessed only by him who possesses it and by Him to whom all things are naked and open. But it is the root of all sins against our neighbour in word or in deed (Jam. i. 14, 15). The man who is acceptable before God, walking uprightly, not backbiting with his tongue, nor doing evil to his neighbour, is he who "speaketh the truth IN HIS HEART." Ps. xv. 2, 3. St Paul speaks of the operation of this Commandment on his own heart as the means of revealing to him the holiness of the Law (Rom. vii. 7). The direct connection of the Commandments of the Second Table with the principle of love between man and man, is affirmed Matt. xxii. 39, 40; Rom. xiii. 9, 10; Gal. v. 14.—On the variations between this and the parallel place in Deut. v. 21, see Note after *v.* 21, §II.

There is a curious interpolation in the Samaritan text following the Tenth Commandment. The Israelites are commanded to set up on Mount Gerizim two great plastered stones with the words of the Law inscribed on them, to build there an Altar, and to sacrifice upon it Burnt-offerings and Peace-offerings. The passage is evidently made up from Deut. xxvii. 2—7, with some expressions from Deut. xi. 30, Gerizim being substituted for Ebal. See on Deut. xxvii. 2—7.

18—21. This narrative is amplified in Deut. v. 22—31. The people had realized the terrors of the voice of Jehovah in the utterance of the Ten Words of the Testimony, and they feared for their lives. Though Moses encouraged them, they were permitted to withdraw and to stand afar off, at their tent doors (see Deut. v. 30). It would appear, according to xix. 24, that Aaron on this occasion accompanied Moses in drawing near to the thick darkness. Cf. xxiv. 18.

hear: but *d* let not God speak with us, lest we die.

20 And Moses said unto the people, Fear not: for God is come to prove you, and that his fear may be before your faces, that ye sin not.

21 And the people stood afar off, and Moses drew near unto the thick darkness where God *was*.

NOTE on Chap. XX. *vv.* 1—17.

On The Ten Commandments.

I. *The Name.* II. *What was written on the Stones?* III. *The Division into Ten.* IV. *The Two Tables.* V. *The Commandments as* A Testimony. VI. *Breadth of their meaning.*

§ I.

The Hebrew name which is rendered in our Version the Ten Commandments (עֲשֶׂרֶת הַדְּבָרִים) occurs in Exod. xxxiv. 28; Deut. iv. 13, x. 4. It literally means *the Ten Words*, as it stands in the margin of our Bible; LXX. οἱ δέκα λόγοι, or τὰ δέκα ῥήματα; Vulg. *decem verba*. But the Hebrew substantive דָּבָר often denotes a *mandate* (Josh. i. 13; Esth. i. 19); and the common English rendering may be therefore justified. In Ex. xxiv. 12, the Ten Commandments are called **the Law, even the Commandment**: the latter word (מִצְוָה) occurs in its plural form in the Second Commandment, Ex. xx. 6; Deut. v. 10. They are elsewhere called the Words of the Covenant (Ex. xxxiv. 28, where the strict rendering would be, *the Words of the Covenant, even the Ten Words*), the Tables of the Covenant (Deut. ix. 9, 11, 15), and simply the Covenant (Deut. iv. 13: 1 K. viii. 21; 2 Chron. vi. 11); also the Two Tables (Deut. ix. 10, 17). But the most frequent name for them in the Old Testament is, the Testimony[1] (הָעֵדוּת, LXX. τὸ μαρτύριον or τὰ μαρτύρια), or the Two Tables of the Testimony[2]. In the New Testament they are called simply the Commandments[3] (αἱ ἐντολαί). The name Decalogue (ὁ δεκάλογος) is found first in Clement of Alexandria, and was commonly used by the Fathers who followed him.

We thus know that the Tables were two, and that the Commandments were ten, in number. But the Scriptures do not, by any direct statements, enable us to determine with precision how the Ten Commandments are severally to be made out, nor how they are to be allotted to the Two Tables. On each of these points various opinions have been held.

§ II.

But there is a question which rightly claims precedence of these: What actually were the Words of Jehovah that were engraven on the Tables of Stone? We have two distinct statements, one in Exodus (xx. 1—17) and one in Deuteronomy (v. 6—21), apparently of equal authority, but differing from each other in several weighty particulars. Each is said, with reiterated emphasis, to contain the words that were actually spoken by the Lord, and written by Him upon the stones[4].

The variations which are of most importance are in the Commandments which we commonly call the Fourth, the Fifth, and the Tenth. The two copies of these are here placed side by side. The expressions in Deuteronomy which differ in the original Hebrew from the corresponding ones in Exodus, are in italics, and the additional clauses are in brackets.

Exodus xx.	Deut. v.
IV. (*vv.* 8—11.)	IV. (*vv.* 12—15.)
Remember the sabbath day, to keep it holy. Six days shalt thou labour, and do all thy work: But the seventh day is the sabbath of the Lord thy God: in it thou shalt not do any work, thou, nor thy son, nor thy daughter, thy manservant, nor thy maidservant, nor thy cattle, nor thy stranger that is within thy gates: For in six days the Lord made heaven and earth, the sea, and all that in them is, and rested the seventh day: wherefore the Lord blessed the sabbath day, and hallowed it.	*Keep* the sabbath day to sanctify it, [*as the* Lord *thy God hath commanded thee.*] Six days thou shalt labour, and do all thy work: But the seventh day is the sabbath of the Lord thy God: in it thou shalt not do any work, thou, nor thy son, nor thy daughter, nor thy manservant, nor thy maidservant, [*nor thine ox, nor thine ass,*] nor any of thy cattle, nor thy stranger that is within thy gates; [*that thy manservant and thy maidservant may rest as well as thou.*] And remember that thou *wast a servant in the land of Egypt, and that the* Lord *thy God brought thee out thence through a mighty hand and by a stretched out*

---

[1] Ex. xvi. 34, xxv. 16, 21, xxx. 6, xl. 20; Lev. xvi. 13, &c. &c.

[2] Ex. xxxi. 18, xxxii. 15, xxxiv. 29.

[3] Matt. xix. 17; Mark x. 19; Luke xviii. 20; Rom. xiii. 9.

[4] Ex. xx. 1, xxiv. 12, xxxi. 18, xxxii. 15, 16; Deut. v. 4, 5, 22, iv. 13, ix. 10.

V. (*v.* 12.)
Honour thy father and thy mother: that thy days may be long upon the land which the LORD thy God giveth thee.

V. (*v.* 16.)
Honour thy father and thy mother. [*as the* LORD *thy God hath commanded thee*]; that thy days may be prolonged, [*and that it may go well with thee*], in the land which the LORD thy God giveth thee.

X. (*v.* 17.)
Thou shalt not covet thy neighbour's house, thou shalt not covet thy neighbour's wife, nor his manservant, nor his maidservant, nor his ox, nor his ass, nor any thing that is thy neighbour's.

X. (*v.* 21)
Neither shalt thou desire thy neighbour's wife, *neither* shalt thou *covet* thy neighbour's house, [*his field*], or his manservant, or his maidservant, his ox, or his ass, or any thing that is thy neighbour's.

In the Fourth Commandment, it will be seen that in Deuteronomy:—

(1) "Keep (שָׁמוֹר) the Sabbath day," is read instead of "Remember (זָכוֹר) the Sabbath day."

(2) Three fresh clauses are inserted:—
"As the LORD thy God hath commanded thee."
"Nor thine ox nor thine ass."
"That thy manservant and thy maidservant may rest as well as thou."

(3) A different reason is given for the Commandment, referring to the deliverance of the Israelites from Egypt, instead of the rest of God after the six works of Creation.

In the Fifth, Deuteronomy inserts the same expression as it does in the Fourth, "as the LORD thy God hath commanded thee;" and also the words, "that it may go well with thee."

In the Tenth, it transposes "thy neighbour's house," and "thy neighbour's wife;" it inserts "his field," and it makes the two parts of the Commandment more distinct by the use of a different verb in the imperative mood in each. The verb rendered *desire* (חָמַד) is the same that is rendered *covet* in Exodus, but the one here rendered *covet* is a different one (אָוָה).

It should also be observed that, in Deut. v. verses 17, 18, 19, 20, 21 are linked together by the copulative conjunction. The few other slight variations do not affect the sense.

It has been generally assumed that the whole of one or other of these copies was written on the Tables. Most commentators have supposed that the original document is in Exodus, and that the author of Deuteronomy wrote from memory, with variations suggested at the time. Others have conceived that Deuteronomy must furnish the more correct form since the Tables must have been in actual existence when the book was written. But neither of these views can be fairly reconciled with the statements in Exodus and Deuteronomy to which reference has been made. If either copy, as a whole, represents what was written on the Tables, it is obvious that the other cannot do so.

A conjecture which seems to deserve respect has been put forth by Ewald. He supposes that the original Commandments were all in the same terse and simple form of expression as appears (both in Exodus and Deuteronomy) in the First, Sixth, Seventh, Eighth, and Ninth, such as would be most suitable for recollection, and that the passages in each copy in which the most important variations are found were comments added when the Books were written. It is not necessary to involve this theory with any question as to the authorship of the Books, or with any doubt as to the comments being the words of God[1] given by Moses as much as the Commandments, strictly so called, that were written on the Tables. In reference to the most important of the differences, that relating to the reason for the observance of the Sabbath day, the thoughts are in no degree discordant, and each sets forth what is entirely worthy of, and consistent with, the Divine Law[2]. Slighter verbal or literal variations, with no important difference of meaning (such as *keep* for *remember*), may perhaps be ascribed to copyists[3].

It may be supposed then that the Ten Words of Jehovah, with the prefatory sentence, were to this effect, assuming that each Table contained Five Commandments. See § IV.

I am Jehovah thy God who have brought thee out of the land of Egypt, out of the house of bondage.

FIRST TABLE.
i. *Thou shalt have no other God[4] before me.*
ii. *Thou shalt not make to thee any graven image.*
iii. *Thou shalt not take the name of Jehovah thy God in vain.*
iv. *Thou shalt remember the Sabbath day, to keep it holy.*
v. *Thou shalt honour thy father and thy mother.*

[1] See Ex. xx. 1.
[2] See the following Note, § III.
[3] What is assumed, on the theory here stated, to be the comment on both the First and Second Commandments ("For I the LORD thy God am a jealous God," &c. See on Ex. xx. 5) occurs in a somewhat different and more diffuse form in Ex. xxxiv. 6, 7. Does not a comparison of the two passages tend to confirm the supposition that the words are not a part of the original Ten Commandments, but that they were quoted here in a condensed form by Moses, as bearing on the two Commandments, when the book of Exodus was put together?
[4] See on Ex. xx. 3.

EXODUS. XX.

SECOND TABLE.
vi. *Thou shalt not kill.*
vii. *Thou shalt not commit adultery.*
viii. *Thou shalt not steal.*
ix. *Thou shalt not bear false witness.*
x. *Thou shalt not covet.*

A practical illustration from the usage of different ages may tend to shew the probability that the Ten Commandments were familiarly known in such a compendious form as this, at a time when they were used not only as the common watchwords of duty, but as the axioms of the Law in its actual operation. In those copies of the Commandments which have been used in different branches of the Church for the instruction of its members, the form has almost always been more or less abbreviated of a part, or the whole, of those which are the most expanded in Exodus and Deuteronomy; namely, the Second, Third, Fourth, Fifth, and Tenth[1]. The earliest book of Christian instruction in which they are given at full length as they stand in Exodus, appears to be "the Prymer in English," of about A.D. 1400, printed in Maskell's 'Monumenta Ritualia" (Vol. II. p. 177). They are also given in full in the Primer of Edward VI. (A.D. 1553). When they were first introduced into our Communion Service in the Second Prayer Book of Edward VI. (A.D. 1552), the words in the introductory sentence, "which have brought thee out of the land of Egypt, out of the house of bondage," were unfortunately omitted, and have not been restored in succeeding editions. But they are not only retained in our Catechism, but are made a special topic of instruction in connection with the Commandments in Nowell's larger Catechism[2].

§ III.

The mode in which the Commandments are divided into Ten in our own Service Book agrees with the most ancient authorities, Jewish as well as Christian, and the usage of the Eastern Church. It appears to be based on the clearest view of the subject matter, as it is set forth in the sacred text[3].

But another arrangement, which is first found distinctly stated in St Augustin[4], demands attention from its having been universally adopted by the Western Church until the Reformation. The Second Commandment is added to the First (or, in some of the abridged forms, omitted altogether), and the number ten is made out by treating the Tenth as two Commandments. St Augustin, following Deuteronomy, and the LXX. in Exodus (see below), makes the Ninth "Thou shalt not covet thy neighbour's wife," and the Tenth "Thou shalt not covet thy neighbour's house," &c.: while others, following the Hebrew text of Exodus, reverse this order. In some forms used by the Western Church the whole paragraph on coveting is kept entire, but it is headed as "the Ninth and Tenth Commandments[5]." The general arrangement here spoken of was used by the Church in Britain before the Reformation[6], and is still retained by the Lutheran as well as the Romish Church.

An arrangement unlike either of these may be traced to the fourth century, is distinctly set forth in the Targum of Palestine (which probably belongs to the seventh century), and has been adopted by Maimonides, Aben-Ezra, and other Jewish authorities down to the present day. The First *Word* is identified with "I am the LORD thy God which brought thee out of the land of Egypt" (which cannot of course be properly called a *Commandment*), and the Second Word is made, as in the arrangement last mentioned, to include what we reckon as the First and Second Commandments.

The subject matter itself seems to suggest grave and obvious objections to the two latter arrangements. There is a clear distinction between polytheism and idolatry which entitles each to a distinct Commandment: and the sin of coveting our neighbour's possessions is essentially the same in its nature, whatever may be the object coveted.

It is worthy of notice in regard to the sequence of the Commandments, that the LXX. in Ex. xx. (according to the Vatican text) and Suidas (s. πλαξὶν) place vii. and viii. before vi., and transpose the *house* and the *wife* in x.; and that Philo places vii. before vi. according to

---

[1] Sulp. Sev. 'Sac. Hist.' lib. I. 'Synopsis Sac. Script.' ascribed to St Athanasius. Suidas s. πλαξίν. King Alfred's 'Laws.' 'The Lutheran Cat.' (in which what are here called the sacred writers' comments are named *appendices*). 'The Institution,' &c. and 'The Erudition,' &c. of Henry VIII. The Catechism of Edward VI. The Douay Catechism. The Catechism of the Greek Church, &c. &c.

[2] p. 23. Edit. Jacobson.

[3] This division is recognized in Philo, 'de Orac.' c. 12, 22, 31; 'Quis rer. div. heres.' c. 35. Joseph.'Ant.' III. 5, § 5. Origen 'Hom. in Exod.' VIII. Jerome 'in Ephes.' VI. 2. Sulp. Sev. 'Sac. Hist.' I. 'Synopsis S.S.' ascribed to Athanasius. Suidas s. πλαξίν. The Catechism of the Greek Church. 'The Institution,' &c. and 'The Eru-

dition,' &c. of Henry VIII. The Primer of 1553, &c. &c.—The testimony of Clement of Alexandria, 'Stromat.' VI. § 137, is ambiguous, and has been quoted both for and against the arrangement; see Suicer s. δεκάλογος, and Kurtz, 'Old Covenant,' III. 124.

[4] 'Quæst. in Exod.' LXXI. Serm. VIII. IX. &c.

[5] The Trent and Lutheran Catechisms.

[6] King Alfred's 'Laws.'—The 'Speculum' of St Edmund, Archbishop of Canterbury (1234—1242), and the 'Treatises' of Richard Hampole (circ. 1340), published by the Early English Text Society.—The Primer of 1400, &c. &c.

the order recognized in Mark x. 19; Luke xviii. 20; Rom. xiii. 9; James ii. 11. The usual order is preserved by the other ancient versions in Exodus, and by the LXX. in Deut. v.; as it is also, as regards vi. and vii., in Matt. v. 21, 27, xix. 18.

§ IV.

The distribution of the Commandments between the Two Tables which is most familiar to us, allotting four to the First Table and six to the Second, is first mentioned by St Augustine, though it is not approved by him. It is based on a distinction that lies on the surface, and that easily adapts itself to modern ethical systems, between our duty towards God and our duty towards our neighbour[1]. The division approved by St Augustine was, in relation to the matter in each Table, the same; but as he united the First and Second Commandments into one, and divided the Tenth into two, he made the First Table to comprise three Commandments, and the Second Table, seven. He mystically associated the first of these numbers with the Persons of the Trinity, and the latter with the Sabbatical institution[2].

But the more symmetrical arrangement which allots five Commandments to each Table is supported by the most ancient authorities[3], and is approved by several modern critics. It is also countenanced by Rom. xiii. 9, where the complete Second Table appears to be spoken of as not including the Fifth Commandment.

Philo places the Fifth Commandment last in the First Table, and calls it a link between the Two Tables. On the reason of this designation of his, see on Ex. xx. 12. The real distinction between the Tables appears to be that the First relates to the duties which arise from our Filial relations, the Second to those which arise from our Fraternal relations[4]. But as the Commandments represent the essence of law, they assume the strict form of law. They are expressed, almost exclusively, in the prohibitory form, because it belongs to law to say what a man shall not do, rather than what he shall do. The Commandments therefore set forth neither of the relations that have been mentioned on the positive side. They contain no injunctions to love God, like that in Deut. vi. 5, x. 12, &c.; nor to love our brethren, like that in Lev. xix. 18; nor do they tell us to *love* our parents.

---

[1] See on Exod. xx. 12.

[2] 'Quæst. in Exod.' 71. The notion is adopted in the 'Speculum' of St Edmund. See p. 337, note 6.

[3] Philo, 'de Orac.' 25; 'Quis rer. div. heres.' 35. Josephus 'Ant.' III. 5, § 8 and § 5. Irenæus, 'Adv. hæres.' II. 24, § 4. Gregor. Naz. 'Carm. Var.' XXXV.

[4] Knobel observes that the subject of the First Table is *pietas*, that of the Second Table, *probitas*.

§ V.

The name most frequently used by Moses for the Decalogue (הָעֵדוּת) signifies something strongly affirmed, literally, *something spoken again and again*: it is therefore properly rendered in our version THE TESTIMONY (see § I.). Taking this in connection with the prohibitory form of the Commandments, the name must have been understood as the Testimony of Jehovah against the tendency to transgress in those to whom the document was addressed. When Moses laid up the completed Book of the Law, of which the Commandments were the central point, by the side of the Ark of the Covenant, his declared purpose was "that it may be there for a witness against thee; for I know thy rebellion and thy stiff neck" (Deut. xxxi. 26, 27)[5].

It was by the Law, as it was represented in these Commandments, that there came "the knowledge of sin[6]." The disturbance of the conscience which results from doing wrong, when there is no expressed law, is a vague discomfort to the person with no clear apprehension as to its cause. But when the voice of the Lord has given forth the Law in words intelligible to the mind, then comes *the knowledge* of sin, as the transgression of righteous obligation to a gracious God[7].

And this knowledge of sin necessarily involves a consciousness of condemnation. Hence the Tables given to Moses were "a ministration of condemnation"—"a ministration of death written and engraven on stones" (2 Cor. iii. 7, 9; cf. Eph. ii. 15). Yet was this ministration of condemnation a true revelation of Him who had redeemed His people in love. and it is, in the truest sense, a demand on them for the tribute of their love[8]. It is love in the creature which alone can obey the Law in reality and with acceptance[9].

The relation in which the condemning strictness of the Law stood to the forgiving mercy of Jehovah was distinctly shewn in the

---

[5] Hengstenberg takes nearly the same view as is here given of the application of the word עֵדוּת, and of the relation of the Mercy seat to the Decalogue. 'Pentateuch,' Vol. II. p. 524.

[6] Rom. iii. 20, vii. 7; cf. note on Ex. xx. 17.

[7] On the mode in which this was figured in the Sacrifices of the Law, see notes on Lev. iv.

[8] "For though the Law, being love, may seem to reveal God who is love, yet is it rather a demand for love than a revelation of love ; and though it might have been, in the light of high intelligence, and where there was no darkening of sin, concluded that love alone could demand love, yet does the mere demand never so speak to sinners; but 'by the Law is the knowledge of sin:' wherefore 'the Law worketh wrath.'" Campbell, 'The Nature of the Atonement,' p. 41. Cf. Rom. vii. 7—14.

[9] Matt. xxii. 37—40 ; Mark xii. 29— 31 ; Luke x. 26, 27 ; Rom. xiii. 8, 10; Gal. v. 4 ; Jam. ii. 8. See on Ex. xx. 2.

symbolism of the Sanctuary. When the Tables of the Law were deposited in the Ark of the Covenant, they were covered by the Mercy seat, which, in accordance with its name, was the sign of the Divine lovingkindness (see Note on ch. xxv. 17). The Cherubim which were on the Mercy seat appear to have figured the highest condition of created intelligence in the act of humble adoration and service, and so to have expressed the condition on which were obtained forgiveness, deliverance from the letter that killeth (2 Cor. iii. 6), and communion with Jehovah. This view of the significance of the Ark and what pertained to it seems aptly to suit the words in which the arrangement of the symbols is prescribed; "and thou shalt put the mercy seat above upon the ark; and in the ark thou shalt put the testimony that I shall give thee. And there I will meet with thee, and I will commune with thee from above the mercy seat, from between the two cherubims which are upon the ark of the testimony," Ex. xxv. 21, 22.

The Ark, as the outward and visible sign of the Covenant between Jehovah and His people, thus expressed, in a way suited to the time and the occasion, the Divine purpose in the Atonement. The Law was the characteristic feature in the dispensation which was then present; and accordingly the essence of the Law was expressed, not in a symbol, but in plain words written by the finger of God. But the sentence of condemnation implied in the Commandments could not be exhibited in its naked severity as the basis of the Covenant. It was enclosed in the Ark, and over it the Divine mercy was symbolized in such shadowy outline as was to edify the faithful believers until the fulness of the time came, when the Son was sent "whom God hath set forth to be a propitiation ($\iota\lambda\alpha\sigma\tau\eta\rho\iota\sigma\nu$, *a mercy seat*)[1] through faith in his blood, to declare his righteousness for the remission of sins that are past, through the forbearance of God; to declare, I say, at this time His righteousness: that He might be just, and the justifier of him that believeth in Jesus" (Rom. iii. 25, 26).

The significance of the whole Sanctuary may be said to be concentrated in the Tables of the Law, and the Mercy seat. The other holy things, with every external arrangement, were subordinated to them[2]. And hence the place in which they were deposited was the Holy of Holies, closely shut off by the vail, entered by no one but the High-priest, and by him only once in the year, Ex. xl. 20, 21; Lev. xvi. 2.

§ VI.

It is to be observed that the Decalogue, in respect to its subject-matter, does not set forth what is local, or temporary, or peculiar to a single nation[3]. Its two Tables are a standing declaration of the true relation between morality and religion for all nations and ages[4]. The Fourth Commandment is, in its principle, no exception to this[5]. The Decalogue belonged to the Israelites, not because the truths expressed in it were exclusively theirs, but because it was revealed to them in a special manner (see on Ex. xx. 2). The breadth of meaning which rightly belongs to it may be compared to that of the Lord's Prayer, which, though it was especially given by Christ to His followers for their own use, contains nothing unsuitable for any believer in One God.

NOTE on CHAP. XX. v. 8.

ON THE SABBATH DAY.

I. *The Sabbath according to the Law;* II. *according to Tradition.* III. *Its connection with the Creation.* IV. *Its relation to Sunday.* V. *Its connection with the deliverance from Egypt.* VI. *Its compass of meaning.*

§ I.

That the formal observance of the Sabbath day originated in the Law of Moses appears to have been the opinion of Philo and of most of the Fathers and Rabbinists[6], and is held by many modern critics[7]. But see note on Gen. ii. 3.

In what way was the Sabbath day to be kept holy in accordance with the Fourth Commandment? It is expressly said that the ordinary work of life should be intermitted by the whole community, not only the masters, servants, and foreign residents[8], but also the cattle; and the period of this intermission

---

[1] See Note on ch. xxv. 17.
[2] See Note at the end of ch. xl. § III.
[3] Philo seems to have been impressed with this when he lays an emphasis on the fact that the Ten Commandments were given by Him who was *the Father of the Universe* (ὁ πατὴρ τῶν ὅλων), *the God of the World* (Θεός κόσμου), 'de decem Orac.' 9, 10.
[4] "It was the boast of Josephus ('Cont. Ap.' II. 17), that whereas other legislators had made religion to be a part of virtue, Moses had made virtue to be a part of religion." Stanley, 'Jewish Church,' Vol. I. 175.
[5] See Note 'On the Sabbath day,' § IV.
[6] Philo, 'de Orac.' c. 20. Justin Martyr, 'Dialog. cum Tryph.' § 19. Irenæus, IV. 16. Tertullian, 'Adv. Jud.' 2, 4. Otho, 'Rabb. Lex.' p. 603.
[7] See Hengst. 'On the Lord's Day,' p. 7; Ewald, 'Alterthüm.' p. 3; 'Hist. of Israel,' I. 576. Hessey, 'Sunday,' Lect. IV., &c. On the word *Remember* in Ex. xx. 8, see note.
[8] See on Ex. xx. 10.

was from the evening of the sixth day of the week to the evening of the seventh[1]. The following occupations are expressly mentioned as unlawful in different parts of the Old Testament; sowing and reaping (Ex. xxxiv. 21), pressing grapes, and bearing burdens of all kinds (Neh. xiii. 15; Jer. xvii. 21), holding of markets and all kinds of trade (Neh. xiii. 15; Amos viii. 5), gathering wood, and kindling a fire for cooking (Ex. xxxv. 3; Num. xv. 32). The Sabbath was to be a day of enjoyment like other festivals (Isa. lviii. 13; Hos. ii. 11), and such restrictions as were imposed could have been unacceptable to none but the disobedient and the avaricious, such as are spoken of in Amos viii. 5, 6.

In the service of the Sanctuary, the Morning and Evening Sacrifices were doubled[2], the Shewbread was changed[3], and, after the courses of the Priests and Levites had been instituted by David, each course in its turn commenced its duties on the Sabbath day[4]. When the Temple was built, there is reason to believe that there was a special musical service for the day[5].

The term *Holy Convocation*, which belongs to the Sabbath day in common with certain other Festival days, would seem to imply that there was a meeting together of the people for a religious purpose[6]. From the mode in which the commands to keep the Sabbath day and to reverence the Sanctuary are associated, it may be inferred with probability that there was such a meeting in the Court of the Sanctuary[7]. At later periods, in places remote from the Temple, we know that it was a custom to resort on this day to public teachers, and to hear the reading of the Old Testament, with addresses of exposition and exhortation, in the Synagogues[8]. It is not unreasonable to suppose that some usage of this kind may have been observed at the Sanctuary itself from the first institution of the Sabbath[9].

[1] See Lev. xxiii. 32.
[2] Num. xxviii. 9; 2 Chro. xxxi. 3; Ezek. xlvi. 4.
[3] Lev. xxiv. 8; 1 Chro. ix. 32; Matt. xii. 4, &c.
[4] 2 K. xi. 5; 2 Chro. xxiii. 4; cf. 1 Chro. ix. 25.
[5] This is favoured by a comparison of the heading of Ps. lxxxi. with v. 3 of the Psalm itself, as well as by the Talmud.
[6] Lev. xxiii. 2, 3.
[7] Lev. xix. 30; Ezek. xxiii. 38.
[8] 2 K. iv. 23; Luke iv. 15, 16; Acts xiii. 14, 15, 27. xv. 21.
[9] There may be references to such a custom Lev. x. 11; Deut. xxxiii. 10. The earliest and best Jewish traditions state that one great object of the Sabbath day was to furnish means and opportunity for spiritual edification. Philo, 'de Orac.' c. 20. 'Vit. Mos.' III. 27. Jos. 'Ant.' XVI. 2. § 3. 'Cont. Ap.' I. 20, II. 18. For rabbinical authorities to the same effect, see Cartwright on Ex. xx. 8, in the 'Critici Sacri.'

Such are the particulars that can be gathered out of the Scriptures as to the mode of observing the Sabbath day. In the time of the Legislator an entire rest from the work of daily life was to reign throughout the Camp: and it may be conjectured that the people assembled before the Altar at the hours of the Morning and Evening Sacrifices for prayer and contemplation, and to listen to the reading of portions of the Divine Law, perhaps from the lips of Moses himself.

The notices of the Sabbath day in the Prophets are most frequently accompanied by complaint or warning respecting its neglect and desecration[10]. But in the time of Isaiah (i. 13) a parade of observing it had become a cloak for hypocrisy, probably under a kindred influence to that which turned the public fasts into occasions for strife and debate (Isa. lviii. 4). These diverse abuses may have co-existed as belonging to two opposite parties in the community, both being in the wrong.

§ II.

In another age, after the Captivity, the Pharisees multiplied the restraints of the Sabbath day to a most burdensome extent. It was forbidden to pluck an ear of corn and rub out the grains to satisfy hunger in passing through a cornfield (Matt. xii. 2); or to relieve the sick (Matt. xii. 10; Luke xiii. 14). It was however permitted to lead an ox or an ass to water, or to lift out an animal that had fallen into a pit (Matt. xii. 11; Luke xiv. 5), to administer circumcision, if the eighth day after the birth of a child fell on a Sabbath (Joh. vii. 22), and to invite guests to a social meal (Luke xiv. 1). According to rabbinical authorities, it was forbidden to travel more than 2000 cubits on the Sabbath[11], to kill the most offensive kinds of vermin, to write two letters of the alphabet, to use a wooden leg or a crutch, to carry a purse, or, for a woman, to carry a seal-ring or a smelling bottle, to wear a high head-dress or a false tooth. Amongst other restraints laid upon animals, the fat-tailed sheep was not allowed to use the little truck on which the tail was borne to save the animal from suffering. These are a portion of 39 prohibitions of the same kind[12].

[10] Is. lvi. 2—6, lviii. 13; Jer. xvii. 21, 27; Ezek. xx. 13, 16, 20; Amos viii. 5, &c.
[11] On the Sabbath-day's journey, see Joseph. 'Ant.' XIII. 8. § 4 with the Note on Ex. xvi. 29: also Walther, 'de Itin. Sabb.' in 'Thes. Philolog.' II. p. 417. Winer, 'R. B.' s. 'Sabbathsweg.'
[12] Mishna, 'de Sabbatho.' We are told by a eulogist of the Talmud that the rabbinical Sabbath was not "a thing of grim austerity" ('Quarterly Rev.' Dec. 1867.) Its austerity was indeed somewhat mitigated by qualifying regulations. Though the Jew could not light a fire on the Sabbath, he was formally permitted, at the latest moment of the eve of the Sabbath, to pack

Connected with this trifling of the Pharisees and the Rabbinists, is the notion that the intention of the Law was, that the Sabbath should be, as nearly as possible, a day of mere inaction. This has been held not only by Jewish writers[1], but by some Christians in the time of S. Chrysostom[2], and by critics of more modern date (Spencer, Vitringa, Le Clerc). Our Lord decides this very point by declaring that there is a kind of work which is proper for the Sabbath day[3]. See the next section.

§ III.

In examining the two distinct grounds for the observance of the Sabbath day which are assigned by Moses[4], the first step is to trace the nature of the connection between the Day and the Creation of the world. What is clearly stated is, that the Day was hallowed by the Divine Law as a memorial of the rest of God when the Creation of the world was completed[5]. Man was to rest because God had rested. But the rest of man can only partially resemble the rest of God. "The Creator of the ends of the earth fainteth not, neither is weary[6]." His work in the world did not cease at the close of the six days, nor has it ever been remitted since[7]. His hand must be ever holding the corners of the earth and the strength of the hills[8]. His rest cannot therefore be like that inaction which belongs to night and sleep, which man, in common with all animals, requires for the restoration of his wasted powers. But yet a man may have conscious experience, after well performed work, of a restful condition that bears an analogy to the occasion on which "God saw every thing that He had made, and, behold, it was very good[9]." And this Sabbath feeling is only to be enjoyed by those whose work, performed in a spirit of trustful dependence, has kept pace with the day during the week; those who obey not only the command, "Remember the Sabbath day," but also the command, "Six days shalt thou labour[10]."

up hot food in such a way as to keep it hot as long as possible ('de Sabb.' IV. 1. 2). Under particular conditions, the sick might be relieved (Mish. 'Joma,' VIII. 6). Fasting on the Sabbath was strictly prohibited (Otho, 'Rab. Lex.' p. 608; cf. Judith viii. 6). Whether or not a Sabbath regulated by rabbinical rules was, on the whole, grimly austere, we need not scruple to call the rules themselves grossly absurd.

[1] Buxtorf. 'Synag. Jud.' CXVI.
[2] 'Hom. in Matt.' XXXI.
[3] Matt. xii. 12; Mark iii. 4, &c.
[4] See Ex. xx. 11; Deut. v. 15; Note 'On the Ten Commandments,' § II.
[5] Ex. xx. 11, xxxi. 17. Cf. Gen. ii. 3.
[6] Is. xl. 28.
[7] See John v. 17.
[8] Ps. xcv. 4, 5.
[9] Gen. i. 31.
[10] Moses (says Philo) ἐκέλευσεν τοὺς μέλλοντας

The true rest of man then is so far like the rest of the Creator, that it is remote in its nature from the sleep of insensibility as it is from the ordinary struggle of the world. The weekly Sabbath, as representing that state, was "a shadow of things to come[11]," a foretaste of the life in which there is to be no more *toilsome fatigue* (πόνος[12]), that life which is the true *keeping of Sabbath* (σαββατισμός) into which our Saviour entered as our forerunner when He ceased from His works on earth, as God had ceased from His works on the seventh day (Heb. iv. 9, 10).

The works of the Creation are described as culminating in the creation of man. The Sabbath crowned the completed works, and as it was revealed to the Israelite, it reminded him of "the fact of his relation to God, of his being made in the image of God; it was to teach him to regard the universe not chiefly as under the government of sun or moon, or as regulated by their courses; but as an order which the unseen God had created, which included Sun, Moon, Stars, Earth, and all the living creatures that inhabit them. The week, then, was especially to raise the Jew above the thought of Time, to make him feel that though he was subject to *its* laws, he yet stood in direct connection with an *eternal* law; with a Being who is, and was, and is to come[13]." Philo aptly calls the day *the imaging forth* (ἐκμαγεῖον) *of the first beginning*. Some of the wisest Jewish teachers (Aben-Ezra, Abarbanel) have said that he who breaks the Sabbath denies the Creation. The Sabbath, in this connection, became to the Israelite the central point of religious observance, and represented every appropriation of time to the public recognition of Jehovah. Hence the injunction to observe it appears to be essentially connected with the warning against idolatry[14].

§ IV.

But this great idea did not exclusively belong to the Israelite, although it was revealed to him, above all men, in its true relation to God and man. Real worship for every man, always and everywhere, is of course based on the truth of a Creator distinct from the Creation. And thus the Law of the Sabbath was the expression of a universal truth. Hence, the Commandment bears its meaning for all mankind. The day which we observe, in accordance with ecclesiastical usage, holds another place in the week, and its connection with

ἐν ταύτῃ ζῆν τῇ πολιτείᾳ, καθάπερ ἐν τοῖς ἄλλοις, καὶ κατὰ τοῦθ' ἕπεσθαι θεῷ, πρὸς μὲν ἔργα τρεπομένους ἐφ' ἡμέρας ἕξ, ἀνέχοντας δὲ καὶ φιλοσοφοῦντας τῇ ἑβδόμῃ καὶ θεωρίαις μὲν τῶν τῆς φύσεως σχολάζοντας, κ.τ.λ. 'de decem Orac.' c. 20.
[11] Col. ii. 16, 17.
[12] Cf. Rev. xiv. 13.
[13] Maurice 'On the Old Testament,' Serm. I.
[14] See Lev. xix. 3. 4; Ezek. xx. 16, 20.

the Creation of the world has thus been put into the background. But the meaning of the Lord's day cannot be separated from the great meaning of the Sabbath. As the Sabbath reminded the believer under the Old Covenant that God had rested after He had created man and breathed into him the breath of life before sin had brought death into the world, so the Sunday now reminds the believer that Christ rested after He had overcome death, that he might restore all who believe in Him to a new life, that they may become the sons of God by adoption[1]. What therefore the Sunday, as a commemoration of the Resurrection, is to the dispensation of Christ, the Sabbath, in respect to its connection with the rest of God, was to the dispention of Moses. On this ground then there is reason enough why the Fourth, as well as the other Commandments, should be addressed to Christian congregations and should hold its place in our Service.

§ V.

It was at a later period that the inspired Legislator set forth a second ground on which obedience to the Commandment was required. It was said to the Israelite that he should observe the Day in order that his manservant and his maidservant might rest as well as he; and the words were added; "and remember that thou wast a servant in the land of Egypt, and that the LORD thy God brought thee out thence through a mighty hand and a stretched out arm: therefore the LORD thy God commanded thee to keep the Sabbath day[2]." By the command that the manservants and the maidservants were to rest on the Day as well as their masters, witness was borne to the equal position which every Israelite might claim in the presence of Jehovah. The Sabbath was thus made a distinguishing badge, a sacramental bond, for the whole people, according to the words, "it is a sign between me and you throughout your generations; that ye may know that I am the LORD that doth sanctify you[3]." The wealthy Israelite, in remembrance of what he himself, or his forefathers, had suffered in Egypt, was to realize the fact on this Day that the poorest of his brethren had enjoyed the same deliverances, and had the same share in the Covenant, as himself. The whole nation, as one man, was to enjoy rest. He who outraged the Sabbath, either by working himself, or by suffering his servants to work, broke the Covenant with Jehovah, and at the same time cut himself off from his people so as to incur the sentence of death[4].

This latter ground for the observance of the Sabbath day furnishes a not less strict analogy with the Sunday than that which has been noticed. What the Sabbath was to "the kingdom of priests, the holy nation[5]," on the score that they had been redeemed from the bondage of Egypt and made free men, such the Sunday is to "the chosen generation, the royal priesthood, the holy nation, the peculiar people[6]," as those whom Christ has redeemed from the bondage of corruption, and brought into the glorious liberty of the children of God[7].

§ VI.

In order rightly to apprehend the compass of the Fourth Commandment in reference to the public worship of the Israelites, it should be kept in view that the Sabbath did not stand by itself, as an insulated observance. Not only did the original ground of the Weekly Sabbath connect it with all true worship, but it formed the centre of an organized system including the Sabbatical year, and the Jubilee year[8]. Besides this, the recurrence of the Sabbatical number in the cycle of yearly festivals is so frequent and distinct, as plainly to indicate a set purpose. Without laying stress on the mystical meaning of the number *seven*, as Philo, Bähr, and others have done, it is evident that the number was the Divinely appointed symbol, repeated again and again in the public services, suggesting the connection between the entire range of the Ceremonial Law and the consecrated Seventh Day. And this may be compared with the important remark of Bähr, that the ritual of the Sabbath day, in spite of the superlative sanctity of the Day, was not, like that of other Festivals, distinguished by offerings or rites of a peculiar kind, but only by a doubling of the common daily sacrifices. It was thus not so much cut off from the Week as marked out as *the Day of Days*, and so symbolized the sanctification of the daily life of the people. In whichever way we regard it, the Fourth Commandment appears to have stood to the Israelite as an injunction in the broadest sense to maintain the national Worship of Jehovah.

---

[1] Rom. iv. 25, vi. 4, viii. 13, 15.
[2] Deut. v. 14, 15.
[3] Ex. xxxi. 13, 17; cf. Lev. xx. 8; Is. lvi. 2, 4; Ezek. xx. 12. 20, xxii. 8, 26.
[4] Ex. xxxi. 14, 15—xxxv. 2; Jer. xvii. 21—27.
[5] Ex. xix. 6.
[6] 1 Pet. ii. 9.
[7] Rom. viii. 21.
[8] Lev. xxv.

22 ¶ And the LORD said unto Moses, Thus thou shalt say unto the children of Israel, Ye have seen that I have talked with you from heaven.

23 Ye shall not make with me gods of silver, neither shall ye make unto you gods of gold.

24 ¶ An altar of earth thou shalt make unto me, and shalt sacrifice thereon thy burnt offerings, and thy peace offerings, thy sheep, and thine oxen: in all places where I record my name I will come unto thee, and I will bless thee.

l Deut. 27. 5.
Josh. 8. 31.
† Heb. *build them with hewing.*

25 And *l* if thou wilt make me an altar of stone, thou shalt not † build it of hewn stone: for if thou lift up thy tool upon it, thou hast polluted it.

26 Neither shalt thou go up by steps unto mine altar, that thy nakedness be not discovered thereon.

CHAPTER XXI.

1 *Laws for menservants.* 5 *For the servant whose ear is bored.* 7 *For womenservants.* 12 *For manslaughter.* 16 *For stealers of men.* 17 *For cursers of parents.* 18 *For smiters.* 22 *For a hurt by chance.* 28 *For an ox that goeth.* 33 *For him that is an occasion of harm.*

NOW these *are* the judgments which thou shalt set before them.

THE BOOK OF THE COVENANT.
Ch. xx. 22—xxiii. 33.
Introductory Note.

Now follows a series of laws, some of them addressed simply to the conscience, like the Ten Commandments, and others having the sanction of a penalty attached. The context seems to make it clear that we may identify this series with what was written by Moses in the book called the BOOK OF THE COVENANT, and read by him in the audience of the people (see xxiv. 4, 7). There has been a difference of opinion as to the compass of matter contained in this Book. But the weight of authority is in favour of its comprising the last five verses of ch. xx. with chaps. xxi, xxii, xxiii (de Wette, Ewald, Hupfeld, Knobel, Keil, Herxheimer, &c.). A few would add the Ten Commandments (Hengst., Kurtz, &c.). Some Jewish Commentators imagine that the BOOK OF THE COVENANT included very considerable portions of Genesis and of the earlier part of Exodus.

Adopting the conclusion as by far the most probable one, that the Book of the Covenant included from ch. xx. 22 to xxiii. 33, it is evident that the document cannot be regarded as a strictly systematic whole. Portions of it were probably traditional rules handed down from the Patriarchs, and retained by the Israelites in Egypt. Probable traces of præ-Mosaic antiquity may be seen in xx. 24—26, xxi. 6, xxiii. 19, &c. Some of the laws relate to habits of fixed abode, not (at least if taken in their strict form) to such a mode of life as that of the Israelites in their march through the Wilderness (see xxii. 5, 6, 29, xxiii. 10, 11): some, especially those relating to slavery, would seem to have been modifications of ancient usages (see on xxi. 20, 21). These more or less ancient maxims may have been associated with notes of such decisions on cases of difference as had been up to this time pronounced by Moses and the judges whom he had appointed by the advice of Jethro. See xviii. 13—26.

In whatever way these laws may have originated, as they are here brought together, they are clearly enforced by Jehovah as conditions of conduct for the covenanted people. The adoption of Patriarchal maxims accords with the spirit of the Mosaic legislation, as expressed in the Fifth Commandment.

CHAP. XX. 22—26. Nothing could be more appropriate as the commencement of the Book of the Covenant than these regulations for public worship.

23. Assuming this to be an old formula, its meaning is brought out more comprehensively in the Second Commandment, and is strengthened by the fact declared in *v.* 22, that Jehovah had now spoken from Heaven.

24—26. These must have been old and accepted rules for the building of altars, and they are not inconsistent with the directions for the construction of the Altar of the Court of the Tabernacle, ch. xxvii. 1—8. There is no good reason to doubt that they were observed in "the Brazen Altar," as it is called, although no reference is made to them in connection with it. That Altar, according to the directions that are given, must indeed have been rather *an altar case*, with a mass of earth or stone within, when it was put to use. See notes on xxvii. 1—8, and cf. Josh. xxii. 26—28.

CHAP. XXI. The Book of the Covenant, continued.

1. *judgments*] *i.e.* decisions of the Law. It is worthy of remark that these judgments

344 EXODUS. XXI. [v. 2—11.

^a Lev. 25. 41. Deut. 15. 12. Jer. 34. 14.

2 ^aIf thou buy an Hebrew servant, six years he shall serve: and in the seventh he shall go out free for nothing.

3 If he came in †by himself, he shall go out by himself: if he were married, then his wife shall go out with him.

† Heb. *with his body.*

4 If his master have given him a wife, and she have born him sons or daughters; the wife and her children shall be her master's, and he shall go out by himself.

† Heb. *saying shall say.*

5 And if the servant †shall plainly say, I love my master, my wife, and my children; I will not go out free:

6 Then his master shall bring him unto the judges; he shall also bring him to the door, or unto the door post; and his master shall bore his ear through with an aul; and he shall serve him for ever.

7 ¶ And if a man sell his daughter to be a maidservant, she shall not go out as the menservants do.

8 If she †please not her master, who hath betrothed her to himself, then shall he let her be redeemed: to sell her unto a strange nation he shall have no power, seeing he hath dealt deceitfully with her.

† Heb. *be evil in the eyes of, &c.*

9 And if he have betrothed her unto his son, he shall deal with her after the manner of daughters.

10 If he take him another *wife*, her food, her raiment, and her duty of marriage, shall he not diminish.

11 And if he do not these three unto her, then shall she go out free without money.

---

begin with some that relate to slavery (*vv.* 2—16); other judgments on the same subject occur in *vv.* 20, 21, 26, 27.

2. A Hebrew might be sold as a bondman in consequence either of debt (Lev. xxv. 39) or of the commission of theft (Ex. xxii. 3). But his servitude could not be enforced for more than six full years. The law is more fully expressed in Deut. xv. 12—18, where it enjoins that the bondman should not be sent away at the end of his period of service without a liberal supply of provisions; and it is further supplemented by other regulations, especially in reference to the Jubilee, in Lev. xxv. 39—43, 47—55. Foreign slaves are expressly spoken of Lev. xxv. 44, 46.

3. If a married man became a bondman, his rights in regard to his wife were respected: but if a single bondman accepted at the hand of his master a bondwoman as his wife, the master did not lose his claim to the woman, or her children, at the expiration of the husband's term of service. Such wives, it may be presumed, were always foreign slaves.

5, 6. But if the bondman loved his wife so as to be unwilling to give her up, or if he was strongly enough attached to his master's service, he might, by submitting to a certain ceremony, prolong his term "for ever;" that is, most probably, till the next Jubilee, when every Hebrew was set free. So Josephus ('Ant.' IV. 8, § 28) and the Rabbinists understood the phrase. See Lev. xxv. 40, 50. The custom of boring the ear as a mark of slavery appears to have been a common one in ancient times, observed in many nations. See Xenoph. 'Anab.' III. 1, § 31; Plaut. 'Pœnul.' v. ii. 21; Juvenal, I. 104; Plut. 'Cicero,' c. 26, &c.

6. *unto the judges*] Literally, *before the gods* (*elohim*). The word does not denote *judges* in a direct way, but it is to be understood as the name of God, in its ordinary plural form, God being the source of all justice. (So Gesen., de Wette, Knobel, Fürst, Herxh., &c.) LXX. πρὸς τὸ κριτήριον τοῦ Θεοῦ. The name in this connection always has the definite article prefixed. See xxii. 8, 9, &c.

7. A man might, in accordance with existing custom, sell his daughter to another man with a view to her becoming an inferior wife, or concubine. In this case, she was not "to go out," like the bondman; that is, she was not to be dismissed at the end of the sixth year. But women who were bound in any other way, would appear to have been under the same conditions as bondmen. See Deut. xv. 17.

8. *shall he let her be redeemed*] More strictly, **he shall cause her to be redeemed**. The meaning seems to be that he should either return her to her father as set free, or find another Hebrew master for her who would grant her the same privileges as she would have had if she had remained with himself. The latter sentence of the verse appears to signify that, although he was not forced to keep literal faith with the woman by making her his concubine, he was not permitted to sell her to a foreigner. Even in the case of a foreign captive who had been accepted as a concubine, and had displeased her master, she could not be sold as a slave,

12 ¶ ᵇHe that smiteth a man, so that he die, shall be surely put to death.

13 And if a man lie not in wait, but God deliver *him* into his hand; then ᶜI will appoint thee a place whither he shall flee.

14 But if a man come presumptuously upon his neighbour, to slay him with guile; thou shalt take him from mine altar, that he may die.

15 ¶ And he that smiteth his father, or his mother, shall be surely put to death.

16 ¶ And he that stealeth a man, and selleth him, or if he be found in his hand, he shall surely be put to death.

17 ¶ And ᵈhe that ǁcurseth his father, or his mother, shall surely be put to death.

18 ¶ And if men strive together, and one smite ǁanother with a stone, or with *his* fist, and he die not, but keepeth *his* bed:

19 If he rise again, and walk abroad upon his staff, then shall he that smote *him* be quit: only he shall pay *for* †the loss of his time, and shall cause *him* to be thoroughly healed.

20 ¶ And if a man smite his servant, or his maid, with a rod, and he die under his hand; he shall be surely †punished.

Marginal notes:
ᵇ Lev. 24. 17.
ᶜ Deut. 19. 3.
ᵈ Lev. 20. 9. Prov. 20. 20. Matt. 15. 4. Mark 7. 10.
ǁ Or, *revileth.*
ǁ Or, *his neighbour.*
† Heb. *[his] ceasing.*
† Heb. *avenged.*

---

but was entitled to her freedom. See Deut. xxi. 14.

11. *if he do not these three unto her*] Most commentators refer these three things to the food, raiment, and duty of marriage, mentioned in *v.* 10. But Knobel and others prefer the interpretation of most of the Rabbinists, which seems on the whole best to suit the context, that the words express a choice of one of three things, in which case their sense is, *if he do neither of these three things*. The man was to give the woman, whom he had purchased from her father, her freedom, unless (i) he caused her to be redeemed by a Hebrew master (*v.* 8); or, (ii) gave her to his son, and treated her as a daughter (*v.* 9); or, (iii) in the event of his taking another wife (*v.* 10), unless he allowed her to retain her place and privileges. These rules (*vv.* 7—11) are to be regarded as mitigations of the then existing usages of concubinage. The form in which they are expressed confirms this view.

12. No distinction is expressly made here or elsewhere between the murder of a free man and that of a bondman. See on *v.* 20. The law was afterwards expressly declared to relate also to foreigners, Lev. xxiv. 17, 21, 22; cf. Gen. ix. 6.

13, 14. There was no place of safety for the guilty murderer, not even the Altar of Jehovah. Thus all superstitious notions connected with the right of sanctuary were excluded. Adonijah and Joab appear to have vainly trusted that the vulgar feeling would protect them, if they took hold of the horns of the Altar on which atonement with blood was made (1 K. i. 50, ii. 28; Lev. iv. 7). But for one who killed a man "at unawares," that is, without intending to do it, the Law afterwards appointed places of refuge, Num. xxxv. 6—34; Deut. iv. 41—43, xix. 2—10; Josh. xx. 2—9. It is very probable that there was some provision answering to the Cities of Refuge, that may have been based upon old usage, in the Camp in the Wilderness.

15, 16, 17. The following offences were to be punished with death:—

Striking a parent, cf. Deut. xxvii. 16.
Cursing a parent, cf. Lev. xx. 9.
Kidnapping, whether with a view to retain the person stolen, or to sell him, cf. Deut. xxiv. 7.

18, 19. If one man injured another in a quarrel so as to oblige him to keep his bed, he who had inflicted the injury was set free from the liability to a criminal charge (such as might be based upon *v.* 12) when the injured man had so far recovered as to be able to walk with a staff: but he was required to compensate the latter for the loss of his time until his recovery was complete, and for the cost of his healing.

20, 21. The Jewish authorities appear to be right in referring this law, like those in *vv.* 26, 27, 32, to foreign slaves (see Lev. xxv. 44—46). All Hebrew bondmen were treated, in regard to life and limb, like freemen, and the Law would take this for granted. The master was permitted to retain the power of chastising his alien slave with a rod, but the indulgence of unbridled temper was so far kept in check by his incurring punishment if the slave died under his hand. If however the slave survived the castigation a day or two, it was assumed that the offence of the master had not been so heinous, and he did not become amenable to the law, because the loss of the slave who, by old custom, was recognized as his property, was accounted, under the circumstances, as a punish-

21 Notwithstanding, if he continue a day or two, he shall not be punished: for he *is* his money.

22 ¶ If men strive, and hurt a woman with child, so that her fruit depart *from her*, and yet no mischief follow: he shall be surely punished, according as the woman's husband will lay upon him; and he shall pay as the judges *determine*.

23 And if *any* mischief follow, then thou shalt give life for life,

24 *ᵉ* Eye for eye, tooth for tooth, hand for hand, foot for foot,

25 Burning for burning, wound for wound, stripe for stripe.

26 ¶ And if a man smite the eye of his servant, or the eye of his maid, that it perish; he shall let him go free for his eye's sake.

27 And if he smite out his manservant's tooth, or his maidservant's tooth; he shall let him go free for his tooth's sake.

28 ¶ If an ox gore a man or a woman, that they die: then *ᶠ* the ox shall be surely stoned, and his flesh shall not be eaten; but the owner of the ox *shall be* quit.

29 But if the ox were wont to push with his horn in time past, and it hath been testified to his owner, and he hath not kept him in, but that he hath killed a man or a woman; the ox shall be stoned, and his owner also shall be put to death.

30 If there be laid on him a sum of money, then he shall give for the ransom of his life whatsoever is laid upon him.

31 Whether he have gored a son, or have gored a daughter, according to this judgment shall it be done unto him.

ᵉ Lev. 24. 20. Deut. 19. 21. Matt. 5. 38.

ᶠ Gen. 9. 5

---

ment. It is not said how the master was to be treated in the event of the immediate death of the slave. It may have been left to the decision of the judges as to whether the case should come under the law of *v*. 12, or some secondary punishment should be inflicted.—The protection here afforded to the life of a slave may seem to us but a slight one; but it is the very earliest trace of such protection in legislation, and it stands in strong and favourable contrast with the old laws of Greece, Rome, and other nations. The same may be said of *vv*. 26, 27, 32. These regulations were most likely, as much as was feasible at the time, to mitigate the cruelty of ancient practice; they were as much as the hardness of the hearts of the people would bear, Matt. xix. 8. See Mr Goldwin Smith's admirable essay, "Does the Bible sanction American Slavery?"

22—25. The sense is rather obscure. The rule would seem to refer to a case in which the wife of a man engaged in a quarrel interfered. If the violence did no more than occasion premature birth, he who inflicted it was punished by a fine to be proposed by the husband, and approved by the magistrates. But if the injury was more serious, so as to affect life or limb, a penalty was to be inflicted in accordance with the law of suffering like for like, the *jus talionis*.—This law is repeated in substance, Lev. xxiv. 19, 20, 21; Deut. xix. 21; cp. Gen. ix. 6. It has its root in a simple conception of justice, and is found in the laws of many ancient nations. It was ascribed to Rhadamanthus (Arist. 'Ethic.' v. 5). It was recognized in the laws of Solon (Diog. Laert. I. 57), in the Laws of the Twelve Tables (Aul. Gell. x. 1; Festus, s. *talio*), by the ancient Indians (Strab. xv. p. 710), and by the Thurians (Diod. Sic. xII. 17). It appears to be regarded in this place as a maxim for the magistrate in awarding the amount of compensation to be paid for the infliction of personal injury. The sum was to be as nearly as possible the worth in money of the power lost by the injured person. This view appears to be in accordance with Jewish tradition (Mishna, 'Baba Kama,' VIII. 1). Michaelis has some good remarks on the *jus talionis* ('Laws of Moses,' Vol. III. p. 448).— Our Lord quotes *v*. 24 as representing the form of the Law, in order to illustrate the distinction between the Letter and the Spirit (Matt. v. 38). The tendency of the teaching of the Scribes and Pharisees was to confound the obligations of the conscience with the external requirements of the Law. The Law, in its place, was still to be "holy and just and good," but its direct purpose was to protect the community, not to guide the heart of the believer, who was not to exact eye for eye, tooth for tooth, but to love his enemies, and to forgive all injuries.

26, 27. When a master inflicted a permanent injury on the person of his bondservant, freedom was the proper equivalent for the disabled or lost member.

28—31. If an ox killed a person, the animal was slain as a tribute to the sanctity of human life (Gen. ix. 6; cf. Gen. iv. 11). It

32 If the ox shall push a manservant or a maidservant; he shall give unto their master thirty shekels of silver, and the ox shall be stoned.

33 ¶ And if a man shall open a pit, or if a man shall dig a pit, and not cover it, and an ox or an ass fall therein;

34 The owner of the pit shall make *it* good, *and* give money unto the owner of them; and the dead *beast* shall be his.

35 ¶ And if one man's ox hurt another's, that he die; then they shall sell the live ox, and divide the money of it; and the dead *ox* also they shall divide.

36 Or if it be known that the ox hath used to push in time past, and his owner hath not kept him in; he shall surely pay ox for ox; and the dead shall be his own.

CHAPTER XXII.

1 *Of theft.* 5 *Of damage.* 7 *Of trespasses.* 14 *Of borrowing.* 16 *Of fornication.* 18 *Of witchcraft.* 19 *Of beastiality.* 20 *Of idolatry.* 21 *Of strangers, widows, and fatherless.* 25 *Of usury.* 26 *Of pledges.* 28 *Of reverence to magistrates.* 29 *Of the firstfruits.*

IF a man shall steal an ox, or a ‖ sheep, and kill it, or sell it; he shall restore five oxen for an ox, and ^a four sheep for a sheep.

‖ Or, *goat.*

^a 2 Sam. 12. 6.

2 ¶ If a thief be found breaking up, and be smitten that he die, *there shall* no blood *be shed* for him.

3 If the sun be risen upon him, *there shall be* blood *shed* for him; *for* he should make full restitution; if he have nothing, then he shall be sold for his theft.

4 If the theft be certainly found in his hand alive, whether it be ox, or ass, or sheep; he shall restore double.

---

was stoned, and its flesh was treated as carrion. In ordinary cases, the owner suffered only the loss of his beast. But if the ox had been previously known to be vicious, the guilty negligence of its owner, in not keeping it under restraint, was reckoned, *prima facie*, as a capital offence. His life might however be commuted for a fine to be determined by the judges; and, as we may infer with probability, to be agreed to by the parents or near relations of the slain person.

32. If the slain person was a slave, the ox was to be stoned to death, and its owner was to pay to the master of the slain person what appears to have been the standard price of a slave, thirty shekels of silver. See on Lev. xxv. 44—46, xxvii. 3.

33, 34. If a man either left his pit (or well) exposed, or dug a new one without protecting it, and an animal fell therein, he was to pay the value of the animal to its owner, but was allowed to appropriate the carcase. The usual mode of protecting a well was probably then, as it is now in the East, by building round it a low circular wall.

35, 36. The dead ox in this case, as well as in the preceding one, must have been worth no more than the price of the hide, as the flesh could not be eaten. See Lev. xvii. 1—6. There is here the same sort of prudent restraint laid upon the owners of vicious animals as in *v.* 29.

CHAP. XXII. **The Book of the Covenant,** continued.

1. The theft of an ox appears to have been regarded as a greater crime than the theft of a sheep, not from the mere consideration of value, but because it shewed a stronger purpose in wickedness to take the larger and more powerful animal. It may have been on similar moral ground that the thief, when he had proved his persistency in crime by adding to his theft the slaughter, or sale, of the animal, was to restore four times its value in the case of a sheep (cf. 2 S. xii. 6), and five times its value in the case of an ox; but if the animal was still in his possession alive (see *v.* 4) he had to make only twofold restitution.

2. *breaking up*] **breaking in.**

3, 4. If a thief, in breaking into a dwelling in the night, was slain, the person who slew him did not incur the guilt of blood; but if the same occurred in daylight, the slayer was guilty in accordance with xxi. 12. The distinction may have been based on the fact that in the light of day there was a fair chance of identifying and apprehending the thief, or, at least, his design would be apparent: but in the darkness of night there could be no reckoning as to how far his purpose might extend, and there would be a great probability of his escaping unrecognized. When a thief was apprehended in the act, he could be forced to make restitution if he had the means, and if not he was to be sold as a bondslave. The latter punishment may be likened to our penal servitude; and, in the case of a Hebrew, it could not be prolonged beyond six years See xxi. 2.

5 ¶ If a man shall cause a field or vineyard to be eaten, and shall put in his beast, and shall feed in another man's field; of the best of his own field, and of the best of his own vineyard, shall he make restitution.

6 ¶ If fire break out, and catch in thorns, so that the stacks of corn, or the standing corn, or the field, be consumed *therewith;* he that kindled the fire shall surely make restitution.

7 ¶ If a man shall deliver unto his neighbour money or stuff to keep, and it be stolen out of the man's house; if the thief be found, let him pay double.

8 If the thief be not found, then the master of the house shall be brought unto the judges, *to see* whether he have put his hand unto his neighbour's goods.

9 For all manner of trespass, *whether it be* for ox, for ass, for sheep, for raiment, *or* for any manner of lost thing, which *another* challengeth to be his, the cause of both parties shall come before the judges; *and* whom the judges shall condemn, he shall pay double unto his neighbour.

10 If a man deliver unto his neighbour an ass, or an ox, or a sheep, or any beast, to keep; and it die, or be hurt, or driven away, no man seeing *it:*

11 *Then* shall an oath of the LORD be between them both, that he hath not put his hand unto his neighbour's goods; and the owner of it shall accept *thereof,* and he shall not make *it* good.

12 And *b* if it be stolen from him, he shall make restitution unto the owner thereof.

b Gen. 31. 39.

13 If it be torn in pieces, *then* let him bring it *for* witness, *and* he shall not make good that which was torn.

14 ¶ And if a man borrow *ought* of his neighbour, and it be hurt, or die, the owner thereof *being* not with it, he shall surely make *it* good.

15 *But* if the owner thereof *be* with it, he shall not make *it* good: if it *be* an hired *thing,* it came for his hire.

16 ¶ And *c* if a man entice a maid that is not betrothed, and lie with her, he shall surely endow her to be his wife.

c Deut. 22. 28.

17 If her father utterly refuse to give her unto him, he shall † pay money according to the dowry of virgins.

† Heb. *weigh.*

---

4. See on *v.* 1.

5. *shall put in his beast, and shall feed*] Rather, **shall let his beast go loose, and it shall feed**. (Thus the LXX., Vulg., Syr., Luther, Zunz, &c.) He who had allowed his beast to stray and consume the pasture or the grapes of his neighbour, had to restore out of the best of his possessions a like quantity of produce, without regard to the quality of that which had been consumed.

7. *pay double*] Cf. *v.* 4.

8. It would appear that if the master of the house could clear himself of imputation, the loss of the pledged article fell upon its owner.

judges] See on xxi. 6.

9. *all manner of trespass*] In every case of theft, he who was accused, and he who had lost the stolen property, were both to appear before the judges (xviii. 25, 26): the convicted thief, under ordinary circumstances, was to pay double. See *vv.* 4, 7.

10—13. This law appears to relate chiefly to herdsmen employed by the owners of cattle. It implies that, if he to whom the creatures were entrusted could prove that he had taken all reasonable care and precaution, the risk of loss or injury fell upon the owner: and if no witness could be produced, the oath of the herdsman himself that he had performed his duty was accepted. But when an animal was stolen (*v.* 12), it was presumed either that the herdsman might have prevented it, or that he could find the thief and bring him to justice (see *v.* 4). When an animal was killed by a wild beast, the keeper had to produce the mangled carcase, not only in proof of the fact, but to shew that he had, by his vigilance and courage, deprived the wild beast of its prey.

14, 15. If a man borrowed, or hired, an animal, it was at his risk, unless the owner accompanied it.

15. *it came for his hire*] These words are obscure, but they probably mean that the sum paid for hiring was regarded as covering the risk of accident.

16, 17. The man who seduced a girl that was not betrothed had to forfeit for her bene-

18 ¶ Thou shalt not suffer a witch to live.

19 ¶ Whosoever lieth with a beast shall surely be put to death.

20 ¶ *d* He that sacrificeth unto *any* god, save unto the LORD only, he shall be utterly destroyed.

21 ¶ *e* Thou shalt neither vex a stranger, nor oppress him: for ye were strangers in the land of Egypt.

22 ¶ *f* Ye shall not afflict any widow, or fatherless child.

23 If thou afflict them in any wise, and they cry at all unto me, I will surely hear their cry;

24 And my wrath shall wax hot, and I will kill you with the sword; and your wives shall be widows, and your children fatherless.

25 ¶ *g* If thou lend money to *any* of my people *that is* poor by thee, thou shalt not be to him as an usurer, neither shalt thou lay upon him usury.

26 If thou at all take thy neighbour's raiment to pledge, thou shalt deliver it unto him by that the sun goeth down:

27 For that *is* his covering only, it *is* his raiment for his skin: wherein shall he sleep? and it shall come to pass, when he crieth unto me, that I will hear; for I *am* gracious.

28 ¶ *h* Thou shalt not revile the ‖ gods, nor curse the ruler of thy people.

29 ¶ Thou shalt not delay *to offer* the † first of thy ripe fruits, and of thy † liquors: *i* the firstborn of thy sons shalt thou give unto me.

d Deut. 13. 13, 14, 15. 1 Mac. 2. 24.
e Lev. 19. 33.
f Zech. 7. 10.
g Lev. 25. 37. Deut. 23. 19. Psal. 15. 5.
h Acts 23. 5.
‖ Or, *judges.*
† Heb. *thy fulness.*
† Heb. *tear.*
i chap. 13. 2, 12. & 34. 19.

---

fit a proper sum for a dowry (see on Deut. xxii. 28, 29), and to marry her, if her father would allow him to do so. The seducer of a betrothed girl was to be stoned. See Deut. xxii. 23, 27.

18. *Thou shalt not suffer a witch to live*] The practice of witchcraft by both sexes is condemned in Lev. xx. 27; Deut. xviii. 9—12. Wizards alone are mentioned Lev. xix. 31. The witch is here named to represent the class. This is the earliest denunciation of witchcraft in the Law. In every form of witchcraft there is an appeal to a power not acting in subordination to the Divine Law. From all such notions and tendencies true worship is designed to deliver us. The practice of witchcraft was therefore an act of rebellion against Jehovah, and, as such, was a capital crime. The passages bearing on the subject in the Prophets, as well as those in the Law, carry a lesson for all ages. Isa. viii. 19, xix. 3, xliv. 25, xlvii. 12, 13, &c.

19. See Lev. xviii. 23.

20. This was probably an old formula, the sense of which, on its ethical side, is comprised in the First and Second Commandments.

shall be utterly destroyed] The Hebrew word here used is *cherem* (*i.e. devoted*). See on Lev. xxvii. 28.

21. *a stranger*] More properly, **a foreigner** (Heb. *geer*), one who dwells in a land to which he does not belong. See on xx. 10. The command is repeated xxiii. 9. See also Lev. xix. 33, 34; Deut. x. 17—19.

22—24. The meaning of the word rendered *afflict*, includes all cold and contemptuous treatment. See Deut. x. 18. The same duty is enforced with the promise of a blessing, Deut. xiv. 29.

25. See on Lev. xxv. 35—43; cf. Deut. xxiii. 19.

26, 27. The law regarding pledges is expanded Deut. xxiv. 6, 10—13.

28. *the gods*] Heb. *elohim.* See on xxi. 6. This passage has been understood in three different ways: (1) Some of the best modern authorities take it as the name of God (as in Gen. i. 1), and this certainly seems best to represent the Hebrew, and to suit the context. So de Wette, Knobel, Schott, Keil, Benisch, &c. (2) Our Version follows the LXX., Vulg., Luther, Cranmer, &c.; it is also countenanced by Philo ('Vit. Mos.' III. 26), and Josephus ('Ant.' IV. 8. § 10; 'Contr. Ap.' II. 34), who make a boast of the liberality of the sentiment as regards the gods of other nations. (3) The word is rendered as *judges* by the Targums, Saadia, the Syriac, Theodoret, Geneva Fr. and Eng., Zunz, Herxh., &c., and this makes good sense, but it is rightly objected that *elohim*, to have the meaning according to which alone it could be so rendered, should have the article prefixed. See on xxi. 6.

curse the ruler, &c.] Acts xxiii. 5.

29, 30. The offering of Firstfruits appears to have been a custom of primitive antiquity, and was connected with the earliest acts of sacrifice. See Gen. iv. 3, 4. The references to it here and in xxiii. 19 had probably been handed down from patriarchal times. The specific law relating to the firstborn of

350 EXODUS. XXIII. [v. 30—9.

30 Likewise shalt thou do with thine oxen, *and* with thy sheep: seven days it shall be with his dam; on the eighth day thou shalt give it me.

31 ¶ And ye shall be holy men unto me: [k] neither shall ye eat *any* flesh *that is* torn of beasts in the field; ye shall cast it to the dogs.

a Lev. 22. 8.
Ezek. 44. 31.

CHAPTER XXIII.

1 *Of slander and false witness.* 3, 6 *Of justice.* 4 *Of charitableness.* 10 *Of the year of rest.* 12 *Of the sabbath.* 13 *Of idolatry.* 14 *Of the three feasts.* 18 *Of the blood and the fat of the sacrifice.* 20 *An Angel is promised, with a blessing, if they obey him.*

THOU shalt not ‖ raise a false report: put not thine hand with the wicked to be an unrighteous witness.

2 ¶ Thou shalt not follow a multitude to *do* evil; neither shalt thou [†]speak in a cause to decline after many to wrest *judgment:*

‖ Or, *receive.*

† Heb. *answer.*

3 ¶ Neither shalt thou countenance a poor man in his cause.

4 ¶ If thou meet thine enemy's ox or his ass going astray, thou shalt surely bring it back to him again.

5 *a* If thou see the ass of him that hateth thee lying under his burden, ‖ and wouldest forbear to help him, thou shalt surely help with him.

6 Thou shalt not wrest the judgment of thy poor in his cause.

7 Keep thee far from a false matter; and the innocent and righteous slay thou not: for I will not justify the wicked.

8 ¶ And *b* thou shalt take no gift: for the gift blindeth [†] the wise, and perverteth the words of the righteous.

9 ¶ Also thou shalt not oppress a stranger: for ye know the [†] heart of a stranger, seeing ye were strangers in the land of Egypt.

a Deut. 22. 4.

‖ Or, *wilt thou cease to help him?* or, *and wouldest cease to leave thy business for him: thou shalt surely leave it to join with him.*

b Deut. 16. 19.
Ecclus. 20. 29.

† Heb. *the seeing.*
† Heb. *soul.*

---

living creatures was brought out in a strong light in connection with the deliverance from Egypt (xiii. 2, 12, 13). Regarding "the eighth day," see Lev. xxii. 27. The form for offering Firstfruits is described Deut. xxvi. 2—11. But besides these usages exclusively referring to Firstfruits, there were others embodying the same religious idea in the rites of the festivals of the Passover and Pentecost. See on Lev. xxiii.

the first of thy ripe fruits, and of thy liquors] The literal rendering of the Hebrew is given in the margin ("thy fulness and thy tear"), and is retained in Luther's version. Firstfruits (בכורים, xxiii. 19) are not here mentioned by name; but the connection clearly shows that they are meant. The latter of the two Hebrew substantives (דמע) does not occur elsewhere. But according to its etymology, it means that which drops like a tear. The LXX. has ἀπαρχὰς ἅλωνος καὶ ληνοῦ σου. Vulg. *decimas tuas et primitias tuas.* These renderings, as well as that in our Bible (which nearly follows Onk. and the Syr.), are of course paraphrases rather than versions.

31. The sanctification of the nation was emphatically symbolized by strictness of diet as regards both the kind of animal, and the mode of slaughtering. See Lev. chaps. xi. and xvii.

CHAP. XXIII. The Book of the Covenant, concluded.

1—3. These four commands, addressed to the conscience without sanction of punishment, are so many illustrations of the Ninth Commandment, mainly in reference to the giving of evidence in legal causes. It is forbidden:—

1. To circulate a false report (cf. Lev. xix. 16).

2. To join hand in hand with another in bearing false witness.

3. To follow a majority in favouring an unrighteous cause.

4. To shew partiality to a man's cause because he is poor (cf. Lev. xix. 15).

2. This verse might be more strictly rendered, *Thou shalt not follow the many to evil; neither shalt thou bear witness in a cause so as to incline after the many to pervert justice.*

3. *countenance*] Rather, **to show partiality to**.

4, 5. So far was the spirit of the Law from encouraging personal revenge that it would not allow a man to neglect an opportunity of saving his enemy from loss. On the apparently different spirit expressed in Deut. xxiii. 6, and on the reference to the subject in Matt. v. 43, see in loc. Cf. Deut. xxii. 1—4.

5. *wouldest forbear to help him*, &c.] The words are rather difficult, but the sense appears to be:—*If thou see the ass of thine enemy lying down under his burden, thou shalt forbear to pass by him; thou shalt help him in loosening the girths of the ass.* The passage is rendered to this effect by Saadia, Gesenius, Knobel, &c.

6—9. These verses comprise four precepts, which are evidently addressed to those in authority as judges:—

10 And ^c six years thou shalt sow thy land, and shalt gather in the fruits thereof:

11 But the seventh *year* thou shalt let it rest and lie still; that the poor of thy people may eat: and what they leave the beasts of the field shall eat. In like manner thou shalt deal with thy vineyard, *and* with thy ‖ olive-yard.

12 ^d Six days thou shalt do thy work, and on the seventh day thou shalt rest: that thine ox and thine ass may rest, and the son of thy handmaid, and the stranger, may be refreshed.

13 And in all *things* that I have said unto you be circumspect: and make no mention of the name of other gods, neither let it be heard out of thy mouth.

14 ¶ ^e Three times thou shalt keep a feast unto me in the year.

marginal notes:
^c Lev. 25. 3
‖ Or, olive trees.
^d chap. 20. 8. Deut. 5. 13. Luke 13. 14.
^e Deut 16. 16.

---

1. To do justice to the poor.—Comparing *v.* 6 with *v.* 3, it was the part of the judge to defend the poor against the oppression of the rich, and the part of the witness to take care lest his feelings of natural pity should tempt him to falsify his evidence.

2. To be cautious of inflicting capital punishment on one whose guilt was not clearly proved.—A doubtful case was rather to be left to God Himself, who would "not justify the wicked," nor suffer him to go unpunished though he might be acquitted by an earthly tribunal. *v.* 7.

3. To take no bribe or present which might in any way pervert judgment (*v.* 8); cf. Num. xvi. 15; 1 S. xii. 3.

4. To vindicate the rights of the stranger (*v.* 9)—rather, the **foreigner**. See on xx. 10. This verse is a repetition of xxii. 21, but the precept is there addressed to the people at large, while it is here addressed to the judges in reference to their official duties. This is Knobel's explanation; but Bleek and others, overlooking the very distinct contexts, take the repetition as merely redundant.—The word rendered *heart* is more strictly *soul* (נפש), and would be better represented here by **feelings**. Cf. on xxviii. 3 and on Lev. xvii. 11.

10—12. This is the first mention of the Sabbatical year; the law for it is given at length Lev. xxv. 2. Both the Sabbatical year and the weekly Sabbath are here spoken of exclusively in their relation to the poor, as bearing testimony to the equality of the people in their Covenant with Jehovah. In the first of these institutions, the proprietor of the soil gave up his rights for the year to the whole community of living creatures, not excepting the beasts: in the latter, the master gave up his claim for the day to the services of his servants and cattle. See Note 'On the Sabbath day,' § V. after ch. xx.

11. *thou shalt let it rest and lie still*] Some understand this expression to relate to the crops, not to the land, so as to mean, *thou shalt leave them* (*i.e.* the crops) *and give them up to the poor*, &c. (Kranold, Hupfeld, Davidson.) The words, if they stood by themselves, might bear this interpretation as well as that given in our version, and neither interpretation is opposed to Lev. xxv. 2—5, where it is said that the land was to remain untilled. But it has been presumed without the least authority that the writer of Leviticus made a mistake, and that the original law, as it is here given, was not intended to prevent the land from being tilled as usual, but only to forbid that the crops should be harvested by the proprietor, in order that the poor might gather them for themselves. See on Lev. xxv. 2. It has also been objected that this original law could not have been written by Moses in the wilderness, where, of course, it could not have been observed, and that this difficulty occurred to the writer of Leviticus, and induced him to prefix the words "when ye come into the land which I give you." But surely this difficulty, if we admit it to have a real existence, would have been avoided by any one writing a clever fictitious narrative with a view to deceive his own, or later ages. It seems easier and more reasonable to regard Moses as having legislated and written with the deep conviction ever in his mind that the promise of the possession of the land made to Abraham was sure of fulfilment. See on *vv.* 20, 31.

12. *may be refreshed*] Literally, *may take breath*.

13. Cf. Deut. iv. 9, vi. 13, 14; Josh. xxii. 5.

14—17. This is the first mention of the three great Yearly Festivals. The Feast of Unleavened Bread, in its connection with the Paschal Lamb, is spoken of in ch. xii., xiii.: but the two others are here first named. The whole three are spoken of as if they were familiarly known to the people. The points that are especially enjoined are that every male Israelite should attend them at the Sanctuary (cf. xxxiv. 23), and that he should take with him an offering for Jehovah. He was, on each occasion, to present himself before his King with his tribute in his hand. That the latter condition belonged to all the Feasts,

352 EXODUS. XXIII. [v. 15—19.

15 *Thou shalt keep the feast of unleavened bread: (thou shalt eat unleavened bread seven days, as I commanded thee, in the time appointed of the month Abib; for in it thou camest out from Egypt: *and none shall appear before me empty:)

16 And the feast of harvest, the firstfruits of thy labours, which thou hast sown in the field: and the feast of ingathering, *which is* in the end of the year, when thou hast gathered in thy labours out of the field.

17 Three times in the year all thy males shall appear before the Lord God.

18 Thou shalt not offer the blood of my sacrifice with leavened bread; neither shall the fat of my ‖ sacrifice remain until the morning.

19 *h* The first of the firstfruits of thy land thou shalt bring into the

chap. 13. 3. & 34. 18.

Deut. 16. 16. Ecclus. 35. 4.

‖ Or. *feast.*

h chap 34. 26.

---

though it is here stated only in regard to the Passover, cannot be doubted. See Deut. xvi. 16.

15, 16. On the Feast of Unleavened Bread, or the Passover, see xii. 1—28, 43—50, xiii. 3—16, xxxiv. 18—20; Lev. xxiii. 4—14. On the Feast of the Firstfruits of Harvest, called also the Feast of Weeks, and the Feast of Pentecost, see xxxiv. 22; Lev. xxiii. 15—21. On the Feast of Ingathering, called also the Feast of Tabernacles, see Lev. xxiii. 34—36, 39—43.

16. *in the end of the year*] Cf. xxxiv. 22. The year here spoken of must have been the civil or agrarian year, which began after harvest, when the ground was prepared for sowing. Cf. Lev. xxiii. 39; Deut. xvi. 13—15. The sacred year began in spring, with the month Abib, or Nisan. See on Exod. xii. 2, and on Lev. xxv. 9.

when thou hast gathered] Rather, **when thou gatherest in**. The Hebrew does not imply that the gathering in was to be completed before the Feast was held. In some years the harvest must have fallen later than in others. It was perhaps rarely completed before the time appointed for the Feast. And hence the fitness of the expression, "which is in the end of the year," as explained in the preceding note.

18, 19. These verses comprise three maxims, each of which, according to the best interpretation, appears to relate to one of the Festivals, in due order, as named in *vv.* 14—17.

18. *the blood of my sacrifice*] It is generally considered that this must refer to the Paschal Lamb. The blood that was sprinkled on the door-posts, or (after the first occasion) on the Altar, emphatically represented "the sacrifice of the Lord's passover." See xii. 7, 11, 13, 22, 23, 27.

the fat of my sacrifice] Strictly, **the fat of my feast**. In the parallel passage xxxiv. 25, what appears to be the equivalent expression is, "the sacrifice of the feast of the passover." It has been inferred with great probability that the *fat of my feast* means not literally the *fat* of the Paschal Lamb, but the *best part* of the feast, that is, the Paschal Lamb itself (Knobel, Keil). This explanation best accords with xii. 10, where there is no mention of the fat. If we take the words in their mere literal sense, they must refer to the fat of the sacrifices in general, which, when the ritual of the sacrifices was arranged, was burnt upon the Altar by the Priests (Lev. i. 8, iii. 3—5).

19. *The first of the firstfruits of thy land*] This most probably means the *best*, or *chief* of the Firstfruits, &c. As the preceding precept appears to refer to the Passover, so it is likely that this refers to Pentecost, as especially to the offering of what are called in *v.* 16 "the firstfruits of thy labours;" that is, the two wave loaves described Lev. xxiii. 17. They are called in Leviticus, " the firstfruits unto the Lord;" and it is reasonable that they should here be designated the *chief* of the Firstfruits. If, with Keil and others, we suppose the precept to relate to the offerings of Firstfruits in general, the command is no more than a repetition of xxii. 29.

Thou shalt not seethe a kid in his mother's milk] This precept is repeated xxxiv. 26; Deut. xiv. 21. There has been much discussion as to its meaning. St Augustine and some more recent commentators have given up the explanation of it in despair. If we are to connect the first of the two preceding precepts with the Passover, and the second with Pentecost, it seems reasonable to connect this with the Feast of Tabernacles. The only explanation which accords with this connection is one which refers to some sort of superstitious custom connected with the harvest. Abarbanel speaks of such a custom, in which a kid was seethed in its mother's milk to propitiate in some way the deities. But the subject is more pointedly illustrated in an ancient commentary on the Pentateuch by a Karaite Jew, from the manuscript of which a quotation is given by Cudworth ('On the Lord's Supper,' p. 36). It is there said to have been a prevalent usage to boil a kid **in its**

v. 20—23.]   EXODUS. XXIII.   353

i ch. 34. 26.
Deut. 14. 21.

house of the LORD thy God. *i*Thou shalt not seethe a kid in his mother's milk.

k chap. 33. 2.

20 ¶ *k*Behold, I send an Angel before thee, to keep thee in the way, and to bring thee into the place which I have prepared.

21 Beware of him, and obey his voice, provoke him not; for he will not pardon your transgressions: for my name *is* in him.

22 But if thou shalt indeed obey his voice, and do all that I speak; then I will be an enemy unto thine enemies, and *l* an adversary unto thine adversaries.

23 *l* For mine Angel shall go before thee, and *m*bring thee in unto the Amorites, and the Hittites, and the Perizzites, and the Canaanites, *and* the Hivites, and the Jebusites: and I will cut them off.

l Or, *I will afflict them that afflict thee.*
l chap. 33. 2.
m Josh. 24. 11.

---

mother's milk, when all the crops were gathered in, and to sprinkle with the milk the fruit trees, fields and gardens, as a charm to improve the crops of the coming year. The explanation based upon this is preferred by Bochart, John Gregory, Grotius, Knobel and others. The command, so understood, is a caution against the practice of magic. See on xxii. 18. But in a matter so doubtful, it is but fair to give such other explanations as seem most worthy of notice.

1. It has been taken as a prohibition of the eating of flesh and milk together (the Targums, Erpenius). This is countenanced by the traditional custom of the Jews ('Mishna,' Cholin VIII. 1; Maimon. 'de Cit. Vel.' 9; Buxtorf, 'Syn. Jud.' p. 596).

2. It has been supposed to forbid the eating of a kid before it has been weaned from its mother—Luther, Calvin, Fagius, &c.

3. It has been referred to a custom now existing among the Arabs, which is certainly of great antiquity, of preparing a gross sort of food by stewing a kid in milk, with the addition of certain ingredients of a stimulating nature, which is commonly called in Arabic, "a kid in his mother's milk." Aben-Ezra, Keil, Thomson ('The Land and the Book,' ch. VIII.), &c.

4. It has been brought into connection with the prohibitions to slaughter a cow and a calf, or a ewe and her lamb, on the same day (Lev. xxii. 28), and to take a bird along with her young in the nest (Deut. xxii. 6). It is thus understood as a protest against cruelty and outraging the order of nature (*ne commisceatur germen cum radicibus*). Theodoret, Vatablus, Ewald, &c. See Bochart, 'Hieroz.' l. II. c. 52.

20—33. These verses appear to form the conclusion of the Book of the Covenant. They contain promises of the constant presence and guidance of Jehovah (*vv.* 20—22), of the driving out of the nations of the Canaanites by degrees (23—30), and of the subsequent enlargement of Hebrew dominion (*v.* 31). But these promises are accompanied by solemn exhortations and threatenings.—Cf. xxxiv. 10—17, where similar promises and warnings are prefixed to the shorter compendium of Law which was written down after the renewal of the Tables.

20, 21. *an Angel...for my name is in him*] The Angel appears to mean the presence and the power of Jehovah Himself, manifested in the work of leading and delivering His people, and maintaining His Covenant with them. Cf. xxxii. 34, xxxiii. 2, 15, 16, and the notes; see also on Gen. xii. 7.

20. *the place which I have prepared*] The promise of the Land may be seen to inspire the legislation and conduct of Moses throughout his career. There is no trace of uncertainty as to the ultimate aim of his mission. He had been called to lead the people to the home prepared for them, according to the promise first made to Abraham, and to discipline them in their passage through the wilderness to become a strong nation.

22. *and an adversary unto thine adversaries*] The rendering in the margin is the better one. Cf. Deut. xx. 4.

23. The nations here mentioned are those only that inhabited the land strictly called the Land of Canaan, lying between the Jordan and the Great Sea. See Num. xxxiv. 2; cf. Exod. xxxiv. 11.

I will cut them off] It has been too absolutely taken for granted that it was the Divine will that the inhabitants of Canaan should be utterly exterminated. We know that, as a matter of fact, great numbers of the Canaanite families lived on, and intermarried with the Israelites (see Judg. i., ii., with such cases as those of the Sidonians, of Araunah, of Uriah, of the family of Rahab, &c.). The national existence of the Canaanites was indeed to be *utterly* destroyed, every trace of their idolatries was to be blotted out, no social intercourse was to be held with them while they served other gods, nor were alliances of any kind to be formed with them. These commands are emphatically repeated and expanded in Deuteronomy (vii.; xii. 1—4, 29—31).

VOL. I.

Z

354 EXODUS. XXIII. [v. 24—31.

^a Deut. 7. 25.

24 Thou shalt not bow down to their gods, nor serve them, nor do after their works: ^a but thou shalt utterly overthrow them, and quite break down their images.

25 And ye shall serve the LORD your God, and he shall bless thy bread, and thy water; and I will take sickness away from the midst of thee.

^o Deut. 7. 14.

26 ¶ ^o There shall nothing cast their young, nor be barren, in thy land: the number of thy days I will fulfil.

27 I will send my fear before thee, and will destroy all the people to whom thou shalt come, and I will make all thine enemies turn their

† Heb. *neck.*

† backs unto thee.

28 And ^p I will send hornets before thee, which shall drive out the Hivite, the Canaanite, and the Hittite, from before thee.

^p Josh. 24. 12.

29 I will not drive them out from before thee in one year; lest the land become desolate, and the beast of the field multiply against thee.

30 By little and little I will drive them out from before thee, until thou be increased, and inherit the land.

31 And I will set thy bounds from the Red sea even unto the sea of the Philistines, and from the desert unto the river: for I will deliver the inhabitants of the land into your hand; and thou shalt drive them out before thee.

They were often broken by the Israelites, who had to suffer for their transgression (Num. xxxiii. 55; Judg. ii. 3). But it is alike contrary to the spirit of the Divine Law, and to the facts bearing on the subject scattered in the history, to suppose that any obstacle was put in the way of well disposed individuals of the denounced nations who left their sins and were willing to join the service of Jehovah. The Law, as it was addressed to the Israelites, never forgets the stranger (rather, **the foreigner**, LXX. προσήλυτος) who had voluntarily come within their gates. See xx. 10. The spiritual blessings of the Covenant were always open to those who sincerely and earnestly desired to possess them. Lev. xix. 34, xxiv. 22. A narrowness and cruelty in this and other respects has been very generally ascribed to the Law of Moses, from which it has been justly vindicated by Salvador, 'Histoire des Institutions de Moïse,' Vol. I. p. 447.

24. Cf. Num. xxxiii. 52; Deut. vii. 5, 16, xii. 29, 30, xx. 18.

27. *destroy*] Rather, **overthrow**. See on *v.* 23; cf. xv. 14; Deut. ii. 25; Josh. ii. 11.

28. *hornets*] Cf. Deut. vii. 20; Josh. xxiv. 12. The Hebrew word is in the singular number, used for the species—**the hornet**. Bochart ('Hieroz.' lib. IV. c. 13) has collected instances from ancient authorities of large bodies of men being driven away by noxious insects and other small creatures; and the author of the Book of Wisdom (xii. 8, 9) with some of the commentators have supposed that hornets are literally meant (see 'Crit. Sac.'). But there seems to be no reasonable doubt that the word is used figuratively for a cause of terror and discouragement. Bees are spoken of in the like sense, Deut. i. 44;

Ps. cxviii. 12. The passage has been thus understood by most critics.

29. *beast of the field*] The term is applied to any wild animal; here it means a destructive one, as it does also Deut. vii. 22: cf. Lev. xxvi. 22; 2 K. xvii. 25; Job v. 22; Ezek. xiv. 15.

31. In *v.* 23, the limits of the Land of Canaan, strictly so called, are indicated; to this, when the Israelites were about to take possession of it, were added the regions of Gilead and Bashan on the left side of the Jordan (Num. xxxii. 33—42; Josh. xiii. 29—32). These two portions made up the Holy Land, of which the limits were recognized, with inconsiderable variations, till the final overthrow of the Jewish polity. But in this verse the utmost extent of Hebrew dominion, as it existed in the time of David and Solomon, is set forth. The kingdom then reached to Eloth and Ezion-geber on the Ælanitic Gulf of the Red Sea (1 K. ix. 26), and to Tiphsah on the "River," that is, the River Euphrates (1 K. iv. 24), having for its western boundary "the Sea of the Philistines," that is, the Mediterranean, and for its southern boundary "the desert," that is, the wildernesses of Shur and Paran (cf. Gen. xv. 18; Deut. i. 7, xi. 24; Josh. i. 4). Hengstenberg thinks that these broad descriptions of the Land are to be taken as rhetorical, and not as the strict terms of the promise ('Pentateuch,' II. p. 217). He considers this to be the right way of meeting those who reject the genuineness of the narrative on the ground of the improbability that Moses should have foretold the extent of the conquests of David and Solomon. But the cavils of such objectors may be met more simply and effectively by urging that if Moses

32 *Thou shalt make no covenant with them, nor with their gods.

33 They shall not dwell in thy land, lest they make thee sin against me: for if thou serve their gods, *it will surely be a snare unto thee.

CHAPTER XXIV.

1 Moses is called up into the mountain. 3 The people promise obedience. 4 Moses buildeth an altar, and twelve pillars. 6 He sprinkleth the blood of the covenant. 9 The glory of God appeareth. 14 Aaron and Hur have the charge of the people. 15 Moses goeth into the mountain, where he continueth forty days and forty nights.

AND he said unto Moses, Come up unto the LORD, thou, and Aaron, Nadab, and Abihu, and seventy of the elders of Israel; and worship ye afar off.

2 And Moses alone shall come near the LORD: but they shall not come nigh; neither shall the people go up with him.

3 ¶ And Moses came and told the people all the words of the LORD, and all the judgments: and all the people answered with one voice, and said, *All the words which the LORD hath said will we do.

4 And Moses wrote all the words of the LORD, and rose up early in the morning, and builded an altar under the hill, and twelve pillars, according to the twelve tribes of Israel.

5 And he sent young men of the children of Israel, which offered burnt offerings, and sacrificed peace offerings of oxen unto the LORD.

6 And Moses took half of the blood, and put *it* in basons; and half of the blood he sprinkled on the altar.

7 And he took the book of the covenant, and read in the audience of the people: and they said, *All that the LORD hath said will we do, and be obedient.

---

was acquainted with the geography of the region (which can hardly be called in question), he might certainly have foreseen that the Hebrew power, when it became very strong in the Land of Canaan, could not fail to exercise domination over all the country from the Euphrates to the Mediterranean and the Red Sea.

CHAP. XXIV.
The Sealing of the Covenant.
1—8.

1, 2. It is not easy to trace the proper connection of these two verses as they stand here. Ewald, with great probability, thinks that their right place is between verses 8 and 9 in this chapter ('Hist. of Israel,' p. 529). It has been suggested that they may relate to what was said to Moses immediately after the utterance of the Ten Commandments, ch. xx. 19 (Knobel).—If they are here placed in due order of time (as Rosenmüller, Keil and others suppose), the direction to Moses contained in them was delivered on the mount (see xx. 21), but its fulfilment was deferred till after he had come down from the mount and done all that is recorded in *vv.* 3—8.

3, 4. The narrative in these verses seems naturally to follow the end of the preceding chapter. Moses leaves the mount and repeats the words of the Book of the Covenant to the people, they give their assent, and the next morning he arranges the ceremony for the formal ratification of the Covenant.

4. *twelve pillars*] As the altar was a symbol of the presence of Jehovah, so these twelve pillars represented the presence of the Twelve Tribes with whom He was making the Covenant. Keil suggests that the pillars were perhaps arranged as boundary stones for the spot consecrated for the occasion.

5. *young men of the children of Israel*] The Targums and Saadia call these *the firstborn sons*. There is no fair ground for this interpretation. Moses was on this occasion performing the office of a priest (the family of Aaron not being yet consecrated), and he employed young men whose strength and skill qualified them to slaughter and prepare the sacrifices. The Law did not regard these acts as necessarily belonging to the priests, and it is probable that they were regarded in the same way in earlier times, when the sacerdotal character belonged especially to the firstborn sons. See on Lev. i. 5, and Exod. xxviii. 1.

burnt offerings...peace offerings] The Burnt offerings figured the dedication of the nation to Jehovah, and the Peace offerings their communion with Jehovah and with each other.

6. *he sprinkled*] Rather, **he cast**. See on Lev. i. 5. The same word is used *v.* 8.

7. *the book of the covenant*] See *v.* 4, and Introd. note on xx. 22. The people had to repeat their assent to the Book of the Covenant before the blood was thrown upon them. Cf. 2 K. xxiii. 2, 21; 2 Chron. xxxiv. 30.

8 And Moses took the blood, and sprinkled *it* on the people, and said, Behold ᶜthe blood of the covenant, which the LORD hath màde with you concerning all these words.

9 ¶ Then went up Moses, and Aaron, Nadab, and Abihu, and seventy of the elders of Israel:

10 And they saw the God of Israel: and *there was* under his feet as it were a paved work of a sapphire stone, and as it were the body of heaven in *his* clearness.

11 And upon the nobles of the children of Israel he laid not his hand: also they saw God, and did eat and drink.

12 ¶ And the LORD said unto Mo-

ᶜ 1 Pet. 1. 2.
Heb. 9. 20.

8. *the blood of the covenant*] It should be observed that the blood which sealed the Covenant was the blood of Burnt offerings and Peace offerings. The Sin offering had not yet been instituted. That more complicated view of human nature which gave to the Sin offering its meaning, had yet to be developed by the Law, which was now only receiving its ratification. The Covenant between Jehovah and His people therefore took precedence of the operation of the Law, by which came the knowledge of sin. Rom. iii. 20; Note on the Ten Commandments, § V.

Half of the blood had been put into basins, and half of it had been cast upon the Altar. The Book of the Covenant was then read, and after that the blood in the basins was cast "upon the people." It was cast either upon the elders, or those who stood foremost; or, as Abarbanel and others have supposed, upon the twelve pillars representing the Twelve Tribes, as the first half had been cast upon the altar, which witnessed the presence of Jehovah. The blood thus divided between the two parties to the Covenant signified the sacramental union between the Lord and His people. Cf. Ps. l. 5; Zech. ix. 11.

The instances from classical antiquity adduced as parallels to this sacrifice of Moses by Bähr, Knobel and Kalisch, in which animals were slaughtered on the making of covenants, are either those in which the animal was slain to signify the punishment due to the party that might break the covenant (Hom. 'Il.' III. 298, XIX. 252; Liv. 'Hist.' I. 24, XXI. 45); those in which confederates dipped their hands, or their weapons, in the same blood (Æsch. 'Sept. c. Theb.' 43; Xenoph. 'Anab.' II. 2, § 9); or those in which the contracting parties tasted each other's blood (Herodot. I. 74, IV. 70; Tac. 'Annal.' XII. 47). All these usages are based upon ideas which are but very superficially related to the subject; they have indeed no true connection whatever with the idea of sacrifice as the seal of a covenant between God and man. See on Ex. xxix. 20.

The Feast of the Peace offerings.
9—11.

9. It would appear that Moses, Aaron with his two sons, and seventy of the elders (xix. 7) went a short distance up the mountain to eat the meal of the Covenant (cf. Gen. xxxi. 43—47), which must have consisted of the flesh of the Peace offerings (*v. 5.*). Joshua is not named here, but he accompanied Moses as his servant. See *v.* 13.

10. *And they saw the God of Israel*] As they ate the sacrificial feast, the presence of Jehovah was manifested to them with special distinctness. In the act of solemn worship, they perceived that he was present with them, as their Lord and their Deliverer. It is idle to speculate, as Keil and others have done, on the mode of this revelation. That no visible form was presented to their bodily eyes, we are expressly informed, Deut. iv. 12; see on xxxiii. 20; cf. Isa. vi. 1.

there was under his feet as it were a paved work of a sapphire stone, and as it were the body of heaven in his clearness] Rather, *under His feet, it was like a work of bright sapphire stone, and like the heaven itself in clearness.* On the sapphire, see xxviii. 18; cf. Ezek. i. 26. The pure blue of the heaven above them lent its influence to help the inner sense to realize the vision which no mortal eye could behold.

11. *he laid not his hand*] i.e. he did not smite them. It was believed that a mortal could not survive the sight of God (Gen. xxxii. 30; Ex. xxxiii. 20; Judg. vi. 22, xiii. 22): but these rulers of Israel were permitted to eat and drink, while they were enjoying in an extraordinary degree the sense of the Divine presence, and took no harm. " When the heads of the people venture to draw near their God, they find his presence no more a source of disturbance and dread, but radiant in all the bright loveliness of supernal glory; a beautiful sign that the higher religion and state of conformity to law, now established, shall work onwards to eternal blessedness." Ewald, ' Hist. of Israel,' Vol. I. p. 529.

Moses goes up to receive the Tables.
12—18.

12. *tables of stone, and a law, and commandments*] Maimonides and many of the Jews understand *the tables of stone* to denote the Ten Commandments; *the law*, the Law written in the Pentateuch; and *the command-*

ses, Come up to me into the mount, and be there: and I will give thee tables of stone, and a law, and commandments which I have written; that thou mayest teach them.

13 And Moses rose up, and his minister Joshua: and Moses went up into the mount of God.

14 And he said unto the elders, Tarry ye here for us, until we come again unto you: and, behold, Aaron and Hur *are* with you: if any man have any matters to do, let him come unto them.

15 And Moses went up into the mount, and a cloud covered the mount.

16 And the glory of the LORD abode upon mount Sinai, and the cloud covered it six days: and the seventh day he called unto Moses out of the midst of the cloud.

17 And the sight of the glory of the LORD *was* like devouring fire on the top of the mount in the eyes of the children of Israel.

18 And Moses went into the midst of the cloud, and gat him up into the mount: and *d* Moses was in the mount forty days and forty nights.

d chap. 34. 28. Deut. 9. 9.

CHAPTER XXV.

1 *What the Israelites must offer for the making of the tabernacle.* 10 *The form of the ark.* 17 *The mercy seat, with the cherubims.* 23 *The table, with the furniture thereof.* 31 *The candlestick, with the instruments thereof.*

AND the LORD spake unto Moses, saying,

---

ments (it should be *the commandment*), the oral or traditional law which was in after ages put into writing in the Mishna and the Gemara. Ewald takes the words to mean the Ten Commandments, and " other sacred books of the Law" ('H. of I.' 1. p. 606). But it is more probable that the Ten Commandments alone are spoken of, and that the meaning is, *the Tables of stone with the Law, even the Commandment.* So Knobel, Keil, Herx. See Note on the Ten Commandments, § I.

that thou mayest teach them] More strictly, **to teach them**. The promise of the Tables is fulfilled after the directions for the Tabernacle have been given, xxxi. 18.

13. *Joshua*] See on *v.* 9; cf. xxxii. 17; xxxiii. 11.

mount of God] See on iii. 1.

14. It need not be supposed that the Elders were required to remain on the very spot where Moses parted with them, but simply that they were to advance no further. Aaron and Hur were to represent the authority of Moses during his absence.

15. *Moses went up*] Moses appears to have left Joshua and gone up alone into the cloud. See *v.* 2.

16. Cf. xix. 18 sq.

18. During this period of forty days, and the second period when the Tables were renewed, Moses neither ate bread nor drank water. Deut. ix. 9; Exod. xxxiv. 28. Elijah in like manner fasted for forty days, when he visited the same spot (1 K. xix. 8). The two who met our Saviour on the Mount of Transfiguration, the one as representing the Law, the other as representing the Prophets, thus shadowed forth in their own experience the Fast of Forty days in the wilderness of Judæa.

THE ARK AND THE TABERNACLE.
CHAP. XXV. XXVI.

Jehovah had redeemed the Israelites from bondage. He had made a Covenant with them and had given them a Law. He had promised, on condition of their obedience, to accept them as His own "peculiar treasure," as "a kingdom of priests and a holy nation" (xix. 5, 6). And now He was ready visibly to testify that He made his abode with them. He claimed to have a dwelling for Himself, which was to be in external form a tent of goats' hair, to take its place among their own tents, formed out of the same material (on Ex. xxvi. 7). The special mark of His presence within the Tent was to be the Ark or chest containing the Ten Commandments on two tables of stone (Ex. xxxi. 18), symbolizing the divine Law of holiness, covered by the Mercy seat, the type of reconciliation.—Moses was divinely taught regarding the construction and arrangement of every part of the Sanctuary. The directions which were given him are comprised in Ex. xxv. 1—xxxi. 11. The account of the performance of the work, expressed generally in the same terms, is given Ex. xxxv. 20—xl. 33.

The meaning of the Tabernacle, with the relation in which it stood to the Tables of the Law, is considered more at length in the Note at the end of ch. xl.

CHAP. XXV. 1—9. Moses is commanded to invite the people to bring their gifts for the construction and service of the Sanctuary and for the dresses of the Priests.

2 Speak unto the children of Israel, that they †bring me an ‖offering: ᵃof every man that giveth it willingly with his heart ye shall take my offering.

3 And this *is* the offering which ye shall take of them; gold, and silver, and brass,

4 And blue, and purple, and scarlet, and ‖fine linen, and goats' *hair*,

† Heb. *take for me.*
‖ Or, *heave offering.*
ᵃ chap. 35. 5.
‖ Or, *silk.*

---

2. *an offering*] The Hebrew word is *tĕrumāh*, which occurs here for the first time. On the marginal rendering "heave offering," see note on Ex. xxix. 27. The word in this place appears to denote no more than *offering*, in its general sense, being equivalent to *korban*. It is used with the same compass of meaning Ex. xxx. 13, xxxv. 5, &c. In Num. xviii. 24, tithes are called a *tĕrumah*.

that giveth it willingly with his heart] Literally, **whose heart shall freely give it**. The public service of Jehovah was to be instituted by freewill offerings, not by an enforced tax. Cf. 1 Chron. xxix. 3, 9, 14; Ezra ii. 68, 69; 2 Cor. viii. 11, 12, ix. 7. On the zeal with which the people responded to the call, see Ex. xxxv. 21—29, xxxvi. 5—7.

my offering] The recipient of the offering is here denoted by the possessive case, according to the common Hebrew idiom. Ex. xxx. 13, xxxv. 5, 21, 24, &c.

3. *gold, and silver, and brass*] The supply of these metals possessed by the Israelites at this time probably included what they had inherited from their forefathers, what they had obtained from the Egyptians (Ex. xii. 35), and what may have been found amongst the spoils of the Amalekites (Ex. xvii. 8—13). But with their abundant flocks and herds, it can hardly be doubted that they had carried on important traffic with the trading caravans that traversed the wilderness, some of which, most likely, in the earliest times were furnished with silver, with the gold of Ophir (or gold of Sheba, as it seems to have been indifferently called), and with the bronze of Phœnicia and Egypt (Gen. xxxvii. 25, 28; Deut. xxxiii. 25; 1 K. ix. 28, x. 15; 1 Chron. xxix. 4; 2 Chron. ix. 14; Job xxii. 24, xxviii. 16; Ps. xlv. 9).—Cf. note on Ex. xxxviii. 24.

brass] The Hebrew word *nĕhosheth* [see on 2 K. xviii. 4] must mean pure copper in such passages as Deut. viii. 9, xxxiii. 25; Job xxviii. 2. But it commonly denotes (as it does most likely in this place) the hardened alloy of copper and tin, more strictly called **bronze** than brass, which was so largely used for weapons and implements before the art of working iron was well understood. On the bronze of the Egyptians see Wilkinson's 'Popular Account,' Vol. I. p. 148, II. p. 152, and De Rougemont, 'Age du Bronze,' p. 180. The latter writer proves that the Egyptians were well acquainted with bronze and with the art of working in all the common metals, except iron, under the fourth dynasty, ages before the time of Abraham.

4. *blue, and purple, and scarlet*] The names of the colours are used for the material which was dyed with them. The Jewish tradition has been very generally received that this material was wool. Cf. Heb. ix. 19 with Lev. xiv. 4, 49, &c. But the question is not quite without difficulty. See on xxviii. 5, and Lev. xix. 19.—The material, having been spun and dyed by the women, appears to have been delivered in the state of yarn. The Egyptians were well skilled in the art of dyeing (Wilkinson, II. p. 83). The weaving and embroidering were left to Aholiab and his assistants, Ex. xxxv., cf. *v.* 25 with *v.* 35. The Egyptians in like manner used to dye the threads of their stuffs before weaving them, and to employ women in spinning, and men in weaving and embroidering. (Wilkinson, 'Ancient Egyptians,' II. p. 79 sq.). Respecting the names of the colours, see Note at the end of the chapter.

fine linen] The word *shēsh*, which is here used, is Egyptian (Birch in Bunsen's 'Egypt,' Vol. V. p. 571). It is rendered by the LXX. βύσσος, which must be allied to *butz*, the name of the "fine linen" of Syria, in Ezek. xxvii. 16, which was that used in the time of Solomon for the hangings of the Temple and for other purposes (1 Chron. xv. 27; 2 Chron. ii. 14, iii. 14, v. 12). That the word *shēsh* denoted the fine flax, or the manufactured linen, for which Egypt was famous [see Ezek. xxvii. 7, where the original word is *shēsh*: but in Prov. vii. 16 "fine linen of Egypt" is a mistranslation, see note in loc.], and which the Egyptians were in the habit of using for dresses of state (Gen. xli. 42); and not *cotton*, as some have imagined, nor *silk* [as the word *shēsh* is rendered Prov. xxxi. 22, and in the margin here and elsewhere], is now clearly proved. Wilkinson, 'Pop. Account,' &c. II. p. 73, and his note to Herodot. II. 86. The *linen cloth* of Persia is mentioned, Esth. i. 6, by its Persian name *karpas* (the parent of κάρπασος and *carbasus*), which in our version is wrongly rendered *green*, as the name of a colour. The occurrence of these three native names, *shēsh*, *butz*, and *karpas*, for the same article produced in three different countries, in strict consistency with the narratives in which they occur, is worthy of remark. The LXX. translates each of the three by βύσσος. Cf. notes on Ex. ix. 31, xxxix. 28. The estimation in which fine linen was held in differ-

5 And rams' skins dyed red, and badgers' skins, and shittim wood,

6 Oil for the light, spices for anointing oil, and for sweet incense,

---

ent ages, before silk was generally known, may be seen 1 Chron. xv. 27; Prov. xxxi. 22; Ezek. xvi. 10, 13; Luke xvi. 19; Rev. xix. 8, 14. If silk is anywhere spoken of in the Hebrew Bible, it is only in Ezek. xvi. 10, where the word is not *shēsh* but *meshi*, which Fuerst thinks may be of Chinese derivation.— It would seem that, for the use of the Tabernacle, the flax was spun by the women, like the coloured wools, and was delivered in the state of thread to be woven by Aholiab and his assistants (Ex. xxxv. 25, 35). The fine linen appears to have been used as the groundwork of the figured curtains of the Tabernacle as well as of the embroidered hangings of the Tent and the Court. See on xxxv. 35.

goats' hair] The hair of the goat has furnished the material for tents to the Roman armies (Virg. 'Georg.' III. 313) and to the Arabs and Eastern Nomads of all ages, as it did to the Israelites in the wilderness. The tent which was to be the chosen dwelling-place of Jehovah was to be formed of the same material as the tents of His people. See Introd. Note.

5. *rams' skins dyed red*] These skins may have been tanned and coloured like the leather now known as red morocco, which is said to have been manufactured in Libya from the remotest antiquity. On the manufacture of leather by the Egyptians, see Wilkinson, 'Pop. Account,' II. pp. 102—106.

badgers' skins] The skins here spoken of were certainly not those of the badger, as was supposed by Luther and Gesenius. That animal is often found in the Holy Land, but it is very rare in the wilderness, if it exists there at all (Tristram, 'N. H.' p. 44). The Hebrew name here used, *tachash*, occurs in the Old Testament only in connection with these skins, which were employed for the outer covering of the Tent of the Tabernacle (Ex. xxvi. 14), and in wrapping up the holy things when they were moved (Num. iv. 8, 10, &c.), and which are mentioned as the material of the shoes of the prophetic impersonation of Jerusalem by Ezekiel (xvi. 10). The word bears a near resemblance to the Arabic *tuchash*, which appears to be the general name given to the seals, dugongs and dolphins found in the Red Sea (Tristram), and, according to some authorities, to the sharks and dog-fish (Fürst). The substance spoken of would thus appear to have been leather formed from the skins of marine animals, which was well adapted as a protection against the weather. Pliny speaks of tents made of seal skins as proof against the stroke of lightning ('H. N.' II. 56), and one of these is said to have been used by Augustus whenever he travelled (Sueton. 'Octav.' 90). The skins of the dolphin and dugong are cut into sandals by the modern Arabs, and this may explain Ezek. xvi. 10. The question seems thus to be determined on pretty certain grounds. But it is remarkable that the LXX., with Josephus, the Vulgate, the Targums, and most of the ancient versions, treat the word *tachash* as the name of ordinary leather, distinguished only by a particular colour. But there is a difference as to whether the colour was black, red, violet, or blue. Most of the ancient authorities, followed by Bochart and Rosenmüller, imagine the colour to have been *hyacinthine*, the first of the three colours in the embroidered work of the Tabernacle [see Note at the end of the Chapter]. From Josephus speaking of the colour of these skins, such as he conceived it to be, as like the heavens ('Ant.' III. 6, § 4), we may infer with confidence that he conceived *hyacinthine* to be *sky-blue*. [Note, § II.]

shittim wood] The word *shittim* is the plural form of *shittah*, which occurs as the name of the growing tree Is. xli. 19. The tree is satisfactorily identified with the *Acacia seyal*, "a gnarled and thorny tree, somewhat like a solitary hawthorn in its habit and manner of growth, but much larger. [See note on Ex. xxvi. 15.] It flourishes in the driest situations, and is scattered more or less numerously over the Sinaitic Peninsula" (Tristram). It is rare in the Holy Land except in the neighbourhood of the Dead Sea, where it appears to have given its name to two places in ancient times. See Num. xxv. 1; Joel iii. 18. It grows in Egypt in some regions at a distance from the coast. The timber is hard and close-grained, of an orange colour with a darker heart, well adapted for cabinet work. The LXX. call it *wood that will not rot*, ξύλα ἄσηπτα. It appears to be the only good wood produced in the wilderness. No other kind of wood was employed in the Tabernacle or its furniture. In the construction of the Temple cedar and fir took its place (1 K. v. 8, vi. 18; 2 Chron. ii. 8). A distinct species of Acacia is mentioned by Dr Robinson, Dr Royle and others, as *A. gummifera*. But Mr Tristram states that the gum arabic of commerce is obtained from the *A. seyal*, and forms an important article of traffic on the shores of the Red Sea, as it did in ancient times. See also Bunsen, v. 414. As the plural form, *shittim*, is always applied to the wood, never being used like the singular *shittah* (Is. xli. 19) for the growing tree, the conjecture will hardly stand that the plural name is to be accounted for from "the tangled thicket into which its stem expands." (Tristram 'H. N.' p. 390; Stanley, 'S. and P.' p. 20; 'Jewish Ch.' I. p. 163; Houghton,

7 Onyx stones, and stones to be set in the *b*ephod, and in the *c*breastplate.

8 And let them make me a sanctuary; that I may dwell among them.

9 According to all that I shew thee, *after* the pattern of the tabernacle, and the pattern of all the instruments thereof, even so shall ye make *it*.

10 ¶ *d*And they shall make an ark of shittim wood: two cubits and a half *shall be* the length thereof, and a cubit and a half the breadth thereof,

b chap. 28. 4.
c chap. 28. 15.
d chap. 37. 1.

'Smith's Dict.' III. 1295; Royle, 'Kitto's Cycl.' III. 841.) See also on Ex. iii. 2.

6. *Oil for the light*] The oil was to be "pure olive oil beaten," see on Ex. xxvii. 20.

spices for anointing oil] What these spices were see Ex. xxx. 22—25.

sweet incense] See Ex. xxx. 34, 35.

7. On the materials and construction of the ephod and breastplate, see ch. xxviii.

8. *sanctuary*] Heb. *mikdash*, *i.e.* a hallowed place. This is the most comprehensive of the words that relate to the place dedicated to Jehovah. It included the Tabernacle with its furniture, its Tent and its Court.

that I may dwell among them] The purpose of the Sanctuary is here definitely declared by the Lord Himself. It was to be the constant witness of His presence amongst His people. xxix. 42—46, xl. 34—38, &c.

9. *According to all that I shew thee*] The Tabernacle and all that pertained to it were to be in strict accordance with the ideas revealed by the Lord to Moses: nothing in the way of form or decoration was to be left to the taste or judgment of the artificers. The command is emphatically repeated *v.* 40, xxvi. 30; cf. Acts vii. 44; Heb. viii. 5.—The word here translated *pattern* is also used in Chronicles to denote the plans for the Temple which were given by David to Solomon (1 Chron. xxviii. 11, **12**, 19); it is elsewhere rendered *form, likeness, similitude,* Deut. iv. 16, 17; Ezek. viii. 3, 10. The revelation to the mind of Moses was, without doubt, such as to suggest the exact appearance of the work to be produced. But there is no need to adopt the materialistic notion of some of the rabbinists, that a Tabernacle in the heavens was set forth before the bodily eyes of the Legislator.

the tabernacle] The Hebrew word *hammishkān*, signifies the dwelling-place. It here denotes the wooden structure, containing the holy place and the most holy place, with the tent which sheltered it. See on xxvi. 1.

The Ark of the Covenant.
xxv. 10—16 (cf. xxxvii. 1—5).

The ARK is uniformly designated in Exodus the ARK OF THE TESTIMONY (xxv. 22, xxvi. 34, xxx. 6, 26, xxxi. 7, xl. 3, &c.); it is so called also Num. iv. 5, vii. 89; Josh. iv. 16: it is called simply THE TESTIMONY Ex. xvi. 34, xxvii. 21; Lev. xvi. 13, xxiv. 3; **Num. xvii.** 10. But in Num. x. 33 it is named THE ARK OF THE COVENANT, and this is its most frequent name in Deuteronomy and the other books of the Old Testament. In some places it is named THE ARK OF THE LORD (Josh. iii. 13, iv. 11, vii. 6; 1 S. iv. 6; 2 S. vi. 9, &c.), THE ARK OF GOD (1 S. iii. 3, iv. 11, v. 1, &c.), THE ARK OF THE STRENGTH OF THE LORD (2 Chron. vi. 41; Ps. cxxxii. 8), and THE HOLY ARK (2 Chron. xxxv. 3). Cf. note on *v.* 16.

The Ark of the Covenant was the central point of the Sanctuary. It was designed to contain the Testimony (xxv. 16, xl. 20; Deut. xxxi. 26), that is, the Tables of the Divine Law, the terms of the Covenant between Jehovah and His people: and it was to support the Mercy seat with its Cherubim, from between which He was to hold communion with them (Ex. xxv. 22). On this account, in these directions for the construction of the Sanctuary, it is named first of all the parts. But on the other hand, in the narrative of the work as it was actually carried out, we find that it was not made till after the Tabernacle (Ex. xxxvii. 1—9). It was more suitable that the receptacle should be first provided to receive and shelter the most sacred of the contents of the Sanctuary as soon as it was completed. The practical order of the works seems to be given in Ex. xxxi. 7—10, and xxxv. 11—19.—On the Golden Altar, see on xxx. 1.—The completion of the Ark is recorded xxxvii. 1—5. On its history, see concluding note on ch. xl.

10. *an ark*] The Hebrew name is *arōn*, which means a box, or coffer (Gen. l. 26; 2 K. xii. 9, 10; 2 Chro. xxiv. 8, &c.). The word *ark* exactly answers to it; but our translators have employed the same to render quite a different word (*tēbāh*), which is used nowhere in the Hebrew Bible except to denote what we familiarly call "the ark" of Noah, and the "ark of bulrushes" (Gen. vi. 14; Ex. ii. 3). In the first instance, there is the same confusion in both the LXX. and the Vulgate, but not in the latter one. The word *tēbāh* is Egyptian, having nearly the same meaning. See on Ex. ii. 3.—Taking the cubit at eighteen inches (see on Gen. vi. 15), the Ark of the Covenant was a box 3 ft. 9 in. long, 2 ft. 3 in. wide, and 2 ft. 3 in. deep.

of shittim wood] It is well observed that if the Ark, which appears to have been preserved till the destruction of Jerusalem (2 Chro. xxxv. 3; Jer. iii. 16), had originated

and a cubit and a half the height thereof.

11 And thou shalt overlay it with pure gold, within and without shalt thou overlay it, and shalt make upon it a crown of gold round about.

12 And thou shalt cast four rings of gold for it, and put *them* in the four corners thereof; and two rings *shall be* in the one side of it, and two rings in the other side of it.

13 And thou shalt make staves *of* shittim wood, and overlay them with gold.

14 And thou shalt put the staves into the rings by the sides of the ark, that the ark may be borne with them.

15 The staves shall be in the rings of the ark: they shall not be taken from it.

16 And thou shalt put into the ark the testimony which I shall give thee.

---

in Palestine, it would not have been made of shittim wood, the wood of the Wilderness (see on v. 5), but either of oak, the best wood of the Holy Land, or of cedar, which took the place of shittim wood in the construction of the Temple (Stanley, 'Jewish Church,' I. p. 163).

11. *overlay it with pure gold*] According to the rabbinists, the Ark was lined and covered with plates of gold. But there is nothing in the original which might not aptly denote the common process of gilding. The Egyptians in early times were acquainted with both the art of gilding and that of covering a substance with thin plates of gold. (Wilkinson's 'Pop. Acc.' II. 145.)

a crown of gold] That is, an edging or **moulding** of gold round the top of the Ark, within which the cover or Mercy seat (v. 17) may have fitted (cf. Ex. xxxvii. 2). There were golden mouldings, called by the same name, to the Table of Shewbread (v. 24, xxxvii. 11, 12) and to the Golden Altar (xxx. 3, xxxvii. 26). The Heb. word *zeer* signifies, according to its etymology, a band, or cincture, and is naturally applied to a crown. Our Version in here rendering it *crown*, follows the Vulgate and some other ancient Versions. But the renderings of the LXX., Josephus, the Targums, Luther, de Wette, Zunz, Wogue, &c., more nearly agree with our word **moulding**, *i.e.* a small cornice, and this answers to the radical meaning of *zeer* as well as *crown* does. See Reland, 'De Spoliis Templi,' c. VII.

12. *four corners thereof*] Rather, **its four bases**, or feet. The Hebrew substantive is rendered *corners* in most of the ancient versions. But the LXX. have κλίτη (which appears to be rather vaguely used to denote *extremities*, cf. vv. 12, 19), and there seems no doubt that the original means *feet* (Aben-Ezra, Abarbanel, Gesen., Fürst, Knobel, &c.). The word may possibly denote the lowest part of each corner: but it is not unlikely that there were low blocks, or plinths, placed under the corners to which the rings were attached (see on v. 26), and that it is to

them the word is here applied. The Ark, when it was carried, must thus have been raised above the shoulders of the bearers. The rings of the Golden Altar were placed immediately under the golden moulding (xxx. 4); but those of the Table of Shewbread were fastened to the feet of the four legs. It has been imagined by some Jewish and other authorities that the Ark was raised on high when it was carried in order to display the most sacred symbol of the Sanctuary. But we may infer, from there being a similar arrangement of the rings on the Table of Shewbread, as well as from the distinctive character of the Ark itself, that this could not have been the case. The Ark of the Covenant of Jehovah was never carried about like the arks of the gentile nations, for display. See Note at the end of chap. xl.

15. *they shall not be taken from it*] This direction was probably given in order that the Ark might not be touched by the hand (cf. 2 S. vi. 6). There is no similar direction regarding the staves of the Tabernacle of Shewbread (v. 27), those of the Golden Altar (xxx. 5), nor those of the Altar of Burnt offering (xxvii. 7). These were of less sanctity than the Ark and might be touched.—The formula in Num. iv. 6, 8, 11, 14, as it is rendered in our version, may seem to contradict the direction here given in regard to the Ark. But it might rather be translated in a more general sense, as, *put the staves in order* (see note in loc.).

16. *the testimony which I shall give thee*] The stone Tables of the Ten Commandments (Ex. xxiv. 12, xxxi. 18, xxxiv. 1, 28) are called the Testimony, or, the Tables of the Testimony (xxxi. 18, xxxii. 15, xxxiv. 29), as the Ark which contained them is called the Ark of the Testimony (see Introd.), and the Tabernacle in which the Ark was placed, the Tabernacle of the Testimony (Ex. xxxviii. 21; Num. i. 50, &c.); they are also called the Tables of the Covenant (Ex. xxxiv. 28; Deut. ix. 9, 11, 15), as the Ark is called the Ark of the Covenant. The meaning of the latter name admits of no doubt: the

17 And thou shalt make a mercy seat *of* pure gold: two cubits and a half *shall be* the length thereof, and a cubit and a half the breadth thereof.

18 And thou shalt make two cherubims *of* gold, *of* beaten work shalt thou make them, in the two ends of the mercy seat.

19 And make one cherub on the one end, and the other cherub on the other end: *even*¹ of the mercy seat shall ye make the cherubims on the two ends thereof.

20 And the cherubims shall stretch forth *their* wings on high, covering the mercy seat with their wings, and their faces *shall look* one to another; toward the mercy seat shall the faces of the cherubims be.

¹ Or, *of the matter of the mercy seat.*

Ten Commandments contained "the word of the Covenant" between Jehovah and His people (Ex. xxxiv. 28; Deut. iv. 13). But there has been a difference regarding the interpretation of the former name, which derives additional importance from its being the name used here and in ch. xl. 20 in immediate connection with the first placing of the Tables within the Ark and under the Mercy seat. The reasons for taking the word Testimony, in its application to the Ten Commandments, as signifying the direct testimony of Jehovah against sin in man, and thus bringing it into connection with Deut. xxxi. 26, 27, is given elsewhere. See Note on the Ten Commandments, after ch. xx. 21.

The Mercy Seat.
xxv. 17—22. (Cf. xxxvii. 6—9.)

17. *a mercy seat of pure gold*] In external form, the Mercy seat was a plate of gold with the cherubim standing on it, the whole beaten out of one solid piece of metal (xxxvii. 7); it was placed upon the Ark and so took the place of a cover. Its Hebrew name is *kapporeth*, and on the true meaning of this word there is a very important difference of opinion. The greater number of recent translators and critics, Jewish and others, with the Arabic amongst the ancient versions, render it as simply *cover*. Our version, following the general voice of antiquity, with Luther, Cranmer, and others of the early translators in modern languages, gives, as we believe, the truer rendering, calling it the Mercy seat. [See Note at the end of the chapter.]

18—20. The way in which the Cherubim of the Mercy seat are here mentioned, with reference to their faces, wings and posture, is in favour of the common Jewish tradition (Otho, 'Rabb. Lex.' p. 129), that they were human figures, each having two wings. They must have been of small size, proportioned to the area of the Mercy seat. On the other notices of Cherubim in the Scriptures, see Note on Gen. iii. 24. Comparing the different references to form in this place, in 2 Sam. xxii. 11 (Ps. xviii. 10), in Ezek. ch. i., x. and in Rev. ch. iv., it would appear that the name *Cherub* was applied to various combinations of animal forms. Similar combinations were made by most ancient peoples in order to represent conceivable combinations of powers, such as are denied to man in his earthly state of existence. It is remarkable that amongst the Egyptians, the Assyrians and the Greeks, as well as the Hebrews, the creatures by very far most frequently introduced into these composite figures, were man, the ox, the lion, and the eagle. These are evidently types of the most important and familiarly known classes of living material beings. The rabbinists recognized this in the Cherubim as described by Ezekiel, which they regarded as representing the whole creation engaged in the worship and service of God (Schoettgen, 'Hor. Heb.' p. 1108). Cf. Rev. iv. 9—11, v. 13. It would be in harmony with this view to suppose that the more strictly human shape of the Cherubim of the Mercy seat represented the highest form of created intelligence engaged in the devout contemplation of the divine Law of love and justice. Cf. 1 Pet. i. 12. They were thus symbols of worship rendered by the creature in the most exalted condition (See Augustin. 'Quæst. in Exod.' cv.).—It is worthy of notice that the golden Cherubim from between which Jehovah spoke to His people bore witness, by their place on the Mercy seat, to His redeeming mercy; while the Cherubim that took their stand with the flaming sword at the gate of Eden, to keep the way to the tree of life, witnessed to His condemnation of sin in man. The most perfect finite intelligence seems thus to be yielding assent to the divine Law in its twofold manifestation.

18. *of beaten work*] *i.e.* elaborately wrought with the hammer.

19. *even of the mercy seat*] Rather, **out of the Mercy seat**. The sense appears to be that the Cherubim and the Mercy seat were to be wrought out of one mass of gold. (Cf. xxxvii. 7.) This meaning agrees with Onkelos, Saadia, and most modern interpreters. But the LXX., Vulg. and Syr. translate the words in question as if the second clause of the verse were, in sense, only a repetition of the first clause.

20. See on *v.* 18.

21 And thou shalt put the mercy seat above upon the ark; and in the ark thou shalt put the testimony that I shall give thee.

22 And there I will meet with thee, and I will commune with thee from above the mercy seat, from *between the two cherubims which *are* upon the ark of the testimony, of all *things* which I will give thee in commandment unto the children of Israel.

23 ¶ ƒThou shalt also make a table *of* shittim wood: two cubits *shall be* the length thereof, and a cubit the breadth thereof, and a cubit and a half the height thereof.

24 And thou shalt overlay it with pure gold, and make thereto a crown of gold round about.

25 And thou shalt make unto it a border of an hand breadth round about, and thou shalt make a golden crown to the border thereof round about.

26 And thou shalt make for it four rings of gold, and put the rings in the four corners that *are* on the four feet thereof.

---

21. *the testimony*] See on *v.* 16. Cf. xl. 20.

22. *I will commune with thee*] See Note on the Ten Commandments, § V.

The Table of Shewbread.

23—30. (Cf. xxxvii. 10—16.)

23. *a table of shittim wood*] This Table is one of the most prominent objects in the triumphal procession sculptured in relief on the Arch of Titus. The most important of the sculptures of the Arch were carefully copied under the direction of Reland in 1710. Since that time they have gone on to decay, so that the engravings of them in his work 'De Spoliis Templi,' &c., are now of great interest and value. Reland has interpreted the sculptures with his accustomed learning and sagacity.

The Shewbread Table with its incense cups and the two Silver Trumpets (Num. x. 2).

The Table which is here represented could not, of course, have been the one made for the Tabernacle. The original Ark of the Testimony was preserved until it disappeared when Jerusalem was captured by the Babylonians: it was never replaced by an Ark of more modern construction. See concluding note on ch. xl. But the Shewbread Table, the Golden Altar, and the Golden Candlestick, were renewed by Solomon for the Temple. Of the Candlestick, ten copies were then made. (1 K. vii. 48, 49; 2 Chro. iv. 19). From the omission of them amongst the spoils carried home from Babylon (Ezra i. 9—11) we may infer that the Table and the Golden Altar with a single Candlestick were re-made by Zerubbabel (see 1 Macc. i. 21, 22), and again by the Maccabees (1 Macc. iv. 49). There cannot therefore be a doubt that the Table and the Candlestick figured on the Arch are those of the Maccabæan times: and it must have been these which are described, and must have been seen, by Josephus ('Ant.' III. 6. § 6, 7; 'B. J.' VII. 5. § 5). It is however most likely that the restorations were made as nearly as possible after the ancient models. In representing the Table it will be seen that the sculptor has exhibited its two ends, in defiance of perspective. The details and size of the figure, and the description of Josephus, appear to agree very nearly with the directions here given to Moses, and to illustrate them in several particulars. Josephus says that the Table was like the so-called Delphic tables, richly ornamented pieces of furniture in use amongst the Romans, which were sometimes, if not always, covered with gold or silver (Martial, XII. 67; Cicero, 'in Verr.' IV. 59; cf. Du Cange, Art. 'Delphica').

24. *overlay it*] See on *v.* 11.

a crown of gold] Rather, **a moulding of gold**. See on *v.* 11. The moulding of the Table is still seen at the ends of the sculptured figure.

25. *a border*] Rather **a framing**, which reached from leg to leg so as to make the Table firm, as well as to adorn it with a second moulding of gold. Two fragments of such a framing are still seen in the sculpture attached to the legs half-way down.

26. *in the four corners that are on the four feet thereof*] The word here rendered *feet* is

27 Over against the border shall the rings be for places of the staves to bear the table.

28 And thou shalt make the staves *of* shittim wood, and overlay them with gold, that the table may be borne with them.

29 And thou shalt make the dishes thereof, and spoons thereof, and covers thereof, and bowls thereof, ¹to cover withal: *of* pure gold shalt thou make them.

¹ Or, *to pour out withal*.

30 And thou shalt set upon the table shewbread before me alway.

31 ¶ ᵍAnd thou shalt make a candlestick *of* pure gold: *of* beaten work shall the candlestick be made: his shaft, and his branches, his bowls, his

ᵍ chap. 37. 17.

---

the common name for the feet of men or animals. Josephus says that the feet of the Table were like those that the Dorians used to put to their couches, which appear to have been famous for their splendour (Ælian, 'Var. Hist.' XII. 29; Athenæus, II. 47). Comparing this with the sculpture, it would seem that the legs terminated in something like the foot of an animal, such as in modern furniture is called *a claw*. The like device often occurs in the ancient Egyptian furniture (Wilkinson, I. pp. 59, 60, 62, &c.). The word here rendered *corner* is not the same as that so rendered in *v.* 12, and it may denote any extreme part. We might thus render the words, **upon the four extremities that are at the four feet.** Josephus speaks of the rings as having been in part attached to the claws themselves. But there is no trace of the rings in the sculpture.

27. *Over against the border*] Rather, **Over against the framing**; that is, the rings were to be placed not upon the framing itself, but at the extremities of the legs answering to each corner of it.

29. *dishes*] The Hebrew word is the same as is employed to denote the large silver vessels which were filled with fine flour and formed part of the offerings of the Princes of Israel in Num. vii. 13 sq., where it is rendered *chargers*. According to its probable etymology, it denoted a deep vessel, and therefore neither of the English words answers well to it: perhaps *bowls* would be nearer the mark. Knobel conjectures that these vessels, which belonged to the Shewbread Table, were used to bring the bread into the Sanctuary; but it is hard to imagine that vessels of sufficient size for such a purpose (Lev. xxiv. 5) were formed of gold. They may possibly have been the measures for the meal used in the loaves.

spoons] The Hebrew word is that used for the small gold **cups** that were filled with frankincense in the offerings of the Princes, Num. vii. 14 sq. The LXX. render it θυΐσκαι =*incense cups*. See on Lev. xxiv. 7. These must be the only vessels which are mentioned by Josephus in connection with the Table— δύο φιάλαι χρύσεαι λιβανωτοῦ πλήρεις ('Ant.' III. c. 6. § 6. c. 10. § 7), and which are represented on the Table in the sculpture.

covers...bowls] According to the best authority these were **flagons** and **chalices**, such as were used for Drink offerings. LXX. σπονδεῖα and κύαθοι. See the next note.

to cover withal] More correctly rendered in the margin, *to pour out withal*. It is strange that our translators in the text should have left Luther and Cranmer, backed as they are by the LXX., the Vulg., the Syriac, the Targums, and the most direct sense of the original words, to follow Saadia and the Talmud. With the exception of some recent Jewish versions, the best modern authorities apply the passage, along with the two last names of vessels, to the rite of the Drink offering, which appears to have regularly accompanied every Meat offering (Lev. xxiii. 18; Num. vi. 15, xxviii. 14, &c.). The subject is important in its bearing upon the meaning of the Shewbread: the corrected rendering of the words tends to shew that it was a true Meat offering [see on Lev. xxiv. 9].—The first part of the verse might thus be rendered:—**And thou shalt make its bowls and its incense-cups and its flagons and its chalices for pouring out** *the Drink offerings*.

30. The Shewbread Table was placed in the Holy Place on the north side (xxvi. 35). Directions for preparing the Shewbread are given in Lev. xxiv. 5—9. It consisted of twelve large cakes of unleavened bread, which were arranged on the Table in two piles, with a golden cup of frankincense on each pile (Jos. 'Ant.' III. 10. § 7). It was renewed every Sabbath day. The stale loaves were given to the priests, and the frankincense appears to have been lighted on the Altar for a memorial [see on Lev. ii. 2]. We may presume that the Drink offering was renewed at the same time. The Shewbread, with all the characteristics and significance of a great national Meat offering, in which the twelve tribes were represented by the twelve cakes, was to stand before Jehovah *perpetually*, in token that He was always graciously accepting the good works of His people, for whom Atonement had been made by the victims offered on the Altar in the Court of the Sanctuary [see notes on Lev. xxiv. 5—9].

knops, and his flowers, shall be of the same.

32 And six branches shall come out of the sides of it; three branches of the candlestick out of the one side, and three branches of the candlestick out of the other side:

33 Three bowls made like unto almonds, *with* a knop and a flower in one branch; and three bowls made like almonds in the other branch, *with* a knop and a flower: so in the six branches that come out of the candlestick.

The Golden Candlestick.
31—39. (Cf. xxxvii. 17—24).

31. *a candlestick of pure gold*] This would more properly be called a lamp-stand than a candlestick. Its purpose was to support seven oil-lamps. Like the Shewbread Table, it is a prominent object amongst the spoils of the Temple sculptured on the Arch of Titus. This figure is copied from Reland [see on *v.* 23].

The size of the Candlestick is nowhere mentioned: but we may form an estimate of it by comparing the figure with that of the Table. It is most likely that the two objects are represented on the same scale. Its height appears to have been about three feet, and its width two feet. The details of the sculpture usefully illustrate the description in the text. But the work and form of the pedestal here represented are not in accordance with Jewish taste or usage at any period. Reland conjectures that the original foot may have been broken off, and lost or stolen when the Candlestick was taken out of the Temple, and that the pedestal in the sculpture was added by some Roman artist to set off the trophy. There are other ancient representations of the Candlestick on gems, in tombs, and on the walls of synagogues. Some of these are copied in Reland's work, and one has lately been discovered by Capt. Wilson in a ruined synagogue in the valley of the Jarmuk. In most of them the stem is supported on three feet, or claws. This arrangement however is supposed to contradict Josephus, who says that the stem rose from a *pedestal*: the word he uses (βάσις) is however not quite free from ambiguity. In general form the other figures of the Candlestick copied by Reland nearly agree with that on the arch except in the limbs being more slender, in which particular they are countenanced by the description in Josephus ('B. J.' VII. 5. § 5). It is likely that the sculptor may have thickened the limbs in his work to give them better effect from the point of view from which spectators would see them.

of beaten work] See on *v.* 18.

his shaft, and his branches, his bowls, his knops, and his flowers] This might rather be rendered, **its base, its stem, its flower cups** [see next verse], **its knobs, and its lilies.**

33. *Three bowls made like unto almonds*] More strictly, **three cups of almond flowers.** These appear to be the cups in immediate contact with the knobs as shewn in the sculpture.

a flower] Most of the old versions render the word as **a lily**, and this rendering well agrees with the sculpture.

the candlestick] Here, and in the two following verses, the word appears to denote *the stem*, as the essential part of the Candlestick. It would seem from *vv.* 33—35 that the ornamentation of the Candlestick consisted of uniform members, each comprising a series of an almond flower, a knob and a lily; that the stem comprised four of these members; that each pair of branches was united to the stem at one of the knobs; and that each branch comprised three members. In comparing the description in the text with the sculptured figure, allowance may be made for some deviation in the sculptor's copy, which was pardonable enough, considering the purpose for which the representation was made.

34 And in the candlestick *shall be* four bowls made like unto almonds, *with* their knops and their flowers.

35 And *there shall be* a knop under two branches of the same, and a knop under two branches of the same, and a knop under two branches of the same, according to the six branches that proceed out of the candlestick.

36 Their knops and their branches shall be of the same: all it *shall be* one beaten work *of* pure gold.

37 And thou shalt make the seven lamps thereof: and they shall ¹light the lamps thereof, that they may give light over against †it.

⁰ Or, *cause to ascend.*
† Heb. *the face of it.*

38 And the tongs thereof, and the snuffdishes thereof, *shall be of* pure gold.

39 *Of* a talent of pure gold shall he make it, with all these vessels.

ʰ Acts 7. 44. Heb. 8. 5.

40 And ʰ look that thou make *them* after their pattern, †which was shewed thee in the mount.

† Heb. *which thou wast caused to see.*

---

37. *seven lamps*] These lamps were probably like those used by the Egyptians and other nations, shallow covered vessels more or less of an oval form, with a mouth at one end from which the wick protruded. This may help us to the simplest explanation of the rather obscure words, "that they may give light over against it." The Candlestick was placed on the south side of the Holy Place (xxvi. 35), with the line of lamps parallel with the wall, or, according to Josephus, somewhat obliquely. If the wick-mouths of the lamps were turned outwards, they would give light over against the Candlestick; that is, towards the north side [see Num. viii. 2].

37. *they shall light*] See marginal rendering and note on Lev. xxiv. 2.

38. *the tongs*] The Hebrew word is the same as in Is. vi. 6. The small tongs for the lamps were used to trim and adjust the wicks.

the snuff-dishes] These were shallow vessels used to receive the burnt fragments of wick removed by the tongs. The same Hebrew word is translated, in accordance with its connection, *fire pans*, xxvii. 3, xxxviii. 3; and *censers*, Num. iv. 14, xvi. 6, &c. For the regulations respecting the Priests' tending the lamps, see xxvii. 20, 21; xxx. 8; Lev. xxiv. 2—4 (with the note); 2 Chro. xiii. 11.

39. *a talent of pure gold*] Amongst the discrepant estimates of the weight of the Hebrew talent, the one that appears to be received most generally would make it about 94 lbs. See on xxxviii. 27.

vessels] Rather, **utensils** [see on xxvii. 19].

Several writers have treated of the symbolism of the lights of the Golden Candlestick with their oil, of its ornamentation with the knobs and flowers, and of its branched form (Bähr, Hengstenberg, Keil, &c.). All these particulars might have been in later times appropriated by the prophetic inspiration as figures illustrative of spiritual truth. See Zech. iv. 1—14; Rev. i. 12, 13, 20. But in any especial connection with the place held by the Candlestick in the Sanctuary, as its plan was revealed to Moses, there appears to be only one peculiar point of symbolism on which stress can be laid—the fact that the lamps were seven in number. The general fashion of the Candlestick and its ornaments might have been a matter of taste; light was of necessity required in the Tabernacle, and wherever light is used in ceremonial observance, it may of course be taken in a general way as a figure of the Light of Truth; but in the Sanctuary of the covenanted people, it must plainly have been understood as expressly significant that the number of the lamps agreed with the number of the Covenant. The Covenant of Jehovah was essentially a Covenant of light.

40. See on *v.* 9.

NOTE ON CHAP. XXV. 4.

ON THE COLOURS OF THE TABERNACLE.

I.

Our version is most probably right in its rendering of the names of the three colours used in the curtains and vails of the Tabernacle. But the subject is a doubtful one. The names of colours in all languages appear to have been very vaguely used, until the progress of science in connection with the decorative arts has rendered greater precision both possible and desirable. Our own word *gray*, as applied not only to the mixture of black and white now so called, but also to the brown dress of the "gray friars" and to the cockchafer (the "gray fly" of Milton); and the Latin *purpureus* as applied to snow, to the swan and the foam of the sea, to the rose, to a beautiful human eye, as well as to the colour now known as purple, may be taken as instances. The ἱμάτιον πορφυροῦν of John xix. 2 is called χλαμύδα κοκκίνην in Matt. xxvii. 28. **Mr.**

Gladstone's essay on the use of the names of colours in Homer furnishes other illustrations[1]. That the Hebrew names were used with not more stedfastness is proved by Mr Bevan in Smith's 'Dict. of the Bible' (Art. 'Colours'). The Hebrew names in the text must however have been applied at the time with distinct denotation in reference to the use of the yarn in the embroidery of the curtains. The uncertainty concerns only our discovering what the colours actually were. The earliest equivalents we have for the Hebrew words are those used by the LXX., which have been adopted by Philo and Josephus, and have been followed by the ancient versions in general. But we are unfortunately far from certain of the purport of the Greek words.

II.

The most important of the three colours mentioned in this place is the one rendered *blue*. The balance of evidence seems to be in favour of its being a pure sky blue. The Hebrew is *tĕkēleth* (תְּכֵלֶת), for which the LXX. have ὑάκινθος, and the Vulgate *Hyacinthus*. As the name of a flower, the Greek word has been taken for the iris, the gladiolus, the delphinium, or the hyacinth: as the name of a precious stone, it evidently could not, as some have supposed, belong to the amethyst, since it is mentioned with the amethyst (ἀμέθυστος) in Rev. xxi. 20; it most likely denoted the sapphire[2]: as the name of a colour, it has been supposed to denote pure blue, purple, violet, black, red or rust colour[3]. Of the different flowers to which the word has been ascribed, it may be remarked that the greater number are blue; for example, the common iris, the larkspur, the wild hyacinth, and the starch hyacinth, which is so abundant in the neighbourhood of Athens. The Hebrew word has been very generally taken to denote either blue, or bluish purple, while "the purple" associated with it has been supposed to have had a stronger red tinge. Philo[4], Josephus[5], and Saadia, with most of the Fathers and the rabbinists, appear to have understood it as the colour of the sky. Philo, who took it to symbolize the air, in the expression which he applies to the air (φύσει γὰρ μέλας), has been reasonably supposed to allude to the dark full tinge which distinguishes the skies of southern latitudes[6].

That the Egyptians in early times used indigo as a blue dye is certain[7], and it is by no means improbable that the Israelites did the same. If, as Wilkinson and others[8] suppose, the blue border of the Israelites' garments was adopted from an Egyptian custom, the facts that the Egyptian borders were certainly dyed with indigo, and that the Hebrew and Greek words expressing the colour of the Israelites' borders (Num. xv. 38) are *tĕkēleth* and ὑάκινθος, favour the notion that these words express the colour obtained from indigo. But the etymology of the Hebrew term is supposed rather to indicate that the colour was procured, like the Tyrian purple, from a shell-fish. It is conceived that while a species of Murex produced the purple, a Buccinum produced the blue[9]. Both colours were obtained by the Tyrians from "the Isles of Elishah," that is, the Isles of the Ægean Sea, where it seems most probable that each must have been obtained from the sea[10]. The art of preparing the dye from the fish is now lost, and this, of course, increases the uncertainty of the question at issue.

It is however likely that *tĕkēleth* was the name of the well-known colour obtained from more than one kind of dye. The inquiry regarding the colour itself has peculiar interest from its having been the predominating colour in the decoration of the Sanctuary. Besides taking its place with the other two colours in the curtains and vails of the Tabernacle, it is found by itself in the loops of the curtains (Ex. xxvi. 4), in the lace of the breastplate of the High Priest (xxviii. 28), in the robe of the ephod (xxviii. 31), and the lace of the mitre (xxviii. 37). In wrapping up the sacred utensils when the host was on the march, blue cloths, purple cloths, and scarlet cloths were used for the various articles according to specific directions (Num. iv.). The national significance of blue appears to be shewn in the blue fringes that have been mentioned (Num. xv. 38; cf. Matt. xxiii. 5).

Several Jewish commentators, followed by Luther and Cranmer, have taken the word *tĕkēleth* to denote *yellow silk*. It is hardly

---

[1] 'Essays on Homer,' Vol. III. p. 457.
[2] Professor Maskelyne considers that the hyacinth of Pliny ('H. N.' XXXVII. 40) and other classical writers was what we call the sapphire, while the stone called sapphire by the ancients was lapis lazuli. 'Edinb. Rev.' No. 253. See note on Ex. xxviii. 18.
[3] See Liddell and Scott's 'Lex.'
[4] 'Vit. Mos.' III. 6.
[5] 'Ant.' III. 7. § 7. See also note on Ex. xxv. 5.

[6] Other grounds for rendering the Hebrew word *sky blue*, rather than *violet* or *bluish purple*, as Gesenius and others have preferred, may be found in Bochart, 'Op.' Vol. III. p. 728, and Bähr, 'Symbolik,' Vol. I. p. 303.
[7] Wilkinson, 'Pop. Acc.' Vol. II. p. 78.
[8] Henstenberg, 'Egypt and the Books of Moses,' Smith, 'The Pentateuch,' p. 302.
[9] Bochart, 'Op.' p. III. 727. Gesenius, s. v. Fürst, s.v. Wilkinson, Note on Herodot. III. 20. Tristram, 'Nat. Hist. of the Bible,' p. 297.
[10] Ezek. xxvii. 7; Jer. x. 9. Cf. Plin. H. N.' IX. 60, *sq.*

necessary to state that the material could not have been silk [see note on Ex. xxv. 4]. The notion that the colour was yellow seems to stand upon a mere hollow conjecture suggested by the natural colour of silk.

III.

Purple is in Heb. *argāmān* (אַרְגָּמָן), in the LXX. πορφύρα. The derivation of the Hebrew word is doubtful, but all authorities seem to be in favour of its signifying the purple obtained from more than one species of shell-fish in the Mediterranean, which became commonly known as the Tyrian purple (Ezek. xxvii. 7, 16). The colour seems to have had a strong red tinge, and to have approached what we call crimson. The fish that produced it has been supposed to be a muscle, but it is hardly to be doubted that it was in fact a Murex, two species of which (*M. brandaris* and *M. trunculus*) might have furnished it (Tristram). Hence the dye was called *murex* by the Latin writers. The colour is mentioned in connection with the Sanctuary only in combination with blue and scarlet in the curtains and vails and in some of the cloths for wrapping (Num. iv. 13). The estimation in which the dye was held may be inferred from Judg. viii. 26; Esth. i. 6; Prov. xxxi. 22.

IV.

Scarlet is in Hebrew *tola'ath shāni* (תּוֹלַעַת שָׁנִי), in LXX. κόκκινος διπλοῦς, and in Vulg. "coccus bistinctus[1]." But the literal translation of the two Hebrew words is *scarlet worm*, while in Lev. xiv. 4, 6, 49, 51, 52, the words are transposed (שְׁנִי תּוֹלַעַת), so as to signify *worm scarlet*. The word *shāni*, by itself, denotes scarlet in Gen. xxxviii. 28, 30; Josh. ii. 18; Prov. xxxi. 21, &c. Ancient and modern authorities agree as to the colour, which is uniformly called scarlet in our version except in Jer. iv. 30, where it is rendered *crimson*. The dye used to produce the colour in the vail of the Temple is called *karmil* (כַּרְמִיל), 2 Chron. ii. 7, 14, iii. 14, where it is rendered *crimson*, though there is no reason to doubt that the colour was the same as the *scarlet* of the Tabernacle. It appears to have been obtained from the *coccus ilicis*, the cochineal insect of the holm oak, which was used in the East before the *coccus cacti*, the well-known cochineal of the prickly pear, was introduced from Mexico. The Arabic name for it is *kermez*, which is evidently related to the Hebrew word *karmil*. The root *karm* exists in our *crimson* and *carmine*. In the use of the Sanctuary, it is found only in the figured curtains and embroidery associated with blue and purple, and in the wrapping cloths (Num. iv. 8). It appears to have had a special connection with the rites of purification in association with hyssop and cedar (Lev. xiv. 4, 6, 49, 51, 52; Num. xix. 6; Heb. ix. 19).

V.

On the whole, there does not seem to be much ground to doubt that our version, in rendering the names of the colours of the woven and embroidered work of the Sanctuary, expresses the most probable conclusions.

The three colours, blue, scarlet and purple, have been recognized all but universally as royal colours, such as were best suited for the decoration of a palace[2]. This fact appears to furnish sufficient ground for their having been appointed as the colours for the embroidery which was to adorn the dwelling-place of Jehovah. Many have, however, imagined that there was some other symbolical significance in them. See Bähr, 'Symbolik,' Vol. I. p. 324; Dr W. L. Alexander in Kitto's 'Cyclo.' Vol. I. p. 541, &c.

NOTE ON CHAP. XXV. 17.

ON THE MERCY SEAT.

The word *kapporeth* (כַּפֹּרֶת) is never applied to anything except the golden cover of the Ark. The root from which it comes, *kāphar* (כָּפַר), without doubt signifies *to cover*, and bears an obvious resemblance to our word *cover*. In one passage of the Old Testament, but in one only, the Hebrew word, in its *Kal* or primitive form, is used in this sense in reference to covering the Ark of Noah with pitch (Gen. vi. 14). In the *Piel* form (*Kipper*, כִּפֶּר) the root is used nearly seventy times, and always in the sense of *forgiving* or *reconciling*, that is of covering up offences. Now a large number of recent authorities, Jewish and others[3], have preferred to take *kapporeth* in the simple sense of *a cover*. Josephus and Saadia give countenance to this rendering. The question thus brought before us is, was the *kapporeth* originally regarded as a mere part of the Ark, or as something having a distinct significance, and a recognized designation, of its own? The inquiry is of great importance, from its bearing on the character

---

[1] The Greek and Latin renderings appear to be based on a mistake in regard to the word שְׁנִי, which, with other vowel points, would mean *twice*.

[2] See Esth. i. 6, viii. 15; 2 S. i. 24; Cant. iii. 10; Jer. x. 9; Ezek. xxiii. 6; Dan. v. 7; Luke xvi. 19; Rev. xviii. 12, &c.

[3] Kimchi, Mendelsohn, de Wette, Gesenius, Schott, Fürst, Zunz, Knobel, Herxheimer, Leeser, Benisch, Sharpe, &c. But amongst the Jewish commentators, Wogue and Kalisch are exceptions.

of the Mosaic ritual. The latter view appears to deserve the preference on these grounds;—

1. In the order of the sacred text, the Mercy seat is described by itself, and is directed to be placed "above upon the Ark" (Ex. xxv. 17—22, xxvi. 34): it is never called *the cover* (or *kapporeth*) *of the Ark*, but is always mentioned as a distinct thing (Ex. xxx. 6, xxxi. 7, xxxv. 12, xxxvii. 6—9, xxxix. 35; Lev. xvi. 13; Num. vii. 89, &c.).

2. The Holy of Holies is called in the first Book of Chronicles (xxviii. 11) *the house of the kapporeth* (בֵּית הַכַּפֹּרֶת); and in Leviticus (xvi. 2) it is called the place *within the vail before the kapporeth, which is upon the Ark*. Such expressions as these seem clearly to indicate that the *kapporeth* could not have been regarded as a mere subordinate part of the Ark.

3. An argument scarcely less strong may be drawn from the relationship of the word *kapporeth* to *kippurim* (כִּפֻּרִים) = *atonements*, in connection with the rites of the Day of Atonement, or (as it is literally) the Day of Atonements. No part of the Sanctuary is so intimately connected with the *kippurim* made on that day by the High Priest as the *kapporeth* (Lev. xvi. 2, 13, 14, 15). The phraseology of these passages is certainly not such as could be well accounted for by the mere position of the *kapporeth* as the cover of the Ark.

4. The general current of the most ancient Jewish tradition evidently favours the derivation of *kapporeth* from *kipper* (כִּפֶּר), the *Piel* form of the verb, which, as it has been already observed, nowhere bears any other meaning than *to atone*, or *to shew mercy*. The oldest authority is the Septuagint, in which the word is rendered ἱλαστήριον ἐπίθημα[1]. Philo speaks of the cover of the Ark being called in the Scripture ἱλαστήριον, as a symbol τῆς ἵλεω τοῦ Θεοῦ δυνάμεως[2]. Rabbinical tradition furnishes evidence to the same effect. The vowel points in the word *kapporeth* (כַּפֹּרֶת) are such as to connect it with the *Piel* form *kipper*, rather than with the *Kal* form *kāphar*. Another argument may be added from the use in the Targums of the same expression as is found 1 Chron. xxviii. 11, *the house of the kapporeth* [see § 2], to answer to "the oracle" (דְּבִיר) in 1 K. vi. 5.

5. We might at once settle the question as to the Mercy seat having a meaning of its own by referring to the passages in the New Testament in which the word ἱλαστήριον occurs (Heb. ix. 5; Rom. iii. 25). But it is satisfactory to have such clear evidence as exists that the New Testament use of the word is not a late or artificial adaptation of it, but a clear and simple application of its original meaning.

[1] Fürst, following certain Jewish authorities, conceives that ἱλαστήριον is a gloss of later date. But this is evidently a mere conjecture of prejudice.
[2] 'Vit. Mos.' III. 8.

CHAPTER XXVI.

1 *The ten curtains of the tabernacle.* 7 *The eleven curtains of goats' hair.* 14 *The covering of rams' skins.* 15 *The boards of the tabernacle, with their sockets and bars.* 31 *The vail for the ark.* 36 *The hanging for the door.*

MOREOVER thou shalt make the tabernacle *with* ten curtains *of* fine twined linen, and blue, and purple, and scarlet: *with* cherubims of †cunning work shalt thou make them.

† Heb. *the work of a cunning workman*, or, *embroiderer*

THE TABERNACLE.

xxvi. 1—37. (xxxvi. 8—38.)

CHAP. XXVI. The Tabernacle was to comprise three main parts, the TABERNACLE, more strictly so-called, its TENT, and its COVERING (Ex. xxxv. 11, xxxix. 33, 34, xl. 19, 34; Num. iii. 25, &c.). These parts are very clearly distinguished in the Hebrew, but they are confounded in many places of the English Version [see on *vv.* 7, 9, &c.], and in still more places of the LXX., the Vulgate, and other versions, ancient and modern. The TABERNACLE itself was to consist of curtains of fine linen woven with coloured figures of Cherubim, and a structure of boards which was to contain the Holy Place and the Most Holy Place; the TENT was to be a true tent of goats' hair cloth to contain and shelter the Tabernacle; the COVERING was to be of red rams' skins and tachash skins [see on xxv. 5], and was spread over the goats' hair tent as an additional protection against the weather. On the external form of the Tabernacle and the arrangement of its parts, see Note at the end of the chap. The account of its completion is given ch. xxxvi. 8—38.

THE TABERNACLE.

xxvi. 1—6. (Cf. xxxvi. 8—13.)

1. *tabernacle*] The Hebrew is *mishkān, i.e.* dwelling-place (Job xviii. 21, xxi. 28; Ps. xlix. 11, Is. xxii. 16, &c. &c.). When it denotes the Dwelling-place of Jehovah, it is

2 The length of one curtain *shall be* eight and twenty cubits, and the breadth of one curtain four cubits: and every one of the curtains shall have one measure.

3 The five curtains shall be coupled together one to another; and *other* five curtains *shall be* coupled one to another.

4 And thou shalt make loops of blue upon the edge of the one curtain from the selvedge in the coupling; and likewise shalt thou make in the uttermost edge of *another* curtain, in the coupling of the second.

5 Fifty loops shalt thou make in the one curtain, and fifty loops shalt thou make in the edge of the curtain that *is* in the coupling of the second; that the loops may take hold one of another.

6 And thou shalt make fifty taches

---

regularly accompanied by the definite article (*hammishkān*). The word tabernacle (which our translators took from the Vulgate) might fitly designate the structure of boards which formed the walls of the Holy Places, but its meaning does not etymologically answer to *mishkān*. The Hebrew word is however uniformly rendered tabernacle in our Bible: the confusion to which reference has been made in the preceding note occurs in rendering the names of the Tent and the Covering.

It should be noticed that in this place *hammishkān* is not used in its full sense as denoting the dwelling-place of Jehovah: it denotes only the tabernacle cloth. It was the textile work which was regarded as the essential part of the Tabernacle, and this is apparent in our version of *v.* 6. The tent-cloth in like manner and for the like reason is called simply the Tent (*v.* 11). The wooden parts of both the Tabernacle and the Tent are evidently mentioned as if they were subordinate to the textile parts.—The word *mishkān* is employed with three distinct ranges of meaning, (1) in its strict sense, comprising the cloth of the Tabernacle with its woodwork (Exod. xxv. 9, xxvi. 30, xxxvi. 13, xl. 18, &c.); (2) in a narrower sense, for the tabernacle-cloth only (Exod. xxvi. 1, 6, xxxv. 11, xxxix. 33, 34, &c.); (3) in a wider sense, for the *Mishkān* with its Tent and Covering (Exod. xxvii. 19, xxxv. 18, &c.).

with ten curtains] Rather, **of ten breadths**. The Hebrew word (*yĕri'ah*) is everywhere in our version rendered *a curtain*. Some corresponding word is used in the Ancient Versions (LXX. αὐλαία, Vulg. *cortina*) and in some modern ones. In such places as Ps. civ. 2, Is. liv. 2, Jer. iv. 20, the Hebrew word is evidently applied to an entire tent-curtain. But in connection with the Sanctuary it always denotes what in English would more strictly be called a breadth. Five of these breadths were united so as to form what, in common usage, we should call a large curtain. (See on *v.* 3.) The word curtain will be used in this, its ordinary sense, in these notes. The two curtains thus formed were coupled together by the loops and taches to make the entire tabernacle-cloth, which is what is here called "the tabernacle." See preceding note.

fine twined linen] *i.e.* the most carefully spun thread of flax, each thread consisting of two or more smaller threads twined together (see Wilkinson, 'Pop. Account,' II. 76). On the original word for *linen*, see on xxv. 4.

blue, and purple, and scarlet] See on xxv. 4.

cherubims] See on xxv. 18.

of cunning work] More properly, **of the work of the skilled weaver**. The coloured figures of Cherubim were to be worked in the loom, as in the manufacture of tapestry and carpets: in the hangings for the Tent they were to be embroidered with the needle [see on *v.* 36]. On the different kinds of workmen employed on the textile fabrics, see on xxxv. 35.

3. Each curtain formed of five breadths (see on *v.* 1), was 42 feet in length and 30 feet in breadth, taking the cubit at 18 inches.

4. This verse is obscure as it stands in our version, nor is it easy to render the original word for word so as to make the sense clear. But the meaning appears to be, *And thou shalt make loops of blue on the selvedge of the one breadth* (*which is*) *on the side* (*of the one curtain*) *at the coupling; and the same shalt thou do in the selvedge of the outside breadth of the other* (*curtain*) *at the coupling*. The "coupling" is the uniting together of the two curtains. This explanation substantially agrees with the Ancient Versions and most of the modern ones.

5. The words "in the edge of the curtain that is in the coupling of the second," mean, *on the edge of the breadth that is at the coupling in the second* (*curtain*).—The word rendered "loops" (*lulaoth*) only occurs here and in xxxvi. 11. It is doubtful whether it has connection with any Semitic root; it is probably of Egyptian origin. Conjectures on the other side may be seen in Gesenius' 'Handwörterbuch,' and Fürst's 'Lex.'

6. *taches of gold*] Each clasp, or *tache*, was to unite two opposite loops. On the Heb. word for *tache*, see p. 375, note 7.

of gold, and couple the curtains together with the taches: and it shall be one tabernacle.

7 ¶ And thou shalt make curtains *of* goats' *hair* to be a covering upon the tabernacle: eleven curtains shalt thou make.

8 The length of one curtain *shall be* thirty cubits, and the breadth of one curtain four cubits: and the eleven curtains *shall be all* of one measure.

9 And thou shalt couple five curtains by themselves, and six curtains by themselves, and shalt double the sixth curtain in the forefront of the tabernacle.

10 And thou shalt make fifty loops on the edge of the one curtain *that is* outmost in the coupling, and fifty loops in the edge of the curtain which coupleth the second.

11 And thou shalt make fifty taches of brass, and put the taches into the loops, and couple the ⁱtent together, ⁱ Or, *covering*
that it may be one.

12 And the remnant that remaineth of the curtains of the tent, the half curtain that remaineth, shall hang over the backside of the tabernacle.

13 And a cubit on the one side, and a cubit on the other side † of that † Heb. *in the remainder,*
which remaineth in the length of the curtains of the tent, it shall hang over or, *surplusage.*
the sides of the tabernacle on this side and on that side, to cover it.

14 And thou shalt make a covering for the tent *of* rams' skins dyed red, and a covering above *of* badgers' skins.

15 ¶ And thou shalt make boards for the tabernacle *of* shittim wood standing up.

---

couple the curtains] *i.e.* couple the two outside breadths mentioned in *v.* 4.

it shall be one tabernacle] The tabernacle-cloth alone is here meant. See on *v.* 1. For the mode in which the tabernacle-cloth was disposed, see Note at the end of the chap., § IV.

The Tent-cloth.

7—13 (xxxvi. 14—18).

7. *curtains*] See on *v.* 1.
of goats' hair] See on xxv. 4.
a covering upon the tabernacle] **a tent over the Tabernacle.** The same Hebrew words are rightly translated xxxvi. 14. The name *ohel*, which is here used, is the regular one for a tent of skins or cloth of any sort. See introd. note to ch. xxv., and Note at the end of this chap. § II.

9. The width of each breadth of the tent-cloth was to be four cubits, the same as that of the breadths of the figured cloth of the Tabernacle (*v.* 2). But the length was to be two cubits more, and there was to be an additional breadth (*v.* 13). One of the curtains (see on *v.* 1) was to comprise five breadths and the other six.

shalt double the sixth curtain in the forefront of the tabernacle] The last word should be **Tent**, not tabernacle. The passage might be rendered, *thou shalt equally divide the sixth breadth at the front of the Tent.* In this way, half a breadth would overhang at the front and half at the back. See *v.* 12, and Note at the end of the chapter.

10. The meaning may be thus given:— *And thou shalt make fifty loops on the selvedge of the outside breadth of the one (curtain) at the coupling, and fifty loops on the selvedge of the outside breadth of the other (curtain) at the coupling.* Cf. note *v.* 4.

11. In the Tent, clasps of bronze were used to unite the loops of the two curtains; in the Tabernacle, clasps of gold, cf. *v.* 6 and on *v.* 37.

couple the tent together] This is the right translation. The "covering," as the alternative for *tent* given in the margin, is wrong. See introd. note to this chap. By "the tent" is here meant the tent-cloth alone. See on *v.* 1.

12. *the half curtain*] See on *v.* 9, and Note at the end of the chapter, § IV.

13. The measure of the entire tabernacle-cloth was 40 cubits by 28; that of the tent-cloth was 44 cubits by 30. When the latter was placed over the former, it spread beyond it at the back and front two cubits (the "half-curtain" *vv.* 9, 12) and at the sides one cubit. See Note at the end of the chapter.

The Covering for the Tent.

v. 14. (Cf. xxxvi. 19.)

14. *rams' skins dyed red*] See on xxv. 5.

badgers' skins] The skin, not of the badger, but of a marine animal called *tachash*, perhaps the dugong or the seal. See on xxv. 5.

The Boards and Bars of the Tabernacle.

15—30 (xxxvi. 20—34).

15. *boards*] There is no reason to doubt that these were simple boards or planks (Vulg.

16 Ten cubits *shall be* the length of a board, and a cubit and a half *shall be* the breadth of one board.

17 Two †tenons *shall there be* in one board, set in order one against another: thus shalt thou make for all the boards of the tabernacle.

18 And thou shalt make the boards for the tabernacle, twenty boards on the south side southward.

19 And thou shalt make forty sockets of silver under the twenty boards; two sockets under one board for his two tenons, and two sockets under another board for his two tenons.

20 And for the second side of the tabernacle on the north side *there shall be* twenty boards:

21 And their forty sockets *of* silver; two sockets under one board, and two sockets under another board.

22 And for the sides of the tabernacle westward thou shalt make six boards.

23 And two boards shalt thou make for the corners of the tabernacle in the two sides.

24 And they shall be †coupled together beneath, and they shall be coupled together above the head of it

† Heb. *hands.*

† Heb. *twinned.*

---

tabulæ), of sufficient thickness for the stability of the structure. They are called *pillars* in Greek (LXX. στῦλοι, Philo and Josephus, κίονες). Bähr adopts the rabbinical notion that they were a cubit in thickness; Josephus, with greater probability, says that they were four fingers.

of shittim wood] The shittah tree (*Acacia seyal*, see on xxv. 5) has been said to be too small to produce boards of the size here described. It has been conjectured that each board was jointed up of several pieces. But Mr Tristram regards this conjecture as needless, and states that there are acacia-trees near Engedi which would produce boards four feet in width ('Nat. Hist. of the Bible,' p. 392). If there are no trees so large in the Peninsula of Sinai at this time, liberal allowance may be made for the diminished capabilities of the region for the production of timber.

17. *tenons*] See Note at the end of the chapter.

18. The dimensions of the wooden part of the Tabernacle are not directly stated; but they are easily made out from the measurement, number and arrangement of the boards, if we estimate each of the corner boards (*v.* 23) as adding half a cubit to the width. The entire length of the structure was thirty cubits in the clear, and its width ten cubits. With this agree Philo ('Vit. Mos.' III. 7), Josephus ('Ant.' III. 6. § 3), and all tradition.

the south side southward] The Hebrew phrase, which also occurs xxvii. 9, xxxvi. 23, xxxviii. 9, is relieved from pleonasm if it is rendered, **the south side on the right.** (Geneva Fr., Zunz, Leeser: cf. Gesen. p. 600.) As the entrance of the Tabernacle was at its east end, the south side, to a person entering it, would be on the *left* hand: but we learn from Josephus ('Ant.' VIII. 3. § 6) that it was usual in speaking of the Temple to identify the south with the right hand and the north with the left hand, the entrance being regarded as the face of the structure and the west end as its back.

19. *sockets*] More literally, **bases.** The same word is rightly rendered "foundations" in Job xxxviii. 6: most versions in this place translate it by some word equivalent to *bases*. Each base weighed a talent, that is, about 94 lbs. (see xxxviii. 27), and must have been a massive block. Nothing is said of the form, but as the tenons of the boards were "set in order one against another" (*v.* 17), the bases may have fitted together so as to make a continuous foundation for the walls of boards, presenting a succession of sockets, or mortices (each base having a single socket), into which the tenons were to fit. This seems to have been the notion of Philo and Josephus [see Note at the end of chapter, § I.]. The bases served not only for ornament but also for a protection of the lower ends of the boards from the decay which would have resulted from contact with the ground. The word *socket* seems to have been adopted from Josephus. The word he uses is στρόφιγξ, which does not answer to the Hebrew etymologically, as the βάσις of the LXX. and Philo does; but there is an obvious resemblance which seems to have struck him between what is here spoken of and the socket (στρόφιγξ) in which the tenon of a door turns to serve as a hinge, according to common Eastern custom.

22. *the sides of the tabernacle westward*] Rather, **the back of the Tabernacle towards the west.** See on *v.* 18.

23. *in the two sides*] Rather, **at the back.** So LXX., Vulg., Luther, de Wette, Zunz, Herxh., &c.

24. The corner boards appear to have been of such width, and so placed, as to add

unto one ring: thus shall it be for them both; they shall be for the two corners.

25 And they shall be eight boards, and their sockets *of* silver, sixteen sockets; two sockets under one board, and two sockets under another board.

26 ¶ And thou shalt make bars *of* shittim wood; five for the boards of the one side of the tabernacle,

27 And five bars for the boards of the other side of the tabernacle, and five bars for the boards of the side of the tabernacle, for the two sides westward.

28 And the middle bar in the midst of the boards shall reach from end to end.

29 And thou shalt overlay the boards with gold, and make their rings *of* gold *for* places for the bars: and thou shalt overlay the bars with gold.

30 And thou shalt rear up the tabernacle *a*according to the fashion thereof which was shewed thee in the mount.

a chap. 25 9, 40. Acts 7. 44 Heb. 8. 5.

31 ¶ And thou shalt make a vail *of* blue, and purple, and scarlet, and fine twined linen of cunning work: with cherubims shall it be made:

32 And thou shalt hang it upon four pillars of shittim *wood* overlaid with gold: their hooks *shall be of* gold, upon the four sockets of silver.

33 ¶ And thou shalt hang up the vail under the taches, that thou mayest

---

a cubit to the width of the structure, making up with the six boards of full width (*v.* 22) ten cubits in the clear (see on *v.* 18). There is no occasion to imagine, as some have done, that each of them consisted of two strips mitered together longitudinally so as to form a corner by itself. They may have been simple boards with the width of half a cubit added to the thickness of the boards of the sides. The boards at the corners were to be coupled together at the top "unto one ring," and at the bottom " unto one ring," and each ring was to be so formed as to receive two bars meeting at a right angle.

26, 27. See on *v.* 28, and Note at the end of the chapter, § I.

27. *for the two sides westward*] **for the back towards the west.** Cf. *v.* 22.

28. *in the midst of the boards*] The middle bar was distinguished from the other bars by its reaching from end to end. The Hebrew might mean either that the *midst* throughout which it ran was the middle between the top and the bottom of the boards, or that it was a passage for it bored through the substance of the wood out of sight. The latter would seem to have been the notion of our translators. See xxxvi. 33. But if we suppose the boards to have been of ordinary thickness [see on *v.* 16], by far the more likely supposition is that the bar was visible and passed through an entire row of rings. In either case, it served to hold the whole wall together. On the probable relation of this middle bar to the others, see Note and woodcut, p. 377.

29. *overlay... with gold*] See on xxv. 11. *their rings*] See on *v.* 28.

30. Cf. xxv. 9, 40.

The Vail and the Holy Places.

31—35. (Cf. xxxvi. 35, 36.)

31. *vail*] The Hebrew word literally means *separation* [see on xxxv. 12].

blue, and purple, and scarlet] See on xxv. 4. *twined linen*] See on *v.* 1.

of cunning work, &c.] **of work of the skilled weaver** [see on *v.* 1, and on xxxv. 35] **shall it be made, with Cherubim.**

cherubims] The vail of the first Temple was in like manner adorned with Cherubim (2 Chron. iii. 14). It is remarkable that Josephus describes the vail of the Tabernacle as woven with flowers and all sorts of ornamental forms, except the figures of living creatures ('Ant.' III. 6. § 4). He himself calls the Cherubim *living creatures* ('Ant.' III. 6. § 5), and he must have known that Ezekiel does so (x. 20). He is thus plainly at variance with the statement in Exodus. But can it be that he describes the vail according to the one which existed in the Temple in his time? If so, we obtain a striking instance of the operation of the superstition with which the Jews in later times, including Josephus himself, interpreted the second commandment (see 'Ant.' VIII. 7. § 5, and note on Ex. xx. 4). It may suggest a thought, if we may conceive that the vail of the Temple which was rent at the Crucifixion had been deprived of its characteristic symbol by the dark prejudices of the chosen people.

32. *pillars of shittim wood,* &c.] Rather, **pillars** of shittim wood overlaid with gold, **their hooks also of gold, upon four bases of silver.** Cf. xxxvi. 36.

33. *under the taches*] These taches are not, as some suppose, the same as the *hooks* of the preceding verse. The Hebrew words

bring in thither within the vail the ark of the testimony: and the vail shall divide unto you between the holy *place* and the most holy.

34 And thou shalt put the mercy seat upon the ark of the testimony in the most holy *place*.

35 And thou shalt set the table without the vail, and the candlestick over against the table on the side of the tabernacle toward the south: and thou shalt put the table on the north side.

36 And thou shalt make an hanging for the door of the tent, *of* blue, and purple, and scarlet, and fine twined linen, wrought with needlework.

37 And thou shalt make for the hanging five pillars *of* shittim *wood*, and overlay them with gold, *and* their hooks *shall be of* gold: and thou shalt cast five sockets of brass for them.

---

are quite different. These are the taches of the tabernacle-cloth (see *v.* 6). On the difficulty of the statement, see Note at the end of the chapter, § I.

34. *mercy seat upon the ark of the testimony*] See on xxv. 10—16. The Samaritan text here inserts the passage regarding the Altar of Incense from ch. xxx. 1—10. The omission of all mention of this altar in this place is strange, but the reading of the Samaritan bears marks of an intended emendation, and cannot represent the original text.

35. *candlestick*] See on xxv. 31.
table] See on xxv. 23.

The Front of the Tent.

36, 37. (Cf. xxxvi. 37, 38.)

36. *hanging*] Rather, **curtain** [see on xxvii. 16].

the door of the tent] **the entrance to the Tent.** The word is *pethach*, that is the opening which it is the office of the door (*deleth*), or as in this place, of the curtain (*māsāk*), to close. The distinction between *door* and *entrance* is generally overlooked in our version. See on Lev. viii. 3.

wrought with needlework] **the work of the embroiderer.** The breadths of the cloth and the vail of the Tabernacle were to be of **the work of the skilled weaver**; the entrance curtain of the Tent and that of the Court (xxvii. 16) were to be of the same materials, but embroidered with the needle, not wrought in figures in the loom. [See on *v.* 1, and on xxxv. 35.]

37. *hanging*] **curtain** as in *v.* 36.
five pillars] These, it should be observed, belonged to the entrance of the Tent, not, in their architectural relation, to the entrance of the Tabernacle [see Note, § III.].
overlay them with gold] See on xxv. 11.
their hooks] See on *v.* 33. These pillars had chapiters (capitals), and fillets (**connecting rods**, see on xxvii. 10), overlaid with gold (xxxvi. 38). Their bases (see on *v.* 19) were of bronze (like the taches of the tent-cloth), not of silver, to mark the inferiority of the Tent to the Tabernacle.

NOTE ON CHAP. XXVI. 1—37.

ON THE CONSTRUCTION OF THE TABERNACLE.

I. *The Mishkān, its Tent and its Covering.*
II. *Common view of the arrangement of the parts.* III. *Mr Fergusson's theory.*
IV. *The place of the tabernacle cloth.*
V. *Symmetry of the proposed arrangement.*
VI. *The Court.*

The chief portions of the structure are described with remarkable clearness in Exodus xxvi. and a second time in ch. xxxvi. It would however seem that those parts only are distinctly mentioned which formed visible features in the completed fabric. Mere details of construction were most probably carried out according to the mechanical usage of the time.

If we take this for granted, the sacred text appears to furnish sufficient information to enable us to realize with confidence the form and the general arrangements of the Tabernacle as well as of its Court. But the subject has been encumbered ever since the time of Philo[1] with certain traditional notions which are opposed not only to the words of Exodus, but to the plainest principles of constructive art.

I.

It has been already stated[2] that three principal parts of the Sanctuary are clearly distinguished in the Hebrew, though they are confounded in most versions. These parts are—

1. THE DWELLING PLACE, or THE TABERNACLE, strictly so called; in Hebrew, *hammishkān* (הַמִּשְׁכָּן) [note on xxvi. 1].
2. The TENT, in Heb. *ohel* (אֹהֶל).
3. The COVERING, in Heb. *mikseh* (מִכְסֶה)

---

[1] 'Vit. Mos.' III. 4 sq.
[2] Introd. Note to chap. xxvi.

1. The materials for THE MISHKĀN were a great cloth of woven work figured with Cherubim measuring forty cubits by twenty-eight cubits, and a quadrangular enclosure of wood, open at one end, ten cubits in height, ten cubits in width and thirty cubits in length. The size of the Tabernacle cloth is indicated beyond the reach of doubt by the number and dimensions of the ten breadths (or "curtains") of which it consisted[1]. The size of the wooden enclosure is made out almost as certainly from the number and measurements of the boards[2].

The boards were set upright, each of them being furnished at its lower extremity with two tenons which fitted into mortices in two heavy bases of silver. The whole of these bases placed side by side probably formed a continuous wall-plinth[3]. The boards were furnished with rings or loops of gold so fixed as to form rows, when the boards were set up, and through these rings bars were thrust. There were five bars for each side of the structure and five for the back[4]. The middle bar of each wall "was to reach from end to end," and this plainly distinguished it from the other four bars. It is inferred with great probability that this middle bar was twice as long as the others, that there were three rows of rings, and that the half of each wall was fastened together by two of the shorter bars, one near the top, the other near the bottom, while the two halves were united into a whole by the middle bar reaching from end to end[5]. Thus each wall must have been furnished with four short bars and one long one. Each of the rings near the top and the bottom of the two corner boards was shaped in some way so as to receive the ends of two bars, one belonging to the back, the other to the side, meeting at a right angle. In this way the walls were "coupled together" at the corners[6].

There is nothing said from which we can decide whether the rings and bars were on the outside or the inside of the wooden structure. From the rich materials of which they were made, it seems not unlikely that they constituted an ornamental feature on the inside. It may be added, that on the inside they would tend to make the structure firm more than on the outside.

So far it is not difficult to see nearly what THE MISHKĀN must have been. But it is not so easy to determine the way in which the great figured cloth that belonged to it was arranged. The question must be considered in connection with the description of the parts of the TENT.

[1] Ex. xxvi. 1—6; xxxvi. 8—13.
[2] See on Ex. xxvi. 18.
[3] See on xxvi. 19.
[4] Ex. xxvi. 26—28; xxxvi. 31—33.
[5] See on Ex. xxvi. 28, and woodcut, p. 377.
[6] Ex. xxvi. 24; xxxvi. 29.

There is another difficulty, by far less easy of solution, which may be stated here. It affects the internal arrangement. The vail which separated the Most Holy Place from the Holy Place was suspended from golden hooks attached to four pillars overlaid with gold, standing upon silver bases. But the position of these pillars is not mentioned in Exodus. It is indeed said that the vail was hung "under the taches[7]." Now the taches of the tabernacle cloth must have been fifteen cubits from the back of the Mishkān, that is, half way between its back and front. But according to Philo, Josephus, and all tradition, supported by every consideration of probability, the vail was ten cubits, not fifteen, from the back, and the Holy of Holies was a cubical chamber of corresponding measurement. The statement that the vail was hung "under the taches" remains unexplained. But this difficulty is by no means such as to be set in opposition to any view that may meet all other conditions expressed or involved in the narrative.

2. The TENT is described as consisting of a great tent-cloth of goats' hair, which, according to the number and dimensions of its breadths, was forty-four cubits by thirty[8], and five pillars overlaid with gold standing on bases of bronze, and furnished with golden hooks from which was suspended the curtain that served to close the entrance of the Tent[9].

3. Of the COVERING of rams' skins and tachash skins, nothing whatever is said except as regards the materials of which it was composed[10].

II.

It has been usual to represent the Tabernacle as consisting of the wooden structure which has been described, with the masses of drapery and skins thrown over it "as a pall is thrown over a coffin." There was first the figured

[7] Ex. xxvi. 33. This is not mentioned in ch. xxxvi., where the manufacture of the parts, and not their arrangement, is spoken of. It has been imagined that the *taches* were the same as the *hooks* from which the vail was actually hung (Ex. xxvi. 32). But the words are quite distinct. The word rendered *tache* is *keres* (קֶרֶס), which is supposed to be derived from a root which signifies to bind; that rendered *hook*, is *vāv* (וָו), which is the name of the Hebrew letter shaped like a hook suited for hanging anything on (ו); its origin is unknown. *Keres* is used only in reference to the taches of the tabernacle-cloth and of the tent-cloth of the Sanctuary (Ex. xxvi. 6, 33, &c.), and *vāv* only in reference to the hooks of the vail and of the tent-curtain.
[8] Ex. xxvi. 7—13; xxxvi. 14—18.
[9] Ex. xxvi. 36, 37; xxxvi. 37, 38.
[10] Ex. xxvi. 14; xxxvi. 19. See on xxv. 5.

cloth recognized as part of THE MISHKĀN, then the goats' hair cloth of the TENT, and then the twofold COVERING of skins.

A modification of this arrangement was suggested by Vater and adopted by Bähr[1], which has the advantage of displaying the figured cloth and of connecting it more strictly with the Mishkān, though in no very graceful or convenient manner. It was supposed that this cloth was strained over the top of the structure like a ceiling and fastened to the top of the boards in some way, so as to hang down and cover the walls on the inside as a tapestry, leaving a cubit at the bases of the boards bare, to show as a sort of skirting.

With the exception of certain expressions in Josephus[2], the whole current of opinion seems to have been in favour of this general arrangement of the parts of the Tabernacle. But it should be kept in view that the subject is one in which tradition cannot be of much value. We may allow that it is just possible, though by no means probable, that some points of detail besides what are actually recorded, or some special knowledge of the meaning of technical terms, may have been handed down from the time of Moses. But in a case of this kind we certainly need not hesitate to set tradition aside, whenever it is in conflict either with the letter of Scripture, or with reasonable probability.

The objections to the common theory are these:—

1. The arrangement proposed makes out the fabric to have been unsightly in its form and to have had a great part of the beauty of its materials entirely concealed.

2. It would be quite impossible to strain drapery over a space of fifteen feet, so as to prevent it from heavily sagging; and no flat roof of such materials could by any means be rendered proof against the weather.

3. It is hard to assign any use to the pins and cords of the Tabernacle[4] (which would be essential in the construction of a tent[3]) if the curtains and skins were merely thrown over the woodwork and allowed to hang down on each side.

4. The shelter of the Mishkān is always called in Hebrew by a name which, in its strict use, can denote nothing but a tent, properly so called, of cloth or skins.

5. An essential part of the Tent was the row of five pillars at its entrance[3]: if we suppose these five pillars to have stood just in front of the Mishkān, they must have been strangely out of symmetry with the four pillars of the vail, and the middle pillar must have stood needlessly and inconveniently in the way of the entrance.

III.

We are indebted to Mr Fergusson[7] for what may be regarded as a satisfactory reconstruction of the Sanctuary in all its main particulars. He holds that what sheltered the Mishkān was actually a Tent of ordinary form, such as common sense and practical experience would suggest as best suited for the purpose.

According to this view the five pillars at the entrance of the tent[3] were graduated as they would naturally be at the entrance of any large tent of the best form, the tallest one being in the middle to support one end of a ridge-pole. It has been already observed that the descriptions in Exodus appear to pass over all particulars of the construction except

---

[1] 'Symbolik,' I. p. 63.
[2] See p. 379.
[3] Ex. xxvi. 37.
[4] See Ex. xxvii. 19; xxxv. 18. The word "tabernacle" (*mishkān*), in these places, evidently includes the Tent as well as the Mishkān itself. See note on Ex. xxvi. 1.
[5] Cf. Jer. x. 20.   [6] Ex. xxvi. 37; xxxvi. 38.
[7] Smith's 'Dict. of the Bible,' Art. *Temple.*—"The Holy Sepulchre and the Temple," 1865.

those which formed visible features in the fabric. On this ground we may be allowed to suppose that there was not only a ridge-pole, but a series of pillars at the back of the Tent corresponding in height with those at the front. Such a ridge-pole, which must have been sixty feet in length[1], would have required support, and this might have been afforded by light rafters resting on the top of the boards, or, as is more in accordance with the usage of tent architecture, by a plain pole in the middle of the structure. Over this framing of wood-work the tent-cloth of goats' hair was strained with its cords and tent-pins in the usual way. There must also have been a back-cloth suspended from the pillars at the back. The heads of the pillars appear to have been united by connecting rods (in our version, "fillets") overlaid with gold. [See xxxvi. 38.]

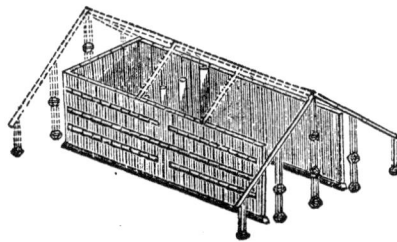

In this cut the woodwork of the Tent and Tabernacle which is described in the text is represented, the assumed positions of the portions that are not described being shown by dotted lines.

Above the tent-cloth of goats' hair was spread the covering of red rams' skins. Mr Fergusson conceives that the covering of tachash skins[2] above this did not cover the whole roof, but served only as "a coping or ridge-piece" to protect the crest of the roof.

[1] Mr Fergusson considers that "the middle bar in the midst of the boards" (Ex. xxvi. 28; xxxvi. 33) was the ridge-pole, and he would render the verse, "And the middle bar which is between the boards shall reach from end to end." But even if this rendering is allowable, we venture to think that the expression "from end to end" cannot, according to the context, refer to the Tent, but only to the wooden part of the Mishkān (see Plan, p. 378). Moreover, the methodical arrangement of the descriptions would be disturbed by the mention of the ridge-pole in Ex. xxvi. 28 and in xxxvi. 33. It could only be introduced in proper order in connection either with the cloth of the Tent (after xxvi. 13 and xxxvi. 18), or with its five pillars (after xxvi. 37 and xxxvi. 36). As however, according to the view here given, there must have been a ridge-pole of some sort, the question involves no essential particular of the construction of the fabric. See on xxvi. 28.

[2] Ex. xxvi. 14; xxxvi. 19. See note on xxv. 5.

IV.

The next inquiry relates to the position of the Tabernacle-cloth of fine linen and coloured yarns.

It is evident that the relation in which the measurement of the tabernacle-cloth stood to that of the tent-cloth had an important bearing on the place of each of them in the structure. The tent-cloth is said to have extended a cubit on each side beyond the tabernacle-cloth[3], and it appears to have extended two cubits at the back and front[4]. It would appear then that the tent-cloth was laid over the tabernacle-cloth so as to allow the excess of the dimensions of the former to be equally divided between the two sides and between the back and front. We may from these particulars infer that the tabernacle-cloth served as a lining to the other, and that they were both extended over the ridge-pole. In this way, the effect would have been produced of an ornamented open roof extending the length of the Tent.

V.

Mr Fergusson has pointed out the very remarkable consistency of the measurements of the different parts, if we accept this mode of putting them together. He assumes the angle formed by the roof to have been a right angle, as a reasonable and usual angle for such a roof, and this brings the only measurements which appear at first sight to be abnormal, into harmony. Every measurement given in the text is a multiple of five cubits, except the width of the tabernacle-cloth, which is twenty-eight cubits, and the length of the tent-cloth, which is forty-four cubits. With a right angle at the ridge, each side of the slope as shewn in this section would be within a

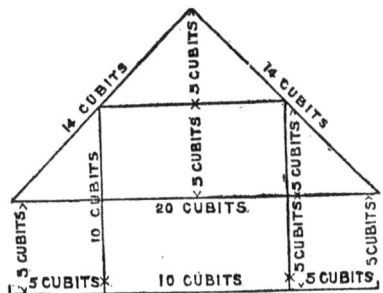

fraction of fourteen cubits (14.08), half the width of the tabernacle-cloth. The slope is here carried just five cubits beyond the wooden walls and to within just five cubits of the ground. The tent-cloth would hang down in a valance on each side, one cubit in depth[5].

[3] Ex. xxvi. 13.
[4] Ex. xxxvi. 9, 13.
[5] Ex. xxvi. 13.

If we allow the tabernacle-cloth, according to this arrangement, to determine the length of the Tent as well as its width, we obtain an area for the structure of forty cubits by twenty. The tent-cloth would of course overhang this at the back and front by two cubits, that is, half a breadth[1]. The wooden structure being placed within the Tent, there would be a space all round it of five cubits in width. This is shown in this Plan, in which one half represents the ground-plan and the other half the extended tent-cloth.

surements which are not directly stated in the text, but are made out by inference from the theory. Each chief measurement of the Temple was just twice that of the Tabernacle. The Most Holy Place, a square of ten cubits in the Tabernacle[4], was one of twenty cubits in the Temple: the Holy Place, in each case, was a corresponding double square. The Porch, which was five cubits deep in the Tabernacle, was ten cubits in the Temple; the side spaces, taking account of the thickness of the walls of the Temple, were re-

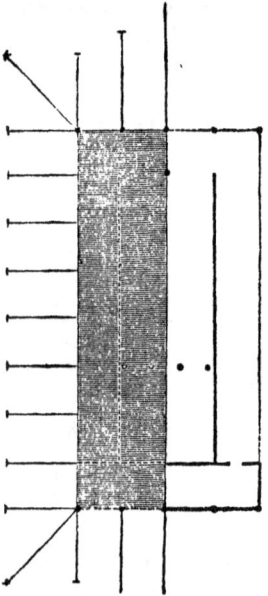

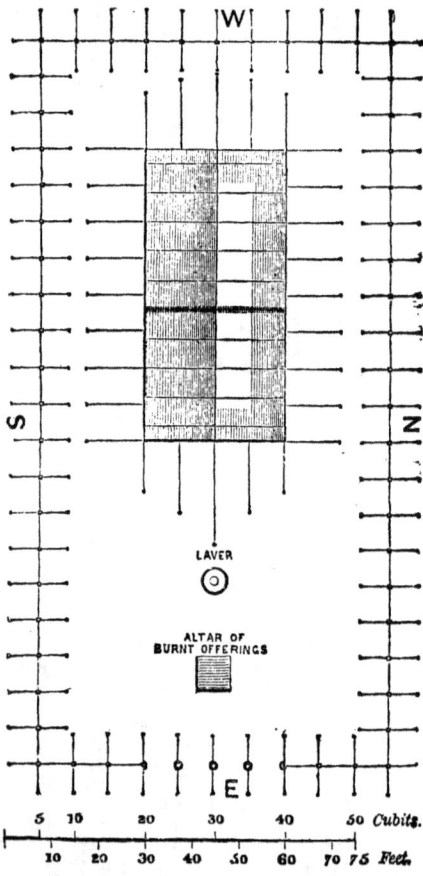

The five pillars, to reach across the front of the Tent, must have stood five cubits apart. Their heads were united by **connecting rods** ("fillets") overlaid with gold (Exod. xxxvi. 38). The space immediately within them, according to Mr Fergusson, formed a porch of five cubits in depth[2]. The spaces at the sides and back may have been wholly or in part covered in for the use of the officiating priests, like the small apartments which in after times skirted three sides of the Temple. It was probably here that those portions of the sacrifices were eaten which were not to be carried out of the sacred precinct[3].

The exact symmetrical relation which the dimensions of the Temple bore to those of the Tabernacle is not only striking in itself, but it bears a strong testimony to the correctness of Mr Fergusson's theory as regards those mea-

spectively five cubits and ten cubits in width; the height of the ridge-pole of the Tabernacle was fifteen cubits, that of the roof of the Holy Place in the Temple thirty cubits[5].

[4] It has already been observed that the length of the Most Holy Place is not given in Exodus; but **ten** cubits is universally accepted on the ground of inference. See § I.

[5] 1 K. vi. 2. The analogy here pointed out seems to shew the fitness of the word *tent* (Heb. *ohel*, wrongly rendered "tabernacle") as applied to the Temple in the vision of Ezekiel xli. 1).

---

[1] Ex. xxvi. 9, 12.
[2] See cut, p. 376.
[3] Lev. vi. 16, 26, &c. We may infer that **priests** also lodged in them from Lev. viii. 33; I S. iii. 2, 3.

Whether we believe the statements of Josephus to contain any elements of genuine tradition or not, it is worth noticing that in certain particulars he strikingly countenances the views of Mr Fergusson. He speaks of the Tabernacle as consisting of three parts. The third part was the Most Holy Place, the second part the Holy Place; and he seems to intimate that the remaining, or first part, was the entrance with its five pillars. He also says that the tent-curtain was so arranged in the front as to be *like a gable and a porch* (ἀετώματι παραπλήσιον καὶ παστάδι)[1].

It may perhaps be doubted whether there is, within the entire range of ancient literature (unless we should except the works of strictly technical writers), a description of any structure more clear and practical than that of the Tabernacle contained in the xxvith and xxxvith chapters of Exodus. Mr Fergusson's testimony on this head deserves to be quoted; "it seems to me clear that it must have been written by some one who had seen the Tabernacle standing. No one could have worked it out in such detail without ocular demonstration of the way in which the parts would fit together."

VI.

The second Plan in the preceding page exhibits the Tabernacle in its Court, with the cords and tent-pins in their proper places, as determined by Mr Fergusson in accordance with the practice of tent-architecture. It will be seen that the width of the Tent is the same as that of the entrance to the Court, which is a coincidence connected with the harmony of the arrangement that well deserves to be noticed.

[1] 'Ant.' III. 6. § 4.

CHAPTER XXVII.

1 *The altar of burnt offering, with the vessels thereof.* 9 *The court of the tabernacle inclosed with hangings and pillars.* 18 *The measure of the court.* 20 *The oil for the lamp.*

AND thou shalt make an altar *of* shittim wood, five cubits long, and five cubits broad; the altar shall be foursquare: and the height thereof *shall be* three cubits.

2 And thou shalt make the horns of it upon the four corners thereof: his horns shall be of the same: and thou shalt overlay it with brass.

3 And thou shalt make his pans to receive his ashes, and his shovels, and his basons, and his fleshhooks, and his firepans: all the vessels thereof thou shalt make *of* brass.

4 And thou shalt make for it a

CHAP. XXVII.

The Altar of Burnt-offering.

1—8. (Cf. xxxviii. 1—7.)

The great Altar which stood in the Court immediately in front of the Tabernacle was commonly called the ALTAR OF BURNT-OFFERING, because on it were burnt the whole Burnt-offerings, and all those parts of the other animal sacrifices which were offered to the Lord. It was also called the BRAZEN ALTAR, because it was covered with bronze, in distinction from the Golden Altar, or Altar of Incense (Exod. xxxix. 38, 39, xl. 5, 6).

1. *an altar*] See Note at the end of ch. xl. § I.

2. *his horns shall be of the same*] These horns were projections pointing upwards in the form either of a small obelisk, or of the horn of an ox. They were to be actually parts of the Altar, not merely superadded to it. On them the blood of the Sin-offering was smeared (Exod. xxix. 12; Lev. iv. 7, viii. 15, ix. 9, xvi. 18). To take hold of them appears to have been regarded as an emphatic mode of laying claim to the right of Sanctuary (Exod. xxi. 14; 1 K. i. 50).

3. *pans to receive his ashes*] Rather **pots** as in xxxviii. 3; 1 K. vii. 45. On the use to which these pots were put in disposing of the ashes of the Altar, see Lev. i. 16.—The Heb. word here rendered *to receive his ashes*, is remarkable. In its derivation it is connected with *fat*, and it is never used in reference to any ashes except those of the Altar. It occurs Num. iv. 13, and Ps. xx. 3; where see margin. But all authorities are agreed as to what it denotes in these places.

his basons] According to the etymology of the name (from *zārak*, to scatter) it is inferred that these vessels were used for receiving the blood of the victims and casting it upon the Altar [see xxiv. 6, Lev. i. 5, &c.].

his fleshhooks] These were for adjusting the pieces of the victim upon the Altar [cf. 1 S. ii. 13].

his firepans] The same word is rendered *snuffdishes*, xxv. 38, xxxvii. 23: *censers*, Lev. x. 1, xvi. 12, Num. iv. 14, xvi. 6, &c. These utensils appear to have been shallow metal vessels which served either to catch the snuff of the lamps when they were trimmed, or to burn small quantities of incense. No-

grate of network *of* brass; and upon the net shalt thou make four brasen rings in the four corners thereof.

5 And thou shalt put it under the compass of the altar beneath, that the net may be even to the midst of the altar.

6 And thou shalt make staves for the altar, staves *of* shittim wood, and overlay them with brass.

7 And the staves shall be put into the rings, and the staves shall be upon the two sides of the altar, to bear it.

8 Hollow with boards shalt thou make it: as †it was shewed thee in the mount, so shall they make *it*.

† Heb. *he shewed.*

9 ¶ And thou shalt make the court of the tabernacle: for the south side southward *there shall be* hangings for the court *of* fine twined linen of an hundred cubits long for one side:

10 And the twenty pillars thereof and their twenty sockets *shall be of* brass; the hooks of the pillars and their fillets *shall be of* silver.

11 And likewise for the north side

---

thing however is said of the burning of incense in immediate connection with the Brazen Altar, and it has been supposed that the firepans were employed merely to carry burning embers from the Brazen Altar to the Altar of Incense, and that this use furnishes their only claim to the name of *censers*. See on Num. xvi. 6.

5. *the compass of the altar*] This appears to have been a shelf, or projecting ledge, of convenient width, carried round the Altar half way between the top and the base, on which the priests probably stood when they tended the fire or arranged the parts of the victims. It was supported all round its outer edge by a vertical net-like grating of bronze that rested on the ground. 'The name is a peculiar one, occurring only in this application and only in one other place, xxxviii. 4. But there appears to be scarcely a doubt as to its meaning.

8. *Hollow with boards*] Slabs, or **planks,** rather than *boards*. The word is that which is used for the stone tables of the Law (xxiv. 12, xxxi. 18), not that applied to the boards of the Tabernacle (xxvi. 15).

There has been considerable difference of opinion regarding some points in the description of the Brazen Altar, but the most probable account of it seems to be this. It was a hollow casing, formed of stout acacia planks covered with plates of bronze, seven feet six in length and width and four feet six in height. Jewish as well as Christian authorities have supposed that, when it was fixed for use, it was filled up with earth or rough stones. If we connect this suggestion with the old rule regarding the Altar of earth and the Altar of stone given in chap. xx. 24, 25, the woodwork might in fact be regarded merely as the case of the Altar on which the victims were actually burned. The shelf round the sides (*v.* 5) was required as a stage for the priests to enable them to carry on their work conveniently on the top of the Altar. Hence it is said of Aaron that he *came down* from the Altar (Lev. ix. 22). According to rabbinical tradition, there was a slope of earth banked up for the priest to ascend to the stage (cf. Ex. xx. 26). Such a slope could only have been at the south side, as the place of ashes was on the east (Lev. i. 16), the west side was opposite the Tabernacle, and on the north the victims appear to have been slain close to the Altar [see on Lev. i. 11]. The rings for the staves for carrying the Altar were attached to the corners of the grating (*v.* 4), which must have been proportionally strong.

The Altar of Solomon's Temple is described 2 Chro. iv. 1. It was twenty cubits in length and breadth and ten cubits in height; so that it was unlike the Altar of the Tabernacle, not only in its magnitude but in its proportions. The Altar erected by Herod is said by Josephus to have been fifty cubits square and fifteen cubits high ('Bell. Jud.' v. 5. § 6).

as it was shewed thee in the mount] See on xxv. 40.

The Court of the Tabernacle.

9—19. (Cf. xxxviii. 9—20.)

9. *the south side southward*] **the south side on the right.** See on xxvi. 18.

fine twined linen] See on xxvi. 1.

10. *sockets*] **bases.** See on xxvi. 19.

fillets] Rather, **connecting rods.** So the Targums. The Hebrew word is peculiar, and may mean any sort of bonds or fastenings. What are spoken of in this place appear to have been curtain-rods of silver connecting the heads of the pillars. The hangings were attached to the pillars by the silver hooks; but the length of the space between the pillars would render it most probable that they were also in some way fastened to these rods. The capitals of the pillars were overlaid with silver, as we learn from chap. xxxviii. **17.**

11. *sockets*] **bases.**

fillets] **connecting rods.**

in length *there shall be* hangings of an hundred *cubits* long, and his twenty pillars and their twenty sockets *of* brass; the hooks of the pillars and their fillets *of* silver.

12 ¶ And *for* the breadth of the court on the west side *shall be* hangings of fifty cubits: their pillars ten, and their sockets ten.

13 And the breadth of the court on the east side eastward *shall be* fifty cubits.

14 The hangings of one side *of the gate shall be* fifteen cubits: their pillars three, and their sockets three.

15 And on the other side *shall be* hangings fifteen *cubits:* their pillars three, and their sockets three.

16 ¶ And for the gate of the court *shall be* an hanging of twenty cubits, *of* blue, and purple, and scarlet, and fine twined linen, wrought with needlework: *and* their pillars *shall be* four, and their sockets four.

17 All the pillars round about the court *shall be* filleted with silver; their hooks *shall be of* silver, and their sockets *of* brass.

18 ¶ The length of the court *shall be* an hundred cubits, and the breadth †fifty every where, and the height five cubits *of* fine twined linen, and their sockets *of* brass.

† Heb. *fifty by fifty.*

19 All the vessels of the tabernacle in all the service thereof, and all the

---

13. *the east side eastward*] **on the front side eastward.** The front [see on xxvi. 18, cf. *v.* 9].

14, 15, 16. See on *v.* 18, note (*c*).

16. *an hanging*] The Hebrew word is not the same as that rendered *hanging* in *vv.* 11, 12, 14, 15, and it would be better represented by **curtain.** It strictly denotes an entrance curtain, which, unlike the hangings at the sides and back of the Court, could be drawn up, or aside, at pleasure. The words are rightly distinguished in our Bible in Num. iii. 26.

wrought with needlework] **the work of the embroiderer.** See on xxvi. 36, xxxv. 35. On the materials, see xxv. 4.

sockets] **bases.**

17. *filleted with silver*] **connected with silver rods.** See on *v.* 10.

18. (*a*) The size and general construction of the Court of the Tabernacle are described in such a way as to leave no important doubt. Its area was one hundred and fifty feet (taking the cubit at eighteen inches) in length, and seventy-five feet in width. It was enclosed by hangings of fine linen suspended from pillars seven feet six inches in height, and standing seven feet six inches apart. These pillars were connected at their heads by silver rods [see on *v.* 10]; they had silver hooks for the attachment of the hangings, and their capitals were overlaid with silver; they stood on bases of bronze. At the east end of the enclosure the linen hangings on each side were continued for twenty-two feet six inches, and the intermediate space of thirty feet was the entrance, which was closed by an embroidered curtain (*vv.* 14, 15, 16). The pillars were kept firm by cords and tent-pins of bronze [see *v.* 19, cf. Num. iii. 26].

(*b*) The position of the Tabernacle in the Court could hardly have been in the middle, as Josephus imagined ('Ant.' III. 6. § 3). It is most probable that its place was, as Philo conceived ('Vit. Mos.' III. 7), equidistant from the west, the north and the south walls of the Court, so as to leave between it and the entrance of the Court a suitable space for the Brazen Altar and the Laver. See Note at the end of ch. xxvi. with the plan of the Court, according to Fergusson, in which the feasibility of this arrangement is strikingly apparent.

(*c*) There has been a difficulty raised regarding the number and distribution of the pillars of the Court. Knobel, taking up the notion of Philo and some other interpreters, supposes that the number was fifty-six, each corner pillar being reckoned both as one for the side and as one for the end. Keil, who contends for sixty as the number, has not made the matter much clearer by his mode of explanation. The mode of stating the numbers involved in the arrangement in *vv.* 10, 11, 12, 14, 15, 16 is perhaps a technical one. Taking it for granted that the number sixty, as given in those verses, is the true one, and that the Court measured precisely one hundred cubits by fifty, the pillars must have stood five cubits apart, which is in accordance with the general symmetry of the Sanctuary [see Note at the end of ch. xxvi. § V.]. If we may suppose the numbers, referring to each side of the enclosure, to have belonged to the spaces between the pillars rather than to the pillars themselves, the statements become clear, in reference both to the sides with their continuous hangings, and to the front where there was the entrance. See Mr Fergusson's plan, p. 378.

19. *All the vessels,* &c.] Our version here follows the Vulgate, and is obviously wrong.

pins thereof, and all the pins of the court, *shall be of* brass.

20 ¶ And thou shalt command the children of Israel, that they bring thee pure oil olive beaten for the light, to cause the lamp [†] to burn always.

† Heb. *to ascend up.*

21 In the tabernacle of the congregation without the vail, which *is* before the testimony, Aaron and his sons shall order it from evening to morning before the LORD: *it shall be* a statute for ever unto their generations on the behalf of the children of Israel.

CHAPTER XXVIII.

1 *Aaron and his sons are set apart for the priest's office.* 2 *Holy garments are appointed.* 6 *The ephod.* 15 *The breastplate with twelve precious stones.* 30 *The Urim and Thummim.* 31 *The robe of the ephod, with pomegranates and bells.* 36 *The plate of the mitre.* 39 *The embroidered coat.* 40 *The garments for Aaron's sons.*

AND take thou unto thee Aaron thy brother, and his sons with him, from among the children of Israel, that he may minister unto me in the priest's office, *even* Aaron, Nadab and

---

We know that the vessels of the Tabernacle were of gold, xxv. 29, 39. The Hebrew word rendered *vessels* means in the broadest sense *utensils*: it is in different places rendered *furniture, stuff, sacks, jewels, weapons,* &c. In the same connection as in this place, it is not incorrectly represented by *instruments*, Num. iii. 8. The verse might be thus translated; **All the tools of the Tabernacle used in all its workmanship, and all its tent-pins, and all the tent-pins of the court, shall be of bronze.**—The working tools of the Sanctuary were most probably such things as axes, knives, hammers, &c. that were employed in making, repairing, setting up and taking down the structure. Cf. Num. iii. 36.

the tabernacle] Heb. *hammishkān.* The word is here to be taken as including both the Mishkān and the Tent, as in Num. i. 51, 53, &c. [see on xxvi. 1].

the pins thereof,...the pins of the court] The Hebrew word is the regular name for tent-pins.

The Lamps of the Sanctuary.
vv. 20, 21.

It is not quite easy to see the reason of the insertion of these verses in this place. The passage, with unimportant verbal alterations, is repeated Lev. xxiv. 2, 3, where it is connected in a natural manner with the rules for the supplying and ordering of the Shewbread. Cf. Exod. xxv. 6, 37; xxxv. 14, xl. 4, 24, 25.

20. *pure oil olive beaten*] The oil was to be of the best kind. It is called *beaten*, because it was obtained by merely bruising the olives in a mortar or mill, without the application of heat. The finest oil is now thus obtained from young fruit freshly gathered, and hence it is sometimes distinguished as " cold drawn." The inferior kind is expressed from unselected fruit, under stronger pressure, with the application of heat.

the lamp] *i.e.* the lamps of the Golden **Candlestick.** [See xxv. 37.]

to burn] The word is literally rendered in the margin *to ascend up.* It should be observed that it does not properly mean to burn in the sense of to consume, and that it is the word regularly used to express the action of fire upon what was offered to Jehovah [see on Lev. i. 9].

always] *i.e.* every night "from evening till morning." Cf. xxx. 8.

21. *the tabernacle of the congregation*] More literally, **the Tent of meeting** [see Note at the end of ch. xl. § II.]. This is the first occurrence of this designation of the Tabernacle.

without the vail, which is before the testimony] *i.e.* the Holy Place [see on xxv. 16].

CHAP. XXVIII.

THE INVESTITURE OF AARON AND HIS SONS.

1—43 (Cf. xxxix. 1—31).

Moses is now commanded to commit all that pertains to the Offerings made to the Lord in the Sanctuary to the exclusive charge of the members of a single family, who were to hold their office from generation to generation. In the patriarchal times, the external rites of worship had generally been conducted by the head of the tribe or family, in accordance with the principle involved in the dedication of the firstborn (Ex. xiii. 2; Num. iii. 12, 13). Moses, as the divinely appointed and acknowledged leader of the nation, had, on a special occasion, appointed those who were to offer sacrifice, and had himself sprinkled the consecrating blood of the victims on the people (xxiv. 5, 6, 8). On the completion of the Tabernacle, after Aaron and his sons had been called to the priesthood, he took chief part in the daily service of the Sanctuary (xl. 23—29, 31, 32) until the consecration of the family of Aaron, on which occasion he appears to have exercised the priest's office for the last time (Lev. viii. 14—29; cf. Ex. xxix. 10—26). The setting apart of the whole tribe of Levi for the entire cycle of religious services is mentioned Num. iii. 5—13, viii. 5—26, xviii. 1—32.

Abihu, Eleazar and Ithamar, Aaron's sons.

2 And thou shalt make holy garments for Aaron thy brother for glory and for beauty.

3 And thou shalt speak unto all *that are* wise hearted, whom I have filled with the spirit of wisdom, that they may make Aaron's garments to consecrate him, that he may minister unto me in the priest's office.

4 And these *are* the garments which they shall make; a breastplate, and an ephod, and a robe, and a broidered coat, a mitre, and a girdle: and they shall make holy garments for Aaron thy brother, and his sons, that he may minister unto me in the priest's office.

5 And they shall take gold, and blue, and purple, and scarlet, and fine linen.

---

1. Nadab and Abihu, the two elder sons of Aaron, had accompanied their father and the seventy Elders when they went a part of the way with Moses up the mountain (xxiv. 1, 9). Soon after their consecration they were destroyed for "offering strange fire before the Lord" (Lev. x. 1, 2). Eleazar and Ithamar are here mentioned for the first time, except in the genealogy, vi. 23. Eleazar succeeded his father in the High-priesthood, and was himself succeeded by his son Phinehas (Judg. xx. 28). But Eli, the next High-priest named in the history, was of the line of Ithamar. The representatives of both families held office at once in the time of David. See 1 Chro. xxiv. 1—3; 2 S. viii. 17.

3. *wise hearted*] The heart was frequently spoken of as the seat of wisdom (Ex. xxxi. 6, xxxv. 10, 25, xxxvi. 1; Job ix. 4; Prov. xi. 29, xvi. 21, 23, &c.). The same notion is traced in the Latin phrase *homo cordatus;* also in the language of Homer, ' Il.' XV. 52; 'Od.'. VII. 82, XVIII. 344. The bowels, as distinguished from the heart, were commonly recognized as the seat of the affections (Gen. xliii. 30; 1 K. iii. 26; Is. lxiii. 15: and, in the Hebrew text, Deut. xiii. 6; 2 S. xxiv. 14, &c. See also Luke i. 78; 2 Cor. vi. 12, vii. 15; Phil. i. 8, ii. 1; Philemon, v. 7, &c.).

the spirit of wisdom] See on xxxi. 3. What may be especially noticed in this place is, that the spirit of wisdom given by the Lord is spoken of as conferring practical skill in the most general sense: those who possess it are called *because* they possess it; they are not first called and then endowed with it.

garments to consecrate him] There is here a solemn recognition of the significance of an appointed official dress. It expresses that the office is not created or defined by the man himself (Heb. v. 4), but that he is *invested* with it according to prescribed institution. The rite of anointing was essentially connected with investiture in the holy garments (xxix. 29, 30; xl. 12—15).—The history of all nations shews the importance of these forms. As time goes on, their "ancient and well-noted face" becomes more and more valuable as a witness against restless longing for change. The following points in this divinely ordained investiture of the Priests of Jehovah seem to be worthy of special notice in our own day:— (1) there was nothing left to individual taste or fancy, every point was authoritatively laid down in minute detail: (2) the High-priest, when performing his highest and holiest functions, was attired in a plain white dress (Lev. xvi. 4): (3) the only garments worn by the other priests "for glory and for beauty" (*v.* 40), when they were engaged in the service of both the Golden Altar and the Brazen Altar (see Lev. vi. 10), were also white, with the exception of the Girdle (*v.* 40): (4) there were no changes in the dresses of the priests at the three Great Festivals, nor any periodical change whatever, except when the High-priest, on the Day of Atonement, put off his robes of office for the dress of white linen.

4. There are here mentioned six articles belonging to the official dress of the High-priest, which are described in the verses that follow; but the description does not follow the order of this enumeration, and it comprises, in addition, the gold plate of the mitre (*v.* 36) and the garments which were common to all the priests.

and his sons] These, it is evident, were the representatives of the family who, in the ages that followed, inherited the High-priesthood in succession. But the sons who were consecrated at this time with Aaron as common priests, are designated in the same way in *v.* 40 and elsewhere.

5. *gold, and blue,* &c.] **the gold and the blue and the scarlet and the fine linen.** The definite article is prefixed to each substantive to denote specially the quantity and the quality of the material required for the dresses. With the exception of the gold, the materials were the **same** as those of the tabernacle-cloth, the vail of the Tabernacle and the entrance-curtain of the Tent (xxvi. 1, 31, 36. See on xxv. 4). The gold was wrought into thin flat wires which could either be woven with the woollen and linen threads, or worked with the needle (**see**

6 ¶ And they shall make the ephod *of* gold, *of* blue, and *of* purple, *of* scarlet, and fine twined linen, with cunning work.

7 It shall have the two shoulder-pieces thereof joined at the two edges thereof; and *so* it shall be joined together.

8 And the ¹curious girdle of the ephod, which *is* upon it, shall be of the same, according to the work thereof; *even of* gold, *of* blue, and purple, and scarlet, and fine twined linen.

9 And thou shalt take two onyx stones, and grave on them the names of the children of Israel:

10 Six of their names on one stone, and *the other* six names of the rest on the other stone, according to their birth.

11 *a* With the work of an engraver in stone, *like* the engravings of a signet, shalt thou engrave the two stones with the names of the children of Israel: thou shalt make them to be set in ouches of gold.

¹ Or, embroidered.

a Wisd 18. 24.

---

xxxix. 3 and on xxxv. 35). In regard to the mixture of linen and woollen threads in the Ephod and other parts of the High-priest's dress, a difficulty seems to present itself in connection with the law which forbad garments of linen and woollen mixed to be worn by the Israelites (Lev. xix. 19; Deut. xxii. 11). It has been conjectured that the coloured threads here mentioned were not woollen but dyed linen (Knobel). But see on Lev. xix. 19.

The Ephod.
6—12 (xxxix. 2—7).

6. *the ephod*] The Hebrew word is here retained, which, according to its etymology, has the same breadth of meaning as our word *vestment*. The garment being worn over the shoulders, the word is rendered by the LXX. ἐπωμίς (which occurs also Ecclus. xlv. 8), and by the Vulgate *superhumerale*. It consisted of blue, purple and scarlet yarn and "fine twined linen" (on xxvi. 1) wrought together in **work of the skilled weaver** (on xxvi. 1 and xxxv. 35). It was the distinctive vestment of the High-priest, to which "the breastplate of judgment" was attached (*vv.* 25—28).

7. From this verse, and from xxxix. 4, it would seem that the Ephod consisted of two principal pieces of cloth, one for the back and the other for the front, joined together by shoulder straps (see on *v.* 27). Below the arms, probably just above the hips, the two pieces were kept in place by a band attached to one of the pieces, which is described in the next verse. Most Jewish authorities have thus understood the description. But Josephus describes the Ephod as a tunic (χιτών) having sleeves ('Ant.' III. 7. § 5). It is just possible that the fashion of it may have changed before the time of the historian. On the respect in which this Ephod of the High-priest was held, see 1 S. ii. 28, xiv. 3, xxi. 9, xxiii. 6, 9, xxx. 7. But an Ephod made of linen appears to have been a recognized garment not only for the common priests (1 S. xxii. 18) but also for those who were even temporarily engaged in the service of the Sanctuary (1 S. ii. 18; 2 S. vi. 14; 1 Chro. xv. 27).

8. *the curious girdle of the ephod, which is upon it, shall be of the same*] The meaning might rather be expressed:—*the band for fastening it, which is upon it, shall be of the same work, of one piece with it.* So de Wette, Knobel, Zunz, Herx., &c. This band being woven on to one of the pieces of the Ephod was passed round the body, and fastened by buttons, or strings, or some other suitable contrivance.

9. *two onyx stones*] The Hebrew name of the stone here spoken of is *shoham*. It is uniformly rendered *onyx* in our Bible and in the Vulgate; Josephus calls it the *sardonyx*. The LXX. and Philo, on the other hand, call it the *beryl*. But the Greek translators are inconsistent in translating the word in different places, so that, as regards this question, no confidence can be placed in them. The stone was most likely one well adapted for engraving; in this respect the onyx is preferable to the beryl See on *v.* 17.

11. *an engraver in stone*] **an artificer in stone.** See on xxxv. 35.

like the engravings of a signet] Cf. *vv.* 21, 36. These words probably refer to a peculiar way of shaping the letters, adapted for engraving on a hard substance.—Seal engraving on precious stones was practised in Egypt from very remote times, and in Mesopotamia, probably, from 2000 A.C.

ouches of gold] The gold settings of the engraved stones are here plainly denoted; but, according to the derivation of the Hebrew word, they seem to have been formed not of solid pieces of metal, but of woven wire, wreathed round the stones in what is called *cloisonnée* work, a sort of filigree, often found in Egyptian ornaments. Mr King conjectures that these stones, as well as those on the breastplate, were "in the form of ovals, or rather ellipses, like the cartouches, containing proper names, in hieroglyphic inscriptions."

12 And thou shalt put the two stones upon the shoulders of the ephod *for* stones of memorial unto the children of Israel: and Aaron shall bear their names before the LORD upon his two shoulders for a memorial.

13 ¶ And thou shalt make ouches *of* gold;

14 And two chains *of* pure gold at the ends; *of* wreathen work shalt thou make them, and fasten the wreathen chains to the ouches.

15 ¶ And thou shalt make the breastplate of judgment with cunning work; after the work of the ephod thou shalt make it; *of* gold, *of* blue, and *of* purple, and *of* scarlet, and *of* fine twined linen, shalt thou make it.

16 Foursquare it shall be *being* doubled; a span *shall be* the length thereof, and a span *shall be* the breadth thereof.

17 And thou shalt †set in it settings of stones, *even* four rows of stones: the first row *shall be* a ‖ sardius, a topaz, and a carbuncle: *this shall be* the first row.

† Heb. *fill in it fillings of stone.*
‖ Or, *ruby*

'Ancient Gems,' p. 136. The same word is used in *vv.* 13, 14, 25, where it seems to express an ornamental gold button, without a stone. The word *ouches* is used by Shakspeare, Spenser, and some of their contemporaries in the general sense of jewels. See Nares' 'Glossary.'

12. *upon the shoulders of the ephod*] *i.e.* upon the **shoulder-pieces** of the ephod. See *v.* 7.

upon his two shoulders] Cf. Isa. ix. 6, xxii. 22. The High-priest had to represent the Twelve Tribes in the presence of Jehovah; and the burden of his office could not be so aptly symbolized anywhere as on his shoulders, the parts of the body fittest for carrying burdens. The figure is familiar enough in all languages. Cf. on *v.* 29.

The Breastplate.
13—30. (Cf. xxxix. 8—21.)

13. *ouches*] See on *v.* 11. These were two in number, to suit the chains mentioned in the next verse. Cf. *v.* 25 and xxxix. 18.

14. *two chains of pure gold at the ends; of wreathen work shalt thou make them*] Rather, two chains of pure gold **shalt thou make of wreathen work, twisted like cords.**—They were more like cords of twisted gold wire than chains in the ordinary sense of the word. Such chains have been found in Egyptian tombs, and some of these were exhibited in the Paris Exhibition of 1867.

15. *the breastplate of judgment*] The meaning of the Hebrew word (*choshen*) rendered *breastplate*, appears to be simply *ornament*. The names given to it in nearly all versions must therefore be regarded as glosses. The LXX., Philo, Josephus and the son of Sirach (Ecclus. xlv. 10) call it λογεῖον, or λόγιον, and the Vulgate *rationale*, in reference to its use as an oracle in making known the judgments of the Lord. It was from this use that it was designated the *Choshen of Judgment*. Symmachus renders the word as a receptacle, or bag (δόχιον), from what appears to have been its form. The names given to it by most modern translators (like our own *breastplate*) relate merely to its place in the dress. It was to be made of a piece of *cunning work* (the work of the skilled weaver, see xxxv. 35), the same in texture and materials as the Ephod. This piece was a cubit (two spans) in length and half a cubit (a span) in width, and it was to be folded together so as to form a square of half a cubit. Whether it was doubled with no other purpose than to give it stability (Rosenmüller, Knobel, Kalisch), or in order to form what was used as a bag (Gesenius, Bähr, Fürst), has been questioned: but the latter appears to be by far the more likely alternative. On the mode in which it was attached to the Ephod, see *v.* 22 sq., and on its probable use as a bag, see Note at the end of the Chapter.

17. *settings*] The same Hebrew word is less aptly rendered "inclosings" in *v.* 20. From xxxix. 13 it appears that they were ouches of *cloisonnée* work, like those mentioned in *v.* 11 as the settings of the gems on the shoulder-pieces of the ephod.

four rows of stones] No very near approach to certainty can be obtained in the identification of these precious stones. In several instances the Hebrew names themselves afford some light on the subject. The oldest external authority to help us is the LXX., and next to it come Josephus ('Ant.' III. 7. § 5; 'Bel. Jud.' V. 5. § 7) and the other old versions, especially the Vulgate. It must however be observed that the Greek and Latin names are not always consistently applied to the same Hebrew word in different places (see on *v.* 9). One point of interest in the inquiry appears to be the etymological identity of several of the names of stones in Hebrew, Greek, Latin and the modern languages of Europe. These names were probably transmitted to the Greeks and Romans by the Phœnician merchants, whose traffic in most of the precious stones

18 And the second row *shall be* an emerald, a sapphire, and a diamond.

19 And the third row a ligure, an agate, and an amethyst.

here mentioned is alluded to by Ezekiel (xxviii. 13). But, unfortunately, the identity of the stone denoted by no means follows from the identity of the name. A name was often given in ancient times to a substance on account of some single characteristic, such as its colour or its hardness. Hence *adamant* was applied to the diamond, to steel, and to other hard bodies: *sapphire* was certainly applied to the lapis-lazuli, and, though not till a much later age, to what we call the sapphire. Hence it is plain that our conclusions on the subject can rarely be quite certain. The field of conjecture in the present inquiry may however be somewhat narrowed from the results of the study of the antique gems of Assyria, Egypt and Ancient Greece. We need not hesitate to exclude those stones which appear to have been unknown to the ancients, and those which are so hard that the ancients did not know how to engrave them. On such grounds, according to Prof. Maskelyne, we must at once reject the diamond, the ruby, the sapphire, the emerald, the topaz, and the chrysoberyl.—The best information on the subject may be found in two articles in the 'Edinb. Rev.' Nos. 253, 254, by Prof. Maskelyne, to whom these notes on the breastplate are greatly indebted.

a sardius] Heb. *odem*, i.e. *the red stone;* LXX. σάρδιον; Vulg. *sardius;* Jos. σαρδόνυξ in one place ('Ant.' III. 7. § 5), but σάρδιον in another ('Bel. Jud.' V. 5. § 7). The Sardian stone, or **sard**, was much used by the ancients for seals; and it is perhaps the stone of all others the best for engraving (see Theophrastus, 'de Lapid.' 8; Pliny, 'H.N.' XXXVII. 23, 31). It is mentioned Ezek. xxviii. 13.

topaz] Heb. *pitdāh;* LXX. and Jos. τοπάζιον; Vulg. *topazius*. The word *topaz* appears to have been formed by metathesis from *pitdāh* (Gesenius, Knobel, Fürst). The *pitdāh* is mentioned by Ezekiel (xxviii. 13); and it is spoken of in Job (xxviii. 19) as a product of Ethiopia, which tends to confirm its identity with the topaz which is said by Strabo (XVI. p. 770), Diodorus (III. 39), and Pliny (XXXVII. 32), to have been obtained from Ethiopia. It was not however the stone now called the topaz: it may have been the peridot, or chrysolite, a stone of a greenish hue.

a carbuncle] Heb. *bāreketh;* LXX. and **Jos.** σμάραγδος, Vulg. *smaragdus*. It was certainly not the carbuncle; it is not improbable that it was the **beryl**, which is a kind of emerald (Plin. XXXVII. 16, Solinus XV. 23). The Greek name sometimes appears as μάραγδος, supposed to be identical with the Sanskrit name of the beryl, *marakata* (Fürst), which plainly appears to be allied to the Heb. *bāreketh*, and probably to our own *emerald*. Gesenius and Liddell and Scott severally ascribe the Hebrew name and the Greek to roots signifying to *glitter*, or *sparkle:* but the characteristic quality thus suggested is not one that particularly distinguishes the beryl amongst precious stones. The *bāreketh* is mentioned Ezek. xxviii. 13.

18. *an emerald*] Heb. *nophek*, i.e. *the glowing stone* (Knobel, Fürst); LXX. and Jos. ἄνθραξ; Vulg. *carbunculus*. There seems no reason to doubt that the garnet, which when cut with a convex face is termed the **carbuncle**, is meant. (See Theoph. 'de Lapid.' 18). The same stone is mentioned Ezek. xxvii. 16, xxviii. 13.

a sapphire] Heb. *sappīr;* LXX. σάπφειρος; Vulg. *sapphirus*. Josephus appears to have transposed this name and the next, and may fairly be regarded as agreeing with the LXX. as to its meaning. It is conceived to have been the sapphire of the Greeks, not only from the identity of the name, but from the evident references to the colour in Exod. xxiv. 10; Ezek. i. 26, x. 1. The name also occurs Job xxviii. 6, 16; Cant. v. 14; Isa. liv. 11; Lam. iv. 7; Ezek. xxviii. 13. Michaelis and others objected to what is now called the sapphire on account of its hardness, and supposed that the lapis-lazuli is most probably meant. The best recent authorities justify this conjecture, in reference not only to the *sappīr* of the Old Testament, but to the sapphire of the Greeks and Romans (see the first note on this verse). According to a Jewish fancy in the Talmud, the Tables of the Law were formed of *sappīr*.

a diamond] Heb. *yahalom*. The etymology of the word is supposed to be similar to that ascribed to the Greek ἀδάμας, so as to give it the meaning of *the unconquerable*. Hence some of the ancient versions, with Aben-Ezra, Abarbanel, and Luther (whom our translators followed), have taken the diamond as the stone denoted. But there is no trace of evidence that the ancients ever acquired the skill to engrave on the diamond, or even that they were acquainted with the stone. The LXX. render *yahalom* by ἴασπις, and the Vulg. by *jaspis:* but these words answer more satisfactorily to the jasper (see on *v.* 20). Some imagine it to be the onyx, which is more likely the *shoham* (*v.* 9): but it may possibly be some other variety of **chalcedony**, or (perhaps) rock crystal. In the uncertainty which exists, the original name **yahalom** might be retained in the version. The word is found in Ezek. xxviii. 13: but it is another word (*shamīr*) which is rendered *diamond* or *adamant* in Jer. xvii. 1; Ezek. iii. 9; Zech. vii. 12.

20 And the fourth row a beryl, and an onyx, and a jasper: they shall be set in gold in their †inclosings.

† Heb. *fillings*.

21 And the stones shall be with the names of the children of Israel, twelve, according to their names, *like* the engravings of a signet; every one with his name shall they be according to the twelve tribes.

22 ¶ And thou shalt make upon the breastplate chains at the ends *of* wreathen work *of* pure gold.

23 And thou shalt make upon the breastplate two rings of gold, and shalt put the two rings on the two ends of the breastplate.

24 And thou shalt put the two wreathen *chains* of gold in the two rings *which are* on the ends of the breastplate.

25 And *the other* two ends of the two wreathen *chains* thou shalt fasten in the two ouches, and put *them* on the shoulderpieces of the ephod before it.

26 ¶ And thou shalt make two rings of gold, and thou shalt put them upon the two ends of the breastplate in the border thereof, which *is* in the side of the ephod inward.

27 And two *other* rings of gold thou shalt make, and shalt put them on the two sides of the ephod underneath, toward the forepart thereof, over against the *other* coupling thereof, above the curious girdle of the ephod.

---

19. *a ligure*] Heb. *leshem*, LXX. and Jos. λιγύριον, Vulg. *ligurius*. According to Theophrastus ('de Lapid.' 29) and Pliny ('H. N.' XXXVII. 11), **amber** came from Liguria, and this would exactly account for the names used by the LXX. and Vulg., if, as is not in any respect improbable, amber is here meant. On the name λυγκούριον, see Liddell and Scott. The *leshem* is not mentioned elsewhere in the Old Testament except in xxxix. 12.

an agate] Heb. *shevoo*, LXX. ἀχάτης, Vulg. *achates*. Josephus appears to have transposed ἀχάτης with the next name: he makes several other changes in the order of the stones in the list given, 'Bel. Jud.' v. 5. § 7. No question has been raised that the agate is here meant. The word *shevoo* occurs only here and xxxix. 12; but another word (*kadkod*) is rendered *agate* in our version, Isa. liv. 12; Ezek. xxvii. 16.

an amethyst] Heb. *achlāmāh*, LXX. and Josephus ἀμέθυστος, Vulg. *amethystus*. Mentioned only here and xxxix. 12.

20. *a beryl*] Heb. *tarshish*, LXX. and Jos. χρυσόλιθος, Vulg. *chrysolithus*. This could hardly have been the beryl (see on v. 17) or the turkois, as Luther and Cranmer imagined. The Hebrew name is reasonably supposed to have been given to the stone because it came from Tarshish. A kind of carbuncle, or garnet, is spoken of by Pliny, called *carchedonius*, in connection with Carthage ('H. N.' XXXVII. 25), and this is supposed by some to be the *tarshish* (Knobel, Fürst). Others suppose that it was what Pliny calls the chrysolite, a brilliant yellow stone (see Plin. XXXVII. 42), which they identify with what is now known as the Spanish topaz (Gesenius, &c.). It would seem to be best, in such uncertainty, to retain the name **tarshish**

in translating. The stone is mentioned Cant. v. 14; Ezek. i. 16, x. 9, xxviii. 13; Dan. x. 6.

an onyx] Heb. *shoham*. Josephus and the Vulgate take it for the onyx (see on *v*. 9); but the LXX., apparently by a copyist's transposition, have βηρύλλιον here, and ὀνύχιον for the next stone. The *shoham* is mentioned Gen. ii. 12; Ex. xxv. 7; 1 Chro. xxix. 2; Job xxviii. 16; Ezek. xxviii. 13.

a jasper] Heb. *yashpeh*. The similarity of the Hebrew name to our word *jasper*, to the Greek ἴασπις, the Latin *jaspis*, and the Arabic *jasb*, is obvious. Josephus and the Vulgate render it as *beryl*, and the LXX. as onyx (but see preceding note). The best authorities take it for jasper (Gesen., Bähr, Knobel, Fürst): it was probably the green jasper. It is mentioned nowhere else except Ex. xxxix. 13; Ezek. xxviii. 13.

their inclosings] **their settings** (see on *v*. 17).

22. *chains at the ends of wreathen work*] **chains of wreathen work, twisted like cords** (see on *v*. 14).

23. *on the two ends of the breastplate*] The extremities spoken of here, and in the next verse, must have been the upper corners of the square. The chains attached to them (*v*. 25) suspended the Breastplate from the ouches of the shoulder-pieces (*vv*. 9, 11, 12).

26. *two rings*] These two rings appear to have been fastened to the Breastplate, near its lower corners upon the inner side, so as to have been out of sight. See on the following two verses.

27. "And two rings of gold shalt thou make and put them on **the two shoulderpieces of the Ephod, low down in the**

28 And they shall bind the breastplate by the rings thereof unto the rings of the ephod with a lace of blue, that *it* may be above the curious girdle of the ephod, and that the breastplate be not loosed from the ephod.

29 And Aaron shall bear the names of the children of Israel in the breastplate of judgment upon his heart, when he goeth in unto the holy *place*, for a memorial before the LORD continually.

30 ¶ And thou shalt put in the breastplate of judgment the Urim and the Thummim; and they shall be upon Aaron's heart, when he goeth in before the LORD: and Aaron shall bear the judgment of the children of Israel upon his heart before the LORD continually.

31 ¶ And thou shalt make the robe of the ephod all *of* blue.

32 And there shall be an hole in the top of it, in the midst thereof: it shall have a binding of woven work round about the hole of it, as it were the hole of an habergeon, that it be not rent.

33 ¶ And *beneath* upon the ‖ hem of it thou shalt make pomegranates *of* blue, and *of* purple, and *of* scarlet,

‖ Or, *skirts.*

---

front of it, near the joining, above the band for fastening it." It would seem that the shoulder-pieces were continued down the front of the Ephod as far as the band (see on *v.* 8); the joining appears to have been the meeting of the extremities of the shoulder-pieces with the band. These rings were attached to the shoulder-pieces just above this joining.

28. *the curious girdle of the ephod*] the band for fastening it (see on *v.* 8). The two lower rings of the Breastplate were to be tied to the rings near the ends of the shoulder-pieces, opposite to which they seem to have been placed, by laces of blue, so as to keep the Breastplate firmly in its place just above the band.

29. The names of the Tribes on the two onyx stones were worn on the shoulders of the High-priest to indicate the burden of the office which he bore (see on *v.* 12); the same names engraved on the stones of the Breastplate were worn over his heart, the seat of the affections, as well as of the intellect (see on *v.* 3), to symbolize the relation of love and of personal interest which the Lord requires to exist between the Priest and the People.

30. *put in the breastplate of judgment the Urim and the Thummim*] It is not questioned that this rendering (which agrees with the Vulgate, Saadia, Luther, and most modern versions) fairly represents the original words; and it most naturally follows that the Urim and the Thummim (whatever they were) were *put into* the bag that was formed by the doubling of the *Choshen* (see on *v.* 15), as the Tables of the Law were *put into* the Ark, the same verb and preposition being used in each case (xxv. 16). Most critics are in favour of this view. But it cannot be denied that the words may also mean, *upon the Breastplate*. So the LXX., the Syriac, de Wette, Knobel. See Note at the end of the Chapter.

the Urim and the Thummim] These were probably some well-known means for casting lots which, from this time forward, were kept in the bag of the *Choshen*. See Note.

The Robe of the Ephod.

31—35. (xxxix. 22—26.)

31. *the robe of the ephod*] The Robe of the Ephod was a frock or robe of the simplest form, woven without seam, wholly of blue (see Note at the end of ch. xxv. § II.). It was put on by being drawn over the head. It appears to have had no sleeves. It probably reached a little below the knees. It must have been visible above and below the Ephod, the variegated texture of which it must have set off as a plain blue groundwork.

32. *And there shall be an hole in the top of it, in the midst thereof*] And its opening for the head shall be in the middle of it. So de Wette, Knobel, Kalisch, Herx., &c. The meaning appears to be that the opening through which the head was to be put should be a mere round hole, not connected with any longitudinal slit before or behind.

of woven work] of the work of the weaver (see on xxvi. 1, xxxv. 35). This was probably a stout binding of woven thread, sewn over the edge of the hole for the head, to strengthen it and preserve it from fraying.

an habergeon] The original word, *tacharah*, is found in Egyptian papyri of the 19th dynasty (Brugsch, 'D. H.,' p. 1579), though its root appears to be Semitic (Gesen. 'Thes.' p. 518). Corselets of linen, such as appear to be here referred to, were well known amongst the Egyptians (Herodot. II. 182, III. 47; Plin. XIX. 2. Cf. Hom. 'Il.' II. 529).

33, 34. The skirt was to be adorned with a border of pomegranates in colours, and a

roundabout the hem thereof; and bells of gold between them round about:

34 A golden bell and a pomegranate, a golden bell and a pomegranate, upon the hem of the robe round about.

35 *b* And it shall be upon Aaron to minister: and his sound shall be heard when he goeth in unto the holy *place* before the LORD, and when he cometh out, that he die not.

36 ¶ And thou shalt make a plate *of* pure gold, and grave upon it, *like* the engravings of a signet, HOLINESS TO THE LORD.

37 And thou shalt put it on a blue lace, that it may be upon the mitre; upon the forefront of the mitre it shall be.

38 And it shall be upon Aaron's forehead, that Aaron may bear the iniquity of the holy things, which the children of Israel shall hallow in all their holy gifts; and it shall be always upon his forehead, that they may be accepted before the LORD.

39 ¶ And thou shalt embroider the coat of fine linen, and thou shalt make the mitre *of* fine linen, and thou shalt make the girdle *of* needlework.

b Ecclus. 45. 9.

---

small golden bell was to be attached to the hem between each two of the pomegranates.

35. *his sound*] Its sound, i.e. the sound of the Robe. Some conceive that the bells furnished a musical offering of praise to the Lord (Knobel, &c.). But it seems more likely that their purpose was that the people, who stood without, when they heard the sound of them within the Tabernacle, might have a sensible proof that the High-priest was performing the sacred rite in their behalf, though he was out of their sight. The bells thus became an incentive to devotional feelings. This accords with very early tradition. See Ecclus. xlv. 9.

that he die not] The bells also bore witness that the High-priest was, at the time of his ministration, duly attired in the dress of his office, and so was not incurring the sentence of death which is referred to again in *v.* 43 in connection with the linen drawers that were worn by the whole body of the priests. An infraction of the laws for the service of the Sanctuary was not merely an act of disobedience; it was a direct insult to the presence of Jehovah from His ordained minister, and justly incurred a sentence of capital punishment. Cf. Ex. xxx. 21; Lev. viii. 35, x. 7.

The Mitre and the Garments of Fine Linen.
36—43. (xxxix. 27—31.)

36. In the narrative of the making of the holy things (xxxix. 28, 30) the Mitre of fine linen is mentioned before the Golden Plate, as having been first completed, and as that to which the plate itself was to be attached. But in these directions the plate is first described, as being the most significant part of the head-dress. For a similar transposition, shewing the strictly practical character of the narrative, see on xxxv. 11.

engravings of a signet] See on *v.* 11.

HOLINESS TO THE LORD] This inscription testified in express words the holiness with which the High-priest was invested in virtue of his sacred calling.

37. *a blue lace*] The plate was fastened upon a blue band or fillet, so tied round the mitre as to shew the plate in front.

the mitre] According to the derivation of the Hebrew word, and from the statement in *v.* 39, this was a twisted band of linen coiled into a cap, to which the name *mitre*, in its original sense, closely answers, but which, in modern usage, would rather be called a *turban*.

38. *bear the iniquity of the holy things*] The Hebrew expression "to bear iniquity" is applied either to one who suffers the penalty of sin (*v.* 43; Lev. v. 1, 17; xvii. 16, xxvi. 41, &c.), or to one who takes away the sin of others (Gen. l. 17; Lev. x. 17, xvi. 22; Num. xxx. 15; 1 S. xv. 25, &c. See on Gen. iv. 13). In several of these passages the verb is rightly rendered to *forgive*.—The iniquity which is spoken of in this place does not mean particular sins actually committed, but that condition of alienation from God in every earthly thing which makes reconciliation and consecration needful. Cf. Num. xviii. 1. It belonged to the High-priest, as the chief atoning mediator between Jehovah and His people (see on *v.* 36), to atone for the holy things that they might be "accepted before the Lord" (cf. Lev. viii. 15, xvi. 20, 33, with the notes): but the common priests also, in their proper functions, had to take their part in making atonement (Lev. iv. 20, v. 10, x. 17, xxii. 16; Num. xviii. 23, &c.).

39. *embroider the coat of fine linen*] This garment appears to have been a long tunic, or cassock. Josephus says that it was worn next the skin, that it reached to the feet, and that it had closely fitting sleeves ('Ant.' III. 7. § 2). The verb translated *embroider* (*shābatz*, a word of very rare occurrence) appears ra-

40 ¶ And for Aaron's sons thou shalt make coats, and thou shalt make for them girdles, and bonnets shalt thou make for them, for glory and for beauty.

41 And thou shalt put them upon Aaron thy brother, and his sons with him; and shalt anoint them, and †consecrate them, and sanctify them, that they may minister unto me in the priest's office.

† Heb. *fill their hand.*

42 And thou shalt make them linen breeches to cover †their nakedness; from the loins even unto the thighs they shall †reach:

† Heb. *flesh of their nakedness.*
† Heb. *be.*

43 And they shall be upon Aaron, and upon his sons, when they come in unto the tabernacle of the congregation, or when they come near unto the altar to minister in the holy *place;* that they bear not iniquity, and die: *it shall be* a statute for ever unto him and his seed after him.

---

ther to mean **weave in diaper work**. The tissue consisted of threads of one and the same colour diapered in checkers, or in some small figure. According to xxxix. 27 such tissue was woven by the ordinary weaver, not by the skilled weaver. (See on xxxv. 35; Gesen. 'Thes.' p. 1356; Fürst, 'Lex.' s. v. Cf. Wilkinson, 'Pop. Account,' Vol. II. p. 86.) It has been inferred from *vv.* 40, 41, and from xxxix. 27, that this and the other linen garments of the High-priest, with the exception of the mitre, did not differ from the dress of the common priests mentioned in the next verse. See Lev. vi. 10; Ezek. xliv. 17.

the mitre of fine linen] See on *v.* 37.

the girdle of needlework] **the girdle of the work of the embroiderer** (xxvi. 1, xxxv. 35). The word translated *girdle* is a different one from that so rendered in *v.* 8 (see note). The name here used (*abnet*) has been supposed to be a Persian word (Gesenius), but it is more likely to be an Egyptian one (Fürst, Brugsch, Birch). It was embroidered in three colours (xxxix. 29). Josephus says that its texture was very loose, so that it resembled the slough of a snake, that it was wound several times round the body, and that its ends ordinarily hung down to the feet, but were thrown over the shoulder when the priest was engaged in his work.

40. *Aaron's sons*] The common priests are here meant. See on *v.* 4. The girdle worn by them is here called by the same name as that of the High-priest (*abnet*), and was probably of the same make. Cf. xxxix. 29. Instead of the mitre consisting of a coil of twisted linen, the common priests wore **caps** of a simple construction which, according to a probable explanation of the name, seem to have been cup-shaped. They were however of fine texture and workmanship (xxxix. 28). The word *bonnet* is, in our present English, less suitable than **cap**. The description of the head-dress of the priests given by Josephus ('Ant.' III. 3. § 6) perhaps indicates a change of form in his day. Cf. on *v.* 7.

for glory and for beauty] See *v.* 2 and the following note.

41—43. The dress of white linen was the strictly sacerdotal dress common to the whole body of priests (Ezek. xliv. 17, 18). These were "for glory and for beauty" not less than *the golden garments* (as they were called by the Jews) which formed the High-priest's dress of state (*v.* 2). The linen suit which the High-priest put on when he went into the Most Holy place on the Day of Atonement, appears to have been regarded with peculiar respect (Lev. xvi. 4, 23; cf. Exod. xxxi. 10), though it is nowhere stated that it was distinguished in its make or texture, except in having a girdle (*abnet*) wholly of white linen, instead of a variegated one.—It may here be observed that the statement in Josephus, that the High-priest wore his golden garments only when he went into the Most Holy place ('Bel. Jud.' v. 5. § 7) is an obvious mistake: the reading is probably corrupt (see Hudson's note).—The ancient Egyptian priests, like the Hebrew priests, wore nothing but white linen garments in the performance of their duties (Herod. II. 37, with Wilkinson's note; Hengst. 'Egypt and the Books of Moses,' p. 145).

43. *in unto the tabernacle*] **into the Tent.** See on xxvi. 1.

that they bear not iniquity, and die] See on *vv.* 35, 38.

NOTE on CHAP. XXVIII. 30.

ON THE URIM AND THE THUMMIM.

I. *Their names.* II. *They were previously known, and distinct from the Breastplate.* III. *Their purpose and history.* IV. *Their origin.* V. *Theories.*

I.

The expression *the Urim and the Thummim* (אֶת־הָאוּרִים וְאֶת־הַתֻּמִּים) appears to mean *the Light and the Truth.* The primary meaning of the latter term is *perfection.* The form of the words is plural; but, according to the Hebrew idiom, this does not necessarily imply a plural sense. The rendering of the LXX. is, ἡ δήλωσις καὶ ἡ ἀλήθεια; that of Symmachus, φωτισμοὶ καὶ τελειότητες; that of the Vulgate, *Doctrina et Veritas*. The other ancient versions substantially agree with one or other of these. In most modern versions, except Luther's (*Licht und Recht*) and de Wette's (*das Licht und die Wahrheit*), the words are untranslated.

II.

From the way in which they are spoken of in Ex. xxviii. 30 and in Lev. viii. 8, compared with Ex. xxviii. 15—21, it would appear, taking a simple view of the words, that the Urim and the Thummim were some material things, and that they were separate from the Breastplate itself, as well as from the gems that were set upon it. It would seem most probable that they were kept in the bag of the Breastplate (Ex. xxviii. 16). And from the definite article being prefixed to each of the names, from their not being described in any way, and from their not being mentioned in the record of the construction of the Breastplate (xxxix. 21), it seems most likely that they were something previously existing and familiarly known. It is true that the Samaritan text says that Moses was *to make* them: but even if we accept this very weak authority, when the statement is compared with the fact that there is no direction given as to form or material, it leaves us to infer that they were no novelty as regards their use.

III.

The purpose of the Urim and the Thummim is clearly enough indicated in Num. xxvii. 21; 1 S. xxviii. 6; and also (as they were evidently regarded as belonging to the Ephod) in 1 S. xxiii. 9—12, xxx. 7, 8, cf. xxii. 14, 15. We are warranted in concluding that they were visible things of some sort by which the will of Jehovah, especially in what related to the wars in which His people were engaged, was made known, and that from this time they were preserved in the bag of the Breastplate of the High-priest, to be borne "upon his heart before the LORD continually" (Ex. xxviii. 30). They were formally delivered by Moses to Aaron (Lev. viii. 8), and subsequently passed on to Eleazar (Num. xx. 28, xxvii. 21). They were esteemed as the crowning glory of the Tribe of Levi (Deut. xxxiii. 8). There is no instance on record of their being consulted after the time of David. They were certainly not in use after the Captivity; and it seems to have become a proverb in reference to a question of inextricable difficulty, that it should not be solved "till there stood up a priest with Urim and Thummim" (Ezra ii. 63; Neh. vii. 65; cf. Hos. iii. 4). Such seem to be all the particulars that can be gathered immediately, or by easy inference, from Holy Scripture, regarding the nature, purpose, and history of the Urim and the Thummim.

IV.

Since the time of Spencer, the opinion has prevailed to a great extent that the Urim and the Thummim were wholly, or in part, of Egyptian origin. With this opinion is connected the notion that they were two small images of precious stone, which appears to have taken its rise from a passage in Philo; τὸ δὲ λογεῖον τετράγωνον διπλοῦν κατεσκευάζετο, ὡσανεὶ βάσις, ἵνα δύο ἀρετὰς ἀγαλματοφορῇ, δήλωσίν τε καὶ ἀλήθειαν ('Vit. Mos.' III. 11). But may not the symbol of the two virtues in the fancy of Philo have been rather the two sides of the *Choshen* than two actual images? Philo's use of the verb ἀγαλματοφορεῖν in other connections may tend to confirm this view. See 'de Confus. Ling.' c. 13; 'de Mundi Opif.' c. 23; but still more to the point is a passage in which he says that the two webs of the *Choshen* were called *Revelation and Truth*.—Ἐπὶ δὲ τοῦ λογείου διττὰ ὑφάσματα καταποικίλλει, προσαγαρεύων τὸ μὲν δήλωσιν τὸ δὲ ἀλήθειαν ('de Monarch.' II. 5. See also 'Legis Alleg.' III. 40, where he substitutes σαφήνεια for δήλωσις). But it is alleged that a close analogy is furnished by the image of sapphire (*lapis lazuli*, see on Ex. xxviii. 18) called *Truth*, that was suspended by a gold chain on the breasts of the Egyptian Judges, with which they touched the lips of acquitted persons (Diod. Sic. I. 48, 75; Ælian, 'Var. Hist.' XIV. 34). That such a custom as this was of old standing in Egypt, is rendered very probable by certain pictures of great antiquity in which the image is represented as a double one, bearing the symbols of *Truth and Justice*. The deity endowed with this dual character was called *Thmei*, and with this name some have connected the word *Thummim*, (Wilkinson, II. p. 205). But this etymology is entirely rejected by Egyptian scholars.—The Egyptian origin of the Urim and the Thummim has been advocated by Spencer, Gesenius, Knobel, Fürst, Hengstenberg, Plumptre (in Smith's 'Dict.' s. v.) and others.

But an argument on the other side seems to be furnished by the connection of the *Teraphim* with the Urim and the Thummim, which may be traced in the Old Testament. It has been suggested on very probable ground that the Teraphim may have been employed as an unauthorized substitute for the Urim and the Thummim[1]. Now we know that the Teraphim belonged to patriarchal times,

---

[1] See Judg. xvii. 5, xviii. 14, 17, 20; Hos. iii. 4; and, as rightly rendered in the margin, 2 K. xxiii. 24; Ezek. xxi. 21; Zech. x. 2: to these may be added, as it stands in the Hebrew, 1 S. xv. 23.

to the Semitic race, and to regions remote from Egypt (see Gen. xxxi. 19, &c.). Is not the supposition as easy that the Urim and the Thummim took the place of what must have been familiarly known to the Patriarchs, and which appear, in a renewal of the old degraded form, to have been in later times confounded with them, as that they were adopted from the Egyptians?

V.

As to the form and material of the Urim and the Thummim, and as to the mode in which they were consulted by the High-priest, there have been many conjectures, some of them very wild and startling. It would be out of place here to go at length into a subject in which there is so little to limit or to regulate the field of conjecture, that anything like certainty is beyond the reach of hope; but the inquiry must not be entirely passed over. We may first observe that the different views which have been taken are based on three distinct theories:—

1. That the Divine Will was manifested through the Urim and the Thummim by some physical effect addressed to the eye or the ear.

2. That they were some ordained symbol which, when the High-priest concentrated his sight and attention on it, became a means of calling forth the prophetic gift.

3. That they were some contrivance for casting lots.

1. Josephus, who identified the stones of the Breastplate with the Urim and the Thummim, says that they signified a favourable answer to the question proposed by shining forth with unusual brilliancy. He adds that they had not been known to exhibit this power for 200 years before his time ('Ant.' III. 8. §9). As regards the mode of the answer, several Jewish, and many Christian, writers, have followed him. The rabbinists adopted the notion, and shewed their usual tendency by exaggerating it. They said that the answer was communicated in detail by particular letters in the inscriptions on the stones shining out in succession, so as to spell the words[1].—Spencer, supposing that the Urim and the Thummim were two images, or Teraphim, imagined that an angel was commissioned to speak through the lips of one of them with an audible voice ('de Leg. Hebr.' lib. III. c. v. §3). Prideaux and others have supposed that an audible voice addressed itself from the Mercy-seat as the High-priest stood before it wearing the Breastplate on his breast ('Connection,' &c., book I.).

2. Some of those who have held the second theory have conceived that the High-priest used to fix his eyes on the gems of the Breastplate until the spirit of Prophecy came upon him and gave him utterance. Others have conjectured that the object of his contemplation was not the gems themselves, but some distinct object with sacred associations, such as a gold plate or gem of some kind inscribed with the name JEHOVAH, attached to the outside of the Breastplate. This theory, in some form, is adopted by the Targum of Palestine, Theodoret, Lightfoot, Kalisch and many others; but it is most fully reasoned out by Plumptre in Smith's 'Dictionary.'

3. Michaelis, Jahn and others, have supposed that the Urim and the Thummim might have been three slips, one with *yes* upon it, one with *no*, and the third plain, and that the slip taken out of the pocket of the Breastplate at hap-hazard by the High-priest was regarded as giving the answer to the question proposed.—Gesenius and Fürst have adopted Spencer's notion, that they were two images, but supposed that they were used in some mode of casting lots.—Winer, following Züllig, imagined that the Urim were diamonds cut in the form of dice, and that the Thummim were rough diamonds (according to the meaning of the word, *entire*) with some sort of marks engraved on them, which the High-priest, when he sought for an answer, took out of the bag and threw down on a table in the Sanctuary, drawing a meaning from the mode in which they fell.

But the theory itself is not necessarily involved in these hollow and vain conjectures as to the material instruments which may have been employed. No attempted explanation seems to be more in accordance with such analogy as the history of the Israelites affords, or more free from objection, than that the Urim and the Thummim were some means of casting lots. That the Lord should have made His will known to His people by such means may indeed run counter to our own habits of thought. But we know that appeals to lots were made under divine authority by the chosen people on the most solemn occasions[2]. The divine will was manifested by circumstances in themselves of as little note, or of as little external connection with the question at issue, as the dampness or the dryness of a fleece laid on the ground (Judg. vi. 36—40). It must have been a truth commonly recognized by the people that though "the lot was cast into the lap, the whole disposing thereof was of the Lord" (Prov. xvi. 33).—The practice of casting lots was not wholly discontinued till it was exer-

---

[1] See Sheringham's note on *Yoma*, in Surenhusius, Vol. II. p. 251, and the notes of Drusius and Cartwright on Ex. xxviii. 30 in the 'Crit. Sac.'

[2] Lev. xvi. 8; Num. xxvi. 55; Josh. vii. 14—18, xiii. 6, xviii. 8; 1 S. xiv. 41, 42; Acts i. 26.

cised in completing the number of the twelve Apostles (Acts i. 26). It seems worthy of remark, that the Urim and the Thummim appear to have fallen into disuse as the prophetic office became more distinct and important in and after the reign of David; and that we hear nothing of the casting of lots in the Apostolic History after the day of Pentecost, when the Holy Ghost was given to lead believers into all truth. In each case, the lower mode of revelation appears to give way to the higher[1].

[1] It has been objected that there is nothing in the etymology of the names of the Urim and the Thummim to justify the conjecture that they were connected with casting lots. But the words in their proper meaning probably referred to the result obtained (*i. e.* the knowledge of the divine will) rather than to the mere material instruments employed.

CHAPTER XXIX.

1 *The sacrifice and ceremonies of consecrating the priests.* 38 *The continual burnt offering.* 45 *God's promise to dwell among the children of Israel.*

AND this *is* the thing that thou shalt do unto them to hallow them, to minister unto me in the priest's office: *a* Take one young bullock, and two rams without blemish,

a Lev. 8. 2. & 9. 2.

2 And unleavened bread, and cakes unleavened tempered with oil, and wafers unleavened anointed with oil: *of* wheaten flour shalt thou make them.

3 And thou shalt put them into one basket, and bring them in the basket, with the bullock and the two rams.

4 And Aaron and his sons thou shalt bring unto the door of the tabernacle of the congregation, and shalt wash them with water.

5 And thou shalt take the garments, and put upon Aaron the coat, and the robe of the ephod, and the ephod, and the breastplate, and gird him with the curious girdle of the ephod:

6 And thou shalt put the mitre upon his head, and put the holy crown upon the mitre.

7 Then shalt thou take the anointing *b* oil, and pour *it* upon his head, and anoint him.

b chap. 30. 25.

8 And thou shalt bring his sons, and put coats upon them.

9 And thou shalt gird them with girdles, Aaron and his sons, and †put the bonnets on them: and the priest's office shall be theirs for a perpetual statute: and thou shalt † *c* consecrate Aaron and his sons.

† Heb. *bind.*
† Heb. *fill the hand of.*
c chap. 28. 41.

10 And thou shalt cause a bullock to be brought before the tabernacle of the congregation: and *d* Aaron and his sons shall put their hands upon the head of the bullock.

d Lev. 1. 4.

11 And thou shalt kill the bullock before the LORD, *by* the door of the tabernacle of the congregation.

12 And thou shalt take of the blood of the bullock, and put *it* upon the horns of the altar with thy finger, and pour all the blood beside the bottom of the altar.

e Lev. 3. 3. ‖ *It seemeth by anatomy, and the Hebrew doctors, to be the midriff.*

13 And *e* thou shalt take all the fat that covereth the inwards, and ‖ the caul *that is* above the liver, and the

---

CHAP. XXIX.

THE CONSECRATION OF THE PRIESTS.

1—37.

The account of the consecration of Aaron and his sons, in accordance with the directions contained in this chapter, is given in Lev. viii., ix. The details of the ceremonies involve many important references to the Law of the Offerings contained in Lev. i.—vii. Most of the notes on these details are therefore given under the narrative of the consecration in Leviticus.

1, 2, 3. See on Lev. viii. 2, 26.

2. *cakes unleavened tempered with oil*] These are called *cakes of oiled bread* in Lev. viii. 26. See on Lev. ii. 4.

4. *door of the tabernacle*] **entrance of the tent.** See on Lev. viii. 3.

wash them] See on Lev. viii. 6.

5, 6. See on Lev. viii. 7, 8, 9; Exod. xxviii. 7, 8, 31—39, xxxix. 30.

6. *the holy crown*] See on xxxix. 30.

7. *the anointing oil*] See Lev. viii. 10—12; Exod. xxx. 22—25.

8. See on Lev. viii. 13: cf. Exod. xxxix. 41.

10—14. See on Lev. viii. 14—17; cf. Lev. iv. 3.

two kidneys, and the fat that *is* upon them, and burn *them* upon the altar.

14 But the flesh of the bullock, and his skin, and his dung, shalt thou burn with fire without the camp: it *is* a sin offering.

15 ¶ Thou shalt also take one ram; and Aaron and his sons shall put their hands upon the head of the ram.

16 And thou shalt slay the ram, and thou shalt take his blood, and sprinkle *it* round about upon the altar.

17 And thou shalt cut the ram in pieces, and wash the inwards of him, and his legs, and put *them* unto his pieces, and ⁂ unto his head.

Or, upon.

18 And thou shalt burn the whole ram upon the altar: it *is* a burnt offering unto the LORD: it *is* a sweet savour, an offering made by fire unto the LORD.

19 ¶ And thou shalt take the other ram; and Aaron and his sons shall put their hands upon the head of the ram.

20 Then shalt thou kill the ram, and take of his blood, and put *it* upon the tip of the right ear of Aaron, and upon the tip of the right ear of his sons, and upon the thumb of their right hand, and upon the great toe of their right foot, and sprinkle the blood upon the altar round about.

21 And thou shalt take of the blood that *is* upon the altar, and of the anointing oil, and sprinkle *it* upon Aaron, and upon his garments, and upon his sons, and upon the garments of his sons with him: and he shall be hallowed, and his garments, and his sons, and his sons' garments with him.

22 Also thou shalt take of the ram the fat and the rump, and the fat that covereth the inwards, and the caul *above* the liver, and the two kidneys, and the fat that *is* upon them, and the right shoulder; for it *is* a ram of consecration:

23 And one loaf of bread, and one cake of oiled bread, and one wafer out of the basket of the unleavened bread that *is* before the LORD:

24 And thou shalt put all in the hands of Aaron, and in the hands of his sons; and shalt ‖wave them *for* a wave offering before the LORD.

‖ *Or, shake to and fro.*

25 And thou shalt receive them of their hands, and burn *them* upon the altar for a burnt offering, for a sweet savour before the LORD: it *is* an offering made by fire unto the LORD.

26 And thou shalt take the breast of the ram of Aaron's consecration, and wave it *for* a wave offering before the LORD: and it shall be thy part.

27 And thou shalt sanctify the breast of the wave offering, and the shoulder of the heave offering, which is waved, and which is heaved up, of the ram of the consecration, *even* of *that* which *is* for Aaron, and of *that* which is for his sons:

28 And it shall be Aaron's and his sons' by a statute for ever from the children of Israel: for it *is* an heave offering: and it shall be an heave offering from the children of Israel of the sacrifice of their peace offerings, *even* their heave offering unto the LORD.

29 ¶ And the holy garments of Aaron shall be his sons' after him, to be anointed therein, and to be consecrated in them.

30 *And* †that son that is priest in his stead shall put them on seven days,

† *Heb. he of his sons.*

15—18. See on Lev. viii. 18—21.

19—28. See on Lev. viii. 22—29.

27. On Waving and Heaving, first mentioned in their connection with the ceremonies of the Altar in this chapter, see preface to Leviticus. It should be noticed that the right shoulder (rather perhaps *the right leg*, see Lev. vii. 32) was to be formally presented to the priests (*vv.* 22, 24), in order to make a recognition of the Law of the Heave-offering, though, on this special occasion, it was not to be eaten like an ordinary heave-offering, but to be made part of the burnt-offering. (*v.* 25.)

28. This law is repeated Lev. vii. 34. **Cf.** Lev. x. 14, 15; Num. vi. 20.

29, 30. See on Lev. viii. 30, 33.

when he cometh into the tabernacle of the congregation to minister in the holy *place*.

31 ¶ And thou shalt take the ram of the consecration, and seethe his flesh in the holy place.

32 And Aaron and his sons shall eat the flesh of the ram, and the *f*bread that *is* in the basket, *by* the door of the tabernacle of the congregation.

f Lev 8. 31.
Matt. 12. 4

33 And they shall eat those things wherewith the atonement was made, to consecrate *and* to sanctify them: but a stranger shall not eat *thereof*, because they *are* holy.

34 And if ought of the flesh of the consecrations, or of the bread, remain unto the morning, then thou shalt burn the remainder with fire: it shall not be eaten, because it *is* holy.

35 And thus shalt thou do unto Aaron, and to his sons, according to all *things* which I have commanded thee: seven days shalt thou consecrate them.

36 And thou shalt offer every day a bullock *for* a sin offering for atonement: and thou shalt cleanse the altar, when thou hast made an atonement for it, and thou shalt anoint it, to sanctify it.

37 Seven days thou shalt make an atonement for the altar, and sanctify it; and it shall be an altar most holy: whatsoever toucheth the altar shall be holy.

38 ¶ Now this *is that* which thou shalt offer upon the altar; *g* two lambs of the first year day by day continually.

g Numb. 28. 3.

39 The one lamb thou shalt offer in the morning; and the other lamb thou shalt offer at even:

40 And with the one lamb a tenth deal of flour mingled with the fourth part of an hin of beaten oil; and the fourth part of an hin of wine *for* a drink offering.

41 And the other lamb thou shalt offer at even, and shalt do thereto according to the meat offering of the morning, and according to the drink offering thereof, for a sweet savour, an offering made by fire unto the LORD.

31—34. See on Lev. viii. 31, 32.

33. *a stranger*] **one of another family,** *i.e.* in this case, one not of the family of Aaron. The Hebrew word (*zār*) is the same as is used xxx. 33, Deut. xxv. 5.

35, 36. See on Lev. viii. 33, 35.

37. See on Lev. viii. 11.

The Continual Burnt-offering.
38—46.

38. *this is that which thou shalt offer*] The primary purpose of the national Altar is here set forth. On it was to be offered "the continual Burnt-offering" (*v.* 42), consisting of a yearling lamb with its meat-offering and its drink-offering, and this was to figure the daily renewal of the consecration of the nation. The victim slain every morning and every evening was an acknowledgment that the life of the people belonged to Jehovah, and the offering of meal was an acknowledgment that all their right works were His due (see on Lev. ii.); while the incense symbolized their daily prayers. (See on xxx. 6—8.)

39. *at even*] Literally, *between the two evenings.* See on xii. 6.

40. *a tenth deal*] *i.e.* the tenth part of an Ephah; it is sometimes called an Omer (Exod. xvi. 36; Num. xxviii. 5. See on Lev. xxiii. 13). The Ephah seems to have been rather less than four gallons and a half (see on Lev. xix. 36); and the tenth deal of flour may have weighed about 3 lbs. 2 oz.

an hin] The word *hin*, which here first occurs, appears to be Egyptian. The measure was one-sixth of an ephah. The quarter of a hin was therefore about a pint and a half. See on Lev. xix. 36.

beaten oil] *i.e.* oil of the best quality. See on xxvii. 20.

wine for a drink-offering] The earliest mention of the Drink-offering is found in connection with Jacob's setting up the stone at Bethel (Gen. xxxv. 14). But it is here first associated with the rites of the Altar. The Law of the Drink-offering is stated Num. xv. 5 sq. Nothing whatever is expressly said in the Old Testament regarding the mode in which the wine was treated: but it would seem probable, from the prohibition that it should not be poured upon the Altar of Incense (Exod. xxx. 9), that it used to be poured on the Altar of Burnt-offering. Josephus ('Ant.' III. 9. § 4) says that it was poured round the Altar ($\pi\epsilon\rho\grave{\iota}$ $\tau\grave{o}\nu$ $\beta\omega\mu\acute{o}\nu$): it may have been cast upon it in the same way as the blood of the Burnt-

42 *This shall be* a continual burnt offering throughout your generations *at* the door of the tabernacle of the congregation before the Lord: where I will meet you, to speak there unto thee.

43 And there I will meet with the children of Israel, and ⁸*the tabernacle* shall be sanctified by my glory.

^{⁸ Or, Israel.}

44 And I will sanctify the tabernacle of the congregation, and the altar: I will sanctify also both Aaron and his sons, to minister to me in the priest's office.

45 ¶ And ʰI will dwell among the children of Israel, and will be their God.

^{ʰ Lev. 26. 12. 2 Cor. 5. 16}

46 And they shall know that I *am* the Lord their God, that brought them forth out of the land of Egypt, that I may dwell among them: I *am* the Lord their God.

CHAPTER XXX.

1 *The altar of incense.* 11 *The ransom of souls.* 17 *The brasen laver.* 22 *The holy anointing oil.* 34 *The composition of the perfume.*

AND thou shalt make an altar to burn incense upon: *of* shittim wood shalt thou make it.

2 A cubit *shall be* the length thereof, and a cubit the breadth thereof; foursquare shall it be: and two cubits *shall be* the height thereof: the horns thereof *shall be* of the same.

3 And thou shalt overlay it with pure gold, the †top thereof, and the ⁱsides thereof round about, and the horns thereof; and thou shalt make unto it a crown of gold round about.

^{† Heb. the roof and the walls. † Heb. walls.}

4 And two golden rings shalt thou make to it under the crown of it, by the two †corners thereof, upon the two sides of it shalt thou make *it;* and

^{† Heb. ribs.}

---

offering and the Peace-offering (see on Lev. i.), or at its foot (ἐs θεμέλια, Ecclus. i. 15. This appears to agree with the patriarchal usage mentioned Gen. xxxv. 14.

42. *at the door of the tabernacle*] **at the entrance of the Tent.**

43. *the (tabernacle) shall be sanctified*] The word *tabernacle* is certainly not the right one to be here supplied. From the context it may be inferred that what is meant is the spot in which Jehovah promises to meet with the assembly of His people, who were not admitted into the *Mishkān* itself, as the priests were (see xxv. 22); that is, the Holy Precinct between the Tabernacle and the Altar. See Lev. x. 17, 18.—This verse should be rendered, **And in that place will I meet with the children of Israel, and it shall be sanctified with my glory.**

44, 45. The purpose of the formal consecration of the Sanctuary and of the priests who served in it was, that the whole nation which Jehovah had set free from its bondage in Egypt might be consecrated in its daily life, and dwell continually in His presence as "a kingdom of priests and an holy nation."

46. Cf. Gen. xvii. 7.

Chap. XXX.
The Altar of Incense.

1—10. (xxxvii. 25—28, xl. 26, 27.) This passage would seem naturally to belong to ch. xxv., where directions are given for the whole of the furniture of the Tabernacle, except the Altar of Incense. No satisfactory reason appears for its occurrence in this place. In the lists of the articles (xxxi. 8, xxxv. 15), and in the record of their construction (xxxvii. 25—28), and of their arrangement in the Sanctuary (xl. 26, 27), the Altar of Incense is mentioned in due order. It should however be observed, that the instructions here given respecting it are distinguished from those relating to the other articles in ch. xxv. in as far as they comprise directions for the mode in which it was to be used (*vv.* 7—10).

The Altar was to be a casing of boards of shittim wood (see on xxv. 5), 18 inches square and three feet in height (taking the cubit as 18 inches), entirely covered with plates of gold. Four "horns" were to project upwards at the corners like those of the Altar of Burnt-offering (xxvii. 2). A moulding of gold was to run round the top. On each of two opposite sides there was to be a gold ring through which the staves were to be put when it was moved from place to place.

3. *a crown of gold*] **a moulding of gold.** See on xxv. 11.

4. *by the two corners thereof*] The Hebrew word does not mean *corners.* See margin. The sense of the first part of the verse appears to be: *And two gold rings shalt thou make for it under its moulding; on its two sides shalt thou make them* (*i.e.* one ring on each side). So de Wette, Knobel, Schott, Wogue. The Ark and the Shewbread Table had each four rings, two for the pole on each side; but the Incense Altar, being shorter,

they shall be for places for the staves to bear it withal.

5 And thou shalt make the staves *of* shittim wood, and overlay them with gold.

6 And thou shalt put it before the vail that *is* by the ark of the testimony, before the mercy seat that *is* over the testimony, where I will meet with thee.

7 And Aaron shall burn thereon ⁺sweet incense every morning: when he dresseth the lamps, he shall burn incense upon it.

8 And when Aaron ⁱlighteth the lamps ⁺at even, he shall burn incense upon it, a perpetual incense before the LORD throughout your generations.

9 Ye shall offer no strange incense thereon, nor burnt sacrifice, nor meat offering; neither shall ye pour drink offering thereon.

10 And Aaron shall make an atonement upon the horns of it once in a year with the blood of the sin offering of atonements: once in the year shall he make atonement upon it throughout your generations: it *is* most holy unto the LORD.

11 ¶ And the LORD spake unto Moses, saying,

12 ᵃWhen thou takest the sum of the children of Israel after ⁺their number, then shall they give every man a ransom for his soul unto the LORD, when thou numberest them; that there be no plague among them, when *thou* numberest them.

⁺ Heb. *incense of spices.*
ⁱ Or, *setteth up.* Heb. *causeth to ascend.*
| Heb. *between the two evens.*
ᵃ Numb. 1. 2, 5.
⁺ Heb. *them that are to be numbered.*

---

was sufficiently supported by a single ring on each side, without risk of its being thrown off its balance.

6. The place for the Altar of Incense was outside the vail, opposite to the Ark of the Covenant and between the Candlestick on the south side and the Shewbread Table on the north (xl. 22—24). It appears to have been regarded as having a more intimate connection with the Holy of Holies than the other things in the Holy Place (see 1 K. vi. 22; Rev. viii. 3; also Heb. ix. 4, if we are to identify it with the θυμιατήριον there mentioned, see on Lev. xvi. 12); and the mention of the Mercy-seat in this verse, if we associate with it the significance of incense as figuring the prayers of the Lord's people (Ps. cxli. 2; Rev. v. 8, viii. 3, 4), seems to furnish additional ground for an inference that the Incense Altar took precedence of the Table of Showbread and the Candlestick.

7. *the lamps*] See on xxvii. 21.

burn incense] The word here and elsewhere applied to the burning of incense is the same as that used xxv. 37. See note.

7, 8. The offering of the Incense accompanied that of the morning and evening sacrifice. The two forms of offering symbolized the spirit of man reaching after communion with Jehovah, both in act and utterance, according to the words of the Psalmist, "Let my prayer be set forth before thee as incense; and the lifting up of my hands as the evening sacrifice." Ps. cxli. 2.

9. By this regulation, the symbolism of the Altar of Incense was kept free from ambiguity. Atonement was made by means of the victim on the Brazen altar in the court outside; the prayers of the reconciled worshippers had their type within the Tabernacle.

10. See on Lev. xvi. 18, 19.

shall he make atonement] rather, **shall atonement be made.**

The Ransom of Souls.

11—16. (xxxviii. 25—28.)

11, 12. The materials for the textile work, the wood, the gold, and the bronze, were to be the free-will offerings of those who could contribute them (xxv. 2, xxxv. 21 sq.). But the silver was to be obtained by an enforced capitation on every adult male Israelite, the poor and the rich having to pay the same (*v.* 15). Hence, in the estimate of the metals collected for the work (xxxviii. 24—31) the gold and the bronze are termed *offerings* (strictly, **wave-offerings**, see preface to Leviticus), while the silver is spoken of as "the silver of them that were numbered." But this payment is brought into its highest relation in being here accounted a spiritual obligation laid on each individual, a tribute expressly exacted by Jehovah. Every man of Israel who would escape a curse (*v.* 12) had in this way to make a practical acknowledgment that he had a share in the Sanctuary, on the occasion of his being recognised as one of the covenanted people (*v.* 16).—Silver was the metal commonly used for current coin. See Gen. xxiii. 16.

12. *When thou takest the sum of the children of Israel*] The silver must have been contributed at this time, along with the other materials, since it was used in the Tabernacle, which was completed on the first day of the first month of the second year after coming

13 This they shall give, every one that passeth among them that are numbered, half a shekel after the shekel of the sanctuary: (*b* a shekel *is* twenty gerahs:) an half shekel *shall be* the offering of the LORD.

14 Every one that passeth among them that are numbered, from twenty years old and above, shall give an offering unto the LORD.

15 The rich shall not †give more, and the poor shall not †give less than half a shekel, when *they* give an offering unto the LORD, to make an atonement for your souls.

16 And thou shalt take the atonement money of the children of Israel, and shalt appoint it for the service of the tabernacle of the congregation; that it may be a memorial unto the children of Israel before the LORD, to make an atonement for your souls.

17 ¶ And the LORD spake unto Moses, saying,

18 Thou shalt also make a laver *of* brass, and his foot *also of* brass, to wash *withal:* and thou shalt put it between the tabernacle of the congregation and the altar, and thou shalt put water therein.

19 For Aaron and his sons shall wash their hands and their feet thereat:

b Lev. 27. 25. Numb. 3. 47. Ezek. 45. 12.

† Heb. *multiply.*
† Heb. *diminish.*

---

out of Egypt (xl. 17). But the command to take the complete census of the nation appears not to have been given until the first day of the second month of that year (Num. i. 1). On comparing the words of Exod. xxx. 12 with those of Num. i. 1—3, we may perhaps infer that the first passage relates to a mere counting of the adult Israelites at the time when the money was taken from each, and that what the latter passage enjoins was a formal enrolment of them according to their genealogies and their order of military service.

a ransom for his soul] What the sincere worshipper thus paid was at once the fruit and the sign of his faith in the goodness of Jehovah, who had redeemed him and brought him into the Covenant. (See Introd. note to ch. xxv.) Hence the payment is rightly called a *ransom* in as much as it involved a personal appropriation of the fact of his redemption. On the word *soul*, see on Lev. xvii. 11.

that there be no plague] *i.e.* that they might not incur punishment for the neglect and contempt of spiritual privileges. Cf. 1 Cor. xi. 27—30; and the Exhortation in our Communion Service.

13. *half a shekel*] The probable weight of silver in the half-shekel would now be worth about 1*s*. 3½*d*. (See on Exod. xxxviii. 25.) *Gerah* is, literally, a *bean*, probably the bean of the carob or locust-tree (Aben-Ezra). It was used as the name of a small weight, as our word *grain* came into use from a grain of wheat. The purpose of the definition of the shekel here given is not quite certain. It might seem to countenance the rabbinical notion that there were two kinds of shekel, the shekel of the Sanctuary consisting of twenty gerahs, and the common shekel. (See on xxxviii. 24.) But it is more likely that the weight is defined rather for the sake of emphasis, to intimate that the just value should be given precisely. The words in question might rather be rendered: "half a shekel after the shekel of the sanctuary, twenty gerahs to the shekel; the half shekel shall be the offering (Heb. *terumah*, as in *vv.* 14, 15; see xxv. 2) to Jehovah."

15. Every Israelite stood in one and the same relation to Jehovah. See on *vv.* 11, 12.

16. *tabernacle of the congregation*] Tent of meeting.

a memorial unto the children of Israel] The silver used in the Tabernacle was a memorial to remind each man of his position before the Lord, as one of the covenanted people.

The Laver of Brass.
17—21. (xxxviii. 8.)

18. *a laver of brass*] The bronze for the Laver and its foot was supplied from the bronze mirrors of the women "who assembled at the door of the tabernacle." The women seem to have voluntarily given up these articles of luxury (see on xxxviii. 8). Bronze mirrors were much used by the ancient Egyptians. Wilkinson, Vol. II. p. 345. No hint is given as to the form of the Laver. It may have been made with an immediate view to use of the simplest and most convenient form. The Brazen Sea and the ten Lavers that served the same purpose in the Temple of Solomon, were elaborately wrought in artistic designs and are minutely described (1 K. vii. 23—29).

tabernacle of the congregation] Tent of meeting.

19. *wash their hands and their feet*] Whenever a priest had to enter the Tabernacle, or to offer a victim on the Altar, he was required to wash his hands and his feet; but on certain solemn occasions he was required to bathe his whole person (xxix. 4; Lev. xvi. 4). The Laver must also have furnished the water for washing those parts of the victims that needed cleansing (Lev. i. 9).

20 When they go into the tabernacle of the congregation, they shall wash with water, that they die not; or when they come near to the altar to minister, to burn offering made by fire unto the LORD:

21 So they shall wash their hands and their feet, that they die not: and it shall be a statute for ever to them, *even* to him and to his seed throughout their generations.

22 ¶ Moreover the LORD spake unto Moses, saying,

23 Take thou also unto thee principal spices, of pure myrrh five hundred *shekels*, and of sweet cinnamon half so much, *even* two hundred and fifty *shekels*, and of sweet calamus two hundred and fifty *shekels*,

24 And of cassia five hundred *shekels*, after the shekel of the sanctuary, and of oil olive an ᶜ hin:

ᶜ chap. 29. 40.

---

20. *tabernacle of the congregation*] **Tent of meeting.**

that they die not] See on xxviii. 35.

to burn offering made by fire unto the LORD] Literally, *to send up in fire an offering to Jehovah*. The verb is the same as in v. 7 and xxv 37.

The Holy Anointing Oil.

22—33. (xxxvii. 29.)

23. *principal spices*] *i.e.* the best spices.

pure myrrh] There cannot be much doubt as to the identity of this substance from its name in different languages (Hebrew, *mōr*; Arabic, *murr*; Greek, σμύρνα; Latin, *myrrha*). It is a gum which comes from the stem of a low, thorny, ragged tree, that grows in Arabia Felix and Eastern Africa, called by botanists *Balsamodendron myrrha*. The word here rendered *pure*, is literally, *freely flowing*, an epithet which is explained by the fact that the best myrrh is said to exude spontaneously from the bark (Plin. 'H. N.' XII. 35; Theophrast. 'de Odorib.' 29), while that of inferior quality oozes out in greater quantity from incisions made in the bark. On the estimation in which myrrh was held, see Cant. i. 13; Matt. ii. 11; on its use as a perfume, Ps. xlv. 8; Prov. vii. 17; Cant. v. 5; and on its use in embalming, John xix. 39. This is the first mention of it in the Hebrew text of the Old Testament, but in our version it is named by mistake in Gen. xxxvii. 25, xliii. 11.

five hundred shekels] Probably rather more than 15¼ lbs. See on xxxviii. 24.

sweet cinnamon] This substance is satisfactorily identified, like the preceding one, on account of its name (Heb. *Kinnamon*; Gr. κιννάμωμον; Lat. *cinnamomum*). It is obtained from a tree allied to the laurel that grows in Ceylon and other islands of the Indian Ocean, known in Botany as the *Cinnamomun zeylanicum*. It is the inner rind of the tree dried in the sun. The origin of the name appears to be found in the Malay language (Ritter, Knobel). Herodotus says that the word is Phœnician, but this means no more than that the Greeks learned it from the Phœnicians. It is probable that Cinnamon was imported from India in very early times by the people of Ophir, and that it was brought with other spices from the south part of Arabia by the trading caravans that visited Egypt and Syria. Hence, even in later times, Cinnamon and other Indian spices were spoken of as productions of the land of the Sabæans (Strabo, XVI. pp. 769, 774, 778). If we accept this explanation, the mention of these spices in Exodus may be taken as the earliest notice we have connected with commerce with the remote East. Cinnamon is elsewhere mentioned in the Scriptures only, Prov. vii. 17; Cant. iv. 14; Rev. xviii. 13.

two hundred and fifty shekels] Probably about 7 lbs. 14 oz. See on xxxviii. 24.

sweet calamus] The word rendered calamus (*kanēh*) is the common Hebrew name for a *stalk*, *reed*, or *cane* (Gen. xli. 5; 1 K. xiv. 15; Ezek. xli. 8). The **fragrant cane** (or *rush*) here spoken of is mentioned in Isa. xliii. 24, in Jer. vi. 20 (where it is called in the Hebrew "**the good cane** from a far country"), and in Cant. iv. 14; Ezek. xxvii. 19, where it is called simply **cane**. It was probably what is now known in India as the Lemon Grass (*Andropogon schoenanthus*). Aromatic reeds were known to the ancients as the produce of India and the region of the Euphrates (Xenophon, 'Anab.' I. 5, § 1; Diosc. 'Mat. Med.' I. 16). The statements that such reeds were produced in the neighbourhood of Libanus (Theophr. 'H. P.' IX. 7; 'C. P.' VI. 18; Polybius, V. 45), near the Lake of Gennesaret (Strabo, XVI. p. 755) and in the Land of the Sabæans (Strabo, XVI. p. 778; cf. Diod. II. 49), may be regarded as some of the many mistakes which have arisen from confounding the country from which a commodity is obtained with that of its original production.

24. *cassia*] The Hebrew name (*kiddāh*) is found elsewhere only in Ezek. xxvii. 19, where it is associated, as it is here, with sweet cane. The word rendered *cassia* in Ps. xlv. 8 is a different one, but it is probable that the same substance is denoted by it. Most of the ancient versions, and all modern authorities, seem to be in favour of *cassia* being the true rendering of *kiddāh*. Cassia is the inner bark

25 And thou shalt make it an oil of holy ointment, an ointment compound after the art of the ¹apothecary: it shall be an holy anointing oil.

26 And thou shalt anoint the tabernacle of the congregation therewith, and the ark of the testimony,

27 And the table and all his vessels, and the candlestick and his vessels, and the altar of incense,

28 And the altar of burnt offering with all his vessels, and the laver and his foot.

29 And thou shalt sanctify them, that they may be most holy: whatsoever toucheth them shall be holy.

30 And thou shalt anoint Aaron and his sons, and consecrate them,

¹ Or, *perfumer*

that *they* may minister unto me in the priest's office.

31 And thou shalt speak unto the children of Israel, saying, This shall be an holy anointing oil unto me throughout your generations.

32 Upon man's flesh shall it not be poured, neither shall ye make *any other* like it, after the composition of it: it *is* holy, *and* it shall be holy unto you.

33 Whosoever compoundeth *any* like it, or whosoever putteth *any* of it upon a stranger, shall even be cut off from his people.

34 ¶ And the LORD said unto Moses, Take unto thee sweet spices, stacte, and onycha, and galbanum;

---

of an Indian tree (*Cinnamonum cassia*), which differs from that which produces cinnamon in the shape of its leaves and some other particulars. It bears a strong resemblance to cinnamon, but it is more pungent, and of coarser texture. It was probably in ancient times, as it is at present, by far less costly than cinnamon, and it may have been on this account that it was used in double quantity.

an hin] Probably about six pints. See on Lev. xix. 36.

25.] *an oil of holy ointment*] rather, **a holy anointing oil**.

after the art of the apothecary] According to Jewish tradition, the essences of the spices were first extracted, and then mixed with the oil (Otho, 'Lex. Rabb.' p. 486). That some such process was employed is probable from the great proportion of solid matter compared with the oil. The preparation of the Anointing Oil, as well as of the Incense, was entrusted to Bezaleel (xxxvii. 29), and the care of preserving it to Eleazar the son of Aaron (Num. iv. 16). In a later age, it was prepared by the sons of the priests (1 Chro. ix. 30).

26—31.] Cf. xl. 9—15. See on Lev. viii. 10—12.

26. *tabernacle of the congregation*] **Tent of meeting.**

29.] See on xxix. 37.

32. *upon man's flesh*] *i.e.* on the persons of those that were not priests who might employ it for such anointing as was usual on festive occasions (Ps. civ. 15; Prov. xxvii. 9; Matt. vi. 17, &c.).

33. *a stranger*] **one of another family.** See on xxix. 33. The Holy Anointing Oil was not even to be used for the anointing of a king. See on 1 K. i. 39.

cut off from his people.] See on Gen. xvii. 14, Exod. xxxi. 14, and Lev. vii. 20.

The Holy Incense.

34—38. (xxxvii. 29.)

34.] The Incense, like the Anointing Oil, consisted of four aromatic ingredients.

stacte] The Hebrew word is *nataph* (*i.e.* a *drop*), which occurs in its simple sense in Job xxxvi. 27. Our version and the Vulgate have adopted the word used by the LXX. (στακτή), which, like the Hebrew, may denote anything that drops, and was applied to the purest kind of myrrh that drops spontaneously from the tree (see on *v.* 23). But the substance here meant, which is nowhere else mentioned in the Old Testament, is generally supposed to be the gum of the Storax-tree (*Styrax officinalis*) found in Syria and the neighbouring countries. The gum was burned as a perfume in the time of Pliny ('H. N.' XII. 40). But it seems by no means unlikely that the *stacte* here mentioned was the gum known as Benzoin, or Gum Benjamin, which is an important ingredient in the incense now used in churches and mosks, and is the produce of another storax-tree (*Styrax benjoin*) that grows in Java and Sumatra. See on *v.* 23. It may be observed that the liquid storax of commerce is obtained from quite a different tree known to botanists as *Liquidambar syraciflua*.

onycha] Heb. *shechēleth* (which appears to mean a *shell*, or *scale*), LXX. ὄνυξ, Vulg. *onycha*. The word does not occur in any other place in the Old Testament. The Greek word was not only applied to the well-known precious stone, the onyx, from its resemblance to the human nail, but to the horny operculum, or cap, of a shell. The operculum of the strombus, or wing-shell, which

v. 35—37.]   EXODUS. XXX.   401

these sweet spices with pure frankincense: of each shall there be a like *weight:*

35 And thou shalt make it a perfume, a confection after the art of the apothecary, ⁺tempered together, pure *and* holy:

36 And thou shalt beat *some* of it very small, and put of it before the testimony in the tabernacle of the congregation, where I will meet with thee: it shall be unto you most holy.

37 And *as for* the perfume which thou shalt make, ye shall not make to yourselves according to the composition thereof: it shall be unto thee holy for the LORD.

⁺ Heb. *salted.*

---

abounds in the Red Sea, is said to be employed at this day in the composition of perfume, and to have been used as a medicine in the Middle Ages under the name of *Blatta Byzantina.* Pliny, most likely referring to the same substance with imperfect knowledge, speaks of a shell called *onyx* that was used both as a perfume and a medicine ('H. N.' XXXII. 46; cf. Dioscorides, 'Mat. Med.' II.11). Its identification with the *shecheleth* of the text seems probable. Saadia uses the word *ladanum*, the name of the gum of the Lada tree (see Plin. 'H. N.' XII. 37). Bochart, on weak ground, imagined that bdellium (Gen. ii. 12) was meant. See Bochart, 'Op.' Vol. III. p. 803; Gesen. 'Thes.' p. 1388.

galbanum] Heb. *chelbenāh;* LXX. χαλβάνη; Vulg. *galbanum.* It is not mentioned elsewhere in the Old Testament. No doubt has been raised as to its identity. Galbanum is now well known in medicine as a gum of a yellowish brown colour, in the form of either grains or masses. It burns with a pungent smell which is agreeable when it is combined with other smells, but not else. It is imported from India, Persia, and Africa; yet, strange to say, the plant from which it comes is not yet certainly known. (See 'English Cyclo.' s. v.)

pure frankincense] Heb. *lebonah;* LXX. λίβανος; Vulg. *thus.* This was the most important of the aromatic gums. Like myrrh, it was regarded by itself as a precious perfume (Cant. iii. 6; Matt. ii. 11), and it was used unmixed with other substances in some of the rites of the Law (Lev. ii. 1. 15, v. 11, vi. 15, &c.). The Hebrew name is improperly rendered *incense* in our Version in Isa. xliii. 23, lx. 6, lxvi. 3; Jer. vi. 20, xvii. 26, xli. 5. It is certain that the supplies of it, as well as of the other spices, were obtained from Southern Arabia (Isa. lx. 6, Jer. vi. 20. Cf. 1 K. x. 1, 2, 10, 15; 2 Chro. ix. 9. 14). The Greek and Latin writers in general speak of its being produced in that region. But they evidently knew but little of the subject, as their descriptions of the plant producing it differ greatly from each other. (Plin. 'H. N.' VI. 32, XII. 31; Diod. Sic. II. 49, V. 41; Theophrast. 'de Plant.' IX. 1; Arrian, 'Perip.' with Stuck's note, p. 49; Dioscor. I. 82; Strabo, XVI. p. 774. Cf. p. 782.) The tree from which it is obtained

VOL. I.

is not found in Arabia, and it was most likely imported from India by the Sabæans, like Cinnamon, Cassia, and Calamus (see on *v.* 23). The tree is now known as the *Boswellia serrata,* or *B. thurifera,* and grows abundantly in the highlands of India, where its native name is *Salai.* The native name of the gum is *olibanum,* and its Arabic name, *looban:* the Hebrew and Greek names seem to have been taken directly from the Arabic. The frankincense of commerce is a different substance, the resin of the spruce and of some other kinds of fir.

35. *after the art of the apothecary*] The four substances were perhaps pounded and thoroughly mixed together, and then fused into a mass.

tempered together] With this rendering, most Versions, modern as well as ancient, and many of the best critics, agree. But, according to its etymology, the Hebrew might mean *seasoned with salt,* or (as it stands in the margin) *salted.* It is thus explained in the Talmud, which has been followed by Maimonides, de Wette, Gesenius, Herxheimer, Kalisch, and Keil. It is urged that this accords with the law that every offering should be accompanied by salt (Lev. ii. 13). But this law appears to refer only to the offerings of what was used as food (see note in loc., and on Lev. xxiv. 7), and Knobel has well observed that the use of salt in incense is contrary to all known analogy, since no such combination is known to have been made in the incense of any people.—Josephus speaks of the incense of the Temple as consisting of thirteen ingredients, but he does not state what they were ('B. J.' v. 5. § 5). A list of them is however given by Maimonides. A change may have been made in the composition in later times.

36. A portion of the mass was to be broken into small pieces and put "before the testimony;" that is opposite to the Ark of the Covenant, on the outside of the vail, conveniently near the Golden Altar on which it was to be lighted. (See on *v.* 6, and on xl. 20.) It may be observed that the incense thus brought into relation with the Ark was styled "most holy," while the Oil is no more than "holy," *v.* 32.

37, 38. Cf. *vv.* 32, 33. The Holy Incense, like the Holy Anointing Oil, was to be

C C

38 Whosoever shall make like unto that, to smell thereto, shall even be cut off from his people.

CHAPTER XXXI.

1 *Bezaleel and Aholiab are called and made meet for the work of the tabernacle.* 12 *The observation of the sabbath is again commanded.* 18 *Moses receiveth the two tables.*

AND the LORD spake unto Moses, saying,

2 See, I have called by name Bezaleel the *a*son of Uri, the son of Hur, of the tribe of Judah:

a 1 Chron. 2. 20.

3 And I have filled him with the spirit of God, in wisdom, and in understanding, and in knowledge, and in all manner of workmanship,

4 To devise cunning works, to work in gold, and in silver, and in brass,

5 And in cutting of stones, to set *them*, and in carving of timber, to work in all manner of workmanship.

6 And I, behold, I have given with him Aholiab, the son of Ahisamach, of the tribe of Dan: and in the hearts of all that are wise hearted I have put

---

kept in the Sanctuary, exclusively for the service of Jehovah.

CHAP. XXXI.

The Call of Bezaleel and Aholiab.
1—11. (xxxv. 30—35.)

2—6. This solemn call of Bezaleel and Aholiab is full of instruction. Their work was to be only that of handicraftsmen. Every thing that they had to do was prescribed in strict and precise detail. There was to be no exercise for their original powers of invention, nor for their taste. Still it was Jehovah Himself who called them by name to their tasks, and the powers which they were now called upon to exercise in their respective crafts, were declared to have been given them by the Holy Spirit. (See on xxviii. 3.) Thus is every effort of skill, every sort of well-ordered labour, when directed to a right end, brought into the very highest sphere of association.

3. *the spirit of God*] Literally, *a spirit of Elohim*. Mr Quarry ('Genesis,' &c. pp. 271—275) endeavours to prove that this expression has a lower meaning than *the spirit of Jehovah* (which stands in our Bible, "the spirit of the LORD"), and he would rather translate it, "a divine spirit." The definite article is wanting in the Hebrew in both cases. Mr Quarry however conceives that the distinction lies in the fact that Jehovah is a proper name, while Elohim is an appellative. But there is certainly no fair ground to infer any difference of meaning from the general use of the two phrases in the sacred text. It is the spirit of Elohim who inspires Balaam (Num. xxiv. 2), Azariah, the son of Oded (2 Chro. xv. 1), and Zechariah, the son of Jehoiada (2 Chro. xxiv. 20), in their prophetic utterances; while it is the Spirit of Jehovah who inspires the Judges for their work as leaders of the people. (Judg. iii. 10, vi. 34, xi. 29.) The Spirit of Jehovah who inspired Saul (1 S. x. 6) is the same as is more frequently called the Spirit of Elohim (1 S. x. 10, xi. 6, &c.). The terms would thus seem to be strictly equivalent.

wisdom] The Hebrew word is derived from a root of which the meaning is *to judge* or *decide*. It is used to denote the proper endowment of the ruler (2 S. xiv. 20; Is. xix. 11), and that of the prophet (Ezek. xxviii. 3, 4; Dan. v. 11); the highest exercise of the mind in a general sense (Job ix. 4, xi. 6, xii. 12, xv. 8), and, as in this place, the prime qualification of the workman in any manner of work. (Exod. xxviii. 3, xxxi. 6, xxxv. 10, 25, 26, 31, 35, xxxvi. 1, 2, &c.) It is, in fact, that "right judgment in all things" for which we specially pray on Whitsun-day. LXX. σοφία; Vulg. *sapientia*.

understanding] The Hebrew word is from a root that signifies *to discern*, or *discriminate;* it denotes the perceptive faculty. LXX. σύνεσις; Vulg. *intelligentia*.

knowledge] *i.e.* experience, a practical acquaintance with facts. LXX. ἐπιστήμη; Vulg. *scientia*.

in all manner of workmanship] *i.e.* not only in the intellectual gifts of wisdom, understanding and knowledge, but in dexterity of hand.

4. *to devise cunning works*] Rather, **to devise works of skill**. The Hebrew phrase is not the same as that rendered "cunning work" in respect to textile fabrics in xxvi. 1.

4—6. There appears to be sufficient reason to identify Hur, the grandfather of Bezaleel, with the Hur who assisted Aaron in supporting the hands of Moses during the battle with Amalek at Rephidim (Ex. xvii. 10), and who was associated with Aaron in the charge of the people while Moses was on the mountain (Ex. xxiv. 14). Josephus says that he was the husband of Miriam ('Ant.' III. 2. §4; VI. § 1). It is thus probable that Bezaleel was related to Moses. He was the chief artificer in metal, stone and wood; he had also to perform the apothecary's work in the composition of the Anointing Oil and the Incense (xxxvii. 29). He had precedence of all the artificers, but Aholiab appears to have had the entire charge of the textile work (xxxv. 35, xxxviii. 23).

wisdom, that they may make all that I have commanded thee;

7 The tabernacle of the congregation, and the ark of the testimony, and the mercy seat that *is* thereupon, and all the †furniture of the tabernacle,

8 And the table and his furniture, and the pure candlestick with all his furniture, and the altar of incense,

9 And the altar of burnt offering with all his furniture, and the laver and his foot,

10 And the cloths of service, and the holy garments for Aaron the priest, and the garments of his sons, to minister in the priest's office,

11 And the anointing oil, and sweet incense for the holy *place:* according to all that I have commanded thee shall they do.

12 ¶ And the LORD spake unto Moses, saying,

13 Speak thou also unto the children of Israel, saying, Verily my sabbaths ye shall keep: for it *is* a sign between me and you throughout your generations; that *ye* may know that I *am* the LORD that doth sanctify you.

14 *b* Ye shall keep the sabbath therefore; for it *is* holy unto you: every one that defileth it shall surely be put to death: for whosoever doeth any work therein, that soul shall be cut off from among his people.

15 Six days may work be done;

† Heb. *vessels*.

b chap. 20. 8. Deut. 5. 12. Ezek. 20. 12.

---

6. *all that are wise hearted*] See on xxviii. 3.

7. *tabernacle*] **Tent**, in both places. *of the congregation*] **of meeting**.

8. *the table and his furniture*] xxv. 23—30. *the pure candlestick*] That is, the candlestick of pure gold; xxv. 31—40. *the altar of incense*] xxx. 1—10.

9. *the altar of burnt offering*] xxvii. 1—8. *the laver*] xxx. 17—21.

10. *And the cloths of service*] Rather, **And the garments of office**; that is, the distinguishing official garments of the Highpriest. LXX. στολαὶ λειτουργικαί. With this agree, more or less clearly, the Syriac, Vulg., Targums, Saadia, Luther, Cranmer, both the Geneva Versions, de Wette, Zunz, Knobel, Kalisch, &c. The three kinds of dress mentioned in this verse appear to be the only ones which were peculiar to the Sanctuary. They were: (1) The richly adorned state robes of the High-priest (see xxviii. 6—38, xxxix. 1 sq.). (2) The "holy garments" of white linen for the High-priest, worn on the most solemn occasion in the year (see Lev. xvi. 4; Ex. xxviii. 39). (3) The garments of white linen for all the priests, worn in their regular ministrations (see xxviii. 40, 41).—From the connection in which the expression rendered "cloths of service" here occurs, and a comparison of this verse with xxxix. 1, it seems strange that any doubt should have arisen as to its meaning. But some Jewish writers have supposed that the wrapping cloths are denoted which are mentioned Num. iv. 6, 7, 11, &c., and our translators appear to have held some similar notion. Gesenius imagined that the inner curtains of the Tabernacle are meant. But neither of these interpretations appears to be supported by a single ancient authority, nor can either of them be well reconciled with the expression, "to do service in the holy place" (xxxv. 19, xxxix. 1, 41). Cf. xxviii. 35.

The Penal Law of the Sabbath.

12—17. (xxxv. 2, 3.)

In the Fourth Commandment the injunction to observe the Seventh Day is addressed to the conscience of the people (see on xx. 8): in this place, the object is to declare an infraction of the Commandment to be a capital offence. The two passages stand in a relation to each other similar to that between Lev. xviii. xix. and Lev. xx. See note on Lev. xviii. 24.—Considering the weighty bearing of the Sabbath upon the Covenant between Jehovah and His people, a solemn sanction of its observance might well form the conclusion of the string of messages which Moses was to deliver on this occasion. But from the repetition of the substance of these verses in the beginning of ch. xxxv. it seems likely (as many commentators have observed) that the penal edict was specially introduced as a caution in reference to the construction of the Tabernacle, lest the people, in their zeal to carry on the work, should be tempted to break the divine Law for the observance of the Day. In this chapter, the edict immediately follows the series of directions given to Moses on Sinai for the work; in ch. xxxv. Moses utters it before he repeats any of the directions to the people.

13. *a sign between me and you,* &c.] Cf. *v.* 17: Ezek. xx. 12, 20. See on Exod. xx. 8.

14. *put to death*] This Law was very soon put into operation in the case of the man who gathered sticks upon the Sabbath-

but in the seventh *is* the sabbath of rest, †holy to the Lord: whosoever doeth *any* work in the sabbath day, he shall surely be put to death.

† Heb. *holiness.*

16 Wherefore the children of Israel shall keep the sabbath, to observe the sabbath throughout their generations, *for* a perpetual covenant.

17 It *is* a sign between me and the children of Israel for ever: for *c in* six days the Lord made heaven and earth, and on the seventh day he rested, and was refreshed.

c Gen. 1. 31. & 2. 2.

18 ¶ And he gave unto Moses, when he had made an end of communing with him upon mount Sinai, *d* two tables of testimony, tables of stone, written with the finger of God.

d Deut. 9. 10.

CHAPTER XXXII.

1 *The people, in the absence of Moses, cause Aaron to make a calf.* 7 *God is angered thereby.* 11 *At the intreaty of Moses he is appeased.* 15 *Moses cometh down with the tables.* 19 *He breaketh them.* 20 *He destroyeth the calf.* 22 *Aaron's excuse for himself.* 25 *Moses causeth the idolaters to be slain.* 30 *He prayeth for the people.*

AND when the people saw that Moses delayed to come down out of the mount, the people gathered themselves together unto Aaron, and said unto him, *a* Up, make us gods, which shall go before us; for *as for*

a Acts 7. 40.

---

day. Death was inflicted by stoning. Num. xv. 35.

cut off from among his people] This is distinctly assigned as a reason why the offender should, or might, be put to death. The passage seems to indicate the distinction between the meaning of the two expressions, *to be cut off from the people*, and *to be put to death*. He who was cut off from the people had, by his offence, put himself out of the terms of the Covenant, and was an outlaw. (See on Lev. xviii. 29.) On such, and on such alone, when the offence was one which affected the well-being of the nation, as it was in this case, death could be inflicted by the public authority.

17. *was refreshed*] Literally, *he took breath*. Cf. xxiii. 12; 2 S. xvi. 14. The application of the word to the Creator, which occurs nowhere else, is remarkable.

18. The directions for the construction of the Sanctuary and its furniture being ended, the Tables of Stone which represented the Covenant between Jehovah and His people, and which, when covered with the Mercy-seat were to give the Sanctuary its significance, are now delivered to Moses in accordance with the promise xxiv. 12; cf. xxxii. 15, 16.

The history of what relates to the construction of the Sanctuary is here interrupted, and is taken up again chap. xxxv. 1.

Chap. XXXII.—XXXIV.

The Golden Calf. The Covenant and the Tables broken and renewed.

The exact coherence of the narrative of all that immediately relates to the construction of the Sanctuary, if we pass on immediately from ch. xxxi. to ch. xxxv., might suggest the probability that these three chapters originally formed a distinct composition. This suggestion is in some degree strengthened, if we take account of some part of the subject matter of ch. xxxiv. (see on xxxiv. 12—27). But this need not involve the question of the Mosaic authorship of the three chapters. The main incidents recorded in them follow in due order of time, and are therefore in their proper place as regards historical sequence.

The Golden Calf, xxxii. 1—6.

The people had, to a great extent, lost the patriarchal faith, and were but imperfectly instructed in the reality of a personal unseen God. Being disappointed at the long absence of Moses, they seem to have imagined that he had deluded them and had probably been destroyed amidst the thunders of the mountain (xxiv. 15—18). They accordingly gave way to their superstitious fears and fell back upon that form of idolatry that was most familiar to them (see on *v*. 4). The narrative of the circumstances is more briefly given by Moses at a later period in one of his addresses to the people (Deut. ix. 8—21, 25—29, x. 1—5, 8—11). It is worthy of remark that Josephus, in his very characteristic chapter on the giving of the Law ('Ant.' III. 5), says nothing whatever of this act of apostasy, though he relates that Moses twice ascended the mountain, and renews his own profession that he is faithfully following the authority of the Holy Scriptures. Philo speaks of the calf as an imitation of the idolatry of Egypt, but he takes no notice of Aaron's share in the sin ('Vit. Mos.' III. 19. 37).

1. *unto Aaron*] The chief authority during the absence of Moses was committed to Aaron and Hur (xxiv. 14).

make us gods] The substantive (*elohim*) is plural in form and may denote *gods*. But according to the Hebrew idiom, the meaning need not be plural, and hence the word is used as the common designation of the true God (Gen. i. 1, &c. See on xxi. 6). It here denotes a god, and should be so rendered

this Moses, the man that brought us up out of the land of Egypt, we wot not what is become of him.

2 And Aaron said unto them, Break off the golden earrings, which *are* in the ears of your wives, of your sons, and of your daughters, and bring *them* unto me.

3 And all the people brake off the golden earrings which *were* in their ears, and brought *them* unto Aaron.

4 *b* And he received *them* at their hand, and fashioned it with a graving tool, after he had made it a molten calf: and they said, These *be* thy gods, O Israel, which brought thee up out of the land of Egypt.

5 And when Aaron saw *it*, he built an altar before it; and Aaron made proclamation, and said, To morrow *is* a feast to the LORD.

6 And they rose up early on the morrow, and offered burnt offerings, and brought peace offerings; and the *c* people sat down to eat and to drink, and rose up to play.

7 ¶ And the LORD said unto Moses, *d* Go, get thee down; for thy

b Psal. 106. 19.
1 Kings 12. 28.

c 1 Cor. 10. 7.

d Deut 9. 12.

(Saadia and most modern interpreters). It is evident that what the Israelites asked for was a visible god. Our version follows the LXX., Vulg., &c.

2. *Break off the golden earrings*] It has been very generally held from early times, that Aaron did not willingly lend himself to the mad design of the multitude; but that, when overcome by their importunity, he asked them to give up such possessions as he knew they would not willingly part with, in the hope of putting a check on them (Augustin. 'Quæst.' 141; Theodoret. 'Quæst.' 66). Assuming this to have been his purpose, he took a wrong measure of their fanaticism, for all the people made the sacrifice at once (*v.* 3). His weakness, in any case, was unpardonable and called for the intercession of Moses (Deut. ix. 20). According to a Jewish tradition found in the later Targums, Aaron was terrified by seeing Hur, his colleague in authority (xxiv. 14), slain by the people because he had ventured to oppose them.

4. *And he received...a molten calf*] The Hebrew is somewhat difficult. The following rendering represents the sense approved by most modern critics;—*and he received the gold at their hand and collected it in a bag and made it a molten calf* (Bochart, Gesenius, Rosenmüller, Fürst, Knobel, Kurtz, &c. with the later Targums). Our version is supported by the LXX., Onkelos, Luther, de Wette, Keil, &c. Other interpreters conceive the latter part of the passage to mean that Aaron *shaped the gold in a mould* (or, *after a pattern*) *and made it a molten calf* (Saadia, Syriac, Vulgate, Aben-Ezra, Michaelis, Zunz, Herx., &c.).

a molten calf] The word *calf* may mean a yearling ox. The Israelites must have been familiar with the ox-worship of the Egyptians; perhaps many of them had witnessed the rites of Mnevis at Heliopolis, almost on the borders of the Land of Goshen, and they could not have been unacquainted with the more famous rites of Apis at Memphis. It is expressly said that they yielded to the idolatry of Egypt while they were in bondage (Josh. xxiv. 14; Ezek. xx. 8, xxiii. 3, 8). The earliest Jewish tradition derives the golden calf from an Egyptian origin (Philo, 'Vit. Mos.' III. 19). It seems most likely that the idolatrous tendency of the people had been contracted from the Egyptians, but that it was qualified by what they still retained of the truths revealed to their forefathers. In the next verse, Aaron appears to speak of the calf as if it was a representative of Jehovah— "To-morrow is a feast to the LORD." They did not, it should be noted, worship a living Mnevis, or Apis, having a proper name, but only the golden type of the animal. The mystical notions connected with the ox by the Egyptian priests may have possessed their minds, and, when expressed in this modified and less gross manner, may have been applied to the LORD, who had really delivered them out of the hand of the Egyptians. Their sin then lay, not in their adopting another god, but in their pretending to worship a visible symbol of Him whom no symbol could represent. The close connection between the calves of Jeroboam and this calf is shewn by the repetition of the formula, "which brought thee up out of the land of Egypt" (1 Kings xii. 28).

These be thy gods] **This is thy god.** See on *v.* 1.

5. *a feast to the LORD*] See on *v.* 4.

6. See 1 Cor. x. 7). Hengstenberg, Kurtz and others have laid a stress upon the similarity of what is briefly described in the words, "the people sat down to eat and drink, and rose up to play," to certain rites of the Egyptians spoken of by Herodotus (II. 60. III. 27). But such orgies were too common amongst ancient idolaters for the remark to be of much worth.

The trial of Moses as a Mediator.
7—35.

The faithfulness of Moses in the office that had been entrusted to him was now to be put

people, which thou broughtest out of the land of Egypt, have corrupted *themselves*:

8 *e* They have turned aside quickly out of the way which I commanded them: they have made them a molten calf, and have worshipped it, and have sacrificed thereunto, and said, These *be* thy gods, O Israel, which have brought thee up out of the land of Egypt.

9 And the LORD said unto Moses, *f* I have seen this people, and, behold, it *is* a stiffnecked people:

10 Now therefore let me alone, that my wrath may wax hot against them, and that I may consume them: and I will make of thee a great nation.

11 *g* And Moses besought † the LORD his God, and said, LORD, why doth thy wrath wax hot against thy people, which thou hast brought forth out of the land of Egypt with great power, and with a mighty hand?

12 *h* Wherefore should the Egyptians speak, and say, For mischief did he bring them out, to slay them in the mountains, and to consume them from the face of the earth? Turn from thy fierce wrath, and repent of this evil against thy people.

13 Remember Abraham, Isaac, and Israel, thy servants, to whom thou swarest by thine own self, and saidst unto them, *i* I will multiply your seed as the stars of heaven, and all this land that I have spoken of will I give unto your seed, and they shall inherit *it* for ever.

14 And the LORD repented of the evil which he thought to do unto his people.

e Deut. 9. 8.
f chap. 33. 3. Deut. 9. 13.
g Psal. 106. 23.
† Heb. *the face of the LORD.*
h Numb. 14. 13.
i Gen. 12. 7. & 15. 7 & 48. 16.

---

to the test. It was to be made manifest whether he loved his own glory better than he loved the brethren who were under his charge; whether he would prefer that he should himself become the founder of a "great nation," or that the LORD'S promise should be fulfilled in the whole people of Israel. As in the trial of Abraham, the object to be attained was not that He who knows the hearts of all men might be assured that the servant whom He had chosen was true and stedfast, but that the faith of the servant might be strengthened and instructed, by its being made known to him what power had been given to him to resist temptation. This may have been especially needful for Moses, in consequence of his natural disposition. See Num. xii. 3; cf. Ex. iii. 11. With this trial of Moses may be compared the third temptation which the evil one was permitted to set before our Saviour. Matt. iv. 8—10.

Moses was tried in a twofold manner. The trial was at first based on the divine communication made to him in the mount respecting the apostasy of the people: on this occasion, he rejects the offer of glory for himself and intercedes for the nation; the exercise was a purely spiritual one, apart from visible fact, and no answer is given to his intercession (see on *v.* 14). But in the second case, stirred up as he was by the facts actually before his eyes, after he had unflinchingly carried out the judgment of God upon the persons of the obstinate idolaters, he not only again intercedes for the nation, but declares himself ready to sacrifice his own salvation for them (*v.* 32). It is thus that the hearts of God's saints in all ages are strengthened beforehand, by inward struggles that are witnessed by no human eye, to fight the battle when outward trials come upon them.—If the wonderful narrative in this passage should appear to any thoughtful reader incoherent or obscure, let him read it again and again and apply to it the key of his own spiritual experience.

On another occasion in the history, when the people had rebelled on account of the report of the ten spies, the trial of Moses' faithfulness was repeated in a very similar manner (Num. xiv. 11—23).

8. *These be thy gods...have brought*] **This is thy god, O Israel, who has brought**—

10. *let me alone*] But Moses did not let the LORD alone; he wrestled, as Jacob had done, until, like Jacob, he obtained the blessing (Gen. xxxii. 24).

12. *repent of this evil*] See on *v.* 14.

13. See Gen. xv. 5, 18, xxii. 17, xxxii. 12.

14. This states the fact that was not revealed to Moses till after his second intercession when he had come down from the mountain and witnessed the sin of the people (*vv.* 30—34). He was then assured that the Lord's love to His ancient people would prevail. God is said, in the language of Scripture, to repent, when his forgiving love is seen by man to blot out the letter of His judgments against sin (2 Sam. xxiv. 16; Joel ii. 13; Jonah iii. 10, &c.); or when the sin of man seems to human sight to have disappointed the purposes of grace (Gen. vi. 6; 1 Sam. xv. 35, &c.). As they exist in the

15 ¶ And Moses turned, and went down from the mount, and the two tables of the testimony *were* in his hand: the tables *were* written on both their sides; on the one side and on the other *were* they written.

k chap. 31. 18.

16 And the *k*tables *were* the work of God, and the writing *was* the writing of God, graven upon the tables.

17 And when Joshua heard the noise of the people as they shouted, he said unto Moses, *There is* a noise of war in the camp.

18 And he said, *It is* not the voice of *them that* shout for mastery, neither *is it* the voice of *them that* cry for

† Heb. *weakness*.

†being overcome: *but* the noise of *them that* sing do I hear.

19 ¶ And it came to pass, as soon as he came nigh unto the camp, that he saw the calf, and the dancing: and Moses' anger waxed hot, and he cast the tables out of his hands, and brake them beneath the mount.

l Deut. 9. 21.

20 *l*And he took the calf which they had made, and burnt *it* in the fire, and ground *it* to powder, and strawed *it* upon the water, and made the children of Israel drink *of it*.

21 And Moses said unto Aaron, What did this people unto thee, that thou hast brought so great a sin upon them?

22 And Aaron said, Let not the anger of my lord wax hot: thou knowest the people, that they *are* set on mischief.

23 For they said unto me, Make us gods, which shall go before us: for *as for* this Moses, the man that brought us up out of the land of Egypt, we wot not what is become of him.

24 And I said unto them, Whosoever hath any gold, let them break *it* off. So they gave *it* me: then I cast it into the fire, and there came out this calf.

25 ¶ And when Moses saw that the people *were* naked; (for Aaron had made them naked unto *their* †shame among †their enemies:)

† Heb. *those that rose up against them*.

26 Then Moses stood in the gate

Eternal Father, wrath and love are essentially ONE, however they may appear to thwart each other to carnal eyes. The awakened conscience is said *to repent*, when, having felt its sin, it feels also the divine forgiveness: it is at this crisis that God, according to the language of Scripture, repents towards the sinner. Thus the repentance of God made known in and through the One true Mediator reciprocates the repentance of the returning sinner, and reveals to him Atonement.

17, 18. Moses does not tell Joshua of the divine communication that had been made to him respecting the apostasy of the people, but only corrects his impression by calling his attention to the kind of noise which they are making.

19. Though Moses had been prepared by the revelation on the Mount, his righteous indignation was stirred up beyond control when the abomination was before his eyes.

20. We need not suppose that each incident is here placed in strict order of time. What is related in this verse must have occupied some time and may have followed the rebuke of Aaron. Moses appears to have thrown the calf into the fire to destroy its form and then to have pounded, or filed, the metal to powder, which he cast into the brook (Deut. ix. 21). He then made the Israelites drink of the water of the brook. The act was of course a symbolical one. The idol was brought to nothing and the people were made to swallow their own sin (cf. Mic. vii. 13, 14). It seems idle to speculate, as many interpreters have done (Rosenmüller, Davidson, Kurtz, &c.), on the means by which the comminution of the gold was effected.

21. Moses, in grave irony, asks Aaron whether the people had offended him in any way to induce him to inflict such an injury on them as to yield to their request.

22. *my lord*] The deference here shown to Moses by Aaron should be noticed. His reference to the character of the people, and his manner of stating what he had done (*v.* 24), are very characteristic of the deprecating language of a weak mind.

23. *Make us gods*] **Make us a god.**

25. *naked*] Rather, **unruly**, or *licentious*. So the LXX., Onk., Syriac, and nearly all critical authorities.

shame among their enemies] Cf. Ps. xliv. 13; Deut. xxviii. 37; Ps. lxxix. 4.

26—29.] The Tribe of Levi, Moses' own Tribe, now distinguished itself by immediately returning to its allegiance and obeying the call to fight on the side of Jehovah. We need not doubt that the 3000 who were slain were those who persisted in resisting Moses: we may perhaps conjecture that they were

of the camp, and said, Who *is* on the LORD's side? *let him come* unto me. And all the sons of Levi gathered themselves together unto him.

27 And he said unto them, Thus saith the LORD God of Israel, Put every man his sword by his side, *and* go in and out from gate to gate throughout the camp, and slay every man his brother, and every man his companion, and every man his neighbour.

28 And the children of Levi did according to the word of Moses: and there fell of the people that day about three thousand men.

29 ¹For Moses had said, †Consecrate yourselves to day to the LORD, even every man upon his son, and upon his brother; that he may bestow upon you a blessing this day.

30 ¶ And it came to pass on the morrow, that Moses said unto the people, Ye have sinned a great sin: and now I will go up unto the LORD; peradventure I shall make an atonement for your sin.

31 And Moses returned unto the LORD, and said, Oh, this people have sinned a great sin, and have made them gods of gold.

32 Yet now, if thou wilt forgive their sin—; and if not, blot me, I pray thee, out of thy book which thou hast written.

33 And the LORD said unto Moses, Whosoever hath sinned against me, him will I blot out of my book.

34 Therefore now go, lead the people unto *the place* of which I have spoken unto thee: behold, mine Angel shall go before thee: nevertheless in the day when I visit I will visit their sin upon them.

<small>¹ Or, *And Moses said, Consecrate yourselves to day to the LORD, because every man hath been against his son, and against his brother, &c.*
† Heb. *Fill your hands.*</small>

---

such as contumaciously refused to drink of the water of the brook (*v.* 20). The spirit of the narrative forbids us to conceive that the act of the Levites was anything like an indiscriminate massacre. An amnesty had first been offered to all in the words, "Who is on the LORD's side?" Those who were forward to draw the sword were directed not to spare their closest relations or friends; but this must plainly have been with an understood qualification as regards the conduct of those who were to be slain. Had it not been so, they who were on the LORD's side would have had to destroy each other. We need not stumble at the bold, simple way in which the statement is made. The Bible does not deign to apologise for itself; and hence at times it affords occasion to gainsayers, who shut their eyes to the spirit while they are captiously looking at disseevered fragments of the letter.

29. *Consecrate yourselves to day to the* LORD] The margin contains the literal rendering. Our version gives the most probable meaning of the Hebrew (see Lev. viii. 22, 27), and is supported by the best authority. The Levites were to prove themselves in a special way the servants of Jehovah, in anticipation of their formal consecration as ministers of the Sanctuary, by manifesting a self-sacrificing zeal in carrying out the divine command, even upon their nearest relatives (cf. Deut. x. 8). Kurtz, adopting the rendering of the Targums, supposes that what the Levites were commanded to do was to offer sacrifices upon the Altar to expiate the blood which they were directed to shed. But this interpretation cannot be well reconciled with the Hebrew, and it is hard to imagine that expiation could be required for what was done in direct obedience to the command of the LORD. It may be added that the Sin-offering, the only kind of sacrifice that would be suitable on such a hypothesis, had not yet been instituted.

31. *returned unto the* LORD] *i.e.* he again ascended the Mount.

gods of gold] **a god of gold.**

32. For a similar form of expression, in which the conclusion is left to be supplied by the mind of the reader, see Dan. iii. 15; Luke xiii. 9, xix. 42; John vi. 62; Rom. ix. 22.—For the same thought, see Rom. ix. 3. It is for such as Moses and St Paul to realize, and to dare to utter, their readiness to be wholly sacrificed for the sake of those whom God has entrusted to their love. This expresses the perfected idea of the whole Burnt-offering.

thy book] The figure is taken from the enrolment of the names of citizens. This is its first occurrence in the Scriptures. See Ps. lxix. 28; Isa. iv. 3; Dan. xii. 1; Luke x. 20; Phil. iv. 3; Rev. iii. 5, &c.

33, 34. Each offender was to suffer for his own sin. On xx. 5 cf. Ezek. xviii. 4, 20. Moses was not to be taken at his word. He was to fulfil his appointed mission of leading on the people towards the Land of Promise.

34. *mine Angel shall go before thee*] See on xxiii. 20, and xxxiii. 3.

35 And the LORD plagued the people, because they made the calf, which Aaron made.

CHAPTER XXXIII.

1 *The Lord refuseth to go as he had promised with the people.* 4 *The people murmur thereat.* 7 *The tabernacle is removed out of the camp.* 9 *The Lord talketh familiarly with Moses.* 12 *Moses desireth to see the glory of God.*

AND the LORD said unto Moses, Depart, *and* go up hence, thou and the people which thou hast brought up out of the land of Egypt, unto the land which I sware unto Abraham, to Isaac, and to Jacob, saying, ^aUnto thy seed will I give it: ^{a Gen. 12. 7.}

2 ^bAnd I will send an angel before thee; and I will drive out the Canaanite, the Amorite, and the Hittite, and the Perizzite, the Hivite, and the Jebusite: ^{b Deut. 7. 22. Josh. 24. 11.}

3 Unto a land flowing with milk and honey: for I will not go up in the midst of thee; for thou *art* a ^cstiffnecked people: lest I consume thee in the way. ^{c chap. 32. Deut. 9. 13.}

in the day when I visit, &c.] This has been supposed to refer to the sentence that was pronounced on the generation of Israelites then living, when they murmured on account of the report of the ten spies, that they should not enter the land (Num. xiv.). On that occasion they were charged with having tempted God "these ten times" (*v.* 22). But though the LORD visited the sin upon those who rebelled, yet He "repented of the evil which He thought to do unto His people." He chastised the individuals, but did not take His blessing from the nation.

35. *and the* LORD] **Thus Jehovah.**

CHAP. XXXIII.

The Conference between Jehovah and His mediator is continued in this Chapter. It had been conceded to Moses that the nation should not be destroyed (see xxxii. 10 sq), and that he should lead them on towards the place of which the LORD had spoken (see xxxii. 34). But the favour was not to be awarded according to the terms of the original promise (xxiii. 20—23). The Covenant on which the promise was based had been broken by the people. Jehovah now therefore declared that though His Angel should go before Moses (xxxii. 34) and should drive out the heathen from the land, He would withhold His own favouring presence, *lest he should consume them in the way* (xxxiii. 2, 3). Thus were the people forcibly warned that His presence could prove a blessing to them only on condition of their keeping their part of the covenant (see on *v.* 3). If they failed in this, His presence would be to them "a consuming fire" (Deut. iv. 24). The people, when they heard the Divine message, mourned and humbled themselves, stripping off their accustomed ornaments in accordance with the command (*vv.* 4—6). Moses now appointed a religious service of a peculiar kind, dedicating a Tent pitched at some distance from the camp, as a meeting-place for Jehovah and himself (*vv.* 7—11). Here he again intercedes with persevering fervour until he obtains the answer, "My presence shall go with thee, and I will give thee rest" (*v.* 14; see note). He then dares to reason on this answer and to prove its necessity, as one man might discuss terms with another (*v.* 11). The answer is at last given in a still clearer and more gracious form: "I will do this thing also that thou hast spoken: for thou hast found grace in my sight, and I know thee by name" (*v.* 17). Having proved himself worthy of his calling as a mediator, both in vindicating the honour of Jehovah and in his self-sacrificing intercession with Jehovah for the nation, he is rewarded by a special vision of the Divine nature: Jehovah reveals Himself to him in His essential character to the utmost point that such revelation is possible to a finite being (*vv.* 18—23).

2. See on iii. 8.

3. *milk and honey*] See on iii. 8.

for I will not go up in the midst of thee] This is the awful qualification with which the possession of the promised Land might have been granted: Jehovah Himself was not to go before the people. According to the Targums, it was the *shekinah* that was to be withheld (see on xiv. 19, 20). Hengstenberg supposes that the Angel promised in xxiii. 20—23 was "the Angel of Jehovah," κατ' ἐξοχήν, the Second Person of the Trinity, in whom Jehovah was essentially present, the same whom Isaiah called "the Angel of His presence" (lxiii. 9) and Malachi, "the Angel of the Covenant" (iii. 1); but that the Angel here mentioned was an ordinary Angel, one commissioned for this service out of the heavenly host (Christology, Vol. I. p. 107). It should however be noted that this Angel is expressly spoken of as *the Angel of Jehovah* in xxxii. 34. But in whatever way we understand the mention of the Angel in this passage as compared with xxiii. 20, the meaning of the threat appears to be that the nation should be put on a level with other nations, to lose its character as the people in special covenant with Jehovah (see on *v.* 16).—On the name *Angel*

4 ¶ And when the people heard these evil tidings, they mourned: and no man did put on him his ornaments.

5 For the LORD had said unto Moses, Say unto the children of Israel, Ye *are* a stiffnecked people: I will come up into the midst of thee in a moment, and consume thee: therefore now put off thy ornaments from thee, that I may know what to do unto thee.

6 And the children of Israel stripped themselves of their ornaments by the mount Horeb.

7 And Moses took the tabernacle, and pitched it without the camp, afar off from the camp, and called it the Tabernacle of the congregation. And it came to pass, *that* every one which sought the LORD went out unto the tabernacle of the congregation, which *was* without the camp.

8 And it came to pass, when Moses went out unto the tabernacle, *that* all the people rose up, and stood every man *at* his tent door, and looked after Moses, until he was gone into the tabernacle.

9 And it came to pass, as Moses entered into the tabernacle, the cloudy pillar descended, and stood *at* the door

---

of Jehovah, see on Gen. ii. 1. Hengstenberg's arguments have been elaborately answered by Kurtz, 'Hist of O. C.' Vol. I. § 50 (2), and Vol. III. § 14 (3).

lest I consume thee in the way] See introd. note to this chap. St Augustine speaks of the mystery that Jehovah should declare Himself to be less merciful than His Angel (Quæst. 150). It would seem that the presence of Jehovah represented the Covenant with its penalties as well as its privileges. See preceding note.

4—6. See introd. note.

5. *I will come up...consume thee*] By far the greater number of versions put this conditionally; **If I were to go up for one moment in the midst of thee, I should consume thee** (see *v.* 3). This rendering seems best to suit the context. Our translators follow the earlier English versions, which are supported by the Syriac, Vulg. and Luther.

that I may know, &c.] **and I shall know by that what to do unto thee.** That is, by that sign of their repentance Jehovah would decide in what way they were to be punished.

6. *by the mount Horeb*] **from mount Horeb** *onwards*. The meaning, according to all the best authorities, appears to be that they ceased to wear their ornaments from the time they were at Mount Horeb.

The Temporary Tent of Meeting.
7—11.

7. *the tabernacle*] The original word signifies **the Tent.** The only word in the Old Testament which ought to be rendered *tabernacle (mishkān)* does not occur once in this narrative (see on xxvi. 1). What is here called The Tent has been understood in three different ways. It has been taken to denote:

1. The Tabernacle constructed according to the pattern showed to Moses in the Mount (our version and the earlier English ones, several Jewish authorities, Knobel, &c.). But if we are in any degree to respect the order of the narrative, the Tabernacle was not made until after the events here recorded (see xl. 2).

2. An old sanctuary, or sacred tent, which the Israelites had previously possessed (Michaelis, Rosenmüller, &c.). But it is incredible that such a structure should not have been spoken of elsewhere, had it existed.

3. A tent appointed for this temporary purpose by Moses, very probably the one in which he was accustomed to dwell. According to the Hebrew idiom, the article may stand for the possessive pronoun, and thus it is most likely that the right rendering is, *his tent*. This is by far the most satisfactory interpretation (LXX., Syriac, Jarchi, Aben-Ezra, Drusius, Grotius, Geneva French, Kurtz, Wogue, &c.).

pitched it without the camp, afar off from the camp] This tent was to be a place for meeting with Jehovah, like the Tabernacle which was about to be constructed. But in order that the people might feel that they had forfeited the Divine presence (see xxv. 8), **the Tent of meeting** (as it should be called, see on xxvii. 21, and Note at the end of Chap. xl.) was placed "afar off from the camp," and the Mediator and his faithful servant Joshua were alone admitted to it (*v.* 11).

8. *the tabernacle*] **the Tent.**

at his tent door] **at the entrance of his tent** (see on xxvi. 36). The people may have stood up either out of respect to Moses, or from doubt as to what was going to occur. But as soon as the cloudy pillar was seen, they joined in worship (*v.* 10).

9. *as Moses entered...talked with Moses*] "As Moses entered into **the Tent**, the cloudy

of the tabernacle, and *the* LORD talked with Moses.

10 And all the people saw the cloudy pillar stand *at* the tabernacle door: and all the people rose up and worshipped, every man *in* his tent door.

11 And the LORD spake unto Moses face to face, as a man speaketh unto his friend. And he turned again into the camp: but his servant Joshua, the son of Nun, a young man, departed not out of the tabernacle.

12 ¶ And Moses said unto the LORD, See, thou sayest unto me, Bring up this people: and thou hast not let me know whom thou wilt send with me. Yet thou hast said, I know thee by name, and thou hast also found grace in my sight.

13 Now therefore, I pray thee, if I have found grace in thy sight, shew me now thy way, that I may know thee, that I may find grace in thy sight: and consider that this nation *is* thy people.

14 And he said, My presence shall go *with thee*, and I will give thee rest.

15 And he said unto him, If thy presence go not *with me*, carry us not up hence.

16 For wherein shall it be known here that I and thy people have found grace in thy sight? *is it* not in that thou goest with us? so shall we be separated, I and thy people, from all the people that *are* upon the face of the earth.

17 And the LORD said unto Moses, I will do this thing also that thou hast spoken: for thou hast found grace in my sight, and I know thee by name.

18 And he said, I beseech thee, shew me thy glory.

---

pillar **came down and stood at the entrance of the Tent and talked with Moses**" (LXX., Vulg., Onk., de Wette, Knobel, &c.). *The Cloudy pillar* is the proper nominative to the verb *talked* (cf. xiii. 21, xix. 9, xxiv. 16, xl. 35).

10. *the tabernacle door*] **the entrance of the Tent.**

rose up and worshipped] or, *began to worship*. The people by this act gave another proof of their penitence.

in his tent door] **at the entrance of his tent.**

11. *face to face*] The meaning of these words is limited by *v.* 20, see note; cf. also Num. xii. 8; Deut. iv. 12.

Joshua] See on xvii. 9.

the tabernacle] **the Tent.**

The Mediator is rewarded.
12—13.

12. *let me know whom thou wilt send with me*] Jehovah had just previously commanded Moses to lead on the people and had promised to send an Angel before him (*v.* 2, xxxii. 34). Moses was now anxious to know who the Angel was to be.

I know thee by name] The LORD had called him by his name, iii. 4; cf. Isa. xliii. 1, xlix. 1.

found grace] xxxii. 10, &c.

13. *thy way*] He desires not to be left in uncertainty, but to be assured, by Jehovah's mode of proceeding, of the reality of the promises that had been made to him.

14.] Ewald considers that this verse should be read interrogatively, "Must my presence go with thee, and shall I give thee rest?" This rendering may make the connection more simple; but it appears to be supported by no other authority. See on xxxiv. 9.

rest] This was the common expression for the possession of the promised Land. Deut. iii. 20; Josh. i. 13, 15, xxii. 4, &c.; cf. Heb. iv. 8.

15, 16] Moses would have preferred that the people should forego the possession of the Land and remain in the wilderness, if they were to be deprived of the presence of Jehovah, as the witness for the Covenant, according to the original promise. It was this which alone **distinguished** (rather than "separated") them from other nations, and which alone would render the Land of Promise a home to be desired.

17. Cf. *v.* 13. His petition for the nation, and his own claims as a mediator, are now granted to the full.

18. *shew me thy glory*] The faithful servant of Jehovah, now assured by the success of his mediation, yearns, with the proper tendency of a devout spirit, for a more intimate communion with his Divine Master than he had yet enjoyed. He seeks for something surpassing all former revelations. He had talked with the LORD "face to face as a man speaketh unto his friend" (*v.* 11; cf. Deut. xxxiv. 10), but it was in the Cloudy pillar: he, and the people with him, had seen "the glory of the LORD," but it was in the form of "devouring fire" (xvi. 7. 10, xxiv. 16, 17):

19 And he said, I will make all my goodness pass before thee, and I will proclaim the name of the Lord before thee; ^dand will be gracious to whom I will be gracious, and will shew mercy on whom I will shew mercy.

20 And he said, Thou canst not see my face: for there shall no man see me, and live.

21 And the Lord said, Behold, *there is* a place by me, and thou shalt stand upon a rock:

22 And it shall come to pass, while my glory passeth by, that I will put thee in a clift of the rock, and will cover thee with my hand while I pass by:

23 And I will take away mine hand, and thou shalt see my back parts: but my face shall not be seen.

CHAPTER XXXIV.

1 *The tables are renewed.* 5 *The name of the LORD proclaimed.* 8 *Moses intreateth God to go with them.* 10 *God maketh a covenant with them, repeating certain duties of the first table.* 28 *Moses after forty days in the mount cometh down with the tables.* 29 *His face shineth, and he covereth it with a vail.*

AND the Lord said unto Moses, ^aHew thee two tables of stone like unto the first: and I will write upon *these* tables the words that were in the first tables, which thou brakest.

2 And be ready in the morning, and come up in the morning unto

^c Rom. 9. 15.

^a Deut. 10. 1.

---

he had even beheld the "similitude" of the Lord in a mystical sense (Num. xii. 8). But he asks now to behold the face of Jehovah in all its essential glory, neither veiled by a cloud nor represented by an Angel.

19, 20] But his request could not be granted in accordance with the conditions of human existence. The glory of the Almighty in its fulness is not to be revealed to the eye of man. A further revelation of the Divine goodness was however possible. Jehovah was to reveal Himself as the gracious One, whose mercy in forgiving iniquity included, and brought into harmony, all the claims of justice (xxxiv. 6, 7; see on xxxii. 14). The promise here given was to be fulfilled on the morrow, when the mediator was to receive the twofold reward of his spiritual wrestling; the covenant was to be renewed with the nation according to its original terms, and he himself was to be permitted to penetrate more deeply into the mysteries of the Divine nature than had ever before been granted to mortal man.

It was vouchsafed to St Paul, as it had been to Moses, to have special "visions and revelations of the Lord" (2 Cor. xii. 1—4). He was "caught up into the third heaven" and heard "unspeakable words which it is not *possible* for a man to utter." But he had, also like Moses, to find the narrow reach of the intellect of man in the region of Godhead. It was long after he had heard the unspeakable words in Paradise that he spoke of the Lord as dwelling "in the light which no man can approach unto, whom no man hath seen nor can see" (1 Tim. vi. 16). He knew of the Mediator greater than Moses (Heb. iii. 5, 6), who being "in the bosom of the Father" had declared Him in a higher sense than He had been declared to Moses, but still it remains true that "no man hath seen God at any time" (John i. 18). However intimate may be our communion with the Holy One, we are still, as long as we are in the flesh, "to see through a glass darkly," waiting for the time when we shall see, with no figure of speech, "face to face" (1 Cor. xiii. 12). Then we know "that we shall be like him, for we shall see him as he is" (1 John iii. 2). It was in a tone of aspiration lower than that of Moses or St Paul, that St Philip said, "Lord, shew us the Father" (John xiv. 8).

19. *will be gracious to whom I will be gracious, and will shew mercy on whom I will shew mercy*] Jehovah declares His own will to be the ground of the grace which He is going to shew the nation. St Paul applies these words to the election of Jacob in order to overthrow the self-righteous boasting of the Jews (Rom. ix. 15).

20. Cf. xix. 21. Such passages as this being clearly in accordance with what we know of the relation of spiritual existence to the human senses, shew how we are to interpret the expressions "face to face" (*v.* 11), "mouth to mouth" (Num. xii. 8), and others of the like kind. See especially xxiv. 10, 11; Isa. vi. 1; and cf. John xiv. 9.

21—23.] The conjectures and traditions on the place of this vision, inconclusive as they must be, are given by Robinson, 'Bib. Res.' Vol. I. p. 153.

Chap. XXXIV.

The Covenant and the Tables are renewed—The second revelation of the Divine Name to Moses.

1—10.

1. *Hew thee*] See *v.* 4. The former tables are called "the work of God," xxxii. 16.

the words that were in the first tables, which thou brakest] These were "the words

mount Sinai, and present thyself there to me in the top of the mount.

^a chap. 19. 12.

3 And no man shall ^bcome up with thee, neither let any man be seen throughout all the mount; neither let the flocks nor herds feed before that mount.

4 ¶ And he hewed two tables of stone like unto the first; and Moses rose up early in the morning, and went up unto mount Sinai, as the LORD had commanded him, and took in his hand the two tables of stone.

5 And the LORD descended in the cloud, and stood with him there, and proclaimed the name of the LORD.

6 And the LORD passed by before him, and proclaimed, The LORD, The LORD God, merciful and gracious, longsuffering, and abundant in goodness and truth,

7 Keeping mercy for thousands, forgiving iniquity and transgression and sin, and that will by no means clear *the guilty;* ^c visiting the iniquity of the fathers upon the children, and upon the children's children, unto the third and to the fourth *generation.*

^c chap. 10. Deut. 5. 9. Jer. 32. 18.

8 And Moses made haste, and bowed his head toward the earth, and worshipped.

9 And he said, If now I have found

---

of the covenant, the ten commandments" (*v.* 28); see Deut. iv. 13, ix. 10, 11, x. 1, 4, and especially Deut. v. 6—22. These passages would seem to leave no room for doubt that what we recognize as the Ten Commandments were inscribed on the second as well as the first pair of Tables. But Göthe, in one of his early works, started the notion that what was written on these Tables was the string of precepts, which may be reckoned as Ten, contained in this chap. *vv.* 12—26. Falsely regarding the Mosaic Covenant as essentially narrow and exclusive, he could not see how an expression of universal morality like the Ten Commandments of Ex. xx. could possibly have formed its basis. Hitzig has taken a similar view. Hengstenberg ('Pent.' Vol. II. p. 31) and Kurtz ('Old Cov.' III. 182) have answered Hitzig at length.—Ewald holds that the Tables mentioned in this verse contained the original Ten Commandments, but that the tables spoken of in *v.* 28 were distinct ones, on which Moses engraved this string of precepts. But this seems an utterly gratuitous supposition.

3. These are similar to the instructions given on the first occasion. See xix. 12, 13.

6, 7. This was the second revelation of the name of the God of Israel to Moses. The first revelation was of Jehovah as the self-existent One, who purposed to deliver His people with a mighty hand (iii. 14); this was of the same Jehovah as a loving Saviour who was now forgiving their sins. The two ideas that mark these revelations are found combined, apart from their historical development, in the Second Commandment, where the Divine unity is shewn on its practical side, in its relation to human obligations (cf. xxxiv. 14). Both in the Commandment and in this passage, the Divine Love is associated with the Divine Justice; but in the former there is a transposition to serve the proper purpose of the Commandments, and the Justice stands before the Love. This is strictly the legal arrangement, brought out in the completed system of the ceremonial Law, in which the Sin-offering, in acknowledgment of the sentence of Justice against sin, was offered before the Burnt-offering and the Peace-offering (see pref. to Leviticus). But in this place the truth appears in its essential order; the retributive Justice of Jehovah is subordinated to, rather it is made a part of, His forgiving Love (see on xxxii. 14). The visitation of God, whatever form it may wear, is in all ages working out purposes of Love towards all His children. The diverse aspects of the Divine nature, to separate which is the tendency of the unregenerate mind of man and of all heathenism, are united in perfect harmony in the Lord Jehovah, of whom the saying is true in all its length and breadth, "God is love" (1 Joh. iv. 8). It was the sense of this in the degree to which it was now revealed to him that caused Moses to bow his head and worship (*v.* 8). But the perfect revelation of the harmony was reserved for the fulness of time when "the Lamb slain from the foundation of the world" was made known to us in the flesh as both our Saviour and our Judge. —Moses quotes the words here pronounced to him in his supplication after the rebellion that arose from the report of the ten spies (Num. xiv. 18).

9. Moses had been assured of the pardon of the people and the perfect restoration of the Covenant (xxxiii. 14, 17): he had just had revealed to him, in a most distinguished manner, the riches of the Divine forgiveness. Yet now, in the earnest travail of his spirit, he supplicates for a repetition of the promise, adding the emphatic petition, that Jehovah would take Israel for his own inheritance (ch. xv. 17). This yearning struggle after assurance

grace in thy sight. O Lord, let my Lord, I pray thee, go among us; for it *is* a stiffnecked people; and pardon our iniquity and our sin, and take us for thine inheritance.

10 ¶ And he said, Behold, ᵈI make a covenant: before all thy people I will do marvels, such as have not been done in all the earth, nor in any nation. and all the people among which thou *art* shall see the work of the Lord: for it *is* a terrible thing that I will do with thee.

11 Observe thou that which I command thee this day: behold, I drive out before thee the Amorite, and the Canaanite, and the Hittite, and the Perizzite, and the Hivite, and the Jebusite.

12 ᵉ Take heed to thyself, lest thou make a covenant with the inhabitants of the land whither thou goest, lest it be for a snare in the midst of thee:

13 But ye shall destroy their altars, break their †images, and cut down their groves:

14 For thou shalt worship no other god: for the Lord, whose name *is* Jealous, *is* a ᶠjealous God.

15 Lest thou make a covenant with the inhabitants of the land, and they go a whoring after their gods, and do sacrifice unto their gods, and *one* call thee, and thou eat of his sacrifice;

16 And thou take of ᵍ their daughters unto thy sons, and their daughters go a whoring after their gods, and make thy sons go a whoring after their gods.

17 Thou shalt make thee no molten gods.

18 ¶ The feast of ʰ unleavened bread shalt thou keep. Seven days thou shalt eat unleavened bread, as I commanded thee, in the time of the month Abib: for in the ⁱ month Abib thou camest out from Egypt.

19 ᵏAll that openeth the matrix *is* mine; and every firstling among thy cattle, *whether* ox or sheep, *that is male.*

20 But the firstling of an ass thou shalt redeem with a ‖ lamb: and if thou redeem *him* not, then shalt thou break his neck. All the firstborn of thy sons thou shalt redeem. And none shall appear before me ⁱ empty.

21 ¶ ᵐ Six days thou shalt work, but on the seventh day thou shalt rest: in earing time and in harvest thou shalt rest.

ᵈ Deut. 5. 2.

ᵉ chap. 23. 32. Deut. 7. 2.

† Heb. *statues.*

ᶠ chap. 20. 5.

ᵍ 1 Kings 11. 2.

ʰ chap. 23. 15.

ⁱ chap. 13. 4.

ᵏ chap. 22. 29. Ezek. 44. 30.

‖ Or, *kid.*

ⁱ chap. 23. 15.

ᵐ chap. 23. 12. Deut. 5. 12. Luke 13. 14.

---

is like the often-repeated utterance of the heart, when it receives a blessing beyond its hopes, " can this be real?" These words of Moses wonderfully commend themselves to the experience of the prayerful spirits of all ages.—A hint may perhaps be gathered from this verse in favour of reading the verbs in xxxiii. 14 (see note) affirmatively rather than interrogatively.

10. *marvels*] These marvels are explained in the following verse. Cf. Deut. vii. 1, &c.

Conditions of the Covenant.
11—27.

11. The names of the nations are the same as occur in the first promise to Moses in iii. 8.

12—27. The precepts contained in these verses are, for the most part, identical in substance with some of those which follow the Ten Commandments and are recorded in "the Book of the Covenant" (xx.—xxiii.; see xxiv. 7). Such a selection of precepts in this place, connected with the account of the restored Covenant and the new Tables, may tend to support the probability that chapters xxxii., xxxiii., xxxiv. originally formed a distinct composition. See introd. note to xxxii.

12. See on xxiii. 32, 33.

13. See on xxiii. 24.

cut down their groves] See Note at the end of the Chap.

14. See on xx. 5.

15, 16] An expansion of *v.* 12 (cf. Deut. xxxi. 16). The unfaithfulness of the nation to its Covenant with Jehovah is here for the first time spoken of as a breach of the marriage bond. The metaphor is, in any case, a natural one, but it seems to gain point, if we suppose it to convey an allusion to the abominations connected with heathen worship, such as are spoken of Num. xxv. 1—3. Cf Lev. xvii. 7, xx. 5, 6; Num. xiv. 33.

15. *eat of his sacrifice*] See Num. xxv. 2.

17. *molten*] See on xx. 4.

18. See xxiii. 15.

19. See on xiii. 2, 12 and Lev. xxvii. 26.

20. See xiii. 13.

shall appear before me empty] See xxiii. 15.

21. See xx. 9, xxiii. 12. There is here added to the Commandment a particular cau-

22 ¶ *And thou shalt observe the feast of weeks, of the firstfruits of wheat harvest, and the feast of ingathering at the †year's end.

23 ¶ °Thrice in the year shall all your men children appear before the Lord God, the God of Israel.

24 For I will cast out the nations before thee, and enlarge thy borders: neither shall any man desire thy land, when thou shalt go up to appear before the Lord thy God thrice in the year.

25 *Thou shalt not offer the blood of my sacrifice with leaven; neither shall the sacrifice of the feast of the passover be left unto the morning.

26 The first of the firstfruits of thy land thou shalt bring unto the house of the Lord thy God. Thou shalt not seethe a *kid in his mother's milk.

27 And the Lord said unto Moses, Write thou *these words: for after the tenor of these words I have made a covenant with thee and with Israel.

28 *And he was there with the Lord forty days and forty nights; he did neither eat bread, nor drink water. And he wrote upon the tables the words of the covenant, the ten †commandments.

29 ¶ And it came to pass, when Moses came down from mount Sinai with the two tables of testimony in Moses' hand, when he came down from the mount, that Moses wist not that the skin of his face shone while he talked with him.

30 And when Aaron and all the children of Israel saw Moses, behold, the skin of his face shone; and they were afraid to come nigh him.

31 And Moses called unto them; and Aaron and all the rulers of the congregation returned unto him: and Moses talked with them.

32 And afterward all the children of Israel came nigh: and he gave them in commandment all that the Lord had spoken with him in mount Sinai.

---

tion respecting those times of year when the land calls for most labour.—The old verb *to ear* (*i.e.* to plough) is genuine English. Though it appears to be cognate with the Latin *arare*, it is certainly not derived from it. The English verb is found Gen. xlv. 6, in Shakespeare ('Rich. II.' III. 2; 'Ant. and Cleo.' I. 4), and elsewhere.

22. See xxiii. 16.
23. See xxiii. 14, 17.
24. *for I will cast out*] See xxiii. 23.
enlarge thy borders] See xxiii. 31; Deut. xii. 20.
neither shall any man desire, &c.] This is the only place in which the promise is given to encourage such as might fear the consequences of obeying the Divine Law in attending to their religious duties. But cf. xxiii. 27.
25, 26.] See xxiii. 18, 19.
27. *Write thou*] Moses is here commanded to make a record in his own writing of the preceding precepts (see on *vv.* 12—27). The Book of the Covenant was written in like manner (xxiv. 4, 7).—On the words " he wrote," in the next verse, see note.

Moses receives the New Tables, comes down from the Mount, and converses with the people.
28—35.
28. Cf. xxiv. 18.

he wrote] According to Hebrew usage, the name of Jehovah *may* be the subject of the verb; that it must be so, is evident from *v.* 1. Cf. xxxii. 16.

29. *the two tables of testimony*] Cf. xxxi. 18.
the skin of his face shone] Cf. Matt. xvii. 2. The brightness of the Eternal Glory, though Moses had witnessed it only in a modified manner (xxxiii. 22, 23), was so reflected in his face, that Aaron and the people were stricken with awe and feared to approach him until he gave them words of encouragement. The Hebrew verb *kāran*, to *shine*, is connected through a simple metaphor with *keren*, a *horn;* and hence Aquila and the Vulgate have rendered the verb *to be horned*. The latter part of the verse in the Vulg. is, *et ignorabat quod cornuta esset facies sua ex consortio sermonis Domini*. From this use of the word *cornuta* has arisen the popular representation of Moses with horns on his forehead.

33—35. St Paul refers to this passage as shewing forth the glory of the Law, though it was but a "ministration of condemnation," and was to be done away, in order to enhance the glory of the Gospel, "the ministration of the spirit," which is concealed by no vail from the eyes of believers, and is to last for ever (2 Cor. iii. 7—15).

33 And *till* Moses had done speaking with them, he put *a vail on his face.

34 But when Moses went in before the LORD to speak with him, he took the vail off, until he came out. And he came out, and spake unto the children of Israel *that* which he was commanded.

35 And the children of Israel saw the face of Moses, that the skin of Moses' face shone: and Moses put the vail upon his face again, until he went in to speak with him.

a 2 Cor. 3. 13.

33. *And till Moses had done*] Our translators give what may seem to be the easiest sense of the original by supplying the word *till*. But the Hebrew rather requires that **when**, not *till*, should be inserted; and this agrees better with *v*. 35 (so the LXX., Vulg., the Targums, Syriac, Saadia, and nearly all modern versions, not excepting Luther and Cranmer). If we adopt this rendering, Moses did not wear the vail when he was speaking to the people, but when he was silent. See on *v*. 35.

34. *Moses went in*] *i.e.* to the Tent of meeting.

35. Our version accords with the Hebrew and all the ancient versions, except the Vulgate, which has this remarkable rendering, for which it is difficult to account unless we may suppose it to represent a different reading in the original:—*videbant faciem egredientis Moysi esse cornutam; sed operiebat ille rursus faciem suam, siquando loquebatur ad eos*. It has been suggested that if we may imagine St Paul to have had such a reading in his mind, it would simplify the use he makes of the passage in 2 Cor. iii. 12—15. But it is not necessary to resort to any such supposition, since St Paul's application of the narrative may be well explained as referring to the simple fact that it was distinctive of the old dispensation that a vail should conceal the glory. There was no occasion to notice the particular that Moses did not wear the vail just in the act of speaking.

NOTE ON CHAP. XXXIV. 13.

THE GROVES.

This is the first reference to what is commonly known as grove-worship. The original word for *grove* in this connection is אֲשֵׁרָה (*ashērāh*), a different one from that so rendered in Gen. xxi. 33 (אֵשֶׁל, *ēshel*). Our translators have followed the sense given in most of the passages in which the word occurs by the LXX., Vulg., and Saadia, and which has been adopted by most Jewish authorities, by Luther, and other modern translators. It was supposed that what the Law commands is the destruction of groves dedicated to the worship of false deities. The allusions to such groves in classical writers are familiar enough. The connection of sacred groves and trees with the worship of the powers of nature may be traced very generally amongst the ancient nations of Asia and Europe (see Humboldt, 'Cosmos,' Vol. II. p. 95, Sabine's translation). But there appear to be insuperable difficulties in the way of thus rendering *ashērāh*. Since the times of Selden and Spencer most critics have taken the word to denote either a personal goddess or some symbolical representation of one.

The following conclusions seem to be fairly deduced from the references to the subject in the Old Testament:

(1) According to the most probable derivation of the name the *ashērāh* represented something that was upright, which was fixed, or planted, in the ground; hence, if it was not a tree, it must have been some sort of upright pillar or monument.

(2) It was formed of wood, and when it was destroyed it was cut down and burned (Deut. vii. 5; Judg. vi. 25, 26; 2 K. xxiii. 6, 15). It might be made of any sort of wood. See note on Deut. xvi. 21.

(3) That it could not be a grove appears from an *ashērāh* having been set up "under every green tree" in Judah in the time of Rehoboam (1 K. xiv. 23), and in Israel in the time of Hoshea (2 K. xvii. 10); from an *ashērāh idol* (not "an idol in a grove," as it stands in our version) having been destroyed and burnt near the brook Kidron by Asa (1 K. xv. 13; 2 Chr. xv. 16); and from a carved image of *the ashērāh* having been set up in the Temple by Manasseh (2 K. xxi. 7), which was brought out by Josiah and burnt and stamped to powder (2 K. xxiii. 6).

The worship of *ashērāh* is found associated with that of Baal (Judg. iii. 7; 1 K. xviii. 19, 2 K. xxi. 3; xxiii. 4), like that of Astarte, or *Ashtoreth* (עַשְׁתֹּרֶת) (Judg. ii. 13, x. 6; 1 S. vii. 4). Hence it has been inferred by de Wette and others that *Ashērāh* was another name for Astarte. This opinion might seem to be countenanced by the LXX. in

2 Chron. xv. 16 (where the Vulgate has *simulacrum Priapi*), and by the Vulgate in Judg. iii. 7. But it has been proved that the words have no etymological connection with each other, and are not likely to have had the same denotation. Movers, resting his main argument upon 2 K. xxiii. 13—15, conceived them to be the names of two distinct deities. On the whole, the most probable result of the inquiry seems to be that while Astarte was the personal name of the goddess, the *ashērāh* was a symbol of her, probably in some one of her characters, wrought in wood in some conventional form. If we suppose it to have symbolized her as a goddess of nature, the conjecture that its form resembled that of the sacred tree of the Assyrians, with which we have become familiar from the monuments of Nineveh[1] (see Fer-gusson, 'Nineveh and Persepolis,' p. 299), gains something in probability.

It has been supposed, on what seems to be good ground, that the image, or rather **pillar** (מַצֵּבָה, *matzēvāh*), spoken of here and elsewhere in the same connection, was a stone pillar, set up in honour of Baal, as the *Ashērāh* was a wooden pillar, set up in honour of Astarte (1 K. xiv. 23; 2 K. xvii. 10, xviii. 4, &c.). But Gesenius rightly observes that these monuments may have lost in later times their original meaning as regards Baal and Astarte, as the *hermæ* of the Greeks did in regard to Hermes. They probably became connected with a debased and superstitious worship of Jehovah, like the figure of the calf (see on xxxii. 4). This perhaps explains the need of the prohibition that an *ashērāh* should be placed near the Altar of Jehovah. See Deut. xvi. 21. (Selden, 'de Diis Syr.' p. 343 sq.; Spencer, 'de Leg. Heb.' lib. II. c. xxvii. §1; Gesenius, 'Thes.' and 'Handwörterbuch,' s.v.; Fürst, 'Lex.' s.v.; Movers, 'Phönizier,' I. p. 560; Keil on 1 Kings xiv. 23.)

[1] It has been conjectured from the sculptured figures that this was an upright stock which was adorned at festive seasons with boughs, flowers, and ribbons. Such might have been the *ashērāh*.

CHAPTER XXXV.

1 *The sabbath.* 4 *The free gifts for the tabernacle.* 20 *The readiness of the people to offer.* 30 *Bezaleel and Aholiab are called to the work.*

AND Moses gathered all the congregation of the children of Israel together, and said unto them, These *are* the words which the LORD hath commanded, that *ye* should do them.

2 *a* Six days shall work be done, but on the seventh day there shall be to you †an holy day, a sabbath of rest to the LORD: whosoever doeth work therein shall be put to death.

3 Ye shall kindle no fire throughout your habitations upon the sabbath day.

4 ¶ And Moses spake unto all the congregation of the children of Israel, saying, This *is* the thing which the LORD commanded, saying,

5 Take ye from among you an offering unto the LORD: *b* whosoever *is* of a willing heart, let him bring it, an offering of the LORD; gold, and silver, and brass,

6 And blue, and purple, and scarlet, and fine linen, and goats' *hair*,

7 And rams' skins dyed red, and badgers' skins, and shittim wood,

8 And oil for the light, and spices for anointing oil, and for the sweet incense,

9 And onyx stones, and stones to be set for the ephod, and for the breastplate.

10 And every wise hearted among you shall come, and make all that the LORD hath commanded;

11 *c* The tabernacle, his tent, and his covering, his taches, and his boards, his bars, his pillars, and his sockets,

a chap. 20. 9.
Lev. 23. 3.
Deut. 5. 12.
Luke 13. 14.
† Heb. *holiness.*

b chap. 2.

c chap. 26. 31.

CHAP. XXXV. The narrative of what relates to the construction of the Sanctuary is now resumed from xxxi. 18.

Moses delivers to the people the messages on the supply of materials for the Sanctuary.

1—19.

1. Moses here addresses the whole people. See xxv. 1; cf. on Lev. viii. 3. On *v.* 2 see on xxxi. 12.

3. This prohibition is here first distinctly expressed, but it is implied xvi. 23.

10. *wise hearted*] See on xxviii. 3.

11. See on xxvi. 1—37. It has been already observed that in the instructions for making the Sanctuary, the Ark of the Covenant, as the principal thing belonging to it, is mentioned first; but in the practical order of the work, as it is here arranged, the

VOL. I.

D D

12 The ark, and the staves thereof, *with* the mercy seat, and the vail of the covering,

13 The table, and his staves, and all his vessels, and the shewbread,

14 The candlestick also for the light, and his furniture, and his lamps, with the oil for the light,

15 *^d* And the incense altar, and his staves, and the anointing oil, and the sweet incense, and the hanging for the door at the entering in of the tabernacle,

16 *^e* The altar of burnt offering, with his brasen grate, his staves, and all his vessels, the laver and his foot,

17 The hangings of the court, his pillars, and their sockets, and the hanging for the door of the court,

18 The pins of the tabernacle, and the pins of the court, and their cords,

19 The cloths of service, to do service in the holy *place*, the holy garments for Aaron the priest, and the garments of his sons, to minister in the priest's office.

20 ¶ And all the congregation of the children of Israel departed from the presence of Moses.

21 And they came, every one whose heart stirred him up, and every one whom his spirit made willing, *and* they brought the LORD's offering to the work of the tabernacle of the congregation, and for all his service, and for the holy garments.

22 And they came, both men and women, as many as were willing hearted, *and* brought bracelets, and earrings, and rings, and tablets, all jewels of gold: and every man that offered *offered* an offering of gold unto the LORD.

23 And every man, with whom was found blue, and purple, and scarlet, and fine linen, and goats' *hair*, and red skins of rams, and badgers' skins, brought *them*.

24 Every one that did offer an offering of silver and brass brought the LORD's offering: and every man, with whom was found shittim wood for any work of the service, brought *it*.

25 And all the women that were

---

^d chap. 30. 1.

^e chap. 27. 1.

Tabernacle with its Tent and covering come first. See on xxv. 10—16.

12. On the Ark and the Mercy Seat, see on xxv. 10—22.

the vail of the covering] The second Hebrew word is not the same as that in the preceding verse, which is rendered *covering*, and denotes the Covering of the Tent (see on xxvi. 14): but it is the one used for the entrance curtains (see on xxvi. 36, xxvii. 16). The same phrase occurs Ex. xxxv. 12, xl. 21; Num. iv. 5.

13, 14. See on xxv. 23—38.

15. *the incense altar*] See on xxx. 1

the anointing oil] See on xxx. 22—33.

the sweet incense] See on xxx. 34—38.

the hanging for the door] **the entrance curtain.** See on xxvi. 36, xxvii. 16.

16. *the altar of burnt offering*] See on xxvii. 1—8.

the laver] See on xxx. 18—21.

17. See on xxvii. 9—18.

18. These were the tent-pins and cords of the Tent of the Tabernacle and those of the pillars of the Court. See Note at the end of Ch. xxvi. The word *Tabernacle* (*mishkān*) is here used for the full name, **the Tabernacle of the Tent of meeting** (see xl. 2, 6, 29, note on xxvi. 1, &c.). It denotes the entire structure.

19. *the cloths of service to do service in the holy place*] Rather;—**the garments of office to do service in the Sanctuary,** &c. See on xxxi. 10.

21. See on xxv. 2.

22. *bracelets*] Rather, **brooches.**

earrings] The Hebrew word signifies a ring, either for the nose (Prov. xi. 22; Isa. iii. 21) or for the ear (xxxii. 2; Gen. xxxv. 4; Judg. viii. 24). That ear-rings, not nose-rings, as some have imagined, are here meant is confirmed by what we know of early Hebrew and Egyptian customs. See Gen. xxxv. 4; Wilkinson, 'Pop. Acc.' I. p. 145, II. p. 338.

rings] **signet rings.**

tablets] It is not certain what the Hebrew word denotes. Gesenius and others have taken it for *gold beads;* but Fürst, with more probability, for **armlets**, in accordance with the Ancient Versions. It is most likely that all the articles mentioned in this verse were of gold. The indulgence of private luxury was thus given up for the honour of the LORD. Cf. xxxviii. 8.

23, 24. See on xxv. 3, 4, 5.

25. See on xxv. 4.

wise hearted did spin with their hands, and brought that which they had spun, *both* of blue, and of purple, *and* of scarlet, and of fine linen.

26 And all the women whose heart stirred them up in wisdom spun goats' *hair*.

27 And the rulers brought onyx stones, and stones to be set, for the ephod, and for the breastplate;

28 And *ᶠspice, and oil for the light, and for the anointing oil, and for the sweet incense.

ᶠ chap. 30. 23.

29 The children of Israel brought a willing offering unto the Lord, every man and woman, whose heart made them willing to bring for all manner of work, which the Lord had commanded to be made by the hand of Moses.

30 ¶ And Moses said unto the children of Israel, See, ᵍthe Lord hath called by name Bezaleel the son of Uri, the son of Hur, of the tribe of Judah;

ᵍ chap. 31. 2.

31 And he hath filled him with the spirit of God, in wisdom, in understanding, and in knowledge, and in all manner of workmanship;

32 And to devise curious works, to work in gold, and in silver, and in brass,

33 And in the cutting of stones, to set *them*, and in carving of wood, to make any manner of cunning work.

34 And he hath put in his heart that he may teach, *both* he, and Aholiab, the son of Ahisamach, of the tribe of Dan.

35 Them hath he filled with wisdom of heart, to work all manner of work, of the engraver, and of the cunning workman, and of the embroiderer, in blue, and in purple, in scarlet, and in fine linen, and of the weaver, *even* of them that do any work, and of those that devise cunning work.

---

27. See on xxviii. 9—20. The precious stones and spices were contributed by the rulers, who were more wealthy than the other Israelites.

28. See on xxx. 22—38.

29. Cf. *v.* 21. Observe the emphatic repetition.

30. Cf. xxxi. 2

31. Cf. xxxi. 3.

32. *to devise curious works*] **to devise works of skill.** Cf. xxxi. 4.

33 *to make any manner of cunning work*] **to work in all manner of works of skill.**

34. "And he hath put **it into his heart to teach, both into his heart and into Aholiab's,**" &c.—They were qualified by the Lord not only to work themselves, but to instruct those who were under them.

35. *of the engraver*] **of the artificer.** The branches of work committed to Bezaleel are here included under the general term **the work of the artificer**: they are distinctly enumerated *vv.* 32, 33 and xxxi. 4, 5. But what was under the charge of Aholiab is here for the first time clearly distinguished into the work of **the skilled weaver**, that of the embroiderer, and that of the weaver.

the cunning workman] **the skilled weaver**, literally, *the reckoner*. He might have been so called because he had nicely to count and calculate the threads in weaving figures in the manner of tapestry or carpet. His **work was** chiefly used in the curtains and vail of the Tabernacle, in the Ephod and the Breastplate (xxvi. 1, 31, xxviii. 6, 15, &c.). It is generally called "cunning work" in our version, but the name is unfortunately not restricted to it.

the embroiderer] He worked with a needle, either shaping his design in stitches of coloured thread, or in pieces of coloured cloth sewn upon the groundwork. His work was employed in the **entrance curtains** of the Tent and the court, and in the girdle of the High-priest (xxvi. 36, xxvii. 16, xxviii. 39).— The Hebrew root *rākam* = to work with a needle, has survived in Arabic, but is not found in Syriac, nor in the Targums. It is a curious fact that through the Arabic have come from the same Semitic root the Spanish *recamare* and the Italian *ricamare*.

the weaver] He appears to have worked in the loom in the ordinary way with materials of only a single colour. The tissues made by him were used for the Robe of the Ephod and its binding and for the coats of the priests (xxviii. 32, xxxix. 22, 27). The distinctions in the kinds of work mentioned in this and the two preceding notes are clearly expressed in the LXX. and are in accordance with Jewish tradition (Bähr, 'Symb.' I. p. 266; Gesenius, 'Thes.' p. 1310).

As the names of the three classes of workers are in the masculine gender, we know that they denote men, while the spinners and dyers were women (*v.* 25). From what we know of the proficiency

CHAPTER XXXVI.

1 *The offerings are delivered to the workmen.* 5 *The liberality of the people is restrained.* 8 *The curtains of cherubims.* 14 *The curtains of goats' hair.* 19 *The covering of skins.* 20 *The boards with their sockets.* 31 *The bars.* 35 *The vail.* 37 *The hanging for the door.*

THEN wrought Bezaleel and Aholiab, and every wise hearted man, in whom the LORD put wisdom and understanding to know how to work all manner of work for the service of the sanctuary, according to all that the LORD had commanded.

2 And Moses called Bezaleel and Aholiab, and every wise hearted man, in whose heart the LORD had put wisdom, *even* every one whose heart stirred him up to come unto the work to do it:

3 And they received of Moses all the offering, which the children of Israel had brought for the work of the service of the sanctuary, to make it *withal.* And they brought yet unto him free offerings every morning.

4 And all the wise men, that wrought all the work of the sanctuary, came every man from his work which they made;

5 ¶ And they spake unto Moses, saying, The people bring much more than enough for the service of the work, which the LORD commanded to make.

6 And Moses gave commandment, and they caused it to be proclaimed throughout the camp, saying, Let neither man nor woman make any more work for the offering of the sanctuary. So the people were restrained from bringing.

7 For the stuff they had was sufficient for all the work to make it, and too much.

8 ¶ *a* And every wise hearted man among them that wrought the work of the tabernacle made ten curtains *of* fine twined linen, and blue, and purple, and scarlet: *with* cherubims of cunning work made he them.   *a* chap. 26. 3, 4.

9 The length of one curtain *was* twenty and eight cubits, and the breadth of one curtain four cubits: the curtains *were* all of one size.

10 And he coupled the five curtains one unto another: and *the other* five curtains he coupled one unto another.

11 And he made loops of blue on the edge of one curtain from the selvedge in the coupling: likewise he made in the uttermost side of *another* curtain, in the coupling of the second.

12 *b* Fifty loops made he in one curtain, and fifty loops made he in the edge of the curtain which *was* in the coupling of the second: the loops held one *curtain* to another.   *b* chap. 26. 10.

13 And he made fifty taches of gold, and coupled the curtains one unto another with the taches: so it became one tabernacle.

---

of the textile arts in Egypt in early times, we need not wonder at the exact division of labour among the Hebrews which the use of the terms in this verse indicates. —It is remarkable in regard to the other arts of construction, that the workman in each of them was called by the general name *artificer* (in Hebrew, literally, *one who cuts*) added to the name of the material in which he worked: thus the carpenter was called an **artificer in wood**; the smith, **an artificer in iron**; the mason, or the lapidary (xxviii. 11), **an artificer in stone**. —The view given in these notes of the three kinds of workers in textile fabrics, is substantially that of Gesenius, Bähr, Fürst, Winer and others. But Knobel and Keil take a different view respecting the embroiderer, and consider that he worked not with a needle but with a loom of some peculiar kind.

CHAP. XXXVI.

Bezaleel, Aholiab, and their assistants are set to work.

1—7.

1. See on xxxi. 3.

4. *the wise men*] *i.e.* the skilful men. See on xxxi. 3.

3, 5—7. See on xxv. 2.

The Tabernacle is made.

8—38.

8—13. See on xxvi. 1—6.

8. *made he them*] Rather, **were they made**. A corresponding change should be made in most of the verses in this Chapter. See on xxxvii. 1—5.

14 ¶ And he made curtains *of* goats' hair for the tent over the tabernacle: eleven curtains he made them.

15 The length of one curtain *was* thirty cubits, and four cubits *was* the breadth of one curtain: the eleven curtains *were* of one size.

16 And he coupled five curtains by themselves, and six curtains by themselves.

17 And he made fifty loops upon the uttermost edge of the curtain in the coupling, and fifty loops made he upon the edge of the curtain which coupleth the second.

18 And he made fifty taches *of* brass to couple the tent together, that it might be one.

19 And he made a covering for the tent *of* rams' skins dyed red, and a covering *of* badgers' skins above *that*.

20 ¶ And he made boards for the tabernacle *of* shittim wood, standing up.

21 The length of a board *was* ten cubits, and the breadth of a board one cubit and a half.

22 One board had two tenons, equally distant one from another: thus did he make for all the boards of the tabernacle.

23 And he made boards for the tabernacle; twenty boards for the south side southward:

24 And forty sockets of silver he made under the twenty boards; two sockets under one board for his two tenons, and two sockets under another board for his two tenons.

25 And for the other side of the tabernacle, *which is* toward the north corner, he made twenty boards,

26 And their forty sockets of silver; two sockets under one board, and two sockets under another board.

27 And for the sides of the tabernacle westward he made six boards.

28 And two boards made he for the corners of the tabernacle in the two sides.

29 And they were †coupled beneath, and coupled together at the head thereof, to one ring: thus he did to both of them in both the corners. † Heb. *twinned.*

30 And there were eight boards; and their sockets *were* sixteen sockets of silver, †under every board two sockets. † Heb. *two sockets, two sockets under one board.*

31 ¶ And he made *c* bars of shittim wood; five for the boards of the one side of the tabernacle, *c* chap. 25. 28. & 30. ¶

32 And five bars for the boards of the other side of the tabernacle, and five bars for the boards of the tabernacle for the sides westward.

33 And he made the middle bar to shoot through the boards from the one end to the other.

34 And he overlaid the boards with gold, and made their rings *of* gold *to be* places for the bars, and overlaid the bars with gold.

35 ¶ And he made a vail *of* blue, and purple, and scarlet, and fine twined linen: *with* cherubims made he it of cunning work.

36 And he made thereunto four pillars *of* shittim *wood*, and overlaid them with gold: their hooks *were of* gold; and he cast for them four sockets of silver.

37 ¶ And he made an hanging for the tabernacle door *of* blue, and purple, and scarlet, and fine twined linen, †of needlework; † Heb. *the work of a needleworker,* or, *embroiderer.*

38 And the five pillars of it with their hooks: and he overlaid their chapiters and their fillets with gold: but their five sockets *were of* brass.

14—18. See on xxvi. 7—13.
19. See on xxvi. 14.
20—34. See on xxvi. 15—29.
22. *equally distant one from another*] **set in order one against another.** See xxvi. 17.
27. *for the sides*] **for the back.** See xxvi. 22.

33. *to shoot through the boards*] rather, **to reach across the boards.** See xxvi. 28.
35, 36. See on xxvi. 31, 32.
37. *an hanging for the tabernacle door*] **an entrance curtain for the entering of the Tent.** See on xxvi. 36.
38. *their chapiters and their fillets*] **their capitals and their connecting rods.**

CHAPTER XXXVII.

1 *The ark.* 6 *The mercy seat with cherubims.* 10 *The table with his vessels.* 17 *The candlestick with his lamps and instruments.* 25 *The altar of incense.* 29 *The anointing oil and sweet incense.*

a chap. 25. 10.

AND Bezaleel made *"the ark of shittim wood: two cubits and a half *was* the length of it, and a cubit and a half the breadth of it, and a cubit and a half the height of it:

2 And he overlaid it with pure gold within and without, and made a crown of gold to it round about.

3 And he cast for it four rings of gold, *to be set* by the four corners of it; even two rings upon the one side of it, and two rings upon the other side of it.

4 And he made staves *of* shittim wood, and overlaid them with gold.

5 And he put the staves into the rings by the sides of the ark, to bear the ark.

b chap. 25. 17.

6 ¶ And he made the *"mercy seat *of* pure gold: two cubits and a half *was* the length thereof, and one cubit and a half the breadth thereof.

7 And he made two cherubims *of* gold, beaten out of one piece made he them, on the two ends of the mercy seat;

¶ Or, *on t of, &c.* ¶ Or, *out of, &c.*

8 One cherub ¶on the end on this side, and another cherub ¶on the *other* end on that side: out of the mercy seat made he the cherubims on the two ends thereof.

9 And the cherubims spread out *their* wings on high, *and* covered with their wings over the mercy seat, with their faces one to another; *even* to the mercy seatward were the faces of the cherubims.

10 ¶ And he made the table *of* shittim wood: two cubits *was* the length thereof, and a cubit the breadth thereof, and a cubit and a half the height thereof:

11 And he overlaid it with pure gold, and made thereunto a crown of gold round about.

12 Also he made thereunto a border of an handbreadth round about; and made a crown of gold for the border thereof round about.

13 And he cast for it four rings of gold, and put the rings upon the four corners that *were* in the four feet thereof.

14 Over against the border were the rings, the places for the staves to bear the table.

15 And he made the staves *of* shittim wood, and overlaid them with gold, to bear the table.

16 And he made the vessels which *were* upon the table, his *"dishes, and his spoons, and his bowls, and his covers ¶to cover withal, *of* pure gold.

c chap. 25. 29.

¶ Or, *to pour out with- al.* *d* chap. 25. 31.

17 ¶ And he made the *"candlestick *of* pure gold: *of* beaten work made he the candlestick; his shaft, and his branch, his bowls, his knops, and his flowers, were of the same:

18 And six branches going out of the sides thereof; three branches of the candlestick out of the one side thereof, and three branches of the candlestick out of the other side thereof:

19 Three bowls made after the

These rods united the heads of the pillars, like the connecting rods of the Court (xxvii. 10). Neither these nor the capitals are mentioned in the instructions in xxvi. 37. See Note at the end of Ch. xxvi.

Chap. XXXVII.
The Furniture of the Tabernacle is made.
1—29.

1—5. See on xxv. 10—16 and on xxxv. 11. It has been observed that the Ark, as the most precious thing made for the Sanctuary, is expressly spoken of as the workmanship of Bezaleel himself. The expression here is quite free from ambiguity; but to prevent misunderstanding, it may be well to observe that in chap. xxxvi. 8, 10, 11, 12, 13, 14, 16, 17, 18, 19, 20, &c., and elsewhere, there is no nominative expressed in the Hebrew, and the verb is used indefinitely, as in the German phrase with *man* and the French one with *on*. In translating into English, it would be better in such cases to use the passive voice. See on xxxvi. 8.

6—9. See on xxv. 17—22.
7. *beaten out of one piece*] See on xxv. **18.**
10—16. See on xxv. 23—30.
17—24. See on xxv. 31—39.

fashion of almonds in one branch, a knop and a flower; and three bowls made like almonds in another branch, a knop and a flower: so throughout the six branches going out of the candlestick.

20 And in the candlestick *were* four bowls made like almonds, his knops, and his flowers:

21 And a knop under two branches of the same, and a knop under two branches of the same, and a knop under two branches of the same, according to the six branches going out of it.

22 Their knops and their branches were of the same: all of it *was* one beaten work *of* pure gold.

23 And he made his seven lamps, and his snuffers, and his snuffdishes, *of* pure gold.

24 *Of* a talent of pure gold made he it, and all the vessels thereof.

25 ¶ *^e*And he made the incense altar *of* shittim wood: the length of it *was* a cubit, and the breadth of it a cubit; *it was* foursquare; and two cubits *was* the height of it; the horns thereof were of the same.

26 And he overlaid it with pure gold, *both* the top of it, and the sides thereof round about, and the horns of it: also he made unto it a crown of gold round about.

27 And he made two rings of gold for it under the crown thereof, by the two corners of it, upon the two sides thereof, to be places for the staves to bear it withal.

e chap. 30. 34.

28 And he made the staves *of* shittim wood, and overlaid them with gold.

29 ¶ And he made *^f*the holy anointing oil, and the pure incense of sweet spices, according to the work of the apothecary.

f chap. 30. 35.

CHAPTER XXXVIII.

1 *The altar of burnt offering.* 8 *The laver of brass.* 9 *The court.* 21 *The sum of that the people offered.*

AND *^a*he made the altar of burnt offering *of* shittim wood: five cubits *was* the length thereof, and five cubits *the* breadth thereof; *it was* foursquare; and three cubits the height thereof.

a chap. 27. 1.

2 And he made the horns thereof on the four corners of it; the horns thereof were of the same: and he overlaid it with brass.

3 And he made all the vessels of the altar, the pots, and the shovels, and the basons, *and* the fleshhooks, and the firepans: all the vessels thereof made he *of* brass.

4 And he made for the altar a brasen grate of network under the compass thereof beneath unto the midst of it.

5 And he cast four rings for the four ends of the grate of brass, *to be* places for the staves.

6 And he made the staves *of* shittim wood, and overlaid them with brass.

7 And he put the staves into the rings on the sides of the altar, to bear it withal; he made the altar hollow with boards.

8 ¶ And he made the laver *of* brass, and the foot of it *of* brass, of

---

25—28. See on xxx. 1—10.
29. See on xxx. 22—38.

CHAP. XXXVIII.
The Brazen Altar, the Laver, and the Court are made.
1—20.

1—7. See on xxvii. 1—8.
8. *the laver*] See on xxx. 18—21. It appears that the metal for this laver was supplied by women, who gave up their bronze mirrors, such as were commonly used in Egypt and elsewhere (Wilkinson, 'Pop. Acc.' II. p. 336). This is generally approved by critics as the simple meaning of the Hebrew,

and it agrees with the ancient versions and the Targums. The other interpretations—one, that the laver was furnished with mirrors for the use of the women who served in the Sanctuary (Michaelis, Bähr); and another, that its sides were adorned with figures in relief of women ranged in a religious procession (Knobel)—only deserve notice from the learning and reputation of their authors. The women who assembled **at the entrance of the Tent of meeting** were most probably devout women who loved the public service of religion. The giving up their mirrors for the use of the Sanctuary was a fit sacrifice for such women to make (cf. **on**

EXODUS. XXXVIII. [v. 9—24.

¹ Or, brasen glasses.
† Heb. assembling ov troops.

the ¹ lookingglasses of *the women* † assembling, which assembled *at* the door of the tabernacle of the congregation.

9 ¶ And he made the court: on the south side southward the hangings of the court *were of* fine twined linen, an hundred cubits:

10 Their pillars *were* twenty, and their brasen sockets twenty; the hooks of the pillars and their fillets *were of* silver.

11 And for the north side *the hangings were* an hundred cubits, their pillars *were* twenty, and their sockets of brass twenty; the hooks of the pillars and their fillets *of* silver.

12 And for the west side *were* hangings of fifty cubits, their pillars ten, and their sockets ten; the hooks of the pillars and their fillets *of* silver.

13 And for the east side eastward fifty cubits.

14 The hangings of the one side *of the gate were* fifteen cubits; their pillars three, and their sockets three.

15 And for the other side of the court gate, on this hand and that hand, *were* hangings of fifteen cubits; their pillars three, and their sockets three.

16 All the hangings of the court round about *were* of fine twined linen.

17 And the sockets for the pillars *were of* brass; the hooks of the pillars and their fillets *of* silver; and the overlaying of their chapiters *of* silver; and all the pillars of the court *were* filleted with silver.

18 And the hanging for the gate of the court *was* needlework, *of* blue, and purple, and scarlet, and fine twined linen: and twenty cubits *was* the length, and the height in the breadth *was* five cubits, answerable to the hangings of the court.

19 And their pillars *were* four, and their sockets *of* brass four; their hooks *of* silver, and the overlaying of their chapiters and their fillets *of* silver.

20 And all the *ᵇ* pins of the tabernacle, and of the court round about, *were of* brass.

ᵇ chap. 27. 19.

21 ¶ This is the sum of the tabernacle, *even* of the tabernacle of testimony, as it was counted, according to the commandment of Moses, *for* the service of the Levites, by the hand of Ithamar, son to Aaron the priest.

22 And Bezaleel the son of Uri, the son of Hur, of the tribe of Judah, made all that the LORD commanded Moses.

23 And with him *was* Aholiab, son of Ahisamach, of the tribe of Dan, an engraver, and a cunning workman, and an embroiderer in blue, and in purple, and in scarlet, and fine linen.

24 All the gold that was occupied

---

xxxv. 22). We know from the instance of Anna (Luke ii. 36) that pious women, in later ages, used to spend much time within the precincts of the Temple. But there seems to be but weak ground for the notion of Hengstenberg and others that these women ever formed a regularly constituted order, like the widows, or deaconesses, of the early Church, and the Nazarites for life in the time of the Prophets (Lam. iv. 7; Amos ii. 11). Hengstenberg conceives that Moses made no specific law on the subject because the institution had been adopted from the customs of the Egyptian temples. The only passages quoted from the Old Testament in support of the existence of such an order of women are 1 Sam. ii. 22, Lam. ii. 21 (Hengst. 'Egypt,' &c. p. 184).

9—20. See on xxvii. 10—19.

18. *the height in the breadth was five cubits*] The meaning seems to be that the height of the curtain answered to the breadth of the stuff of which it was formed; *i.e.* five cubits. See xxvii. 18.

The sum of the metals used in the Sanctuary.
21—31.

21. "This is the **reckoning** of the Tabernacle, **the Tabernacle of the Testimony** (see on xxv. 16) **as it was reckoned up** according to the *commandment* of Moses, by the service of the Levites, by the hand of Ithamar," &c. The weight of the metals was taken by the Levites, under the direction of Ithamar.

23. *an engraver*] **an artificer.**—*a cunning workman*] **a skilled weaver.** See on xxxv. 35

24. *of the holy place*] Rather, **of the Sanctuary.** The gold was employed not only in the Holy Place, but in the Most Holy

for the work in all the work of the holy *place*, even the gold of the offering, was twenty and nine talents, and seven hundred and thirty shekels, after the shekel of the sanctuary.

25 And the silver of them that were numbered of the congregation *was* an hundred talents, and a thousand seven hundred and threescore and fifteen shekels, after the shekel of the sanctuary:

26 A bekah for † every man, *that is*, half a shekel, after the shekel of the sanctuary, for every one that went to be numbered, from twenty years old and upward, for six hundred thousand and three thousand and five hundred and fifty *men*.

27 And of the hundred talents of silver were cast the sockets of the sanctuary, and the sockets of the vail; an hundred sockets of the hundred talents, a talent for a socket.

28 And of the thousand seven

† Heb. *a poll*.

Place and in the entrance to the Tent (xxxvi. 38).

the gold of the offering] **the gold of the wave offering** (see pref. to Leviticus).

talents...the shekel of the sanctuary] The Shekel was the common standard of weight and value with the Hebrews: but what its weight was in early times, as compared with our standard, is a matter on which there has been much difference of opinion. There is however no particular reason to suppose that the Hebrew standard underwent much alteration in the course of ages; and in regard to later times, we have three distinct elements of calculation which lead to a tolerably harmonious result. (*a*) According to the rabbinists, the shekel weighed 320 barley grains, which are equal to about 214 English grains, the weight of which was originally taken from a grain of wheat. (*b*) There are several silver shekels in existence coined in the Maccabean times (see 1 Macc. xv. 6), and, making allowance for wear, each of these appears to have weighed 220 grains. (*c*) The LXX., when they do not retain the original name in the form σίκλος, render it by δίδραχμον (Gen. xxiii. 15; Ex. xxi. 32, xxx. 13, 15; Lev. xxvii. 3; Num. iii. 47, &c.): they also render *bekah*, the half shekel, by δραχμή (see *v*. 26). Now the Macedonian didrachmon, with which they must have been familiar, weighed 218 grains. It hence appears that we cannot be far wrong in estimating the shekel at 220 English grains (just over half an ounce avoirdupois) and its value in silver as 2*s*. 7*d*.—The statement of Josephus ('Ant.' III. 8. § 2), that the shekel was equal to four Attic drachms (252 grains) is evidently a rough estimate: and still further from accuracy is his turning the fifty shekels of 2 K. xv. 20 into fifty drachms ('Ant.' IX. 11. § 1)—A question is raised as to the meaning of the term, "a shekel of the sanctuary." The rabbinists speak of a common shekel of half the weight of the shekel of the sanctuary. But there is no sufficient reason to suppose that such a distinction existed in ancient times, and the Shekel of the Sanctuary (or, *the Holy Shekel*) would seem to denote no more than an *exact* Shekel, "after the king's weight" (2 S. xiv. 26), "current money of the merchant" (Gen. xxiii. 16).

In the reign of Joash, a collection similar to the one here mentioned, apparently at the same rate of capitation, was made for the repairs of the Temple (2 Chron. xxiv. 9). The tax of later times, called *didrachma* (Matt. xvii. 27), which has often been connected with this passage of Exodus, and which was recognized by our Lord as having the same solemn meaning as this payment of half a shekel, was not, like this one and that of Joash, a collection for a special occasion, but a yearly tax for the support of the Temple, of a whole shekel (δίδραχμον).—See on xxx. 13.

The Talent (Heb. *kikkār*, LXX. τάλαντον) contained 3000 shekels, as may be gathered from *vv*. 25, 26. According to the computation here adopted, the Hebrew Talent was 94⅔ lbs. avoirdupois. The Greek (Æginetan) Talent, from which the LXX. and most succeeding versions have taken the name *talent*, was 82¼ lbs. The original word, *kikkār*, would denote a circular mass, and nearly the same word, *kerker*, was in use amongst the Egyptians for a mass of metal cast in the form of a massive ring with its weight stamped upon it.

26. *A bekah*] Literally, *a half*: the words "half a shekel," &c. appear to be inserted only for emphasis, to enforce the accuracy to be observed in the payment. See on xxx. 13, where there is a similar expression, and cf. xxx. 15.—Respecting the capitation and the numbering of the people, see on xxx. 12. There must have been, in addition to the sum of the half shekels, the free-will offerings of silver (see xxxv. 24), of which no reckoning is here made. They may perhaps have been amongst what was returned to the donors as being more than enough (xxxvi. 7).

27. *sockets*] **bases**. See on xxvi. 19.

28. The hooks, chapiters and fillets here spoken of belonged to the pillars of the Court. See xxvii. 10, 17.

hundred seventy and five *shekels* he made hooks for the pillars, and overlaid their chapiters, and filleted them.

29 And the brass of the offering *was* seventy talents, and two thousand and four hundred shekels.

30 And therewith he made the sockets to the door of the tabernacle of the congregation, and the brasen altar, and the brasen grate for it, and all the vessels of the altar,

31 And the sockets of the court round about, and the sockets of the court gate, and all the pins of the tabernacle, and all the pins of the court round about.

CHAPTER XXXIX.

1 *The cloths of service and holy garments.* 2 *The ephod.* 8 *The breastplate.* 22 *The robe of the ephod.* 27 *The coats, mitre, and girdle of fine linen.* 30 *The plate of the holy crown.* 32 *All is viewed and approved by Moses.*

AND of the blue, and purple, and scarlet, they made cloths of service, to do service in the holy *place*,

---

30. *sockets to the door of the tabernacle of the congregation*] **bases for the entrance of the Tent of meeting.** See xxvi. 37.

the brasen altar] See xxvii. 1—8.

31. *the sockets of the court*] See xxvii. 10, 17.

the pins of the tabernacle...the pins of the court] See on xxvii. 19.

According to the estimate of the shekel that has here been adopted, the weight of the metals mentioned in this chapter would be nearly as follows, in avoirdupois weight:—

Gold, 1 ton 4 cwt. 2 qrs. 13 lbs.
Silver, 4 tons 4 cwt. 2 qrs. 20 lbs.
Bronze, 2 tons 19 cwt. 2 qrs. 11 lbs.

The value of the gold, if pure, in our money would be £175075. 13*s*., and of the silver £38034. 15*s*. 10*d*. The quantities of the precious metals come quite within the limits of probability, if we consider the condition of the Israelites when they left Egypt (see introd. note to Exod. and on xxv. 3), and the object for which the collection was made. There is no reasonable ground to call in question the substantial accuracy of the statements of Strabo (XVI. p. 778) and Diodorus (III. 45) regarding the great stores of gold collected by the Arab tribes near the Ælanitic Gulf, and they were probably still more abundant at this time when the tribes must have come into frequent contact with the Israelites. There may be no trace of native gold in those regions at present; but the entire exhaustion of natural supplies of the precious metals is too familiarly known to need more than a bare notice in this place (see 'Bib. Atlas' of the S. P. C. K. p. 38). Bähr, Knobel and others have remarked that the quantities collected for the Tabernacle are insignificant when compared with the hoards of gold and silver collected in the East in recent, as well as ancient, times. In communities in which there is not much commercial stir, and in consequence not much use for a circulating medium, the precious metals will be more readily accumulated either for a great national object, as in this case, or for the gratification of a ruler. The enormous wealth of the sovereigns, and also of the temples, of India, a century ago, taking the most moderate statements, may furnish examples. As instances in ancient times, we may refer to the accounts of gold in the temple of Belus (Diod. Sic. II. 9; cf. Herodot. I. 183); of the wealth of Sardanapalus (Ctesias, edit. Bähr, p. 431); and of the spoils taken by Cyrus (Plin. 'H. N.' XXXIII. 15, 47) and by Alexander (Diod. Sic. XVII. 66). All reasonable allowance may be made for exaggeration in these statements, and the argument, in its connection with well ascertained facts, will still be left amply strong enough for our purpose. For more examples, see Bähr, 'Symbolik,' I. p. 259; Knobel on Ex. xxv. and xxxviii.

It is worthy of notice that silver, in the time of Homer, appears to have been more precious than gold amongst the Greeks (Gladstone, 'Juventus Mundi,' p. 531). The treasures of Thrace and Laurium were then unknown. But it seems to have been otherwise with the Asiatic nations. The word *silver* (according to Pictet) is Sanscrit. This would tend to shew that the metal was known to the Aryan race before the Germanic nations migrated to the West. The forefathers of the Greeks and Romans probably lost all knowledge of it, and when they again met with it, they gave it quite a different name (ἀργύριον, *argentum*). This same argument may be applied to other metals. But what distinguishes silver is, that it was at first obtained by the people of Southern Europe from sparing, and, perhaps, distant sources. We know that the quantity of silver at Rome was very greatly increased by the contributions obtained in the Punic Wars (Niebuhr, 'Hist. of Rome,' Vol. III. p. 613). By this time Spain had begun to yield its supply. The Hebrews and Egyptians probably obtained the metal in the earliest times both from Asia and Africa.

CHAP. XXXIX.
The Priests' Dresses are made.
1—31.

1. See on xxviii. 5. The fine linen is omitted in this verse, but is mentioned in the next.

[v. 2—21.] EXODUS. XXXIX. 427

^a chap. 31. 10. & 35. 19.

and ^amade the holy garments for Aaron; as the LORD commanded Moses.

2 And he made the ephod *of* gold, blue, and purple, and scarlet, and fine twined linen.

3 And they did beat the gold into thin plates, and cut *it into* wires, to work *it* in the blue, and in the purple, and in the scarlet, and in the fine linen, *with* cunning work.

4 They made shoulderpieces for it, to couple *it* together: by the two edges was it coupled together.

5 And the curious girdle of his ephod, that *was* upon it, *was* of the same, according to the work thereof; *of* gold, blue, and purple, and scarlet, and fine twined linen; as the LORD commanded Moses.

^b chap. 28 9.

6 ¶ ^bAnd they wrought onyx stones inclosed in ouches of gold, graven, as signets are graven, with the names of the children of Israel.

7 And he put them on the shoulders of the ephod, *that they should be* stones

^c chap. 28. 12.

for a ^cmemorial to the children of Israel; as the LORD commanded Moses.

8 ¶ And he made the breastplate *of* cunning work, like the work of the ephod; *of* gold, blue, and purple, and scarlet, and fine twined linen.

9 It was foursquare; they made the breastplate double: a span *was* the length thereof, and a span the breadth thereof, *being* doubled.

10 And they set in it four rows of

¹ Or, *ruby*.

stones: *the first* row *was* a ¹sardius, a topaz, and a carbuncle: this *was* the first row.

11 And the second row, an emerald, a sapphire, and a diamond.

12 And the third row, a ligure, an agate, and an amethyst.

13 And the fourth row, a beryl, an onyx, and a jasper: *they were* inclosed in ouches of gold in their inclosings.

14 And the stones *were* according to the names of the children of Israel, twelve, according to their names, *like* the engravings of a signet, every one with his name, according to the twelve tribes.

15 And they made upon the breastplate chains at the ends, *of* wreathen work *of* pure gold.

16 And they made two ouches *of* gold, and two gold rings; and put the two rings in the two ends of the breastplate.

17 And they put the two wreathen chains of gold in the two rings on the ends of the breastplate.

18 And the two ends of the two wreathen chains they fastened in the two ouches, and put them on the shoulderpieces of the ephod, before it.

19 And they made two rings of gold, and put *them* on the two ends of the breastplate, upon the border of it, which *was* on the side of the ephod inward.

20 And they made two *other* golden rings, and put them on the two sides of the ephod underneath, toward the forepart of it, over against the *other* coupling thereof, above the curious girdle of the ephod.

21 And they did bind the breastplate by his rings unto the rings of the

---

cloths of service] more properly, **the garments of office.** On these and the Holy Garments, see on xxxi. 10.

2. *the ephod*] See on xxviii. 6 sq.

3. *the gold*] See on xxviii. 5.

with cunning work] **with work of the skilled weaver.** See on xxvi. 1, xxxv. 35.

5. *the curious girdle*] See on xxviii. 8.

6, 7. See on xxviii. 9—12.

8. *the breastplate*] See on xxviii. 15, 16.

10—13. On the precious stones, see on xxviii. 17—20.

13. *in their inclosings*] Rather, **in their settings.** See on xxviii. 11, 17.

15. *chains at the ends, of wreathen work*] **chains of wreathen work twisted.** See on xxviii. 14.

16. See on xxviii. 13, 23.

19. See on xxviii. 26, 27.

20. "And they made **two rings of gold** and put them on the **two shoulder-pieces of the Ephod, low down in the front of it, near the joining, above the band for fastening it.**" See on xxviii. 27.

21. See on xxviii. 28.

ephod with a lace of blue, that it might be above the curious girdle of the ephod, and that the breastplate might not be loosed from the ephod; as the Lord commanded Moses.

22 ¶ And he made the robe of the ephod *of* woven work, all *of* blue.

23 And *there was* an hole in the midst of the robe, as the hole of an habergeon, *with* a band round about the hole, that it should not rend.

24 And they made upon the hems of the robe pomegranates *of* blue, and purple, and scarlet, *and* twined *linen*.

25 And they made *d*bells *of* pure gold, and put the bells between the pomegranates upon the hem of the robe, round about between the pomegranates;

26 A bell and a pomegranate, a bell and a pomegranate, round about the hem of the robe to minister *in;* as the Lord commanded Moses.

27 ¶ And they made coats *of* fine linen *of* woven work for Aaron, and for his sons,

28 And a mitre *of* fine linen, and goodly bonnets *of* fine linen, and *e*linen breeches *of* fine twined linen,

29 And a girdle *of* fine twined linen, and blue, and purple, and scarlet, *of* needlework; as the Lord commanded Moses.

30 ¶ And they made the plate of the holy crown *of* pure gold, and wrote upon it a writing, *like to* the engravings of a signet, *f*HOLINESS TO THE LORD.

31 And they tied unto it a lace of blue, to fasten *it* on high upon the mitre; as the Lord commanded Moses.

32 ¶ Thus was all the work of the tabernacle of the tent of the congregation finished: and the children of Israel did according to all that the Lord commanded Moses, so did they.

33 ¶ And they brought the tabernacle unto Moses, the tent, and all his furniture, his taches, his boards, his bars, and his pillars, and his sockets,

34 And the covering of rams' skins dyed red, and the covering of badgers' skins, and the vail of the covering,

35 The ark of the testimony, and the staves thereof, and the mercy seat,

36 The table, *and* all the vessels thereof, and the shewbread,

37 The pure candlestick, *with* the lamps thereof, *even with* the lamps to be set in order, and all the vessels thereof, and the oil for light,

38 And the golden altar, and the anointing oil, and †the sweet incense, and the hanging for the tabernacle door,

39 The brasen altar, and his grate of brass, his staves, and all his vessels, the laver and his foot,

40 The hangings of the court, his pillars, and his sockets, and the hanging for the court gate, his cords, and his pins, and all the vessels of the service of the tabernacle, for the tent of the congregation,

41 The cloths of service to do service in the holy *place,* and the holy garments for Aaron the priest, and his sons' garments, to minister in the priest's office.

42 According to all that the Lord commanded Moses, so the children of Israel made all the work.

43 And Moses did look upon all the work, and, behold, they had done it as the Lord had commanded, even so had they done it: and Moses blessed them.

22—26. See on xxviii. 31—35.
27. See on xxviii. 40, 41.
28. *a mitre*] See on xxviii. 37.
bonnets] See on xxviii. 40.
breeches] See on xxviii. 42.
29. *a girdle*] See on xxviii. 40.
30. *the holy crown of pure gold*] Cf. xxix. 6. See on xxviii. 36.

HOLINESS TO THE LORD] See on xxviii. 36.

The whole work of the Sanctuary is submitted to Moses and approved.
32—43.

33—38. See on xxxv. 11—15, and on xxvi. 1.
39, 40. See on xxxv. 16—18.
41. See *vv.* 1, 27, xxxi. 10.

CHAPTER XL.

The tabernacle is commanded to be reared, 9 and anointed. 13 Aaron and his sons to be sanctified. 16 Moses performeth all things accordingly. 34 A cloud covereth the tabernacle.

AND the LORD spake unto Moses, saying,

2 On the first day of the first month shalt thou set up the tabernacle of the tent of the congregation.

3 And thou shalt put therein the ark of the testimony, and cover the ark with the vail.

4 And *a* thou shalt bring in the table, and set in order †the things that are to be set in order upon it; and thou shalt bring in the candlestick, and light the lamps thereof.

5 And thou shalt set the altar of gold for the incense before the ark of the testimony, and put the hanging of the door to the tabernacle.

6 And thou shalt set the altar of the burnt offering before the door of the tabernacle of the tent of the congregation.

7 And thou shalt set the laver between the tent of the congregation and the altar, and shalt put water therein.

8 And thou shalt set up the court round about, and hang up the hanging at the court gate.

9 And thou shalt take the anointing oil, and anoint the tabernacle, and all that *is* therein, and shalt hallow it, and all the vessels thereof: and it shall be holy.

10 And thou shalt anoint the altar of the burnt offering, and all his vessels, and sanctify the altar: and it shall be an altar †most holy.

11 And thou shalt anoint the laver and his foot, and sanctify it.

12 And thou shalt bring Aaron and his sons unto the door of the tabernacle of the congregation, and wash them with water.

13 And thou shalt put upon Aaron the holy garments, and anoint him, and sanctify him; that he may minister unto me in the priest's office.

14 And thou shalt bring his sons, and clothe them with coats:

15 And thou shalt anoint them, as thou didst anoint their father, that they may minister unto me in the priest's office: for their anointing shall surely be an everlasting priesthood throughout their generations.

a chap. 26. 35.
† Heb. *the order thereof.*

† Heb. *holiness of holinesses.*

CHAP. XL.
Moses is commanded to arrange the holy things, and to anoint them and the priests.
1—11.

2. *On the first day of the first month*] See *v.* 17.

4. *the things that are to be set in order*] The directions given in Lev. xxiv. 5—9 are here presupposed, and must have been issued before this chapter was written.

5. *before the ark*] See on xxx. 6.
the hanging of the door to the tabernacle] **the curtain at the entrance of the Tabernacle.**

6. *before the door of the tabernacle of the tent of the congregation*] **before the entrance of the Tabernacle of the Tent of meeting.**

7, 8. See Note at the end of Ch. xxvi. § VI.

8. *hang up the hanging*] **hang up the entrance curtain.**

9—11. The directions to anoint and consecrate the Tabernacle and the Priests had been previously given xxx. 26—31. They are here repeated in a summary form. The anointing is described Lev. viii. 10—12.

9. *vessels*] **utensils**. The name includes the whole of the furniture of the Tabernacle. See on xxvii. 19.

10. *vessels*] **utensils**.
most holy] In the preceding verse the Tabernacle and its utensils are said to be rendered *holy* by the anointing; the Altar and its utensils are here, and in xxx. 10, said to be *most holy*. The term *most holy* must not in this case be taken as expressing a higher degree of holiness than that which belonged to the Tabernacle; it is only used for emphasis, as a caution (it has been conjectured) in reference to the position of the Altar exposing it to the chance of being touched by the people when they assembled in the Court, while they were not permitted to enter the Tabernacle. The Tabernacle itself, with all that belonged to it, is called *most holy* in xxx. 29.

12. *the door of the tabernacle of the congregation*] **the entrance of the Tent of meeting.** The directions in *vv.* 12—15 had been previously given xxix. 4—9, xxx. 30; the ceremony is described Lev. viii. 5, 6.

16 Thus did Moses: according to all that the Lord commanded him, so did he.

17 ¶ And it came to pass in the first month in the second year, on the first *day* of the month, *that* the ^btabernacle was reared up.

18 And Moses reared up the tabernacle, and fastened his sockets, and set up the boards thereof, and put in the bars thereof, and reared up his pillars.

19 And he spread abroad the tent over the tabernacle, and put the covering of the tent above upon it; as the Lord commanded Moses.

20 ¶ And he took and put the testimony into the ark, and set the staves on the ark, and put the mercy seat above upon the ark:

21 And he brought the ark into the tabernacle, and ^c set up the vail of the covering, and covered the ark of the testimony; as the Lord commanded Moses.

22 ¶ And he put the table in the tent of the congregation, upon the side of the tabernacle northward, without the vail.

23 And he set the bread in order upon it before the Lord; as the Lord had commanded Moses.

a Numb. v. 1.

c chap. 35. 12.

Moses puts the Tabernacle in order.
17—33.

17. *on the first day of the month*] That is, on the first of the month Nisan (xii. 2, xiii. 4), one year, wanting fourteen days, after the departure of the Israelites from Egypt. They had been nearly three months in reaching the foot of Mount Sinai (xix. 1); Moses had spent eighty days on the mountain (xxiv. 18, xxxiv. 28), and some time must be allowed for what is related in chap. xxiv., as well as for the interval between the two periods which Moses spent on the mountain (xxxiii. 1—23). The construction of the Tabernacle and its furniture would thus appear to have occupied something less than half a year. Bleek's objection to this period as too short for the completion of such a work ('Introd. to O. T.' Vol. I. p. 247) is worth nothing if we duly consider the interest which the whole people must have felt in it, and the nature of the structure, so unlike one of solid masonry.

19. The tent cloth was spread over the tabernacle cloth, and the covering of skins was put over the tent cloth. See xxvi. 1, 6, 11, 14; and Note at the end of Ch. xxvi. § II.

20. *the testimony*] *i.e.* the Tables of stone with the Ten Commandments engraved on them (see xxv. 16, xxxi. 18). Nothing else is said to have been put into the Ark. These were found there by themselves in the time of Solomon (1 K. viii. 9; 2 Chron. v. 10). The Pot of Manna was "laid up before the testimony" (Ex. xvi. 34); Aaron's rod was also placed "before the testimony" (Num. xvii. 10); and the Book of the Law was put at "the side of the Ark" (Deut. xxxi. 26). The expression "before the testimony" appears to mean the space immediately in front of the Ark. Most interpreters hold that the Pot of Manna and Aaron's rod were placed between the Ark and the Vail. It is however said in the Epistle to the Hebrews that the Ark contained "the golden pot that had manna, and Aaron's rod that budded, and the tables of the covenant" (ix. 4). From this statement, and from the mode of expression in Kings and Chronicles (which appears to indicate that the fact of the Ark's containing nothing at that time but the Tables was unexpected), it would seem that the other articles were at some period put within the Ark; and this accords with some rabbinical traditions. It has however been conjectured that "before the testimony" may mean the space within the Ark, at the back of which the Tables are supposed to have been placed. But from a comparison of Ex. xxx. 36 with xl. 5, it appears that the two expressions "before the testimony," and "before the ark of the testimony," are equivalent and denote the space in front of the Ark, even extending to the outside of the Vail. Besides this, it is plain that Aaron's Rod, when it was brought "before the testimony," was merely restored to the place "before the Lord in the tabernacle of witness," where it was first placed along with the other rods (Num. xvii.; cf. *v.* 7 with *v.* 10). These considerations, added to the presumption from Ex. xxv. 16, xl. 20, that nothing but the Tables were put into the Ark, seem to afford sufficient evidence that the articles in question were not at first placed within it, but in front of it. It is very probable that the pot and the rod had been put into the Ark before it was taken by the Philistines, but that they were not sent back with the Ark and the Tables. 1 Sam. iv. 11, vi. 11.

the mercy seat] See on xxv. 21.

21. *the vail of the covering*] See on xxxv. 12.

22—24. See on xxv. 23—29, and Lev. xxiv. 5—9.

23. *he set the bread in order*] Moses performed these priestly functions (see on xxviii. 1) of setting the Bread on the Table, lighting

24 ¶ And he put the candlestick in the tent of the congregation, over against the table, on the side of the tabernacle southward.

25 And he lighted the lamps before the LORD; as the LORD commanded Moses.

26 ¶ And he put the golden altar in the tent of the congregation before the vail:

27 And he burnt sweet incense thereon; as the LORD commanded Moses.

28 ¶ And he set up the hanging *at* the door of the tabernacle.

29 And he put the altar of burnt offering *by* the door of the tabernacle of the tent of the congregation, and offered upon it the burnt offering and the meat offering; as the ^d LORD commanded Moses.

30 ¶ And he set the laver between the tent of the congregation and the altar, and put water there, to wash *withal*.

31 And Moses and Aaron and his sons washed their hands and their feet thereat:

32 When they went into the tent of the congregation, and when they came near unto the altar, they washed; as the LORD commanded Moses.

33 And he reared up the court round about the tabernacle and the altar, and set up the hanging of the court gate. So Moses finished the work.

34 ¶ ^e Then a cloud covered the tent of the congregation, and the glory of the LORD filled the tabernacle.

e Numb. 9. 15. 1 Kings 8. 10.

35 And Moses was not able to enter into the tent of the congregation, because the cloud abode thereon, and the glory of the LORD filled the tabernacle.

36 And when the cloud was taken up from over the tabernacle, the children of Israel [†] went onward in all their journeys:

† Heb. *journeyed*

37 But if the cloud were not taken up, then they journeyed not till the day that it was taken up.

38 For the cloud of the LORD *was* upon the tabernacle by day, and fire was on it by night, in the sight of all the house of Israel, throughout all their journeys.

---

the Lamps (*v.* 25), burning Incense (*v.* 27), and offering the Daily Sacrifice (*v.* 29), before the holy things with which they were performed were anointed. The things had been made expressly for the service of Jehovah, by His command, and in this fact lay their essential sanctity, of which the anointing was only the seal and symbol. Aaron and his sons, on similar ground, having had the divine call, took part in the service of the Sanctuary as soon as the work was completed (*v.* 31). But Moses took part with them, and most likely took the lead, until they were consecrated and invested (Lev. viii.) and publicly set apart for the office. See on Lev. viii. 14.

26. *before the vail*] that is, opposite to the Ark, in the middle between the Table of Shewbread on the North and the Candlestick on the South (see on xxx. 36).

28. *set up the hanging,* &c.] **put up the curtain at the entrance to the Tabernacle.**

29. *by the door*] **at the entrance.** It is here evident that the term denoted a broad space in front of the Tabernacle. See Plan, p. 378.

31, 32. See xxx. 18—21.

33. *set up the hanging*] **put up the curtain.** See on xxvi. 36.

The glory of the Lord is manifested on the completed work.

34—38.

34, 35. On the distinction between the Tent as the outer shelter and the Tabernacle as the *dwelling-place* of Jehovah, which is very clear in these verses, see on xxvi. 1. The glory appeared as a light within and as a cloud on the outside.

35. Cf. the entrance of the High-priest into the Holy of Holies on the Day of Atonement, Lev. xvi. 2, 13. For special appearances of this glory in the Tabernacle, see Num. xiv. 10, xvi. 19, 42; cf. Ex. xvi. 10; 1 K. viii. 10, 11.

36—38. This is more fully described Num. ix. 15—23, x. 11, 12, 34.

The Tabernacle, after it had accompanied the Israelites in their wanderings in the wilderness, was most probably first set up in the Holy Land at Gilgal (Josh. iv. 19, v. 10, ix. 6, x. 6, 43). But before the death of

Joshua, it was erected at Shiloh (Josh. xviii. 1, xix. 51). Here it remained as the national Sanctuary throughout the time of the Judges (Josh. xviii. 8, xxi. 2, xxii. 19; Judg. xviii. 31, xxi. 19; 1 S. i. 3, iv. 3). But its external construction was at this time somewhat changed, and *doors*, strictly so called, had taken the place of the entrance curtain (1 S. iii. 15): hence it seems to have been sometimes called *the Temple* (1 S. i. 9, iii. 3), the name by which the structure of Solomon was afterwards commonly known. After the time of Eli it was removed to Nob in the canton of Benjamin, not far from Jerusalem (1 S. xxi. 1—9). From thence, in the time of David, it was removed to Gibeon (1 Chro. xvi. 39, xxi. 29; 2 Chro. i. 3; 1 K. iii. 4, ix. 2). It was brought from Gibeon to Jerusalem by Solomon (1 K. viii. 4). After this, it disappears in the narrative of Scripture. When the Temple of Solomon was built, "the Tabernacle of the Tent" had entirely performed its work; it had protected the Ark of the Covenant during the migrations of the people until they were settled in the Land, and the promise was fulfilled, that the Lord would choose out a place for Himself in which His name should be preserved and His service should be maintained (Deut. xii. 14, 21, xiv. 24).

In accordance with its dignity as the most sacred object in the Sanctuary, the original Ark of the Covenant constructed by Moses was preserved and transferred from the Tabernacle to the Temple. The Golden Altar, the Candlestick and the Shewbread table were renewed by Solomon. They were subsequently renewed by Zerubbabel, and lastly by the Maccabees (see on xxv. 23). But the Ark was preserved in the Temple until Jerusalem was taken by the forces of Nebuchadnezzar (2 Chro. xxxv. 3; Jer. iii. 16). It was never replaced in the Second Temple. (Jos. 'Bell. Jud.' v. 5. § 5; Tacitus, 'Hist.' v. 9). According to a rabbinical tradition, its place was occupied by a block of stone.

NOTE ON CHAP. XL.

ON THE SANCTUARY AS A WHOLE.

I. *The Altar and the Tabernacle.* II. *Names of the Tabernacle.* III. *Order of the Sacred things.* IV. *The Ark and its belongings.* V. *Allegorical explanations.* VI. *Originality of the Tabernacle.*

I.

The two chief objects within the Court were the Brazen Altar and the Tabernacle. As sacrificial worship was no new thing, there is nothing said or intimated as to the purpose of the Altar, either in the instructions for the Sanctuary or in the record of its completion[1]. The intention was merely to provide a *single* Altar of suitable construction for the offerings of the whole nation in such juxtaposition with the Tabernacle as to suit the order of the inspired ritual.

But the Tabernacle was an entirely new matter belonging to the dispensation of the Mosaic Covenant. Its purpose was therefore distinctly set forth at this time. It was to be the symbolical dwelling-place of Jehovah, where He was to meet with His people or their representatives. His own words were: "Let them make me a sanctuary that I may dwell among them."—"I will meet you, to speak there unto thee, and there will I meet with the Children of Israel[2]."

II.

The name most frequently given to the Tabernacle in our Version is, "The Tabernacle (or Tent[3]) of the congregation[4]." But the latter word in Hebrew (מוֹעֵד) signifies *meeting*, in its most general sense, and is always used without the article. The better rendering of the name is **The Tabernacle** (or **The Tent**) **of meeting**, and the idea connected with it is that of Jehovah meeting with either Moses, or the priests, or (in only a few cases[5]) with the people gathered into a congregation at the entrance of the Tent. The English translation is not supported by the old Versions, nor by the best critical authorities. The complete designation is given as "the Tabernacle of the Tent of meeting." Ex. xl. 1, 29, &c.

The Tabernacle is also called, **The Tabernacle** (or **The Tent**) **of the Testimony**[6]. Now this designation evidently relates to the Tabernacle as the depository of the Testimony[7], that is, the Tables of the Law. It has been preferred by the LXX. (ἡ σκηνὴ τοῦ μαρτυρίου) and the Vulgate (*tabernaculum testimonii*), to render not only the Hebrew, which strictly answers to it, but also the name in more common use, which means The Tabernacle of **meeting**. It occurs in the New Testament, Acts vii. 44; Rev. xv. 5.

---

[1] Ex. xxvii. 1—8, xxxviii. 1—7. See note on Ex. xx. 24.
[2] Ex. xxv. 8, xxix. 42, 43. See also Ex. xxvii. 21, xxviii. 12.
[3] On the words *Tabernacle* and *Tent*, in some cases used indifferently for the whole structure, see on xxvi. 1.
[4] Ex. xxvii. 21, xxviii. 43, xxix. 4, 10, 11, 30, xxx. 16, 18, 20, 36, xxxi. 7, xxxv. 21, xl. 2, 6, 7, 12; Lev. i. 1, 3, 5, &c. &c.
[5] Lev. viii. 3. 4; Num. x. 3: cf. Ex. xxxiii. 7.
[6] The Hebrew word (עֵדֻת), in this connection, always has the article. Ex. xxxviii. 21; Num. i. 50, 53, ix. 15, x. 11, xvii. 7, 8, xviii. 2.
[7] See Note on Ex. xx. 1—17, § V.

The second name, of itself, suggests that the Tabernacle owed its character and significance to the Ark with its sacred contents and the Mercy-seat that covered it. Above the Mercy-seat, in a concentrated sense, was the spot where Jehovah communed with His people[1]. The furniture of the Holy Place held a subordinate position, and all its symbolism pointed to the truth which had its deepest and fullest expression in the Ark. In the form and materials of the Tabernacle itself there appears to have been nothing, either in its wood-work or its curtains, but what was most convenient for the arrangement and protection of the holy things and most becoming for beauty. It was in fact a regal Tent[2], in which the Ark symbolized the constant presence of Jehovah, who now condescended to dwell amongst the people whom He had redeemed.

III.

The order in which the chief facts connected with the construction of the Sanctuary are related in the sacred narrative, closely corresponds with the essential relation in which the several parts stand to each other. The Ten Commandments are uttered by the voice of Jehovah from the summit of Mount Sinai, with every circumstance that can show their solemn importance[3]: a short practical compendium of the Law, called the Book of the Covenant[4], is written out by Moses for the occasion: after the Covenant is sealed by sprinkling on the people the blood of Burnt-offerings and Peace-offerings, a mysterious manifestation of the Divine presence is made to Moses, Aaron and the Elders[5]: Moses is then summoned to the Mount and receives instructions first for making the Ark that was to contain the tables of the Ten Commandments with the Mercy-seat that was to cover them[6], next for the holy things that were to be placed in the Holy Place, and not till then, for the Tabernacle with its Tent and its Covering[7]: after this, the Brazen Altar and the Court are described[8], and directions are given for the consecration of those who had to minister at the Altar and the Tabernacle[9]: what may be regarded as a supplementary section relating to the Golden Altar[10] and some other things, is followed by the appointment of the workmen and a repetition of the Law for the observance of the Sabbath-day[1]. These practical instructions being completed, the precious gift of the Tables of the Law is put into the hands of Moses[2]. This arrangement of the particulars is the more noticeable, because the articles are named in reversed order in the account of the construction of the work[3].

IV.

The Ten Commandments conveyed no new revelation in the details of their subject matter. Every duty enjoined in them may be found expressed in no obscure terms in the earlier portion of the Pentateuch. But the old truths were now for the first time embodied and proclaimed to the people in connection with their lately recovered freedom. Hence they were put into new relations with other truths, and were combined with them in expressing the will of Jehovah. The tables of the Testimony did not however, by themselves, form the central point of the Sanctuary. It required the complete Ark that contained them, with the Mercy-seat that covered them, to convey the true meaning of the Covenant that was based on the name of Jehovah as it was revealed to Moses[4].

We may regard then the sacred contents of the Tabernacle as figuring what was peculiar to the Covenant of which Moses was the Mediator, the closer union of God with Israel and their consequent election as "a kingdom of priests, an holy nation[5]:" while the Brazen Altar in the Court not only bore witness for the old sacrificial worship by which the Patriarchs had drawn nigh to God, but formed an essential part of the Sanctuary, signifying, by its now more fully developed system of Sacrifices[6] in connection with the Tabernacle, those ideas of Sin and Atonement, which were first distinctly brought out by the revelation of the Law and the sanctification of the nation[7].

V.

Keeping strictly to the conclusions that appear clearly to follow from the sacred narrative, there seems to be neither occasion nor place for those allegorical explanations of the Tabernacle which are so often found in commentators, both Jewish and Christian. Philo[8], Josephus[9], Theodoret[10], Jerome[11], with other Fathers, and some of the Rabbinists, supposed

---

[1] Ex. xxv. 22.
[2] See Note on chap. xxvi.
[3] Ex. xix, xx.
[4] See on Ex. xx. 22.
[5] Ex. xxiv. According to the Epistle to the Hebrews, the Book was sprinkled as well as the people; see Heb. ix. 19.
[6] See on Ex. xxv. 10—16.
[7] See Note on Ex. xxvi.
[8] Ex. xxvii.
[9] Ex. xxviii, xxix.
[10] See on Ex. xxx. 1.

[1] Ex. xxxi. 1—17. [2] Ex. xxxi. 18.
[3] Ex. xxxvi, xxxvii.
[4] Ex. xxxiv. 6, 7. See Note on ch. xx. § VI.
[5] Ex. xix. 6.
[6] See Lev. i.—vii.
[7] See notes on Lev. iv.
[8] 'Vit. Mos.' III. 6.
[9] 'Ant.' III. 7. § 7. Cf. 'Bel. Jud.' v. 5. § 4, where the same explanation is applied to the Temple.
[10] 'Quæst. in Exod.' 60.
[11] 'Epist.' LXIV. § 9.

that the structure was a type of the material universe of heaven and earth which the Lord had created as an abode for Himself. It appears however that no two of these writers agree together in the application of this theory to the several parts. Bähr[1], following in this general track, has elaborated with curious ingenuity an explanation of almost every recorded particular in the description of Moses.—In other lines of speculation, the Tabernacle has been taken as a symbol of human nature (Luther), and as a prophetic type of the Christian Church (Cocceius).

VI.

It has been usual, especially since the time of Spencer, to seek out parallels from heathen antiquity for the Tabernacle itself, but more particularly for the Ark of the Covenant. The Tabernacle has been compared with several moveable temples of which there are notices in ancient writers, the most remarkable of which seems to be "the Sacred Tent" ($\dot{\eta}$ $\dot{\iota}\epsilon\rho\grave{a}$ $\sigma\kappa\eta\nu\dot{\eta}$) of the Carthaginians mentioned by Diodorus[2].

The Ark of the Covenant has been most generally likened to the arks, or moveable shrines, which are represented on Egyptian monuments[3]. The Egyptian arks were carried in a similar manner by poles resting on men's shoulders, and some of them had on the cover two winged figures not unlike what we conceive the golden Cherubim to have been. Thus far the similarity is striking. But there were points of great dissimilarity. Between the winged figures on the Egyptian arks there was placed the material symbol of a deity, and the arks themselves were carried about in religious processions, so as to make a show in the eyes of the people. We know not what they contained. As regards the Ark of the Covenant, the absence of any symbol of God was one of its great characteristics. It was never carried in a ceremonial procession: when it was moved from one place to another, it was closely packed up, concealed from the eyes even of the Levites who bore it[4]. When the Tabernacle was pitched, the Ark was never exhibited, but was kept in solemn darkness. Rest, it is evident, was its appointed condition. It was occasionally moved out of its place in the Holy of Holies, but only as long as the nation was without a settled capital, and had something of the character of an army on the march. During this period it accompanied the army on several occasions[1]. But it had been foretold that the time should come when the Sanctuary was to be fixed[2], and when this was fulfilled, we are told that "the Ark had rest[3]." It was never again moved till the capture of Jerusalem by the forces of Nebuchadnezzar[4]. Not less, we may fairly suppose, was it distinguished from all other arks in the simple grandeur of its purpose: it was constructed to contain the plain text of the Ten Commandments written on stone in words that were intelligible to all.

Such resemblances to foreign patterns as have been mentioned are without doubt interesting; but it should always be kept in view that they are extremely superficial. The Israelites could hardly have been in contact with the Egyptians for so long a period without learning much of their arts and customs. It is most likely that they were in the habit of using the same tools and modes of construction. In order to attain a given end they probably used similar mechanical contrivances. There are certain points of likeness in the descriptions of Moses and what we know of Egyptian art, which would clearly prove that the Israelites had dwelt in Egypt[5]. But on the whole, it seems wonderful that there is so little in the Sanctuary to remind us of any foreign association. Besides such distinctions as might naturally be ascribed to the difference between an idol's temple and a structure meant to express the Covenant between the unseen Lord and His people, there is in the Tabernacle an originality, both in its general arrangement and in its details, which is by far more striking than any resemblance that may be traced between it and heathen models.

---

[1] 'Symbolik,' Vol. I. p. 75.
[2] Lib. xx. 65: others are mentioned by Knobel.
[3] Wilkinson, 'Pop. Acc.' Vol. I. p. 267.—The articles in Smith's and Kitto's Dictionaries.— Smith, 'The Pentateuch,' p. 260, &c. &c.— On the arks of other ancient nations, see Bähr, 'Symbolik,' Vol. I. 399, and Knobel, p. 262.
[4] Num. iv. 5, 6, 19, 20.

[1] 1 S. iv. 3, xiv. 18; 2 S. xi. 11.
[2] Deut. xii. 10, 11.
[3] 1 Chro. vi. 31; cf. xvi. 1.
[4] See concluding note on Exod. xl.—It is strange that Knobel and others should regard such occasions as are described Josh. vi. 8, 2 S. vi. 12--16, as of the nature of ceremonial processions.
[5] Hengstenberg has not stated the argument too confidently in his 'Egypt and the Books of Moses,' but he has certainly brought some very fanciful instances to its support.

NOTE ON THE ROUTE OF THE ISRAELITES FROM RAMESES TO SINAI. F. C. C.

(Chaps. XVI. XVII. XIX.)

The commentary on the first nineteen chapters of Exodus had been some time in print, when the results of the survey of the western districts of the Sinaitic peninsula were communicated to the writer. Some conclusions to which he had been led by the researches of travellers, of which the fullest account is given in Ritter's work on Sinai and Palestine (see Band 1. p. 517—638), were materially affected by the information which he received from Captain Wilson, of the Royal Engineers, who with Captain Palmer, R. E., conducted the survey, and from the Rev. F. W. Holland, who accompanied the expedition, and had previously spent much time in exploring the Peninsula, of which he has prepared a valuable map, published by the Geographical Society.

The first part of the route, from Rameses to Elim, is not affected by these new sources of information, and the notes remain untouched. It may, however, be convenient to touch briefly on this portion in order to present a clear and connected view of the circumstances which may have determined the direction of the march. The first two days' march brought the Israelites from Rameses to Etham. Rameses was the general name of the district in the time of Jacob; the principal city built by the Israelites was probably situate on the ancient canal at some distance from the frontier. Etham was on the edge of the wilderness, at the point where the road towards Palestine branched off; and the direction of the journey was turned southwards, towards the encampment by the sea at Baal-zephon. See xii. 37, xiii. 20, xiv. 2, 3. Etham, which is probably identical with Pithom, is held by the writer of this note to correspond to the ancient Heroopolis, the frontier city of Egypt, near the southern extremity of Lake Timsah. The journey from this place to Suez would occupy sufficient time for a communication to be made to Pharaoh, and for the rapid march of his army[1]. The Israelites

[1] The subjoined sketch, prepared by the Rev. S. Clark, shows the route of the Israelites from Rameses to 'Ayún Músa, and the probable extent of the Red Sea north of its present bed in the time of Moses. Mr Clark identifies Etham with a spot near Serapeum.

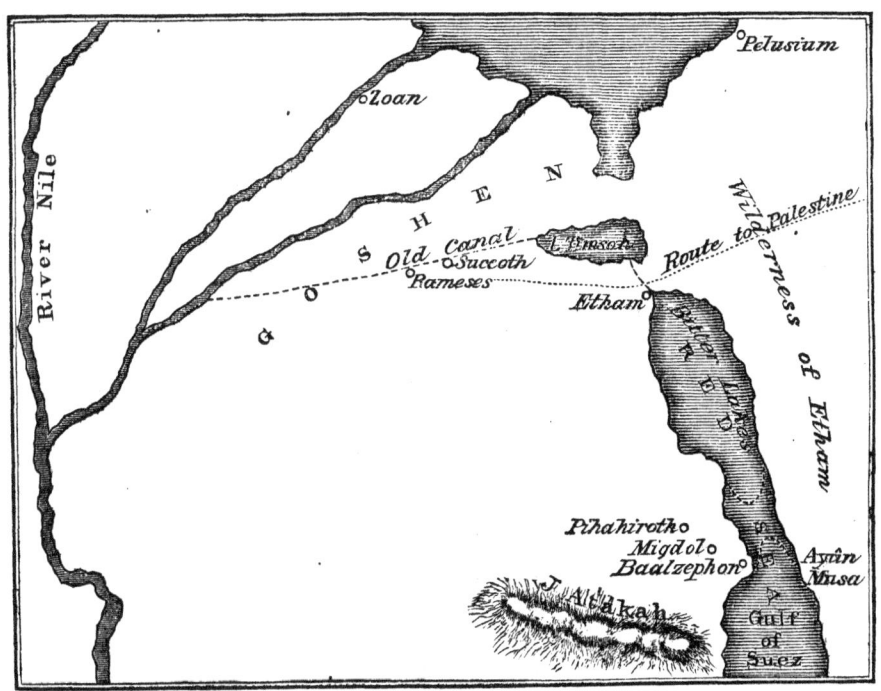

must have had a considerable start in order to reach the encampment of Suez before they were overtaken, but they could scarcely have been so near to Suez when at Etham as the site fixed upon by Robinson would bring them, or the passage could have been effected without interruption. That passage took place, as nearly all modern critics admit, near Suez, where sands of considerable extent were passable when "the Lord caused the sea to go back by a strong east wind," which blew all the night; see c. xiv. 21. After crossing the sea the Israelites would naturally make their first station at 'Ayún Músa, where they would find an ample supply of water: passing thence by Marah they reached Elim, when they encamped under the palm-trees, by the waters. Elim is generally identified with the Wady Gharandel. It is probable that the Israelites remained there several days and then advanced to the station on the Red Sea, near the headland called Ras-Selima, or, as in the map, Ras Abu Zenimeh.

The difference of opinions as to the course pursued by the Israelites up to this point is limited to questions of secondary importance; but from Elim two principal routes lead to Sinai, one by El Markha and Wady Feiran, the other, less circuitous, through a succession of Wadys on the north-east. Both these routes are reported by Captain Wilson, R.E. to be practicable even for a large host like that of the Israelites: the former is the more easy of transit; the latter has the advantage of an abundant supply of excellent water at the beginning of the journey. At the one end of the route it may be regarded as settled that the station by Ras-Selima was the starting-point, if not for the whole host, yet for the head-quarters of the Israelites. At the other extremity the reasons which will be adduced appear to prove that Ras Sufsafeh was the summit from which the Law was delivered, and the Wady er Rahah the wilderness of Sinai on which the people were assembled to hear it.

The facts stated in Exodus and in the itinerary in Numbers xxxiii. are these. The first station was in the wilderness of Sin, which lay between Elim and Sinai. The people remained there some days: we find no complaint of want of water, but they suffered from want of food, and were supplied first with quails and then with manna. From this wilderness they advanced, encamping first at Dophkah, then at Alush; thence they went to Rephidim, where they found no water until it was supplied by a miracle from the rock of Horeb. At Rephidim they were attacked by the Amalekites. Their next encampment was in the wilderness of Sinai. Some fifteen days elapsed between the first encampment in the wilderness of Sin and their arrival at the Mount of God: compare xvi. 1, and xix. 1.

We may first consider the claims of the more direct route, advocated with great ability by Knobel, whose view has been adopted by Keil, and is accepted in the foot-notes of this commentary. It has been fully described by Burckhardt, Robinson and other travellers, whose accounts are generally corroborated by Captains Wilson and Palmer and by Mr Holland.

From Ras Abu Zenimeh this route passes through several Wadys to a wide undulating plain, the Debbet er Ramleh. This desert is identified by Knobel with the wilderness of Sin. It corresponds in many striking particulars with the accounts of that wilderness: bare, wild, and desolate, it would offer no refreshment to the Israelites after their first long and laborious march. It lies, properly speaking, between Elim and the Sinaitic group in which greenstone and porphyry take the place of the sandstone of the desert. The word Debbet moreover corresponds exactly in meaning to Sin[1]; and at Wady Nasb, the first station on this route, there is a copious supply of water: a circumstance which, combined with the supply of quails and manna, gives a probable reason for the delay of some days in this wilderness. From Wady Nasb the road passes by Sarábit el Khadim. At this place the Egyptians worked mines of great extent, and the remains of buildings with numerous inscriptions prove that it was occupied by an Egyptian colony before the time of Moses. The existence of this settlement presents conflicting arguments for and against the selection of this route by Moses. On the one hand it may be reasoned that he would avoid coming into contact with Egyptians, especially since this must have been a military station, and a conflict would seem inevitable, since the sojourn in the district extended over some days. On the other hand it is admitted that the Egyptians would keep the entire route from Ras Selima in good order, and take great care to protect the sources of water: nor considering that the whole colony, as Captain Wilson states, could not consist of more than 1000 men, is it at all probable that they would attempt to arrest the advance of the vast host of the Israelites; especially if, as may be assumed, they had received information of the destruction of Pharaoh's host in the Red Sea.

The road from Sarábit el Khadim is extremely rough; but, as military authorities affirm, not impracticable even for light waggons, such as the Israelites probably used. Dophkah is assumed by Knobel to be in the Wady Sih, both names having the same meaning[2]. Alush,

---

[1] Freytag, in his Arabic lexicon, s. v. explains the former to mean "arena æquabilis et plana," the latter Sin, or Sinin, "arena elatior et longius protensa per regionis superficiem," a most exact description of this district.

[2] سيح, *sih*, flowing waters, the same being the meaning of دفق, *dafaka*, from which דפקה was probably derived.

EXODUS. XVI. XVII. XIX.

Country through which the Israelites must have passed on their way to Mount Sinai.

according to the same critic, may be the Wady el 'Esh, where there is a spring of good water: a journey of two hours from this point ends in the Wady es Sheikh.

The correspondence of the sites and even of the names on this route, and of the circumstances of the journey, presents a strong if not conclusive argument in its favour, nor is the argument affected by any discoveries made in the late survey. The notes on the text are therefore left in their original form; the writer still retaining, though with some diffidence in face of the opinions of the explorers, his conviction that Knobel is right, so far as this part of the route is concerned.

We have now to consider the other main route. The first day's journey from Ras Abu Zenimeh southwards leads through a narrow slip of barren sand to the open plain of El Markha. From this a Wady at once opens on the east, leading to the Wady Feiran. This route is most unlikely to have been selected by the Israelites: it would have brought them into contact with Egyptians in a district occupied by that people for centuries, nor do the narrow passes present any features corresponding to the wilderness of Sin. On the south, however, a very even and tolerably wide tract of desert land extends through El Markha, and at its southern extremity, by a sudden turn eastwards, through the Wady Feiran just described. This tract is identified by the conductors of the survey and by Mr Holland with the wilderness of Sin. They consider it to be the route which Moses would naturally have followed having once reached the station by Ras Selima. The chief objection to this view is that there are no springs of water in the district; to which it is answered that the Israelites who had waggons (see Num. vii. 3) and oxen would of course bring with them a supply, which might suffice for a rapid march until they reached the upper part of the Wady Feiran. The march however was not rapid, since there was a considerable delay, probably a whole week, in the wilderness of Sin. The route then passes north east of Mount Serbal, till it meets the Wady Sheikh, from which point two routes lead to Er Rahah and Ras-Sufsafeh; the one direct, but rough at the upper end; the other circuitous, but well adapted for the march and encampment of the Israelites. In Wady es Sheikh about midway this route meets the upper route previously described.

The question on which the explorers differ is one of great importance. It touches the site of Rephidim, where the Israelites first suffered for want of water, and where they defeated the Amalekites. Captains Wilson and Palmer hold that the battle was fought in the Wady Feiran, under Mount Serbal. Mr. Holland places Rephidim at the pass of Al Watiyeh, at the eastern end of Wady es Sheikh, to the north of the point where it joins the Wady ed Deir, which leads to Sinai.

If indeed the Israelites passed through Wady Feiran, it seems improbable that they should not have come into collision with the natives. From El Hesweh it is a well-watered district, winding for a considerable distance through defiles which could be easily defended by a people who had been trained for warfare by centuries of fierce struggles with the Egyptians: on the adjoining highlands towards Jebel Serbal remains of curious buildings, which undoubtedly belong to a very ancient period, still attest the presence of a numerous population along this route[1]. The site of the battle with the Amalekites is fixed by Captain Wilson near the ancient city of Feiran. The hill on which Moses witnessed the combat is supposed by Dr Stanley, 'S. and P.' p. 41, to be the rocky eminence which commands the palm-grove, on which in early Christian times stood the church and palace of the bishops of Paran. Captain Wilson holds it to be the Jebel Tahûneh, on the opposite side of the Wady. The whole of the Wady Feiran may have been cleared of the Amalekites by the decisive victory; after which the Israelites halted some time, with their head-quarters under the palm-groves, when they were visited by Jethro. This view assumes the identification of the Mount of God where Moses encamped in the wilderness, c. xviii. 5, with Mount Serbal, a conjecture of Ritter's which seems open to grave objection, since the Mount of God in Exodus is in all probability the group of Sinai, and the term "wilderness" is scarcely applicable to the palm-groves of Feiran. From this place the Israelites might have proceeded to the Wady er Rahah, either by Wady es Sheikh, the longer route, but presenting no impediments; or by the W. Solaf, which though rugged in part is not impracticable, and in Captain Wilson's opinion would most probably have been pursued.

Mr Holland, on the other hand, believes that the Israelites passed through the Wady Feiran without encountering opposition, and that they then traversed the Wady es Sheikh; Rephidim he places at the pass, called El

[1] Mr Holland describes them in a paper read at the Church Congress, 1869. After careful examination he came to the conclusion that they were probably the tombs and store-houses of the ancient Amalekites. They evidently were the work of a large and powerful people who inhabited the peninsula at a very early period. There are indications that they were, to some extent, an agricultural, as well as a pastoral people, a point of great importance in its bearings upon the probable condition of the neighbourhood of Mount Sinai at the time of the Exodus. See Introduction, p. 245. The Egyptian names of the old inhabitants were Anu and Mentu.

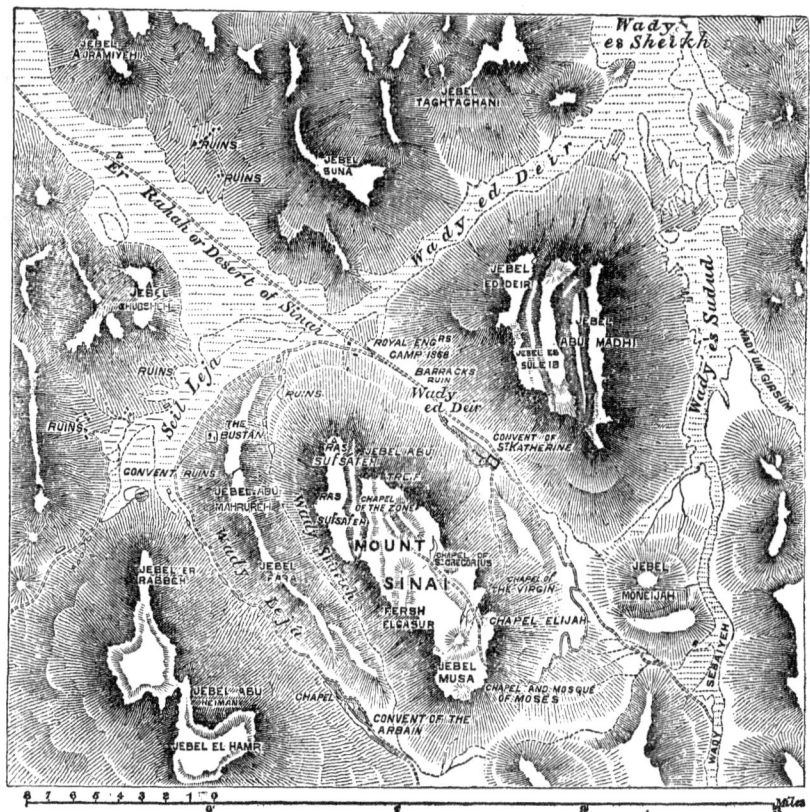

Group of Mount Sinai from the Ordnance Survey[1].

Watîyeh; it is shut in by perpendicular rocks on either side. The Amalekites holding this defile would be in a position of great strength: and their choice of this point for the attack is well accounted for, supposing the Israelites to have reached it without previous molestation. It commands the entrance to the Wadys surrounding the central group of Sinai, on and about which the Bedouins pasture their flocks during the summer. All the requirements of the narrative appear to be satisfied by this assumption. On the north is a large plain destitute of water for the encampment of the Israelites; there is a conspicuous hill to the north of the defile commanding the battle-field, presenting a bare cliff, such as we may suppose the rock to have been which Moses struck with his rod. On the south of the pass is another plain sufficient for the encampment of the Amalekites, within easy reach of an abundant supply of water. At the foot of the hill on which Moses most probably sat, if this be Rephidim, the Arabs point out a rock, which they call "the seat of the prophet Moses."

Taking all points into consideration we feel constrained to adopt one of the following alternatives. If, as the explorers hold, the Israelites passed through the Wady Feiran, the conflict with the Amalekites must have taken place on the spot fixed upon by Captains Wilson

---

[1] The engravings which accompany this note were supplied by General Sir Henry James, F.R.S.

The first is an accurate representation of a raised model of that group, together with the adjoining Wadys, which is at the Topographical department. The model is on the scale of six inches to the mile, and represents the natural features in their true proportions.

The other is taken from a photograph, which represents the northern end of the Sinaitic group, with Ras-Sufsafeh in the centre, and the extensive plain of the Wady Rahah in front.

and Palmer. If however the battle field was at El Watiyeh the Israelites may have reached it by the upper route, which meets the lower about midway in the Wady es Sheikh. The arguments appear to the writer to preponderate in favour of this view, which accepts all the facts ascertained by the Expedition of Survey, and presents a series of coincidences of great weight in the settlement of the question.

From this point the writer accepts without hesitation the conclusion to which all the persons concerned in the Survey unanimously arrive touching the encampment of the Israelites in the wilderness of Sinai. The representation of the Sinaitic group here given will enable the reader to judge of the weight of the arguments which led to that conclusion.

The opinion which formerly appeared to the writer to be sustained by the strongest evidence identified Jebel Musa with the peak of Sinai. This view was advocated by Ritter. He supposed that on the south of Jebel Musa there is a plain of great extent, the Wady Sebaiyeh, in which the Israelites could assemble in front of the mount. The pyramidal height of Jebel Musa is described as rising over it like a monolithic wall of granite, a sheer precipice of 2000 feet; on the summit the mosque, the Christian chapel, and even the so-called stone of Moses, are seen distinctly from the plain; which Wellsted, Vol. II. p. 34, describes in terms which might have seemed conclusive.

"We crossed a large plain terminating in a broad and extensive valley. It has been objected to the identification of Jebel Musa with Mount Sinai, that the narrow valleys and ravines contiguous to it could not have contained the immense multitude of Israelites. *In this valley however there is more than ample space for them:* while at the same time at its termination Mount Sinai stands forth in naked majesty." A traveller who spent some time in the neighbourhood lately informed the writer of this note that the description is quite accurate, and that it is the only plain where the host could have been assembled. Tischendorf, who notices the extent of the plain, specially adapted for so great an event, observes that "the situation supplies an excellent illustration of the words in c. xix. 12, 'that ye go not up unto the mount, nor touch the border of it;' for in this plain the mountain can be touched in the literal sense, rising sheer from the plain, standing before the eye from base to summit as a whole;" and again, "Seldom could one so properly be said to stand at the nether part of the mount as in the plain at the foot of Sinai looking upwards to the granite summit 2000 feet high."

The view of Jebel Musa is admitted to be singularly striking. Lepsius says of the ascent that it lies between vast heights and rocks of the wildest and grandest character, giving the impression of an approach to a spot of historical interest. The ascent from the chapel of Elijah occupies about three-quarters of an hour to the summit, a height of 7,530 to 7,548 feet. On the top is a level space 70 or 80 feet in width. Travellers give different accounts of the view from this spot. Seetzen and Burckhardt could see nothing; when they visited it the whole district was covered with a dense mist. Robinson speaks slightingly of the effect: and Ruppell says that the view is shut in by higher mountains on all sides except the north, on which he looked over a vast expanse including the desert of Er Ramleh, which is identified in these notes with the wilderness of Sin. Wellsted, however, who explored the district with unusual care, gives a most impressive description of the view. Vol. II. p. 97. He ascended the mount in very clear weather in January 1833, and took accurate trigonometrical measurements over an extent of 90 miles. "The view comprehends a vast circle. The gulphs of Suez and Akaba were distinctly visible, and from the dark blue waters of the latter the island of Tiran, sacred to Isis, rears itself. Mount Agrib on the other side points to the land of bondage. Before me is St Catherine, its bare conical peak now capped with snow. In magnificence and striking effect few parts of the world can surpass the wild naked scenery everywhere met with in the mountain-chain which girds the sea-coast of Arabia. Several years wholly passed in cruising along its shores have rendered all its varieties familiar to me, but I trace no resemblance to any other in that before me: it has a character of its own. Mount Sinai itself and the hills which compose the district in its immediate vicinity, rise in sharp, isolated conical peaks. From their steep and shattered sides huge masses have been splintered, leaving fissures rather than valleys between their remaining portions. These form the highest part of the range of mountains that, spread over the peninsula, are very generally in the winter months covered with snow, the melting of which occasions the torrents which everywhere devastate the plains below. The peculiarities of its conical formation render this district yet more distinct from the adjoining heights which appear in successive ridges beyond it, while the valleys between them are so narrow that they can scarcely be perceived. No villages and castles as in Europe here animate the picture: no forests, lakes, or falls of water break the silence and monotony of the scene. All has the appearance of a vast and desolate wilderness either grey, or darkly brown, or wholly black. Few who stand on the summit of Mount Sinai, and gaze from its fearful height upon the dreary wilderness below, will fail to be impressed with the fitness of the whole scene for the sublime and awful dispensation, which an almost universal tradition declares to have been revealed there." Schubert's description, quoted by Ritter, 'Sinai,' p. 587, fully corroborates this account. "The summit of the mount was reached, a holy place to the mightier half of the nations of the earth, to Jews, Moslems and Christians. The view from its height of 7000 feet extends over a circle of more than 360 miles in diameter, and 1600 miles in circumference: a rugged outline of a desert panorama of terrible beauty under the blue vault of the purest and brightest heaven of Arabia. No other place comes near to it in all this. On the east and west the eye catches glimpses of the girdle of sea which encircles the highlands of the Peninsula: beyond it are seen the ranges of Arabian and Egyptian heights. In the space between no green meadow, no cultivated field, no wood, no brook, no village, no Alpine hut. Only storm and thunder resound in the wilderness of Sinai, else for ever silent: a chain of rock standing as on the third day of creation when as yet there was no grass, no tree upon the earth: a mass of granite, unmingled with later formations; none of its abrupt deep ravines are filled up with sandstone, or chalk, or other alluvial deposits: strata of Greywacke and Basalt run like black veins for leagues through its walls and peaks. Here on such a spot as this was the law given, which pointed to Christ by whom it was fulfilled."

The accuracy of these descriptions is borne out by the accounts of other travellers. Thus Henniker quoted by Dr Stanley, 'S. P.' p. 12: "The view from Jebel Musa (where the particular aspect of the infinite complication of jagged peaks and varied ridges is seen with the greatest perfection) is as if Arabia Petræa were an ocean of lava, which, whilst its waves were running mountains high, had suddenly stood still."

Unfortunately for this hypothesis the raised model, from which the plan is taken, proves that the valley immediately below Jebel Musa could not have held a considerable portion of the Israelites; it is, as Dean Stanley describes it, rough, uneven, and narrow. It is proved, moreover, that there is no level plain in the Wady Sebaiyeh on which the Israelites could be assembled within sight of the summit of Jebel Musa, which however is visible at many points between the entrance of the Wady (which lies to the south-east) and its farthest end, a distance of nearly seven miles. This circumstance, which rests on the authority of military surveyors, seems conclusive. Jebel Musa, the loftiest and grandest summit of the group, may have been included in the tremendous manifestations of divine power, but the announcement of the Law must have taken place elsewhere.

On the northern extremity however there is a concurrence of circumstances in favour of Ras Sufsafeh. At its foot lies the plain Wady ed Deir extending to the north-east, meeting the Wady es Sheikh, which has been above

The Mountains of Sinai, Ras Sufsafeh in the centre. The foreground is the extensive plain of Wady Rahah.
(Photograph by the Ordnance Survey.)

identified with Rephidim, and immediately in front the far wider plain Er Rahah; to the left a plain of greater extent than was previously supposed, the Seil Leja. From every part of these two Wadys the granite rock of Ras Sufsafeh is distinctly visible, and there is space for the entire host of the Israelites, taking the highest calculation of their numbers. This fact, of cardinal importance in the question, is attested by the military officers who conducted the survey.

Indeed Sir Henry James concurs with those officers in the opinion that no spot in the world can be pointed out which combines in a more remarkable manner the conditions of a commanding height, and of a plain in every part of which the sights and sounds described in Exodus would reach an assembled multitude of more than two million souls. The description of Ras Sufsafeh, the central height in the subjoined engraving, taken from the photographs, presents many remarkable coincidences; and though inferior in height to the peak of Jebel Musa, it satisfies the main conditions of the narrative.

Dean Stanley, 'S. P.' p. 42—44, has drawn out, with his usual felicity of expression, the most striking characteristics of the scenery. He observes that the existence of such a plain in front of such a cliff is so remarkable a coincidence with the sacred narrative, as to furnish a strong internal argument, not only of its identity with the scene, but of the scene itself having been described by an eye-witness. He then dilates upon other not less impressive circumstances. The awful and lengthened approach as to some natural sanctuary; the plain not broken and narrowly shut in, like almost all others in the range, but presenting a long retiring sweep against which the people could remove and stand afar off; the cliff rising like a huge altar in front of the whole congregation, and visible against the sky in lonely grandeur from end to end of the whole plain, the very image of the "mount that might be touched," and from which the "voice" of God might be heard far and wide over the stillness of the plain below, widened at that point to the utmost extent by the confluence of all the contiguous valleys; the place where beyond all other parts of the Peninsula is the adytum withdrawn as if in the end of the world from all the stir and confusion of earthly things. We are also indebted to Dean Stanley for noting other details which are fully borne out by the late exploration, and scarcely leave room for doubt as to the exact point of the delivery of the Law. A small eminence at the entrance of the convent valley is marked by the name of Aaron, from which he is believed to have witnessed the festival of the golden calf; a tradition which fixes the locality of the encampment on Wady Rahah. Two other points meet here and nowhere else; first Moses is described as descending the mountain without seeing the people, the shout strikes the ear of his companion before they ascertain the cause; the view breaks on him suddenly as he draws nigh to the camp, and he throws down the tables and dashes them in pieces "beneath the mount:" now any one descending the mountain path by which Ras Sufsafeh is accessible (according to Captain Wilson in three-quarters of an hour to a practised mountaineer) through the oblique gullies which flank it, would hear the sounds borne through the silence of the plain, but would not see the plain itself until he emerged from the lateral Wady; and when he did so he would be immediately under the precipitous cliff of Sufsafeh. The brook which came down from the mount is probably identified with that which flows through the Seil Leja.

Taking all these circumstances into consideration it seems impossible to resist the conclusion that the Law was delivered on Ras Sufsafeh, to the Israelites encamped in the plain below.

ESSAY I.

ON THE BEARINGS OF EGYPTIAN HISTORY UPON THE PENTATEUCH.

1. Sources of Egyptian history. 2. General results. 3. List of Pharaohs from 12th to 20th Dynasty. 4. Time of Abram's visit; objections and proofs; Story of the two Brothers; Benihassan; Story of Saneha; presents to Abram. 5. Time of Joseph; invasion of Hyksos; inquiry into Manetho's statements; era of Set Nubte. 6. Apepi or Apophis not the Pharaoh of Joseph. 7. Connection of 12th Dynasty with On. 8. Tomb of Chnumhotep; Egyptian nomes. 9. Egyptian irrigation; labyrinth under Amenemha III. 10. Probable condition of the Israelites under the Hyksos. 11. Inquiry into date of Exodus. 12. Amosis or Aahmes I., a new king, a conqueror, builder of ports, &c., employs forced labourers. 13. Chronology, dates examined. 14. Last year of Thotmes II.; probable date of the Exodus. 15. Amenophis I. 16. Thotmes I. 17. Thotmes II.; events of reign; character of Queen Hatasou. 18. Campaigns of Thotmes III. concluded 40 years after decease of Thotmes II. 19. Objections considered. 20. Amenophis II. and Thotmes IV. 21. Amenophis III. and the Queen Tei. 22. Religious revolution in Egypt. 23. Statements of Manetho, Cheremon, Lysimachus, and Diodorus. 24. The identification of Rameses II. with the Pharaoh of Moses considered. 25. State of Palestine under the early Judges. 26. Campaigns of Seti I. against the Cheta. 27. Rameses II., length of reign, first campaign in Syria. 28. Fortresses built or enlarged. 29. Employment of Aperu identified with Hebrew captives. 30. Alliance of Rameses with Cheta. 31. State of Palestine described in Egyptian Papyrus. 32. State of Goshen at the same time incompatible with occupation by Israelites. 33. Reign of Merneptah; events and dates coincide with the first hypothesis in this Essay. 34. Rameses III.

---

(1) Our knowledge of early Egyptian history is derived chiefly from monumental inscriptions and papyri, which have been deciphered within the last few years; partly also from fragments of Manetho, and from the accounts of Greeks who visited Egypt after the close of the Old Testament history.[1]

The historical notices drawn from the last source have little independent value. Facts of importance, corroborated by modern researches, are recorded by Herodotus, Diodorus, and other Greeks, but they are mixed with legends, disfigured by manifest forgeries, and their statements, so far as regards the chronology, are irreconcileable with contemporary inscriptions.

The fragments of Manetho[2] have a higher value. He was a priest, conversant with the literature of ancient Egypt, and had access to monuments which, under the Ptolemies, were for the most part in a state of perfect preservation. The original history perished at a very early period, and is only known from extracts in Josephus. The catalogue of Kings begins with gods, and continues through thirty dynasties of mortals, ending with Nectanebo 343 B.C. The list is derived from authentic sources, but there are numerous errors and mis-statements attributable in part to the ignorance or carelessness of transcribers. This remark applies to names, but still more to dates, which are seldom confirmed, and often contradicted, by the monuments.[3]

The facts drawn from old Egyptian documents are to be found in the first volume of Bunsen's 'Egypt.' The extracts in Josephus are taken from the Αἰγυπτιακά; the catalogue of dynasties is preserved by Syncellus, 800 A.D., in two widely-differing recensions, one from the lost 'Chronographia' of Julius Africanus, 220 A.D., the other from the 'Chronicon' of Eusebius, of which we have now the Armenian version.

---

[1] The principal object of this dissertation is to bring the latest discoveries to bear upon biblical questions, reference is therefore seldom made to works of great value already well known to all students. It is right to observe that it was printed in 1868; a few references have been made in the notes, and two or three in the text, to works which have appeared before the last revision in 1870.

[2] The best account of Manetho is given by Rev. H. Browne in Kitto's 'Cyclopædia.' All the frag-

[3] The regnal years of many kings are deter-

ments are of the highest importance. Some refer to past transactions, and are chiefly valuable as showing what view the Egyptians took of their ancient history, more especially of the succession and character of their ancient kings.[4] Other inscriptions relate to contemporary events, which they describe for the most part in highly coloured and inflated language, but apparently without careless or wilful misstatement of the facts.

(2.) From these monuments the history of a large portion of the ancient and middle empire, with which alone we are now concerned, has been constructed, though not without long intervals of partial or total obscurity. The earliest part of that history has lately been investigated with great care, and the results given in a work by M. de Rougé,[5] to which reference will frequently be made in the following pages. The names of nearly all the Pharaohs of the first six dynasties have been found, together with notices which prove the extent and complete organisation of their kingdom.

The interval between the sixth and the eleventh dynasties is of uncertain duration. No light is thrown upon it by contemporary monuments. M. de Rougé[6] considers it probable that "the royal families placed here in the lists of Manetho do but represent sovereigns of a part of the country, contemporary with other Pharaohs."

The twelfth dynasty again stands out in clear and strong relief. The Pharaohs were lords of all Egypt; their monuments represent the highest development of sculpture and architecture, and the main events of their reigns are recorded in numerous inscriptions. Some facts of importance have also been lately ascertained in reference to the early kings of the thirteenth dynasty, proving that they too were masters of all Egypt, and therefore that the invasion of the Shepherd kings could not have taken place at the time formerly assumed by Lepsius.[7]

The interval between the fourth king of the thirteenth dynasty and the last of the seventeenth is a period of confusion and disturbance. The monuments supply no data by which the order of events and the chronology can be determined, or even probably conjectured. That Egypt during that time was invaded by the Hyksos, who were masters of the north, has been proved by the researches of M. Mariette: part of the country appears to have been governed throughout the period by contemporary dynasties, ending with Rasekenen; but the most complete list of the ancestors of Seti I. gives the name of no Pharaoh between Amenemha, the last king but one of the twelfth dynasty, and Aahmes, or Amosis, the first of the eighteenth.

From the beginning of the eighteenth dynasty, when the Hyksos were expelled by Aahmes I., the monumental history of Egypt is tolerably complete; the succession of nearly all the Pharaohs and the principal events in the reigns of the most distinguished are distinctly recorded. The chronology, however, is uncertain; the regnal years are often found on the monuments, but without even an approximation to completeness; with one exception, to be noticed presently, no general era, or computation of lengthened periods, is based on the authority of ancient inscriptions.

(3.) The subjoined list embraces the whole period within which the Israelites and their ancestors are assumed by any scholars to have been in contact with Egypt before or soon after the settlement in Canaan.

12th Dynasty.—Amenemha, Osirtasin I., Amenemha II., Osirtasin II., Osirtasin III., Amenemha III., Amenemha IV., and a Queen, Ra-Sebek-Nefrou.

13th Dynasty.—A series of Pharaohs bearing a general name, Sebek-hotep.

14th to 17th Dynasty.—Hyksos, and Egyptians; the last of the Hyksos, Apepi, or Apophis; the last of the contemporary Egyptians, Ta-aaken Rasekenen.

18th Dynasty. — Aahmes I. (Nefertari Queen), Amenhotep I., Thotmes I. (Aahmes Regent), Thotmes II., Thotmes III., Amenhotep II., Thotmes IV., Amenhotep III., Amenhotep IV. (who took the name Khun-Aten), three other kings not recognised as legitimate, Horemheb.

19th Dynasty.—Rameses I., Seti I., Rameses II., Merneptah I, Seti II. or Merneptah II., Amemmeses, Siptah, and Tauser.

20th Dynasty.—Rameses III., twelve kings bearing the name Rameses with special designations.

(4.) The first contact with Egypt is generally admitted,[8] and may be here assumed to have

---

mined from contemporary inscriptions. The discrepancies in Manetho are so numerous that they can scarcely be accounted for by errors of transcription.
[4] The two most important documents referring to the past are the Turin Papyrus (published by Lepsius, 'Auswahl,' 1842, and 'Kœnigsbuch,' 1858), and the list of kings lately discovered in the temple of Abydos by M. Mariette. It is printed in the 'Zeitschrift,' 1864, by M. de Rougé, 'Recherches,' pl. ii., and by M. Mariette, 'Fouilles,' vol. ii. It represents Seti I., accompanied by his son Rameses II., in the act of rendering homage to seventy-six of his ancestors, beginning with Mena or Menes.
[5] 'Recherches sur les Monuments qu'on peut attribuer aux six premières Dynasties de Manethon.' Paris, 1866.
[6] 'Recherches,' p. iv. This statement is again made in M. de Rougé's 'Exposé de l'État actuel des Études égyptiennes,' 1867. See p. 17.

[7] See M. de Rougé, 'Recherches,' pp. vi. vii.
[8] Lepsius is the only exception. All other scholars in England, France, and Germany, are

UPON THE PENTATEUCH.

taken place before the eighteenth dynasty: the first question to be considered is whether the visit of Abram, and the immigration of the Israelites, are to be referred to the period of disturbance and general misery which followed the invasion of the Hyksos, and lasted till their expulsion, or to the earlier period when Egypt was united and prosperous under its native sovereigns.

The natural impression made by the narrative in the Book of Genesis would certainly be that the transactions which it sets before us so fully and distinctly, belong to the earlier period. The account of Abram's visit (Gen. xii. 10-20) is very brief, but it evidently represents Egypt as in a condition of great prosperity. It was the resort of foreigners in times of famine. Pharaoh and his princes are rich and luxurious, nor are there any indications of war or intestine troubles.

It has, however, been argued that some facts in this short narrative point rather to the habits of a nomad and half-savage race, than to the polished and civilised Pharaohs of the ancient empire. It is urged that representations of camels are not found on Egyptian monuments; but they formed part of the property which Abram acquired by the favour of Pharaoh. It is, however, known that long before that period the Pharaohs were masters of a large part of the Peninsula of Sinai, and of the intervening district, nor is it likely that they would have kept up their communications without using the 'ships of the desert.' Camels were not likely to be represented on the sepulchral monuments at Benihassan,[9] far from the frontiers of Egypt; they were not used in the interior of the country, and were probably regarded as unclean.

Two objections of more importance rest on the supposed habits and feelings of the early Egyptian kings: late discoveries have converted these objections into strong arguments in favour of the earlier date.

The fear which Abram felt lest his wife should be taken from him, and that he should be slain for her sake, would seem to indicate wild and savage habits, such as can scarcely be attributed to native Egyptians. But in the story of the two brothers,[10] the Pharaoh of the time, acting on the advice of his counsellors, sends two armies to fetch a beautiful woman by force and then to murder her husband. The story is full of wild superstitions, but the portraiture of manners is remarkably simple and graphic, and it unquestionably represents the feelings of the Egyptians at the time of their highest civilisation. It belongs to the age of Rameses II., and the act is attributed not to a tyrant and oppressor, but to a Pharaoh beloved by his people, and passing into heaven at his decease.

Another curious coincidence has been pointed out by M. Chabas, 'Les Papyrus hiératiques de Berlin,' p. xiv. In a very ancient papyrus of Berlin, referring to the 12th dynasty, the wife and children of a foreigner are confiscated as a matter of course, and become the property of the king. M. Chabas observes, "C'est ainsi qu'à une époque probablement un peu postérieure à celle des événements que raconte notre papyrus, Abraham se vit enlever sa femme Saraï, qui fut placée dans la maison du Roi."

It is again objected that Abram was not likely to be admitted into the presence, much less into the favour, of a native Egyptian king, whereas a nomad of kindred origin and similar habits might willingly receive him.

We have, however, two distinct and absolute proofs that under the twelfth dynasty a personage of the race, habits, and position of Abram would be welcomed under such circumstances as those described in Genesis.

In the sepulchral monuments at Benihassan, and in the tomb of the Governor of the province, a man of the highest rank, nearly related to the reigning Pharaoh, Osirtasin II., is found one of the most interesting and best known pictures of the ancient empire. It represents the arrival of a nomad chief, with his family and dependents, to render homage and seek the protection of the prince. These foreigners are called Amu,[11] a name which was given

---

so far agreed, they place the visit of Abraham before the eighteenth dynasty. Dr. Ebers places the visit of Abraham before the Hyksos, and that of Joseph some time after their expulsion. This involves, according to his calculations, an interval of some eight or ten centuries between Abraham and Joseph. The arguments by which he shows that neither could have visited Egypt during the Hyksos period corroborate the position taken in this dissertation. Dr. Ebers' work, 'Ægypten und die Bücher Moses,' published a few months since, reached me after this dissertation was ready for the press. Reference will be made to it in the notes.

[9] We have no other monuments which represent the habits of Egypt under the twelfth dynasty. There are no representations of camels on monuments of the Ptolemaic or the Roman period, when they were of course well known to the Egyptians. Ebers supposes that it was contrary to the rules of Egyptian art to represent these uncouth forms. This is possible, but scarcely probable, since the giraffe and other strange animals are common on the monuments. It is more probable that they were held unclean.

[10] This curious story, the earliest fiction in existence, is among the select Papyri in the British Museum: it is called the Papyrus d'Orbiney: a fac-simile is published by the Trustees of the Museum: it contains nineteen pages of hieratic writing, remarkably clear and legible: the style is simple, and presents fewer difficulties than any similar document. It has been translated in part by Mr. Goodwin, Mr. Le Page Renouf, and M. de Rougé. The story abounds throughout with illustrations of the narrative in the Pentateuch.

[11] The word is applied to pastoral nomads,

specially to the native tribes on the north-west of Egypt and in Palestine of Semitic descent. The chief is called the Hak, or prince, corresponding to Sheich, as used chiefly of heads of tribes: his name is Abshah.[12] The features of the family, their colour, and their costume, a rich tunic, or "coat of many colours," are thoroughly Semitic. It is to be observed also that, although they are represented as suppliants, making lowly obeisance, and bringing the customary gifts, yet the prince receives them as persons of some distinction: a scribe who presents them holds a tablet describing their number and purpose, and a slave behind the governor bears his sandals, which were only taken off on ceremonial occasions.

Not less striking is the evidence drawn from one of the oldest papyri in existence, lately translated by Mr. Goodwin. He calls it the Story of Saneha: the events which it relates belong to the reigns of the first two kings of the twelfth dynasty, Amenemhe and Osirtasin. Saneha (*i.e.* son of the Sycomore, a name probably given or assumed on his adoption by the Egyptians) was, like the chief above described, an Amu; he was not only received into the service of the Pharaoh, but rose to high rank, and, even after a long residence as a fugitive in a foreign land, he was restored to favour, made "a counsellor among the officers, set among the chosen ones: precedence is accorded to him among the courtiers, he is installed in the house of a prince, and prepares his sepulchre among the tombs of the chief officers." Mr. Goodwin points out the resemblance between this narrative and the history of Abraham; but it proves something more, for it shows that to an Egyptian of that early age the circumstances in the history of Abraham and of Joseph which are often regarded as improbable would appear most natural, facts if not of frequent, yet of certain occurrence.

M. Chabas, in a treatise on the same papyrus, observes—"Ce narrateur devint le favori de ce monarque (*sc.* Asirtasin) et fut pendant quelque temps préposé à l'administration de l'Égypte, *pour en développer les ressources*. Ce détail nous rappelle le rôle que, selon l'Écriture, Pharaon attribua au patriarche Joseph."

It may also be argued that such a reception was far less likely to be accorded to either of these Patriarchs at any later period. The little that is positively known of the Hyksos, the masters of Tanis, indicates a certain harshness and even ferocity of character;[13] nor after their expulsion were the kings either of the eighteenth or nineteenth dynasty likely to look with favour upon foreigners bearing, as may be probably inferred, a close resemblance to them in features and language. The presents too which the Pharaoh made to Abram include sheep, oxen, asses, and slaves, all of which are frequently represented on the early monuments, and specially at Benihassan,[14]—a fact the more important to be noticed since V. Bohlen and others ventured to deny that either sheep or asses were common in Egypt: the ass was looked upon as unclean under the middle and later Empire, as Typhonian, and would not probably have been presented to a favoured stranger. The omission of horses is remarkable. The Hyksos, admitted to be Arabians, probably brought the horse into Egypt, and no animal was more prized by the later Pharaohs; but it was wholly unknown, so far as we can judge from the monuments, to the Egyptians of the twelfth or any earlier dynasty.[15]

In fact, the notices of Abram's visit to Egypt agree so entirely with all that is certainly known of the Egyptians under the twelfth dynasty, and differ in so many material points from what is known from the monuments or early tradition of the Hyksos, and of the Middle Empire, that critics of very opposite schools have concurred in adopting the earlier date, notwithstanding the difficulty presented by their acceptance of the chronology of Manetho as given by Africanus or Josephus. For my own part I regard it as all but cer-

---

and specially those of Arabia and Palestine. It is an Egyptian word, derived from Amu (⸺ 𓆰𓎛𓏥), a herdsman's scourge. The word Shasous, which will occur frequently, is also applied to nomads, but probably with reference to their wandering habits, equivalent to Bedouins. Hyksos is not the name of a people, but of the dynasty, and probably means Prince of the Shasous. M. Chabas objects to this etymology, but it is generally accepted, and rests on strong grounds.

[12] Some have thought that the name is identical with Abraham, an opinion which is undoubtedly incorrect; but there is a very remarkable resemblance between the names, both in form and meaning: since "shah" means sand, and "raham" means multitude. When Abshah was received, Abraham would not be rejected.

[13] This alludes particularly to the hard, sullen features, wholly unlike those of Egyptian princes, found on the lately-discovered monuments which represent the Hyksos at Tanis. See 'Rev. Archéologique,' 1861, p. 105. Dr. Ebers gives the head of the Sphinx from M. Mariette, l. c. 208.

[14] Sheep are represented on the Pyramids—in one inscription 3208 as the property of an individual. Asses of great size and beauty are found in many pictures at Benihassan. I believe, but may be mistaken, that they occur comparatively seldom on the monuments of later periods.

[15] V. Bohlen infers from this omission that Genesis could not have been written by an author conversant with Egyptian manners.. The true inference is that he describes exactly what took place at the time which he gives an account of. It is very probable that horses were first introduced under the 12th dynasty, after the reign of Osirtasin. From that time the intercourse with Asia appears to have been constant

tain that Abraham visited Egypt in some reign between the middle of the eleventh and the thirteenth dynasty, and most probably under one of the earliest Pharaohs of the twelfth.

(5.) The history of Joseph belongs to a period about two centuries later.[16] The duration of the twelfth dynasty is estimated at 213 years; and as the monuments were numerous and complete in Manetho's time, it is probable that the regnal years are drawn from them, and that the numbers are tolerably correct. It has been lately proved beyond all doubt that the invasion of the Hyksos could not have taken place immediately afterwards, as was formerly supposed. Colossal figures of great beauty, and inscriptions, have been found at Tanis, the head-quarters of the Hyksos, which prove that the fourth king of the thirteenth dynasty was still in undisturbed possession of that city; and monumental notices of even later kings are found, both at Tanis and in other parts of Egypt, scarcely reconcileable with the presence of the Arabian invaders.[17]

So far as the monuments and other Egyptian documents are concerned, we are at liberty to place the visit of Joseph either towards the end of the twelfth dynasty, the earlier portion of the thirteenth, or under the first Hyksos.

We are bound to give special attention to this last alternative; it was maintained by all ancient writers, and is accepted, with few but important exceptions, by modern critics. Thus Syncellus: "It is asserted unanimously by all that Joseph ruled over Egypt in the time of Apophis:" Eusebius, speaking of the seventeenth (Shepherd) dynasty, says κατὰ τούτους Αἰγυπτίων βασιλεὺς Ἰωσὴφ δείκνυται. This unanimous consent, however, refers only to Josephus and to those who drew their information exclusively from his account of Manetho's work. It depended wholly upon chronological calculations, and it is of course quite clear that, if the Shepherd dynasty had lasted some 800 years, all the narrative in Genesis would have fallen within it.

This necessitates a brief inquiry into the grounds for the statements in Manetho.

We have first an account of a dynasty of six Shepherd kings: their names in Josephus are Salatis, Beon, Apachnas, Apophis, Jannes, Assir. The general accuracy of this list may be admitted, transposing one name only, viz., Apophis, who is known to have been the last of the Shepherd kings. The late discoveries of M. Mariette at Tanis have given us contemporary authority for the first name. It is Semitic, old Arabian probably (Σάλατις = שַׁלִּיט mighty, ruler), but the Egyptians transcribe it accurately and give the full title, with the invariable adjuncts of Egyptian etiquette, "the Good Deity, star of both worlds, Son of the Sun, Set Shalti,[18] beloved by Sutech, Lord of Avaris." So that Salatis, the first of the Shepherd dynasty, assumed at once the state and title of the Pharaohs, and at least claimed to be sovereign of all Egypt. The second name Beon or "Benon," the more correct reading of Africanus, is also found.[19] Like many other words it has probably the same meaning[20] in Semitic and Egyptian, Son of the Eye, i.e. the beloved one. The order of the three last names is proved by the Turin Papyrus, and by the well-ascertained position of Apophis.

Up to this point we have a solid foundation, six kings, foreigners, two bearing Semitic names, and recognised by ancient Egyptian documents. The duration of the dynasty may have been between two and three centuries.

But in addition to these kings, Manetho, according to Josephus, states that a dynasty or dynasties of Shepherds ruled over all Egypt upwards of 500 years. Africanus gives two dynasties, one lasting 284 years, the other 518. For this statement, however, no evidence is adduced. Not a single name is given by Josephus. The Turin Papyrus has no indication of the dynasty. The monuments are absolutely silent. The statement, indeed, is in glaring contradiction to the fact that Salatis was the first and Apophis the last of the Shepherd kings. It involves an admission of the most improbable of all assumptions, for which not a shadow of resemblance can be found in ancient or modern history,—an assumption that, after a total suspension of the national life lasting from five to ten centuries, after a complete overthrow of their government, institutions, and religion, the Egyptians reverted to the exact point of civilisation in which the invaders found them, speaking and writing their own language without a trace of foreign infusion,[21] worshipping the old gods with the old rites, retaining their old theology,

---

[16] The dates are not certain, but Isaac was born some years after Abraham's visit to Egypt, li ed 180 years (Gen. xxxv. 28), and died before Joseph was sold by his brethren.

[17] See M. de Rougé, 'Recherches,' p. vii. We owe these important facts to M. Mariette.

[18] The group is noticeable

It is found also in a mutilated form in the Turin Papyrus.

[19] In the Papyrus Sallier 1, pl. 1, l. 7.

[20] בן עין. The Egyptian is Beben-an, which Dr. Ebers derives from Ben, "son," and "an," the eye. The Egyptians have the well-known Hebrew and classical term, "child of the eye" for "darling."

[21] The strong infusion of Semitic belongs to the age of Rameses II. The inscriptions of the eighteenth dynasty are nearly free from it. A very remarkable confirmation of the above statements is found in the account of the mummy of Aah-hotep, mother of Ahmes I., given by M. Mariette, 'Musée de Boulaq,' p. 254:—"L'Égypte est revenue sous la xviime dynastie avec la plus singulière persistance au style de la xime."

and recognising in the descendants of their old Pharaohs the inheritors of all their titles and prerogatives. It seems quite incredible that such a statement should have been adopted, as adopted it has been by critics remarkable for sagacity, and some for caution approaching to scepticism. It is the only ground for the assumption that Joseph must needs have visited Egypt while it was under the dominion of the Hyksos.

We do not attach much importance to the chronology of this remote period, so far as it rests on Egyptian documents: it is to a great extent conjectural, and incapable of proof or disproof. But it is a remarkable fact that the only inscription on Egyptian monuments of any age which mentions an era distinct from the regnal year of the actual sovereign, is found on a monument referring to the Hyksos. The importance of this inscription was pointed out by M. de Rougé,[22] and it has been carefully examined by M. Chabas. The personage who set up the tablet was an official of high rank, Governor of Tanis under Rameses II. The date which he gives is the four hundredth year from the era of Set Nubte, *i.e.* Set the golden, under the reign of a Hyksos king, Set-aa-Pehti, *i.e.* Set the mighty and victorious. There is of course a wide field for conjecture here. The reign of Rameses was a very long one (see further on, p. 464), and the Hyksos king is not positively identified. We may consider it as almost certain that the Egyptian governor, a descendant of the Hyksos, believed that 400 years had elapsed between the era of Set and some year in the reign of Rameses. When, again, we consider the analogy of all ancient eras, and the natural course of events, we are all but forced to infer that this era must coincide with the formal recognition of Set as the chief object of worship to the dynasty. If the Papyrus Sallier were our only authority, that recognition might be assigned to Apophis; but the late discovery of the style and title of the first of the Shepherd Kings, Salatis the beloved of Set,[23] proves that the establishment of Set worship at Tanis was far more ancient, contemporary in fact with the inauguration of the Shepherd dynasty.

The inferences from these facts tally very remarkably with the chronology which upon the whole appears to be best supported by Biblical and documental evidence. The end of the reign of Rameses is most probably about 1340 B.C. From this, 400 years would bring us to the middle of the eighteenth century, about 1750 B.C. The expulsion of the Hyksos being taken about 1500, we have thus 250 years for their dynasty, and 250 more would bring us to the time of Abraham. Such arguments are of course open to objections, nor are they given here as conclusive, but they have weight when they harmonize with a system resting on wholly independent grounds. One point at least is clear: if the date is accepted it involves a considerable reduction in the length of the period assigned by Lepsius and Brugsch to the dynasties preceding the age of Rameses.

(6.) But the name of Apophis is specially mentioned as that of the king by whom Joseph was received. The question whether this is possible or probable may now be decided by the positive evidence of contemporary inscriptions,[24] and of the ancient papyrus, Sallier 1.

We know now that Apophis was the contemporary of Rasekenen, the immediate predecessor of Aahmes I., and that Aahmes captured Avaris, the capital or chief fortress of Apophis, and afterwards drove out all the adherents of the hostile dynasty, pursuing them as far as Palestine.

This fact is conclusive. Joseph was a very young man when he came first under the notice of Pharaoh, and lived to an advanced age, 110 years, the utmost limit, as has been lately shown,[5] of Egyptian life. He would therefore have long outlived Apophis, but no one supposes that he could have lived a prosperous and powerful man after the extermination of the dynasty by which he was raised to the highest rank in the state. Nor do other notices of the Pharaoh of Joseph at all accord with what is known of Apophis.

Apophis was not, properly speaking, Lord of all Egypt. Upper Egypt was governed by an independent dynasty; and the very terms which describe the extent of his influence prove the limits of his dominion. Rasekenen, his antagonist, retained possession of the Thebaid to the end of his life, and buildings of great extent were erected by him in Memphis and Thebes after the termination of a successful campaign against Apophis.[26] The

---

[22] 'Revue Archéologique,' Feb. 1864. M. Mariette sent a copy to the same Review, March, 1865. M. Chabas has two articles on it printed in the 'Zeitschrift,' April and May, 1865. The tablet was found in a mass of ruins in the sanctuary of the great temple at San, *i e.* Tanis.

[23] It is probable that Set-aa-pehti, *i.e.* Set the mighty and victorious, was either the Egyptian translation of the Semitic Set-Shalt, Set the mighty ruler, or a second title borne in accordance with Egyptian usage.

[24] The inscriptions are found in the sepulchres of officers who served under Ra-sekenen and the first Pharaohs of the eighteenth dynasty. They are given by Lepsius, 'Denkmäler,' and have been explained by M. de Rougé (whose treatise on the tomb of Aahmes marked a crisis in the advance of Egyptian studies), and are quoted repeatedly in M. Brugsch's 'Histoire d'Égypte.'

[25] By Mr. Goodwin, in the second part of the 'Mélanges égyptologiques' of M. Chabas. The argument is good for Egypt, not for the patriarchs, living the simple life and breathing the pure air of the desert.

[26] See Brugsch, 'Die Geographie des alten

Pharaoh of Joseph was certainly in a different position.

We have also evidence touching the general condition of Egypt under the dynasty or which Apophis was the most powerful king, and to whose reign the notice specially applies. The account given by Manetho of their devastations is probably exaggerated. It is certain that they did not deface the monuments to the extent which is generally supposed. The pyramids, the obelisk at Heliopolis, colossal figures and inscriptions even at Tanis (see above), and monuments in Middle and Upper Egypt, still bear witness in their favour. The Labyrinth in the Fayoum, and the great temples at Memphis and Heliopolis, were certainly left by them uninjured. Still the impression made by their ravages upon the Egyptians was profound: the name by which they were designated means pestilential deadly enemies.[27] From an inscription at Karnak,[28] we find that, under the nineteenth dynasty, when the Egyptians would describe a period of dreadful calamity, they could find no precedent so strong and apt as that of the Shepherd Kings. "One had not seen anything like it even in the time of the kings of Lower Egypt, when the land of Egypt was in their power, when wretchedness prevailed, in the time when the kings of Upper Egypt had not power to repel them." The account in the Papyrus Sallier I. quite agrees with this, showing that the reign of Apophis was cruel and oppressive throughout, and occupied towards the end, as we have seen, by an internecine war.

Again, no fact about Apophis is more certain than that he repudiated the national religion.[29] The testimony of the Papyrus Sallier is clear and explicit: "the King Apepi adopted Sutech as his God, he did not serve any God which was in the whole land." Sutech, or Set, in later ages the representative of the evil principle Typhon, is identified, and was certainly confounded with Baal of the Phœnicians. The only monument[30] on which the name of Apophis is found calls him "the beloved of Sutech:" an appellation, as we have seen, borne by the first Shepherd king, and probably common to all the dynasty. If we accept the probable tradition of Porphyry ('de Abst.' 11, 55), that Aahmes I. suppressed human sacrifices offered under the Shepherd kings at Heliopolis, the form of worship must have been Typhonian, and in all probability of Phœnician origin.[31]

Each and all of these points are quite irreconcileable with the account in Genesis. The Pharaoh of Joseph was unquestionably Lord of all Egypt: the country was in a state of great prosperity: the religion, all the usages and institutions of the Pharaoh and his courtiers, were those of ancient Egypt. There is not a single fact[32] in the history of Joseph which is not illustrated by the inscriptions and sculptures of the best and most prosperous periods of Egypt; not one which gives the least indication of the predominance of a foreign religion, habits, or race.[33]

The question, however, still remains, if Joseph did not enter Egypt when the Shepherds were there, did his visit and the immigration of the Israelites take place before or after that period? We may assume that it did not occur at a later time. With very few exceptions, critics agree that the Israelites were in Egypt at the accession of the eighteenth dynasty. If before, we have still to inquire at what time.

This part of the inquiry is beset with considerable difficulties. We have no means of ascertaining the duration of the interval between the last sovereign of the twelfth dynasty and the invasion of the Shepherds. The titles of forty-eight kings of the thirteenth dynasty are given in the papyrus of Turin; and the names of three of them bear a very remark-

---

Ægyptens,' p. 180. M. Chabas in a treatise, 'Les Pasteurs en Égypte,' published within the last two months, assumes that three Pharaohs bore the name Ra-sekenen, Ra the conqueror. If this were granted, it would leave all other arguments untouched.

[27] See M. Chabas, 'Mél. égypt.,' i.

[28] See 'Revue Archéologique' for July and August, 1867. M. de Rougé gives a full account of the inscription, which has been lately published by M. Duemichen, 'Historische Inschriften.' I observe that the reference to the Shepherd kings is adopted by Dr. Ebers, 'Ægypten,' &c., p. 207.

[29] The name Apepi, the Egyptian form of the word, signifies the great serpent, the enemy of Ra and Osiris. It was probably given to this king, or assumed by him, to mark his antagonism to the old national religion. It has, however, been shown by M. de Rougé, 'Recherches,' p. 9 and p. 45, that the worship of Sutech, or Set, as the tutelary god of lower Egypt, dates from the ancient empire. The peculiarity of Apepi, and probably of his predecessors, would seem to be his exclusive devotion to this deity, who represented force and destruction.

[30] The inscription is given by Burton, 'Excerpta Hieroglyphica,' at San (i.e. Tanis), No. 7, pl. xv.; and by Brugsch, 'Geog. Inschr.,' p. 88, No. 576. Like Salatis, Apepi takes the style of a legitimate Pharaoh.

[31] Sutech is identified with Baal in numerous inscriptions, and is represented specially as the chief deity of the Cheta, masters of northern Syria under the nineteenth dynasty.

[32] This statement is strongly corroborated by the work of Dr. Ebers.

[33] It must be remembered that in Joseph's time the Egyptians would not eat with shepherds; they were an abomination to them. This, of itself, is almost, if not quite, conclusive against the supposition that he was at the court of a Shepherd king. M. Chabas has shown this to be a true and monumental designation of the invaders.

F F

able resemblance to the name given by Pharaoh to Joseph.[34] There appear to be good grounds for the opinion that they were driven out of Lower Egypt, and retained a partial and precarious hold on Middle or Upper Egypt within a century or two after their accession; and if so, Joseph, at the latest, may have lived under one of the early kings, such as the Sebekhotep, whose colossal statue in the Louvre belongs to the best age of Egyptian art, and evidently also to a period of unbroken prosperity.

It is however scarcely possible to resist the impression made by monuments of the twelfth dynasty, which seem to connect the history of Abraham, as we have already seen (p. 446), and still more specially that of Joseph, with this most important and interesting period of Egypt.

(7.) We have the fact that the princes of this great dynasty stood in very special relation to On or Heliopolis. The temple there was built by Osirtasin I., whose name and official title, Osirtasin Cheperkara, stand out in clear and perfect characters on the oldest and most beautiful obelisk of Egypt, still standing at On, the only but certain evidence of the magnificence of the temple. The priest of that city and temple, judging from the general usage of the ancient Pharaohs,[35] was in all probability a near relative of the sovereign. We have abundant notices on the monuments of that dynasty which agree with the intimations of Genesis; proving, on the one hand, that the forms of worship were purely Egyptian, and, on the other hand, that the fundamental principles which underlie those forms, and which belong, as we may not doubt, to the primeval religion of humanity, were still distinctly recognised, although they were blended with speculation and superstitious errors:[36] they were moreover associated with a system which, on many essential points, inculcated a sound and even delicate morality. In the priest of On a Shepherd king would have seen the antagonist of his own special superstition, the last man in Egypt whom he would have brought into connection with his favourite and prime minister: to an Osirtasin and to Joseph himself the alliance would present every inducement of policy, interest, and suitableness.

(8.) The tombs at Benihassan have already supplied us with illustrations of the history of Abraham, which are equally applicable to that of Joseph. The inscriptions, which describe the character of Chnumhotep (a near relative and favourite of Osirtasin I. and his immediate successor), and the recorded events of his government, remind the reader irresistibly of the young Hebrew. It is said of him[37] "he injured no little child : he oppressed no widow: he detained for his own purpose no fisherman: took from his work no shepherd: no overseer's men were taken. There was no beggar in his days : no one starved in his time. When years of famine occurred he ploughed all the lands of the district producing abundant food: no one was starved in it: he treated the widow as a woman with a husband to protect her." The mention of famine, and of unusual precautions to guard against its recurrence, together with other obvious traits of resemblance, led some critics a few years since to see in Chnumhotep the Egyptian original of Joseph. At present the antecedents and connections of that personage are too well known to admit of any confusion; but the probability must be admitted that a king, belonging to a dynasty which sought and rewarded such characteristics in the great officers of state, should have advanced Joseph to a position such as the Bible describes, such too as the old Egyptian papyrus already quoted (p. 446) shows to have been then within the reach of a foreigner.

(9.) There are still more specific reasons for fixing on this period. According to Genesis, one permanent consequence of the visitation was a new division of all Egypt, a redistribution of the land and property: probably, as is pointed out by the Bishop of Ely,[38] a necessary and politic measure, after the complete break-down of the ancient system. Now we are told by Herodotus and Diodorus that an ancient Egyptian king so divided the lands, and that the same system continued to their time. This king must evidently have belonged to a native dynasty: had the division been made by a foreigner and invader, it

---

[34] Viz. Zaf., *i.e.* food. See note on the name Zafnath Paaneah.

[35] See M. de Rougé, 'Recherches,' p. 34. Nearly all the chief priests bear the titles Suten sa or Suten rech — son, grandson, or relative of the king. Ewald justly observes that Heliopolis was, so to speak, the true sacerdotal city and university of Northern Egypt. Geschichte, ii., p. 51.

[36] See especially Lepsius, 'Ælteste Texte des Todtenbuchs.' The earliest known text of the seventeenth chapter of the Ritual belongs to the eleventh dynasty. Its importance is recognised as the most ancient statement of Egyptian views as to the origin and government of the universe. It undoubtedly indicates the previous existence of a pure Monotheism, of which it retains the great principles, the unity, eternity, self-existence of the unknown Deity. Each age witnessed some corruption and amplification of the ancient religion, and corresponding interpolations of the old texts. The very earliest has several glosses, and the text taken apart from them approaches very nearly to the truth as revealed in the Bible.

[37] Lepsius, 'Denkmäler,' ii. pl. 122. Dr. Birch, who gives an interlinear translation in Bunsen's 'Egypt,' vol. v. p. 726-729.

[38] See notes on Genesis.

would have been swept away when the line of the so-called legitimate Pharaohs was restored. Those two historians indeed attribute the division to the sovereign called Sesostris by Herodotus, and Sesoosis by Diodorus: an appellation which was afterwards appropriated to Rameses II., or perhaps to his father, Seti I. But it is well known that the exploits of the great sovereigns who preceded Rameses II. were transferred to him by popular tradition:[39] it is certain also that the division into nomes, and the exemption of the priestly lands from taxation, were anterior to him by many centuries. The system appears to have been coeval with the monarchy, certainly with the pyramids, but in all probability was modified, and extended, if not completed, under the great Pharaohs of the twelfth dynasty. No occasion can be pointed out more likely to have suggested it, and to have enabled the Pharaoh to accomplish it, than that described in Genesis.

Again, we learn from Egyptian sources that, under Amenemha III., in some respects the greatest king of this noble dynasty, whose reign is separated from the first by an interval of some two centuries (see above), a work of extraordinary magnitude and importance was undertaken and completed: one that proves at once the terror caused by the previous liability to famines, and the enormous resources, skill, and forethought of the Pharaoh. Amenemha III. first established a complete system of dykes, canals, locks, and reservoirs, by which the inundations of the Nile were henceforth regulated.[40] The immense artificial lake of Mœris in the Fayoum was made by his orders; it communicated with the Nile by a canal, received the overflowing waters at the time of the inundation, and secured the complete irrigation of the adjoining nomes in the dry season. M. Linant de Bellefonds,[41] to whose industry and ability we are indebted fo: ascertaining the exact site and extent of this lake, observes that the restoration of this magnificent work would be one of the greatest benefits that could be conferred on modern Egypt. Under Amenemha III. also the great labyrinth, the most stupendous work of that great age, was erected. This building was probably connected with the same series of events: it consisted of a vast number of halls and buildings, in which the representatives of the Egyptian nomes were assembled periodically to consult on subjects of national interest; and certainly not without a special view to the conservation of a system which afforded the best—indeed the only real—security against the recurrence of the most formidable calamity to which this people could be exposed. At no period would an Egyptian king have such special reasons for undertaking these works: at none would he have such peculiar opportunities of carrying them into effect — the reasons enforced by the seven years of famine, and the means supplied by the reconstruction of the territorial organisation, which placed the whole resources of the nation at the disposal of this Pharaoh.[42]

In the absence of positive evidence for or against any hypotheses, these coincidences may justify us in regarding it at least as a very probable conjecture that the visit of Abraham may have taken place under the first king of the dynasty, and that of Joseph under Amenemha III., the Pharaoh who is represented on the lately-discovered table of Abydos as the last great king of all Egypt in the ancient empire, and, as such, receiving divine honours from his descendant Rameses.

(10.) But if Joseph and the Israelites were received and treated with great favour by the native dynasty, it may seem improbable that they should have remained undisturbed under the Shepherd kings. We have of course no conclusive evidence either for or against the objection; but we have facts enough to show that it is quite possible that they may have occupied a relative position under the foreigners not differing widely from that in which the invasion found them. There can be no doubt that the invaders directed their assault at once against the great cities of Egypt; both to enrich themselves with the spoil, and to secure their dominion over the lands. We may also feel pretty confident that they overthrew the national forms of worship, although, as we have above shown,

---

[39] Josephus expressly states that Manetho gives the name of Sesostris to the third king of the twelfth dynasty, whom he represents as conqueror of Asia. The researches of M. Mariette have lately shown that Rameses II. was in the habit of appropriating the exploits of his predecessors, and substituting his own name on the monuments (see below, p. 465) This evil habit was adopted by his son Merneptan.

[40] See Brugsch, 'Histoire d'Égypte,' p. 69. Lepsius found a Nilometer of Amenemha and several accurate notices of the height of the inundations under the twelfth and thirteenth dynasties at Semneh and Kumme.

[41] 'Mémoire sur le Lac Mœris:' Alexandrie, 1843. Mœris is not the name of a king, but the Egyptian word "mer," a lake or reservoir. Fayoum is the Arabic corruption of the Coptic ⲪⲒⲞⲘ, an old Egyptian word, "the sea." According to Ptolemy, near the lake was a place called Bakkhis or Banchis. M. Brugsch identifies this with a place called Pi-aneh, "the house of life," which is found on the monuments in connexion with Sebek, the tutelary deity of the district. See 'Geographie des Alten Ægyptens,' p. 233. This name has a special interest for its bearing upon Joseph's Egyptian name Zafnath Paaneah, "the food of life."

[42] The copper mines at Wady Mughara were worked under this prince; there is a curious notice of the expedition in Brugsch, 'H. E.,' p. 69. See also 'Introduction' to Exodus.

there is no evidence that they destroyed or defaced the temples. The Israelites, then a small colony lately established, would offer no temptation to their cupidity; no buildings, no temples, no elaborate ritual which could provoke their animosity. It must also be borne in mind that all historians are agreed that the invasion of the Hyksos was most probably preceded by peaceful visits of the chieftains of Arabia and the adjoining districts of Palestine, of which we have numerous traces in early monuments; from them they may have learned at once to appreciate the riches of Egypt, and to ascertain the state of the country. The jealousy with which such visitors were watched is distinctly noted in Genesis: every nomad company might be suspected of a desire to see the nakedness— that is, to spy the assailable approaches to the land; a jealousy of which also we have distinct notices in the story of Saneha and the inscriptions of Benihassan. But when the fathers of those invaders visited Egypt in the time of the great famine, which, as we know from other documents,[43] would draw them, with their flocks and herds, to the frontier, the person with whom they were brought into contact, and for whom they would feel the deepest reverence, was the master of the granaries, the distributor of food. Joseph could not be unknown by name or by character to the early Hyksos, who were little likely to disturb the kindred and descendants of the man to whom they were indebted for their lives. It is also evident that the rapid multiplication of the Israelites might be favoured by the withdrawal of the native princes from their immediate neighbourhood: they would be relieved from a superintendence ever vigilant and suspicious. It is not, however, necessary to assume any special favour shown to the Israelites by the Shepherds; the absence of any motive for cruel and oppressive treatment is obvious, and suffices for the removal of all objection on this score to the historical combination we have proposed.

(11.) We are now in a position to consider the question at what period in Egyptian history the Exodus took place. Some points of importance may be assumed as all but certain, there being no difference of opinion between Egyptologers. (1.) At whatever period the Israelites came into Egypt, they were settled in the district assigned to them when the first sovereign of the eighteenth dynasty conquered and expelled the Shepherd dynasty. (2.) The Exodus is admitted to have taken place under the eighteenth or nineteenth dynasty, under which is a question to be settled, but certainly under the one or the other. (3.) The dates referring to this period are still generally uncertain, they rest on doubtful calculations; it may suffice to quote the words of M. de Rougé, adopted by M. Chabas, 'Mélanges égyptologiques,' ii. p. 112: "On restera dans la limite du probable en plaçant Seti I. vers 1500, et le commencement de la 17ᵉ dynastie vers le 18ᵉ siècle. Mais il n'y aurait nullement à s'étonner si l'on s'était trompé de *deux cents ans* dans cette estimation, tant les documents sont viciés dans l'histoire. ou incomplets sur les monuments." In a work of great interest and importance published lately by M. Chabas, he reiterates this assertion, and rejects all the dates derived from astronomical notices. See 'Voyage d'un Égyptien,' p. 26.[44] This uncertainty must always be borne in mind: the dates derived from Egyptian monuments may be implicitly relied upon so far as they go, but, with one exception already noticed, they never refer to any general epoch, and do not supply materials for a complete chronological arrangement of events under either of the dynasties with which we are at present concerned.

Egyptian scholars have hitherto been divided between two opinions, some recognising in Aahmes, or Amosis, the first sovereign of the eighteenth dynasty, the first persecutor of the Israelites, and in one of his descendants the Pharaoh of the Exodus; others regarding the third sovereign of the nineteenth dynasty, *i.e.* Rameses II., the Sesostris of the Greeks, and his son Merneptah, or his grandson Seti, as the contemporaries of Moses. We will examine the grounds on which each of these opinions rests; and proceeding in order of time will first inquire into the claims of the eighteenth dynasty

(12.) The circumstances under which Aahmes I. the Amosis of Josephus, obtained possession of Lower Egypt, make it extremely probable that he should have adopted such measures towards the Israelites as are described in the beginning of Exodus.

His accession constitutes one of the most important epochs in Egyptian history; with it terminates the broken and confused period of the ancient Empire; with it begins a continuous series of events under successive dynasties. Previous to his accession, or shortly afterwards, he married an Ethiopian Princess, Nefertari, whose name and portrait are found on many monuments,[45] in which she

---

[43] See the account of the admission of Edomites under Merneptah, *infra*, p. 486.

[44] A single clear notice of a solar eclipse would settle a vast number of questions. M. Chabas has completely shown that hitherto none has been found (see 'Zeitschrift,' May, 1868). On the various attempts to establish a system on astronomical calculations, see Mr. Browne in Kitto's 'Cyclopædia,' vol. iii. p. 52.

[45] One of the most striking portraits of Nefertari is the first plate in the third volume of Lepsius' 'Denkmäler.' See also a coloured tablet in the British Museum. She is there represented as jet black, but not with negro features. She was probably of the higher Nubian race. It has been observed that the portraits of the earlier

is represented as a personage of singular distinction, daughter, wife, sister, and mother of kings, and worshipped centuries after her death as a tutelary deity. It is inferred, with great probability, that this alliance with Ethiopia, which under the ancient empire had furnished large contingents of auxiliary troops to Egypt,[46] supplied Aahmes with resources which enabled him soon after his accession to undertake an expedition against the Northern dynasty. That expedition was completely successful: it terminated the struggle. A contemporary inscription on the tomb of one of his chief officers (the naval captain Ahmes), gives an account of the siege of Avaris, of a battle fought in its vicinity, and of the capture of that city, the stronghold of Apepi. It also informs us that the expulsion of the enemy was followed by an expedition to the borders of Canaan, when Sarouhen was taken by storm.[47]

It is at once clear that the expressions used in Exodus to describe the Pharaoh by whom the Israelites were first persecuted, apply, in the fullest and most literal sense, to this sovereign. To the people of the greater part of Egypt, and most especially to the inhabitants of the North, he was emphatically "a new king:" of him it might be said, as of no native king, succeeding without a struggle (as was most especially the case of Rameses II.), "he arose up over" Egypt; he was, in the true sense of the word, like the Norman William, *a conqueror*. The name of Joseph, whether as a minister of the ejected dynasty, or of one more ancient than that, would probably be unknown to him. Nor can there be any reasonable doubt as to the feelings with which a king in his position must have regarded the Israelites. There is no question as to his finding them in Goshen; that is admitted by all.[48] They were there as the subjects, apparently the favoured subjects, of the expelled dynasty, under whom they retained undisturbed possession of the richest district of Egypt, commanding the western approach to the very heart of the land. The first point that would naturally strike him would be their number (Exod. i. 9), which, after the expulsion of his enemies, would bear an alarming proportion to the native population of the Delta. A prudent man under such circumstances would not be likely to provoke rebellion by proceeding to extremities, but nothing is more probable than that he should do just what Moses tells us the new king actually did, deal with them craftily, prevent their increase, utilise their labour, and cut off all communication with foreigners. The most advantageous employment which would suggest itself would of course be the construction of strongly-fortified depositaries of provisions and arms near the eastern frontier. The line of fortresses was enlarged and strengthened by Rameses II., but that king was not the original founder. Traces are found which prove the existence both of the canal and of several forts under the ancient empire.[49] One of these forts, bearing the name Pa-chtum en Zaru, is mentioned in the monumental annals of Thotmes III. It is identified by M. Brugsch with the Pithom of the Exodus.[50] The name signifies "the fortress of foreigners or sojourners," *i.e.* a fortress either built by foreigners or assigned to immigrants as a

---

kings of the dynasty bear distinct traces of black blood. Rosellini gives a portrait of Amenophis I. (whom, however, he confounds with Aahmes), in which he is represented as a black. 'Monum. R.,' pl. xxix. At Karnak there is a representation of the shrine of Nefertari borne by twelve priests; she is there associated with Rameses II., after an interval of some three centuries.

[46] M. de Rougé gives a very curious account of the organisation of a negro army, under Pepi, of the sixth dynasty. As in our Indian possessions, these alien troops were drilled and commanded by native Egyptians. See 'Recherches,' p. 123.

[47] This is a very important point. It shows the inaccuracy of the account given by Josephus from Manetho, and, before this inscription was known, adopted by Egyptian scholars, viz., that the war between upper and lower Egypt continued to the third or fourth reign of the eighteenth dynasty. There can be no question as to the correctness of the contemporary inscription. Ptolemy, a priest of Mendes, quoted by Apion (ap. Clem. Alex. 'Sor.,' I, 21, p. 178, ed. Potter), says of Amosis that he κατέσκαψε τὴν Αὔαριν. He was better informed than Manetho. M. de Rougé justly claims the credit of having proved this capital point (question capitale). See the 'Report on Egyptian Studies' for 1867, p. 18; and compare M. Chabas, 'Les Pasteurs en Egypte,' 1868, where the whole inscription is translated.

[48] *E.g.* by M. de Rougé, Brugsch, &c.

[49] An officer who fled from Egypt in the reign of Osirtasin speaks of a wall which the king had built to keep off the Sakti, *i.e.* Asiatic invaders. See the story of Saneha; and Chabas, 'Voyage d'un Égyptien,' p. 293; and on the Sakti, p. 321. Dr. Ebers, l. c. p. 81, entirely corroborates the view taken by the writer. He shows that the line, previously existing, must have been strengthened by one of the earliest kings of the eighteenth dynasty, and completed in all probability by the fortress, called the fort, or the "close" of Zar. The word rendered "fort," viz. chetem, is retained in Coptic, as ⲩⲧⲉⲗ, or ⲧⲱⲗ, to shut. This fort is very specially the key of Egypt, ἡ κλεὶς τῆς Αἰγύπτου, the frontier station for the armies of the Pharaohs, and for Asiatic immigrants.

[50] This identification is not accepted by M. Chabas, who gives another and more probable etymology for the Hebrew Pithom, viz. the sanctuary of Tum. But it is probable, indeed all but certain, that the fortress and the sanctuary were contiguous, and formed together the principal rendezvous of the Egyptian troops and foreign embassies on the frontier. On the name Raamses, see infra, under Rameses.

residence.[51] We learn from Genesis that Raamses was the name of the district in the time of Jacob, and from the Egyptian monuments that one of the sons of Aahmes was named Rames; probable grounds are thus found for the designation of the second fort built at the same time. It is also well known that during the latter part of his reign Aahmes was occupied in building and repairing the cities of Northern Egypt. In an inscription lately deciphered,[52] dated in his twenty-second year, certain Fenchu are stated to be employed in the transport of blocks of limestone from the quarries of Rufu (the Troja of Strabo) to Memphis and other cities. These Fenchu are unquestionably aliens, either mercenaries or forced labourers. According to Brugsch, the name means "bearers of the shepherd's staff;" and he describes their occupation as precisely corresponding to that of the Israelites.[53] No proper name for the Israelites is found on the monuments of the eighteenth dynasty;[54] during which period all Egyptologers admit their presence in Egypt: they could certainly not be designated more exactly whether we regard the name or the occupation of these Fenchu.

(13.) It has been shown that little dependence can be placed on systems of Egyptian chronology, yet it may be observed that either of those which are most generally accepted is quite reconcileable with this hypothesis.

Two dates, which differ very widely, are given, not as certain, but approximative and probable.

Brugsch, following Lepsius, fixes the accession of Aahmes I. at 1706 B.C. This would be in very near accordance with Hebrew history if the dates drawn from notices in the Book of Judges were accepted in preference to that given in 1 Kings vi. The last year of Thotmes II., which, as will be shown, is very probably that of the Exodus, falls on the same system in 1647 B.C. Now, the interval between the building of the Temple, about 1010 A.C., and the Exodus, is calculated to amount to 638 years by the advocates of the longer chronology: certainly a most remarkable coincidence, the more so since neither Brugsch nor the other Egyptian chronologers adopt that date for the Exodus.

The other date, given also approximately, is 1525 B.C. for Aahmes I., and 1463 for the last year of Thotmes II. This accords pretty nearly with the shorter interval of 480 years given in 1 Kings vi. 1.

This later date has been lately supported in a very remarkable way by a discovery which, if it could be absolutely relied upon, would settle the chronology.[55] Thotmes III. built a temple at Elephantine: it has been destroyed within the last few years by the natives, but on one stone found near the ruins the name of the king is distinctly read; on another stone is an inscription stating that the 28th of the month Epiphi was the festival of the rising of Sothis, *i. e.* Sirius. From this M. Biot calculates the date, which he fixes as 1445 B.C. Now the reign of Thotmes III. lasted about forty-eight years; the temple was probably built towards the end of his reign, which up to the last seven years was occupied in foreign warfare; we should thus get the date from 1485 to 1492 for the last year of Thotmes II.,

---

[51] This is a point of considerable importance, brought out by Brugsch in the third volume of the 'Geographische Inschriften,' p. 21. He says, "I believe that I am nearer than formerly to the trace of the meaning of this name. The old Egyptian Zaru, or Zalu, is evidently related to the Coptic ⲭⲱⲓⲗⲓ, whence ⲡⲉⲣⲉⲭⲱⲓⲗⲓ, peregrinus, advena."

[52] See Brugsch, 'Zeitschrift' for November, 1867.

[53] Brugsch observes, "With this name is designated the pastoral and nomad tribes of Semitic origin, who lived in the neighbourhood of Egypt, and who are to be thought of as standing to Egypt in the same relation as the Jews," l. c. p. 92. This is the more important since Brugsch does not connect the narrative of Exodus with this period.

[54] On the name "Aperu," supposed to represent Hebrews, see further on. It is found first in papyri of a later date, under the nineteenth dynasty.

[55] This date has given occasion to much controversy. It is utterly irreconcileable with the system of some chronologers. Lepsius at once met it with the assumption that the Egyptian sculptor committed the error of adding a line, the effect of which would be to alter the calculations to the extent of 130 years. He was followed by Bunsen, and, though with some misgiving, by Brugsch. If any answer were needed, it might be given in the words of M. de Rougé: "Ce n'est pas ainsi qu'on peut lever une difficulté de cette gravité : le monument aujourd'hui à Paris est comme gravure de la plus grande beauté ; il appartient du reste à l'époque où les inscriptions présentent la correction la plus parfaite." See also M. Chabas, M.E. ii. p. 18. A more serious objection has since been raised and defended with great ability by M. Chabas. The inscription which gives the official name of Thotmes III., and that which gives the name of the month on which the calculation is based, are on different stones, and cannot be proved to refer to the same date. The latter may possibly refer to additions to the temple. M. Chabas writes with a strong bias, so much so that he even attempts to explain away the well-known phrase for the coming forth or heliacal rising of Sothis ; and Mr. Goodwin, a very high authority, does not consider that he has proved his points. In the present state of the question, all that we are entitled to assume is that the inscriptions may probably refer to the same time, viz. that of the erection of the temple, and give a date which presents a very striking coincidence with that taken from the statement in 1 Kings vi.

a date exactly in accordance with that derived from 1 Kings vi. 1.[56]

In the present state of inquiry it is sufficient to point out the singular accordance between two very different systems of Biblical and Egyptian chronology, whichever may be ultimately adopted.

(14.) Assuming for the present that the persecution of the Israelites began under Aahmes I., the question still remains under which of his successors the Exodus took place. In the absence of monumental evidence the question cannot be decisively settled, but there appear to be substantial grounds for the conclusion that it occurred at the close of the reign of Thotmes II.

The length of the interval between the accession of Aahmes I. and of Thotmes III. cannot be accurately determined. The calculations of Brugsch (which are quite irrespective of our question) give an interval of eighty-one years. According to Josephus, Manetho gives 100 years 5 months for the period between the expulsion of the shepherds and the accession of the Pharaoh whom he calls Mephramuthosis. These dates are wholly uncertain, each recension of Manetho giving different numbers; but the interval probably extended over one hundred years. This coincides very closely with the period required by the Scriptural narrative: some years elapsed before the birth of Moses, eighty years between his birth and the Exodus.

(15.) The events of the succeeding reigns under which Moses must have lived, assuming the correctness of this hypothesis, accord with inferences suggested by the brief narrative of Exodus, and also with notices in Josephus, which though of a legendary character may have some foundation in facts. On the death of Aahmes the government appears to have been in the hands of Nefertari, the Ethiopian princess, either as sovereign, or more probably as regent.[57] Little was known of Amenophis (or Amenhotep) her son, until the following facts were elicited from contemporary monuments. Ahmes, the naval officer already mentioned, went with Amenophis in an expedition into Ethiopia against an insurgent chieftain. The expedition was successful. Josephus gives a long and evidently legendary account of an expedition of Moses into Ethiopia. As a member of the royal household, the adopted child of the King's sister, he would naturally accompany his master; while gratitude to his benefactress would of course give additional impetus to his efforts against an Ethiopian rebel. Amenophis was undoubtedly an able and prosperous king, leaving a great name, and worshipped as a god in after ages.

The circumstances which led to the flight of Moses may have taken place at the close of this reign.[58] Syncellus mentions a tradition that Moses left the court after the death of Amosis and of his daughter, whom he calls Pharie: it is more probable that this occurred some years later, since Moses could not have reached manhood when Aahmes died. At the death of Amenophis he would be about forty. It has been represented as improbable that the adopted son of Pharaoh's daughter found no protector when he slew an Egyptian subject, a most unreasonable objection even if the princess were still living; her death would of course leave him friendless.

(16.) During the reign of Thotmes I., Moses, on this supposition, must have been in Midian, but the events are not without bearings upon his history. The reign was one of great prosperity. The complete subjugation of the district between Upper Egypt and Nubia Proper is attested by the inscription previously quoted and by another found by the Prussian expedition on the rock opposite the island of Tombos.[59] The latter years of his reign[60] were employed in a war of greater interest. We learn from the sepulchral inscription already mentioned that he invaded Mesopotamia, won a great victory, and brought back an immense number of captives. A great advance was thus made in the condition of Egypt. Its

---

[56] A very curious corroboration of this hypothesis may be drawn from some calculations of Mr. Goodwin in the 'Zeitschrift' for 1867, p. 78. He shows that, if certain data be admitted, one of the following dates would fall within the reign of Thotmes III., viz. 1481, 1480, 1479, 1478. He says, "According to the system of some of the chronologists this would suit the reign of Thotmes III." It certainly suits that chronology of the Bible which appears most probable to the writer of this Essay. On grounds quite independent of the astronomical calculation, he would have us go back 120 years, and take 1601, 1600, 1599, 1598 as the date, fixing the accession of Thotmes III. as 1623, 1622, 1621, or 1620. This, as he points out, agrees very nearly with the date of Brugsch, viz. 1625 A.C. It certainly agrees also with the system of those chronologers who adopt the longer interval.

[57] It is an obvious conjecture that such an association may have had some influence upon the feelings of Moses when in later years he married an Ethiopian.

[58] All the recensions of Manetho give thirteen years for Chebron, i.e. Nefertari (see above), and twenty-one for Amenophis. Moses is said to have been forty years old at the time of his flight. The coincidence of dates is perfect, as he was in all probability born a few years before the death of Aahmes.

[59] Ethiopia was henceforth governed by princes of the blood royal. A list of twenty, bearing the style Prince Royal of Cush, beginning with this reign, is drawn from the monuments. The first bears the name Me-Mes, an odd coincidence. See 'Exc.' on Moses.

[60] The duration of the reign is uncertain; the monuments give no information, and the dates of Manetho are in utter confusion.

permaι.ent resources were increased by the acquisition of Nubia, the land of gold,[61] and henceforth we find the Pharaohs in possession of numerous chariots, which, though not unknown,[62] are not represented on early monuments. We have here every indication of national greatness.

(17.) On the death of Thotmes I. the government was once more for some years in the hands of a woman. His wife and sister Aahmes,[63] called Amessis by Josephus, was regent or sovereign, according to Manetho, for upwards of twenty years. Thotmes II.[64] showed energy in the beginning of his reign; he carried on a successful war against the Shasous, the nomad tribes on the north-eastern frontier. No other notice is found of his acts on the monuments. His reign was probably short and certainly inglorious. The following facts are however certain from contemporary monuments.[65] He was married to his sister Hatasou;[66] after his decease, of which the circumstances are unknown, she succeeded him as Queen Regnant. His death was immediately followed by a general revolt of the confederated nations on the north of Palestine, which had been conquered by his father: no attempt was made to recover the lost ascendancy of Egypt until the 22nd year of Thotmes III.

Certainly no conjunction of circumstances can be conceived which would adjust itself more naturally to the Scriptural narrative, if we assume that the Exodus took place at this time. In a history drawn entirely from public inscriptions and monuments, no one would expect to find records of events humiliating to the national pride: a period of heavy and disgraceful calamity would present but a blank.[67] Now the reigns of all other early kings in this great dynasty were prosperous and glorious, filled with great events attested by numerous monuments. This king succeeded to a great place; his first years were brilliant, he cleared his frontiers: there is no indication of rebellion or of foreign invasion, and yet the last years are a complete blank: there is a sudden and complete collapse:[68] he dies, no son succeeding: his throne is long occupied by a woman: and no effort is made to regain the former possessions of Egypt for more than twenty years. We have ample space for the events which preceded the Exodus; we find the conditions presupposed in the accounts of the mission of Moses, and the results which might have been anticipated from calamities which, though not sufficient to crush the nation, would cripple its resources, and for a time subdue its spirit.

Assuming for the present the truth of this hypothesis, we may consider what might be the probable course of events. On the return of Moses from Midian, in the eightieth year of his age, and therefore towards the close of the reign of Thotmes II., he found the Pharaoh in lower Egypt, probably at Zoan (see Psalm lxxviii. 12), *i.e.* Tanis, or as the Egyptians call it Avaris, the city captured by his ancestor The residence of the court for a great part of the year would naturally be in that district. The upper country was quiet after the conquest of Nubia, whereas the territory occupied by the Israelites required watching, and the neighbouring Shasous, or Bedouins, caused constant alarms. The character of the king as described in Exodus was at once weak and obstinate, cruel and capricious,

---

[61] Nub is the well-known Egyptian name for gold.

[62] The war chariot of Aahmes I. is expressly mentioned in the inscription at Elkab.

[63] In these reigns there are several instances of marriages between brother and sister. M. de Rougé observes that it does not appear to have been a custom under the early Pharaohs.—'Recherches,' p. 62.

[64] The joint reigns of Amesses and Mephres, or Misaphris, are computed at thirty-five or thirty-three years in the tables of Bunsen, from Josephus and Africanus. Eusebius omits both Thotmes I. and Amesses. We may not place any reliance on the numbers of Manetho, but they were probably taken from old monuments, and, though often corrupted and distorted, may occasionally be correct. In this case they coincide very strikingly with the narrative of Exodus, allowing an interval of some forty years between the decease of Amenophis and of Thotmes II.

[65] According to the monuments, Thotmes II., his wife Hatasou, and Thotmes III., were children of the same parent or parents. If the joint reigns of Amesses and Thotmes II. extended over thirty years, or even a much shorter period, Thotmes III. could not have been the son of Thotmes I., since he was a mere child at the death of Thotmes II. He is represented as a boy of some ten or twelve years old, sitting on the knees of Hatasou, on the monuments. If we might assume that Thotmes II. and his wife were children of Thotmes I. and Amesses, and that Thotmes III. was a son of Amesses by another husband, this would meet the difficulty. It is certain that Thotmes II. was son of Thotmes I. See 'Denkmäler,' iii. pl. xvi. a. l. 7.

[66] This is probably the true reading of the name, which means "chief of the illustrious." The phonetic value of one of the signs is disputed by Mr. Goodwin, but is shown to be correct by Renouf and Lauth.

[67] M. de Rougé, speaking of the name Aperu (see further on), observes, "C'est la seule trace que la captivité d'Israel aura laissée probablement sur les monuments: il n'est pas à penser que les Égyptiens y aient jamais consigné ni le souvenir des plaies, ni celui de la catastrophe terrible de la Mer Rouge; car leurs monuments ne consacrent que bien rarement le souvenir de leurs défaites." See also the memoir lately published (1869), 'Moïse et les Hébreux,' p. 2.

[68] M. Brugsch says strongly and truly, "as it seems, all that had been previously conquered was completely lost.—'Geographie,' i. p. 54.

UPON THE PENTATEUCH.

such a character as is calculated to provoke or accelerate great national calamities. Nor can we lose sight altogether of the queen. She was a very remarkable woman, daughter, sister, and wife of kings, with the antecedents of her mother and grandmother, both of whom had been regents, and she was able to retain the government of the nation during the prolonged minority of the greatest and most energetic king of the dynasty. Such a woman may well have helped her brother and husband to "harden his heart," after each ague fit of misgiving and terror. That she was a woman of strong religious prejudices is proved by her own inscriptions: as such she could not but be revolted by the insults heaped upon the soothsayers, priests, temples, and idols of Egypt. When her heart was crushed by the loss of her first-born son, we can conceive the mingled feelings which would send her to the king, if not to suggest, yet to strengthen his resolution to make one more effort to save his kingdom from disgrace, and to avenge the long series of calamities upon Israel.[69] These are of course but conjectures, but they rest upon facts distinctly recorded on contemporary Egyptian monuments, and they harmonize thoroughly with the narrative of Exodus.

The history of the next reign supplies some remarkable coincidences.

(18.) Thotmes III. remained in reluctant subjection to his sister at least seventeen years.[70] On taking possession of the throne he defaced her titles on the monuments, and reckoned his own reign from the death of his predecessor, without any notice of the intervening period. It may be inferred from this that her rule was distasteful to the people, associated, it may be, with national disasters. It is certain that during her regency there was a general revolt and confederacy of the nations on the north-west of Egypt from Palestine to Mesopotamia.

It was not until the twenty-second year of his reign—a date, as will appear, of singular importance in this inquiry—that Thotmes III. began a series of expeditions unparalleled for extent and grandeur in Egyptian history.[71]

The following facts are clearly proved.

The king left Zaru, or Pithom, early in the year, and advanced without encountering any opposition to Sarouhen on the southern frontier of Palestine. He was detained by the siege of Gaza, which he took early in the spring of the following year. On the 16th of Pachon, early in March, at a fort named Souhem, he heard of the advance of the allied kings of all the districts between the Euphrates and the Mediterranean. The decisive battle was fought at Megiddo, the earliest and one of the most important of the conflicts in that great battle-field of Western Asia. The allies were completely defeated, the dead covered the plain, horses and chariots[72] in vast numbers were taken, and on the following day the chiefs, who had fled to Megiddo, came to offer submission and tributes, consisting of gold, silver, bronze, lapis-lazuli, coffers of precious metals, chariots plated with gold and silver, magnificent vases of Phœnician workmanship, a harp of bronze inlaid with gold, ivory, perfumes, and wine. The proofs of an advanced civilisation in the nations then dominant in Palestine accord with all the representations in Scripture. The point, however, of main importance in the present inquiry is that the power of the confederacy which gave unity and strength to the people of Canaan was completely broken by Thotmes III., just seventeen years before the date when, on the hypothesis we are now considering, the Israelites entered Palestine.

The incursions of Thotmes continued without intermission during this interval. We have accounts of repeated invasions of Phœnicia, conquests over the Rutens[73] in Mesopotamia, where the king established a fortress or military colony: we find the great names of Assur, Babel, Nineveh, Shinear, the Remenen, or Armenians, and most frequently of the Cheta, the sons of Heth, the Hittites of Scripture.[74]

---

[69] The inscriptions on her obelisk, the most beautiful now remaining at Thebes, give a strong impression of this queen's character. She speaks of her favour with Ammon, boasts of her gracious and popular manners, and is represented in this, and also in other monuments, in masculine attire, including *a beard*. See the inscriptions in the 'Zeitschrift' for 1865, p. 34, and Brugsch, 'Recueil,' ii. p. 79.

[70] Dr. Birch finds a higher date for the joint government, twenty-one years.

[71] A full account of these expeditions was inscribed on the walls of a temple dedicated to Ammon after his last return to Egypt. They are given by Lepsius in the 'Denkmäler,' vol. iii., and in the 'Auswahl;' some are published by Brugsch, 'Recueil,' and by M. de Rougé, 'Étude sur divers monuments du règne de Toutmès III,' 1861. Mr. Birch first encountered, and to a great extent overcame, the formidable difficulties of decipherment and translation. His labours, and those of M. de Rougé and Brugsch, have made them accessible to students.

[72] 892 chariots are mentioned; a very curious coincidence with the statement in Judges v., where we are told that Jabin, in the same battlefield, had 900 chariots.

[73] [hieroglyphs], Rutennu, as M. Chabas has proved, designates the northern Syrians. The name may be read Lutennu, or even Ludennu, and is identified with Lud by M. de Rougemont, 'Age du Bronze.' The presence of Egyptians in Mesopotamia under the eighteenth dynasty, and in the time of Thotmes III., is proved by scarabæi found at Arban, on the Cabus, a tributary of the Euphrates.

[74] M. Chabas denies the identity of the Hittites with the Cheta, chiefly on philological grounds, since the names, of which several are given, indi

One object was steadily pursued by the king during these campaigns. In accordance with the ancient policy of the Pharaohs,[75] but as it would seem because such a measure was especially important at that time, and probably one main motive for the repeated razzias, Thotmes brought an immense number of captives into Egypt. These are his own words:[76] "I made a great offering to Ammon in recognition of the first victory which he granted me, filling his domain with slaves, to make him stuffs of various materials, to labour and cultivate the lands, to make harvests, to fill the habitation of Father Ammon."[77] At Abd el Kurna, in the temple before mentioned, there is a well-known picture of such captives employed in making bricks. It is an admirable illustration of the labours of the Israelites, whom it was formerly supposed to represent: the inscription, however, states that they are "captives taken by his Majesty to build the temple of his Father Ammon."

We have now to call special attention to this fact. The wars of Thotmes III. were terminated by the complete overthrow of all his foes in Syria and Mesopotamia in the fortieth year of his reign. No question is raised about this date. But according to our present hypothesis this took place exactly forty years after the Exodus, immediately before the entrance of the Israelites into Palestine.

They would then have found the country in a state of utter prostration. With the exception of such strongholds as might be retained by the Egyptians to command the road into Syria, the petty kings would keep each his own fortress, with no common head, no powerful ally, accustomed to see their neighbours and kinsmen beaten and subjugated, and, though warlike, well supplied with arms, and occupying forts well-nigh impregnable,[78] yet habituated to defeat, and liable, as the Scriptural narrative describes them, to wild fits of panic at the approach of a new foe. If again, as there is reason to believe, the kings of Bashan, and other districts east of the Jordan, were among the confederates defeated on his first invasion by Thotmes, it would account for their exhaustion, and the extreme terror of the princes of Midian and Moab.[79]

(19.) It may be asked how could the Israelites during that period escape the notice of the king? It is certain that the high road, always followed by the Egyptian armies, ran along the coast of the Mediterranean till it turned off towards Megiddo. The Israelites were in the desert of Tih, a district not easily accessible and offering no temptation to a conqueror whose energies were concentrated in a desperate war. Had they remained in the peninsula of Sinai they would have been within his reach, for its western district was subject to Egypt from a very early period.[80] It is possible that their flight might have been one motive for an expedition which, as we learn from an inscription in the Wady Mughara, was undertaken by the forces of Hatasou and Thotmes in the sixteenth year of their joint reign.

A far more serious objection rests on the improbability that the powerful kings of the eighteenth and nineteenth dynasties would have permitted the invasion or the continued occupation of Palestine by the Israelites.

We might answer in the first place that this objection applies to every other date suggested by chronologers. The very latest date assumes that the Exodus took place under the son or grandson of Rameses II., and that the Israelites passed the Jordan in the time of Rameses III. But that Pharaoh was one of the most powerful sovereigns of Egypt, and it is certain that his descendants, the princes of the twentieth dynasty, retained command of the communications by land and water with Mesopotamia. This is proved by

---

cate a different origin. Most Egyptologers, however, retain the older view, which is defended by very convincing arguments by M. de Rougé. It is confirmed also by the Assyrian inscriptions, which make the Khati or Hatti occupy the country between the Mediterranean and Carchemish, their frontier city in the times of Tiglath Pileser I., see Rawlinson's 'Ancient Monarchies,' vol. ii. pp. 315, 317, and Menant, 'Syllabaire Assyrien,' p. 155, who identifies them with the Hittites. The identification of the Remenen is proposed by Brugsch.

[75] We have a very early record of this policy in the reign of Pepi, of the sixth dynasty. See M. de Rougé, 'Recherches,' p. 128.

[76] See Brugsch, 'Recueil de Monuments Égyptiens,' vol. i. p. 53.

[77] See Brugsch, 'Recueil,' i. p. 53.

[78] The history of the siege of Gaza, which lasted more than a year, may account for the Egyptians leaving so many cities untouched, retaining a partial or entire independence. This applies to campaigns under the nineteenth and twentieth dynasties.

[79] This gives a peculiar force and suitableness to the words of Balaam, twice repeated, "God brought them out of Egypt. He hath, as it were, the strength of an unicorn." Num. xxiii. 22, xxiv. 8.

[80] The intercourse between Egypt and the west of the peninsula began under Snefru, the last Pharaoh of the third dynasty. He defeated the Anu, the ancient inhabitants, and founded a colony at the Wady Mughara. The most ancient monument in existence records this event. The copper-mines there were worked under Chufu (Cheops) and other sovereigns of the fourth and following dynasties. We read of a formal inspection by Pepi. See M. de Rougé, 'Recherches,' pp. 7, 30, 31, 42, 81, 115. The mines were worked under Amenemha, twelfth dynasty, and the influence or sovereignty of Egypt continued unbroken till long after the Exodus. M. Chabas shows that under the twentieth dynasty the communications were regularly carried on

an inscription of great interest and importance, well known to Egyptian scholars, which belongs to the reign of Rameses XII., towards the close of the dynasty. M. de Rougé[81] says, "Elle suppose une domination encore incontestée sur la Mesopotamie, des relations amicales entre les princes d'Asie et le Pharaon, ainsi que des routes habituellement parcourues par le commerce." However it may be accounted for, it is certain that during the whole period between Joshua and Rehoboam the Israelites were not disturbed in the possession of the strongholds of Palestine, although the Pharaohs, as we have just seen, retained an undisputed supremacy in Western Asia up to the time of Samuel or Saul.

There are, however, facts, which, though seldom noticed, are sufficiently obvious, and may enable us to understand the policy of the Pharaohs.

It is clear, even from the history of the campaigns of Thotmes III., that at the end of each campaign the Egyptians withdrew their forces altogether from the countries which they overran, content with the plunder, and especially the capture of prisoners, with the submission of the chiefs, and the tributes which they were secure of exacting. This might be a result of the constitution of the Egyptian armies. The Calasirians and Hermotybians, the warrior caste, had settled homes to which they would certainly choose to return, probably each year after the subsidence of the inundation, when their labours would be required for the cultivation of the fields. We have no trace of permanent occupancy of foreign stations, excepting one in Mesopotamia, another at the copper-mines in the Wady Mughara, and perhaps of a few fortresses on the route through Syria. A rapid campaign directed against the nations to the north of Palestine, who were in a state of chronic insurrection, and threw off the yoke at every opportunity, would give an Egyptian king neither the leisure nor the inclination to assail the strongholds occupied by the Israelites. It must also be borne in mind that the Israelites attacked the most powerful enemies of Egypt, the Hittites and Amorites, and that, whereas their conquest certainly did not result in the establishment of a formidable empire, it was an effectual check to the restoration and consolidation of the powers which Thotmes had overthrown. We do not find notices of many incursions under the immediate successors of Thotmes. That which is recorded, under Amenophis II., appears from the inscription[82] to have been carried on by sea. The three invasions under the nineteenth and twentieth dynasties, by Seti I., Rameses II., and Rameses III., had each the same general object, and was pursued on the same system and with the same general results, although as we shall find presently a considerable number of Israelites were probably carried into captivity by the two last-named kings.

If the date which is here assumed be correct, we shall expect that those events which are ascertained from later Egyptian monuments of the eighteenth and nineteenth dynasties will harmonise with it. An absolute contradiction would be fatal to the hypothesis, which of course will be materially strengthened by general and special coincidences.

(20.) The reign of Thotmes III. was followed by a period of great prosperity. The supremacy of Egypt in Western Asia was unbroken, certainly during the two following reigns. Is this general statement compatible with the conquest of Palestine by the Israelites? To answer this question we must look closely at the events in each reign, not forgetting that, as we have already shown, a general supremacy was undoubtedly retained from the accession of the nineteenth to the termination of the twentieth dynasty: that is throughout the period which all chronologers hold to have extended to the end of the book of Judges.

Immediately after the accession of Amenophis II. he undertook an expedition against the Rutens. He appears to have advanced as far as Nineveh; he certainly returned to Egypt with the trophies of a great victory. An inscription at Amada in Nubia, quoted by M. Brugsch, 'H. E.,' p. 111, and by M. Chabas, 'Voyage d'un Égyptien,' p. 194, states that this king slew seven princes of the confederates at Tachis (a city in Syria), and that "they were hung head downwards on the prow of his Majesty's ship."

These facts are of considerable importance. They show that the whole energies of the Pharaohs were directed against the confederates on the north of Palestine, whose defeat and prostration would of course effectually prevent them from marching into Palestine either to support their allies, or to avenge

---

[81] 'Journal Asiatique,' 5th series, vol. viii. p. 204.

[82] The word used in reference to the invasions of Asia in the reigns of Amenophis II. and III., is ⸻, which indicates a naval expedition. See 'Denkmäler,' iii. pl. 82. M. Chabas, who quotes the inscription, 'Voyage d'un Égyptien,' p. 194, refers, of course by oversight, to Amenophis I. It is a point of much importance in this inquiry to have this intimation of the transport of troops to Phœnicia by water. It is more than probable that the Egyptians had a considerable navy under the vigorous administration of the early kings of this dynasty. We have, in fact, the representation of the transport of chariots and horses on ships in the tomb of Ahmes at El Kab, which belongs to this very period. See Rosellini, M. C., pl. cx., and Duemichen, 'Fleet of an Egyptian Queen,' taf. xxviii. 5.

their fall before Joshua. The mention of the ship of war has a special interest. It is obvious that, as the Pharaohs were the undisputed masters of the sea after the conquest of Phœnicia under Thotmes III., the most ready and effectual way of transporting their troops would be by ships.[83] We have not sufficient data to prove that they did adopt this mode of carrying on their communications, but there are other indications which make it extremely probable. The word used in the inscriptions which record invasions of Asia under Amenophis III. is specially if not exclusively used of naval expeditions. (See note 82.) It has been shown very lately by a contemporary inscription that at a far earlier period, under the sixth dynasty, the Pharaoh Pepi sent large forces by sea against the Herusha, probably Asiatics. See De Rougé, 'Recherches,' p. 126. The rapid march of an Egyptian army along the coast of Palestine some seven or eight years after the passage over the Jordan would not present any considerable difficulty, directed as it was against the confederates of the Amorites, but every semblance of a difficulty disappears if the expedition was by sea.

Under Thotmes IV. we have no notice of Asiatic war. The tributes were probably paid without any further attempt at resistance during that reign, which, though undistinguished and probably short, does not appear to have been a period of disturbance.[84]

(21.) The reign of Amenophis III. was long and prosperous. His supremacy in Syria and Mesopotamia was uncontested; but though the inscriptions speak of expeditions into the Soudan, and of tributes brought from all nations, there is no indication of Asiatic warfare. It was a period of almost uninterrupted peace. There is no probability that the struggles in Palestine would have attracted the attention or called for the interposition of a monarch engaged in magnificent works which surpass in beauty and rival in extent those which were completed under any succeeding dynasty.

There are, however, facts which may perhaps justify a conjecture that the relations between Egypt and the Israelites underwent some modification in the interval after the occupation of Palestine which corresponds to this period. In 1 Chron. iv. 17, we read that Mered, of the tribe of Judah, founded two families, one by an Egyptian wife Bithia, who is called a daughter of Pharaoh. This family was settled at Eshtemoa, on the hilly district of Judah, south of Hebron, now Isemna; the ruins indicate the site of a considerable city. The exact place of Ezra, the father of Mered, in the genealogy is uncertain, but it belongs apparently to the second generation from Caleb. Now we have the fact that Amenophis III. was married to a very remarkable personage who was not of royal parentage and not an Egyptian by creed. Under her influence Amenophis IV., her son (whose strongly marked features have a Semitic, not to say Jewish character),[85] completely revolutionised the religion of Egypt, more especially attacking its most loathsome form, the phallus-worship of Khem. The names of this princess, Tei, and of her parents, Iuaa and Tuaa, bear a singularly near resemblance to that of Mered's wife.[86]

(22.) However this may be, the few known facts of Egyptian history from the accession of Amenophis IV., or Khu-n-Aten (*i.e.* Glory of the Sunbeam), are readily adjusted to the early annals of the Judges. For a few years the ascendancy of Egypt in Mesopotamia was unimpaired. The Rutens and their allies were kept in submission; no indication of an occupation of Palestine by Egypt or its opponents is to be found: then comes a time of internal struggle and confusion, during which all the Asiatics threw off the yoke. We have here a place for the invasion of Cushan Rishathaim, the King of Mesopotamia; which must have taken place about a century after the death of Joshua. The

---

[83] It is to be observed that the current of the Riviera di Ponente runs along the Delta and thence to the coast of Palestine or Syria, carrying with it so much of the Nile mud as to fill up the harbours. The sea voyage would be easy and rapid. We find notice of the transport of corn from Egypt to the land of the Kheta under Merneptah. 'Histor. Ins.,' iii. 24.

[84] Some scholars hold that the Exodus took place at the close of this reign. This theory is supported by ingenious arguments, but is scarcely reconcileable with the condition of Egypt at the beginning of the next reign, nor does it present the coincidences which are drawn from the reign of Thotmes II. and his successors.

[85] The most striking portraits of this king are in Prisse, 'Monuments,' pl. x., and in the 'Denkmäler III.;' all the portraits have the strongest character of individuality, wild, dreamy, fanatic, with features in some points unlike those of his predecessors, and approaching closely to the Hebrew type. Ewald recognises and attaches much importance to the traces of an attempt to introduce a more spiritual form of religion at this period: see 'Geschichte,' v. I. ii., p. 51, note, 2nd edition.

[86] In Egyptian, 𓂋𓏏𓇌𓏏. The name Bithia, exactly transcribed, would be 𓃀𓏏𓇌𓏏. The name of the father of Tei, 𓇋𓅱𓄿𓀀, Iua, is markedly Jewish. See the inscription in Brugsch, 'Geographische Inscriften,' i., taf. ix., No. 333. In a work lately published (1868), 'The Fleet of an Egyptian Queen,' M. Duemichen points out the resemblance and apparent connection between Aten and אדון, Lord, observing that the hieroglyphic group is certainly used with reference to this Semitic name of God. See explanation of pl. III.

growth of the power of the Moabites, and of the nomads bearing the general denomination of Shasous in Egyptian, of Amalek, Edom, Ammon, &c., in Hebrew, was a natural result of the expulsion of the Mesopotamians on the one side, and the prostration of Egypt on the other.[87] In the mean time the Cheta were gradually acquiring the ascendancy from Cilicia to the Euphrates,[88] occupying the strongholds in Syria, and encroaching gradually on the borders of Palestine, a position which, notwithstanding repeated and triumphant invasions of their own territory, they occupied during the whole period of the nineteenth and apparently also the twentieth dynasties.

The duration assigned by M. Brugsch to the eighteenth dynasty from the decease of Thotmes III. is about 100 years. The corresponding period, on the hypothesis we are now considering, brings us near to the occupation of Palestine by Eglon King of Moab. It will be observed that, although the results of comparison of Egyptian and Hebrew annals are, and must be to a great extent conjectural, inasmuch as no direct or distinct notice of the events preceding the Exodus or following the occupation of Palestine by the Israelites is found on Egyptian monuments, and no notice of Egyptian history occurs in the books of Joshua, Judges, and Samuel, yet the conjectures rest on data established beyond all contradiction. They do not profess to do more than show that the two series of events dovetail, and mutually sustain and explain each other: the coincidences, whether they be held complete and convincing or not, are unsought; they forced themselves on the writer's attention, and gradually led him to give a decided preference to the hypothesis which has been here defended, over that which is at present generally supported by Egyptian scholars.

(23.) We have now to consider what arguments favourable or unfavourable to this hypothesis are drawn from Manetho and other documents known to us through the medium of Greek. Here we must carefully distinguish between facts borne out by contemporary monuments, and statements which, whether correctly or incorrectly represented by the translators and epitomizers, are contradicted or not corroborated by such authority.

The Exodus is assumed by all ancient chronologers, who derived their information from Egyptian sources, to have taken place under the eighteenth dynasty.[89] Josephus, who regards the expulsion of the Hyksos to be but a confused tradition of the departure of the Israelites, places it under the first king whom he calls Tethmosis; Africanus, who follows Ptolemy the Mendesian, under Amos, i.e. Amosis, or Aahmes. Eusebius brings the transaction lower down, but still long before the nineteenth dynasty, viz. under Achencherses or Achencheres, i. e. probably Khunaten, the son of Amenophis III. This opinion is said by Syncellus to be avowedly in contradiction to all other authorities. Eusebius was probably led to it by the evident indications of great disturbances under that reign, and by the tradition that emigrations of considerable extent took place soon afterwards.[90]

Passing to Manetho's own statements, we find that he represents the kings of the Thebaid and of Upper Egypt as engaged in a great and long-continued warfare with the Hyksos: he asserts that the king, Misphragmuthosis, drove them out of all the other districts in Egypt, and confined them within the vast enclosure of Avaris. His son Tethmosis besieged the city with an immense army, and, being unable to capture it, made a treaty with them, permitting their departure: they are said to have gone forth with their furniture and their cattle, forming a host not less than 240,000 in number, then to have traversed the desert between Egypt and Syria, and at last, fearing the Assyrians, at that time masters of Asia, to have settled in Judæa, where they built the city of Jerusalem.

Setting the account which has been given in these pages side by side with the statement of Manetho, we see at once the character of his history, and the corroboration which it supplies to what has been advanced.

(1) A war of considerable duration was carried on between the kings of Upper Egypt and the Shepherds. Here Manetho and the monuments agree. (2) The king whom Manetho calls Misphragmuthosis achieved great successes in war, but did not capture Avaris. It is true that the Shepherds were attacked by the first king of the dynasty, but untrue that Avaris was not captured by him. Here we have a partial agreement, but the name of the king is not correct. (3) Certain enemies of the Egyptians were in possession of a limited district under his successor. The monuments are silent, but from the Pentateuch we know that the Israelites occupied Goshen at this time, as nearly all Egyptian scholars agree. (4) These enemies left Egypt by permission, traversed Syria, and occupied Palestine. Their forces amounted to 240,000. The monuments are silent. We have the Scriptural account with scarcely a variation.

---

[87] It is also to be remarked that the Rutens, or Assyrians, were so weakened towards the end of the eighteenth dynasty that they lost the ascendancy; a fact sufficiently explained by the overthrow of Cushan Rishathaim.

[88] See Brugsch, 'H. E.,' p. 127, and M. Chabas, 'Voyage,' p. 325.

[89] All the passages are collected in the first volume of Bunsen's 'Egypt.'

[90] Viz. the expulsion of Danaus and his settlement at Argos. See the statement of Diodorus, p. 462.

The principal inference bearing on our present subject is that all these notices refer to the same period, viz. the early years of the eighteenth dynasty.

In another work Manetho gives what may have been in his time the Egyptian account of the Exodus: it is utterly worthless, and, as nearly all critics have observed, was evidently invented by a person who had the Scripture narrative before him.[91] It represents the Israelites as lepers, and identifies Moses with Osarsiph,[92] a priest of Heliopolis, evidently Joseph. The Egyptian king, in whose reign the enemies first made themselves masters of all Egypt, committing atrocities far beyond those attributed to the Hyksos, is called Amenophis. According to this strange figment, Amenophis committed his son Sethos, called also Rhamses, to the charge of some private individual, and retired into Ethiopia, whence he returned with a great army, and finally ejected the lepers and their allies the Shepherds from Egypt, pursuing them unto the borders of Syria.

All names and events are here in hopeless confusion: but each name and each event is found, though under very different circumstances, either in Egyptian or in sacred history. Osarsiph and Moses, the character of the Mosaic law, the prevalence of leprosy, the connection of Osarsiph with Heliopolis, are taken from Scripture: the names of Avaris, Amenophis, Sethos, Rhamses, from Egyptian monuments. The expulsion of the Shepherds by an Egyptian king with forces brought from Ethiopia is, as we have seen, historical. Amenophis himself, the son of Amosis, made an expedition into Ethiopia. There was a religious aspect of the struggle between the Shepherds and the Egyptians. No inference of any value can be drawn from the whole narrative in favour of either hypothesis now under consideration. On the one side the names of Sethos and Rameses would point to the nineteenth dynasty, but it is scarcely conceivable that a man having the least acquaintance with Egyptian history should have confounded Sethos and his son, or have represented Amenophis as the father of Sesostris. On the other side, the name of Amenophis would point distinctly to the eighteenth dynasty, and the whole narrative might get into the shape which it here assumes, if the facts above proved, and the combinations which we have assumed, had been manipulated by an Egyptian priest under the Ptolemies.

The story told by Chæremon (see Josephus c. Apion, i. 32) is a modification of this. The Israelites are led by Moses and Joseph, whose Egyptian names are said to be Tisithen and Peteseph.[93] They join an army of 300,000 men, whom Amenophis had left at Pelusium, because he did not wish to bring them into Egypt. Amenophis retreated into Ethiopia, where he had a son named Mepenes, who, when he became a man, drove the Jews into Syria, and recalled his father Amenophis from Ethiopia.

An extract from Lysimachus, given also by Josephus, is a mere corruption of the Scriptural narrative, invented under the Ptolemies. It names Bocchoris (B.C. 721) as the Pharaoh of the Exodus: a striking instance of contemptuous disregard of all historical probabilities.

Diodorus has two accounts:[94] in one (c. xxxiv. 1) the adherents of Antiochus Sidetes represent the Jews as a despicable race expelled from Egypt, hateful to the gods on account of foul cutaneous diseases; in the other (c. xl. 1) he relates that in ancient times a pestilence which raged in Egypt was ascribed to the wrath of the gods on account of the multitude of aliens who with their strange worship were offensive to the gods of the land. The aliens were therefore expelled. The most distinguished among them betook themselves to Greece and other adjoining regions, among whom were Danaus and Cadmus. The main body, however, retired into the country afterwards called Judæa, which at that time was a desert. This colony was led by Moses.

From what source Diodorus derived this latter statement is quite uncertain, but the colouring is Egyptian. It undoubtedly points to an earlier period than the nineteenth dynasty; most probably to that assigned by Eusebius to the emigration into Palestine and Greece, viz. the latter reigns of the eighteenth dynasty.

As a general result from this part of our inquiry, we find that, with two exceptions, all the names and transactions noticed by Manetho, and by Greek writers, whether heathen or Christian, harmonise with the course of events under the eighteenth dynasty. One exception is simply noticeable for its absurdity, bringing the Exodus down to the eighth century and the twenty-fourth dynasty: the other is more important since it introduces the names of Sethos and Rameses, but under circumstances and in a relationship which evince either an entire ignorance or a wilful perversion of the best known facts of Egyptian history.

One argument remains of which the importance will not be questioned. Critics of the most opposite schools who have carefully

---

[91] See Browne, 'Ordo Sæclorum,' p. 581.

[92] There is an evident reference to one or both of Joseph's names. The last syllable, Siph, answers to seph, and also to Zaf, food. Osir means rich, powerful, &c.; Osersiph, rich in food.

[93] Seph, the last syllable of Joseph's Hebrew, and the first of his Egyptian name, seems to have left a permanent impression, and that a very natural one, as meaning "food." See Essay II.

[94] See Browne, 'Ordo Sæclorum,' p. 581.

considered the bearings of the facts drawn from Egyptian sources upon the narrative of Exodus, concur in the conclusion that the accession of the eighteenth dynasty was the beginning of the persecution, and that the Exodus took place in some reign before the accession of the nineteenth. Thus Knobel, Winer, and Ewald.

(24.) We have now to consider whether the facts, admitted by all Egyptologers and attested by monuments and other documents of unquestionable authority, which appertain to the history of the 19th dynasty, accord with the hypothesis here adopted, or whether we should acquiesce in the conclusion to which eminent scholars have been led;[95] that which identifies Rameses II. with the first persecutor of the Israelites, and places the Exodus under his son Merneptah. It may be well to say at once that the reader might accept that conclusion without repugnance: on certain conditions it may be reconciled with the narrative of Exodus, which some at least of its chief supporters accept as an authentic document, if not as the production of Moses. It is, however, a question to be determined not by authority, but by circumstantial evidence. It is now universally admitted that no monuments of this or of any other period make mention of the events which preceded or immediately followed the departure of the Israelites.[96] In the following pages every fact bearing upon this question will be fairly and fully stated, together with the arguments on both sides.

(25.) We have first to inquire into the known or probable condition of Palestine during the interval between the early Judges and the time of Deborah and Barak. It is an interval of considerable duration, extending over some two centuries, if we take the numbers in the book of Judges literally,[97] and covering certainly as much time as is occupied by the annals of Egypt between Amenophis III. and the later kings of the nineteenth dynasty.

During the whole of that period it is distinctly stated that the Israelites were not in exclusive possession of Palestine; they dwelt among the Canaanites, Hittites, and Amorites, and Perizzites, and Hivites, and Jebusites. (Judges iii. 5.) Many of the most important strongholds were occupied by these nations, including nearly all those which are mentioned in the records of Seti and Rameses II.[98] Generally speaking, the open country was retained by the Amorites, against whose iron chariotry the Israelites could not make head even in Judah (Judges i. 19). The whole district from the southern frontier upward belonged to them, and was apparently called, as we find it even in inscriptions of the twentieth dynasty, the land of the Amorites.[99] This was the case even when the land was at rest: in some portions of Palestine the Israelites brought the inhabitants into partial subjection and made them tributaries, but the process was slow, alternating with many disasters, and not completed until a very late period, long after that which is now under consideration. When the Israelites were themselves brought under subjection the whole country was in a state described incidentally in the song of Deborah: the highways were unoccupied, the villages ceased, there was war in the gates, *i.e.* the strongholds were blockaded; while not a spear or shield was to be seen among 40,000 in Israel (Judges v. 6).

It is clear therefore that an Egyptian army traversing Palestine at any part of this time would not encounter Israelitish forces in the open field: Israel had no chariotry, no horses, and would not be concerned with expeditions which were invariably directed against its own enemies in Syria.[100]

We have now to remark the very exact correspondence between the Hebrew and

---

[95] M. de Rougé says in his 'Report on Egyptian Studies,' 1867, p. 27, "Les rapports de temps et de noms ont fait penser à M. de Rougé que Rameses II. devait être considéré également comme le Pharaon sous lequel Moïse dut fuir l'Égypte et dont le très-long règne força le législateur futur des Hébreux à un très-long exil. À défaut d'un texte précis qui manque dans la Bible, cette conjecture rend bien compte des faits, et elle a été généralement adoptée." It has in fact been adopted by Egyptian scholars in Germany, France, and England. The sobriety and reserve with which M. de Rougé states this conjecture, to which he attaches great value, stand out in strong contrast to the confidence with which it is maintained as a proved fact by most of his followers.

[96] See the statement of M. de Rougé quoted above, note 67.

[97] The numbers in Judges iii. are a long but uncertain time from the conquest under Joshua, x, Cushan Rishathaim, 8 years; peace, 40 years; Eglon, 18 years; rest, 80 years; Philistines, x; *i.e.* $146 + x + x$. Brugsch calculates the interval between Amenophis III. and Merneptah at 200 years. The elements of uncertainty on both sides are considerable, but the general correspondence is noteworthy.

[98] *E.g.*, Jerusalem, Bethshean, Taanach, Dor, Megiddo, Zidon, Bethshemesh, Bethanath. Gaza and the other four cities in the district were evidently recovered during this period by the Philistines. Compare Judges i. 18 with iii. 3 and 31. In the inscriptions of the nineteenth dynasty, I cannot find any Palestinian city which the book of Judges represents as occupied by Israelites in the period after the conquest.

[99] See *e.g.* Duemichen, 'Hist. Inschriften,' pl. xxviii., xxix.

[100] The strongholds which the Egyptians, under Seti and Rameses II., had occasion to attack, and some of which they appear to have garrisoned, were, with scarcely an exception, in the possession of Canaanites or Hittites. See note 98.

Egyptian notices of the power predominant in Western Asia.

The Assyrians, called Rutens by the Egyptians, were masters of the north of Syria, and of all the countries extending from Cilicia to Mesopotamia, when that district was invaded by the early kings of the eighteenth dynasty.[101] Their influence in the confederacy opposed to Egypt was gradually superseded. Up to the time when Seti I. invaded Syria, *i.e.* according to our computation about 150 years after the Exodus, they were the leaders of the confederacy, which was then broken, dispersed, and for a season crushed by repeated defeats. M. Chabas observes (p. 328) that under Rameses II. they disappear altogether, they are not even mentioned in the great campaign of his 5th year. Their name is found on a small number of monuments belonging to later reigns, but there is no indication that they had recovered their former importance.

In accordance with this we find that their last appearance in Palestine was soon after its occupation by the Israelites, when Cushan Rishathaim was finally expelled by Othniel the nephew of Caleb.

Nothing more probable than that such an event should have occurred under the eighteenth dynasty (see above, p. 460); its occurrence at the late period which the acceptance of the other chronological system would involve is inconceivable.

In place of the Rutens or Assyrians we find the Cheta in possession of Syria at the accession of Seti I. The identification of this people with the Hittites of Scripture has been questioned, chiefly on philological grounds,[102] by M. Chabas; but is still generally admitted by Egyptian scholars, and appears to rest on very sufficient evidence. It is certain that the Hittites, Canaanites, Zidonians, and Amorites, formed part of the confederacy opposed to Seti and Rameses II. We learn from the book of Judges (i. 26) that the country north of Palestine was called the land of the Hittites, that Phœnicia retained its independence, and further, that at the close of the period the whole country was in subjection to Jabin King of Canaan, the captain of whose host was "Sisera,[103] which dwelt in Harosheth of the Gentiles."

Taking now the contemporary history of Egypt derived exclusively from public inscriptions, we have the following coincidences:—

(26.) In the first year of his reign Seti marched against the Shasous, who a that time occupied, or were masters of, the countries from Pithom to Pakanana.[104] He defeated them with great slaughter, and advanced into Mesopotamia. On a second invasion he again traversed the territory occupied by the Shasous and took several forts.

The word Shasous, as we have before seen, was a general denomination for the warlike tribes who at various times overran Palestine. About the time which the synchronism of Egyptian and Hebrew history, on our hypothesis, assigns to Seti and the Israelites, we find Eglon King of Moab in combination with the children of Ammon and Amalek, master of the country. At any time within the period, as we have also observed, the opponents whom the Pharaohs would encounter in Palestine would come under the same general designation.

The fortresses named in the inscriptions which refer to this campaign were one and all occupied by the enemies of Israel.

The Shasous conquered by Seti were in alliance with the Syrians and the Rutens: both mentioned as foes or oppressors of the Israelites.

The great object of Seti and his successor was to conquer Syria, and to occupy its principal city called Kadesh, which is probably identified by Egyptologers with Edessa, or Ems, on the Orontes.

At the close of this reign Egypt was dominant in Syria, and held some fortresses, but the power of the Cheta was unbroken, and we have no traces whatever of a permanent occupation of Palestine. As in the time of Shamgar, the Israelites were in the state described as that of Seti's foes in the inscriptions, either hidden in caves or entrenched in inaccessible strongholds.[105] The principal effect of the invasion, so far as the Hebrews were concerned, would be a diminution in the power and resources of their foes.

The transactions in the reign of Rameses II. will require very special attention. We shall best arrive at a conclusion by considering each point in detail which may tell for or against either hypothesis.

(27.) Rameses Merammon, the Sesostris[106] of

---

[101] For proofs see M. Brugsch, 'H. E. and G.,' and the dissertation by M. Chabas, 'Voyage d'un Égyptien,' p. 318-332.

[102] *I.e.*, from the comparison of Chetan names (of which seventeen are preserved in the treaty between Rameses II. and Khetasar) with the names of Hittites found in the Bible.

[103] The name is evidently *Chetan*; it has the most marked characteristic of the names collected by M. Chabas (see note 74), viz. the termination Sera or *Sar*: see further on.

[104] It is questioned whether this means a fort in Syria or Canaan.

[105] See Brugsch, 'Recueil I.,' pl. xlv. e: "throwing away their bows they fled to *caves* in terror from his majesty." The word "caves" here is Hebrew, [hieroglyphs], magaratha = בערות.

[106] This is generally held, but is not certain. Dr. G. Ebers doubts whether Herodotus does not refer the name to Seti I., and suggests that the hieroglyphic group may perhaps be read Sesetres, or Sesetresu, which comes very near Sesostris. See 'Egypten und die Bücher Moses,' i. p. 79. 1868.

the Greeks, succeeded Seti I. It was supposed until very lately that he was very young, a mere lad, on his accession; but the researches of M. Mariette [107] have brought to light the curious and interesting fact that he had been associated with his father from infancy in the royal dignity, and that he had been admitted to the full prerogatives of a Pharaoh long before the death of Seti: in the first year after that event he is represented as surrounded with a family of twenty-seven princes and as many princesses. This is important in its bearings on Egyptian chronology. There is no doubt that he reigned full sixty-seven years, a date found lately on a monument at Tanis, but from what epoch the year is dated remains uncertain; probably from an epoch long anterior to his father's decease.[108] The argument is of still more importance in its bearing upon another biblical question. Of no king in the whole series of Pharaohs could it be asserted, in such direct contradiction of well-known facts, that he was a *new king*, rising up over Egypt: of none can it be proved more certainly that he did not at once make an entire change in the policy of this kingdom. The argument upon which much stress is laid, viz. that his lengthened reign accords with the notices in Exodus, falls with the assumption that he outlived his father some sixty-seven years.

In the 5th year of his sole reign Rameses invaded Syria. In the neighbourhood of Kadesh, on the Orontes, he defeated the confederates, who as usual had revolted when their conqueror died. The battle would almost seem to be the only one in which the king distinguished himself; it is described on numerous monuments, and forms the subject of what is called the epic poem of Pentaour.[109] The campaign was successful: one of the most important results for this inquiry was the capture, and perhaps the occupation, of some fortresses in Palestine. We have the name of Sharem, or Shalem; it is doubtful whether this is to be identified with Jerusalem; if so, it was, as we know, long after the conquest, in possession of the Jebusites; Maram and Dapur, in the land of the Amorites, are also mentioned: Bethanath, still occupied by Canaanites (see Judges i. 33); and lastly Askelon. The notices of Askelon in Judges show that it was taken at first by the Israelites (i. 18), and imply probably that it came again into the occupation of the Philistines some time later, perhaps in the time of Shamgar. See Judges iii. 31.

So far the argument remains stationary. The condition of Palestine under Rameses continues as under Seti, quite in agreement with that which we find in the 3rd chapter of Judges; Egypt commanding the high roads, occupying some fortresses taken principally from the Canaanites, but concentrating its forces and developing all its energies in its attempt to retain supremacy in Syria. We should of course expect to find among the numerous prisoners of war brought back by Rameses some Israelites, if, as we have assumed, they were then dwelling, though not dominant, in the land.

(28.) It was after the king's return to Egypt that the events occurred upon which the hypothesis rests that he reduced the Israelites of Goshen to bondage. Diodorus relates that he constructed a line of fortifications from Pelusium to Heliopolis. It is, however, proved by the monuments that such a line existed under the ancient empire, and that it had been enlarged and strengthened by his father Seti. It is also known that in the latter years of his reign Rameses effaced his father's name and substituted his own on many of the principal constructions of Egypt;[110] still there can be no reasonable doubt that he employed vast numbers of captives in the fortresses which

---

[107] 'Fouilles exécutées en Égypte, en Nubie, et au Soudan, d'après les ordres de S. A. le Viceroi d'Égypte, par Auguste Mariette Bey.' Paris, 1867. The second volume, in two parts, contains text and plates; the first volume is not yet published. The most important inscription, from the temple at Abydos, has been carefully analysed by M. Maspero, 1867. It belongs to the first year of the sole reign of Rameses II., who is represented as associated from his infancy with his father, and formally crowned while yet a boy. Compare Maspero, p. 29, with Mariette, p. 15. Mariette's work throws an unexpected and curious light on the character of Rameses, and on the state of Egyptian art towards the end of his reign. In the earlier inscriptions Rameses expresses the highest veneration and gratitude to his father; in the latter he effaces the name of Seti, and substitutes his own. The earlier portions of the building and inscriptions are remarkable for beauty and breadth of style; the later sculptures are incorrect, and the style detestable. See 'Fouilles,' especially p. 99. Since this note was printed, M. Mariette has withdrawn the volume here quoted from circulation, and substituted another, in which much valuable matter is suppressed.

[108] This materially affects the argument to which M. de Rougé has always attached special importance (see above, note 95). Moses could not have been born until some years after the beginning of the persecution, *i.e.*, according to M. de Rougé, Brugsch, and others, after the Syrian campaign; when Rameses is now proved to have been at least in the maturity of middle life. We thus lose the space of eighty years required by the Biblical narrative before the Exodus.

[109] This curious and important document was first explained and afterwards translated by M. de Rougé, M. Chabas, and Mr. Goodwin. The translation in Brugsch, 'Histoire d'Égypte,' p. 140, is that of M. de Rougé. The original exists in a hieratic papyrus, Sallier III., in the Select Papyri of the British Museum, and more or less complete in hieroglyphic inscriptions at Karnak and Abu Simbel.

[110] See note [107].

G G

he enlarged, or erected on the banks of the great canal, now called the Wady Tumilat. Among these fortresses two are mentioned specially, the fort of Zaru and Pe-Ramesses. These are assumed by Brugsch to be the Pithom and Rameses of Exodus. The question is fully discussed in another part of this work. Here it is enough to observe that these two cities or forts existed previously. That which Brugsch calls Pithom, but of which the true name in Egyptian is Pa-Chetem en Zalou, was at least as old as the time of Thotmes III. Pithom itself, the Pa-Tum of the inscriptions, the Πάτουμος of Herodotus, may have been, and probably was, in its immediate neighbourhood, but it is nowhere mentioned in connexion with Rameses. The case is much stronger for the other city.[111] Pa-Ramessou, or A-Ramessou, *i.e.* the residence of Rameses, was undoubtedly enlarged by this king: it was a city of the highest importance, the capital of a rich district, the residence of the sovereign, where he received foreign embassies, reviewed his troops, and held a magnificent court. Still it is proved by contemporary documents that it was not founded by Rameses. In the fifth year of his reign, before the great works for the defence of the frontier were constructed, Rameses received the ambassadors of the Cheta in this city, which, according to M. Brugsch, is mentioned by name in the reign of Seti.[112]

Considering, however, the great importance of this citadel, to which additions were made continually under his reign, we should expect that a large number of captives would be employed in the works, and among the captives brought into Egypt at the end of the Syrian campaign Israelites would naturally be looked for. Although it was the usual policy of Rameses to employ prisoners in the parts of his dominions most remote from their own country, there were obvious reasons why this system should be departed from in their case: there was a grim irony, quite in keeping with Egyptian character, in reducing Israelites to servitude on the scene of their forefathers' oppression; and their escape, difficult under all circumstances, could be, and, as we shall see, actually was, guarded against by measures of peculiar stringency.

(29.) Now, that Israelites were actually employed then and there has been, though not really proved, yet shown to be so probable that nearly all Egyptian scholars accept it as a fact. M. Chabas[113] first called attention to the circumstance that the Egyptian word "Aperu" corresponds very closely to "Hebrews," the name by which the Israelites were perhaps best known to foreigners. The transcription is not quite accurate: the letter "p" is by no means the proper representation of the Hebrew "b," nor have I found any conclusive example of a substitution;[114] but the general acquiescence of Egyptologers may be regarded as a sufficient ground for admitting the identification.

Still the question remains whether these Hebrews were in the condition described in Exodus, inhabitants of the district in which

---

[111] The identity of this city with Rameses is the main, in fact the only substantial argument for making Moses the contemporary of Rameses II. Even were it admitted that the name, in the exact form which it takes in Exodus, was first given by Rameses, the argument, though strong, would not be conclusive, for all hold that the names of places may have been altered at successive revisions of the Pentateuch, the new and well-known name being substituted for the old, when a modern editor would give a note. The argument, moreover, has no weight at all when urged by critics who suppose that the Pentateuch was written after the Israelites were connected with Egypt under Solomon, or later. In that case the names of the district and city would of course have been taken from actual usage. I believe the truth to be as stated in the text.

[112] Brugsch, 'H. E.,' p. 156.

[113] See 'Melanges Egyptologiques,' i. p. 42-54, and ii., on Rameses and Pithom.

[114] After a repeated examination of the Semitic names transcribed on Egyptian documents, I find no instance upon which full reliance can be placed. Many names occur in which the B is represented by the Egyptian homophones. The Egyptian "p" represents the "ph" of the Hebrews. Mr. Birch concurs in this statement. The word 𓂝𓊪𓂋, Aper, or Apher, occurs in the annals of Thotmes III. twice in an inscription at Karnak. See M. de Rougé, 'Album Photographique,' pl. lii., and is transcribed by M. de Rougé, עפרה. The exact and proper transcription of the Aperu would be עפרי, not עברי. A still stronger objection, which seems indeed insurmountable, is suggested by one account of these Aperu. In the inscription at Hamamat, under Rameses IV. (see further on), they are called Aperu n na petu Anu, *i.e.* Aperu of the Anu. The Anu are often mentioned as a warlike race in Nubia, who rebelled frequently against the Pharaohs. They are here written with a group which always represents bowmen, whether auxiliaries or enemies.

𓉻𓎡𓏥𓀘𓂋𓏤𓏪𓌙

The inference is almost irresistible that these Aperu, and, if these, the others also, were Nubians, condemned to work in the quarries. See Brugsch, 'Geog. Inschriften,' iii. p. 77; and on the Anu, see the 'Excursus II.,' article Anamim. It seems after all doubtful whether Aperu is a proper name, or simply denotes workmen. Maspero says that they were, as one knows, the servants of the temple. 'Essai,' p. 22. Neither Birch nor Brugsch give this in their Dictionaries, but the etymology points to such a meaning, "Aper, to supply or prepare," and Maspero is a good authority. Aperu is given as a variant of Shennin, attendants in the Ritual, c. lxxviii. 37.

they were employed, or prisoners of war. The former alternative is generally assumed: a close examination of the original documents seems decidedly to point to the latter.

Four Egyptian documents give an account of these Aperu. Two belong to the reign of Rameses II. They are official documents of very peculiar interest. One of them was written by a certain Kawisar, an officer of the commissariat at Pa-Ramesson. He reports that he has executed his orders, which were to distribute corn to the soldiers and to the Aperu, or Apuriu, who are employed in drawing stones for the great Bekken (*i.e.* fortified enclosure) of Pa-Ramesson: the corn was delivered to a general of mercenary troops; the distribution was made monthly. In another report (which however does not mention the Aperu) he speaks of large supplies of fish for the city.

The obvious inference from this account would seem to be that persons employed in such labours, fed by rations, and under military superintendence, were captives, and not inhabitants of the district.[115] The name "Kawisar" resembles the well-known names of Cheta: Chetan officers are found in the service of Rameses, and such a man was peculiarly qualified for the office, both as a natural enemy of the Hebrews and as familiar with their language.[116]

The second document has special claims to attention, since M. Chabas has shown that it is probably the original report addressed by a scribe Keniamen to an officer of high rank, the Kazana, or General Hui,[117] of the household of Rameses. It proves that strict injunctions were given to provide food for the officers of the garrison and also for the "Aperu" who drew stones for the Pharaoh Rameses Merammon in a district south of Memphis

This is a strong corroboration of the conclusion that, if Israelites, they were prisoners of war. The Israelites of the Exodus, from first to last, are represented as forced to labour in their own district under Egyptian taskmasters, who were certainly not soldiers and with a complete national organization of superintendents.

The other documents complete the argument. Aperu were employed in considerable numbers in reigns which all admit to be posterior to the Exodus. In a document of great importance, of which M. Chabas gives an account (see 'Voyage d'un Égyptien,' p. 211), we find a body of 2083 Aperu residing upon a domain of Rameses III. under the command of officers of rank called Marinas: from the signs attached to these names it is evident that they were not subjects but captives.[118] Here, again, the inference is natural that they were brought by Rameses III. on his return from a campaign in Syria. (See further on.) Another notice (see note 114) is found under Rameses IV.: 800 Aperu were employed in the quarries of Hamamat, accompanied, as in all the cases where they are mentioned, by an armed force, generally a detachment of mercenaries. With regard to the Aperu in both reigns, M. Chabas supposes that they may have remained after the Exodus as mercenaries. It may be so; if so, the same explanation would apply to the Aperu under Rameses II.; but it scarcely agrees with the descriptions of their condition, and it seems very improbable that any considerable number of Israelites should have wished or dared to stay, or that their presence would have been tolerated by the Egyptians at all for a long time after the Exodus.

It is to be observed that in every case, far from wishing to diminish the numbers of these labourers, the Egyptian kings took great pains for their maintenance; they were valuable as slaves, not objects of suspicion as disaffected and dangerous subjects.

(30.) Reverting now to the condition of Western Asia, we find that during the latter years of this reign the Cheta retained their position as the dominant power in Syria. In the twenty-first year of Rameses he made a formal treaty [119]

---

[115] This inference is in fact the first which would suggest itself to a scholar looking at any of these documents. M. Brugsch observes (in the third part of his great work on Egyptian Geography, published in 1860, see p. 77), "This name, as the determinative shows, evidently belonged to a foreign people, who had been taken prisoners in the Egyptian campaigns, and condemned to work in the quarries, a custom noticed by all ancient writers on Egypt, and especially with reference to Rameses II."

[116] In the 'Mél. Egypt.' M. Chabas assumes that the name is Semitic. He has since taken much pains (see 'Voy. E.', pp. 326-330) to prove that the Chetan names are altogether of a different origin. The argument stands good in the form above proposed, whichever view is taken.

[117] M. Chabas treats this as a proper name. M. de Rougé shows that it is equivalent to קצין, and means general of cavalry. See 'Revue Archéologique,' Août, 1867. The name Hui is Egyptian, and is found under the ancient empire. This does not support Dr. Ebers' statement, that the cavalry was always under the management of Semitics in this time. See 'Ægypten,' &c., p. 229.

[118] In addition to the stake, which denotes foreigners or slaves, they have for a determinative "a leg in a trap." This is used sometimes for dwellers in general; but the proper meaning, as given by Birch ('Dict. Hier.'), is "entrap, ravish, trample;" and Ebers gives the same meaning to the word which is used in this passage.

[119] This curious document is printed in Brugsch's 'Recueil.' It has been translated, first by Brugsch, and lately by M. Chabas, 'Voyage d'un Égyptien.' Among the terms is one, to which both parties evidently attached great im-

with Chetasar, their king; both parties treating on terms of equality and pledging themselves to perpetual amity. The alliance was confirmed by the marriage of Rameses with the daughter of Chetasar. Between two great powers thus evenly balanced Palestine might be, and probably was, in a state of comparative tranquillity for a period corresponding with the uncertain interval between Eglon and Shamgar. At the close of that interval, which would cover the time of Rameses and extend into the reign of Merneptah, the sacred history represents the south of Palestine as occupied, for the first time after the Exodus, by the Philistines, and the north completely subjugated by Jabin King of Canaan.

(31.) Notices are found in papyri of this period which give some notion of the state of Palestine. The most important is that which was first analysed by Mr. Goodwin, and has since been translated and explained with remarkable ingenuity and learning by M. Chabas.[120] It recites the adventures of an officer of cavalry employed, as it would seem, on a mission into Syria towards the end of the reign of Rameses II. Whether the adventures are real, or, as M. de Rougé[121] and others maintain, the narrative is fictitious, composed for the instruction of students preparing for military service, may be uncertain, but the notices, so far as they go, are valuable, and were probably derived from persons who had been engaged in the campaigns of Rameses. A considerable number of names have been identified, some with certainty, others with more or less of probability, with cities well known from the Scriptural narrative. It is, however, to be remarked, that of these a very small proportion, and those for the most part very doubtful, belong to the interior of Palestine; and that these lie almost exclusively on the high-road, followed, as we have before seen, by the Egyptian armies. The traveller is represented in the first part of the narrative as proceeding at once to Syria,[122] where the transactions occur which occupy the greater part of the story.[123] That country was held by the Cheta, but it was in a state of general disorganisation, overrun by Shasous, and the supremacy of Egypt was evidently recognised. On his return the officer crossed the Jordan, and touched apparently at some places[124] in the north of Palestine; this part of the journey was beset by almost insurmountable difficulties: the country seems to have been almost impassable to a charioteer; until he entered Megiddo (which, as we before saw, was in possession of the Canaanites in the time of the early Judges) he had to encounter the Shasous, from whom he escapes by a precipitate flight, not without serious detriment to his person and property. The description reminds the reader of all the notices in the book of Judges which refer to periods when the Israelites were driven to their fastnesses, or hiding in caves, while the open country, or the passes, were infested by robber hordes from the adjoining deserts. At Joppa, where the authority of Egypt appears to be recognised, the journey seems to come to an end. No mention is made of Israelites in this papyrus, none indeed was to be expected:[125] the only designation for the inhabitants with whom the officer came into contact was Shasous—that which the Egyptians gave to all the nomad and pastoral tribes, probably including the Hebrews, who occupied the countries between their frontiers and Syria.

(32.) One point of great importance in reference to this and the succeeding reigns, in which the events recorded in Exodus are so generally assumed to have occurred, remains to be considered. The collection of papyri in the British Museum, of which the principal have been published by the trustees, belong for the most part to this period. They were written either under Rameses II. or his immediate successors. They indicate a very considerable development of Egyptian literature. The writing is legible, and the composition includes a varied treatment of many distinct subjects, giving a tolerably complete idea of the social and political condition of the people, especially of those employed in the district adjoining Pa-Ramesson. It was quite natural to expect that, if the Israelites were settled in Goshen, or had been very lately expelled, when those documents were written, some notices of them would be found, some allusions at least to the events preceding the Exodus. Accordingly a writer,[1.6] to whose industry and ingenuity we are indebted for some of the first attempts to decipher and

portance, viz. the mutual extradition of fugitives. Stress is laid upon this as bearing upon the narrative in Exodus, but with little cause: it was a condition not likely to be omitted, under any circumstances, between the owners of immense numbers of slaves and the rulers of disaffected districts.

[120] Under the attractive title, 'Voyage d'un Égyptien en Syrie, en Phénicie, en Palestine, &c., au 14ᵐᵉ siècle avant notre ère.' 1866.

[121] See 'Revue Archéologique,' Août, 1867, p. 100, note 1.

[122] This is noticed by M. Chabas, p. 96; it accords with the view above stated, that the communications between Egypt and Syria were most commonly by sea.

[123] At least three sections, from p. 18 to p. 23.

[124] The places named in the first part of the fourth section are in great confusion, and, though evidently Palestinian, are not clearly identified.

[125] M. Chabas ('Voyage,' p. 220) draws an argument against the presence of Israelites from the mention of camels as used for food; but the explanation of the passage is doubtful, and the Shasous named in it were nomads of the desert, who, as M. Chabas observes, ate camel's flesh.

[126] Mr. Dunbar Heath, 'Papyri of the Exodus.

explain the select papyri, believed, and for a time persuaded others, that he found abundance of such notices. He speaks of a true, original, and varied picture of many of the very actors in the Exodus, a Jannes mentioned five times, a Moses twice, a Balaam son of Zippor, and the sudden and mysterious death of a prince royal, &c. Since his work was written all the passages adduced by him have been carefully investigated,[127] and every indication of the presence of the Israelites has disappeared. The absence of such indications supplies, if not a conclusive, yet a very strong argument against the hypothesis which they were adduced to support. It may be added that the descriptions of that part of Egypt which had been occupied by the Israelites happen to be both full and graphic in these documents, and they represent it as remarkably rich, fertile, and prosperous, the centre of an extensive commerce, occupied by a vast native population, a land of unceasing festivities and enjoyment, such as the district might well be some centuries after the departure of the Israelites, such as it certainly was not during the period of their cruel persecution, and of the long series of plagues which fell on their oppressors.

(33.) We now come to the reign of Merneptah, in which M. Brugsch, and many distinguished scholars, consider that the Exodus took place. Merneptah succeeded his father Rameses II., and is said to have reigned twenty years.[128] The notices of this Pharaoh in M. Brugsch's 'Histoire d'Égypte' are but scanty; few monuments were erected in his reign; even his father's tomb was left unfinished; and the indications of a decline in art, and exhaustion of national resources observable towards the close of his father's reign, are numerous and strong. There are not, however, on the monuments, or in the papyri of that period, any notices of internal disturbances towards the end of his reign; it can be shown that the eastern frontier was vigilantly guarded, and nomad tribes admitted under due precautions to feed their cattle in the extensive district occupied by the herds of Pharaoh.[1-9]

The beginning of this reign was, however, signalised by the complete discomfiture of an invasion, which presents some points of peculiar interest in reference to general history as well as to our present inquiry.[130] The names of the confederates are partly African (not negro, but Libyan), and partly Asiatic or European; if M. de Rougé's conclusions are admitted, they consisted of Tyrrhenians or Etrurians, Siculi, Sardinians, Achæans, and Lycians, the first appearance of these well-known names in history. None of the names here mentioned enter into the register of ancient people given in the tenth of Genesis.[131] They were therefore evidently unknown to Moses, who must, however, have had his attention specially drawn to them had he returned to Egypt at that time. The ravages committed by these invaders on the north-west of Egypt are described in language which has an important bearing on a point already discussed; "nothing," the king says, "has been seen like it even in the times of the kings of lower Egypt, when the whole country was in their power and reduced to a state of desolation."

Merneptah appears to have conducted the campaign with considerable ability: he boasts of the supplies of corn by which he saved his people in some districts from perishing by famine, and of a successful incursion into the enemies' territories: unlike the Pharaoh of the Exodus, who led his own army and perished with it in the Red Sea,[132] but like Louis XIV., of whom the reader is constantly reminded in this ostentatious period, Merneptah did not expose his sacred person to the chances of war: "his grandeur was chained to the bank of the river by the divine command." The result was a complete victory, the enemies were driven out of Egypt, vast numbers of prisoners and spoils of great value rewarded the conquerors, obelisks were erected to commemorate the event, and the customary self-laudations of the Pharaoh were accepted and echoed by a grateful people. M. de Rougé observes that the terms in which the Egyptian writer[133] de-

---

[127] See Mr. Goodwin's article in the 'Cambridge Essays' for 1858. This remarkable essay attracted little notice in England, but made an epoch in one of the most difficult and important branches of Egyptian studies. This opinion is completely confirmed by M. Chabas and M. de Rougé, 'Moïse et les Hébreux,' p. 6.

[128] This is quite uncertain: different recensions of Manetho give nineteen and forty years. The highest regnal year in Egyptian documents is the seventh.

[1-9] See 'Excursus II.,' p. 1. The passage here referred to is quoted and translated by M. Chabas, 'Mél. Égypt.,' ii. p. 155, from the papyrus in the British Museum, Anastasi vi. pl. iv. l. 13.

[130] M. de Rougé gives a full account of the inscription at Karnak (since published by M. Duemichen) which describes this invasion. See 'Revue Archéologique,' Juillet et Août, 1867. The general tenour was known to M. Brugsch; see 'H. E.,' p. 172. The identifications of M. de Rougé are maintained with equal learning and acuteness, and, as I have observed (since this note was written), they are for the most part accepted by Dr. Ebers, p. 154.

[131] It is more than probable that every name in that register was known in Egypt, in Phœnicia, or Assyria, before Moses wrote; names not mentioned by him were first known in Egypt under the nineteenth dynasty. If the register had been written under the kings, as M. Ewald assumes, the absence of these great names is inconceivable.

[132] See notes on Exodus.

[133] 'Revue Archéologique,' l. c. M. Rougé

scribes his triumph are in striking opposition to the severity with which late historians have judged his character.

M. Brugsch lays some stress on an inscription which proves that Merneptah lost a son who is named on a monument at Tanis.[134] This he connects with the death of Pharaoh's first-born; but it is evident from that inscription that Merneptah lived some time after his son's death, certainly a longer time than can be reconciled with the account in Exodus.

The little that is actually known of the later years of this Pharaoh militates against the assumption that they were disturbed by a series of tremendous losses. The papyri written about that time or a few years later represent the district of Rameses or Goshen as enjoying peace and remarkable prosperity (see above), and there is reason to believe that the Cheta and Egypt were still in alliance (see the last note): a state of affairs which ensured peace on the eastern frontier.

On the other hand, the facts thus made known, and the probable inferences from them, harmonise with the account of the condition of Palestine in Judges iii. and iv. Jabin, king of Canaan, obtained the complete mastery of the north at the close of the period. The designation of this king is obscure; Canaan can scarcely be the name of the whole country or of the whole people descended from the son of Ham. It is possible that Jabin may have taken his title from the great fortress in the north, Pakanana, of which mention is repeatedly made in the campaigns of Seti and Rameses II., retaining that title after his occupation of Hazor. In that case he was a Cheta, whether or not we are to identify that people with the Hittites. The name of the captain of his host, Sisera, is still more striking. It bears the closest possible resemblance to the principal Chetan names in the treaty with Rameses, of which one main characteristic is the termination Sar (see note 103). Sisera's position is altogether peculiar, and the most natural explanation of it is that he was the chief of the confederates of Syria, and as such commanding the forces of Jabin. The number of chariots, 900, as I have already remarked, corresponds most remarkably with the 892 taken by Thotmes III., after defeating the confederates of Syria on the same battle-field of Megiddo.

The important question of dates has still to be considered. The chronology even of this comparatively late period may still be regarded as open to question: but at present nearly all, if not all, Egyptian scholars consider it certain that the year 1320 occurred in the reign of Merneptah. This rests on calculations too lengthy and difficult to be here discussed: the agreement of scholars may suffice, especially as no one assigns an earlier date to the reign. But we have thus very little more than 300 years, at the utmost 320, between the Exodus and the building of the temple. When we deduct from this number the 40 years in the wilderness and some 30 years up to the death of Joshua on the one hand, and on the other at least 100 from the death of Eli to the building of the temple, we get only 150 years for the whole period of the Judges, including the long government of Eli: little more in short than 100 years for the interval between Joshua and Eli. The events which the most sceptical criticism accepts as historical can by no possibility be compressed within so limited an interval: 200 years is the very least that any manipulation of the narrative can elicit for those transactions; the contradiction is fatal either to the hypothesis of Egyptologers or to the Hebrew records, *i.e.* either to a conjecture resting on coincidences which scarcely bear a searching criticism, or to written documents which all scholars admit to contain a series of authentic transactions. On the other hand, if the reign of Merneptah be assumed to coincide, as we have shown to be probable, with the ascendancy of the Chetan Jabin or Sisera, we have as elsewhere a very near approximation to complete agreement: Hebrew chronologers fixing the date of the temple building at 1010, and the defeat of Jabin somewhere about 1320.[135]

(34.) Little is known of the interval between Merneptah and Rameses III.: that it was a period of weakness and disturbance is tolerably certain, and as such it may supply arguments for either hypothesis, for the Israelites would be left in peace whether they were in the wilderness or in Palestine: if the calculations of Brugsch and other scholars can be depended upon, the duration of the interval was some 33 years, nor can there be much room for doubt, since the dates of Merneptah and Ra-

---

translates the passage addressed to Merneptah, 'Bonheur extrême dans ton retour à Thèbes en vainqueur. On traine ton char avec les mains. Les chefs garrottés sont devant toi, et tu vas les conduire à ton père Amon, mari de sa mère.' Anastasi, iv. pl. v. l. 1, 2.

[134] The defunct prince is represented in the act of offering a libation and incense to Suteh, the god of Avaris. The deity wears a crown exactly resembling that of the Chetan king. It is curious, and may indicate special amity between Merneptah and that family, with which his own was nearly connected: he may have been a son of the Chetan princess married by Rameses II. in the twenty-second year of his reign.

[135] This odd coincidence is unsought. The dates, 1340 for Jabin, 1320 for Barak, are given by Browne, 'Ordo Sæclorum,' p. 281. Thenius, ' Exegetisches Handbuch,' vol. iii. p. 469, gives 1429 for the death of Joshua, adding, "Von da bis 1188 Othniel, Ehud, Jair, Deborah und Barak, Gideon, Abimelech, Thola, Jair" (a misprint for Jephtha). This leads nearly to the same conclusion, and gives ample scope for the events of the scriptural narrative.

meses III. are generally accepted. The importance of this calculation will be shown presently.

Rameses III. was the last Egyptian king whose reign was signalised by great victories in Syria. The events are recorded in numerous inscriptions at Medinet Abou, published by M. Duemichen: a manuscript of great extent in the possession of Mr. Harris [136] has not yet been printed, but the contents so far as can be ascertained confirm the inscriptions, especially in the historical details. The first years were occupied by wars with the same confederation of Libyans and Mediterraneans who had been repulsed by Merneptah: these wars began in the fifth and were terminated in the twelfth year of his reign. We have, moreover, notices of an expedition into Syria in the eighth year, probably in the interval between two campaigns in Africa. A decisive battle was fought in Northern Syria, in which the Cheta are represented as undergoing a complete defeat.[137] A long list of places attacked or taken in this campaign is given by M. Brugsch ('Geographische Inschriften,' vol. ii. p. 75), and some are identified with names well known in Scripture. Of these by far the larger number belong to Syria,[138] and the general result from the notices of the war in the inscription would seem to be that this Pharaoh, like his predecessors, · traversed Palestine rapidly,[139] not diverging from the usual high road, nor losing time in the siege of strongholds occupied by a people who were certainly not confederates of his formidable enemies. Among the conquered chiefs represented on the walls of Medinet Abou are found the king of the Cheta and the king of the Amorites: from other notices it is known that both designations at that period belong to the district north of Palestine.

Bringing these facts to bear upon the two hypotheses, we observe that, on the assumption that the Exodus took place under Merneptah, the campaign of Rameses III. would exactly coincide with the entrance of Joshua and inasmuch as this king reigned at least twenty-six years,[140] the conquest of Canaan would have been begun and nearly completed while his ascendancy was undisputed. The improbability is obvious.

On the other hand, we have the following indications in support of the opposite hypothesis. Accepting the Aperu as Hebrews, we find that a considerable number, evidently prisoners of war, were employed on the royal domain in this reign, and in the quarries of Hamamat under his immediate successor (see note 114). We observe also that after the overthrow of Jabin the peace of Palestine was undisturbed, as might be expected after the discomfiture of the Chetan confederacy, when the Pharaohs were occupied with the internal affairs of Egypt.[141] The outbreak of the Midianites, described in the sixth of Judges, took place some years later, and was probably a result of the increasing weakness of the monarchy. It will be remembered, however, that the general ascendancy of Egypt in Syria and Mesopotamia was unimpaired to the very end of the twentieth dynasty, an era which, according to all systems of chronology, synchronises with the termination of the period embraced in the book of Judges. Palestine in the mean time went through a series of alternate struggles and successes. That Israel was not crushed or absorbed by the great empires between whom its little territory lay, and by whom it was ultimately subjugated, may be attributed, under God's providence, to their mutual rivalry and nearly balanced power; it was frequently overrun by nomad hordes and conterminous nations, Midianites, Amalekites, Ammonites, and· Philistines; but the character of the people was gradually matured, and prepared for the vast development of its resources and institutions under

---

[136] This is one of the most beautiful and interesting of existing papyri; it may be hoped that it will be ere long in the British Museum, and published and translated by Dr. Birch, a scholar to whom Egyptian students are under the very deepest obligation.

[137] Rameses III. employed a large fleet in this war, and of course transported the greater part of his forces into Syria by sea. See Brugsch and De Rougé.

[138] The only names which are held to belong to Palestine proper are each and all questionable: Jamnia, Azer, Duma, Hebron, alone are identified by Brugsch; the last is more probably the name of a city often mentioned in the inscriptions referring to Northern Syria. A repeated examination of the names in this list, and of those which occur in Duemichen's inscriptions, confirm my impression that Rameses did not occupy Palestine either before or after his Syrian campaign; some few places he may probably have captured on his way. If, however, Chibur or Hebron be the city in Judæa, it would be a strong argument that Rameses III. found the Hebrews there; the Canaanitish name was Kirjath Arba; the old name given at its first building before Abraham, was probably restored after the conquest.

[139] The Philistines were in possession of their five cities in the time of Rameses III., and are represented among his captives: see Brugsch, 'G. I.,' ii. pl. xi. This agrees with the notices of a considerable advance of the Philistines in Judges iii. They probably retook the cities which had been conquered by Joshua.

[140] The date 26 is found in the Serapeum of Memphis: Brugsch, 'H. E.,' p. 193.

[141] Numerous inscriptions and some papyri prove that Rameses III. and his successors were employed in developing the resources of Egypt, and in building palaces and temples. Rameses IV., his son, boasts that he had erected as many monuments in a few years as Rameses II. had done in his long reign. M. de Rougé, 'Études égypt.,' p. 29.

Saul, David, and Solomon, in whose reigns it vindicated its claim to equality with the contemporary empires in Africa and Asia.

It would be too much to expect that the conclusions to which the writer of this dissertation has been irresistibly led will be accepted by those who are satisfied with a system which rests on the authority of many great names; but the greatest care has been taken throughout to separate the facts, which are positively ascertained, from the inferences which must to a certain extent vary according to the state of the reader's mind, his judgment, or his prepossessions. Those facts are stated with all possible care, and with as much of completeness as is compatible with the limits of an Excursus. They have been submitted to the judgment of scholars, and have an independent value; nor, although every year brings important additions to our knowledge of the texts and of their interpretation, is it to be feared that what has hitherto been gained will be overthrown, or the fair and legitimate inferences be considerably modified. The truth of the scriptural narrative does not need such support, but some important links are supplied; the series and meaning of events are better understood in the light thrown upon them by contemporary documents which present coincidences and suggest combinations hitherto unknown, or imperfectly appreciated, by the students of Holy Writ.

Since this Essay was printed, two points of great importance to the argument have been illustrated. (1.) In the work lately published by Duemichen, 'The Fleet of an Egyptian Queen from the seventeenth century before our Era,' we have an account of an expedition into Poumt, *i.e.* Arabia. It proves that a considerable navy was fitted out early under the 18th dynasty: on one plate (xxviii.) the gradual improvement in ship-building is shown by drawings from the 6th, 12th, 17th, and 18th dynasties; on two ships the transport of horses and chariots is represented. (2.) M. Lieblein has published in the last number of the 'Revue Archéologique' (October, 1868) a letter to M. de Rougé, in which he gives very strong reasons for bringing down the date of Rameses II. to the twelfth century. Without accepting all his conclusions, we can scarcely resist the impression that the lowest date hitherto assigned to the 18th dynasty is remarkably confirmed by his arguments. See also 'Zeitschrift,' 1869, p. 122, where the same writer fixes the date of Rameses II. at 1134 B.C. This argument, however, rests on genealogical calculations, which are always open to objection.

The writer has lately ascertained that the copper-mines in the peninsula of Sinai were not worked by the Egyptians from the time when they obtained supplies of copper from Syria, *i.e.* from the reign of Tothmosis I.[142] to the seventeenth year of Tothmosis III., when an expedition was sent under military escort—the last occasion on which the presence of Egyptians is noticed. There were therefore no Egyptians settled on the peninsula at the date assigned to the Exodus in this Essay. This important fact is established, though without reference to the Exodus, in an essay by Dr. Gensler, in the Egyptian 'Zeitschrift,' for October and November, 1870.

---

[142] This transcription now appears to the writer preferable to that which has been adopted in these Essays.

SUMMARY VIEW, ETC. 473

A SUMMARY VIEW OF THE TRANSACTIONS ATTESTED BY EGYPTIAN MONUMENTS, AND OF THEIR CONNECTION WITH HEBREW HISTORY.

Dynasties.	Transactions known from Contemporary Monuments.	Connection with Scriptural History.	
		According to this Excursus.	According to Brugsch and others.
XIIth Dynasty: seven Pharaohs, from Amenemha I. to Amenemha IV., and a queen regnant.	A period of great prosperity; foreigners, especially from Western Asia, received and promoted under the early kings; and under the later kings works of extraordinary magnitude executed to secure the irrigation of Egypt, and to guard against the recurrence of famine.	Abraham received and favoured. Joseph saves Egypt from famine; the Pharaoh master of the resources of Egypt.	
XIIIth to XVIIth Dynasty:	The early Pharaohs still masters of Egypt. Invasion of the Hyksos. Salatis master of Avaris, i.e. Tanis, or Zoan. Egypt divided: the worship of Set, Sutech, or Baal, established by the Hyksos in the north; wars between the Theban dynasty and Apepi or Apophis, the last king of the Hyksos.	The Israelites in Goshen rapidly increasing and occupying the whole district, but in a condition of dependence, or partial servitude.	Abraham in Egypt under the Hyksos. Joseph minister of Apophis.
XVIIIth Dynasty: Aahmes I. (Amosis)	Aahmes I. or Amosis captures Avaris and expels the Hyksos. Buildings of great extent undertaken or completed with the aid of forced labourers or mercenaries. The worship of the Theban deities re-established.	Beginning of a systematic persecution of the Israelites, who are employed as forced labourers in restoring or building forts and magazines in their own district.	The Israelites are supposed to remain during the whole period of the 18th dynasty in undisturbed possession of the district of Goshen.
Nefertari.	The Egyptian Queen, a Nubian by birth, possessed of great influence, both before and after the death of Aahmes.	Moses saved and adopted by an Egyptian princess.	
Amenotep I. or Amenophis.	Expeditions into Ethiopia: the Queen-sister in power; succeeding as Regent.	Flight of Moses into Midian.	
Thotmes I.	Expeditions into Nubia and Mesopotamia; immense increase of the Egyptian power.		
Thotmes II. and Hatasou.	First part of the reign prosperous; no indication of foreign or intestine war; latter part of the reign a blank, followed by a general revolt of the confederates in Syria. Hatasou, queen regnant, and retaining power for seventeen or twenty-two years.	Return of Moses, the Exodus, destruction of Pharaoh and his army.	

SUMMARY VIEW OF TRANSACTIONS

Dynasties.	Transactions known from Contemporary Monuments.	Connection with Scriptural History	
		According to this Excursus.	According to Brugsch and others.
Thotmes III.	First attempt to recover the ascendancy in Syria in the 22nd year. Wars: repeated incursions into Palestine, Phœnicia, Syria, and Mesopotamia, terminating in the fortieth year of this reign.	The Israelites in the wilderness; entrance into Palestine of Joshua in the fortieth year after the Exodus.	
Amenotep (Amenophis) II.	Expedition into Syria by sea: overthrow of the confederated nations to the north of Palestine.	Progress of the Israelites in Palestine.	
Thotmes IV.	A reign without notable occurrences.		
Amenotep III.	A prosperous reign; supremacy maintained in Syria and Mesopotamia: no intimations of warfare in Palestine: the Queen Tei of foreign origin favours a new and purer form of religion.		
Amenotep IV. or Khu-en-Aten. Princes not considered legitimate.	The religious revolution completed: followed by a period of disturbance and exhaustion.	Cushan Rishathaim in Palestine.	
Horemheb.	End of eighteenth dynasty.		
XIXth Dynasty: Rameses I.	No considerable events; notices of war with the Cheta, who from this time are dominant in Syria.	The interval between Cushan Rishathaim, and Jabin, extends to the latter reigns in this dynasty. Palestine remains, to a great extent, in the possession of the Amorites and other people of Canaan; sometimes overrun by neighbouring people, and towards the close of the period subject to the Philistines in the south, and the Cheta, or Hittites, in the north.	
Seti I.	The Shasous or Nomads from Egypt to Syria, and the Cheta and nations of Mesopotamia, broken and subdued by a series of invasions. The empire reaches its highest point of civilisation and power.		
Rameses II.	During many years Rameses II. is co-regent with his father with royal dignity. On his accession as sole monarch, he invades Syria, defeats the Cheta, with whose king, however, he afterwards contracts an alliance on equal terms, marrying his daughter. Captives are employed in great numbers in building, restoring, or enlarging fortresses, cities, and temples; among them Aperu at Pa-Rameses and Memphis. The reign lasts sixty-seven years, but the date of its commencement, whether from his father's death, or his admission to royalty, is uncertain.		First beginning of the persecution of the Israelites; the birth, early life, and exile of Moses.
Merneptah.	Beginning of reign signalised by victory over Libyan and Mediterranean invaders: no expeditions into Asia: general state of amity with the Cheta: eastern frontier of Egypt carefully guarded: indications of unbroken peace and prosperity in the district about Pa-Rameses.	..	The plagues of Egypt, followed by the Exodus.

ATTESTED BY EGYPTIAN MONUMENTS. 475

Dynasties.	Transactions known from Contemporary Monuments.	Connection with Scriptural History	
		According to this Excursus.	According to Brugsch and others.
Seti II., Siptah; is close of XIXth Dynasty.	A period not distinguished by foreign wars: letters, however, flourish, and the nation appears to be peaceful and contented.	Palestine in a state of depression, Philistines in the south, Jabin in the north; revolt against Jabin, overthrow of Sisera, war against Jabin continued for some years.	The Israelites in the wilderness.
XXth Dynasty: Rameses III.	A long series of successful wars in Africa and Asia: Palestine traversed, Syria invaded, and the Cheta overthrown. The reign lasts at least twenty-seven years. Aperu employed on the royal domains.	Israelites recover possession of Palestine after the overthrow of Jabin.	The conquest of Palestine begun under Joshua.
Rameses IV.	A peaceful reign occupied chiefly in great buildings. Aperu, captives of war, employed in the quarries.		
Rameses V. to XI.	A period of uncertain duration, the reigns generally short and undistinguished.	The events recorded in the book of Judges after the time of Deborah and Barak.	The entire series of events from the passage over the Jordan to the close of the book of Judges.
Rameses XII.	In this reign the Egyptians retain an acknowledged pre-eminence in Syria and Mesopotamia.		
Rameses XIII.	Close of the twentieth dynasty.		

(476)

ESSAY II.

ON EGYPTIAN WORDS IN THE PENTATEUCH.

ONE important result of late Egyptian researches is the establishment of a complete system of transcription of Hebrew and Egyptian characters. At present no doubt remains as to the exact correspondence of the Hebrew letters with phonetic signs, or groups of common occurrence in papyri and monumental inscriptions. An attempt will be here made to bring this result to bear upon the transcription and explanation of the names, titles, and other words of Egyptian origin in the Pentateuch.[1] In the first place, the Hebrew word will be represented in those Egyptian characters which are accepted by all Egyptologers as the exact, and for the most part the invariable, equivalents. In the next place, the meaning of the Egyptian words thus represented will be investigated. In no case will any doubtful transcription be admitted: nor will any meaning be proposed for which conclusive authority cannot be produced from monuments or papyri of the 18th, 19th, and 20th dynasties, or from still earlier periods. If the interpretation thus elicited give a clear, complete, and satisfactory meaning, one in perfect accordance with the context, and the evident intention of the writer of the Pentateuch, there can be no question as to its value, whether in regard to the bearings upon the exegesis of the Book or upon the question of authorship. It is highly improbable that any Hebrew born and brought up in Palestine, within the period extending from the Exodus to the accession of Solomon, would have had the knowledge of the Egyptian language which will thus be shown to have been possessed by the writer; it is certain that no author would have given the words without any explanation, or even indication, of their meaning, had he not known that his readers would be equally familiar with them.

The following table, which gives the Hebrew characters and the corresponding phonetic signs or letters in Egyptian, will enable the reader to judge for himself of the accuracy of the transcription. The transcription in Roman characters is that which has been lately proposed by M. de Rougé, and accepted by Lepsius, Brugsch, and other Egyptologers. See 'Zeitschrift für Ægyptische Sprache,' &c., 1866.

---

[1] This Essay was printed in 1868. Since that time Dr. Ebers' work has appeared, to which allusion is occasionally made in the notes.

Hebrew	Egyptian.	Conventional Transcription.	The nearest equivalent in ordinary characters.
א		a, or a	a
ב		b	b
ג		ḳ	g
ד		t	d
ה		h	h
ו		u	u
ח		ḥ, or χ	h, or ch, hard
ט		+ t	t, or th
י		i	i, or ee
כ		k	k
ל		l, or r	l, or r
מ		m	m
נ		n	n
ס		s	s
ע		ā	a, o, or ao
פ		p, or f	p, ph, or f
צ		t	z, or ts
ק		ḳ	k
ר		r	r
ש		s	sh, or s
ת		t	th, or t

In addition to the phonetic letters in this list there are many homophones, and syllabic signs, representing the combination of two or more letters. Full lists of these are given by Mr. Birch in the first and last volumes of the latest edition of Bunsen's 'Egypt;' and by M. de Rougé, in the 'Chrestomathie,' now in course of publication. These signs will be explained when they occur in this excursus: they are especially important in eference to the names of places and official designations.

It must be borne in mind that the vowels are of secondary importance both in Hebrew and Egyptian. They might be disregarded in the transcription were it not that certain affinities between some consonants and vowels are observable in both languages.

The first name in the Bible of purely Egyptian origin, form, and meaning, is Pharaoh.

פַּרְעֹה

The vocalisation and diacritic points show that the Hebrews read this Par-aoh, not Pa-raoh. This is important, since the name, whatever it might signify, was well known as the proper official designation of the kings of Egypt, and its correct pronunciation must have been familiar to the translators of the Pentateuch, and probably also to the punctuators of the Bible. The cuneiform inscriptions have the same division, Pir-u, not Pi-ru.

The transcription gives one of these forms:

(Pa Ra), or, adopting a syllabic form of very common occurrence, ⌷ i. e.

Per, or Phar, פַּר, and the elongated form

which more exactly represents עַ, we have

(Par-aoh), or one of the ordinary variants of this well-known word.

The first of these transcriptions gives a clear and not improbable meaning, viz., 'The Sun.' Ra is the well-known designation of the sun from sunrise to sunset; and it is certain that the King of Egypt was regarded as the favourite or living representative of Ra: the question is, whether this was the usual and formal designation of the king, recognised by his subjects and known to foreigners.

Several arguments are used in support of this assumption.

1. From a very early period, long before the Hebrews came into contact with the Egyptians, the sign ☉, pronounced Ra, was the first and most prominent word in the cartouche, or ring, which contained the official name of every Pharaoh, that is, the name which he assumed at his accession.

But this word was not read apart from the other words in the ring, in most cases it was read at the end, not at the beginning of the designation; it had not the article prefixed, and could not therefore be pronounced Pa Ra, or Pharaoh.

2. The king is always called Si Ra, son of Ra. This designation comes between the two rings. It is very ancient, being first borne by Chafra or Chephren. See M. de Rougé, 'Recherches,' p. 56.

But this is in reality an argument against the assumption. The king was not likely to be called both Son of Ra, and The Ra.

3. The word Pa Ra actually occurs as a title of Merneptah Hotephima, the son of Rameses II., in a contemporary papyrus, Anastasi, VI. Pl. v. l. 2.

The sovereign, living, sound, and mighty, *the good Sun* of the whole land.

But "the good Sun" here is not a title, properly speaking. It is simply one of the numerous epithets applied by the Egyptians to their king; a fact sufficiently evident from the addition of the adjective good.[2] The title in this passage is the first word, however, that may be read and explained.

4. A stronger argument is drawn from the Papyrus Rollin (No. 1888), which gives an account of the trial and execution of a sorcerer under Rameses III. It is explained by M. Chabas, in his curious and valuable work, 'Le Papyrus magique d'Harris.' He writes thus (p. 173, n. 2), " , Pera, le Soleil, Memph. φρα, Heb. בְּרָעָה, designation ordinaire des rois d'Egypt." This seems conclusive, considering the high authority which always attaches to M. Chabas' opinion. It must, however, be observed that no other passage is adduced, nor, so far as I am aware, can be adduced, in support of the statement that it is the ordinary designation of the sovereign; and in this passage the word is understood by Mr. Deveria, and by M. Pleyte (who has lately published the papyrus) to mean "the Sun God," to whom the frustration of the sorcerer is attributed.[3] It is true that the kings of Egypt were called "Horus," or the "Crowned Hawk" (the Sun God, as symbol of victory), a title taken at their accession, and borne upon their standard; but this was equivalent to the epithet Si Ra, Son of Ra, and constitutes, therefore, an argument against the assumption, which, if not disproved, must be regarded as not proven.

We have now to consider the other and well-known form, , more commonly as above, in the title of Merneptah, . If the transcription Per-ao, or Phar-ao, can be relied upon, of which we have presently to consider the evidence, the proof of the identity of the title with Pha-

---

[2] Thus Rameses II. is called "Ra, the life of the world," not as an appellation, but an epithet. Mariette, 'Abydos,' pl. 18, l. 36.

[3] Mr. Goodwin observes, "I am now convinced that Pa-Ra in the Rollin Papyrus means the Sun, or God, and not, as I supposed ten years ago when I first deciphered that papyrus, the king or Pharaoh." Mr. Goodwin's remarks, quoted in these notes, are taken from a letter lately received on this Essay, which was forwarded to him by the writer in 1868.

raoh will be conclusive, for the following reasons:—

The regular title of the King of Egypt, the title, *i. e.*, as distinguished from honorary epithets, by which it is always accompanied, is ⌐⌐, written also ⌐⌐, and ⌐⌐, or ⌐⌐⌐⌐. These forms occur very frequently under the ancient Empire, in the inscriptions of the Denkmæler of Lepsius, and in those examined and illustrated by M. de Rougé, 'Recherches sur les Monuments qu'on peut attribuer aux six premières Dynasties de Manéthon.' The simpler form is more commonly found in the earlier inscriptions. On monuments of the 19th and following dynasties the latter is almost exclusively used. The meaning of the group is not questioned, viz., the great house, or the great double house, *i. e.*, the royal palace: nor is it doubted that it stands absolutely for the sovereign. It is further to be observed that whenever the sovereign is spoken of as such, not by his proper name, or by his distinctive official name, this and no other designation is found. In official letters, in reports and in treaties, this designation generally precedes the proper and official names: in narratives, when the name of the king is not given, it is used precisely in the same way as Pharaoh in the Bible.[4] There can be no doubt but that this was the title which to Egyptians and foreigners represented the person of the king.

It is perhaps difficult to present the full force of this argument; but no one can look through the Papyrus D'Orbiney, or other papyri of the 19th and 20th dynasties, without feeling that, so far as the usage is concerned, we have in this group the exact equivalent of Pharaoh. It is the group which would necessarily be used if Genesis were translated into ancient Egyptian. Pharaoh alone would represent to a Hebrew the central group in the Egyptian formula:—"His majesty *the Sovereign*, full of life, health, and might."

But the transcription presents a difficulty, which for a long time prevented Egyptian scholars from recognising the identity of the designations. The group ⌐⌐ is undoubtedly equivalent to פִּ, or "Pi" in the names of cities, as in Pithom, Pihahiroth, &c. M. de Rougé, however, and M. Brugsch, men of the highest eminence among Egyptologers, whose authority on such a point is especially important, hold that the original and proper pronunciation of ⌐⌐ was "per," or "pere," in Hebrew פֶּר.[5] It is possible that the r, by the common process of phonetic decay, was gradually disused in a word of common occurrence, but it may have been, and probably was, retained in a title of such dignity, especially as it preceded the vowel sound "a o."

Another difficulty is presented by the dual form. If ⌐⌐⌐⌐ actually represented two distinct houses, it would be read either Pere pere or Pere-ti: but as representing not a numerical dual, but a form of majesty, the old pronunciation might be, and probably was, retained unchanged. M. Brugsch (D. H., p. 452) gives several instances which seem to prove that though the sign of the house-plan ⌐⌐ is doubled, it was pronounced in the singular. However this may be, it is a sufficient answer to the objection that the original form, as we have already seen, the form most commonly found in inscriptions unquestionably much older than the Pentateuch, was ⌐⌐ ⎯⎯[6], of which the nearest possible transcription in Hebrew is פַּרְעֹה, Pharaoh.

Another argument, which may be regarded as conclusive, has been adduced by M. C. Lenormant, and Professor Lauth, a distinguished Egyptologer. It is clear that

---

[4] The word occurs ten times in seven lines of the Papyrus D'Orbiney, from p. x. l. 9, to p. xi. l. 4. It has almost invariably the addition of ⌐⌐, living, sound, and mighty; and is generally preceded by "(henef)," his majesty.

[5] See 'Chrestomathie Égyptienne,' p. 79, and 'Dictionnaire Hiéroglyphique,' pp. 452, 482-3. This is questioned by M. Page Renouf, a very high authority; but a reference to Mr. Birch's Dictionary, in Bunsen's 'Egypt,' vol. v. p. 464, will shew the invariable connection between ⌐⌐ and ⎯⎯, and one variant at least of ⌐⌐ for ⌐ points in the same direction. I believe M. de Rougé to be, as usual, right in his conclusion. See also M. Chabas, 'Pap. Mag. Harris,' p. 48, and 'Mél. Ég.' ii. p. 204. The group ⌐⌐ ⎯⎯ ⌐⌐ is found in ancient inscriptions, and proves the phonetic value of the shorter form. Mr. Goodwin observes, "there can be no doubt that ⌐⌐ was originally par:" he adds, "I agree with your remark that in such a title the pronunciation would very probably be retained."

[6] Thus, for instance, M. de Rougé renders ⌐⌐ ⎯⎯ suten rech (*i.e.*, near relative, perhaps grandson), du Pharaon, 'Rech.' p. 97. Numerous inscriptions in the Denkmæler, Abt. II., leave no doubt as to the usage. I find that Dr. Ebers adopts the same view, and considers it as unquestionably correct, p. 264. Thus also Duemichen, who gives an example from the time of Thotmes III. See 'Fleet of an Egyptian Queen,' pl. iii.

IN THE PENTATEUCH.

this transcription exactly explains the assertion of Horapollo, 1, 61; viz. that οἶκος μέγας, "the great house," is the true meaning of the hieroglyphic group which formally represents the Egyptian king, and which therefore is the equivalent of the Hebrew Pharaoh.

Other derivations of the word have been proposed, more or less unsatisfactory. The late Duke of Northumberland suggested that it might be identified with the Uræus (in Egyptian ⟨hiero⟩, arāt), the basilisk or the diadem of every Pharaoh. To this the objections are insuperable. The transcription is inexact; the word is never found as a royal designation; and when the sign stands alone it represents a female deity.

The identification with the Coptic ⲡⲟⲩⲣⲟ was natural. It is the general designation of a king; but it appears to represent Pa-Oer, a word constantly employed in the texts to represent a prince, whether native or foreign, but which is never applied to the Pharaoh. Mr. Birch has lately shown the writer two passages in the 5th volume of the Denkmæler, pl. 53, in which ⟨hiero⟩, or ⟨hiero⟩, appears to stand for Pharaoh. It would seem, however, to be a proper name, not a title or general designation.

פוֹטִיפֶרַע, Potiphera,
and
פוֹטִיפַר, Potiphar.

The first part of both names is admitted to correspond to the Egyptian ⟨hiero⟩, Pa-ti, "the given," i.e., a person devoted to, dependent upon, &c. Instances are given by Champollion (not in the Grammar, but in the Précis), and by Rosellini, who says that the form occurs frequently in the name ⟨hiero⟩, Patipara, of which פוֹטִיפֶרַע is an exact transcription. The name signified "devoted to Ra," the most natural designation for the High Priest of On or Heliopolis, the head-quarters of Sun worship. This derivation is well known and universally accepted. It may perhaps be used as an additional argument that ⟨hiero⟩, Pa Ra, represented the Sun-God, not the Sovereign.

The other name presents more difficulty. Gesenius and others assume that Potiphar is simply an abbreviation or a variant of Potiphera. This is very improbable. The transcription of Egyptian words in Hebrew is now admitted by scholars to be exceedingly accurate, and the omission of the characteristic letter ā, ⟨hiero⟩, ע, would be without a parallel. The meaning of the word must be "devoted to Par," or Phar. If the transcription of ⟨hiero⟩, פַר, Phar, be accepted (see above), Potiphar would signify devoted to, or dependent upon the house or palace, and would be written in Egyptian ⟨hiero⟩ Though this name does not occur in the texts it seems to be in accordance with the usage of the language,[7] and is a very suitable designation for the captain of Pharaoh's bodyguard. The priest thus takes his name from the deity to whose service he is attached, the courtier from his master's house.

אָסְנַת
Asenath, wife of Joseph.

The first syllable may be transcribed by ⟨hiero⟩, the exact phonetic equivalent, or by either of two well-known groups ⟨hiero⟩, "as,"[8] or ⟨hiero⟩, the name of Isis, which has the same phonetic value.

The second part may be read ⟨hiero⟩, with the determinative ⟨hiero⟩ or any of the numerous variants. It represents the goddess Neit, or Neith, the Athene of Greece.

The combination of these transcriptions, whichever is adopted, gives a clear meaning in accordance with Egyptian usage.

As-Neit would mean favourite of Neith, or Minerva: the word "as" signifies precious, sacred, or consecrated.

⟨hiero⟩ would mean Isis-Neith. The double name seems strange, but it was not uncommon in Egypt thus to combine the names of two Deities in one proper name. The first example of a man's name taken from

---

[7] We have χerp-pere, mer-pere = housesteward, major-domo: common titles under the ancient empire. I must add that Mr. Goodwin does not admit the probability of this transcription, which needs the support of ancient inscriptions.

[8] Mr. Goodwin has lately proposed a different reading for this sign, viz., "sheps," and he is followed by Brugsch; but both M. Le Page Renouf and Professor Lauth have since *proved* that "as" is the true value in the older texts. See 'Zeitschrift für Ægyptische Sprache,' &c., 1868, pp. 42 and 45. Thus also Maspero, 'Essai,' p. 16. Since this was printed, I have observed ⟨hiero⟩ as a variant in Mariette's 'Fouilles d'Abydos.' Mr. Goodwin now says he can only admit that the group is a polyphone, and may have both values. He adds that he considers the combination Isis Neit supplies a much more plausible explanation.

the gods, given by Champollion in the Grammar, p. 135, combines the two divine names Hor Phre, a second in the same page combines Chons and Thot. It is a strong argument in support of this explanation that a Priest of On would naturally give to his daughter the name of a Deity specially connected with the locality. The principal objects of worship, next to the Sun-God, were Seb and Nut (not Neit), who were honoured as the parents of Osiris and *Isis*, the two tutelary Deities. See Brugsch 'Geographische Inschriften,' vol. i. p. 255. Isis moreover was a name commonly given to women, and most likely to be borne by a daughter of Potiphera. It is also to be remarked that there was a close connection between Isis and Neith. Isis was worshipped at Sais in the temple of Neith, under the name As-ta-oert, Isis the Great. See Brugsch, l. c., p. 245.

The connection of Joseph with this family would seem to have had lasting and very serious consequences. Asenath may, or may not, have adopted her husband's faith—probably she did so; but, like the wives of Jacob, she may not have separated herself altogether from her father's influence, or have cast away altogether the traditional superstitions of her family. It is natural to refer the idolatry of the Ephraimites to this origin. Mnevis, the black bull, was worshipped at On as a local Deity, the living representative of the God Tum, the unseen principle and first cause of all existence.

The question whether a priest of On would be disposed to give his daughter to a Hebrew, the favourite and prime minister of Pharaoh, ought not to be regarded as a difficulty. There was nothing to create a scruple. The worship of Jehovah was certainly not known at that age to Egyptians in its exclusive character. Foreigners, especially of Semitic origin, were received with honour, and raised to the highest rank by the greatest sovereigns of the ancient Empire,[9] and the descendant of Abraham, who had been admitted to the intimacy of a former Pharaoh, would be acknowledged as of noble birth. The circumcision of Joseph would be a strong recommendation: it was a sign of consecration and purity to which the Egyptian priests attached peculiar importance. If the rite were previously known as an Egyptian custom, more especially in priestly and royal families, it would mark Joseph both to Pharaoh and Potiphar as specially qualified for the alliance. If it were previously unknown, no person was more likely than Joseph to have introduced it among the Egyptians; and this is possibly the true solution of an acknowledged difficulty. The first distinct representation of the rite is found on a monument of the 19th dynasty, long after the time of Joseph: two sons of Rameses II. are pictured as undergoing it. See M. Chabas' art. in 'Revue Archéologique,' 1861, p. 298. The word [hieroglyphs], "sabu" (which is translated "circumcise" by Champollion, and after him by Mr. Birch, D. H.), is not found with that sense in any ancient inscription.[10] A passage in the 'Funeral Ritual' (c. xvii. l. 23, ed. Leps.) is supposed by M. de Rougé to refer to circumcision, but the meaning is very doubtful, nor if his explanation were accepted, would it be conclusive: for although portions of the chapter are undoubtedly older than Joseph, the passage is a gloss of doubtful antiquity, and is omitted in the ancient copy lately published by M. Lepsius. See 'Aelteste Texte, Sarkophag 1 des Mentuhotep,' pl. 1, l. 16, 17.

צפנת פענח
Zaphnath Paaneah.—Gen. xli. 45.

The history of the attempts to explain this designation of Joseph is curious and instructive. The most natural process before the hieroglyphic inscriptions were deciphered was to compare the Hebrew form with the Coptic: no explanation was derived from this source which was generally satisfactory to scholars, and most interpreters resorted to the Septuagint, which gives several forms all differing from the Hebrew. Gesenius holds that the Hebrew writer must have modified the Egyptian words in order to bring them into accordance with his own language: a singular assumption, since the word is completely inexplicable in Hebrew. It will be found that an exact transcription of the Hebrew letters gives a clear sense in Egyptian.

The word stands thus—

[hieroglyphs], z f n t p anch.

---

[10] M. Brugsch gives no such meaning in his dictionary. Mr. Goodwin adds, in the letter lately received by me; the meaning adopted by Birch from Champollion's Dictionary is probably based only on the Copic ⲥⲉⲃⲓ, and is of little authority. Ebers gives another word [hieroglyphs] or [hieroglyphs], which he translates "circumcise." Brugsch and Birch have no such meaning, nor do I find any example. A stronger but not conclusive argument is drawn from the well-known hieroglyphic for *mt*. The representations, however, to which Ebers alludes, and the mummies which have been examined, are much later than the time of Joseph.

---

[9] This curious fact is proved beyond all doubt by the 'Story of Saneha,' a hieratic papyrus of extreme antiquity, lately translated by Mr. Goodwin. See especially pp. 39 and 43. It is also to be observed that Saneha, Son of the Sycomore, was a name probably given to the foreigner on his adoption by the Egyptians.

The letter ץ is invariably transcribed by ⌐ or ⌐, and most commonly by the latter. ⌐ is the nearest form for ף, △ could only be represented in Hebrew by נת or נט; and in the Pentateuch △ is generally transcribed by ת, as in Pithom and Asenath. No doubt can be entertained about the remaining letters: all scholars would accept the identification of the Egyptian word here given with the Hebrew. In fact every letter in this transcription rests on the unanimous authority of Egyptian scholars, and is confirmed by a vast number of unmistakable words in ancient inscriptions and papyri.

The meaning is quite clear. The first syllable ⌐ "zaf," is a word of very common occurrence, both in this simple form, and with explanatory signs called determinatives, as a "bushel," or a "widgeon," indicating abundance.[11] Its well-ascertained meaning is "food," especially "corn," or "grain," in general. A few instances will show this usage, and serve to illustrate the biblical account of Joseph's position. Under the early dynasties of the ancient empire the officer of state who received the tributes in kind and had the superintendence of the public granaries bore the title "master of the house of ('zaf' or 'zafa') provisions." M. de Rougé gives the names of three officers who bore this title. Ptah-ases, the son-in-law of a Pharaoh of the 4th dynasty, Chafra or Chefren, was called "mer set zafa," which M. de Rougé renders "chargé de la maison des provisions de bouche." This remark on the office is important, the more so since he does not connect the word with the history of Joseph. "Les tributs versés en nature rendaient cette fonction très importante, ainsi qu'on peut le voir par l'histoire de Joseph."[12] The grandson and chief minister of Nepherkara bore the same title, l. c. p. 86. Another great official of the same early age held the three offices, master of the arsenals, of the Treasury, and of the depôts of provisions, "zaf." De Rougé renders the last title, "chef des lieux des offrandes, des denrées," p. 87. From the last passage it is also clear that the granaries throughout Egypt were under the superintendence of one great officer of state. M. de Rougé observes, "Ces trois titres pouvaient constituer une sorte de ministère des finances."

The next word △, "nt" is the preposition "of," used very commonly on the early monuments. Two examples may be found in Egyptian words quoted by M. de Rougé on the last passage which has been discussed.

The meaning of "Anch" is not questioned. It signifies "life," or with the article it may mean "the living." Thus one name of Memphis is ta-anch for the land of life or of the living.[13]

The meaning, therefore, of the whole name, the only meaning which it could bear to an Egyptian, and of course to a Hebrew of the age of Moses, is "the food of life" or "the food of the living." No question can be raised as to the appropriateness of this designation: it only remains to show that the word "zaf" was likely to be applied to a person. To this it is a complete answer that it occurs in the rings of three Pharaohs of the 13th dynasty. See Brugsch, 'Histoire d'Egypte,' pl. viii., nos. 162, 164, and 167; or Lepsius, 'Königsbuch,' taf. xix 282, 284.[14]

We have now to consider the remarkable reading of the Septuagint. The Egyptian was a living language, though it had undergone considerable modifications, when the Pentateuch was translated, and it is evident from Jerome's account that the Jews in Egypt attached a definite meaning to the word ψονθομ φανηχ, which on their authority he renders salvator mundi. The latter part corresponds with the interpretation above given. Life, or the living, is the equivalent of "the world." The first part is more difficult to explain. The transcription of ψονθ would give ⌐, p-sont, i.e., "foundation." It might possibly be used in the sense of "support," "sustentation;" but I am not aware that any example of such a meaning can be adduced.[15]

---

[11] This complete form is ⌐. The last two signs are not phonetic; they represent a widgeon or duck, and bread.

[12] See 'Recherches,' p. 69.

[13] Jablonski, 'Opuscula,' tom. i. p. 210, suggests from the Coptic ⲥⲱϣ ⲛⲧⲉ ⲡⲉⲛⲉϥ, caput mundi; La Crozius, ⲥⲱϣ ⲛⲧⲉ ⲡⲱⲛ⌐, thus agreeing with the transcription here given so far as the last part is concerned. There can, however, be no doubt that ⌐ represents ףצ; whereas the phonetic value of the Egyptian sign for head differs from it considerably.

[14] The transcription of Brugsch is more accurate, ⌐. Traces of the word are found in other rings, probably also in the name of a Pharaoh of much earlier date. See De Rougé, 'Recherches,' p. 155. In choosing the name, Pharaoh might possibly have had some regard to the name Joseph; seph and zaph bear a near resemblance.

[15] Gesenius renders the word "the support of life;" but the imperfect knowledge of hiero

Another transcription of the Greek form may be suggested; one more exact, since it retains the consonants without any modification.

𓋴𓏏𓐍𓈖𓏌𓀀𓇳, Psntmnānch.

The meaning would be "he who gives joy to the world." This name has a strong Egyptian colouring. It occurs precisely in the same form as that of a royal favourite under the 5th dynasty, 𓋴𓏏𓐍𓈖𓀀𓇳, sntm het, or, as M. de Rougé reads, "senotem het," "delighting the heart." The example shows, also, that the construction is correct: "senotem" is a transitive form, and does not require or admit a preposition. It may be observed that the same root occurs in the names of two princes of the 21st dynasty. (See Brugsch, H. E., Pl. xiv., Nos. 299 and 302.)

One or other of these forms may have been before the minds of the Greek translator—probably the latter; but the reading of the LXX is uncertain, and there is no reason whatever for departing from the simple, intelligible, and well-ascertained sense of the words which is elicited by transcription of the Hebrew.

אַבְרֵךְ

This word, which Gesenius (Thes. *s. v.*) calls "vox perdubia," has never had a satisfactory explanation. It is admitted to be Egyptian, though, as usual, Gesenius supposes that it was modified in the transcription in order to give it a Hebrew character. The explanation suggested by Rosellini, and adopted by Gesenius, is ⲁⲡⲉⲣⲉⲕ, *i.e.* incline or bow the head. This, however, is inadmissible. The transposition of the two words ⲣⲉⲕ and ⲁⲡⲉ is not in accordance with old Egyptian usage. ⲁⲡⲉ may possibly be the true sound of the hieroglyphic for head 𓁶 (see De

---

glyphics in his time led him to the error of identifying "sont" with 𓋴𓏏𓈖𓏤, to which it bears no real resemblance. I have since found the name Sont-ur, *i.e.* the "great foundation," as that of a high priest at Thebes. See Mariette, 'Fouilles,' pl. vii. l. 12. The LXX. may therefore have meant to represent Pa-sont-om-Paanch (om = † *i.e.* am, or ami), belonging to the support of the world. A good sense, but not so good as that given by the Hebrew. Mr. Goodwin considers the transcription of the LXX, which is given above, to be very probable. He translates it "making life pleasant," which is equivalent in meaning. He observes also that the article in old Egyptian would not have been written, but probably it was often supplied in reading and speaking. This applies to the preceding account of the Hebrew form.

Rougé, 'Recherches,' p. 91, n. 2.), but it would not be correctly transcribed by אַב. ⲡⲉⲕ is not found in the sense "bow" or "incline" in old Egyptian.

The exact transcription is 𓂝𓃀𓂋𓎡.

If this give a meaning exactly applicable, there can be no need of further inquiry.

The context tells us, not, as is commonly assumed, that a herald went before Joseph, addressing the people, but "they cried before him," *i.e.* the people or the attendants shouted out with reference to Joseph, "Abrek."

But ab-rek is the imperative, and the emphatic imperative, of the verb "Ab," which is a word specially used in reference to public demonstrations of rejoicing. Thus, in an inscription of Rameses II. we find *Ab*-sen-nek, "they rejoice before thee:" and in another of later date, "the world is in a state of rejoicing," in *Ab* ni. The termination "rek" is equivalent to the Hebrew לְךָ, as M. Chabas has pointed out in explaining the word mai-rek, *i.e.* come.[16] 'Voyage d'un Égyptien,' p. 285.

The chief objection to this explanation is that the verb is in the singular number, addressing an individual, not a multitude. But it seems quite natural that the attendants should address Joseph, calling upon him to rejoice, together with all the people, in his deliverance and exaltation. Some support may be found for this explanation in the fact that subject princes address the Pharaoh in the same form, hotep-rek. See the vignette to the Stèle Pianchi in Mariette's 'Fouilles d'Abydos.'

Another transcription, which comes very near to the Hebrew, would give Ab Rekh, *i.e.* "pure" and "wise:" but it is unlikely to have been used as an exclamation.[17]

מֹשֶׁה, Moses.

In examining the form which this name would properly assume in Egyptian, we must bear in mind the following points:—1. The letter שׁ is generally represented by 𓈙 *i.e.* sh and its homophones, but in very ancient transcriptions, and specially in monuments of the 18th and 19th dynasties, it corresponds in proper names to 𓇋, s. Thus we find 𓊪𓏏𓂋𓊃𓏏𓁗, Āstharta, for עַשְׁתֹּרֶת,

---

[16] It is especially used in exclamations, thus: harek—stand up, see 'Br. D. H.,' p. 814, equivalent to "up with you." The form occurs repeatedly in the texts.

[17] In the 'Æg. Zeitschrift' for 1869, p. 1869, the Egyptian Ap-Rech, i.e. Chief of the Wise. The transcription is not accurate, p for b, and ch for h.

⸺ ⸺, Askelna, for אשקלון, Askalon, and ⸺ ⸺, Pulistha, for פלשת. M. Brugsch, a high authority in all such questions, gives ס or שׁ as the corresponding letters to the Egyptian ⸺ (See 'Geographische Inschriften,' p. 15). This is a point of importance, considering the remarkable accuracy of the transcriptions in the Pentateuch.

2. The final letter ה is adequately represented by a vowel sound, either \\ = *i*, or more commonly by ⸺, *u*, corresponding to the Hebrew ו.

3. The vowel sound in *Mo* is not represented either in Hebrew or Egyptian, but in the transcription a preference should be given to the vowel *o*, which appears from Coptic and Greek to be associated with the consonants *Ms*.

4. It is also to be observed that Moses undoubtedly lays the stress on the verb "draw out," not on the noun "water." The name in Egyptian ought to bear the sense "drawn out," "brought forth." The verb may have borne the same sense in Hebrew also (a fact of extremely common occurrence), but if the writer knew Egyptian he certainly would not have chosen a word for which that language does not supply a natural interpretation.

Among transcriptions which are probable or possible, one exactly fulfils all these conditions. The word ⸺, *m s u*, unquestionably corresponds in form to the Hebrew, letter for letter, on the principles laid down above. The vowel sound, which is required for the first syllable, may be assumed to have been *o*, and this for several reasons. The syllable ⸺ occurs in many names of the 18th dynasty, and is always transcribed by Manetho or his Greek translators by *mos*; thus we find Amosis and Thotmosis.

The question of equal importance as to the meaning remains to be answered.

The explanation, suggested first as it would seem by Gesenius (Thes. *s. v.*) "child" or "son," is quite accurate so far as it goes. Mesu, or Moses, undoubtedly does bear that signification, and may be rendered exactly by "son." But if we had no other information as to the original and common sense of the verb from which it is derived, this interpretation, which contradicts the statement in Exodus, would present an insuperable difficulty, unless we were satisfied with the usual evasion that the word was altered so as to adapt it to a Hebrew etymology. The difficulty, however, is entirely removed when the original meaning, as well as usage, of the word in Egyptian is examined. In his 'Hieroglyphic Dictionary' M. Brugsch shows that the sense "drawing out" is the original one. It is taken from the work of the potter (p. 705). It there means "produce," "bring forth," and, as M. Brugsch affirms in another passage (p. 698), the derivation of משה from the Hebrew root משה, traxit, extraxit, suitably also in the sense "extraxit e ventre matris," would preserve the true sense of the Egyptian.[18]

The word used by Moses may of course be Semitic; although it must be observed that it occurs only in this passage, and in one other which is evidently taken from it, Ps. xviii. 17 (repeated 2 Sam. xxii. 17); but at any rate it is so exceedingly rare that we can best account for its selection by Moses by the supposition that it came exceedingly near to, or exactly represented, the Egyptian. It is far from improbable that it was, in fact, a simple transcription of words, which must have been perfectly intelligible to the Israelites of that age. What the Egyptian princess said—and her words were not likely to be forgotten or misrepresented by her adopted son—was this: "I give him the name Moses —'brought forth'—because I brought him forth from the water."[19]

The probability that this was actually the Egyptian name of Moses comes very near a certainty when we learn that it was very common under the Middle Empire. In the select papyri (Anastasi, vi. p. 3, l. 4)[20] it occurs as the names of a keeper of goats, the superintendent of the "house of measures," where corn was measured or weighed. It was also borne by a prince of the blood-royal of Egypt who held the office of Viceroy of Nubia under the nineteenth dynasty. There is no reason for identifying either of these persons with Moses, but the coincidences with the biblical history and with the legends in Josephus and other writers are curious. This ascertained use of the word appears to give it a very decided preference over two other senses suggested by a faithful transcription. The

---

[18] A family of words closely resembling, or identical with, משה מֹשֶׁה, is found in Egyptian. See Brugsch D. H., p. 711, *s. v.* ⸺

[19] In the Egyptian the translation would run thus:

⸺

Au set hi tat naf pa ran Mesu em tat pe·un mesna su emta pa mu.

[20] See Brugsch, D. H., p. 1162.

word ⟨hieroglyph⟩ ' *i.e.* masi, in the sense "to bring," is common, not only as the instances given by Birch and Brugsch would lead us to suppose, in reference to tributes, but to the simple transfer of objects.[21] It would be quite intelligible in Egyptian were we to read, "She called his name *Masi*, saying because I brought (masi) him out of the waters." It is, however, doubtful whether such a proper name would be in accordance with Egyptian usage. Again, it might be possible, with our present knowledge of Egyptian, to give a more plausible etymology derived from the word "water," than either of those which Jablonski and other scholars formerly proposed. The phonetic value of the group ⟨hieroglyph⟩ is admitted to be Mu, or Mo, and ⟨hieroglyph⟩, shi, denotes a child. Mo-shi, a water-child, would not be an impossible transcription or rendering, were it justified by Egyptian usage. Still it is clear that the stress is laid, not on the noun, but on the verb, and there appears no reason to depart from the simple and natural explanation which has been given above.

It may, however, appear to require some additional evidence that Moses should have used an Egyptian word, or have selected, to say the least, a very unusual Hebrew word to represent it. Here we may call attention to a fact which has hitherto been unnoticed. In that part of the narrative which deals specially with Egyptian matters, words are constantly used which are either of Egyptian origin or common to Hebrew and Egyptian. The following instances are taken from one verse, that in which Moses gives the history of his exposure. His mother made him an ark of bulrushes. The word "ark," תבה (of which Rödiger says, "falsi sunt, qui etymon in linguis Semiticis quæreret"), is admitted to be Egyptian. It is, indeed, very common in the sense "chest" or "coffer," also in the sense "cradle," ⟨hieroglyph⟩, teb, with several variants. (Birch D. N., p. 5359; Br. D.H., 1628.) The Septuagint retains the Hebrew θίβιν, doubtless as a well-known Egyptian word. The material of which this ark was made is called גֹּמֶא. Brugsch ('Dict. Hier.,' p. 145) identifies this word with the Coptic ⲕⲁⲙ, "juncus quo fiunt funes." Brugsch shows, moreover, that it was specially used for making the light boats of the Nile.

He gives the word ⟨hieroglyph⟩ ⲕⲁⲙ, papyrus myopea, p. 1452. See also p. 2320, where a basket of green papyrus (kam nat) is mentioned.

Again, "when she made it, she *daubed* it with *slime*." The word חפר is used in the original both for the process and the material. This corresponds exactly with the original meaning and use of the Egyptian word ⟨hieroglyph⟩, which has the same letters, though, as is very commonly the case, in a different order. The Hebrew is ch-m-r, the Egyptian m-r-ch. Brugsch ('Dict. Hier.,' p. 769) says, "Die Grundbedeutung der Wurzel Merh ist 'beschmieren, bestreichen, überzeichen etwas mit einem feuchten gegenstande." Mr. Goodwin has very lately shown the identity of the words. "The root appears again in ⲙⲉⲣϩⲉ, ⲙⲉⲃⲣⲉϩⲓ, bitumen, pitch, in Hebrew חמר."—'Zeits.,' 1867, p. 86. Whether Moses had this word in mind may, of course, be questioned, but it is evidently the most suitable that could be suggested.

The next word, "pitch," is common to Hebrew and Egyptian. זפת, ⟨hieroglyph⟩, or ⟨hieroglyph⟩, sft. The Egyptian word is very common; the Hebrew occurs only twice in the Bible, but is well known in Arabic, and was probably common to Egyptian and Hebrew.

Jochebed then placed the ark in "the flags." The Hebrew is סוף, for which no plausible etymology has been suggested, nor is the word found in any Semitic language. It answers, however, very nearly to the Egyptian name for a species of papyrus found in marshy places and on the banks of rivers. The word was written either ⟨hieroglyph⟩ (Sallier, 1, 4, 9), *i.e.*, tufi, or ⟨hieroglyph⟩, also to be read "tufi." The Coptic equivalent is ⲭⲟⲟⲥ, which indicates a predominance of the sibilant sound common to dentals. It seems probable that it was also written with ⟨hieroglyph⟩, "z," both because of the Coptic form, and because ⟨hieroglyph⟩, "tzet" (which seems to be an abbreviation), also means papyrus. In that case "tufi" would be translated "zufi" = סוף. The identification of the Egyptian and Hebrew is so probable as to approximate to a certainty. In the last number of Brugsch's Dictionary, published since this was printed, I find that he also identifies tufi, ⲭⲟⲟⲥ and סוף, p. 1580.

Lastly, we read "by the river's brink." על שפת היאר. The form and meaning are Egyptian. It is well known that יאר is

---

[21] It is used for bringing a harp to a man in a tavern. See 'Stele Pianchi ap. Brugsch, D. H.,' p. 157. Brugsch writes the word Masib, but Birch gives Masi, which seems correct. The leg is not phonetic, but determinative.

Egyptian. The Nile has two names: the sacred name Hapi, and the common name, meaning "river," which is here exactly transcribed [hieroglyphs], Aor. The word שָׂפָה, i.e. "lip," for "brink," is sufficiently common in Hebrew, but it is interesting to find in a papyrus of the 19th dynasty precisely the same word with the same meaning. "I sat down by the *lip* of the river, [hieroglyphs], i.e. "spot Atur." Atur is another form of "Aor." The same idiom occurs in the 'Funeral Ritual,' c. ii. 3, l. 2.

It would be very difficult to resist the impression that this verse was written by a man equally familiar with both languages, or, on the other hand, to admit the possibility that coincidences coming so near together were purely accidental, as they must have been in the mouth of a Palestinian Jew.

One more instance of equal interest is taken from the 1st chapter of Exodus, ver. 11. We there read that the Egyptians set שָׂרֵי מִסִּים, "sari massim," over Israel. The words are both common in Hebrew, but they are also common in Egyptian, and precisely in the same signification. Birch gives [hieroglyphs], mās, tribute. 'Dictionary of Hieroglyphics,' *s. v.* The official name "ser" is still more striking. It is common in the sense "chieftain," but we find it specially applied to the officer appointed by Tothmosis III. to superintend the work of captives employed in making bricks. In the inscription on the well-known picture which represents the processes, we find the proper official designation of the overseers,[22] who were armed with heavy whips, and also of the chief superintendent. He is called [hieroglyphs],[23] of which the Hebrew שַׂר, "ser," is the exact transcription. His rank is denoted by the long staff, and by the determinative, viz. the head and neck of a giraffe. Had this title occurred first under the 19th dynasty it might have been regarded as Semitic (for a vast number of military and civil titles were then introduced into Egypt); but occurring, as it does, under the 18th dynasty, it is unquestionably Egyptian. It is found, indeed, in inscriptions far more ancient, *e. g.* under Pepi of the 6th dynasty. See De Rougé, 'Recherches,' p. 118. We have, in any case, a proof that in relating Egyptian transactions Moses either used the native Egyptian word, or that he

adopted the Hebrew word which expressed it most exactly both in meaning and form.

פִּתֹם, Pithom. This city was formerly identified by Brugsch with the fort of Djar, *Pachtum* n Zar. This was a point of importance, since it is certain that that fort or city was in existence early in the 18th dynasty, before the accession of Tothmosis III., the grandson of Amosis I., to whom its erection may be unhesitatingly ascribed. The fortress in question is shown, on grounds which appear conclusive, to have been known at a later period by the name Heroopolis, near the ruins of Mukfar, or Abn Kasheb. See Brugsch, 'Geographie des Alten Ægyptens,' p. 263. The word Pithom, however, does not correspond to the Egyptian form with sufficient accuracy, and it is now admitted to be identical with [hieroglyphs], Pe-tum, the house, *i. e.* dwelling or temple of Tum. Still the conclusions drawn by Brugsch do not lose their interest, since it has lately been shown that this place was in the immediate vicinity of the fortress, and was in all probability built at the same time as the adjoining sanctuary, giving name to the whole set of edifices, or it might have been a second name of the same place. Thus On is called Pitum, with the same meaning, "house of Tum." This is probably the true explanation. The passage translated by M. Chabas, 'Mét. Égypt.,' ii., p. 155, shows that certain nomads of Atema (or, as the name should be transcribed, Edom) applied to the guards of Merneptah Hotephima, the son of Rameses, for permission to feed their cattle in the district adjoining the fortress, to which that sovereign had then given his own name. The place of conference was the great reservoir at Pithom. From this we learn that Pithom was on the frontier of the desert. The name here used for reservoir in the papyrus is Semitic, [hieroglyphs], as Chabas transcribes it Bere-koavota, *i. e.* בְּרֵכוֹת, cisterns or reservoirs: a curious illustration of the biblical narrative, built as the place was by Israelites, and probably occupied by them up to the date of the Exodus. In the time of Merneptah there is no indication of their presence, nor is it at all probable that had the Delta at that time been in the state supposed by Brugsch (see 'Histoire d'Égypte,' p. 174), the king would have admitted a nomad tribe into the district.

אֵתָם, Etham. Exod. xiii. 20. The transcription of this name comes exceedingly near to Pithom. [hieroglyphs], A-tum, [hieroglyphs] Pitum. The meaning is

---

[22] [hieroglyphs] The meaning of the group is the head work-givers, the eye denoting superintendence.

[23] In the eleventh line of the inscription, which is read from right to left. See Brugsch, 'Histoire d'Égypte,' p. 106.

identical, ⌂ *i.e.* A, and ⌐ per, mean "house," "dwelling," and are applied indifferently as designations of one and the same locality: thus Pi Ramessu and A-Ramessu (Chab., 'Mél. Ég.') Etham and Pithom are to be rendered "house of Tum." The site of Etham was on the extreme border of the desert, such, as we have seen, must have been the site of Pithom. The identification of the two names which M. Chabas ('Voy. Ég.,' p. 286) proposes as probable, may therefore be regarded as all but certain. The LXX. give Ὀθώμ, or Ὀθώμ, for Etham. This represents the Egyptian exactly, for the ⌐ corresponds generally to O. In Numbers xxxiii. 6, 7, they give Βουθάν, or, as it should be read, Βουθάμ. The Βου, as in the well-known Busiris for Pe-bsiri, represents the Egyptian ⌐ (not the article, but the group for "house" or Pe): this corroborates the argument for the identification.

The derivation proposed by Jablonski, and accepted by Forster, viz. At-iom, *not-sea*, may illustrate the shifts to which men of learning were formerly driven by their ignorance of the ancient language of Egypt.

רַעְמְסֵס, Gen. xlvii. 11; רַעַמְסֵס, Exod. i. 11. In the former passage the name "Rameses" is that of a district; in the latter, "Raamses," it is the name of a city. The pointing of the former name is preferable. The first syllable רַע is the exact transcription of ⌐, Ra, the well-known name of the Sun-God. The second part of the word, מְסֵס, represents with equal fidelity the Egyptian 𓐍𓊪𓊪, "meses." This latter part is a reduplicated form of the very common word 𓐍𓊪, "mes," a child. It occurs in the name Rameses, which was borne by two Pharaohs of the 19th, and by all the kings of the 20th dynasty. In the name of the sovereign the meaning of the word is either "Ra begat," or "Ra begat him." Hence it is inferred that the name both of the district and of the city must have been derived from that of the king.

It is, however, clear that the writer of the Pentateuch represents the name as that of the district at the time of its occupation by the Israelites, that is, at a time admitted by all to be ages before the 19th dynasty. Had the passage in Genesis occurred in a papyrus of the age of the Exodus, it would have been held as a sufficient proof that the name must have been ancient; nor is there any reason to doubt the statement, or to suppose that the name was simply given as that by which the district was known at the time when Moses wrote. The only question is whether it was a name likely to be given to a place or district at an early age, in accordance with Egyptian usage.

Late researches have shown that "Ra," the first part of the word, entered very commonly into names of places, districts, and cities under the ancient empire: far more commonly than at a later period. Thus we find, from inscriptions in the tomb of Tei (son-in-law of a Pharaoh of the 5th dynasty, An, or Ranuser), that not less than four cities, or districts, in his government were called Ra-asket, Ra-shephet, Ra-Seket, and Ra-hotep (De Rougé, 'Recherches,' p. 94; see also p. 72, where M. de R. observes that the frequent notices of Ra have been much overlooked). Under a preceding Pharaoh we meet with Ra-heb, *i.e.*, festival of Ra; this was a royal residence. Such names might be expected to be found very frequently in the country about On, which was called Pe-Ra, Es-Ra, Nes-Ra, and Aa-Ra. (See Brugsch, 'Geog.,' Nos. 1213, 1214.)

Ra-meses may therefore well have been the old name of the district: whether it represents the original form, "Ra-messon," with the sense "Ra the self-begetting," an ancient appellation of Ra in the Ritual; or Ra-meses, "Ra the creator, former, or begotten," a sense equally suitable and harmonizing with Egyptian notions; or "Ra-mesu," children of Ra. The Egyptians called themselves children of Ra, *i.e.*, Ra-mesu, from the earliest times; it was probably their characteristic name as distinguished from foreigners: this appears from a well-known inscription on the tomb of Seti Merneptah, the father of Rameses II. A city, of which the site is unknown, bore the name Mis-Ra:[24] nor is it at all improbable that this is connected with the name given to the Egyptians in the Bible, viz., Mizraim.[25] That some district should have borne the name, and, if any district, that which was peculiarly associated with the earliest forms of Sun worship, presents no improbability,[26] nothing which can justify us in questioning the accuracy of Moses.

The same arguments apply to the name of the city of Rameses. It was a name very naturally given to the capital of the district. The certain fact that Rameses II. gave his own name to a fortress of considerable extent in this district, as well as to others in different parts of Egypt, has been regarded by Egyptologers as a

---

[24] See Brugsch, 'Geog.,' No. 1517.
[25] This has been suggested by M. Rougemont, 'Age de Bronze,' and is supported by M. Rheinisch. Dr. Ebers rejects, but does not disprove, the identification. In an Essay lately published by Mr. Birch, on the trilingual inscription of San, he observes that Mizraim is supposed by some to represent the common Egyptian word for Egypt, viz. ta-meri. This requires two transpositions, mer-ta and met-ra.
[26] This is, in fact, admitted even by M. Chabas, 'Mél. égypt.,' ii. p. 125.

IN THE PENTATEUCH.

conclusive proof that it could not have borne the name previously. It should, however, be observed that Moses does not call the city, or arsenal, Pi Ramessu, but simply Rameses. The word Pi, or its equivalent *A*, signifying house or residence, so far as I can ascertain, is never omitted in the Egyptian designations of places named after the king. It is found in all the names given by M. Chabas, ' Mél. Ég.,' ii p. 126. It is extremely unlikely that it should have been omitted by Moses in the very same sentence in which he gives the full and accurate transcription of Pithom. Again, the name which the fortress bore after its enlargement by Rameses was invariably that of the Sovereign, who is not called in Egyptian documents Rameses simply, but Rameses Meiamon, or Meramon. This is not conclusive, but it adds some weight to the argument. It is known, moreover, that the fortress was in existence at the beginning of the reign of Rameses, and apparently bearing the name Rameses.[27] In addition to these facts we find that Amosis, or Aahmes, to whom the building of several cities in the Delta is attributed by contemporary monuments, gave the name "Rames" to one of his own sons. It has been observed above, that in the names of early kings, the Greeks transcribe Mes by Moses, which points to a duplicate *s* in Egyptian. It may not be assumed that the name of the city was taken from this prince, but the probability that the same, or that a similar name should be given to both at the same time, is sufficiently obvious. It may be added that Ramesses was likely to be the true name of one of the treasure cities built by Aahmes, because the king was a restorer of the worship of Ra. He was a great builder, and had special reasons for fortifying the Eastern district, which previously bore the name Rameses. It is also certain that Egyptian cities often took their name from a district, in which case the prefix "Pi" is not used.[28]

One argument of great weight remains to be considered. The city of Rameses Meiamon, with its parks, lakes, and the whole adjoining district, was the centre of a great Egyptian population, a place of festivities; whereas, at the time described in the Pentateuch, the two fortresses built by the Israelites were in the district which they occupied, and of which there is no indication whatever that they were dispossessed. In the time of Rameses it was a rich, fertile, and beautiful district, described as the abode of happiness, where all alike, rich and poor, lived in peace and plenty; but in the time of Moses it was the abode of a suffering race, resounding not with the jubilant shouts of Egyptians, but with the groans and execrations of an oppressed population. A stronger contrast can scarcely be drawn than that of the state of the district at the Exodus and that which it presented under Rameses II. and his successors.

פִּיהַחִירֹת, Pihahiroth. It is not certain that the word is Egyptian. If so, it may, like some other names, have been adopted and modified either by the Israelites or other Semitic occupants of the district. There appear to be indications of the name in one of the Select Papyri (Anast. iii. 1, 2), in which the scribe Penbesa gives an account of a visit of Rameses to the adjoining district. The passage is translated by M. Chabas, 'Mél. Égypt.,' ii. p. 133. Garlands of flowers were sent from a place called 〈hieroglyphs〉, *i.e. Pehir*: from the determinatives, it appears that the place was on a river or reservoir. Chabas, however, connects the word 〈hieroglyphs〉 "hir," with the Hebrew חוֹר. We may, therefore, translate Pihahiroth (regarding it as partly Egyptian, partly Semitic) "the house of wells, the watering-place in the desert."

M. Brugsch, however, compares Pihahiroth with the name of a place called "Pehuret," but of which nothing is known. 'Geog.,' p. 298.

גֹּשֶׁן. There can be no doubt that this name is Egyptian, although, as the Israelites occupied the district during the whole period of their sojourn, the form may have been modified. No probable interpretation is supplied by the Coptic, nor does any name exactly corresponding to Goshen appear on the monuments. It is, however, to be remarked that three Egyptian nomes, situate in the Delta, and extending over great part of the district of Goshen, bore each a name beginning with the word *Ka, i.e.* a bull. This word would be represented in Hebrew by the first syllable of Goshen. The Egyptian for bull is written either with 〈hieroglyph〉 or 〈hieroglyph〉 (see Birch, D. H., p. 417, 〈hieroglyphs〉, *ga*), and the regular transcription of 〈hieroglyph〉 (〈hieroglyph〉 being a homophone) is ג, *g*. The vowel sound is vague, but the Greek transcription of Ka-kem is κωχώμη. See Brugsch, 'Geographie,' Index. We may accept "go" as the transcription of the first syllable without any hesitation. That of the second remains doubtful.

If, again, we can depend upon the transcription of M. Brugsch, the name of the 12th

---

[27] Brugsch, 'Histoire d'Égypte,' p. 156. "Les papyrus mentionnent ces deux endroits existants déjà sous Sethos I. par leurs noms égyptiens."

[28] Thus the fortress of Zar is found without the prefix in numerous inscriptions. See Brugsch, Geog.,' p. 260, and Nos. 1263, 1267, taf. xlvii. Dr. Haigh suggests that a synonym of Zar may be read Ka-sen, or Kashen; but his arguments are not very satisfactory. See 'Zeits.' 1861, p. 47.

nomos in Lower Egypt was Ka-she, of which the Hebrew transcription would be נשֶׁה. This comes exceedingly near to the form now in question. The Egyptian ideographs to which Brugsch gives this phonetic value, represent a bull and a leaping calf.[29] See Brugsch, 'Geographie des Alten Ægyptens,' p. 253. The name of the principal city in the district was She-nefer, *i.e.* "the sacred calf," a name which has an obvious and striking bearing upon the history of the Israelites. From another notice it is proved that this city, Neter-she, was situate in a district adjoining that of which *Zar* was the capital. But Zar, or, as it is written more fully, "the fortress of Zar," was close to Pithom, and was formerly identified with it by Brugsch. So that there is sufficient reason to assume that the Egyptian name of the district may have been pronounced Goshe. It is of course possible that the name Goshen may have represented to the Israelites an adjoining district beginning with the word Ka; or that some name even nearer than "Goshe" may have been in use. Ka-kem, *i.e.* the black bull, appears to have been the origin of the LXX. and Coptic ⲔⲈⲤⲈⲘ. The monumental inscriptions in Lower Egypt are scanty.

The bull represented in the names of these districts was Mnevis, worshipped specially at On as the living representative of Tum, the unknown principle and source of all existence. See Brugsch, *l. c.*

גרשׁם. Gershom. Moses explains this name to mean a sojourner in a strange land, Exodus ii. 22. Gesenius finding no Hebrew authority for this meaning of שׁם, assumes a double error, viz. that the writer took שׁם, "there,"

to be the equivalent of a strange land, and that he was ignorant of the true derivation from גרשׁ, banished. The Egyptian gives a complete etymology. The first syllable is common to both languages: גר is the exact equivalent and transcription of 𓎼𓂋 𓀀 or 𓎼𓂋, dweller, or sojourner. The word is preserved in Coptic in the form ϢⲰⲂⲒ, in which Ϣ = 𓎼 and ⲗ = . Moses, as we have seen, usually takes a word common to both languages. The second syllable שׁם is pure Egyptian, retained in the Coptic in the common word ϢⲈⲘⲘⲞ, shemmo, a foreigner, or a foreign land. Thus in this passage the Coptic version of ארץ נכריה, a foreign land, is ⲞⲨⲔⲀϨⲒ ⲚϢⲈⲘⲘⲞ. The meaning to an Egyptian would be exactly what the Hebrew expresses "a dweller in a foreign land." The Coptic, according to Brugsch, D. H., is the equivalent of "shumer," a bow, used commonly as the hieroglyphic of "foreigners."

Genesis xli. 2, אחו, LXX. ἄχει, Coptic ⲀⲬⲒ. The word has long been recognised as Egyptian. It occurs only in this passage and in Job viii. 11, where it is used in parallelism with נמא (see above, p. 485), and described as a water plant. The old Egyptian corresponds exactly, 𓇋𓏤𓆰, as a verb to be green, to grow and flower. The determinative points to herbage by a stream. Another form of the word 𓇋𓏤, *axu*, is used for reeds, rushes. &c. The radical meaning is bright luxuriant growth.

In the Introduction to Exodus the attention of scholars was specially called to a list of words taken from the first fifteen chapters of Exodus, which contain the history of the transactions in Egypt. They are either ἅπαξ λεγόμενα, or peculiar to the Pentateuch, occurring, if at all elsewhere, only in the Psalms of later date, which recapitulate the history. Nearly all are words which are found in Egyptian documents of unquestioned antiquity, either older or not much later than Moses. C. i. 7. שָׁרַץ. In Pentateuch only, except in Psalm cv., taken from this passage, the root is found in Arabic and Æthiopic. The Egyptian 𓋴𓈎 s written with all the dentals, *e.g.*, with 𓂧, which is the exact equivalent of ץ.[1] It exactly corre-

sponds to the Æthiopian ሠረጸ, pullulavit; the 𓊪 represents the impulsive mood, equivalent to Hiphil. This accounts for שָׁרַץ being followed by the objective of the object produced.

פרה, not an uncommon word, but far more frequently found in the Pentateuch (nineteen times) than elsewhere (eleven times altogether): the Eg. root is per, *i.e.*, come forth, grow abundantly, corn and all kinds of grain.

11. שָׂרֵי מִסִּים, see above, p. 486.

13. בפרך occurs once only, Ez. xxxiv. 4 out of the Pent.

16. הָאָבְנַיִם, the two stones. The meaning is purely conjectural; there is no trace of the expression in Hebrew, or of the usage to which it is supposed to refer in Palestine. The root 𓃀, ben, is fo—

---

[29] The leaping calf is the D. of *Ab*, "thirst." I do not find the value assigned to it by Brugsch.

[1] Thus de Rougé, Chr. p. 103. Br. D. H. s. v.

IN THE PENTATEUCH.

in many derivatives in Egyptian; it has the sense to roll, twist, turn, &c.; also to produce, engender. Brugsch connects it with אופן. Possibly it may have some connexion with the very doubtful Hebrew.

C. ii. 3. תבה, ark. 27 times in the Pentateuch, not found elsewhere. It is only used of the ark of Noah, and of the cradle of Moses. It has no Semitic root or equivalent, the Arabic being derived entirely from this passage. In Egyptian it is a common word in the sense of chest, coffer, and *cradle*.

נמא, a word found in Job and Isaiah; but from Egyptian, see above.

זפת, pitch, occurs twice only out of Pentateuch, Isaiah xxxiv. 9; xxxv. 9: common in Egyptian, see above. יאר, the Nile, long known as Egyptian.

5. רחץ, wash, a common word, but used in Egyptian rakat, and recht in the same sense.

10. משה, "to draw forth," only here and in the 18th Psalm; no satisfactory etymology in Semitic; but common in the form mesu, and with variants in the sense bring forth, draw forth, &c. See above.

16. רהט, once only in Cant. i. 17.

iii. 2. סנה, only in Exodus and Deut.; shown in note *ad loc.* to be Egyptian in the sense "thorny acacia."

7. תבן, straw, common in the Pentateuch, rare elsewhere. In Egyptian tebn means "chaff." Pap. Sall. 4, p. 5. קש, stalk, not uncommon in Hebrew, but Egyptian in exactly the same form and sense.

9. שעה, look to, trust in; very rare in this sense. שרי occurs nine times in Pent., thirty times in Job, very rare in later books.

vi. 25. The father-in-law and the son of Eleazer both bear Egyptian names, Putiel, "devoted to El." Phineas occurs under Rameses II.

vii. 3. On the names of magicians and sorcerers see note on this chapter, at the end.

להט, d. λ., and v. 22, לט, correspond to Egyptian words for magic and medical formulæ.

27. צפרדע, zeparda, frog; only found in Exodus and in one Psalm taken from it. It is a purely local name, adopted by the Arabs in Egypt. The radicals of which it is composed occur in a modified form in the Egyptian for "tadpole," hefennu, or hefenr:

[hieroglyph] , and [hieroglyph] , which Brugsch renders "tadpoles," giving as the Arabic equivalent ولد ضفدع the young dofda. The word has also the secondary meaning 100,000 or an indefinite number. The interchange of aspirates and sibilants is common, indeed regular in Zend and Sanscrit, in Greek and Latin. Another word comes even nearer, [hieroglyph] , tsfdt, which has the exact correspondents of ע, ח, and ד; the word means snake or "viper," but appears to be generic for reptiles. It is to be observed also that

[hieroglyph] , hefed, means to squat; a very probable etymology.

19. אגם: found in Isaiah, but uncommon. No satisfactory etymology is given, nor does the word occur in the same sense in the cognate languages. In this passage four words are given, rivers, streams, agammim, and generally every reservoir or collection of water. "Agam" may be assumed to be a well known local term. I find no exact Egyptian equivalent, and the Hebrews probably modified that which they adopted. But

[hieroglyph] , chnum, le puits, la citerne, Brugsch, D. H., p. 1100, would answer the conditions of an exact correspondence in sense, and resemblance in sound. A well 120 cubits deep is mentioned in an inscription quoted p. 246. Another word occurs in the Ritual, 99, 26, which comes nearer in form, viz., Achem, which is mentioned in connexion with the Nile, but the meaning is uncertain.

viii. 3. The combination of these words, shown above to be probably Egyptian, is remarkable, שרץ היאר צפרדעים. It is an instance of the custom of Moses, in describing Egyptian events, to use words either purely Egyptian or common to the two languages.

תנור, oven. The word is not uncommon, but occurs more frequently in the Pentateuch than elsewhere. The etymology is uncertain. The Coptic ⲑⲣⲓⲣ, or ⲧⲣⲓⲣ, comes very near; the permutation of ⲡ and ⲛ is common. The Egyptian supplies "nennu," to bake or roast, D. H., p. 784, and "hir," an oven; combined, the two words give all the elements, but the connection is scarcely probable. The old Egyptian must have had a form from which the Coptic certainly, and probably the Hebrew also, was derived.

14. תמר, in the sense "heap," is peculiar to this passage.

16. כנים: the word occurs six times in this passage, and nowhere else, except in Ps. cv. 31, which is taken from it. No probable Hebrew root is suggested, nor is the word extant in the Semitic dialects. The Arabic Chaldee and Syriac translators use a word quite distinct from it. The Egyptian has no name for an insect corresponding to this, but it has the root "ken," [hieroglyph] , in the sense force and abundance, a sense which in one word is developed into multitudinous [hieroglyph] , one of the commonest words in the language; and in another,

HH 5

△ 𒐚 , takes the sense plague, calamity, &c. The Coptic has ⲭⲛⲉ, percussit. This sense is further determined in one variant by the sign ⟨⟩ , which associates the plague with a bad smell and corruption. One passage quoted by Brugsch is curious, since it points to a periodical visitation: "The year did not bring the plague (ken) at the usual time." This quotation gives a peculiar force to the exclamation of Pharaoh's magicians, "It is the finger of God:" they recognised it as a severe visitation. The word is identified by Brugsch with the Egyptian 𓆼𓏤𓄑𓆰 , chenemms, the mosquito. It is retained in the Coptic ϣⲟⲗⲙⲉⲉ, κώνωψ, culex. See D. H., p. 1103.

21. העָרֹב: the word occurs nowhere but in the description of this plague, seven times here, and twice in Psalms lxxviii. 45, and cv. 31. The Semitic root ערב is very common, but is nowhere connected with insects or a plague of any kind. A late Egyptian word, 𓃀𓏤𓆣 , Abeb, i.e. a beetle, resembles the Hebrew in form, and is connected with several words, 𓇋𓏤, 𓃀𓏤, 𓃀𓃀, which represent species of flies: as for instance 𓄿𓆫 , D. H., p. 183, Champollion Gr., p. 74, which evidently denotes a venomous fly. It is possible either that the Hebrews, adopting the Egyptian word, accommodated it to their own common root, or that the middle letter ר may have been, for the same reason, substituted for ב in the transcription. The oldest forms of ר and ב, i.e. 𓐍 𓐍 , are scarcely distinguishable; and even in the Samaritan, which adds a line to the b, they are easily confused, 𓐍 𓐍 . The Coptic Pentateuch uses the word aϥ, ⲛⲓⲁϥ, adding ⲛⲟⲩϩⲟⲣ. "dog," to express the κυνόμυια of the LXX. This conjecture is somewhat confirmed by the affinity thus brought out with זְבוּב, the fly, especially "the fly that is in the uttermost parts of the rivers of Egypt," Isaiah vii. 18.

23. פְּדוּת, separation, not found elsewhere in this sense: it is from Semitic.

ix. 8. פִיחַ, ἅ. λ. Gesenius derives it from פּוּחַ = נפח. If this probable connection be correct, the word would be common to the Egyptian and Hebrew, nef, nefu, to breathe, or blow.

כַּבְשָׁן occurs only in the Pentateuch. The Arabic has قبس, ignem extudit, which may, or may not, be the root. No Semitic etymology is satisfactory. The Chaldee, Syriac, and Arabic employ a different word

I find no Egyptian equivalent; the nearest in form and sense is 𓊽𓎡𓃀𓊃 , χabs, a burning lamp. Perhaps △𓏏𓃀𓄑 , to bake, of which כָּפַן would be the transcription, may have had a variant nearer to the Hebrew. The word is used in a late variant in the sense of baking bricks, or more probably "using a lime kiln." A curious word lately discovered by Mr. Birch, very probably gives the true form 𓎡𓃀𓊃𓐍𓏤 , kabusa, in Coptic ⲭⲃⲃⲉⲥ, ἄνθραξ, carbo. 'Egypt. Zeitschrift,' 1868, p. 121. Mr. Birch writes ⲭⲁⲓⲃⲉⲥ; Peyron gives ⲭⲃⲃⲉⲥ; and ⲭⲃⲉⲥ.—Lex. Copt. This meets the two conditions of agreement in sense and radical letters.

9. אָבָק, "fine dust," is a very rare word, twice in the Pentateuch, four times in later books.

שְׁחִין, A. V. boils. The word occurs in Job ii. 7, and in reference to Hezekiah. Gesenius compares the Arabic سخن, to be hot, used specially of fever heat: but the word never occurs in connection with eruptions. A Coptic MS., quoted by Peyron, renders this and the word פרה which follows ⲭⲛⲟⲩϥ ⲃⲉⲣⲃⲉⲣ, in which the radical letters partly correspond with the Hebrew, ⲭ often = שׁ . Possibly the Egyptian came nearer still. The true derivation, however, appears to be ⲍⲱⲍ, prurire, of which the Egyptian form was 𓈖𓄿△𓃀𓊪 , to scratch, a word which occurs frequently in early papyri. The exact transcription is χaku. A variant somewhat nearer probably existed, or the Hebrews may have adopted and modified it, substituting, as in many words, sh for χ, and ch for k.

פרה. = ⲃⲉⲣⲃⲉⲣ, see last note.

אֲבַעְבֻּעֹת, ἅ. λ. The assumed root, בוּעַ, is not extant. Egyptian has 𓏏𓏤𓈖 baba, Cop. ⲃⲉⲃⲉ, overflow. The א presents no difficulty.

15. כחר, cut off. In this sense it occurs once in Zechariah, otherwise only here and in Job iv. 7; xv. 28; xxii. 20. The Coptic ⲕⲱⲡⲧ caedere, abscindere, is connected with the root △𓏤 , כח , 𓐍𓐍𓏤 , cut, △𓏤𓊃𓈖 , engrave, carve; still nearer is ϭⲉⲧϭⲱⲧ, concidere, caedere.

31. פִּשְׁתָּה, flax, a common word, is probably Egyptian. No satisfactory Semitic

etymology is proposed; the Arabic has فشر, to which Fuerst gives the sense "carminari," without authority as it would seem: nor is the meaning assigned to it by Gesenius supported by Arabic Lexicographers. A glance at Freytag will show how utterly unconnected the meaning is with flax. Gesenius observes that it is found in Avicenna. I believe that in Syriac and Arabic it is merely a derivative meaning. Gesenius observes that the word does not occur in any Semitic dialect. He had good reason to reject the conjectures of Forster; he would probably not have hesitated to adopt the etymology suggested by the Egyptian [hieroglyphs], Pek, flax, linen, and linen stuffs. It is a very common word, known first from the Rosetta stone. The change of "k" to "sh" is normal. Brugsch, p. 515, compares it with פשתה.

נבעל ἅ. λ. The assumed root נבע does not occur in any Semitic dialect. In Egyptian [hieroglyphs], gabu, blossom, corresponds very nearly. 'D. H.,' p. 755.

32. כסמת, "spelt," occurs very seldom. The Arabic which resembles it is uncommon, كرسنة; it is used by Saadia in translating Is. xxviii. 25. Freytag gives كرسنة, vicia, vetch, but without a root, and it evidently is a strange word, probably a compound word, and of Egyptian origin.

[hieroglyphs], sim, Coptic ϹΙΜ, is a general name for herbs, and is used in the Coptic Version of v. 25. A compound word of uncertain meaning, but denoting some vegetable food, is found in the 'Ritual,' c. 124, 4: [hieroglyphs], chersemau, which corresponds very nearly to the Hebrew grain [hieroglyphs], kemetta, or kemdut, written also [hieroglyphs], means a kind of corn, represented [hieroglyphs] on the Sarcophagus of Seti; Bon., p. 2, B. 1. 43; B. 43; D. H., p. 1497.

32. אפילת, ἅ. λ. No Semitic root is found; that suggested by Gesenius is unsatisfactory, افل has the sense deficit, latuit, whence G. elicits the meaning, late in season, tender. In Egyptian [hieroglyphs], pirt, or pilt. Brugsch renders the word "jeunes plantes qui viennent de pousser," the exact meaning of the Hebrew.

xii. 11. פסח, passover. The Semitic derivations are doubtful, see note *in loc.* The Egyptian [hieroglyphs], pesh-t, corresponds very nearly in form, and exactly in meaning and construction. Champollion, Gr. p. 446, gives two examples, to extend the arms or wings over a person, protecting him.

15. שאר, leaven; the word occurs only in this chapter. Gesenius compares סיר, to boil. In Egyptian [hieroglyphs], with variants pronounced seri, means "seethe," "seething pot." It is connected with seru, cheese, or buttermilk. There can be little doubt of the connexion with the Hebrew, and the Egyptian probably supplies the true root. חמץ, leavened dough, does not occur in the same sense out of the Pentateuch, unless it is in Amos iv. 5, when it seems rather to mean "spoil." The Coptic has ϨΜΧ, acid, which, corresponding with it exactly in form and nearly in sense, implies an Egyptian root; but it may be taken from the Arabic. The Egyptian for fermentation does not seem to be connected with it, [hieroglyphs], stf; which is represented by the Coptic ϹΒ̄ΗΤΕ, see Chabas 'Mél.' ii. p. 219; though the radical letters might be brought under the common law of transmutation between aspirants and sibilants.

22. סף, basin, or, according to some, "threshold," see note *in loc.* The latter sense is somewhat confirmed by the Eg. [hieroglyphs], sep, a step, or threshold.

Considerable additions may be made to this list, which will probably form the basis of a separate treatise. Enough has been said to show that Moses habitually uses words which existed in Egyptian, and for the most part cannot be shown to have a true Semitic etymology.

Since the preceding pages were finally revised for the press the writer has received the 'Journal Asiatique' for March and April, 1870. It contains an article by M. Harkavy, entitled, "Les Mots Égyptiens de la Bible." It does not include proper names. In some important points the writer has the satisfaction of finding his conclusions supported by this Egyptologer, who appears not to have seen these Essays, which were sent to Paris towards the end of last year. The following derivations are partly new and of much interest.

Gen. xli. 43. M. Harkavy adopts Ap-rech, chief of the Rech, or men of learning; a derivation noticed above, p. 483. He defends the transcription of *p* by *b*, and *ch* by *k*, and certainly shows that in words common to Hebrew and Egyptian they are sometimes interchanged. He gives also what appears to be the true equivalent of בנים, see above, p. 491, viz. Chenemms.

Gen. xli. 2, Achu. The same derivation as that given above.

xli. 8. Chartummim, magicians. In a note, p. 109, M. Harkavy observes: "Un savant distingué, qui a lu notre travail, remarque qu'il avait pensé au radical *tem* qui signifie prononcer, énoncer, avec la particule *cher*. L'initiale *cher* forme en effet des titres avec d'autres mots." The reader will find this derivation stated and defended in the note at the end of Exodus, c. vii., p. 279. It was mentioned by the writer to some scholars both in England and Paris, by whom it was approved.

טנא, tena, a sacred basket. The derivation has been given in note on Exod. xvi.

Exod. vii. 11, 22. Mr. Harkavy derives לט להט from Rech-chet, a magician, or man of learning. The writer prefers the etymology proposed, p. 276.

Gen. xlix. 5, מברות, rendered habitation, probably equivalent to Macher, a granary.

Gen. xii. et passim, "Pharaoh." The derivation proposed above is defended.

Gen. xli. 45. Zaphnath Paaneh. M. Harkavy gives the same value to the first syllable, Zaph, food, and to the word Paaneh, life. For the middle syllable he proposes net, saviour. The transcription given above still appears preferable to the writer, who is glad to find M. H. in accord with him in regard to the more important terms, food and life.

The derivations of Shesh and Pak, fine linen, have been already noted.

END OF PART I.